CONTENTS

PREFACE

There are few courses offered at the secondary level which better prepare students for a rich, fulfilling life than one on modern Western civilization. Throughout the course, students will cross paths with great minds, such as Newton, Descartes, and Freud, marvel at works of art created by Delacroix, Van Gogh, and Picasso, and be enthralled by the writings of Voltaire, Shelley, and Zola. They will experience the triumphs and failures of great leaders from Napoléon to Garibaldi, from Stalin to Churchill. They will also re-live the challenges posed by scientific, industrial, political, and cultural revolutions. Perhaps most importantly, students will come to realize that they are part of the ever-evolving time continuum which will go on unravelling long after they have closed the pages of this book and moved on to varied careers.

Such a wide-ranging course carries with it the inherent danger of overwhelming the students. Attempting to cover too much information can leave the students understanding too little, and hence the true value of the course is lost. A course in modern Western civilization must be seen as the beginning of a journey which will enlighten and enrich the lives of those who embark upon it. Seen as an end in itself, such a course becomes a mine field with the potential to destroy even the keenest students' curiosity about the past. The richness and diversity of this period in history are simply too vast to be covered in detail in a single course. Rather, students and teachers must approach the course with the realistic aim of opening many doors to the past and the hope that several of these doors will lead to paths of inquiry to be followed over a lifetime.

A common complaint about texts which attempt to cover broad spans of history is that they are too extensive. Our approach in this text has been to develop fewer concepts and ideas, and to develop them in enough detail to make them understandable. Furthermore, in an attempt to broaden our understanding of the past, this text has given more space to social history, the arts, to the impact of Europe on the wider world, and to the impact of the world on European history and culture. To bring these new elements to the students has meant making some concessions; for instance, some major events may have been outlined rather than dealt with in detail. Students who have a particular interest in the event covered are encouraged, however, to pursue the topic in more depth independently.

From the book's inception, it has been our intent to draw upon the expertise of a variety of leading Canadian scholars. In doing so, we have been able to compile a text which provides a refreshing look at the past 500 years, based on up-to-date research. At times, teachers may find long held beliefs challenged, as recent interpretations alter our understanding of history.

Impact: Western Civilization and the Wider World opens with a general introduction to the study of history, with a focus on various philosophies of history and the concept of historiography. The intent of the opening chapter is to challenge students to think about history not as a listing of dates and facts but as a discipline which requires careful analysis and is open to debate. The text concludes with an epilogue that attempts to draw together the past 500 years by introducing students to the concept of post-modernism. By assisting them in understanding why the modern era is over, the text should enable students to make sense of the material covered in the course and the rapidly changing world in which they live.

In an attempt to enliven the study of history, we have incorporated a number of new features in this text. The chapters on social history provide students with a window on the daily lives of earlier Europeans and help them to understand the past in a broader context. The chapters dealing with globalization, which began with the voyages of Columbus, provide a more accurate picture of the forces that shaped modern Western civilization. Finally, the historiographical questions found at the end of each chapter provide students with an intellectual challenge as they are given the opportunity to respond to interpretations of history. In the end, we hope that both teachers and students find *Impact: Western Civilization and the Wider World* an enjoyable book to read and a valuable learning tool.

Garfield Gini-Newman

Cynthia Grenier

ACKNOWLEDGEMENTS

When first approached by McGraw-Hill Ryerson with the idea of writing a text on modern Western civilization, our first impulse was to return to the format that made *Odyssey Through the Ages* such a successful text. Once again, the building of a strong team proved the key to developing a solid text on European history. Little did we know at the outset how exciting and invigorating working with the assembled team would be. Nor could we have foreseen the manner in which the text would evolve, for many of the features that have been incorporated are the product of a highly successful collaborative effort between ourselves, the contributing authors, reviewers, and the editorial team at McGraw-Hill Ryerson.

Thanks goes to all those who were a part of the team. Firstly, the contributing authors provided superb material to work with and invaluable assistance in photo research and the development of feature studies. David Higgs of the University of Toronto supplied fascinating details of the history of the eighteenth century. Douglas Lorimer of Wilfrid Laurier University provided much food for thought with his provocative chapters on the nineteenth century. The period from the outset of World War I to the eve of World War II offers students new insights into this era thanks to the work of Gilbert Allardyce from the University of New Brunswick. Sonia Riddoch of Queen's University supplied superb and up-to-date coverage of the post-war period.

Many others also played a crucial role in the development of the text. Thanks to Gerry King and Phyllis Evans, both librarians at Vaughan Secondary School, for their patience and unfailing willingness to help. In the crunch, Usha Doshi provided much-needed assistance in pulling together the timelines and wrote several key feature studies. Her diligence and perseverance are much appreciated.

A very special group of young people played an instrumental role in the development of this text. The following students from Vaughan Secondary School were with us throughout the project in the capacity of student editors, helping to ensure the material was both interesting and readable. These include Kathryn Brundage, Joel Fishbane, Henry Leyderman, Fern Bojarski, Laura Levine, David Gram, and Suzan Krepostman.

Other reviewers who made valuable suggestions are Ian Andrews of Oromocto High School, New Brunswick, and John Barecroft of the Simcoe County Board of Education.

Several people were instrumental in providing personal insights into events of the twentieth century. We want to express our gratitude to Daniel Ovsey and his family for providing details of life under the Stalin regime, to Frane and Eda Kruh of Zagorje, Slovenia, and Silva Gini for their personal insights into life during and after the rule of Tito in Yugoslavia.

As always, the team at McGraw-Hill Ryerson has provided superb guidance and support throughout. Thanks to Janice Matthews for her support through difficult times and her faith in our ideas. Also thanks to Crystal Shortt for her patience and understanding in the light of tight deadlines and her skill in guiding such a complex text. Far more people have been involved at some point in the creation of *Impact: Western Civilization and the Wider World*. To all those who have not been mentioned we also wish to express our sincerest gratitude.

Garfield Gini-Newman
Cynthia Grenier

I reserve my greatest thanks for my wife, Laura Gini-Newman, who provides me with support, patience, and understanding. Her insightful comments, constructive suggestions, and genuine enthusiasm have inspired, challenged, and improved my writing.

As I watch my two boys, Mathew and Geoffrey, grow I am continually reminded that children are our greatest resource and inspiration. My commitment to a safer, more tolerant world for my children underlies all that I do, for I am convinced that an understanding of the past can help guide us in the future. This text is dedicated to my children; that they may know a world of harmony rather than discord, and of tolerance rather than prejudice.

Garfield Gini-Newman

I would like to gratefully acknowledge the love and support of my family: my mother, Alexander, Emily, and Kristine.

Also, to my dearest friend, R.W.R. Sockman, thank you for providing me with laughter, joy, and a garden in which to rest.

Cynthia Grenier

Understanding the Nature of Historical Studies

The Canadian classroom in the 1990s is vastly different from that of previous generations. Take a look around you: chances are you will see students from a wide variety of ethnic backgrounds and religious beliefs. Students will be aspiring to become lawyers, entrepreneurs, mechanics, doctors, beauticians, teachers, artists, technicians, etc. This dynamic blend of students in our schools is forcing teachers to rethink the teaching of history in order to transmit a balanced view of history which is appealing and relevant to the majority of the students.

Until very recently, European history was taught from a Eurocentric point of view. Major events in non-Western countries have often received little attention, except where Europeans are directly involved and, even then, the focus tends to be on Europe's influence on the rest of the world. Much is known, for example, of the impact of the Spanish in North, Central, and South America following the arrival of Columbus and of the impact of the Dutch, German, and English settlers in Africa. Far less is written about the impact of non-European cultures on Europe. How, for example, were countries such as Spain, France, Germany, and England changed as a result of their contact with other cultures? What impact did non-Western societies have on the diet, art, politics, or economics of European nations? Do you ever ponder the impact that tomatoes, corn, potatoes, or coffee from America had on Western civilization? Think of the influence of the Iroquois Confederacy on the U.S. Constitution.

As we become a global village, it becomes essential that the study of history not be done in isolation. The focus of this book will be on major events in European history, the impact of Europe on the wider world, and the impact of non-European countries on European culture, politics, and economics.

History is relevant to everyone. Whether your interests lie in the field of mathematics and science, art and literature, folklore, economics, philosophy, or the daily lives of people in past societies, the study of history can help to enrich your understanding and appreciation of the world around you. History involves more than economic wealth, political power, and military strength: it is concerned with the triumphs and failures of humanity, with our advancements and setbacks, and our continual search to understand ourselves, our world, and our spirituality. Consequently, this book deals with the history of modern Western civilization encompassing aspects of daily life, music, art, literature, economics, technological advancements, and intellectual trends. The book has been designed to introduce you to the wide scope of historical studies, to challenge your intellect, feed your curiosity, and inspire you to develop a fuller understanding of the world in which you live.

What Is History?

In 1066, William the Conqueror seized control of England after King Harald died from an arrow wound in the eye; in 1434 the Italian city states signed the Treaty of Lodi, beginning a period of peace which would last over half a century; in 1517, a Catholic monk named Martin Luther posted his *Ninety-Five Theses* on the church door in Wittenburg, and in 1816 Mary Shelley published her famous novel *Frankenstein*. A common misconception among students is that, by memorizing facts such as these, they will do well in a history course and that the sign of a good historian is the ability to recall the important names, dates, and events in history. Were this true, historians would be nothing more than clerks recording historical data. In

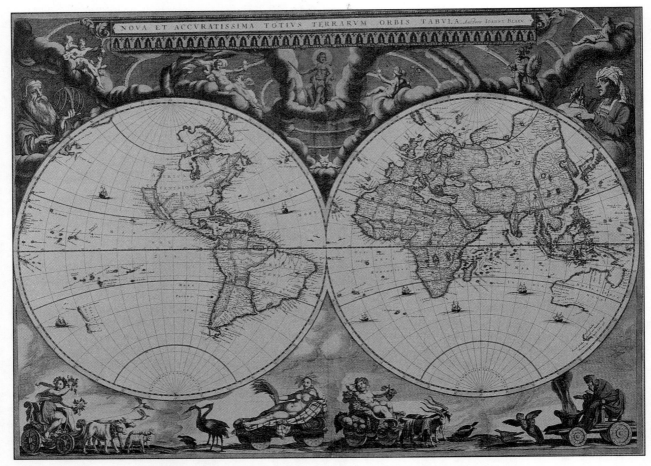

This map from 1662 shows the world as it was then known by Europeans.

fact, the study of history requires the ability to read and write critically, to carry out research and, especially, to think creatively and analytically. Attempting to memorize countless names, dates, and events can be a futile task if the knowledge of the past learned by students of history is not used for a constructive end such as detecting trends or coming to understand the human experience.

History is the study of change over time; without change there is no history. Consider, for example, the anthropologist who embarks on a detailed study of the Efe, a semi-nomadic people in the tropical rain forests of Central Africa, known to outsiders as Pygmies. After studying the Efe for several years, the anthropologist returns to Canada where she writes a report describing in detail the customs, clothing, food, architecture, religious practices, and political structure. Years later, the anthropologist decides to return to Central Africa to study any changes among the Efe and to write a contemporary history of the group. Surprisingly, she discovers that the Efe have undergone no change: all aspects of life have remained exactly as the anthropologist perceived them years before. What would she write about? Obviously there would be no history to record because there had been no change. Apply this unlikely scenario to European society: if Europeans dressed the same, ate the same food, had the same culture as in the eighteenth century, there would be very little for historians to write about.

Thus, the first lesson for the student of history to learn is that the foundation for historical studies is the study of change over time and that the primary question asked by historians is "Why?" History is the attempt to understand the underlying causes and consequences of events. Using historical data for this purpose gives history purpose and relevance.

How can the study of history help to enrich our lives? Imagine living in a society in which no one knew any history; in which we knew nothing of our ancestors or the events that brought us to this period in time. English historian Arthur Marwick suggests: "A society without memory and self-knowledge would be a society adrift." We would suffer from cultural amnesia and therefore be unable to truly understand who we are and where we are heading. French anthropologist Claude Lévi-Strauss argues that those who ignore history condemn themselves to know nothing about the present because historical development alone permits us to evaluate elements of the present.

Some people think that history is about those with power and wealth and that preliterate societies have no history. A good understanding of history must encompass people and society. To suggest that women have no history because until recently they had no power, or that Native Canadians had no history until Europeans began studying their societies is absurd. As historians have come to broaden their definition of history to garner a more accurate understanding of historical developments, it has become increasingly evident that history requires drawing on a wide variety of resources, including written works as well as art, music, archaeology, anthropology, folk tales, dance, religious practices, food, government, family relations, etc. By studying various aspects of the past—and by not limiting the study of history to written records— we have a much greater opportunity to understand our present.

When first introduced to the study of history, students often assume that what is written by historians is fact. Students are seldom asked to consider a historian's point of view or to understand the influence of the historian's culture on history. History is shaped by those who write it as well as by those who live it. British historian E. H. Carr wrote that "When we attempt to answer the question 'What is History?' our answer consciously or unconsciously reflects our own position in time and forms part of our answer to the broader question of what view we take of the society in which we live."

The study of various schools of historical thought or the perspective from which different historians write is referred to as *historiography*. Historians drawing on the same body of information may reach completely different conclusions. Historiography increases the complexity of the study of history but it helps to draw informed and reasoned conclusions about the past regardless of the varying schools of thought adopted by historians.

Throughout the chapters of this book, you will find many instances in which various views of the past are presented. When you encounter references to different views on a historical issue, pause and reflect on the various positions as a historian would do. Critically think of how historians use evidence of the past to support their historical views.

Dealing with Historical Time Periods

One of the difficulties teachers often face when designing a history course is preparing an effective package. All too often, courses begin at a fairly arbitrary starting point. For example, where should a course in modern European history begin? Is the Enlightenment a logical starting point for the course? How about the French Revolution? The difficulty with beginning with either of these events is that the foundation for our understanding of the changes that occurred in Europe over the past 250 years lies in the period preceding the eighteenth century. A clear picture of Europe's medieval heritage is essential; the agrarian society, which was highly religious—often superstitious and violent—contrasts sharply with the refined urban society of the Renaissance.

The Renaissance was a period of revolutionary changes in thought. Humanism, individualism, and the quest for knowledge allowed overseas exploration to occur, challenged the power of the Catholic Church, and produced the Scientific Revolution. When the reason and logic of the Scientific Revolution were applied to society, the foundations for the Enlightenment were laid and a revolution in politics, government, and economics was close at hand. It is this concept of a time continuum that is essential to perceiving the full picture of history. Also important is the realization that just as major developments of the past were the product of preceding events, the trends and events of today

The medical practice of leeching, as it was about to be done on this woman, remained common throughout the eighteenth century.

———————— ⚔ ————————

are presently shaping the developments of the future.

As students of history, we must understand that history is studied but not defined in time periods (such as the Renaissance, the Industrial Revolution, the Age of Romanticism); history does not unfold "in packages" and often the periods identified by historians overlap. The Renaissance, which was largely an Italian phenomenon, began to fade by the mid-sixteenth century while the Reformation was transforming much of Europe north of the Alps. Similarly, while the French Revolution brought radical change to much of Europe, the Industrial Revolution was transforming England. Historical time periods are only organizers to help understand the past.

Contrasting Views of History

Most historians assume that history is not a random series of events but is moving in some kind of ordered direction. According to ancient Greek and Roman scholars, history was an inevitable cyclical progression descending from prosperity to adversity and eventually rising again from adversity to prosperity. Nineteenth-century scholars tended to regard history as progressive, while twentieth-century scholars tend to question the concept of continual forward progress

in history. Being able to understand history in a broad context helps to establish a relevance to our present and future lives. Consider, for example, how important understanding history is in negotiating fair and equitable agreements with a nation's indigenous peoples.

Italian Renaissance writer Niccolò Machiavelli captured the essence of the classical view of history in his famous work *The Prince*. At the end of the fifteenth century, the Italian city-states were in decline after having experienced the glory of the Renaissance. Foreign powers were invading cities such as Florence, Rome, and Milan, leading to chaos. Machiavelli wrote *The Prince* as a guide to restoring the city's grandeur. Machiavelli expresses the classical view of history when he writes: "And if, as I said, the Israelites had to be enslaved in Egypt for Moses to emerge as their leader; if the Persians had to be oppressed by the Medes so that the greatness of Cyrus could be recognized; if the Athenians had to be scattered to demonstrate the excellence of Theseus, then, at the present time, in order to discover the worth of an Italian spirit, Italy had to be brought to her present extremity." Thus, Machiavelli viewed history as cyclical, holding out great hope for a return to prosperity for Florence. He did not, however, view history as necessarily progressive: he did not believe that each time a society returned to a golden age, it would have progressed further than the golden age which had preceded it. A progressive view of history did not emerge until the eighteenth-century period known as the Enlightenment.

Giambattista Vico, a renowned Italian philosopher of the eighteenth century, produced the most revolutionary theory of history in more than one thousand years. His *New Science*, first published in 1725, was a truly original historical work that contradicted the view of his contemporaries and helped establish a basis for the modern study of history. Vico argued that since we are ourselves the creators of history, we can know it with certainty. This idea is an important foundation of modern historiography because it defines what historians study (past human actions) and states their aim (to recover human thinking).

The major aim of Vico's *New Science* was to discover the universal laws of history. The pursuit of this aim resulted in Vico's theory of an "ideal and eternal history," which is the "schematic account of the successive ages through which nations have run their course, and of the *ricorsi* [alternate courses] in which subsequent ages have repeated the patterns of those which came before." In other words, the "ideal" is the universal traits of all cultures and the "eternal" is the commonality and permanence of these traits through the rise and fall of all nations.

Vico's unique view of human history as progressing spirally developed from his theory of an ideal and eternal history. The idea that humanity could have been rational, virtuous, and wise from the beginning was totally rejected by Vico. He also rejected the idea of progress as being a causal process, asserting instead that humanity moves forward slowly and painfully to reach maturity only after turmoil, oppression, and bitter conflict. Vico believed that human progress was based on building upon the ideas of past cultures.

Summarizing his view of the rise and fall of nations, Vico wrote: "Men first feel necessity, then look to utility, next attend to comfort, still later amuse themselves with pleasure, then grow dissolute in luxury and finally go mad and waste their substance."

History as Progressive

In the early eighteenth century, theories of human perfectibility and progress were shaping the writing of history. Many intellectuals wanted to see a pattern in the course of historical change because they were convinced that history is going somewhere and that the miseries suffered by humanity were not in vain but were part of the inevitable process of achieving some morally satisfactory goal. This view of history as progressive has survived into the twentieth century. E. H. Carr defines history as "progress through the transmission of acquired skills from one generation to another." In defence of his progressive view of history, Carr wrote: "Everything that happens has a cause or causes, and could not have happened differently unless something in the cause or causes had also been different."

For many students of history in the late twentieth century, the view of history as progress is quite appealing. North Americans have experienced uprecedented economic growth since the end of World War II; there have been countless medical and technological breakthroughs; and individual rights are being protected. It would be difficult not to perceive progress in the twentieth century.

The obvious problem with believing that history is progressive is that the historian must place a value judgment on events. How many technological advances of the twentieth century have brought with them negative side effects (e.g. increased stress, pollution)? When reflecting on progress, we must first establish what we mean by progress and, secondly, we must acknowledge that others may not share our view. Thus, although historians may be able to discern trends and patterns in history, which help us respond to issues of the present and future, conclusions regarding the progress of humanity will forever remain subjective.

Reflections

The insights into the past provided by history can act as our guide to the future. As you read about the people, places, events, and trends that constitute Modern European history, consider what history is teaching you about yourself and the society in which you live. History is about the spirit of the past: in the face of the Mona Lisa lives the essence of the Renaissance; in the writings of Voltaire lives the spirit of the Enlightenment; the Scientific Revolution lives in our understanding of the universe and the human body; and in the memory of those who died in senseless wars and at the hands of ruthless oppressors lives a constant reminder of the inhumanity we are capable of. The study of history is the study of the triumphs and failures that have brought us to this point in the time continuum and helps us to make sense of the world in which we live. In the study of history lives the spirit of hope that some day the lessons to be learned from the past may enable us to live harmoniously in a truly global village.

UNIT I

The Birth of Modern Europe

Beginning in the fifteenth century, Europe embarked on a course of change that would radically transform its culture and society and have profound implications the world over. Leaving behind its medieval past, feudal laws, limited world view, and devout religious beliefs, Europeans looked to the classical age of Greece and Rome for a new inspiration. A broadening world view brought about by the crusades gave Europeans the courage and desire to explore the world. Driven by an emerging capitalist economic order, they set out to increase their wealth by exploiting the peoples and resources of newly found lands. By the end of the eighteenth century many European powers including Britain, France, Spain, Holland, and Portugal had established extensive overseas empires, many of which were peopled by enslaved Africans who had been imported to work the mines or plantations of the European colonies.

In Europe, humanism, which placed a heavy emphasis on human achievement and potential, would lead to revolutions in art, religion, science, and ultimately in politics. Armed with the radical ideas of the French *philosophes*, the Third Estate (those from neither the Church nor the nobility: the majority of the people) in France would lead a revolution at the end of the eighteenth century that would shake European society to its foundations and irrevocably alter the political map of Europe.

Between 1500 and 1800, Europe radically changed from its medieval past. Gone were the petty kingdoms and the dominance of the Roman Catholic Church. In its place was a new, modern Europe with a global outlook and on the verge of an industrial revolution. Driven by a faith in human ability to know and understand all and to be able to perfect society, Europeans of the eighteenth century were more brazen and self-assured of the superiority of their civilization than ever before.

	Political/Military	INTELLECTUAL	Cultural
1517		Martin Luther posts his *Ninety Five Theses* on church door	
1529	Henry VIII is forced to appeal to Parliament during his struggle with the papacy		
1543		Copernicus: *On the Revolutions of the Celestial Spheres*	
1598	France's Henry IV proclaims the Edict of Nantes		
1618	Thirty Years' War begins		
1628	Cardinal Richelieu becomes Louis XIII's first minister	Harvey: *On the Motion of the Heart and Blood in Animals*	
1629	Charles I suspends Parliament, beginning 11 years of tyranny		
1632		Galileo: *Dialogues on the Two Chief Systems of the World*	
1642	Charles I storms Parliament on horseback, starting English civil war		
1643	Louis XIV's rule of France begins		
1648	Thirty Years' War ends		
1649	Charles I is beheaded by Parliament		
1660	Charles II leads England as a constitutional monarch		
1682	Louis XIV declares that the papacy has no power in France		
1685	James II ascends the throne in England		
1688	Revolution in England: William of Orange seizes the throne		
1712			Alexander Pope: *The Rape of the Lock*
1713	Treaty of Utrecht		
1715	Louis XIV's rule of France ends		
1717		Prussia becomes first European state to institute compulsory education	
1719			Antoine Watteau: *Pilrimage to Cythera* completed
1726			Jonathan Swift: *Gulliver's Travels*
1734			J.S. Bach: *Christmas Oratorio*
			Samuel Johnson: *Plan for Dictionary*
1746			Handel: *The Messiah*
1748	Peace of Aix-la-Chapelle	Montesquieu: *Spirit of the Law*	
1756	Seven Years' War begins		
1758		Helvetius: *Concerning the Mind*	
1761		Rousseau: *The Social Contract*	
1763	Seven Years' War ends Treaty of Paris		
1764		Beccaria: *Essay on Crimes and Punishments*	
1776		Adam Smith: *An Inquiry into the nature and causes of the Wealth of Nations*	
1778			Jean-Jacques Rouseau dies
1784			Jacques-Louis David: *Oath of the Horatii*
1787			Mozart: *Don Giovanni*
1788	England begins shipping convicts to the penal colony of Australia		
1789	French Revolution begins		
1791	Abolition of slavery in France		
1793	Louis XVI of France is executed		
1794	French Revolution ends		
1799	Napoléon leads coup d'état		
1804	Napoléon's conquest of Europe begins		
1808			Beethoven: *Symphony No. 5*
1814	Napoléon's conquest of Europe ends		
1815	Congress of Vienna Treaty is signed		
1822			

1

The Foundations of Modern Europe

❧ CHAPTER HIGHLIGHTS

- An understanding of humanism as a new way of thinking

- The impact of the Reformation as a revolutionary change in the structure and ideals of Western religion

- The nature and the impact of the Scientific Revolution on European thought and life

- The transformation in politics leading to the age of absolutism

- The importance of England as the anti-absolutist state of Europe and its move towards constitutional monarchy

Medieval Europe was a world of stone castles and towering Gothic cathedrals that stand as a testimony to the violent and deeply religious nature of the age. Society was agricultural and isolated from the outside world. Travel and trade were very limited. The lives of most Europeans were dominated by the Catholic Church and the feudal obligations that tied them to the land and the landowners, or feudal lords.

During the thirteenth and fourteenth centuries, several developments would hurtle Europe from its medieval past. Among these occurrences were the Crusades which opened up trade routes to the Middle and Far East; the rebirth of classical thoughts and ideas spurred by the rediscovery of ancient texts; the increasing disillusionment with the Catholic Church resulting from corruption and nepotism; a dramatic increase in trade and an accompanying rise in towns as centres of

trade; and the initial voyages of exploration led by explorers such as Henry the Navigator from Portugal. These developments in medieval Europe would eventually transform the world as well.

The Renaissance and Reformation Periods

The Renaissance, which is generally accepted as the period between 1350 and 1550, is characterized by profound changes in attitudes and ideas and the resulting artistic and intellectual achievements attained. The French term *renaissance* means rebirth and is applied to this period of European history because of the renewed focus on ancient Greco-Roman thinkers, such as Plato, Aristotle, and Cicero, as well as a renewed interest in

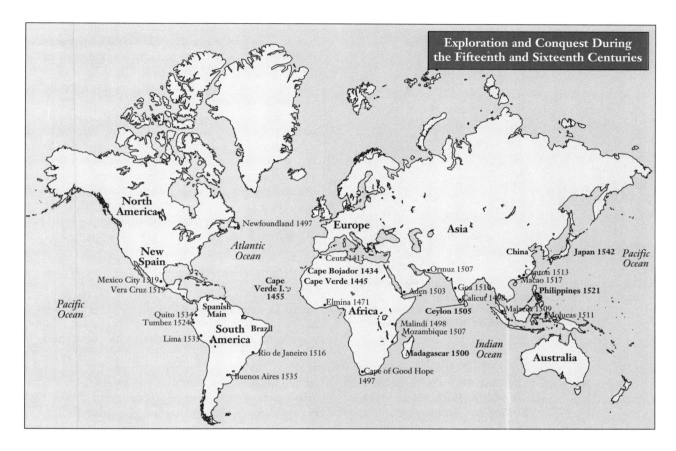

Greco-Roman culture. During the Middle Ages, the absolute authority of God was emphasized, and classical (Greco-Roman) ideas and art forms were rejected as pagan. The fourteenth century brought not only renewed interest in classicism but a renewed focus on the study of humans and human achievement. Humanism was the greatest lasting legacy of the Renaissance.

Humanism

Humanists were concerned with the study of grammar, rhetoric, poetry, history, and moral philosophy. Considered one of the earliest humanists, Francesco Petrarca (1304–1374) stressed the importance of the earthly love of women: he believed it would lead men to love God as the creator of women. Petrarch's emphasis on earthly, physical love is typical of the Renaissance.

Humanism is also reflected in the architecture of the Renaissance: fountains and immaculate gardens began to adorn the grounds of the wealthy. Whereas Gothic cathedrals were the crowning glory of medieval architecture, Renaissance churches were much less grandiose, built on a more human scale. The most impressive buildings of the Renaissance were the homes of wealthy merchants or palazzi.

The influence of humanism is also evident in the paintings and sculptures of the Renaissance. The works of Michelangelo Buonarroti fused classical style with Christian themes. His famous sculpture, *David*, and his paintings on the ceiling of the Sistine Chapel represent the pinnacle of the Renaissance. Although the themes are biblical, these works are centred on human physical and spiritual beauty, respectively. The *Mona Lisa*, by Leonardo da Vinci, is perhaps the most famous painting of the Renaissance.

The Reformation

The Reformation period would ultimately divide Europe along religious lines. Among the causes that

The Doge's Palace, in Venice, Italy, is typical of Renaissance architecture. Wealthy Italian merchants and bankers spent large sums of money building elaborate palazzi in the cities where they did business.

triggered it were the new ideas of the Renaissance. Many of the leading proponents of reform in the Catholic Church, such as **Martin Luther**, were greatly influenced by the humanist philosophy of the Renaissance. Reformers rejected the opulence and extravagance of the papacy and were critical of the formalism of religious practice, favouring instead a simpler, more human style of religion. They wished to bring about a religious revival, which was to be rooted in widespread education using vernacular, everyday language rather than the cultured Latin. They also challenged the concept of the Church as the intermediary between God and the individual, instead stressing that humans could come to God on their own.

The drastic changes that rocked the Christian world throughout the sixteenth century were also the product of the prevalent socio-economic and political conditions in Northern Europe. During the early years of the sixteenth century, food shortages and famines were frequent. The rich became less rich and the poor became much poorer. The time was right for a societal revolution.

Martin Luther's Reformation

The revolution that eventually transformed Europe and the Western world was spearheaded by Martin Luther. Luther's first confrontation with the Catholic Church came on October 31, 1517, when he posted his *Ninety-Five Theses* (written in Latin) on the door of the university church in Wittenberg. These 95 statements attacked abuses within the Church and eventually led to Luther's excommunication in 1520. Undeterred and under the protection of Elector Frederick III of Saxony, Luther formulated the doctrine of Lutheranism, according to which the Lutheran Church would have no saints, relics, fasts, nor monasteries and would allow the clergy to marry. Underlying Lutheran doctrine is the conviction that God is merciful and that salvation is granted through His mercy. It is interesting to note that Luther, a cleric, married a former nun, Katarina von Bora, who supported him in all his endeavours.

The Reformation Spreads

By 1530, the attack on the Catholic Church begun by Martin Luther had spread to many areas throughout Europe. In each area, people of conviction led the struggle to establish new reformed churches. In Switzerland, Ulrich Zwingli laid the foundations for the Anabaptist movement. In Geneva, John Calvin's ideas on the reformation of the Church eventually spread to France (Huguenots), Scotland (Presbyterians), Holland (Dutch Reformed Church); and impacted on Germany (Baptists), and England (Anglicans and Puritans). The religious revolution initiated by Luther in 1517 enveloped most of Europe; it would be carried to overseas colonies as well.

The Wars of Religion

Battles between Catholics and Protestant reformers raged in many countries of Europe for over a century. In France, a series of three weak monarchs between 1559 and 1589 left the country vulnerable and prone to civil war. Many members of the nobility abandoned Catholicism in favour of Calvinism as a symbol of their independence from the king. As it was assumed that peaceful coexistence between people of different faiths was impossible, the Reformation in France ultimately led to a return to the feudal conditions of earlier centuries.

The religious divisions that split France in the sixteenth century often led to violent clashes. In 1561, a Catholic baker guarding the consecrated Eucharistic bread, or Host, at the Paris church of Saint-Médard, was attacked by a crowd of Protestants. As they beat

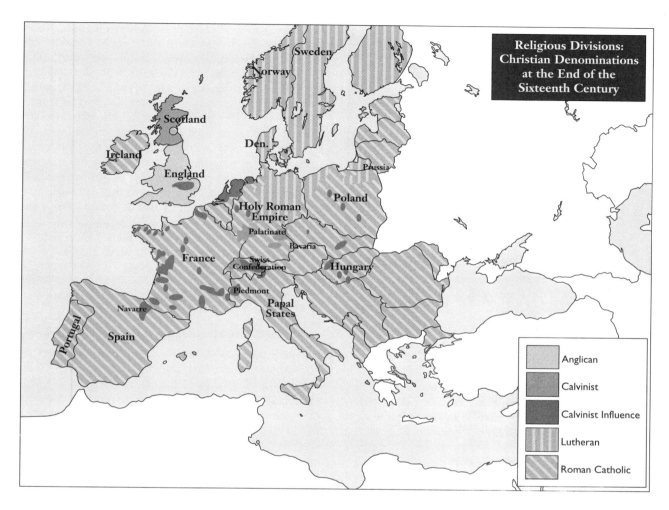

Religious Divisions: Christian Denominations at the End of the Sixteenth Century

Legend:
- Anglican
- Calvinist
- Calvinist Influence
- Lutheran
- Roman Catholic

him to death, the crowd chanted: "Does your God of paste protect you now from the pains of death?" In the same year, an angry mob of Catholics seized a group of just-released Protestant prisoners, killed them, and burned their bodies. Similar acts of violence became frequent across France as Huguenots (French Calvinists) were tortured, maimed, and murdered.

Religious violence in France finally came to an end in 1589 with the ascent to the throne of Henry IV of Navarre. Wanting, above all else, a united France, Henry IV chose to sacrifice religious principles out of political necessity. Upon ascending to the throne, he converted to Catholicism, renouncing his Protestant faith. This decision helped to unite the majority of the French people, who were Catholic, behind the king. In a further move to end religious tensions in France,

Henry IV published the Edict of Nantes in 1598, which granted the Huguenots freedom of conscience and public worship in 200 fortified towns throughout France. Henry IV's strong leadership and his wise political moves united France and restored internal peace.

Other areas of Europe also experienced religious wars as Catholics and Protestants struggled to control the minds and souls of the people. In the Netherlands, civil war between Catholics and Protestants raged from 1568 to 1578. During the sixteenth century, the Netherlands, which were part of the Spanish empire, comprised 17 self-governing provinces. By the 1560s, Calvinism had taken root and a large number of the people had become enriched through trade. This largely middle-class population practised Calvinism's moral gravity, with its emphasis on labour as opposed

Violence and atrocities were endemic to Europe during the sixteenth century, when wars of religion divided many countries. This engraving shows citizens of Haarlem, in the Netherlands, being decapitated or hung by the Spanish during the ten years of civil war.

to leisure. The Spanish adherence to the Catholic faith clashed with Calvinism in the Netherlands and led to years of conflict and war, after which the 17 provinces were divided: the ten southern provinces became the Spanish Netherlands (today Belgium) and Protestants were forced to convert to Catholicism or leave. The seven northern provinces, led by Holland, declared their independence from Spain in 1581 and became the United Provinces of the Netherlands (today the Netherlands).

The Thirty Years' War

In Central Europe, religious divisions culminated in the ***Thirty Years' War*** (1618–1648). In 1555, the Peace of Augsburg recognized the independent powers of German princes (despite the fact that Charles V, king of Spain and Germanic emperor, held the title of Holy Roman Emperor). The prince would now impose his religion on his subjects. This agreement, however, was strictly limited to Lutheranism and Catholicism.

Toward the end of the sixteenth century, Calvinism was making substantial gains in Central Europe and tensions were on the rise between Catholics and Lutherans. When Ferdinand of Styria (now part of Austria) became king of Bohemia in 1617,

he began closing Protestant churches. The Bohemians, who were Czech and German, enjoyed considerable religious freedom whether they were Lutheran, Catholic, or Calvinist and consequently were outraged by Ferdinand's decisions. On May 23, 1618, angry Protestants hurled two of Ferdinand's officials from a castle window. Despite the 25 m fall, the two men survived; Catholics claimed it was due to divine intervention, Protestants claimed it was because they landed on a pile of horse manure. This act ignited a war that was to last 30 years and engulfed Central Europe as well as Denmark, Sweden, Finland, France, Spain, and Holland. It was a devastating war that exhausted many European countries, especially German states and, in the end, settled little. The Thirty Years' War did, however, bring an end to the religious strife that had decimated Europe for over a century. France emerged from the war as the dominant European power of the seventeenth century.

The Scientific Revolution

Europe's break with its medieval past extended far beyond the realm of art, religion, or politics. Its effect was felt in all aspects of life, particularly in scientific thought. From the middle of the sixteenth century to the beginning of the eighteenth, a revolution in science would challenge our long-held perception of ourselves and the universe, and would radically alter the course of European history. Those who took part in this Scientific Revolution are numerous and the contributions they made are far-reaching. Our intent here is to explore the manner in which the Scientific Revolution changed the perception of the world.

The Revolution in Astronomy

Scientific observation was not new to the sixteenth century. What was new were the methods and questions that scientists were asking. The scientific mind of the Middle Ages sought answers that would fit preconceived notions about the universe. For example, it was assumed that a planet follows a circular orbit because the circle was a perfect pattern created by God. Similarly, medieval scientists held firmly to the view that the earth was the centre of the universe and the reason objects fell to the earth when dropped was because they sought the place of greatest heaviness in the universe: the earth. Such notions held scientific progress in check for centuries. Just as the Renaissance

Francis Bacon's *Novum Organum*

Francis Bacon was clearly a product of the English Renaissance. Well versed in politics, literature, and philosophy, Bacon earned a lasting reputation for his work in science. Rejecting the deductive methods of the Middle Ages, Bacon stressed the importance of direct observation in ascertaining truth. His *Novum Organum*, which was published in 1620, was an attempt at replacing Aristotle's *Organon*. Bacon's work explores the faulty traditional methods of science and proposes a method of inquiry that is still largely the basis of scientific study today. Bacon outlined an inductive method based on the direct observation of nature. Foreshadowing the Scientific Revolution of the seventeenth century, Francis Bacon believed that knowledge was the basis of power, as it would allow for human control of nature. Below are several of the aphorisms which made up the *Novum Organum*. As you read these statements, consider the challenge they presented to intellectuals of the seventeenth century and their continued importance for us as we approach the twenty-first century.

MAN, as the minister and interpreter of nature, does and understands as much as his observations on the order of nature, either with regard to things or the mind, permit him, and neither knows nor is capable of more.

Knowledge and human power are synonymous, since the ignorance of the cause frustrates the effect; for nature is only subdued by submission, and that which in contemplative philosophy corresponds with the cause in practical science becomes the rule.

Even the effects already discovered are due to chance and experiment, rather than to the sciences; for our present sciences are nothing more than peculiar arrangements of matters already discovered, and not methods for discovery or plans for new operations.

There is another powerful and great cause of the little advancement of the sciences, which is this: it is impossible to advance properly in the course when the goal is not properly fixed. But the real and legitimate goal of the sciences, is the endowment of human life with new inventions and riches. The great crowd of teachers know nothing of this, but consist of dictatorial hirelings: unless it so happen that some artisan of an acute genius, and ambitious of fame, gives up his time to a new discovery, which is generally attended with a loss of property. The majority, so far from proposing to themselves the augmentations of the mass of arts and sciences, make no other use of an inquiry into the mass already before them, than is afforded by the conversion of it to some use in their lectures, or to gain, or to the acquirement of a name, or the like.

Others with more cunning imagine and consider that, if secondary causes

be unknown, everything may more easily be referred to the Divine hand and wand, a matter, as they think, of the greatest consequence to religion, but which can only really mean that God wishes to be gratified by means of falsehood. Others fear, from past example, lest motion and change in philosophy should terminate in an attack upon religion. Lastly, there are others who appear anxious lest there should be something discovered in the investigation of nature to overthrow, or at least shake, religion, particularly among the unlearned. The two last apprehensions appear to resemble animal instinct, as if men were diffident, in the bottom of their minds and secret meditations, of the strength of religion and the empire of faith over the senses, and therefore feared that some danger awaited them from an inquiry into nature. But anyone who properly considers the subject will find natural philosophy to be, after the Word of God, the surest remedy against superstition, and the most approved support of faith. She is, therefore, rightly bestowed upon religion as a most faithful attendant, for the one exhibits the will and the other the power of God.

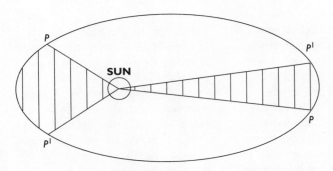

Kepler's second law of planetary motion is illustrated here.
P and P¹ are any two points on the orbit between which
the planet passes in equal lengths of time.

(Chambers, M. et al. *The Western Experience*, Vol. II (1991). Alfred A. Knopf, N.Y.
Reprinted with permission of McGraw-Hill, Inc.)

revolutionized art and religion through a rebirth of classicism and a focus on humanism, these changes would ultimately revolutionize science. Central to this revolution would be the use of experimentation to develop new scientific theories.

Among the first to challenge traditional views of the universe was a Polish scientist named **Nicolaus Copernicus**. His great work *On the Revolutions of the Celestial Spheres*, published in 1543, created quite a stir among many Europeans. Drawing inspiration from the work of Aristarchus of Samos (a Greek philosopher of the third century B.C.E.), Copernicus put forward the revolutionary idea of a heliocentric universe: the planets revolved around the sun rather than the earth. Copernicus's theory further suggested that the earth rotated on its own axis every 24 hours and that the moon revolved around the earth. As revolutionary as Copernicus's ideas were, he was in many ways quite a conservative thinker, basing his conclusions on philosophical deductions rather than astronomical observations.

Galileo Galilei, the great Florentine astronomer born in the late sixteenth century, gathered impressive astronomical evidence to support the ideas of Copernicus. The Church had declared the idea of a heliocentric universe to be "absurd in philosophy and formally heretical" and in 1616 placed Copernicus's book on its *Index* of banned books. Pope Paul V ordered Galileo not to teach or defend his theories. In defiance of the Church order, Galileo eventually published his findings in 1632, in a book entitled *Dialogue on the Two Chief Systems of the World*. Galileo's actions caused him to be brought before the **Holy Inquisition** (a Roman Catholic institution for punishing heretics), where he was coerced into recanting his beliefs, and was then confined to his house for life. The Church thus silenced one of the most brilliant astronomers of all times.

It required the genius of **Johannes Kepler** and **Isaac Newton** building upon the ideas of Copernicus and Galileo to finally arrive at an understanding of how the universe functions. Kepler was a German contemporary of Galileo. Convinced that Copernicus was right, Kepler observed planetary motion and mathematically formulated the laws that govern the solar system. Kepler thus arrived at three universal laws of planetary motion.

Kepler's first law states that planets move in elliptical orbits, with the sun at one focus of the ellipses. This law disproved Galileo's concept of circular orbits. Expressed in common language. Kepler's second law states that, as a planet draws closer to the sun, it moves faster; as it moves farther from the sun, it moves more slowly. The second law challenged the traditional notion that heavenly motion is steady and unchanging. Kepler's third law states the relationship among the movements of all planets as opposed to the motion of an individual planet. This law states that the square of the ratio of the time it takes any two planets to complete their orbit equals the cube of the ratio of these planets' average distance from the sun. This simply means that the size of a planet's orbit is proportional to the time required for one revolution around the sun.

Isaac Newton, an English scientist born in 1642, was to provide the great synthesis that would draw together the discoveries made during the preceding century. Incorporating into one coherent system the concepts of Copernicus, Galileo, and Kepler, Newton formulated his famous Three Laws of Motion: (I) if no force acts on an object, it will remain at rest or maintain its constant motion in a straight line; (II) every change of motion or acceleration of a body is directly proportional to the force that caused the change and inversely proportional to the object's mass; and (III) for every action force, there is an equal reaction force in the opposite direction.

Thus, the work begun in Poland by Copernicus, continued in Italy by Galileo, and in Germany by

Kepler, had been completed in England by Newton during the last two decades of the seventeenth century. All of Europe had witnessed a quiet revolution in ideas that would have a lasting and profound impact.

The Revolution in Anatomy

In the same year Copernicus published his famous work, the Belgian anatomist Andreas Vesalius published his *On the Structure of the Human Body*, a work that would revolutionize anatomy. Vesalius, through careful dissection of human bodies, discovered several errors in the work of Galen (the Greek anatomist of the second century B.C.E.) resulting from the fact that Galen had based his deductions on human anatomy on animal dissections. Vesalius, however, never completely abandoned Galen's theories.

Vesalius found that there were two kinds of blood in the body: venous and arterial. Venous blood, which was drawn into the right chamber of the heart and seeped through a thick wall (septum), was enriched by the "vital spirits" (of Galen) from the air before passing on to the arteries. As he could find no passageway through the septum, he concluded that the mighty power of God was able to make blood pass through the solid walls of the heart. In spite of these seemingly naïve thoughts, Vesalius remains a great anatomist of his time.

William Harvey, a brilliant English physician, was not satisfied with Vesalius resorting to divine power to explain the workings of the heart. The result of his work on the heart—much like Newton's—was to provide a synthesis of many of the ideas about human anatomy, which he published in *On the Motion of the Heart and Blood in Animals* in 1628. Harvey described the heart as a pump rather than as a filtration plant, as it had been traditionally described.

Harvey also discovered that in a single hour the heart pumped out more than a person's mass in blood and therefore the veins would burst if the blood was not somehow circulating. Harvey wrote: "I began to think whether there might not be a motion, as it were a circle." Despite its obvious logic, his discovery of the circulation of the blood would take almost half a century to win acceptance. Harvey's work opened up a whole new set of questions and problems regarding blood and human anatomy.

The Scientific Revolution was, in many ways, a watershed in European history. The new discoveries of scientists initially shocked European society, but they

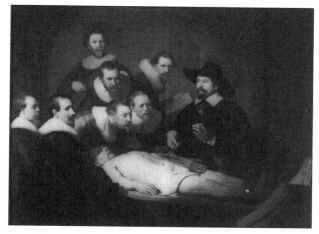

The work of scientists such as Vesalius and Harvey generated much public interest in the study of anatomy. This interest is reflected in Rembrandt's famous painting *The Anatomy Lesson of Dr. Nicolaes Tulp*.

laid the foundations for revolutions in politics, culture, and religion. The new ideas seemed to openly challenge the Bible. In the end, science and religion would be reconciled with God emerging as the great mechanic who had designed and built the intricate universe that humans were only beginning to understand.

The Age of Absolutism

The Scientific Revolution during the sixteenth and seventeenth centuries coincided with an equally important revolution in politics.

Louis XIV and Absolutism

The greatest ruler of the seventeenth century was ***Louis XIV***. He has often been portrayed as the incarnation of all that is bad, perhaps from our twentieth-century insistence on equality. We should set Louis XIV in the proper historical context so that we can better understand his actions.

Before studying the reign of Louis XIV, it is important to have a clear understanding of the concept of ***absolutism***. In the absolutist state, kings claimed to rule by divine right: they were accountable to no one but God. Absolutist monarchs were not limited in their actions by parliaments or representative bodies; they controlled all competing interest groups and regulated all religious sects. Crucial to the success of an absolute monarch was his ability to gain control over the nobility, which had historically posed the greatest threat to the crown.

Prior to the age of absolutism, European monarchs fought wars using temporary armies raised by feudal lords. Once the war was over, these soldiers would return to their occupations. Relying on the nobility for military support was always risky for medieval monarchs: it could lead to internal strife should the nobility withhold its support or challenge the monarchy. Absolute monarchs avoided such problems by creating permanent standing armies recruited, paid, and trained by the state. They also employed secret police to watch over potentially troublesome subjects.

Louis XIV is said to have exclaimed *"L'état, c'est moi!"* ("I am the state!") This phrase exemplifies the absolutist belief that the monarchy was a personification of the state; a concept best illustrated by the experience of France under the reign of Louis XIV.

Foundations of Absolutism in France

Louis XIV inherited rather than created absolutism. During the reign of his father, Louis XIII, **Cardinal Richelieu** was appointed to the council of ministers and, by 1628, had risen to be first minister of the French crown. Richelieu reflected the increasing secularization of the seventeenth century. Although a Roman Catholic bishop, his first loyalty was to the French state. Richelieu used his appointment and influence over the young king Louis XIII to promote the French monarchy as the embodiment of the French state. During his tenure as first minister, Richelieu laid the basis for French absolutism, thereby paving the way for French cultural domination in Europe in the late seventeenth century.

In an attempt to subordinate all groups to the French crown, Richelieu repeatedly challenged and alienated the nobility, levelling their castles and crushing aristocratic conspiracies with summary executions. To centralize control under the crown, Richelieu divided the country into 32 districts, each of which had a royal intendant with extensive powers over justice, the police, and finances. These intendants, drawn largely from the upper middle class or minor nobility, were appointed directly by the monarch to ensure that royal orders were enforced and that the power of the regional nobility was weakened.

Both Cardinal Richelieu and Louis XIII died in 1643 and were succeeded respectively by Jules Mazarin and the child-king Louis XIV. Mazarin's attempt to deal with the increasing financial problems of the crown by raising taxes led to the civil wars known as the Fronde (a word that means "slingshot" or "catapult" in French, and which came to mean "revolt"). When, in 1648, Mazarin attempted to increase government revenues, a bitter civil war broke out between the monarchy and the *frondeurs* (nobility and upper-middle-class). The violence continued intermittently for 12 years.

Perhaps the most important and lasting impact of the Fronde was the political education it provided the young Louis XIV. Louis never forgot the trauma he suffered as a young boy when he and his mother were threatened and at times treated as prisoners by aristocratic rebels. The 12 years of the Fronde convinced Louis that the only alternative to chaos and anarchy was absolute monarchy.

The Reign of the Sun King

During his long reign, 1643–1715, Louis XIV was able to take France to the pinnacle of absolutism, creating the most centralized nation-state in Europe, which gave birth to a new French sense of nationhood. Feudal regionalism and dominance of the Church were replaced with national pride. Louis XIV came to symbolize this new spirit of French culture and became the embodiment of the French state. The title of Sun King was appropriate: everything in France revolved around the person of Louis XIV.

Consolidating Power

When Louis XIV reached the age of 23, he began to centralize power under his control. He created a standing army, which was maintained in peacetime. In 1666, Louis appointed François le Tellier as secretary of war, who created the first modern army. Louis took personal command of the army and directly supervised all aspects and details of military affairs. The army created by le Tellier was modern not only in the sense that it was permanent and professional but also in its training and administration. Gone was the ancient practice of soldiers living off the countryside. This was replaced by a commissariat which was responsible for feeding the troops. Also, an ambulance corps was designed to look after the wounded, uniforms and weapons were standardized, and a rational system of recruitment, training, discipline, and promotion was put into place. This new military machine would allow France to dominate European politics for decades.

Louis XIV also moved quickly to centralize government. The day-to-day governing of France in the seventeenth century was largely carried out by three councils: the Court of State, the Court of Finances, and the Court of Dispatches, which was responsible for the administration of law. By presiding over all the councils and meeting with all high government officials at least once a week, Louis XIV retained absolute control over the government.

To ensure loyalty to himself at all levels of government, Louis XIV used bribery to guarantee that provincial governors sympathetic to the king were elected. He also reduced their term to three years so that any governors who were not loyal could not remain in power long enough to undermine his authority. Furthermore, Louis XIV insisted that all laws receive his approval before being passed. The bureaucracy created by Louis was staffed largely by the upper middle class, depriving the nobility of their traditional role in government. The modern bureaucratic state was born, dominated by middle-class professionals who were paid a salary by the government and whose loyalty was to the state.

Louis XIV's efforts to centralize power under the crown challenged the authority of the Catholic Church in France and a power struggle ensued, with the papacy maintaining its ascendancy. In 1682, Louis XIV produced four articles, which essentially stripped the papacy of its power in France. Eventually, the articles were annulled: Louis having made his point was now willing to return the power. The papacy would never again issue church laws pertaining to French social, political, or economic issues: Louis XIV had won control over the Catholic Church in France. Louis's next centralizing move, in 1685, was to revoke the Edict of Nantes (1598), in which Henri IV granted religious freedom to the Huguenots (French Protestants). More than religious intolerance, this move represented a manoeuvre to unite church and state under the leadership of the king.

The opulence and splendour of the court of Louis XIV are captured in this painting. The king (seated) is shown with his son, grandson, and great-grandson, all of whom Louis outlived.

Colbert's Economic Reforms

French absolutism owed much to the financial genius of *Jean-Baptiste Colbert*, who was appointed controller-general by Louis XIV. Colbert operated on the central principle of *mercantilism*, a system is which the government regulates economic activity based on the premise that international power is a product of its wealth. Colbert believed that France's economic success depended on self-sufficiency. He encouraged the creation of new domestic industries (such as silk, cotton, and tapestries) and discouraged imports of goods in an attempt to limit the export of money.

One of Colbert's greatest achievements was the creation of a powerful merchant marine which was crucial to ensure France's positive balance of trade. In 1661 France had only 18 seaworthy vessels but within 20 years it had 276 frigates, galleys, and ships. Many of these vessels were used to develop trade between France and its colonies in the Caribbean and North America. The Caribbean Islands supplied resources, such as sugar cane, while Canada was rich in minerals, fish, furs, and prime agricultural land.

Under Colbert, the colonization of New France was encouraged. In 1684, the French explorer Robert Cavelier de La Salle claimed the territories along the

During the reign of Louis XIV, the Palace of Versailles was in a state of perpetual expansion.

Mississippi and its delta for France; the territory was appropriately called Louisiana. Overseas colonies not only provided vital natural resources, they also were potential markets for manufactured French goods. When Jean Talon, the first and greatest intendant of New France (French possessions in the St. Lawrence, Great Lakes, and Mississippi Valley during Colbert's time), suggested means to help make the colony more self-sufficient by encouraging the establishment of local industry, he was rebuked by the crown for failing to understand the role the colony was to play in the French empire.

The primary goal of Colbert's domestic taxation policy was to provide more money for the royal treasury. By reducing income tax (paid by the rich) and increasing indirect taxes such as road tolls, milling, and shipping taxes, Colbert shifted the tax burden to the poor, believing if the rich had more money left in their pockets they would spend it on productive goods, thereby benefiting the French economy.

Colbert attempted to improve domestic trade by reducing internal tariffs. Each time a good crossed one of the numerous zones created by Louis XIV, a tariff was placed on it, making the cost of internally traded goods very expensive. (By the time a product crossed the country it would have been hit by 30 to 40 tariffs.) These tariffs were important sources of revenue for the

zones and consequently most of them refused to accept the reduced-tariff plan.

The Palace of Versailles

The *Palace of Versailles* stands today as a monument to the grandeur and absolutism of Louis XIV's reign. His desire to establish a new court that would reflect his power and prestige prompted him to build a palace on the outskirts of the small town of Versailles, about 30 km from Paris. No expense was spared during the building of Versailles, which took nearly 20 years to complete. The opulence of the palace was to reflect the power of the state.

Prior to the construction of Versailles, European palaces had been decorated with exquisite wood carvings. Versailles was to be different: wood was replaced with marble and gold, and the new French Provincial style was introduced, with white walls trimmed with gold paint. Elaborate tapestries adorned so many of the walls that a factory in Gobelins was created specifically to meet the needs of the new palace. The most famous room in the palace is the Hall of Mirrors. This stunning room, with mirrors covering one long wall, huge windows looking out on the famous gardens along the other wall, and dozens of chandeliers, became a symbol of French power. The palace contained an ornate two-story chapel decorated with baroque paintings and could house 900 members of the nobility.

The 365 hectares of gardens at Versailles, much like the palace, reflected the power of the king. The endless, manicured gardens, with their perfectly trimmed hedges and carefully sculpted fountains, created a seemingly perfect landscape: a reflection of the perfectibility possible under the rule of the Sun King. At Versailles, order and reason presumably reigned supreme, under the absolute rule of the king.

The grandeur of Versailles made it the envy of every European monarch; the goal of virtually all members of the French nobility was to live at the Palace of Versailles, which became one of Louis XIV's important tools in gaining control of the French nobility. By granting pensions and extending invitations to live at Versailles, the French aristocracy surrendered its power and accepted the absolute rule of the king. Versailles also welcomed French intellectuals, artists, musicians, and writers as visitors or dwellers. The construction of a magnificent palace thus helped to further Louis XIV's image as the embodiment of the French state.

Peter the Great: Russian Hero or Tyrant?

It is often said that history is largely the creation of those who write it. This certainly seems to be true when one reads the numerous and varying accounts of the role played by Peter the Great in Russian history. Some see him as a super-human hero who transformed Russia into a modern state; others maintain that the price paid in human costs was far too high. We seem to face a paradox in assessing the contributions of the absolute monarchs of the seventeenth and eighteenth centuries. What we can be certain of is that, during these two centuries, Russia turned from its feudal past to head down the road of Westernization. Peter's role in bringing about this transition was instrumental.

Peter the Great's reign began in 1682, when, at the age of ten, he was proclaimed the first czar of Russia. By 1696, with his mother and older half-brother both dead, Peter was able to establish himself as the absolute sovereign of Russia. Immediately, Peter set to work reforming Russia despite staunch opposition from his family, court circles, and government officials. Finding little support among the Russian elite, the czar chose to fill important posts based on merit rather than origin or rank.

Peter the Great believed firmly that Russian progress lay in developing closer ties with Western Europe. In March 1697, he sent a group of 250 Russians to visit numerous European countries where it was hoped they would learn a great deal of everything, from shipbuilding and navigation to crafts, technical skills, and manners. His interest in the West was so great that Peter the Great travelled abroad incognito as Peter Mikhailov. As a result of the 18 months spent abroad, the Russian emissaries not only learned a great deal but also managed to recruit over 750 foreigners to serve in Russia. Isaac Newton was among those who took up the czar's invitation to visit

Russia. Peter also realized the value in maintaining and developing ties with Eastern Europe and Asian countries. Young men were encouraged to learn Turkish, Persian, and even Japanese, and emissaries were sent to Mongolia and China.

Peter the Great's desire to westernize Russia can most clearly be seen in the educational and cultural reforms he implemented. Schools, such as the School of Mathematics and Navigation, were created to train specialists; the Academy of Sciences was created as the pinnacle of learning in Russia. Also, a minimum education was stressed for service in the czar's government and education became compulsory for the gentry. Peter also brought Western culture to Russia by encouraging Western dress and manners, often meeting with stiff resistance from the people. Perhaps the clearest sign of Peter's attempt to westernize Russia was his demand that beards be shaven "for the glory and comeliness of the state and the military profession."

Like all other absolute monarchs, Peter the Great faced the constant challenge of raising enough revenue to meet his needs. And, like all other absolute monarchs, he never found an effective method of raising revenues. Peter's only recourse was to raise taxes on the Russian masses who were already heavily overburdened. By adding new taxes or increasing existing taxes, 550 percent more was wrung from the Russian people in 1724 than in 1680. This was done by taxing almost everything, including beehives, mills, fisheries, bath houses, beards—even the number of corners in a house!

Peter the Great was ruthless with those who opposed him. Prior to his journey to the West, a group known as the *streltsy* (musketeer regiment in Moscow), plotted to depose Peter and put his more conservative elder half sister, Sophia, on the throne. Although the conspiracy was uncovered and defused, Peter had over one thousand *streltsy* tortured and executed and their bodies put

on display as a lesson to the public. His wife, Eudoxia, and his half sister, who had sympathized with the rebels because they defended tradition and religion, were forced to become nuns.

Probably the best summary of the changes brought to Russia by Peter the Great was penned by the Russian historian Mikhail Pogodin, who wrote:

Yes, Peter the Great did much for Russia....We cannot open our eyes, cannot make a move, cannot turn in any direction without encountering him everywhere...

We wake up. What day is today? January 1, 1841—Peter the Great ordered us to count years from the birth of Christ....

It is time to dress—our clothing is made according to the fashion established by Peter the First, our uniform according to his model. The cloth is woven in a factory which he created; the wool is shorn from the sheep which he started to raise.

A book strikes our eyes—Peter the Great introduced this script and himself cut out the letters. You begin to read it—this language became a written language, a literary language, at the time of Peter the First, superseding the earlier church language.

Newspapers are brought in—Peter the Great introduced them.

At dinner, all the courses, from salted herring, through potatoes which he ordered grown, to wine made from grapes which he began to cultivate, will speak to you of Peter the Great.

Let us go to the university—the first secular school was founded by Peter the Great.

You decide to travel abroad—following the example of Peter the Great; you will be received well—Peter the Great placed Russia among the European states and began to instill respect for her....

Louis XIV's Legacy

By the time Louis XIV died in 1715, after an amazing 73-year reign, France had become an extremely strong nation-state. Feudal lords and the Catholic Church had surrendered much of their power to the king. France had gained the stature of Europe's leading cultural and military power and a strong sense of nationhood had emerged: people saw themselves as French rather than as from a particular region. Also, by 1715, France had established an extensive overseas empire that provided the resources and markets to make France an economic power. But one problem would continue to haunt the French crown: debt. Financing numerous wars, paying a professional army, pensions to the nobility, and maintaining the elaborate court at Versailles put a strain on the royal treasury. The increasing tax burden of the lower classes would create a crisis in the eighteenth century that the monarchy could not survive.

England:
The Anti-Absolutist State

In sharp contrast to the absolute monarchy of France and other European states, England, by 1688, was governed by a constitutional monarchy, in which Parliament had achieved supremacy over the crown. Many blame the crown's loss of power on the incompetence of the Stuart kings who ruled for the first half of the seventeenth century but the Tudor monarchs of the sixteenth century were responsible as well.

As early as 1529, Henry VIII was forced to appeal to Parliament for support in his struggle against the papacy over his divorce. This elevated the power of Parliament and set a precedent in English government. Henry's daughter, Elizabeth I, failed to deal with the rise of Puritanism (which challenged the state religion), thus failing to establish the religious unity Louis XIV had managed to secure in France. Elizabeth was forced repeatedly to ask Parliament for tax increases to finance Britain's ongoing war with Spain, and Parliament was becoming increasingly reluctant to comply.

Finally, the absence of a standing army left the monarchy dependent on the questionable loyalty of the militia, which was controlled by the nobility.

Consequently, when James I came to the throne in 1603, England was essentially an absolute state governed by a constitutional monarchy. The struggle between the crown and Parliament for supremacy would dominate English politics for most of the seventeenth century.

The Reign of James I

James I (also James VI of Scotland), son of Mary Queen of Scots, inherited the English throne when his cousin Elizabeth died childless in 1603. The financial problems he inherited as well as his lavish spending habits soon led to a crisis and James was forced to appeal to Parliament for an increase in taxes of 1 million pounds. When Parliament granted an increase of only £200 000, James was forced to look for other methods to increase revenues. James I renewed long-forgotten dues that required people to pay the crown in order for their children to marry, angering the common folk; he sold titles (such as baron, earl, and duke), angering the nobility; he sold monopolies, angering the merchants; and he devised a plan to force people to lend money to the crown or face a fine.

James I also projected a negative image among the people: he was known to be very bright, but fascinated with witches (he wrote a book entitled *Demonology*); he was known to be lazy; it was said that he lavished money on court favourites. His reputation earned him the title of "the wisest fool in Christendom." During his 22-year reign, James was in constant conflict with Parliament over his policies. Under his son Charles, the conflict would escalate.

Charles I and the English Civil War

When ***Charles I*** came to the throne in 1625, his stubborn nature and refusal to compromise quickly earned him Parliament's dislike and led to a debate on the constitutional powers of the crown and Parliament. Parliament's refusal to grant the tax increases requested by Charles led to what is known as the Eleven Years of Tyranny. In 1629, Charles I suspended Parliament, bringing England the closest it would ever come to absolutism. The ongoing war in Ireland had drained the treasury to the point where Charles, in 1640, was forced to recall Parliament for its support to finance the war.

Once Parliament was recalled, Charles I was forced to deal with hostile and rebellious parliamentarians who attempted to thwart the king's endeavours to raise money. After two years of continual conflicts, Charles I stormed Parliament with 1500 horsemen in an attempt to arrest his major opponents in the House of Commons. Most of the parliamentarians managed to escape through the windows and were able to gather support for the civil war that soon erupted. From 1643 to 1649, Royalists (supporters of the monarchy) and Roundheads (supporters of Parliament) battled for control of the government. In 1646, Charles I was captured by the parliamentarians, who attempted to negotiate with him but he stubbornly refused to compromise. Feeling they had no alternative, the parliamentarians charged Charles I with treason. On January 30, 1649 the English king Charles I was beheaded.

Following the execution of Charles I, England was governed as a parliamentary republic from 1649 to 1658, under the leadership of Oliver Cromwell. The government put in place in 1649 was not radically different from the previous one except for the absence of a monarch. Divisions among parliamentarians over issues such as control of the army and religious toleration left England a divided nation. Cromwell refused the crown when it was offered to him and his death in 1658 left England without a ruler. Despite the honourable efforts of his son, Richard, his lack of experience failed to earn him the respect and following of the English people.

Finally, frustrated by disunity, Charles II, son of the beheaded Charles I, who sought refuge in France, was invited back to the throne 11 years after his father's execution. But the terms of the invitation made it impossible for him or any English monarch to pass laws or raise revenues without Parliament's approval. Accepting his role as a constitutional monarch, Charles II ruled effectively despite his known pro-French and pro-Catholic feelings.

James II came to the throne on 1685 following the death of his brother (Charles II). He immediately made it known that he intended to restore the Roman Catholic faith and revive the power of the English monarch. This tactless and confrontational behaviour alienated the English people and prompted a group of prominent citizens to oppose him. The Dutch monarch, William of Orange, who had a claim to the throne through marriage to his wife, Mary, was asked by the parliamentarians to invade England and seize the throne. William entered England at the head of 15 000 troops and James II fled to Europe without offering any resistance. This event, during which not a single shot was fired, has come to be known as the Glorious Revolution. William and Mary accepted the crown of England as constitutional monarchs and governed jointly. To ensure that no future monarch would attempt to govern without Parliament, the English passed the Bill of Rights in 1689, which outlined the powers and rights of Parliament: "That the pretended power of suspending of laws, or the execution of laws, by regal [royal] authority, without consent of Parliament, is illegal."

Whereas France and other European states had developed into absolute monarchies by the end of the seventeenth century, English government had evolved to the point where the monarchy would play a limited and increasingly symbolic role in favour of Parliament, which gained supreme power.

Reflections

The revolutionary changes in science, politics, religion, and culture that took place between 1400 and 1715 transformed Europe from a warring feudal society into a series of modern nation-states. The renewed emphasis on humans and human achievement allowed for tremendous intellectual and artistic growth while challenging the individual's relationship to God, place in the universe, and loyalty to the crown. By the early eighteenth century, Europe's interaction with cultures around the world and its own revolutions at home had laid the foundations for radical future changes that would reshape the Western world.

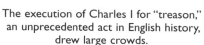

The execution of Charles I for "treason," an unprecedented act in English history, drew large crowds.

Key Concepts, Figures, and Events

Martin Luther   Johannes Kepler   Cardinal Richelieu
Thirty Years' War   Isaac Newton   Jean-Baptiste Colbert
Nicolaus Copernicus   William Harvey   Palace of Versailles
Galileo Galilei   Louis XIV   Charles I
Holy Inquisition   Absolutism

Topics for Further Thought

1. The Renaissance was an era quite different from the centuries which preceded it. How were the attitudes and ideals of the Renaissance different from the medieval age? What evidence is there in our society that Renaissance ideals continue to have an influence?

2. From the end of the Middle Ages through our own century, a common theme in Western civilization has been the increasing secularization of society. To what degree do you think religion limited scientific and intellectual growth in the sixteenth and seventeenth centuries? How did some intellectuals attempt to reconcile science and religion?

3. The Palace of Versailles was more than the grandest palace in Europe, it was a symbol of the power of Louis XIV. How did the architecture and landscaping at Versailles reflect the concept of absolutism? Do you think moving the court from Paris to Versailles was an astute political decision? Explain and support your answer.

4. During the seventeenth century, Europe was governed by monarchs. By the beginning of the twentieth century, virtually all of Europe's monarchs had fallen. Today, Britain is one of the few remaining monarchies. Has the longevity of the British monarchy resulted from the limits placed on it by the constitution? Do you think the British monarchy would also have eventually fallen had the kings of the seventeenth century established absolute rule?

Topics for Further Research

1. The Reformation splintered Christianity into many factions. Research one of the following leaders of the Reformation and prepare a brief biographical sketch and an assessment of his role in the Reformation.

John Calvin   Ulrich Zwingli
Martin Luther   Menno Simons

2. The Thirty Years' War had widespread impact on the people of Europe. Research the contributions and/or impact of the war by the following individuals or countries:

Sweden   France
Gustavus II Adolphus   Prussia

3. The economic policies of Colbert would be challenged in later centuries by prominent economists such as Adam Smith. Prepare a summary of the economic policies advocated by Colbert. Conduct research into current economic theory and compare your research to Colbert's policies. Were his policies sound for increasing the wealth of the French nation-state? You may want to speak to the school's economics teacher before doing your research.

4. In this chapter, you have read about the absolute rule of Louis XIV of France and the anti-absolutist government of England. Using what you have learned about these countries as a framework, research one of the following countries. Explain the nature of its government, culture, and society.

Spain	The Netherlands
Russia	Austria
Sweden	Prussia

Responding to Ideas

1. Following the Reformation, for one century Europe was ravaged by numerous religious wars. Peace was finally restored in 1648 with the Treaty of Westphalia, which established the sovereignty of nations. For 350 years, the Treaty of Westphalia has shaped international politics. Now, as the twentieth century draws to a close, interventionism seems to be replacing the concept of exclusive sovereignty. To what degree might a shift away from the principles set out in the Treaty of Westphalia benefit the world and to what degree might it create new dangers?

2. One of Louis XIV's biographers, François Bluche, wrote in the prologue to *Louis XIV*: "Voltaire, a great man, had no difficulty in identifying the greatness in Louis XIV. 'It must be acknowledged,' he tells us, 'that Louis always had a sense of exaltation in his soul, which drove him to great things'. This sense of greatness has been much denigrated in these times of ours, obsessed as they are by an illusion of equality and indulgent of instincts for levelling." Does Louis XIV deserve credit for shaping the history of Europe or was he a product of his age?

2

The Enlightenment, 1700 – 1789

CHAPTER HIGHLIGHTS

- Living standards, population growth, and advances in agriculture

- The nature of class structure, dynasticism, and the aspirations of the nobility after the death of Louis XIV

- The attempt by European nations to achieve a balance of power and their inability to sustain peace

- The change in intellectual and religious outlook

The period before the outbreak of the French Revolution in 1789 is commonly called the *ancien régime*; the term is also used when referring to prerevolutionary Europe. Politically, it refers to government by absolute monarchies supported by aristocratically led armies. Socially, the *ancien régime* meant a rigid class hierarchy dominated by aristocratic elites with hereditary privileges. In prerevolutionary Europe, the urban labour force was organized into **guilds**; the rural labour force consisted of the peasantry, which was subject to heavy feudal dues.

Economically, the *ancien régime* relied on overseas colonies to enrich state treasuries. Otherwise, the hallmarks of the early eighteenth century were scarcity of food, a low level of iron production, and rudimentary financial institutions.

Eighteenth-century European society was, for the most part, very conservative and focused on the past. But there were forces at work which, by the end of the century, would bring sweeping changes. In Britain, France, and Holland, a growing middle class would emerge as an agent of political and economic change. A rising population would create enormous pressures on the food supply, jobs, and available land, leading to heightened tensions among the classes. Leading intellectuals would lay the foundations for political, economic, and social change in Europe.

In this chapter, we will examine the forces that converged in 1789 to bring about one of the most significant revolutions in European history. By the end of the eighteenth century, Europe would have made a definite break with its past to be hurled forward into a modern age.

European Society in the Eighteenth Century

Population Growth

An important feature of eighteenth-century Europe was the steady rise in population, which went largely undetected due to the lack of accurate record-keeping and calculations that we have in the twentieth century. It is estimated that Europe's population stood at approximately 100 million in 1700. A century later, the population is estimated to have grown to 190 million; by 1850, it had reached 260 million.

A decline in the number of deaths, combined with large rural families led to a rapidly expanding population. Why? On the one hand, there were fewer wars and fewer epidemics in the eighteenth century than in previous centuries. As well, improved hygiene and sanitation led to a decline in fatal illnesses. On the other hand, there was an improved food supply: changes in methods of agricultural production increased grain production, and the introduction of the potato from South America provided a stable food supply. On a single hectare, enough potatoes could be grown to feed a family for one year. Europeans were now able to support larger families.

The rise in population led to increased demands for food, jobs, goods, and services. More people came to live in the countryside than the countryside could sustain, leading to migration to towns and cities. The population explosion also produced an increasingly larger body of socially and politically discontented people. As these pressures and demands grew, the *ancien régime* literally outgrew its bounds, paving the way for a revolution that would shake traditional European society to its very foundations.

Land Use and Agriculture

In eighteenth-century Europe, most of the population lived in small villages and worked the land. However, the nature of agriculture was not the same: the climate, especially rainfall, determined what could be grown successfully. Southern Europe tends to be dry, with sparse rain for several months of the year. Coastal areas of Northern Europe have a much higher annual rainfall, allowing for more intensive agriculture.

As well as by climate, agriculture was affected by the managerial skills of landowners. The use of natural fertilizers and the rotation of crops to replenish the soil were practised; however, yields were still low.

Many estates belonged to aristocrats who spent much of their lives at court. They appointed agents to manage their estates and were often uninterested in the details of daily agricultural practice. Farms owned by resident farmers were generally better managed. Small farms or mere scraps of land that might not provide for one family were held by poorer peasants. There were also day labourers who owned no land or who were permitted to grow some crops for their own consumption on condition that they work for somebody else.

Over the course of the eighteenth century, agriculture was becoming increasingly commercialized, especially on large estates, as landlords sought ways to earn more profits from their land. Most of the agricultural innovations had their origins in England and the Netherlands, where landlords were willing to experiment and finance the experiments of others. English agriculturalist Jethro Tull (1674–1741), for example, introduced the use of the steel plow, which overturned the soil more deeply, and the seed drill, which improved planting. Charles Townsend learned from the Dutch how to utilize sandy soils by applying fertilizers. He also instituted a new system of crop rotation using turnips, barley, wheat, and clover. Using this method, no field was left fallow; instead, crops that produced feed for livestock and replenished the soil were rotated. As a result of this innovation, there was more food available for both animals and human beings. These and several other agricultural innovations created what has become known as the ***Agricultural Revolution***. Although its origins lie in the Netherlands

Censorship has long been an issue in Western society. Here, magicians burn their books as St. Paul looks on with the Bible in hand.

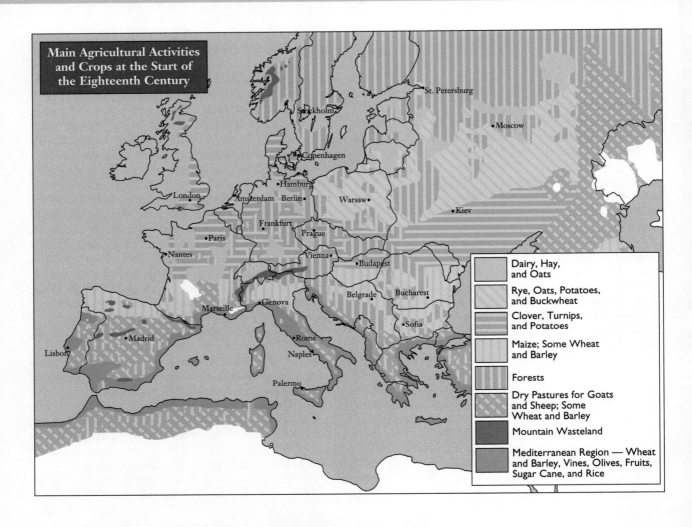

Main Agricultural Activities and Crops at the Start of the Eighteenth Century

Legend:
- Dairy, Hay, and Oats
- Rye, Oats, Potatoes, and Buckwheat
- Clover, Turnips, and Potatoes
- Maize; Some Wheat and Barley
- Forests
- Dry Pastures for Goats and Sheep; Some Wheat and Barley
- Mountain Wasteland
- Mediterranean Region — Wheat and Barley, Vines, Olives, Fruits, Sugar Cane, and Rice

and Great Britain, the impact of this revolution would extend throughout Europe.

Innovations in agriculture led to radical changes in land distribution. For example, in areas where small strips of land were held by poor peasants, it was virtually impossible to coordinate the kind of crop rotation introduced by Townsend. In some areas of Europe and throughout Britain, landlords, intent on earning higher profits from their land, abandoned the centuries-old system of land division. Exercising their right to control land previously rented to peasants, many landlords by the mid-eighteenth century began reclaiming common land and rented strips, creating large fenced-in block fields. This movement by landlords to consolidate their

land is known as *enclosure*. The fields were then farmed using more efficient and profitable methods of agriculture, with the aim of producing a surplus to be sold on the open market. This often resulted in riots and caused much economic and social strife in the countryside.

The Agricultural Revolution and the enclosure movement were most common in Europe west of the Elbe River. Britain and the Netherlands led the way in agricultural reform, while France led the way in agricultural improvement but practised limited enclosure. In Prussia, Austria, Poland, and Russia the great landlords did little to improve agricultural production, choosing to squeeze more labour from the serfs rather than productivity from the soil.

Politics and Dynasticism in Eighteenth-Century Europe

In 1715, more than seven out of ten West Europeans still lived in a world of rural concerns over crops and **tithes** (one tenth of one's income for the Church), the health of livestock, and changes in the climate. Much of the land of the European continent was owned by nobles, members of privileged families who believed themselves to be superior to farmers and merchants because they claimed to be descendants of warriors. In an age of generalized violence and vague notions of international law, those who won in battle received generous rewards from the monarchs. Nobles enjoyed profits from the crops and other products of the land, and demanded obedience from those who worked on their property.

While some peasant farmers owned their land, many others paid rent to a noble, or worked for wages on land owned by religious institutions or a middle-class landowner. In much of Central and Eastern Europe, peasants could not legally negotiate the price of their labour: they were serfs, not free to move away from designated areas without permission of the land-lord. Serfs were obliged by law to provide labour—sometimes as much as four or five days per week—to the owner.

When Louis XIV died in 1715, most of Europe was governed by monarchs who presided over an empire or kingdom in which nobles enjoyed privileges as landowners, judges, officials, and military officers. Although kings and emperors bestowed nobility titles, they were often unhappy with the nobility's greed and demands for protection of their privileges. The eighteenth century saw a broad weakening of the social authority of nobles in many parts of Europe, especially in France. The French Revolution (1789) ended the absolutist monarchy in France and dealt a final blow to the privileges of the nobility.

Government in the Eighteenth Century

At the beginning of the eighteenth century, Europe was mainly a patchwork of kingdoms and states comprised of the subjects, or vassals, who owed allegiance to a ruling family known as a dynasty. This family provided a form of hereditary rule by the eldest son. Loyalty to the dynasty and its religion was the basis of political and social existence beyond the immediate linkage of family to its locality. In their proclamations to their subjects, rulers frequently invoked obedience, talking of paternal concern for children.

The idea of a nation-state, which would demand unwavering loyalty from its citizens, would come in the nineteenth century. European politics in the eighteenth century were still largely a matter of the dynastic ambitions of powerful ruling families served by nobles. Much attention was given to military strength and the funds to pay for it. Not much attention was given to public opinion, except in Britain and Holland, where there were effective representative assemblies under a constitutional monarchy.

The entourage of the ruler, the royal court, was the place where the ambitious wished to be admitted in order to get power and rewards. Rulers were human and obviously fallible: a favourite today could be disgraced tomorrow. Rulers could be children with limited authority, they could become sick, or even insane, like George III of Great Britain (who ruled from 1760 to 1792) or Queen Maria I of Portugal (who ruled from 1777 to 1792). The royal courts of the eighteenth century were cauldrons of personal intrigue where the nobility jockeyed for favouritism with an eye on the heir to the throne. Monarchies were neither public nor accountable institutions; rather, they were constrained by tradition, religious morality and, to some extent, by obedience to legal precedents. They could also be arbitrary and impetuous.

Royal courts were a cultural model of elegance and luxury in which aristocratic women played a significant role. The French court at Versailles was imitated by lesser rulers. The court setting was a splendid palace decorated with chandeliers, mirrors, and gilt carvings to trumpet the magnificence and glory of the sovereign. It was also the home of many individuals with the time and education to address matters of general social concern.

The death of the Sun King Louis XIV, in September 1715, at 76, marked the end of an era. Hardly any of those he ruled over were old enough to remember conditions before his reign. He was followed by a regent, who ruled on behalf of the infant great grandson who was to be the new king Louis XV (and rule from 1723 to 1774). The Regency (1715–1722), while Louis was too young to rule, was a time of desire for novelty and change.

The Lisbon Earthquake

 Beginning at 9:30 a.m. on November 1, 1755, one of the greatest natural catastrophes in the history of modern Europe occurred. Known as the Lisbon Earthquake, the disaster lasted only about 10 minutes, but in the end would account for the destruction of much of Lisbon and the death of thousands of people. The earthquake that struck was actually three distinct shocks, each separated by about an interval of one minute. By the end of the three shocks, the bright, sunny day had been transformed into a hellish nightmare as a cloud of suffocating dust settled and numerous fires broke out around the city. To complete the disaster, one hour after the three shocks, the waters of the Tagus River poured over their banks, wreaking further havoc and destruction on the city of Lisbon. In the end, it is estimated that between 30 000 and 40 000 people lost their lives as a result of the Lisbon Earthquake and the resulting fires. Numerous people died seeking refuge in churches which came to be engulfed in the ensuing fires that were fanned by a northeast wind and lasted nearly a week.

Prior to the earthquake, Lisbon had been a staggeringly rich city, made wealthy by its leading role in commercial overseas trade. Unfortunately, the fires resulting from the earthquake consumed much of the wealth that might have otherwise been recovered. The extent of the losses suffered are illustrated by the loss suffered by the Marquês de Louriçal. At his palace were lost 200 paintings including works by Titian and Rubens; a library of 18 000 books, 1000 original manuscripts, and a vast collection of maps and charts of Portuguese voyages of discovery.

The terror experienced by the Portuguese on All Saints Day of 1755 would not soon be forgotten. Attempts to rebuild the city and put the disaster behind them would be hampered by the numerous aftershocks, estimated at 30 in the week following and up to 500 over the next year. The horror of the catastrophe suffered by Lisbon on that fateful day is captured in a poem by Voltaire from which the following extract is taken.

OH WRETCHED man, earth-fated to be cursed;
Abyss of plagues, and miseries the worst!
Horrors on horrors, griefs on griefs must show,
That man's the victim of unceasing woe,
And lamentations which inspire my strain,
Prove that philosophy is false and vain.
Approach in crowds, and meditate awhile
Yon shattered walls, and view each ruined pile,
Women and children heaped up mountain high,
Limbs crushed which under ponderous marble lie;
Wretches unnumbered in the pangs of death,
Who mangled, torn, and panting for their breath,
Buried beneath their sinking roofs expire,
And end their wretched lives in torments dire.
Say, when you hear their piteous, half-formed cries,
Or from their ashes see the smoke arise,
Say, will you then eternal laws maintain,
Which God to cruelties like these constrain?
Whilst you these facts replete with horror view,
Will you maintain death to their crimes was due?
And can you then impute a sinful deed
To babes who on their mother's bosoms bleed?
Was then more vice in fallen Lisbon found,
Than Paris, where voluptuous joys abound?
Was less debauchery to London known,
Closes my life, worms shall my flesh devour.

Europe after Louis XIV

At the death of Louis XIV, the main family "teams" in the struggle to increase territories and wealth were the Spanish Bourbons, the French Bourbons, the Hanoverians in Britain, the Habsburgs in Central Europe, with their capital in Vienna, and the Romanovs in Russia, with their capital in Moscow soon to move to Saint Petersburg. One of the newest contending teams was the Hohenzollern family of Prussia, whose head had only recently (1701) been recognized as a king by the Holy Roman Emperor. The whole of Southeastern Europe was particularly conscious of a great non-Christian power, that of the Ottomans, with their capital in Constantinople. The Ottomans were overlords of much of the Balkans and also the Middle East and North Africa. There were smaller European dynasties in existence, like the Braganza family that ruled in Portugal, the House of Savoy in Northern Italy and the Bourbons of Naples, the Orange family in the Netherlands, the Wasa in Stockholm, and the families who ruled in the small German states. These smaller dynasties could not provoke the major dynasties without great danger to themselves. They constantly sought to make alliances with the major states or to profit from opportunities from unforeseen events, victories, or defeats.

Major Arenas of European Conflict During the Eighteenth Century

The years 1715 to 1815 saw the emergence of the cluster of great powers that would dominate nineteenth-century Europe. Above all, Russia became a major power in Eastern Europe and German-speaking Prussia grew in importance in Central Europe. Britain and France fought a global duel for control of the seas, which Britain won. Although overextended, Austria remained influential in Central European politics. The Southern European monarchies of Spain, Portugal, and the Italian states were of little weight. The Dutch, Danes, and Swedes were also now secondary powers. A number of smaller states disappeared as they were absorbed into larger units, like Weimar in the German states. However, the great powers were too closely matched in resources and strength to be able to ignore the lesser states and they made frequent overtures to them for collaboration.

French Hegemony Thwarted

Louis XIV wished to extend his authority in Europe. In response to his aspirations, an alliance of the British, Dutch, and others was formed, leading to battles in Northwestern Europe. In 1704, the Duke of Marlborough, commander of an Anglo-Dutch army, won a great victory over French and Bavarian opponents. In the same year, the British navy fighting in the Mediterranean captured Gibraltar and, in 1708, the Mediterranean island of Minorca. Although the French and Spanish fleets had been outclassed by their Anglo-Dutch adversaries at sea, the maritime allies could not prevail in land war in Spain.

After prolonged negotiations, the Peace of Utrecht was signed in April 1713. Under this treaty, the Bourbon king of Spain, Philip V, (who ruled from 1700 to 1746) kept his throne and the Spanish empire but he ceded both Gibraltar and Minorca to Britain and he renounced any claim for himself or his descendants to the French throne.

The Treaty of Utrecht had implications beyond Europe: Louis XIV returned Hudson Bay to Britain and gave up Acadia (Nova Scotia) as well as claims to Newfoundland and the Caribbean island of Saint Kitts. The British received an annual contract, the *Asiento*, to provide the Spanish empire with slaves, an agreement later extended to the Austrian emperor.

Austria was now a power balanced between its interests in Eastern Europe, especially the Balkans and the frontier lands held by the Turkish **Ottoman Empire**, and those in Central and Western Europe, especially Italy and the German states. By the Treaty of Karlowitz (1699), the Turks had already given up most of Hungary and Transylvania to Austria. The war of 1716–1718 led the Turks to surrender Northern Serbia to Austria. Some Austrian gains were lost in the 1730s but the extension of Habsburg authority over new possessions made Austria one of the great European powers on land, a position it would enjoy until World War I.

Eighteenth-century diplomats gave no thought to the wishes of local populations as they discussed land grabs, takeovers, and changes in rulers. However, representatives of the great powers were attentive to the balance of power: their primary aim was to ensure that no one European power should eliminate the others.

By the early decades of the eighteenth century, three powers dominated Europe: Great Britain had become the foremost naval power, Austria had become a formidable land force, and France had acquired

considerable strength both on land and at sea. The British navy, which had achieved supremacy over any maritime rivals in the Atlantic by the mid-1700s, was being challenged by the French, who tried to rebuild their war fleet. By 1739, France had 50 major warships and Britain had 80. Despite the rivalry, there were no serious conflicts in the 1720s and 1730s between the two countries. Conflict between Britain and France did loom over their trading and colonial interests overseas. In an effort to protect its overseas interests, Britain allied itself with France's continental adversary: Austria. Meanwhile, France found support in the other dominant Germanic power: Prussia. Consequently, despite the absence of open conflict, the first half of the eighteenth century was a period of uneasy peace in Europe.

War of the Austrian Succession

The European calm of the early eighteenth century was broken when Maria Theresa became the new Austrian Empress in 1740. The young king of Prussia, Frederick II—better known as Frederick the Great—reacted to her ascension to the throne by overrunning the valued Austrian province of Silesia. Despite various efforts, the Austrians were never able to force Frederick to give up his conquest. This conflict was the first in a series of major European conflicts in the eighteenth century. The ensuing war, which pitted the Anglo-Austrian troops against Franco-Bavarian and Prussian troops, is known as the War of the Austrian Succession.

Peace of Aix-la-Chapelle

The 1748 Peace of Aix-la-Chapelle confirmed the state of affairs in much of Europe. Abroad, the British exchanged Madras in India to get the Louisbourg fortress in Canada from the French. There was to be an undeclared war in North America as the French and British tried to map out their boundaries and zones of authority. Also, at this time both France and Britain entered agreements with Amerindian groups in North America to fight their enemies. Britain, egged on by greedy American colonists, seized many French ships and was aggressive in its response to French diplomacy. This ongoing hostility erupted into open war in 1756.

Seven Years' War: A World War

Meanwhile, in Europe, old alliances changed in response to new rulers and ambitions. In early 1756, Britain and Prussia signed an agreement not to attack each other; then France and Austria signed a defensive alliance. In June of that year, France seized the Mediterranean island of Minorca, which was under British occupation; in August, Prussian troops of Frederick the Great invaded Saxony (a great military success but a diplomatic failure since it united the Austrians and Russians against him). However, Frederick did not give up Silesia, which he had snatched from Austria. Despite a desperate series of battles, the Prussian state survived undefeated. Thus, Europe's major naval and land-based powers were pitted against each other in a war that would have worldwide repercussions, especially for North America.

The *Seven Years' War* was caused by Britain's efforts to strengthen its global naval supremacy and by Russia's expansion in Eastern Europe. It was the first war in which conflicts between two European powers—the French and the British—were fought outside the Continent: in North America, West Africa, the Caribbean, and India. In India, Robert Clive's forces prevailed over the French at Plassey (NW India) in 1757. The result was a steady build-up of British influence over the fractious Indian rulers in the centre of the Subcontinent. In Canada, many strategic points were captured by the British between 1758 and 1762: Louisbourg, Quebec City, and Montreal.

The global nature of the Seven Years' War is evident in the events leading up to the fall of New France. In September 1759, while Generals James Wolfe and Louis Joseph de Montcalm were locked in battle on the Plains of Abraham near Quebec City, two major battles took place: one near Lagos (in Portugal) and the other at Quiberon Bay (in France), which decimated the French fleet on the Atlantic and established the clear supremacy of the British fleet. The removal of the French from the Atlantic cut off the supply line of French troops in New France, thus sealing the fate of New France.

As a result of the loss of a strong navy, the French also lost coastal trading posts in West Africa, disrupting the shipment of African slaves to the West Indian sugar islands. Guadeloupe, Martinique, and other West Indian islands were also seized by the British following the French naval losses at Lagos and Quiberon Bay.

Treaty of Paris

Peace was made in February 1763 at Paris. At the diplomatic table, France showed little interest in reclaiming New France, choosing instead to retain only the small islands of St. Pierre and Miquelon, off Newfoundland, and secure the return of Guadeloupe. The great French writer Voltaire scoffed at the English for relinquishing the rich Guadeloupe to keep the vast but non-productive New France, claiming that they had won nothing more than a land of ice and snow. French colonists who remained after the Treaty of Paris were abandoned by France and would have to rely on themselves to preserve their culture and heritage. This struggle for cultural preservation continues to this day in the form of Quebec nationalism and the sovereignty movement.

In India, France retained only a few coastal trading posts in a zone of clear British influence. France

The emphasis on rational thought is reflected in the orderly design of Bath, England. These townhouses were built during the eighteenth century.

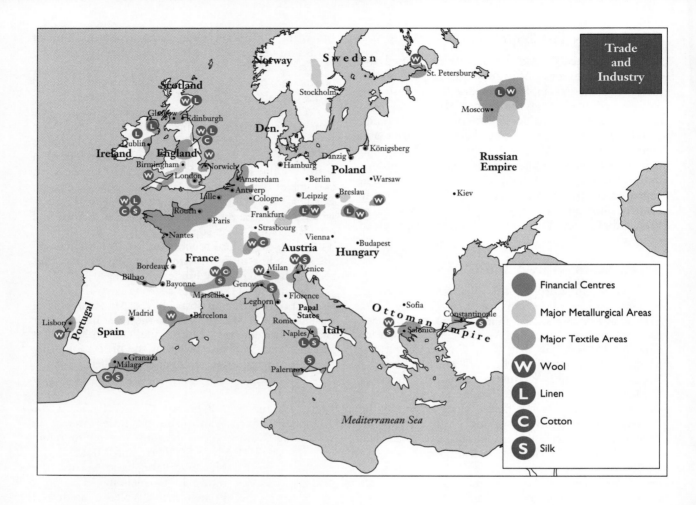

Turks and Poles

From 1763 until the French Revolution in 1789, the major international concerns of France, Spain, and Britain had little to do with Eastern Europe. British attention was fixed on its American colonies in open rebellion (they would ultimately succeed in securing their independence after the American Revolution).

In Eastern Europe, Russia, Prussia, and Austria were intent on grabbing land from weaker neighbours. Poland lost a third of its territory at the time of the first partition (1772–1773). Russia was expanding into Siberia and Central Asia. By the treaty of Kutchuk-Kainardji of 1774, Turkey also lost land and influence to Russia in the Black Sea. That treaty ended a Russo-Turkish war that had raged from 1768. Russia kept up a steady pressure against the *Sublime Porte*, as the Turkish Ottoman Government was called. Catherine II of Russia annexed the Crimean peninsula in 1783, giving Russia a powerful naval base on the Black Sea from which to menace the Ottoman capital of Constantinople.

The Russo-Turkish War of 1787–1792 was an unsuccessful attempt by the Turks to strike back against the relentless Russian expansionism into Southeastern Europe. By the Treaty of Jassy (1792)

did manage to keep the valuable West Indian sugar islands. From a global perspective, the Seven Years' War marked the maritime supremacy of the British navy.

Russia further secured its position at Ottoman expense on the northern shore of the Black Sea.

By the 1780s, the balance of power within Continental Europe was not significantly altered from that of 20 years earlier. Russia and Austria now looked toward Poland and the Balkans for their territorial expansion. Despite several major conflicts little change in European boundaries had occurred. But significant changes had occurred on the high seas, where Britain had clearly established itself as the dominant power, a position it would capitalize on during the next century, when nearly 25 percent of the globe's surface would come under British control.

The Enlightenment

In the eighteenth century, vessels moved by the force of the wind or the muscle power of human rowers; animals dragged wheeled passenger vehicles much as they had since Roman times. It still took weeks to move from one side of Europe to the other, and months to cross oceans. Eighteenth-century minds, however, moved more freely than travellers: a change of outlook, known as the *Enlightenment*, was fundamental to modern secular thought about the relations between the individual and society.

Most people thought of their own needs and those of their loved ones; however, there were also those who thought of the welfare of society as a whole. In medieval times, those who transmitted the message of morality and compassion were the clergy. During the Renaissance and Reformation, increasing numbers of educated individuals thought about the problems of society in ways that were not exclusively related to Christian teachings. They were what we now call "intellectuals," a nineteenth-century word for people who make public issues matters of private concern. Thinkers of the Enlightenment were called *philosophes* (French for "philosophers").

The Enlightenment dealt with the relations between individuals and the state (rather than between family, professional, or religious groups and the state). It was a period that exalted freedom of thought and debate over obedience to tradition and belief. In the economic realm, Enlightenment thinkers praised the action of the free market and advocated an end to medieval guilds that restrained membership in professions. The Enlightenment proclaimed optimism about the possibility of improving the material and moral quality of the lives of Europeans and, indeed, of spreading this message to the wider world.

The Enlightenment was expressed in works in French, English, Italian, and German. Books were translated and read in the written European languages. While Britain and France were home to several of the most illustrious minds of the eighteenth century, other areas of Europe took on the ideas of the Enlightenment, sometimes reformulating the issues in their own terms.

Many absolutist monarchs were ambivalent about too much literacy among their populations. Social theorists hostile to change said that a population needed only sufficient education to do its job. It was argued that book learning would only breed dissatisfaction with rural life. During the eighteenth century, however, government advisers became convinced that a literate population was an advantage. In Portugal in 1759, the establishment of primary schools was ordered in every jurisdiction. By 1800, there were 850 such schools for boys and 24 for girls in the two biggest cities. Girls in bourgeois families were encouraged to read extensively.

Literacy and Book Production

The history of ideas can be called "intellectual history." Before 1456 (when the first book was printed using movable type), literate Europeans copied texts and records by hand on parchment or paper, scratched on slate, and engraved on monuments. Ownership of an individual handwritten scroll or entire book was limited to a small minority. Not all European people used the same alphabet or shared the same cultural background. With the invention of printing, it became possible to produce numerous copies of the same text, resulting in more common bonds among people.

In Western Europe after 1500, there was an increase in the number of writers and readers of the new books, which favoured the diffusion of the ideas of exceptional thinkers to a broad public. During the Enlightenment, information was typically transmitted on a printed page in a leather-bound book with few if any illustrations. There were also newspapers, called gazettes (from the Italian word for the small coin used to pay for them). At the end of the eighteenth century, gazettes were published from Lisbon to Moscow.

Insights into the Eighteenth Century:
The Letters of Madame de Graffigny

Madame de Graffigny was an extraordinary woman of the eighteenth century. Her vast body of work, which included a novel, plays, and over 2500 letters, is a rich window into daily life during the Enlightenment, in particular into the condition of women during this period. Born Françoise d'Happoncourt in 1695, Madame de Graffigny married François Huguet de Graffigny, an abusive man who drank heavily and gambled. When her husband died at a relatively young age, he left her with virtually no money. Using her ingenuity and the generosity of others, Madame de Graffigny was able not only to survive but to establish herself as a major writer of her day. After staying with Voltaire and Madame du Chatelet at Cirey for a couple of months, she moved to Paris, where she pursued a literary career.

In 1747, Madame de Graffigny published her highly successful novel *Letters of a Peruvian Woman*, which became a best-seller and was reprinted 46 times over the next 30 years. Although *Letters of a Peruvian Woman* fell out of favour with the reading public during the nineteenth century, it is currently enjoying renewed success, often used as mandatory reading in university courses. The novel tells the story of Inca princess Zilia, who is taken to France. What makes this novel a compelling read is de Graffigny's brilliant use of the main character to create "a radically new type of epistolary heroine, a model for the age of Enlightenment." When she learns she is to be brought to France, Zilia announces "I seek enlightenment with an urgency that consumes me." Once in France and accustomed to the language, Zilia becomes de Graffigny's voice of social satire. Through her main character, de Graffigny is critical of the superficiality of women's education and of the institution of marriage into which women are thrust at too early an age and without proper preparation.

The greatest insights into life in the eighteenth century are contained in the 2500 letters Madame de

Graffigny wrote to her close friend François Antoine Devaux over a 25-year period. In these letters, de Graffigny and Devaux shared their thoughts on everything, pushing their platonic friendship to the limit. In one letter de Graffigny pleaded, "Tell me what you've drunk, eaten, peed. I'll be glad to know everything." Through the vast body of correspondence, we can learn a great deal about life in the eighteenth century: from problems related to travel (how far one can go before changing horses, when it is advisable to travel with a friend) to what it meant to Madame de Graffigny to feel cold, ill, poorly housed, or lacking money. Letters written upon her arrival in Paris give detailed impressions of the city, including bridges, palaces, and so on.

This vast body of information relating to life in the eighteenth century is being painstakingly transcribed from the original manuscript and translated by a team of 16 editors at the University of Toronto. Headed by Professor Alan Dainard and Professor David Smith of the French Department, and the project's editorial assistant, Marion Filipiuk, the de Graffigny Project will ultimately yield 14 volumes of her correspondence, which will surely become a standard primary source for scholars in many disciplines.

Freemasons

Freemasonry was a fraternal order of free thinkers that was particularly influential in eighteenth-century Europe. The origins of freemasonry have always been shrouded in mystery but according to legend the founders of this secret society, the Craft, were the builders of the ancient Jewish Temple in Jerusalem, long before the Common Era, which was destroyed during the Roman period, but its remains (the Wailing Wall) continue to be venerated. Modern historians associate the origin of freemasonry with the Templars, a military order of Catholic monks sent to Jerusalem in the twelfth century, during the Crusades.

The historical record of freemasonry, however, started in the rooms of a London public bar near the Anglican Cathedral of Saint Paul in June of 1717. Freemasons supported freedom of belief, speech, and thought as well as the open market. They spread the leading ideas of the Enlightenment.

By the end of the *ancien régime* in 1789 (year of the French Revolution), almost every medium-sized town in Europe had one or more masonic lodges. The basic concepts of the Enlightenment were shared among the members.

Overview of the Enlightenment

The Enlightenment was not accepted to the same degree in all parts of Europe. In blasphemers Portugal, Spain, and Italy, the Enlightenment had to confront religious censorship and the ever-vigilant Inquisition, set up to purge society of heretics and their books. Britain, France, Holland, and Denmark had fewer constraints on debates over religious authority, or the "fit" between theological explanations of the universe and the new scientific revelations. In the German states and the Austrian Empire there were barriers to the publication of criticisms of the state and open discussions of new philosophical notions were frowned upon. East of the Elbe River there were fewer towns, lesser levels of literacy, and scant tradition of resistance to authority, while in European areas under Ottoman rule, there was almost no possibility of encountering the main works of the Enlightenment. In short, the Enlightenment did not take root everywhere in Europe at the same time; even within different countries, there were often gaps in knowledge and different ideas among men and women, peasants, priests and intellectuals.

Science captured the imagination of many during the eighteenth century as shown in this painting by Joseph Wright.

In due course, the optimistic attitude of the Enlightenment would reveal itself as an inadequate explanation for the social upheavals of the French Revolution and the Napoleonic era. Enlightened calls for change and improvements met with the resistance of those who were satisfied with traditional ways. Many Christians, particularly Catholics, saw the Enlightenment as an attack on their beliefs. The French poet, playwright, historian, and journalist of the mid-eighteenth century, Voltaire, was particularly disliked by conservatives for his anticlerical sarcasm.

This shift from a government centred on a monarch who was consecrated by the Church to a government, where public policy emerged from educated officials guided by a concern for the welfare of the masses, was an important part of the birth of the modern democracy formulated in the French Revolution.

The Enlightenment lent itself to conflicting interpretations and opinions. It effectively criticized unquestioning obedience to authority, whether royal or religious. Above all, it praised the merit of free inquiry and debate as the best way to reach the truth. Perhaps Enlightenment thinkers were too optimistic about the applicability of an arithmetical and strictly logical rationality to human affairs: they left little or no room for the emotions and moral convictions of individuals. There was a certain arrogance in the unflinching commitment of the leading Enlightenment thinkers to the notion of progress. Rational optimism is a hallmark of the Enlightenment.

Religion During the Enlightenment

By 1715, Europe was peopled by some 18 million Protestants in Britain, the Low Countries, Switzerland, and Scandinavia. There were 73 million Catholics from the Mediterranean to Poland, and some 24 million Orthodox in the Balkans, Russia, and in the Ottoman Empire. Small Jewish communities existed in different parts of Europe under severe legal repression, except in Holland. This religious balance remained much the same over the next century.

Respect for the supernatural was eroded during the Enlightenment. French physician Julien de la Mettrie (1709–1751) wrote a book proposing that humans are machines, albeit "machines that feel, but without any soul that shall outlive the life of the body." Such unflinching atheism was still rare in the eighteenth century. Prior to the contributions of modern science to a fuller understanding of the universe, it was virtually impossible for individuals to distance themselves from the Christian assumption of a divine plan for humanity, recorded in the Holy Scriptures.

Deism, a term derived from the Latin word for God (*Deus*), was a philosophical trend that advocated the simplification of rituals. Deists believed that God did not participate directly in human affairs; instead, God was a superior organizing intelligence in the universe. Deism had many followers in the eighteenth century since it permitted criticism of particular or outdated rituals, but retained the idea of a supreme, divine moral power in the universe.

Eighteenth-century thinkers renewed the interest in the moral and religious systems of the ancient Greeks and Romans. Roman philosopher Lucretius (98–55 B.C.E.) postulated ethical values foreign to the Middle Eastern faiths of Judaism, Christianity, and Islam. Eighteenth-century intellectuals de-emphasized miracles and superstitions that seemed ridiculous in the age of reason, but they stressed religious tolerance. A phrase often heard during the Enlightenment was "My mind is my church," which expressed a belief in God while moving away from the intolerance of the earlier centuries. In response to the rational religion of intellectuals, there arose counter-movements, like the one led by John Wesley. Wesleyans, also known as Methodists, emphasized emotion over reason. They found their greatest appeal among the poor and the lower middle class, who drew emotional support from their highly charged religious meetings.

Major Intellectual Figures of the Enlightenment

Who were the most important original thinkers of the Enlightenment as an international movement? During the eighteenth century, there was widespread interest in the main ideas of *John Locke*, Isaac Newton, *Montesquieu*, Voltaire, Rousseau, Diderot, Kant, and Condorcet among others. Numerous editions of their works were published. During the nineteenth century, historians became interested in the writings of obscure thinkers, such as the Italian Giambattista Vico (see Prologue).

In recent years, scholars have tried to discover how the Enlightenment affected the daily life of people. In conversation and correspondence, new attitudes entered into the daily relations of men and women, servants and employers, rich and poor, town and country dwellers, and even between different cultures and races.

John Locke (1632–1704)

English philosopher John Locke, in his *Essay Concerning Human Understanding* (1690), dealt with the relationship of what he called "innate ideas" to human thought, language, and the limits of human understanding. In his *Essay*, he called for clarity of language against "those who will not take care about the meaning of their own words and will not suffer the significance of their expressions to be inquired into."

Once the meaning of words was established, Locke discussed those experiences that lead to the elaboration of simple and complex ideas. While *Essay* is theoretical, its purpose was to make the reader attentive to evidence and critical of all that is believed on external authority.

Locke defended the right to own property as fundamental to a well-ordered society. He defended the need for elected governments in order to uphold freedom and tolerance. For him, people's decision to leave the "state of nature" was based on the assumption that they would enjoy a better life by entering into a well-ordered society, in which good government would look after its people, or else the people had the right to overthrow the government and elect new leaders.

Locke's ideas are most clearly illustrated in the Constitution of the United States, which guarantees its citizens the "right to life, liberty, and the pursuit of happiness." By contrast, the British North America Act, which was Canada's only Constitution from 1867 to 1982, guaranteed Canadians "peace, order, and good government."

Montesquieu (1689–1755)

Just as Newton (see Chapter 1) formulated the laws of physics as governing nature, some thinkers sought to understand the laws that govern human societies. The Baron de Montesquieu was a judge in the Court of Appeal of Bordeaux, a wine-growing region in Southwestern France. He was a writer and also an amateur scientist. In *The Persian Letters* (1721) he commented satirically on Western institutions through the eyes of Muslim Persian visitors to France writing home. Montesquieu had never been to Persia (today Iran) and he made factually incorrect statements about Islam. His aim was to make French readers look at their own country with the kind of detachment that a foreigner who has a different religion and different attitudes on freedom and sexuality might feel about a newly encountered land. Montesquieu's book conveys the idea that laws and social customs are a product of the different conditions that exist in each society.

Montesquieu's *Spirit of the Laws* (1748) was probably the most influential work on social policy during the first half of the eighteenth century. It set out to prove that law derives from differing circumstances and social systems, that laws are "the necessary relationships deriving from the nature of things." And the nature of things was largely a consequence of politics: whether one lived in a small republic (illustrated from the classical writings) where virtue was present, or in an aristocracy in which the defence of honour by the nobility guided public activity, or in a monarchy in which authority was concentrated in an individual. Montesquieu's ideas were drawn from classical writings and from Asia, notably China and the Islamic world. His arguments tended to show that, in France, a republic was not feasible: France was too large for a republic. He also thought that an overly strong monarch could become despotic and arbitrary. He implied that a monarchy, tempered by aristocracy—represented by the judicial nobility of which Montesquieu was a member—was the best form of government.

The novelty of Montesquieu's thought was its wide scope over space and time. He showed the good and the bad in *all* political systems; he pondered the effects of climate, of social and sexual customs (such as monogamy or polygamy); he referred to skilled economic minorities. Montesquieu provided an excellent summary of the knowledge of his time.

Voltaire (1694–1778)

Voltaire was the pen name of François Marie Arouet, born in Paris, the son of a prominent notary. Voltaire was a hypochondriac who lived a long life, encompassing the reign of Louis XIV and Louis XV up to the start of the reign of Louis XVI (the king who would be decapitated during the French Revolution). Voltaire's life was marked by much controversy and great international fame. His contemporaries enjoyed his tragedies, histories, and poetry but we know him for his political campaigns, his satirical writings, and his questioning of religious authority. Voltaire was sharp, deft, and witty; he constantly defended tolerance and attacked religious pieties.

Voltaire resisted his father's plans to make him study law. He instead travelled to Holland, where he completed *Oedipus*, a play based on a Greek myth. He had already been put in the state prison in central Paris, called the Bastille, because of saucy verses directed against the Duke of Orléans, who was the regent for the child king Louis XV. As a young man of 25, he quarreled with an aristocrat and

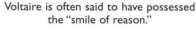

Voltaire is often said to have possessed the "smile of reason."

The Marquise du Châtelet:

Extraordinary Woman of the Enlightenment

The ideals of the Enlightenment did little to free most women of the eighteenth century from the restraints of a traditionally male-dominated society. Although salons provided women the opportunity to engage in intellectual discourse, they were seldom given the same respect as their male counterparts. Yet, despite the male chauvinism of the age, some women were able to leave their mark on this period in history. One such woman was the Marquise du Châtelet.

The Marquise du Châtelet had been married at a young age to one of the most prominent and powerful generals in the French army. The wide gulf in years and lack of similar interests may have been the factors that prevented a loving relationship. What developed instead was an understanding that allowed the Marquise du Châtelet to pursue her interests in mathematics and science and to carry on a lengthy romance with the famous writer Voltaire.

The Marquise du Châtelet was a truly extraordinary woman of many talents and nearly inexhaustible energy. In 1739, she and Voltaire made a trip to the Netherlands in order to resolve an outstanding lawsuit over one of her husband's estates. While on this trip, the Marquise spent three hours each day taking instructions in algebra from a tutor, spent another three hours a day working on algebraic equations by herself, and took a crash course in law from two university professors so that she would be able to understand the intricacies of the lawsuit. Despite this rigorous schedule, she found the time to begin translating Sophocles' play *Oedipus Rex*, which, when published, would become a classic in French theatre for over a century. Also, while in the Netherlands, the Marquise hired a tutor to teach her Flemish, a language she could read and understand after only a month's instruction.

After four months in the Netherlands, the lawsuit was won and the Marquise du Châtelet and Voltaire were ready to return to France. Once at home, the Marquise returned to her usual pattern of attending balls, fêtes, galas, dinner parties, and banquets in the evening, sleeping for two or three hours at sunrise, clearing her head by working through complex mathematical equations before breakfast, and devoting her days to the serious study of science. In the fall of 1739, she began a study of the philosophy and scientific theories of the famous German scientist Gottfried Leibniz. By April 1740 she had completed *Institutions de Physique*, a book that explained the theories of Leibniz with brilliance, clarity, and precision. Châtelet's *Institutions* was greeted with much excitement among the intellectuals of France and helped to solidify her growing reputation as one of the leading intellectuals of her day. Despite her gender and the male chauvinism of the era, the Marquise du Châtelet was regarded as one of the great minds of the Enlightenment who helped to advance the frontiers of human thought.

was beaten up by his servants. By his early 50s, Voltaire had a personal sense of grievance against capricious government and the arrogance of rich aristocrats. He went to England to avoid stirring up more trouble.

England was at that time less populous than France and its language was little known on the Continent. Voltaire stayed there for three years and met a number of famous writers and intellectuals such as Jonathan Swift, Alexander Pope, and Viscount Bolingbroke. He subsequently wrote a book entitled *Philosophical Letters* (1734) in which he praised English law, tolerance of various religions, science, and philosophy. Much of this was exaggerated, aimed at a critique of France. The book was condemned by the Paris Court of Appeal. That year, Voltaire published a book that introduced Newton to a French-reading audience and popularized Newton's ideas.

By the age of 40, Voltaire was an established public figure. Living with the Marquise du Châtelet at her chateau in Eastern France, he read widely and started publication of a history entitled *The Century of Louis XIV*, which was to be a success.

In 1750, Voltaire was invited to Germany by the Prussian king Frederick the Great, who wanted to foster a society of advanced thinkers in Berlin. Voltaire had been in correspondence with him for 14 years. His journey to Berlin began a long exile from Paris, where he was afraid of being punished for his writings. His stay with Frederick the Great lasted for two years, but they clashed due to the Prussian's despotic temperament.

During the 1750s and 1760s, Voltaire became increasingly concerned with crusades on behalf of victims of injustice. The most notable was Jean Calas, a Protestant from Toulouse in Southwestern France, put to death in a cruel, drawn-out public execution (1762) for the alleged murder of his own son, allegedly in order to prevent him from converting to Catholicism. Voltaire wrote a famous treatise on tolerance. Calas had been found guilty by the bigoted local Catholic judiciary. Three years after the execution, a court edict in 1765 recognized the unproven nature of the Calas conviction.

In the following year, Voltaire was appalled by the July 1768 execution of the Chevalier de la Barre at Abbeville, a 19-year-old noble accused of mocking the Procession of the Sacrament and using obscene words while miming other rituals. The punishment was to apologize, bare-headed, wearing a coarse shirt while holding a heavy torch of "ardent wax" (that would sputter and scald) at the main door of the Saint Wulfran Church. He then was to be taken to the place of execution in a cart with a placard on his chest and back reading "impious." There, on his knees, he was to confess his crime of blasphemy in a loud voice. Then his tongue was to be cut out by the executioner and his right hand struck off. Finally, he was to be burned alive. During the execution, there was a modification in the program: his head was cut off before the burning. Into the flames also went a copy of Voltaire's *Philosophical Dictionary*.

In the ritualism and savagery of the sentence, we see the judicial attitude toward blasphemy. The book burning showed the prevalent judicial opinion of Enlightenment ideas. Voltaire campaigned against the horror and senseless cruelty of such punishments. Henceforth he used a famous sign-off to all his letters, "*Écrasez l'infâme*" ("Crush infamy"), which he used until the end of his life.

Voltaire has been accused of anti-Semitism and disrespect for Christian rituals. He also mocked the ceremonies of many religions and he was consistently anticlerical.

The second half of the seventeenth century has been described as the historical revolution, meaning that true sources and accounts of the past began to emerge. Instead of myths and legends, readers asked for evidence of what had taken place in previous centuries. In his *Essay on the Manners and Spirit of Nations* and discourses written between 1753 and 1756, Voltaire would show how "a historian must limit himself and select from these immense collections which serve only to confuse. They constitute a vast storehouse from which you take what is necessary for your own purposes... There is more writing in the archives of a single convent than in the annals of the Roman Empire." Or, again: "Woe to details! Posterity neglects them all; they are a kind of vermin that undermines large works. Whatever characterizes the century, what caused its overturns, what will matter a hundred years hence—that is what I want to set down today."

Voltaire was resolutely against looking to the past as being a better time. Although well-versed in the classics, he believed that it was more important to study the recent past, which is "essential for us to know," than to investigate a remote antiquity, which "only serves to satisfy our curiosity." Voltaire believed that, under Louis XIV, "a general revolution took place in our arts, minds and customs, as in our government, which will serve as an eternal token of the true glory of our century." He claimed that France under Louis XIV inspired England, brought good taste to Germany, the sciences to Russia, and revived Italy. The king was praised for ruling without a prime minister, for putting his revenues in order, for improving the army, for increasing commerce, and for reforming the laws. He criticized the forced exile of the Huguenots for its economic consequences but he wrote about the king: "Louis XIV did more good for his country than 20 of his predecessors together."

Voltaire died in Paris in 1778, upon returning from the triumphal staging of his last play. Few writers had the profound effect on their contemporaries as did Voltaire.

Helvétius (1715–1771)

Claude Adrien Helvétius came from an affluent intellectual Parisian family. Educated at a fashionable school in Paris he encountered the ideas of leading intellectuals such as John Locke. Later he would correspond with Voltaire. Writers often met and discussed new ideas at **salons**, where guests were invited by a hostess. Helvétius went to the salon of Madame Geoffrin, who entertained writers and thinkers as well as officials.

Helvétius published *Concerning the Mind* in 1758, which simplified and extended the ideas of Locke and other previous thinkers. The book was organized around several basic points. First, physical sensibility and memory are the two causes of ideas. Intellectual judgment is the ability to feel and to remember. This idea had already been put forth by La Mettrie in *L'homme machine* (1748) and by the Abbé Condillac in his 1754 *Treatise on Sensations*. Second, judgments derive from our interests, understood as above, and these vary with the individual, time, and social situation. Third, all normal individuals are capable of great ideas: differences in intellectual capacity result from social conditions. Helvétius believed life was the pursuit of human happiness and that this could best be achieved under a reasonable government motivated by the desire for utilitarianism and a desire to improve the life of the citizens.

When *Concerning the Mind* was published it caused a giant scandal and was read all over Europe.

His second book, *Concerning Man*, was censored in France but a Russian prince paid to publish it at the Hague in Holland.

The *Encyclopedia*

By the middle of the eighteenth century, the production and sale of books was a flourishing trade, especially in Northern Europe. The most important single publishing venture of the Enlightenment was doubtless the *Encyclopedia*, published in France between 1751 and 1772 in 28 volumes. The chief editors were the mathematician Jean d'Alembert and the social critic Denis Diderot. Among the contributors were Montesquieu, Voltaire, Rousseau, and virtually every leading French intellectual of the time. The *Encyclopedia* contained a great variety of topics including government, the social system, and religion. It summarized and praised the advances in biology and chemistry. It also used scientific knowledge to support its contributors' scorn of Christianity. In its attempt to encapsulate human knowledge and to elevate the triumphs of the human mind, the *Encyclopedia*, more than any other work of the eighteenth century, embodies the ideals of the Enlightenment.

Beccaria (1738–1794)

Cesare Beccaria, a nobleman from Milan, had strong views on the need to change the way the accused were treated by the criminal system. He associated with a group of writers who believed that harsh punishment did nothing to reform the individual. Beccaria enjoyed discussions generated by the intellectual periodical called, typically, *The Café*, because the café was a place where people might drink the new beverage of coffee that was now being imported into Europe and discuss new ideas. Unlike the salon, the café did not require a special invitation and the atmosphere was more casual.

Discussions with other lawyers and officials led Beccaria to write *Essay on Crimes and Punishments*, published in 1766. It called for an end to judicial torture of suspects and of capital punishment and it met with huge international success.

Beccaria was not alone in these ideas: Jacques Pierre Brissot (1754–1793) thought that death should never be used as a punishment, save against a major enemy of the state; ironically, he himself would be decapitated on a political charge during the French Revolution. Others proposed that torture had no result other than to enable strong rogues to resist, and weak innocents to plead guilty in order to end their torment. The 1766 French translation spread the fame of Beccaria throughout Europe. Many of the so-called "enlightened" rulers, such as Frederick the Great of Prussia, Maria Theresa and Joseph II of the Habsburg Empire, and the Grand Duke Leopold of Tuscany, all expressed admiration and a desire to follow the wise suggestions in Beccaria's book. Catherine the Great of Russia invited Beccaria to take up residence at her court. English philosopher Jeremy Bentham, who sought the greatest good for the greatest number, described Beccaria in glowing terms: "Oh my master! First evangelist of reason!" Bentham admired the moral earnestness, or what he called the "censoriousness," of Beccaria's book.

Beccaria was lavishly praised by enlightened foreigners but the monk Facchini published a book denouncing him as an enemy of religion. The Venetian Inquisition also attacked his book, mistakenly attributing it to another author—an example of how the "justice" system made mistakes. The Spanish translation was forbidden by the Council for Civil Censure, even for the readers with a special licence to read "dangerous" books: many in Europe were still in favour of torturing and executing criminals.

Rousseau (1712–1778)

Jean-Jacques Rousseau was one of the greatest European minds of the eighteenth century. He was concerned with the moral reform of society. Personally, he was an eccentric and a loner who detested salons. Rousseau is often described as a harbinger of modernity and the man of the Enlightenment closest to the most radical phase of the French Revolution. We return to this theme in Chapter 5, but we should keep in mind that he had been dead for 11 years when the Estates-General (the prerevolutionary French legislature, consisting of representatives of the three estates: clergy, nobility, and middle class) met in May of 1789, a meeting that represents the start of the French Revolution.

Rousseau could not accept the Enlightenment notion that the world was improving. He exemplified a moral indignation and sense of spiritual superiority that echoed the Calvinism of his Swiss childhood in Geneva, where he was born on June 25, 1712. His father was a journeyman watchmaker who acquired Swiss citizenship, a privilege not normally granted to the foreign-born, even after generations of residency. His father abandoned him when he was ten. Rousseau was then apprenticed to an engraver who treated him badly. At 16, he began to travel, abandoning the Protestant city of Geneva, capital of a republic of 25 000 inhabitants in 1760.

Rousseau wrote his famous *The Social Contract* (1761), several operas, *The New Héloise*, a love story set in the Alps, and *Confessions*, considered by many literary scholars to be the first modern autobiography. He had various love affairs, the most important being with a woman ten years his senior, Madame de Warens, who helped to perfect his education. In 1741–1742, he went to Paris and took up with the chambermaid at the hotel, Thérèse Levasseur, with whom he had five children, all of whom were abandoned to an orphanage.

Rousseau had converted to Catholicism as a teenager but his world view had an obvious Protestant influence: he looked down on luxury and had a strong sense of individual responsibility. He thought that

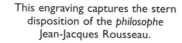

This engraving captures the stern disposition of the *philosophe* Jean-Jacques Rousseau.

French life was too artificial, salon conversation too glib, manners too elaborate, the theatre too frivolous, and religion too exterior. But he was a music teacher and he wrote music articles for the *Encyclopedia*, including a new system of musical notation.

In 1749, Rousseau submitted to the Dijon Academy's competition his essay on the effects of the progress of civilization upon morals. Rousseau argued that "...our minds have been corrupted in proportion as our arts and sciences have made advances toward their perfection." Rousseau confronted the Enlightenment idea of progress head on, lauding the superiority of the "savage" state over the civilized. The Academy awarded him the prize and printed his contribution, which made him famous.

The second discourse, published in 1754, is concerned with the contrast between egotistical self love, or *amour propre*, and the love of oneself, or *amour de soi-même*, which is a healthy instinct for self-preservation. Rousseau thus contrasted biological drives with those produced by society.

In 1756, a new patroness entered his life, Madame d'Épinay. He lived with her for six years in semi-retirement, breaking off contact with Diderot and Parisian friends; eventually he broke with his benefactress too. In this period, he wrote an attack on *philosophes* Voltaire and d'Alembert.

Early in the 1760s, Rousseau published his famous treatise *The Social Contract*, and a book on education, *Émile*. They met with immediate success; however, in 1762, both books were condemned by the Paris parliament as contrary to the government and to religion, whereupon Rousseau fled to Switzerland. After three years in Switzerland, Rousseau went to England, where he was helped by English philosopher David Hume. He began to write his autobiography, *Confessions*, a title which seems to be a reference to the classic work of Saint Augustine (fifth century), of which books 1 to 9 are autobiographical. By 1767, Rousseau had fallen out with Hume and he returned to Paris, where he completed *Confessions*. By 1777, his obvious mental instability made city life unbearable to him. Friends found him a country cottage near Ermonville, where he moved in 1778 and died soon after.

Rousseau's Impact

Rousseau acknowledged that his introspection and self-analysis fuelled much of his work. He was attracted by the idea of childhood innocence corrupted by adulthood and sexuality. This contrast between innocence and experience was for him a paradigm of human life. Earlier humans seemed purer, less corrupt, and closer to nature, whereas the "adult" present was urban, brittle, and artificial.

Contemporaries of a conservative cast of mind instantly perceived the threat in this notion. Edmund Burke said of Rousseau that he was "a ferocious, low-minded, hard-hearted father, devoid of fine general feelings." Young Napoléon Bonaparte submitted an essay to the Lyon Academy, in which he asked "Oh Rousseau, why did you live for only 60 years! In the interests of virtue, you should have lived forever!" However, when Napoléon declared himself First Consul in a coup in 1799, he said to the nobleman who had provided Rousseau's last refuge: "Your Rousseau is a fool—he has led us to this pretty pass!"

Radical contemporaries of Rousseau became interested in his novel ideas. In the provincial city of Arras, a young man who was 20 when Rousseau died avidly devoured *The Social Contract*. He was Maximilien de Robespierre, future leader of the Jacobins during the French Revolution. Another man who read Rousseau was Brissot de Warville, a leading figure of another revolutionary faction: the Girondins. Still another was Jean-Paul Marat, an army doctor who, like Rousseau, grew up in a Protestant environment, and who would become an advocate of the poor, or "*sans-culottes*."

Rousseau put forward a new concept of political authority, which he called the "general will," and which was more than the will of the majority since it could never condone immorality. Unlike the notion of the divine right of kings, and the notion of the rule of reason, Rousseau's ideas lead to representative democracy.

Luxury and Consumerism in the Eighteenth Century

One form of thought at odds with the Christian ideal of frugality and charity was the Enlightenment campaign in favour of luxury. Voltaire observed that "the superfluous is necessary." He meant that consumerism created jobs and stimulated commerce. Investigation of and commentary on the effects of economic activity increased substantially in the eighteenth century. Writers known as physiocrats, led by Dr. François Quesnay (1694–1774), believed that the rural economy was the root of national wealth. Quesnay coined the famous phrase "*Laissez faire, laissez passer*" in praise of a more open marketplace. The article on luxury in the *Encyclopedia* reads:

> Without luxury, there is less exchange of goods and less commerce; without commerce, nations cannot be as populous. A nation whose work force consists only of agricultural laborers will have a smaller population than that which supports also sailors and textile workers.... Every government, unless it is founded on equality and property in

common, has and must have as one of its mainsprings the citizen's desire to accumulate wealth.

Adam Smith

Theoretical analysis of the factors that affect the economy was on the increase in the eighteenth century. Perhaps the most famous economist of the time, *Adam Smith* was a proponent of free trade whose work was translated into many European languages before 1800. He was a Scottish economist of remarkable intellect. His writings clearly reflect the intellectual, social, and economic conditions of the time. They not only contained a powerful message but indeed prophesied a new order that would reshape the world in economic and social terms. His *An Inquiry into the nature and causes of the Wealth of Nations* (1776) emphasized the need for free trade, espoused a labour-value theory, and postulated the "invisible hand of competition," which regulated the economy through supply and demand. Unlike many of his contemporaries, whose fame came posthumously, Smith's brilliant work earned him fame during his own lifetime.

The arguments Smith advanced in *The Wealth of Nations* held great appeal for his contemporaries as it seemed to justify their self-interested pursuit of gain by showing that such activity was beneficial to society at large. Smith's *The Wealth of Nations* was concerned with a type of economy that was capitalist in nature, and his purpose was to explain the laws that govern its operation.

Literary Forms of Preromanticism

Like philosophers, many writers also searched for what made them different from other people. They had confidence in intuition and emotionalism over the demands of logic. This mood has sometimes been called preromanticism. It was also part of the emphasis on the special character of each nation that would be strongly enunciated after the revolutionary and Napoleonic wars. That stress was central to nationalism. Often this was a reaction against Cartesianism: the predominance of logic. (Cartesianism is named after the seventeenth-century philosopher and mathematician René Descartes, who called for logic and clarity in speech and thought.)

Von Herder

An exponent of the different characteristics of peoples, or of national character as some say, was *Johann Gottfried von Herder* (1744–1803). He attended university in Northeastern Prussia in Germany at Königsberg. In 1764–1769, the young von Herder went to Riga, capital of Latvia. Riga was for him what Geneva was to Rousseau: a small, idealized city-state where he did not live but which remained with him as a construct in his mind about morality and patriotic spirit. He had gone to Latvia in order to avoid the experience of the brutalizing military service in the Prussian army. He next moved to France in 1769, where he hoped to draft a constitution for Russia as Rousseau had done for Poland. In his work *Ideas on the Philosophy of the History of Mankind*, he said that the future of humanity lay with what he characterized as "the tireless, peaceful Slavs." Paris contrasted sharply with Riga and von Herder, unlike most of the East European intelligentsia, did not admire French culture. When the opportunity presented itself, he left Paris for Strasbourg. There he met the great German writer Johann Wolfgang von Goethe (1749–1832), who recommended him for a job as a librarian in the German-speaking duchy of Weimar. Von Herder remained there until his death in 1803.

Using the ducal library and with leisure to read and reflect, von Herder wrote down his ideas on national character—today we would say ethnic identity. He became conscious of his German culture when living in cities where another language predominated. He thought of his Germanness not in terms of loyalty to a particular ruler or dynasty nor as a citizen of a state, but to a language and culture.

This engraving reflects the shift in society from a warrior nobility to a wealthy merchant class. Note how the man is rejecting the armour of the past in favour of the fruits of trade.

In fact, von Herder was opposed to the individual-, liberal-contract theory of society advocated by the *philosophes*, which said that the legitimacy of established order resulted from the satisfaction of individual interests under the limitations of natural law and reason. He was influenced by Rousseau and perhaps also by the new forms of emotional religiosity that flourished in the eighteenth century (e.g. Pietism, a late-seventeenth-century movement against the clerical despotism and creed-bound theology of the Lutheran Church). Von Herder emphasized feelings, emotions, and the need for shared sentiments.

Von Herder believed that essential force (in German *Kraft*) was the cultural glue that bonded individuals in a community and that the core of this bond was language. He wrote: "Each nation speaks in the manner it thinks, and thinks in the manner it speaks." To him, a people without a common language was an absurdity. He opposed what linguistic specialists call interference, or what we might call mixing of idioms (as when English-speaking Montrealers say *métro* or people from England say "tube" for subway). Von Herder thought that cultures could and should remain pure, that a people removed from its original habitat is weakened and degenerated. He studied folk poetry: poetry that sprang from the creativity of working people and responded directly to the eternal questions of human existence.

Some of von Herder's ideas would be echoed in the nationalism of the nineteenth century, and they caused great suffering to ethnic minorities in countries where one or more than one language was spoken.

Condorcet (1743–1794)

The Marquis de Condorcet is often referred to as the last of the *philosophes*. He marked the end of the universalizing, rationalistic Enlightenment and died in prison, probably by suicide, while awaiting execution by the new "rational" decapitating machine called the guillotine. He had been a critic of royal government and he welcomed the 1789 Revolution enthusiastically. He was a distinguished mathematician who believed that the calm application of reason would bring about a better world. By temperament, he could not understand the geometry of jealousy, the algebra of spite, the calculus of ambition, and the arithmetic of greed. He was forced into hiding by his political enemies and it

was during that period (1793–1794) that he wrote what is sometimes called the testament of the Enlightenment, *Sketch for a Historical Picture of the Progress of the Human Mind*, an intellectual history of humanity through time divided into ten epochs, in which the main enemies of clear thinking were priests of the various religions who kept their own power and wealth through the ignorance and subservience of the masses. In the tenth and last epoch, Condorcet hailed the triumph of Enlightenment.

Reflections

The Enlightenment was as much a general attitude as a set of specific programs. In some parts of Europe, it was most apparent as a demand for more rational government: standardization of weights and measures, free markets in grain and other commodities, better training for officials, more open justice, and an end to judicial torture. In Catholic countries, the Enlightenment was often seen as an enemy of faith.

The opposition was never simple or clear-cut. Eighteenth-century churchmen were seriously affected by the prevailing mental climate of rationalism, deductive thinking, and mistrust of emotionalism. Many archbishops, bishops, and parish priests looked down on such traditional activities as the veneration of relics, the adoration of particular statues of saints or the Virgin Mary, the burning candles at altars, ostentatious forms of piety such as vigils, self-flagellation, or attending numerous masses.

In predominantly Protestant lands, the clergy were equally disapproving of highly emotional forms of worship like those of the Wesleyans in England. The faithful often shrieked, tore at their clothes, and wept and went into convulsions at John Wesley's outdoor sermons. These activities were seen as a distortion of the Christian message.

The Enlightenment had an indirect effect in weakening some traditional forms of belief. The archbishop of a small town in Southern Italy, asked by his bishop about the condition of faith in Francavilla in 1783, replied:

> In this town, foolish credulity in demoniacal manifestations and in the superstitions to undo their effects prevail quite strongly. That ignorant people

believe in them is not surpising, but that a few ecclesiastics, and especially monks, encourage these false beliefs and superstitions—whether out of ignorance or out of malice—is displeasing to all good people.

Such an answer revealed that Enlightenment values had spread far from the salons of a few fashionable *philosophes*.

The eighteenth-century clergy, both Catholic and Protestant, was generally too elitist and distant from the poorest part of the population to fully understand their need for solace for their agony over the meaning of life. And the percentage of the European population living at the poverty line was steadily increasing from 1770 onward.

Key Concepts, Figures, and Events

Ancien Régime	Agricultural Revolution	Ottoman Empire
Seven Years' War	Enlightenment	*Philosophes*
Freemasonry	Voltaire	John Locke
Baron de Montesquieu	Cesare Beccaria	Jean-Jacques Rousseau
Adam Smith	Johann Gottfried von Herder	

Topics for Further Thought

1. The eighteenth century brought about significant change in Western Europe, particularly in France. While the events of 1789 highlighted the break with the past, the winds of change were evident prior to the French Revolution. Explain the nature of change that was evident in France prior to 1789. Be sure to discuss religious, economic, political, and social change.

2. The Enlightenment was an age dominated by the ideas of numerous intellectuals, few of whom actually put their philosophy into action. How were the ideas and the ideals of the eighteenth century in stark contrast to the reality of life? In responding to this question, consider the division of wealth, power, and court life versus life among the peasantry and urban poor.

3. During the seventeenth century, while England placed constitutional limits on the power of their monarch, in France, Louis XIV created an absolute monarchy. How did this bring about the ultimate demise of the monarchy in

France? In countries where monarchs refused to relinquish some of their power, they were eventually overthrown. What does this suggest about the nature of despotism and the stability of such governments?

4. When studying the early history of Canada, we cannot get a clear understanding of the events that shaped our destiny without being aware of the events occurring in Europe. To what degree was the history of North America in the eighteenth century determined by European ambitions? Were colonies and colonists in North America mere pawns in European diplomacy? Do you think this contributed to the American Revolution?

5. When studying the ideas of the Enlightenment, we see a theme that has been common in European history since the Renaissance: a secular move toward faith in progress and human achievement. To what degree is the Enlightenment an extension of humanism and to what degree are reason and logic applied to society?

6. The ideals of the Enlightenment were embraced with varying degrees of vigour in different parts of Europe. The most hostile opposition came from those who saw the Enlightenment as an attack on the authority of the Church. Did the ideas of the *philosophes* undermine the authority of the Church? Could the intellectuals of the eighteenth century have worked in harmony with religious authorities in reforming society?

7. Voltaire has been described as the "architect of the Enlightenment" who possessed the "smile of reason." Reflecting on the ideals of the eighteenth-century *philosophes* and the work of Voltaire, do you believe that he was the embodiment of the Enlightenment?

8. Both Rousseau and von Herder were clearly products of the eighteenth century, and yet both expressed ideas in their writings which stood in stark contrast to many other intellectuals of their age. To what degree were Rousseau and von Herder harbingers of change that would sweep over Europe in the late eighteenth and nineteenth centuries?

Topics for Further Research

1. Since the eighteenth century, Europe has experienced a steady growth in population. Several factors account for this growth. Research one of the factors as it relates to the eighteenth century:

New Foods   Disease and Medicine
Hygiene   Agricultural Expansion

2. Change in agriculture was one of the important factors which reshaped European economies and cultures in the eighteenth century. Research the nature of agriculture (division of land, use of technology, crops) during the eighteenth century in one of the following countries:

Italian States   German States
France   Spain
Great Britain   The Netherlands
Russia

3. During the eighteenth century, many colourful monarchs sat on the thrones of Europe. Prepare a biographical sketch of one of the following monarchs:

George III of Britain
Maria I of Portugal
Catherine the Great of Russia
Philip V of Spain
Louis XV of France
Frederick the Great of Prussia

4. The ideas of many brilliant intellectuals dominate our study of the Enlightenment. Try to get behind the ideas of the *philosophes* by preparing a biographical sketch of one of the following:

Rousseau   Von Herder
Locke   Montesquieu
Smith   Diderot
Condorcet

Responding to Ideas

1. The essential character and importance of the Enlightenment continue to be a topic of debate among historians. American historian Peter Gay, in an article entitled "The Unity of the French Enlightenment," described what he saw as the primary challenge faced by intellectuals of the eighteenth century and their response. He wrote: "The philosophes' crisis was a crisis of freedom. They felt the anxiety and exhilaration of the explorer who stands before the unknown." Gay argues that the 1760s were a time of turmoil when the beginnings of industrialization and modern politics were issuing a challenge to the *ancien régime*. Gay notes: "In this time of trouble, the philosophes added to their sense of power over the environment, a sense of mission.... The philosophes grew more radical, more combative, more convinced than ever that they were the prophets of a new age...." Gay's interpretation places a heavy emphasis on the role of the *philosophes* in bringing about the radical change in French society at the end of the eighteenth century. What evidence from this chapter supports Gay's interpretation? Are there other factors worthy of more attention in explaining the changes that brought an end to the *ancien régime*?

2. Frank Manuel, a historian of ideas, argues that the *philosophes* of the eighteenth century introduced a new moral outlook that was particularly modern. In *The Age of Reason*, Manuel summarized: "Although the philosophes did not solve the problem of the existence of evil and suffering in the world, they did manage to establish in European society a general consensus about conduct which is evil, a moral attitude which still sustains us... the eighteenth-century men of letters did formulate a set of moral principles which to this day remain basic to any discussion of human rights." Considering the values of our contemporary society, do you believe that Manuel gives a naïve and overly optimistic view of the Enlightenment, or has he accurately described the importance of the *philosophes* in shaping the morality of the modern world?

CHAPTER
3
Daily Life
During the Enlightenment

A poor woodcutter lived with his wife and two children on the edge of a large forest. The boy was called Hansel and the girl Gretel. The woodcutter did not have much food around the house and, when a great famine devastated the entire country, he could no longer provide enough for his family's daily meals. One night, as he was lying in bed and thinking about his worries, he began tossing and turning. Then he sighed and said to his wife: "What's to become of us? How can we feed our poor children when we don't have enough for ourselves?"

"I'll tell you what," answered his wife. "Early tomorrow morning, we'll take the children out into the forest where it is most dense. We'll build a fire and give them each a piece of bread. Then we'll go about our work and leave them alone. They won't find their way back home and we'll be rid of them."

• • •

It was now the third morning since they had left their house.... At noon, they saw a beautiful bird.... They followed it until they came to a little house that was made of bread. Moreover, it had cake for a roof and pure sugar for windows....

Suddenly, the door opened and a very old woman leaning on a crutch came slinking out of the house.... The old woman... only pretended to be friendly. She was really a wicked witch on the lookout for children.... As soon as she had any children in her power, she would kill, cook, and eat them.... Now, witches have red eyes and cannot see very far, but they have a keen sense of smell, like animals, and can detect when humans are near them.

This well-known tale provides many insights into the peasant world of the eighteenth century. Recorded in early nineteenth-century Germany, "Hansel and Gretel" is one of the 211 folk tales compiled by the Grimm brothers, Jacob and Wilhelm. Grimm's fairy tales not only have helped to preserve the rich oral tradition of the German peasantry, they also depict life among the lower classes prior to the Industrial Revolution. For example, it is evident from the "Hansel and Gretel" extracts that hunger was a constant threat to the poor and that witchcraft and superstition were an important element of life in the eighteenth century. Among the middle and upper classes, though, the eighteenth century was an age of reason.

The Value of Social History

The value in studying **social history** is hotly debated among historians. Some maintain that history is about power, about great leaders and wars that redefine political boundaries and shape economic fortunes. They contend that studying the lives of the poor and weak is of little significance, to say nothing of how people dressed, what they ate, how they spent their leisure time, or how working women contributed to the economy of the eighteenth century.

Social history has gained popularity over the past few decades as people become interested in broad historical trends and attempt to understand the way ordinary people perceived the world in which they lived. One of the great challenges we face in studying history is being able to divorce ourselves from our present so as not to slip into the assumption that people in the past thought like we do today. We must constantly remind ourselves that the past is an unfamiliar place that can cause us culture shock. A common entry in any eighteenth-century book of proverbs was: "He who is snotty, let him blow his nose." Lack of understanding of such a proverb illustrates the gap between the eighteenth-century mindset and ours.

To emphasize great events and the daily life of the elite is to come to deal only with the surface of the past. The impact of the rural community and the contributions made by women of all classes are accepted facts. Our lives are shaped as much by the social trends and developments of the past centuries as by intellectual developments, political movements, and economic theories. Moreover, the study of daily life adds a human dimension—which can also be fascinating.

Tales such as "Little Red Riding Hood" reflect the dominant themes in peasant literature.

The Enlightenment and Social History

The eighteenth century was a truly transitional period during which ideas were far ahead of actions. It was an age of salons and intellectual giants that contrasted with an impoverished peasantry and growing crime. Prior to the eighteenth century, few talked of social or political equality or the inherent rights of all people. By contrast, the twentieth century is undoubtedly a democratic age in which all human beings are believed to have equal and inalienable rights. Also, while the eighteenth century was an age of elite culture dominated by the aristocracy, of operas, limited literacy, and distinct fashions for upper and lower classes, the twentieth century is an age of mass culture dominated by the middle class where compulsory education ensures widespread literacy, television is the dominant medium, and fashion trends are shared by all classes.

It is to the eighteenth century that we must look for the seeds of change in the nineteenth and twentieth centuries. Eighteenth century intellectuals, such as Voltaire, Rousseau, and Diderot, talked of a new age, an age which was to be born with the French Revolution. By the end of the eighteenth century, Europe had started on the road to revolutionary

Madame Geoffrin's salon attracted some of the leading intellectuals of the age. This staged portrait, which shows a famous actor reading to a group of intellectuals and nobles, was painted in 1755.

change, which could be seen in all aspects of life. Perceptions of class would be radically altered by Enlightenment ideals as were views regarding children, family, and even crime and punishment. This chapter explores various aspects of social history in Europe during the eighteenth century, including the daily life of the upper and lower classes, cities and city life, crime and punishment, and the changing role of women.

Daily Life Among Europe's Upper and Middle Classes

The Salon

During the eighteenth century the *salon*, a room where an intellectually oriented hostess would entertain selected guests, became the dominant symbol of the Enlightenment; a place where men and women of the intelligentsia came together to exchange their views on politics, literature, and a wide range of other topics. Created in early seventeenth-century France by the Marquise de Rambouillet, whose ill health prevented her from venturing far from her famous *chambre bleue* (blue room), the salon grew in popularity and reached its zenith in the second half of the eighteenth century. Smaller than the traditional formal great halls for entertainment, the salon offered guests a casual atmosphere in which they could mingle and converse freely. Intellectually, the salon provided a sheltered outlet for views that were condemned by the courts of Europe. Voltaire, shunned by Louis XV for his critical views of the Church and the monarchy, received numerous invitations to express his views at Parisian salons.

Prerevolutionary France was a very rigid hierarchical society in which class determined who held an important post. Salons allowed both men and women a degree of social mobility, for they involved mixed elements of the nobility, bourgeoisie, and intelligentsia. The social equality promoted by the *philosophes* of the eighteenth century was embraced by the salons as they were open to all who were well-mannered, famous, talented, rich, or important in some way: class and origins were less important than one's merits.

The *philosophes* argued for expanded women's rights, including better educational opportunities, claiming the prejudice against women was the sign of a barbaric society. In the salons, women participated equally with men, sharing their works and opinions. Some met and married men of superior rank or wealth, while others used the salon as a base from which they were able to influence kings, ministers, political policy, and literary and artistic tastes. Madame Geoffrin's salon counted Diderot and Montesquieu among its many famous guests. Another famous salon was run by the Marquise du Deffand and her niece Julie de Lespinasse. Historians Bonnie Anderson and Judith Zinsser described their salon as follows:

> ...from 1754 to 1764, these women maintained one of the most brilliant salons in Europe. Part of the attraction was the contrast between the two: aunt and illegitimate niece; one in her sixties, the other in her twenties; one known for her love affairs, the other a virgin; blind patroness and sighted protegee; the cynic and the romantic. Their salon became one of the ornaments of Enlightenment culture, and an invitation to the famous yellow drawing room was prized.

Despite the decline of the salon by the nineteenth century, it was an important element in the transition from the dominance of upper-class culture of previous centuries to the more middle-class culture of the nineteenth and twentieth centuries.

Good Taste and Good Manners: The Signs of Distinction

The salons of the eighteenth century drew a wide variety of people from different backgrounds and social classes. Wealth and brilliance began to join birth in determining distinction in society. The importance of good taste was also a new dimension of the eighteenth century. The Middle Ages had placed courtliness above all other qualities; the Renaissance had added conversing and civility as important qualities; the Enlightenment elevated good taste to a primary social virtue. Taste defined what a person truly was, rather than being merely a superficial attribute. Thus, the prominent sign of distinction in the eighteenth century was good taste in art, fashion, and particularly food and manners.

During the eighteenth century rules of etiquette and the nature of banqueting underwent important changes. Previously, many dishes were placed on the table at once, as we would today in a buffet. In 1742, the book of recipes and etiquette *Nouveau cuisinier royal et bourgeois* suggested that, for a dinner party for six to eight people, at least three courses be served, each with at least seven dishes per course. The same source suggested that, for a dinner party for 25 people, 27 dishes per course be served, making a total of 81 dishes. The need for this many dishes was to cater to a diversity of tastes.

The eighteenth-century practice of seating men at one end of the table and women at the other gave way to an alternating pattern. As a result, the boisterous toasts of the men became more refined. Other changes at the dinner table reflected a growing sense of individualism. During the Middle Ages two or three people took sips from the same soup bowl and ate meat from a single platter, dipped their bread and meat in the same sauceboats, and drank from a single cup passed around the table. By the eighteenth century, diners had their own bowl, plate, fork, knife, and spoon. No longer was it acceptable for people to share utensils or eat from the same plate.

John Trusler's *The Honours of the Table*, published in 1788, outlined proper table manners: "It is vulgar to eat your soup with your nose in the plate. You must avoid smelling the meat while it is on the fork.... It is exceedingly rude to scratch any part of your body, to spit, or blow your nose... to lean your elbows on the table, to sit too far from it, to pick your teeth before the dishes are removed." Trusler went on to suggest that if you needed to go to the toilet during the meal, you should slip away unobserved and return without announcing where you had been. The former practice of keeping a chamber pot in or just outside the dining room was discontinued for its vulgarity.

The scientific and technological changes of the previous century affected nearly every aspect of life, including food quality and preparation. At the beginning of the century, the way people lived and ate was still quite similar to that of their medieval predecessors. By the end of the century, homemakers had access to a wide array of kitchen equipment, including tools, pots, dishes, and glasses. Often, technological developments in one area brought changes in others; for example, improvements in rolling sheet iron led to better kitchen utensils and allowed for finer flour to be produced, thereby improving the quality of bread. Advances in agriculture brought great improvements to people's diets. Up until the beginning of the eighteenth century, cattle had to be killed before winter, as winter feeding practices had not been developed. Consequently, salted meat was a prominent part of people's diet. With the development of winter feeding practices originating in Holland, cattle could be kept year-round, allowing for fresh meat on the table in all seasons and less chance for improperly preserved meat to spoil.

With fresh meat available year-round and increased consumption of sugar, which made food more palatable, many of the old spices and flavourings common in previous centuries fell out of fashion. So too did the emphasis on appearance over taste. People of the medieval period placed a great deal of importance on the visual aspect of food: they served large birds

This painting captures the elaborate dress worn by both men and women of the late seventeenth century as well as the mounds of food served at banquets.

Eating Habits in Eighteenth-Century England

The eighteenth century brought many changes to the eating habits of the English. Manners, food—even mealtimes—changed. At the beginning of the century, the upper classes generally had breakfast between 9:00 and 10:00 a.m. and dinner between 2:00 and 3:00 p.m. As the century progressed, dinner was more commonly eaten between 6:00 and 7:00 p.m., leaving a long gap in the middle of the day. This led to the custom of tea being served with light sandwiches or scones around 4:00 p.m. The sandwich was introduced in the eighteenth century when the Earl of Sandwich was busy at a gambling table and asked a servant to put some meat between two slices of bread so that he would not have to leave the table.

Other changes to the English diet included pudding, replacing cereal pottage as a starchy filler. By the 1740s, roast beef and plum pudding had become a national dish. One foreign visitor wrote: "They bake them in the oven, they boil them with meat, they make them fifty-several ways: BLESSED BE HE THAT INVENTED PUDDING, for it is a manna that hits the palates of all sorts of people...."

During the late seventeenth century, coffee, chocolate, and tea became popular drinks in England. Chocolate was initially mixed with wine and later water. Coffee and tea, both recognized as stimulant drugs, were quite expensive and therefore were drunk primarily by the wealthy. To safeguard against theft, tea and coffee were often kept in a locked caddy. The introduction of tea, coffee, and chocolate created a need for special new cups, pots, kettles, and urns, spawning a new industry in pottery and metalware. Throughout the eighteenth century, serving tea became an increasingly elegant ceremony involving the household's finest silverware and china.

Below are three recipes common among all classes in England in the eighteenth century:

Barley Gruel

1.1 L water
50 g pearl barley
25 g raisins
25 g currants
2.5 mL ground mace
30 mL sugar
50 mL white wine

Put the water in a saucepan with the barley, raisins, currants, and mace and boil until the water is reduced by half and the barley is tender. Stir in the sugar and white wine, and serve.

Fried Celery

150 g flour
2.5 mL salt
1.5 mL nutmeg
2 egg yolks
125 mL white wine
1 bunch of celery stalks
clarified butter

To make the batter, mix the flour, salt, and nutmeg in a bowl, make a well in the centre, and drop in the egg yolks with 15 mL of the wine. Mix, stirring in the flour, then gradually add the remaining wine. Leave to stand.

Cut the celery into 12.5 mm lengths and simmer in boiling water until almost tender. Drain well and pat dry. Dip each piece in the batter to completely coat, then fry in hot clarified butter for about 2 minutes on each side until golden.

Strawberry Fritters

450 g large strawberries
175 g flour
50 g white sugar
10 mL nutmeg
2 eggs, well beaten
225 mL whipping cream
vegetable oil for deep frying
icing sugar to finish

The strawberries must be dry to begin. Leave the stems on for easier handling. In a bowl, mix the flour, sugar, and nutmeg. Make a well and drop in the eggs and cream. Stir until all the flour and sugar are mixed in. Let the batter stand for an hour or two. Dip each strawberry in batter until it is completely coated, and fry a few at a time in hot oil. Your oil must be hot enough to puff them, but not so hot as to brown them too quickly. Drain on absorbent paper and keep hot. Pile them in a pyramid in a warmed dish and sprinkle with icing sugar.

complete with all their feathers. Birds such as swan, stork, peacock, and cormorant, more renowned for their splendour than their flavour, disappeared from eighteenth-century cookbooks. Medieval cookbooks often advised cooks to add saffron or other ingredients to enhance colour; eighteenth-century cookbooks refer to the natural colour of foods when properly cooked, placing emphasis on the quality of the food rather than on appearance.

Family Life

Women in the Eighteenth Century

Despite the prominent role some women played in hosting the salons of Europe, the Enlightenment did little to change the traditional role of women in society. Enlightenment thinkers advocated the inalienable rights of men—be they slaves, Indians, Jews, or the poor—but, overall, they did not extend these rights to women. Although some argued against the prejudices shown toward women, it was more common for men of the eighteenth century to defend the view that women were inferior to men in that they lacked in the crucial faculties of reason and ethics. Contrary to the logic, rationality, and egalitarianism of the age, the ideal woman of the Enlightenment was no different from the ideal woman of past centuries: silent, obedient, subservient, modest, and chaste. Rousseau wrote about intelligent women in his popular novel *Emile* (1762):

> I would a thousand times rather have a homely girl, simply brought up, than a learned lady and a wit who make a literary circle of my house and install herself as its president. A female wit is a scourge to her husband, her children, her friends, her servants, to everybody. From the lofty height of her genius, she scorns every womanly duty, and she is always trying to make a man of herself....

Voltaire had little to say on the subject of women's education or role in society, although he did write to a friend concerning the intellect of his mistress, the Marquise du Châtelet: "Emilie, in truth, is the divine mistress, endowed with beauty, wit, compassion and all of the other womanly virtues. Yet I frequently wish she were less learned and her mind less sharp."

Women of the lower classes were often sent away to work as servants in wealthy households. For their extensive duties, which included cleaning, cooking, shopping, and caring for children, women received little if any pay, their wages often being sent directly to their parents. Young women also had to endure frequent beatings at the hands of an ungrateful mistress or unwanted sexual advances from the master, his sons, or his friends. Sexual abuse of servant girls and women was widespread throughout Europe. The upper classes exploited them and the women had no legal protection. When a girl would become pregnant as a result of abuse, she would be quickly fired and, often having no other recourse, would be forced to fend for herself through petty thievery or prostitution. An angry Parisian prostitute described the plight of many young women like herself by saying: "What are we? Most of us are unfortunate women, without origins, without education, servants and maids for the most part."

Family, Marriage, and Children

During the 1700s, the nuclear family was the norm. Because couples were on their own immediately after marriage, it was quite common among the majority of Europeans in the late seventeenth and early eighteenth centuries to marry relatively late: the average age of both men and women marrying for the first time was 27 years. Many people never married at all.

Infant mortality, high among the upper classes, was disturbingly common among the lower classes. Prey to numerous diseases, cold, and hunger, surviving infancy was a challenge many children could not meet. Those who did survive often succumbed to childhood illnesses or accidents. The death of children was so expected in Europe prior to the twentieth century that it was common for parents to give successive sons the same name to ensure one survived to adulthood carrying the father's name. The famous English historian Edward Gibbon was the first of six boys to be named after his father; none of the others survived the rigours of childhood.

Prior to the eighteenth century, children were born into a world of constraints. Swaddling, an ancient practice, involved wrapping and immobilizing the baby. As a result, babies were easier to care for, often placed on a board while the mother went about her business, and seemed to be much more subdued and less prone to crying. Tight bonnets were used to help shape the child's head in conformity with aesthetic ideals. By the eighteenth century, both these practices were condemned as being harmful to the development of the child. But the practice among the middle and

This touching portrait captures a child's first steps, as the mother, godmother, and nurse watch in delight.

⚓

upper classes of hiring a wet-nurse to breast-feed their children continued throughout the century. Upper-class women regarded breast-feeding as crude and beneath their station in life.

The care given infants is indicative of the attitude toward children in the eighteenth century. Although it was important to have children so they could carry on the family line, children were treated with great indifference by their parents. Showing outward signs of love and affection was uncommon, creating a vast psychological gulf between parents and children. Unfortunately for many children, this indifference often led to physical abuse, as the only attention they received from their parents were attempts to discipline them. Susannah Wesley proudly proclaimed that her children were "taught to fear the rod and to cry softly, by which means they escaped the abundance of correction they might otherwise have had, and that most odious noise of the crying of children was rarely heard in the house."

Education

During the eighteenth century, there was a significant rise in formal education. Compulsory education for children aged 7 to 12 arose during the late seventeenth century, at the beginning of the Enlightenment. Both England and France established such schools to teach basic literacy and religion to the children of the poor. Prussia was the first European state to institute compulsory education, marking an important development for universal education in 1717. Despite these advances in the eighteenth century, many children failed to receive any formal education; their education came informally from their parents beginning at the age of seven or eight, when young boys would accompany their fathers into the fields and young girls would begin learning the essentials of housekeeping. By the age of 12, young boys would be apprenticed to a master, from whom they would learn a trade, or they would find employment with a neighbour working in the fields. At the same age, young girls would be sent out as servants as described earlier.

Culture of the Unenlightened During the Eighteenth Century

Culture among the middle and upper classes during the eighteenth century was characterized by a flood of new ideas concerning politics, economics, morals and religion, and the nature of humans. Intellectuals proposed radical new ideas that often challenged society as Europeans knew it. Enlightenment thinkers de-emphasized miracles and superstitions that often made religion seem ridiculous in an age of reason. A common sentiment among *philosophes* of the eighteenth century can be expressed by the phrase "My mind is my church": while retaining a belief in God, dogmatism and intolerance were frowned upon by intellectuals of the Enlightenment.

This emphasis on reason and attack on superstition clearly distinguished the enlightened middle and upper classes from the unenlightened masses. When a child of the lower class was baptized, parents often resorted to magic to ensure the health of the child. Once the priest had left the church, the child was rolled on the altar to strengthen its muscles and protect it against rickets, and the godparents were expected to

England's Experimental Penal Colony

 Australia has a unique colonial past for, unlike other British colonies such as Canada, it was not initially settled by free colonists seeking a better life in a new land; instead, Australia's first white settlers were convicts. For over half a century, British ships crowded with petty thieves, rebels, and other outcasts, made the long and arduous journey to the new British colony in the South Pacific.

Transporting criminals was an idea that went back almost as far as England's overseas empire. To many English, the idea of forced exile had many merits, including the permanent removal of felons from Britain and granting criminals their life. The transportation of criminals had the added bonus of providing the English colonies with a large labour force that could do the work most English people disliked, such as clearing land and building roads.

Beginning in 1618, convicts were transported to England's new colonies in the Americas; in 1717, England passed a law making transportation official by imposing penalties of seven years in the Americas for minor offences to 14 years for capital offences. Between 1717 and 1776, 40 000 felons were transported to the American colonies.

England's rising crime rate and the increasing opposition to executing petty criminals contributed to drastic crowding in British jails during the latter part of the eighteenth century. These problems were compounded by the outbreak of the American Revolution and the subsequent loss of the Thirteen Colonies. With the outbreak of the Revolution, England lost its major outlet for transported felons, precipitating a crisis in England's jails. To relieve the pressure from the jails, the English government decided to house criminals selected for transport in the old ships anchored in the Thames River and other southern ports until they could decide what to do with them. These hulks, their masts and rigging gone but still floating, were seen to be inhabitable by the authorities and therefore a suitable alternative to jails. By 1790, the number of convicts on these floating jails was increasing by 1000 per year. The threat of disease was disturbing and problems with security were beginning to alarm many English citizens. The British government found the answer to the dilemma in the newly acquired colony of Australia.

In 1788, England began transporting criminals to the penal colony of Botany Bay in Australia. Among the first shipload were petty thieves, highway robbers, muggers, cattle and sheep thieves, swindlers, and forgers. None of those transported on the first voyage were murderers or rapists. They were petty criminals who often stole out of necessity: the second oldest convict to be transported on the first voyage was 70-year-old Elizabeth Beckford, imprisoned for seven years for stealing 12 pounds of Gloucester cheese. Later voyages would include criminals as well as political activists such as the weaver Thomas Holden, who was transported in 1812 for his activities as an early trade unionist.

A total of about 160 000 men, women, and children were transported to Australia. By the time the last shipload of convicts sailed for Australia in 1868, many free settlers had arrived to populate the colony along with freed convicts. Over time, new aristocrats would emerge, copying the social trends of England and gradually creating a distinctive Australian culture that for decades would try to ignore its origins.

kiss under the belfry to help guard the child against stammering and muteness.

Cats figured prominently in the superstitions and folklore of the eighteenth century. Believed to be agents of the devil, cats were often seen as witches who had been transformed and went about casting spells on innocent victims. Some of the common beliefs about cats were that if one were to enter a bakery, the bread would not rise; if a cat was buried alive, it could clear a field of weeds; a cat lying on a man's bed was the devil waiting to carry off the soul to hell; and a new house could be protected by enclosing cats within its walls. Unlike some members of the middle and upper classes, who emphasized reason and intellect, the lower classes' daily lives were guided by superstition and folklore.

Leisure Among the Unenlightened

Members of the middle and upper classes spent much of their leisure time in cafés and salons listening to music, poetry, and discussing ideas; the lower classes did so in pubs, where they drank, gossiped, and discussed brochures. By the eighteenth century, wine—usually adulterated or watered down—was fast becoming the favourite drink in Europe while in England, gin had become the drink of the poor. The booklets and brochures read aloud in the pubs by the few who were literate were generally of three types: religious booklets of Bible stories and tales of saints' lives; almanacs, which included how-to-live guides on cleanliness, nourishment, and potions for illness; and entertainment literature, comprising tales, fables, and satires in which hunger, sex, and oppression were the most common themes.

The year was filled with holidays that allowed for much merrymaking, eating, drinking, dressing up, and playing games. The festivities provided a time for the young to meet and for adults to enjoy a break from the daily grind in the fields. The highlights of the year's holidays occurred between the spring sowing and summer harvest or in the early autumn once the harvest was completed.

Entertainment among the lower classes included numerous blood sports, such as bull-baiting, where a pack of dogs was set loose on a tied-up bull, or cock-fighting. Torture of animals, especially cats, was also a popular amusement throughout Europe. Children would attach cats to poles and roast them over bonfires, and an English crowd once shaved a cat to look like a priest, dressed it in a miniature monk's habit, and hanged it from the gallows. Torture of cats was so common that expressions such as "as patient as a cat whose claws are being pulled out" were often used. By the end of the eighteenth century, enlightened reformers and moralists were denouncing such cruelties, although nothing was said about the blood sports of the gentry, such as fox hunting.

Crime and Punishment in the Eighteenth Century

One of the great social concerns of the eighteenth century was the rising crime rate. Scottish reformer Patrick Colquhoun's *Treatise on the Police of the Metropolis* (1797) suggested that 115 000 people in London (approximately one in eight citizens) were living off crime. Among those included in this "criminal class" were obvious criminals, such as thieves, muggers, forgers, as well as scavengers, bear-baiters, and gypsies, who had no clear connection to crime. Similarly, Colquhoun's treatise suggests that the estimated 50 000 prostitutes who worked the streets of London included many women of the lower class who simply lived with a man out of wedlock. Regardless of the accuracy of Colquhoun's data, his work does reflect the sense among the middle and upper classes that England was plagued by crime.

Throughout the eighteenth century, many retained the old belief that public hangings acted as an effective deterrent to crime. It was common for parents to take their children to a hanging and afterwards flog them so that they would not forget the example they had seen. The hanging of a famous criminal often drew crowds of 25 000 to 30 000 people, who were unruly and jostled for the best seats on the grandstand. After the criminal had died, the body was handed over to the Royal College of Physicians, often despite requests from the family to claim the body for proper burial.

Moralists and reformers of the eighteenth century increasingly protested against execution for petty crime, such as forgery or theft. In fact between 1749 and 1799 the percentage of executions for capital convictions declined from 69.3 percent to 15.7 percent. As a result of the drastic decline in executions and the increase in the number of crimes committed, England's jails by the end of the century were bursting at the seams. Even the enlightened sensibilities of the eighteenth century never led anyone to believe that jails could reform criminals. Instead, England's prisons have been described as "incubators of crime."

Historian Robert Hughes noted: "There was no attempt to classify or segregate prisoners by age, sex, or gravity of crime. Women were thrown in the same common ward as men, first offenders with hardened criminals, inoffensive civil debtors with muggers, clerkly forgers with murderers, ten year old boys with homosexual rapists." With crime believed to be on the rise, executions becoming less popular, and jails costing a great deal of money and being overcrowded, England sought an alternative for its penal system. The alternative resulted from Captain James Cook's chance discovery of *Australia* for the Europeans in 1770. Beginning in 1788 and continuing for over half a century, England relieved pressure on its overcrowded jails by shipping thousands of convicts to Australia. These would be the first European settlers of Australia.

Reflections

The eighteenth century was an important transitional period in the history of modern Europe. The belief in progress brought about by the Scientific Revolution was applied to society and politics, leading prominent intellectuals to postulate a better world where a belief in the dignity of humans replaced the static class structure of previous centuries. While these ideas dominated the discussions in the salons of Europe, the masses, who remained exploited, uneducated, and largely unenlightened, clung to ancient superstitions and prejudices. Eventually, the ideas of the elite would trickle down to the common people, providing the inspiration for the French Revolution. In studying the social history of the eighteenth century, we sense a degree of familiarity with our own society.

Key Concepts, Figures, and Events

Social History　　　　　Salon　　　　　Australia

Topics for Further Thought

1. The study of social history presents historians with unique challenges and potentially great rewards. How has this chapter on the social history of the eighteenth century helped to enrich and expand your understanding of the forces that have shaped modern European history? Should you wish to pursue a more in-depth study of an aspect of social history from this period, what are some of the challenges you would face?

2. At the outset of this chapter, it was suggested that the eighteenth century was a transitional period in modern European history. How do the changes in social and cultural history from this period support this statement?

3. Salons, which originated in the seventeenth century, had their greatest impact during the Enlightenment. Assess the importance of salons on the intellectual growth of the eighteenth century. How did salons reflect the ideals of the Enlightenment?

Topics for Further Research

1. Carry out further research on aspects of daily life in the eighteenth century. Based on your research, prepare two accounts of historical fiction that outline a typical day in the life of i) a man or woman of the middle or upper class and ii) a man or woman of the lower class (either urban or rural).

2. Despite continuing restrictions imposed on women in European society of the eighteenth century, several women achieved prominence during this century for their work in a variety of fields. Select and research a prominent woman from the eighteenth century. Based on your research, write a short essay or report describing her life, accomplishments, and impact on the Enlightenment.

3. Australia's unique colonial past makes it of particular interest to students of the eighteenth and nineteenth centuries. Do further research to find out how successfully Australia relieved the pressure from English jails and assess the impact of Australia's past as a penal colony on shaping its national culture and identity.

Responding to Ideas

1. One of the central ideas of the Enlightenment was that of equality and the assumption that humans had certain basic rights. Yet historians Bonnie Anderson and Judith Zinsser described women's place in eighteenth century as follows: "Even the most brilliant, even those supported by their families rarely escaped the traditional expectations about a woman's life, the roles these expectations prescribed, and the practical hazards of being female. When choices had to be made, their own desires and their scholarship suffered." To what degree do the ideals of the Enlightenment and the reality faced by most women in the eighteenth century support the idea that this period was a transition to the twentieth century, when women have gained a fuller role in Western culture?

2. Historian Robert Darnton suggests that there is much to be learned from the stories of *Mother Goose*. A close examination of these stories in their original form can shed much light on the lives of the common people of the eighteenth century. Review a few of your favourite *Mother Goose* stories before responding to the following statement by Darnton. In your response, explain what you believe can be learned by carefully studying the stories you have selected. "The peasants of early modern France inhabited a world of stepmothers and orphans, of inexorable, unending toil, and of brutal emotions, both raw and repressed. The human condition has changed so much since then that we can hardly imagine the way it appeared to people whose lives were nasty, brutish, and short. That is why we need to reread *Mother Goose*."

Eighteenth-Century Europe and the Wider World

❧ CHAPTER HIGHLIGHTS

- An overview of the history of European knowledge of the "outside world"

- The development of maritime technology and of a new economic ideology for overseas trade and colonization

- The African origins of slavery as a product of the European search for wealth

- The reciprocal nature of the Grand Exchange

- The impact of religious and intellectual attitudes toward non-European peoples

- The development and success of the abolitionist movement

The year 1992 marked the 500th anniversary of the discovery of North America by *Christopher Columbus*. The voyage of Columbus was one of many European voyages of discovery that occurred between 1487 and 1780. During these three centuries of exploration and colonization, Europe was to undergo profound changes in its economic system while altering the histories of diverse peoples worldwide. The driving force behind European expansion between 1492 and 1780 was the quest for new markets and sources of raw materials to fuel the emerging capitalist economy. In their quest for riches, Europeans showed little concern for the personal well-being or the preservation of the culture and heritage of the peoples encountered.

European Knowledge of the Wider World up to 1700

From antiquity, Europeans had only fragmentary knowledge of Asia and Africa: the Greek historian Herodotus (480–425 B.C.E.) recorded improbable accounts of Africans in his *Histories*; Roman trade goods have been excavated in Eastern India; and the Venetian adventurer Marco Polo, who lived in Asia from 1271 to 1295, heard from Chinese informants about the existence of the Japanese islands.

The available information about other continents increased quite quickly from around 1500 C.E. onward. The earliest known settlement in North

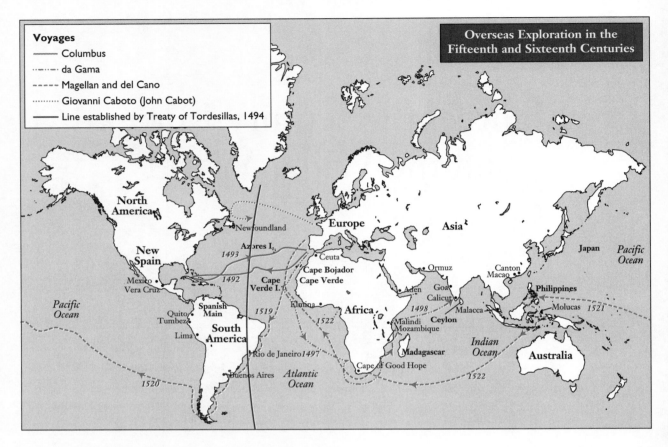

America was by Norsemen at L'Anse aux Meadows, Newfoundland, around 1000 C.E. Following this failed settlement, contact with North America seems to have been forgotten until new links were made by Europeans with the Americas beginning in 1492 with the voyages of Christopher Columbus.

The initial big push in exploration came from vessels based on the Iberian peninsula (Spain and Portugal). Indeed, Cape Rock in Portugal is the most westerly point of the European continent. Italian seamen such as Christopher Columbus and Giovanni Caboto (known as John Cabot in English), sought employment from the kings of Spain and Portugal, not from the Italian states. The questions of the adequacy of Ptolomean geography—the idea that the world was a central land mass surrounded by sea—and of the shape of the globe, were most hotly debated in Madrid and in Lisbon. Consequently, it was in Spain and Portugal that explorers were most likely to find investors willing to finance risky overseas exploration.

Only during the course of the fifteenth century did people gradually come to realize that the world was round and that a new continent lay between East and West. If you sailed westward from Europe, it was not Asia you encountered but the Americas. Between America and Asia lay the largest world ocean, the Pacific. From 1500 Portugal, Spain, France, Holland, England, and Scandinavia established a network of sea-linked capitalist relations with the Americas and Asia.

European voyages on the Pacific provided knowledge of the west coast of the Americas from Tierra del Fuego to Alaska. Australia was discovered by the Portuguese in the sixteenth century, explored by the Dutch in 1606, and settled by the British from 1770 onward. Although there were inland areas of Africa and North America where Europeans had never set foot, by 1800 the major land masses of the world were known. No single European power ever fully controlled all of these sea lanes and markets. Europeans collectively established a global, capitalist economic system.

Maritime Technology and the Emergence of Capitalism

Europeans took the world lead in the design and production of long-distance ocean-going vessels. Technological changes during the fifteenth century allowed for greater distances to be travelled with much less risk. Among the changes that helped to revolutionize sea travel in the fifteenth century were changes in sails; the use of the Catalan rudder, which was mounted on the sternpost instead of two side rudder oars; compasses; nautical charts; and pilot's books. Navigation of the open seas became possible: no longer was it necessary to be constantly within sight of land, nor were clear skies essential for navigation.

By the sixteenth century, the economic system in Europe relied on the organization of capital, labour, and raw materials to produce surplus wealth. This new economic system, capitalism, provided the impetus for powerful merchants to sponsor voyages of exploration and colonization. This brought about a radical change in the nature of long-distance trade: from the predominance of luxury items to raw, unprocessed goods that could be refined by European manufacturers. Finished goods would, in turn, be used in trade with the regions supplying the raw materials. Thus, as European countries adopted the capitalist mode of production, their economies became increasingly tied to the use of inexpensive raw materials and labour from various parts of the world.

In parts of the world that were not able to resist the European intrusion because they were too sparsely populated or because the local peoples were not strong enough, settlers set up colonies of immigrants. An interrelationship between the colony and the home markets in Europe often developed: Europeans might work in "transformation industries," where colonial raw materials were reworked, as in the case of spinning cotton to make cloth.

Capitalism operated on a global scale because sea lanes made transactions easier than across land routes. The distribution of tasks and rewards permitted some nations to exploit others. Military potential was also important to the resolution of conflict in focal points of the world economy. During the seventeenth and eighteenth centuries, there was great impetus in European naval gunnery and shipbuilding. The big players (Britain, France, Holland) are often called the "core" states who interacted and exploited the weakness of less advanced economies overseas and weaker military states.

Searching for Wealth

The richness of Asian, African, and American natural resources meant that, from the sixteenth century onward, clashes between European powers would take place on a global level. All Europeans wanted bullion at a time when the credit mechanisms of international trade did not yet exist; spices were equivalent to precious metals. Portuguese expansion in the fifteenth century saw landfall on the uninhabited volcanic islands of Madeira and the Azores in the Atlantic, and also the steady exploration of the West African Coast; they established trading stations and purchased slaves brought to them for sale by local rulers. The Portuguese sought to reach India by sailing around the Cape of Good Hope. Vasco da Gama arrived on the west coast of the Indian Subcontinent in 1498.

In the Americas, Spanish conquistadors initially looked for gold and silver but also settled and enslaved the local people for agricultural and mining work. This intrusion caused the spread of European diseases, such as the common cold and smallpox, which would exterminate many Amerindian groups. Between 1508 and 1511, Puerto Rico, Jamaica, and Cuba were occupied. The Spaniards found some gold (exhausted by 1515) on Hispaniola (today Haiti and the Dominican Republic) and settled in Cuba, where they established agricultural estates. They soon discovered that there were wealthier peoples on the mainland. In 1519, Hernán Cortés conquered Mexico and with his men found a rich city. Francisco Pizarro conquered Peru in 1532.

Within 30 years of the landfall of Christopher Columbus, the Spanish discovered the largest concentrations of precious metals in the Americas, the Aztec Empire with its capital in what is now Mexico City, and the Inca empire of Peru. These were highly developed Amerindian societies with sophisticated knowledge of astronomy, masonry construction, and agriculture. Both civilizations were doomed to military defeat accompanied by a population collapse induced by epidemic disease and intermarriage with their conquerors.

The rivalry between Spain and Portugal over the control of newly discovered lands caused tensions which the papacy tried to forestall with the *Treaty of Tordesillas* (1494), which was to divide the respective areas of exploration according to a line of longitude

North American natives were often depicted in classical form during the eighteenth century, as seen in this engraving.

———————— ⚔ ————————

some 370 Portuguese leagues west of the Azores. The idea was that the Portuguese would continue to move southward along the Atlantic Coast of Africa, where they might encounter new islands, and the Spanish would do the same in the Americas. However, the treaty was drawn before the shape of South America was completely known, leaving Brazil (which protrudes into the Atlantic) on the Portuguese side.

Brazil, which later became the largest and most populous country of South America, appeared in the early days of exploration to offer lesser rewards than sedentary civilizations with dense populations. The first export from Brazil was a kind of wood that gave a red dye. Only later did Brazil become the largest exporter of coffee.

Central America was crucial for access from the Atlantic to the Pacific Coast of South America before the construction of the Panama Canal (1881–1914). The first expedition to the Panama-Colombia border took place between 1509 and 1513: great mule trains carried goods from one side to the other. Trade fairs such as Portobello were major exchange points in any Pacific-Atlantic trade. Fortresses such as El Moro in San Juan de Puerto Rico provided protected anchorage for the Spanish fleet. The fortress at Acapulco on the Pacific Coast of Mexico protected the fleets that crossed to Manila and the Philippine Islands. The

protection was needed against pirates from the Northern European powers who had realized that the easiest way to get bullion was to steal it after the Spanish had collected it for shipment to the royal treasury.

The Spanish concentrated more on settlement than trade. They started to enslave the native peoples wherever they landed. The Taino of Puerto Rico became extinct within 100 years of the Spanish conquest. Native peoples were largely destroyed by European diseases against which they had no immunity. Karen Kuperman noted in *Settling With the Indians*: "European diseases did more than European technology to vanquish the American Indian in the early years of colonization."

The abuses of enslavement helped decimate the Amerindian populations: places like the silver mines of Potosí in what is now Bolivia (discovered in 1545) effectively functioned as death camps. Priests and royal officials tried to prevent the worst abuses but the greed of the settlers and the complicity of many royal governors were too strong for them to successfully protect the native peoples.

Africans were imported to replace Amerindian labour. The African slave trade persisted for three centuries, shipping millions of Africans under inhuman conditions to work on plantations in the Americas.

African Origins of Slavery

Although trade in people was not new in either Africa or Europe, the scale of the trade was. Between 1701 and 1801, over 6 million people were forcibly removed from Africa to supply the demand for slaves in Europe and the Americas. Slavery rested on European demand for colonial goods. Slavery was practised in traditional African society long before the advent of the Europeans. Arabs from North Africa had many slaves. The coastal tribes were predatory and went inland to capture people from smaller settlements. The earliest market was the line of the Sahel and Sub-Saharan peoples exchanging slaves for gold. The principal sources of slaves were criminals sold as punishment, individuals sold by family at a time of famine, those kidnapped by slaving bands of merchants, and prisoners of war.

Slavers in the early days felt no need to apologize for their occupation. Indeed slavers could invoke religion as a reason for what they were doing: baptizing whole shiploads of puzzled Africans, and declaring that

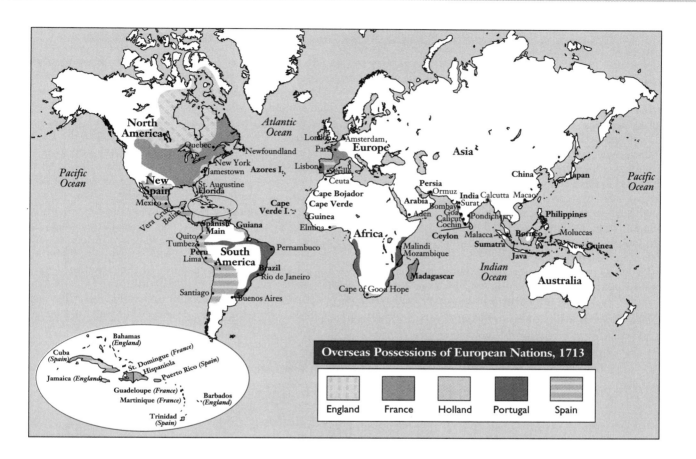

Overseas Possessions of European Nations, 1713

England | France | Holland | Portugal | Spain

they should be grateful for slavery because it led them to Jesus, their saviour.

The earliest coastal stations were places where business was done with traders coming from the interior. Europeans quickly learned that the most efficient way to obtain slaves was to trade on the coast with African middlemen who specialized in selling their neighbours in exchange for trade goods and metals.

As the Spanish need for slaves grew, so too did the maritime trade in humans, especially from the coast of Guinea. The *Asiento* (monopoly on the supply of cargoes) was first given in 1595 to supply 38 000 slaves in nine years. The slave trade across the Atlantic in the sixteenth century was dominated by the Spanish and the Portuguese, but in the seventeenth century it was dominated by the Dutch. British and Danish ships began participating in the eighteenth century. The

trade in captives was gradually abolished in the nineteenth century, as was slavery itself. The last great emancipation of slaves took place in Brazil in 1888. (The East European equivalent, the freeing of Rumanian serfs, was a little earlier, in 1864.)

As early as 1501, there were Africans on Hispaniola, but only in 1518 did the slave trade proper begin with the landing of the first cargo of African captives. It took between 35 and 50 days to cross from the west coast of Africa to Brazil—somewhat less to Cuba. The Dutch joined the slave trade after their independence from Spain. In 1626, the French built the fort of Saint Louis in Senegal, marking their entry into the slave trade, to supply their sugar islands with labour. The English took a Portuguese castle on the coast and began to supply Barbados with slaves. In 1663, the commercial association called Royal

Adventurers of England was formed, with its slaves branded "dy," for Duke of York, on the chest. Using the coins made from the Guinea Coast gold was to advertise the company: a gold coin worth 21 shillings was called a guinea. In 1672, the Adventurers were replaced by the Royal African Company, a sign of the state approval of this line of endeavour.

Who was most reprehensible in the slave trade: the rulers who sold other Africans, the slave traders and their crews, or the investors in Europe who enjoyed the profits? Indeed it was Europeans, for it was they who introduced chattel slavery, they who provided an insatiable market for slaves, and they who created and encouraged a century of civil wars between African kingdoms, which produced the prisoners to be sold into slavery. The net result of the exploitation of Africans as slaves was massive depopulation, particularly of young males, and the underdevelopment of Africa. No contribution to Africa's infrastructure was made, only cheap manufactured goods were exchanged for slaves, thus contributing to Africa's Third World status today.

Trading Companies

The novelty in the Dutch, English, and French efforts in the expansion of Europe was the trading company. The northern countries had a well-developed commercial system, in which certain cities financed and organized long-distance enterprises. The family capitalism that had been typical of the Hansa traders in the Baltic or the Italian merchant republics could not marshal enough money to mount the new endeavours, so companies were formed: the East India Company (1600) in England to trade for spices with the Indian Malabar Coast; the United East India Company (1602) in the Netherlands, which was set up as a trading post at the Cape of Good Hope to trade with Indonesia and Malaya; the French East India Company (1604) in Northwestern France (port of Lorient); and the Dutch United West India Company (1621) in the Netherlands, which dealt in furs and slaves. The last-named company sent Henry Hudson to explore Northern Canada.

The Grand Exchange

When Columbus set sail on his return visit to the Americas in 1493, he could not have known the profound implications this voyage would have on the world. To begin with, items aboard his ships would initiate a revolution that would change the diet of the entire world forever. Aboard the 17 ships were seeds, fruit trees, and livestock. These proved to be the tip of the iceberg in terms of the foods that would be exchanged between the Old World and the New World.

Over the next few centuries, the variety of food eaten by people the world over would increase by what is called the Grand Exchange.

Sunflowers, native to the Great Plains of North America, were exported to Europe, where they thrived in cold Northern Europe, and provided Russians with a welcome new cooking oil. In return, wheat, barley, and oats from Europe and the Middle East arrived in North America, eventually making the Great Plains the "breadbasket of the world."

Other important crops of the Grand Exchange include coffee from Africa, which became one of the Caribbean's and Brazil's most important crops, and the nutritious cacao chocolate, which was exported from tropical America to Europe and from which cocoa and chocolate are made. As well, tomatoes from Mexico, known to Europeans as the "apples of love," came to be favoured by Italian chefs. Peanuts, potatoes,

vanilla, corn, hot peppers, and tobacco are a few of the numerous other crops that arrived in Europe, and eventually Asia, enriching the diet of all classes. In addition to the grains mentioned earlier, cattle, horses, poultry, and pigs were all exported from Europe to the New World where they have become staples in the diet of all Americans.

When you next sit down to eat a meal, think about the origin of the foods you are eating and try to imagine your diet had the Grand Exchange in foods not taken place. While European contact brought disease and exploitation to millions of Amerindians, we must not lose sight of the beneficial results. Primary among these is a richer and more varied diet for people worldwide.

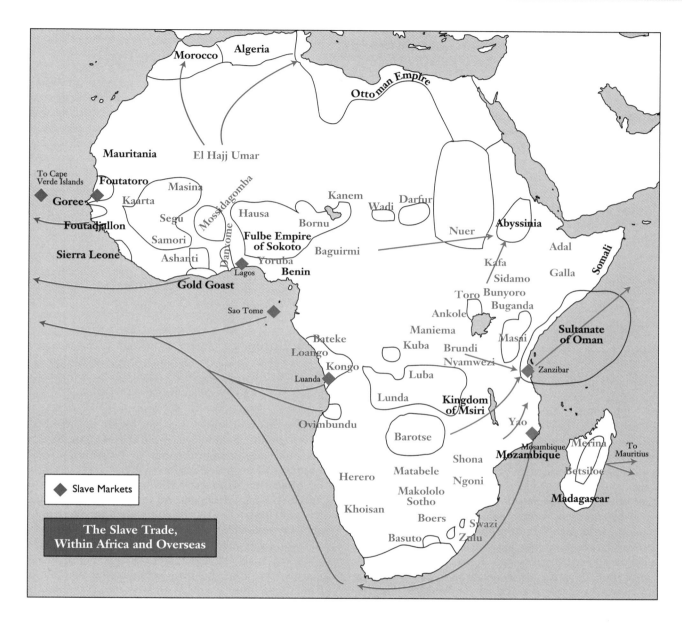

The Slave Trade, Within Africa and Overseas

◆ Slave Markets

Set up by government initiative, these companies became the cutting edge of economic exploitation overseas. These great joint stock companies had an unprecedented development after 1600. In many cases, they were awarded monopoly rights, exemptions from taxation, the right to own land, and so forth.

No country better displayed those characteristics than the Netherlands. The ambassador of Louis XIV to the Hague from 1672 to 1679 compared the modest but comfortable existence of the merchants of Amsterdam with the rituals of the French court at Versailles:

It must be granted that this little republic can now be numbered among the mightiest powers of Europe. In this we have reason to admire the fruits of industry, shipping, and trade for these are the sources from which all their wealth flows with an abundance which is all the more remarkable because, until now, the skill and ability of Holland have kept this flow almost completely away from the other nations of Europe.

In 1594, the Far Company was formed in Amsterdam. It was composed of nine merchant members. Although not a big commercial success, it would have enormous impact in European expansionism: the link of maritime exploration, trading posts, and large-scale rather than individual capitalism. The Far Company decided that the Portuguese, despite the claims of their king to be "lords of the conquest, navigation and commerce of Ethiopia, India, Arabia, and Persia" as king Manuel had put it in 1501, were actually strained to the limits to maintain their trading network in the Indian Ocean. To celebrate the dawn of a new century and a new contender, the Dutch fleet engaged Portuguese ships off Java and won, despite the reputation of the Portuguese gunners. From now on, the Dutch would carry the war against the Spanish crown (at the time linked with that of Portugal) not only in the Netherlands but far away across the ocean. This was perhaps the first true world war because European quarrels were settled on distant oceans.

The Dutch began to absorb products from the colonial territories into their economy: Delft porcelain patterns owed a lot to models brought from the Orient; the Dutch specialization in tobacco was a result of the colonies, as was the start of the chocolate and liqueur businesses. These products brought from overseas and treated at home gave work to Dutch people and were then re-exported. When sailing outward-bound, the Dutch carried salt fish from the herring of the North Sea, as well as woolen goods and other European products to be used in their holdings in the West Indies, Java, South Africa, and Ceylon, which they had wrested from the Portuguese and which would be snatched from them by the English.

By the eighteenth century, all the European maritime powers gave special attention to ship design, training of sailors, and protection of shipping routes from pirates.

Reciprocal Nature of the Grand Exchange

The passing of knowledge from Europe to the wider world was always a two-way process. In many parts of the world, other societies were becoming familiar with the arrival of exotic individuals. On screens painted in Japan, which are a source of information about the first contacts with the Portuguese, we see blacks represented, the first Africans ever seen in that part of the world. On the beach in Acapulco, Mexico a monument was put up in the twentieth century to the Japanese envoy sent on an embassy to Europe at the start of the seventeenth century who crossed there on his way to Europe. Several years later, he would again cross Mexico on his return voyage to Japan with news of the nature of European societies. A hundred years before, Montezuma, the Aztec ruler of Mexico captured by Hernán Cortés, liked to ask his Spanish page boy many questions about Spain.

New Foods

The greatest impact Columbus had on the world was not his initial contact in 1492 but rather his return visit in 1493, when he brought with him horses, pigs, wheat, chickpeas, vegetable seeds, and fruit trees. Later Europeans would bring chickens, barley, oats, and rye as well as coffee and sugar from Africa. The flow of foodstuffs was equally great from North and South America to Europe, Africa, and China.

Maize (corn) entered the peasant food chain in Northern Spain, Portugal, and Italy in the form of animal food and was also ground into flour. Tomatoes, which were also first encountered by Spaniards in the valley of Mexico, became a staple of the peasant diet in Northern Spain, Portugal, and Italy. Columbus noted in Cuba that corn was tasty either boiled, roasted, or ground into flour. The Spaniards took corn to the Philippines in the sixteenth century, and Chinese merchants there brought it to China. The Portuguese took it to Africa, where it was widely cultivated and used on the slave ships.

Another New World crop that made a big impact on European diet was the potato. They were used to provision ships returning to Europe and, by 1573, the Seville poorhouse was buying them for the inmates.

A Taste for Sweetness

European colonization of the Americas led to one of the great revolutions in cuisine. Prior to Columbus's return voyage in 1493, sugar cane was unknown in the Americas and produced in limited quantities in the Old World. Until the seventeenth century, sugar remained a luxury, affordable only by the European elite. After 1700, Europeans established colonies in the Caribbean and South America, where vast quantities of sugar cane could be grown, so the price declined to levels low enough for sugar to become a regular part of the average European's diet. In England, the per capita consumption of sugar increased 20 times between 1663 and 1775, an indication of its popularity and its increased use along with the rise in consumption of coffee, tea, and chocolate.

Sugar was introduced into Europe by returning Crusaders. Europeans began to import sugar to be used as a medicine and, in very wealthy households, as an expensive additive for foods and drinks. At this time, sugar was so highly priced that it was considered a suitable gift for princes to send to each other. The appeal of sugar lies in the fact that it is a very powerful sweetener and does not leave an aftertaste like maple or honey. Furthermore, sugar is a better preservative than honey; it can be easily transported and stored.

Since the seventeenth century, sugar has been produced in increasingly large quantities and the price has steadily declined. Before it became a commonplace food item, white sugar, especially when served from a silver caster, was a subtle way of showing off one's wealth; so was icing a cake. By the nineteenth and twentieth centuries, the use of sugar had reached such heights that some began to question its effects on health, although there were always those who argued: "That which preserves apples and plums, will also preserve livers and lungs."

The arrival of the nineteenth century and the Industrial Revolution brought another use for sugar and consequently another dramatic

---

African slaves on sugar plantations in the Caribbean worked long, hard days.

increase in its consumption. The rise of a new urban working class who worked long hours in factories—and had no garden or forest from which to get food—created a need for foods that were inexpensive and easy to prepare. Often, these foods were insufficient to sustain the level of work demanded of the labourers. A remedy common among the English working class was to drink several cups of tea every day. The sugar, although it did not nourish, was a calorie-rich stimulant that warmed the body and dulled hunger pangs. As the nineteenth century progressed, factory-prepared foods became an increasingly larger part of many people's diet. Food manufactures relied heavily on sugar to both preserve foods and bring out flavour.

Only in the late twentieth century, with its emphasis on health, weight, and appearance, and scientific confirmation of the ill-effects of a sugar-heavy diet, have North Americans and Europeans begun to relinquish their love affair with sugar. After three centuries, the decline in the price of sugar is no longer met with a rise in consumption; in fact, recent studies show that in the Western world, the per capita consumption of sugar has begun to decline.

Knowledge of the potato went to Spain's Italian possessions and spread to France, Germany, and Britain. There was an initial resistance to potatoes although enlightened monarchs of the eighteenth century encouraged its use as a food source. Potatoes were nutritious, grew on land not suitable for other crops, and took pressure off the demand for wheat, which was more expensive to cultivate.

Other New World foods to enter the European diet were chocolate, peanuts, vanilla, pineapple, lima beans, and peppers sweet and hot. "Retransmission" by Europeans from one area of the world to another was rapid: pineapples, papaya, and sweet potatoes had been taken across the Pacific to Asia within a century. Manioc, rice, yams, cowpeas, and a variety of citrus fruits not previously known to Africa were taken there before 1700. Coffee, a plant which originated in Arabia, was taken to South America and the second Spanish governor of Colombia took the first cows to the New World to provide milk and meat. As well, by the sixteenth century, the turkey, native to North and Central America, was well domesticated in Western Europe.

Sugar cane was planted in the New World as early as 1506. Arabs had cultivated sugar in the Mediterranean area at least from 750 C.E. in Palestine, and then in Egypt and Sicily. In 1550, there were at least five sugar plantations in Brazil and by 1623 the number had jumped to more than 350. By 1580, sugar plantations of Northeastern Brazil were the major source of revenue there. Europe was avid for a sweetener other than the traditional honey. When the Dutch attacked the Portuguese colony of Pernambuco during the seventeenth century, the motivation was to take over this rich source of revenue. Coffee, tea, sugar, and spices were soon generating revenues. They also provided new sources of taxation for governments. The diet of the average European was now healthier and more varied than it had been a few centuries earlier.

The Amerindians

In North America, the first European description of the native peoples spoke of *Skraelings* in the Norse sagas. This word has a derogatory connotation. Columbus informed Spanish monarchs Ferdinand and Isabella that he had found people in the new lands who were "very well built, of handsome bodies and faces."

He thought that he had arrived in India, so he and his Spanish sailors called them Indians.

In 1534, Jacques Cartier came to Canada from Saint-Malo in Normandy. Upon his return to France, he took some Amerindians with him who, after causing much diversion to the French court, sickened and died. When Cartier returned to Canada, he claimed that they were alive and well, having married into great families, and were so happy in France that they had no desire to return to their families. The native people were likely not convinced of this. They were not happy when the French established a fort at which a number of men remained for the winter: the French were attacked and wiped out. The following winter, another group tried to survive, but this time it was scurvy that caused sickness and death. (They did not know about stewing the bark and needles of white cedar to get vitamin C as the native people did.) Later, French renegades and *coureurs de bois* (fur traders) who learned the survival skills of the Amerindians extended the knowledge of native customs among the immigrants from France.

Samuel de Champlain, the French explorer who, as commander of a Spanish vessel, had visited the West Indies, Mexico, Colombia, and Panama, and then explored the St. Lawrence River and founded Montreal for France, collected systematic information about Indians. Etienne Brulé discovered two of the Great Lakes and was the first European to see the site of what is today Toronto.

The religion of the newcomers was, of course, Christianity. Saint Augustine, an early Christian philosopher (354–430) who had lived in North Africa, warned against racial discrimination in his *City of God*:

> Whoever is born anywhere as a human being, that is, as a rational mortal creature, however strange he may appear to our senses in bodily form or colour or motion or utterance, or in any faculty, part or quality of his nature whatsoever, let no true believer have any doubt that such an individual is descended from the one man who was first created.

Unfortunately, the egalitarianism that had characterized early Christianity was not extended to Africans or Amerindians as their conquerors **proselytized** (converted them to the new faith). The medieval mind understood nature to be static, or unchanging. As late as the nineteenth century, English scientists and theologians egocentrically assumed that, if all humanity (meaning Europe) was created at the same time as recounted in the Bible, it meant that those who were unlike the Europeans must have degenerated. Moreover, the cause of this supposed degeneration was sin.

A controversy over whether Amerindians were either rational or capable of understanding Christianity existed even before the famous debate of 1550–1551 between Bartolomé de Las Casas and *Juan Ginés de Sepúlveda*. Las Casas (1474–1566) was a native of Seville who, at age 40, became a missionary priest known as Fray Bartolomé de Las Casas and devoted his life to the fight for justice for Amerindian people and to condemn the "robbery, evil, and injustice perpetrated against them." He was opposed by Sepúlveda (1490–1573) who was a learned humanist and Aristotelian thinker. The ancient Greek philosopher Aristotle taught that some individuals are slaves by nature, and Sepúlveda held that, as children are inferior to adults and women to men, or monkeys to humans, so Indians are "naturally" inferior to Spaniards. He argued that the conquest of uncivilized and barbaric peoples by a pious and most just king such as the Emperor Charles V was sufficient reason for his defence of their enslavement. The issues were referred to theologians in 1550 but they reached no final decision. Consequently, the Church did not call for an absolute end of Amerindian slavery.

Debates such as the Las Casas-Sepúlveda drew support from different factions of Spanish society: whereas the **conquistadors**, or Spanish conquerors, wanted to enslave and exploit the Amerindians as agricultural labourers and miners, the clergy defended them against cruelty and set up schools to educate them according to Christian values. In 1511, a Dominican priest, Antonio de Montesinos, warned the Spanish settlers of Hispaniola that they were in mortal sin, "for the cruelty and tyranny you use in dealing with these innocent people." He went on to ask them: "Tell me, by what right or justice do you keep these Indians in such cruel and horrible servitude? On what authority have you waged a detestable war against these people, who dwelt quietly and peacefully on their own land?"

Pope Paul III, in 1537, ordered members of the clergy to "Go ye and teach all nations. All, without exception, for all are capable of receiving the doctrines of the faith." Paul III denounced as satanic any effort to hinder the preaching of salvation by attempting to "publish abroad that the Indians of the West and the South, and other peoples of whom we have recent knowledge, should be treated as dumb brutes created for our service, pretending that they are incapable of receiving the Catholic Faith. The Indians are truly men."

Spanish settlers also viewed the world through medieval eyes: they believed that God stood above the saints, who were above the believers; below these were the unbelievers, such as Hindus, Jews, Moslems, Buddhists, animists—who were, however, clearly humans. Then they believed in a world between humans and beasts: that of hermaphrodites and witches, in which they included the Amerindians. The latter could be enslaved because of the natural right of the higher rank to be served by inferiors, as argued by Aristotle, and expounded by John Major, a Scottish intellectual living in Paris who argued much like Sepúlveda. A distinction was made between the animals on Noah's Ark (a vessel described in the Old Testament as carrying all the animal species in creation to safety at the time of the Great Flood) and those not listed, such as mermaids, unicorns, phoenixes, and unknown New World species such as the turkey, quetzal, raccoon, opossum, llama, coyote, and bison.

There was no certainty among Europeans about the origin of Amerindians, although it was obvious from their appearance that they were more like Asians than

European depictions of non-Europeans in the eighteenth century often reflected misconceptions and were based more on Enlightenment ideals than reality, as seen in William Vincent's *The Indian Queen*.

The Indian Queen

Africans. French writer Pierre d'Avity, in the 1630s, gave the following composite account of Amerindians drawn from various visitors:

> They are as handsome young men and beautiful young women as may be seen in France. They are great runners and swimmers, and the women too have a marvellous disposition. ...not at all malicious but literal, have a good mind and clear one so far as discerning common and sensible matters, deducing their reasons with gracefulness, always employing some pleasing comparison. They have a very good memory for material matters, such as having seen you, the qualities of a place where they have been, or what one did in their presence some twenty or thirty years ago.

Franciscans and Jesuits were active missionaries among Amerindians in the seventeenth century. They observed that the Indians thought Frenchmen were weaker, and that the heavy body hair of Europeans was ugly. Father Garnier in 1648 called for "suitable" Holy Pictures for missionary work that represented Christ and Saints without beards or curly hair.

The accounts of Amerindians by those who had met them, or those who read about them, were not always consistent. We can see that there were to be both good and bad characteristics in what was said of them over the centuries. In time, the view of Amerindians as inferior subhuman beings was repudiated and they came to be regarded as fully human, although a younger civilization. Unfortunately, by the time this view was accepted, the Amerindian population had been decimated by disease and European atrocity. Racism continues to plague the survivors as they struggle to maintain their culture and heritage in the European world system. Guatemalan activist Rigoberta Manchú won the Nobel Peace Prize in 1992 for her heroism in defending the Maya of Guatemala against genocide by the government.

Evolving Nature of the European World System

Europeans of the Atlantic Coast were gradually becoming accustomed to the idea of constant contact with great empires beyond the seas. Sometimes they encountered cultures more sophisticated and ancient than the European. All of these peoples were at some level being absorbed into a global trading system, in which Europeans bought and sold goods in different parts of the world: cotton and pepper—and later opium—from India to China, Chinese porcelain and tea to Europe, European brandy and reshipped tobacco from Latin America for furs from Amerindians in North America, and so forth. Everywhere, Europeans pressed forward, convinced of their ideas on progress and the superiority of their religion.

Within this world system lay the seeds of conflict between Europeans. Western Europe is a relatively small part of the world but it contains a rich variety of rival states with a great deal of diversity in social customs and systems of government.

By 1800, it was evident that Spain and Portugal had failed to take full control of the world system they had pioneered. The Iberian legacy was evident in the predominance of Catholicism and in the use of the Spanish and Portuguese languages in America. But Spain and Portugal did not have much of an influence in the realm of economics. The Dutch had also slowed down after 1700. They lost some of their overseas markets to newcomers and political infighting between the provinces caused a certain decline in their vigour. With the dawn of the nineteenth century, the British were beginning a period of global authority that would end with World War I.

The Abolition of Slavery

Despite the widespread acceptance of slavery prior to the eighteenth century, not all people were completely indifferent to the spectacle of cruelty, exploitation, and death that was the slave trade. The long-term problems of slave life, including the use of flogging and other physical punishments to keep the slaves from running away or rebelling, followed on the heels of the appalling conditions on the slave ships. The horrors of the crossing from Africa to the Americas lasted a few weeks but the spiritual and physical mutilation of slavery could last for a lifetime.

During the Enlightenment, calls for an end to slavery became increasingly common. The European movement for an end to African slavery and to the slave trade in the eighteenth century coincided with efforts to ensure better treatment of Amerindians, Asians, and Pacific Islanders. Although the efforts of governments and churches were often disobeyed by settlers, in the eighteenth century, indigenous peoples were understood not to be legally open to exploitation. But not blacks. The history of slavery reveals that during the eighteenth century the numbers of Africans shipped rose to higher annual levels than previously despite many calls for an end to slavery.

As the scale of the slave trade built up, churches increasingly offered support for the practice of slavery. The French Bishop Bossuet in 1690 wrote that trading slaves was permissible under the law of Man and God, quoting works of Saint Paul for support. Protestant leaders in the Dutch church, as well as the Protestant bishops of the Anglican church, were just as ready to justify slavery. There were also many who justified slavery on the basis that blacks were stronger and more resistant to the climatic and working conditions of the colonial plantations. The immorality of such ideas is obvious. Others argued that, if the slave trade were to be legally terminated, it would continue illegally because it was so profitable. In fact, slavery was never highly profitable: the best returns by the eighteenth century are estimated to be in the 5 to 10 percent range. One could make the same profits in other commerce without the same hardships and risks. However, there was always the hope for an unusually profitable trip which might reward the trader handsomely.

Abolitionist Movement

During the eighteenth century, the ***abolitionist movement***, or movement to abolish slavery, gained momentum, especially among Quakers in the United States and in humanitarian circles in England and France. The most famous European work written against slavery in the eighteenth century was that by ***Abbé Guillaume-Thomas-François Raynal*** (1713–1796). Raynal never left Europe and composed his survey of world conditions of slavery entirely from books. The fact that his work, *Philosophical and Political History of the Commercial Establishments of Europeans in the Two Indies* (1770–1781), appeared in three editions and some 50 printings in a variety of languages is indicative of the worldwide interest in the issue of slavery.

Raynal, who had already published several books on Dutch and English history and one of political commentary, was influenced by Rousseau's ideas on freedom. His famous book was essentially a compilation of other works. It gave a negative overview of the European world system. Raynal was not uniformly hostile to what Europeans had done in the world; rather, he thought that commerce had brought arts and sciences to formerly barbarian lands, an idea he shared with Montesquieu. He thought that colonization of uninhabited places was acceptable; however, if a foreign territory was occupied by a local population, only hospitality could be asked of those who dwelt there. He said that the Chinese were quite justified in trying to exclude the Europeans, who were such dangerous guests. European settlers who lived in the colonies, he went on, were vicious and quite likely to disobey their rulers in the homelands. He believed in intermarriage as a means to end competition between groups of different racial origins. Raynal discussed the Iberians, the English, the Dutch, the French, and the North Americans. His book had 48 maps and numerous statistics, of perhaps questionable accuracy, but they attempted to put issues into a quantifiable form. Raynal generally espoused the notion that the discovery of the East and West Indies had been a catastrophe for much of humanity.

Leading physiocrats (those who believed the inherent natural order governing society was based on nature) were vocal in their support of the book. So too were other intellectuals. As a result of the interest and support garnered by Raynal's ideas, organizations to end slavery sprang up. For example, political reformer Jacques Pierre Brissot founded a club in Paris, the Society of Friends of the Blacks, in imitation of one in England to bring together people interested in struggling to end slavery. The club attracted leading intellectuals such as Condorcet, abbé Sieyès, LaFayette, and others. It aimed to win over influential and powerful people. On the other hand, promoters hired by slave owners met in a luxurious house located on a fashionable square.

Slavery favoured the growth of European nations by solving the acute labour shortage in America. The production of sugar, cotton, and tobacco enabling enormous wealth to be made, required human labour on an industrial scale. Thus, millions of Africans were enslaved for the benefit of manufacturing and commercial interests in Europe.

Slavery was abolished in France on September 27, 1791 and in the French colonies by decrees issued between 1792 and 1794 against the opposition of French colonists. In 1793, the Assembly of the newly formed province of Upper Canada passed an act "to prevent the further introduction of slaves, and to limit the term of contracts for servitude." But slavery for those who were already slaves persisted in Upper Canada into the first decades of the nineteenth century. There were very few if any slaves in Upper Canada by the time that emancipation was enacted in England in 1834.

However, unlike in Canada, in the French tropical colonies there were big economic interests involved in plantation agriculture. Haiti had undergone an insurrection led by Toussaint L'Ouverture, a former slave who had read Raynal and had an understanding of the imperial expansion and trade of Europe. L'Ouverture was tricked and captured by the French in 1802 and taken to France, where he died in prison the following year. Bitter fighting continued, leading to the independence of the country with a black majority in 1804.

In North America, slavery was abolished in Mexico in 1829 but it persisted in the South of the United States and was the cause of the Civil War, which raged from 1861 to 1866 before an end was put to slavery. In some European colonies in Africa during the nineteenth century, working conditions on plantations were indistinguishable from those of slavery. In the twentieth century, the enslavement of Africans began to be universally regarded as a crime against humanity.

Numbers of Africans Shipped to Slavery

Conservative estimates of Africans shipped to slavery range between 2.5 and 3 million; higher estimates range between 9 and 14 million. The imprecision results from the high death rates and the poor record-keeping of slavers. American scholar Philip D. Curtin calculated the grand total of Africans taken by sea for the whole period of the slave trade as 9.5 million, of which 1 percent went to Europe, 6.8 percent to Canada and the U.S., 42.2 percent to the Caribbean, and 49.1 percent to Latin America.

By the time slavery was abolished by all European powers, much of the world had been irrevocably altered. Heavy depopulation, particularly of young males, had weakened African communities and states. Meanwhile indigenous peoples decimated in the Caribbean due to exploitation and disease, were replaced by African slaves. In Latin America and the Caribbean, present-day populations reflect the blending of European settlers with indigenous peoples and African slaves. Consequently, racism has not constituted a problem as it has in the U.S. and Canada, where British settlers did not mix with the indigenous populations but segregated them.

Islam

Islam, which in Arabic means literally "to surrender to the will of God," is a major world religion founded in Arabia by the Prophet Muhammad in the seventh century of the Common Era. Islam is a religion that is practised, more than being a set of beliefs. Those who practise Islam, who accept God's commandments as revealed to the Prophet in the Koran, are called Muslims. Islam flourished and expanded to such a degree that, by about 1500, Europe was surrounded and threatened by it, especially the Catholic Church. One of the great victories of Christians over Muslims in the Middle Ages had been that of Charles Martel at Tours in France in 732 C.E., which turned back the Muslim invasion from Spain. Islamic armies were pushed back over the Pyrenees Mountains into Spain, which the Muslims had conquered coming from North Africa in 711.

Martel's victory over the Moors, as the Spanish and Portuguese called North African Muslims, or Berbers, held back the Islamic occupation of Western—and Christian—Europe. In Eastern Europe, the threat remained: Orthodox Christians still had vivid memories of the fall of Constantinople (today Istanbul), in 1453, which marked the fall of the Byzantine Empire, a Christian power for the previous 1000 years.

Some of the important consequences of the Muslim victory at Constantinople were that classical (Greek and Roman) manuscripts were transferred to the West, mainly to Italy, contributing to the Renaissance. It also shifted the legal succession of the Byzantine emperor and the leadership of the Orthodox Church to Moscow and the Russian caesar, or czar; and, finally, by losing access to the Black Sea, Europe was deprived of a land route to India, which strengthened interest in the maritime route around Africa and led to numerous voyages of exploration beginning in the late fifteenth century.

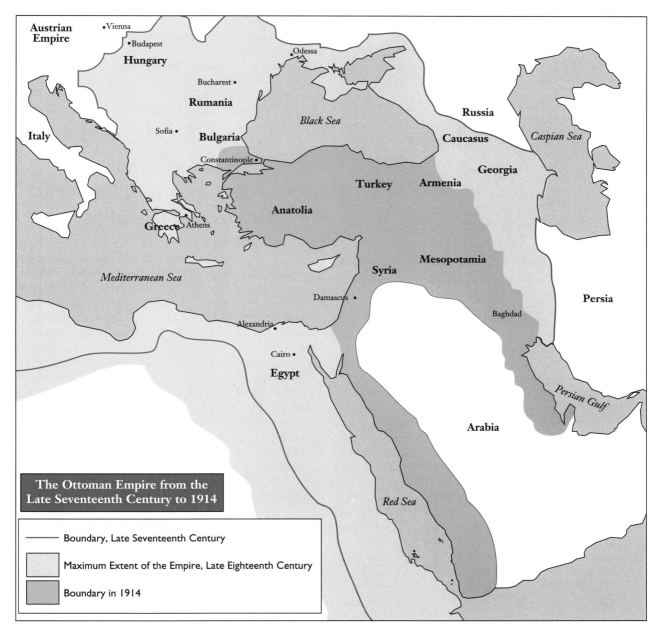

The **Ottoman Empire**, ruled by the Turks, was the dominant power of the Eastern Mediterranean from the sixteenth to the nineteenth century. Muslim—and vigorous—the Ottoman Empire represented a threat to Eastern Europe. The Turks were at the walls of Vienna in 1529, and again in 1682. In the sixteenth century, the West was aware of three major Muslim empires: the Ottoman Empire, which had replaced Christian Byzantium; the Savvafid Empire, which had replaced Zoroastrianism in Persia (today Iran); and the Mogul Empire, which had established itself over Hindu India.

What were the reasons for the strength of Islamic societies, in particular the Turks? This question

Daniel Defoe's Robinson Crusoe and his companion Friday lived an idyllic life on their deserted Pacific island.

greatly interested Western observers, who sought to find the weak spots of such dangerous adversaries with their long history of menace over Christendom. The answer included the superiority of their military, which performed better in the field than the more undisciplined feudal armies of the Europeans. The Ottomans also had a more efficient bureaucracy than that of the West in the seventeenth century—in particular the fact that the office and property reverted to the state at the end of a tenure instead of being inherited by relatives as in the West. In true Islamic tradition, new appointments were given on grounds of ability rather than birth. Ottoman bureaucracy was thus open to men of talent of diverse origins instead of being restricted to those of Turkish descent, leading to a more competently and efficiently run state.

The great flaw of the Ottoman Empire was perhaps the excessively exploitive treatment of the peasantry, which prevented the improvement of agriculture and the accumulation of capital that would stimulate demand and purchasing power for town artisans and growth of a business class. Excessive taxation kept the artisan and commercial class weak. There was also a decline in leadership quality and, altogether, the once-feared Ottoman Empire gradually weakened. By 1800, Europeans were calling the Ottoman Empire "the Sick Man of Europe."

Another significant weakness of the Ottomans was in the failure during the sixteenth to nineteenth centuries to develop artillery and in particular ships to carry naval gunnery. The armed strength of the Muslim rulers lay in land armies. That was true even in the relatively calm waters of the Mediterranean. Thus, by the beginning of the nineteenth century, Islam had ceased to pose a threat to Europe.

Europeans' Images of Non-Europeans: The Pacific Ocean and Island Idylls

The maritime explorations of Europeans continued throughout the eighteenth century. French officer and navigator Louis Antoine de Bougainville, who had been an aide-de-camp to general Montcalm when the French were defeated at the battle of the Plains of Abraham in Quebec in 1759, subsequently sailed the Pacific and published *Account of a Voyage Around the World*. Like the reports of Captain Cook, the English seaman who explored Hawaii, Australia, New Guinea, New Zealand, and other Pacific islands for the British, Bougainville described people with different moral and political systems in an idyllic tropical setting.

Cook's and Bougainville's chronicles added to the picture of tropical life on Pacific islands already spread by **Daniel Defoe's** book *The Life and Strange Surprising Adventures of Robinson Crusoe* (1719), based on the true story of Selkirk, a brutal Scottish sailor who was marooned by shipmates on an uninhabited island off the coast of Chile in 1704. He survived for four years before being picked up by a passing ship. Defoe never met Selkirk, and in any event he changed the story: Robinson Crusoe is not abandoned but shipwrecked, and he is able to hold on to European civilization from the wreckage. He has a dog, a set of carpenter's tools (products of European technology), some ink to write with (to record his thoughts), some rum to enjoy, but also a Christian Bible to study. As he looks at the island, he contemplates the wonders of God's creation. He also has a human companion whom he names Friday (the day on which he saves him from cannibals). Friday becomes the non-white deferential servant who accepts as natural the authority of the European.

Robinson Crusoe is the most famous of Defoe's 607 publications. It was translated into most European languages during the eighteenth century. Others also wrote on this archetypal situation of Europeans adapting to an abundant environment outside of the trappings of civilization. Johann Rudolph Wyss's *The Swiss Family Robinson* (1813) had an entire family adapting to a castaway situation. In 1903, Henry Devere Stacpool wrote a novel about children growing up on an island without adults, which provided the plot for a famous movie in the late 1940s and, in a remake, in the 1970s: *The Blue Lagoon*. Western society's fascination with remote tropical islands remains strong to this day as made evident by their popularity with tourists seeking to escape city life.

European Exploration of the Pacific

During the last decades of the eighteenth century, Europeans explored and mapped the Pacific Northwest. Russian expeditions searched the shores of the Pacific and Arctic for animals with fur that could be sold and, in the 1780s, Russians began to settle in Alaska. English vessels under Captain Vancouver and others explored the west coast of Canada in the years 1791 to 1795. The Spanish sailed north from California, then part of Mexico, and a detachment of soldiers commanded by a lieutenant wintered on the west coast of Vancouver Island. More elaborate expeditions intended to make scientific and ethnographic observations for the Spanish crown sailed up the American coast commanded by Alejandro Malaspina and Dionisio Alcalá Galiano. This Russian, British, and Spanish naval activity led to the acquisition of more accurate knowledge of the contours of the North Pacific. By 1800, the configuration of the five continents was known. Artifacts from the inhabitants of those areas, as well as descriptions of the family life and activities of the inhabitants, were taken back to Europe and given much attention.

European artists had painted non-Europeans from the earliest days of the overseas explorations. These were used to make prints or engravings to accompany travel accounts and were highly subjective, like the depictions of cannibalism or of jewels and rich fabrics suggesting an exotic land of pleasures.

This early depiction of the peoples of the Americas includes classical figures and mythological creatures.

China

No one foreign society affected the eighteenth-century European mind more than China. Jesuit accounts provided the first favourable descriptions since those of Italian merchant Marco Polo in the thirteenth century. Italian Jesuits such as Matteo Ricci reached Beijing at the start of the seventeenth century. They gained Chinese acceptance as a result of the assistance they provided toward calendar reform, improvements in artillery, and the advice in negotiations with the Russians, leading to the Sino-Russian treaty of 1689. Christianity was officially tolerated in China at the end of the seventeenth century. However, in 1724, the Chinese Emperor, like the Japanese a century earlier, forbade the teaching of the European religion.

Jesuits stayed on as technical assistants in Beijing until the dissolution of their order in 1773. Serious books about China were published, of which the most successful was that by the Frenchman Jean-Baptiste du Halde, which gave a positive view of China. He described the Chinese emperors as being wise monarchs who took advice from knowledgeable officials. In short, supporters of the Enlightenment held China as an "empire of benevolent reason." Leibniz hoped there would be a true communication of Enlightenment between China and Europe. Despite the missionary intentions of the Jesuits, their search for similarities between Christian and Chinese beliefs was taken as being in favour of deism. (Deism is a belief in God without accepting any particular religion.)

Europeans were impressed by the fact that, aside from the Imperial dynasty and the descendants of the revered Chinese philosopher Confucius (551–479 B.C.E.), there was no hereditary nobility in China. Voltaire was quite well informed about China and Japan from travellers' accounts. He went so far as to say that the Chinese Empire was the best in the world. He said of

Gulliver's Travels

 One of the most enduring tales of the eighteenth century is *Gulliver's Travels*. Over 250 years after it was written, this satirical story remains a popular children's story; repeatedly reprinted in various abridged versions and made into numerous films, including Disney's *Gulliver Mickey*. Ironically, the story penned by Jonathan Swift was not intended to be merely an intriguing tale of a man lost at sea, swept onto the shores of a land inhabited by the tiny people of Lilliput. Instead it was intended as an attack on the liberal thinkers of the day, who sought to limit the powers of king and Church. Unlike the other satirists with whom he is often compared (Voltaire, Charles Dickens, Mark Twain) Swift was a staunch conservative who gazed back upon the past and glorified it, often remaining oblivious to the merits of the changing world in which he lived and to the problems of a world that was quickly being left behind. If one takes the time to read *Gulliver's Travels* in its entirety a clear change in tone becomes evident: the first part, dealing with Lilliput, is reasonably good-natured; the second part, dealing with Brobingnag, is noticeably more bitter; while the final part shows Swift's anger as he seems to turn completely against humanity. The selections below are brief extracts taken from Parts I and IV of *Gulliver's Travels*. Note in the second extract how Swift, despite his general criticisms, extols the virtues of English civilization.

Part I

On the fifth of November, which was the beginning of summer in those parts, the weather being very hazy, the seamen spyed a rock, within half a cable's length of the ship; but the wind was so strong, that we were driven directly upon it, and immediately split. Six of the crew, of whom I was one, having let down the boat into the sea, made a shift to get clear of the ship, and the rock. We rowed by my computation, about three leagues, till we were able to work no longer, being already spent with labour while we were in the ship. We therefore trusted ourselves to the mercy of the waves; and in about half an hour the boat was overset by a sudden flurry from the north. What became of my companions in the boat, as well as of those who escaped on the rock, or were left in the vessel, I cannot tell; but conclude they were all lost.

I got to the shore, which I conjectured was about eight o'clock in the evening. I then advanced forward near half a mile, but could not discover any sign of houses or inhabitants; at least I was in so weak a condition, that I did not observe them. I was extremely tired, and with that, and the heat of the weather, and about half a pint of brandy that I drank as I left the ship, I found myself much inclined to sleep. I lay down on the grass, which was very short and soft; where I slept sounder than ever I remember to have done in my life, and as I reckoned, above nine hours; for when I awaked it was just day-light. I attempted to rise, but was not able to stir: For as I happened to lie on my back, I found my arms and legs were strongly fastened on each side to the ground; and my hair, which was long and thick, tied down in the same manner. I likewise felt several slender ligatures across my body, from my armpits to my thighs. I could only look upwards; the sun began to grow hot, and the light offended my eyes. I heard a confused noise about me, but in the posture I lay, could see nothing except the sky. In a little time I felt something alive moving on my left leg, which advancing gently forward over my breast, came almost up to my chin; when bending my eyes downwards as much as I could, I perceived it to be a human creature not six inches high, with a bow and arrow in his hands, and a quiver at his back. In the mean time, I felt at least forty more of the same kind (as I conjectured) following the first.

I was in the utmost astonishment, and roared so loud, that they all ran back in a fright; and some of them, as I was afterwards told, were hurt with the falls they got by leaping from my sides upon the ground. However, they soon returned; and one of them, who ventured so far as to get a full sight of my face, lifting up his hands and eyes by way of admiration, cryed out in a shrill, but distinct voice, *Hekinah Degul*: The others repeated the same words several times, but I then knew not what they meant.

...The next morning at sunrise we continued our march, and arrived within two hundred yards of the city gates about noon. The emperor, and all his court, came out to meet us; but his great officers would by no means suffer his majesty to endanger his person by mounting on my body.

The great gate fronting to the north was about four foot high, and almost two foot wide, through which I could easily creep. On each side of the gate was a small window not above six inches from the ground: into that on the left side, the king's smiths conveyed fourscore and eleven chains, like those that hang to a lady's watch in Europe, and almost as large, which were locked to my left leg with six and thirty padlocks. Over against this temple, on the other side of the great highway, at twenty foot distance, there was a turret at least five foot high. Here the emperor ascended with many principal lords of his court, to have an opportunity of viewing me, as I was told for I could not see them.

Part IV

But I had another reason, which made me less forward to enlarge his majesty's dominions by my discoveries. To say the truth, I had conceived a few scruples with relation to the distributive justice of princes upon those occasions. For instance, a crew of pirates are driven by a storm they know not whither; at length a boy discovers land from the topmast; they go on shore to rob and plunder; they see a harmless people, are entertained with kindness; they give the country a new name; they take formal possession of it for their king; they set up a rotten plank, or a stone, for a memorial; they murder two or three dozen of the natives, bring away a couple more, by force, for a sample; return home and get their pardon. Here commences a new dominion acquired with a title by divine right. Ships are sent with the first opportunity; the natives driven out or destroyed; their princes tortured to discover their gold; a free licence given to all acts of inhumanity and lust, the earth reeking with the blood of its inhabitants: and this execrable crew of butchers, employed in so pious an expedition, is a modern colony, sent to convert and civilize an idolatrous and barbarous people!

But this description, I confess, does by no means affect the British nation, who may be an example to the whole world for their wisdom, care, and justice in planting colonies: their liberal endowments for the advancement of religion and learning; their Christianity; their caution in stocking their provinces with people of sober lives and conversations, from this the mother kingdom; their strict regard to the distribution of justice, in supplying the civil administration through all their colonies with officers of the greatest abilities, utter strangers to corruption; and, to crown all, by sending the most vigilant and virtuous governors, who have no other views than the happiness of the people over whom they preside, and the honour of the king their master.

Confucius, whose ethical precepts were deeply rooted in Chinese culture, "I have read his books attentively and made extracts from them: I found they spoke only of the purest morality... he appeals only to virtue, he preaches no miracles; there is nothing in them of religious allegory."

Voltaire's knowledge of non-European societies and the destruction of his *Philosophical Dictionary* (burned at the stake with the innocent teenager Chevalier de la Barre) led him to deride the Judeo-Christian chronology of the world as given in the Bible.

French economist and physician François Quesnay, founder of the physiocrats, published a book entitled *Chinese Despotism* (1767) by which he understood despotism as meaning the domination of natural law, which he believed led the Chinese to be more dependent on agriculture than any other nation. Quesnay knew from the writings of visitors to China that the tithe on crops was the principal tax base, and the Chinese Emperor performed solemn rites to mark the phases of the agricultural year. Quesnay even prevailed on Louis XV to guide the plow at the symbolic act of the 1756 spring tilling. For the physiocrats, a powerful Chinese emperor such as Kang H'si was the ideal enlightened, paternalistic ruler.

Western Europeans were fascinated by other systems of writing: Egyptian hieroglyphs, Babylonian and Persian cuneiform writing, or early Greek script had not been deciphered. The obvious antiquity of Chinese civilization astonished students of the chronology laid down by Western scholars of the Bible. Chinese was an ancient writing still in use. Some Europeans had learned some spoken Chinese for use in trading but without any knowledge of script or grammar.

Again, the Jesuits were the forerunners in making the language accessible to Westerners through books. Fourmont, who studied with a young Chinese sent to Europe by the Jesuits, published in 1719 the first book on the 214 radicals in the Chinese language, and this was followed by dictionaries. Joseph de Guignes studied the language in the second half of the century and suggested that the Chinese might have crossed into North America by a land bridge from Asia. Another theory held that the Chinese descended from the Egyptians.

This speculation about historical evidence and records permitted the elaboration of much more complex views of the early history of other civilizations than could be extrapolated from Biblical authority and the knowledge of the Greek and Roman classics. Baron Melchior Grimm (1723–1807), the German-born writer and critic who produced a literary review, wrote in 1776 about this passion for China:

> The Chinese Empire has become in our time the object of special attention and of special study: the missionaries first fascinated public opinion by rose-coloured reports from that distant land, too distant to be able to contradict their falsehoods. Then the philosophers took it up and drew from them whatever could be of use in denouncing and removing the evils they observed in their own country. Thus, this country became in a short time the home of wisdom, virtue, and good faith; its government the best possible, and the longest established, its morality the loftiest and the most beautiful in the known world; its laws, its policy, its arts, and its industry were likewise such as to serve as a model for all nations of the earth.

China's Influence on Interior Decoration in Europe

Interest in China went as far as to influence interior decoration. *Chinoiserie* is the name of the European style and objects that imitated the Chinese. As artisans attempted to recreate a version of an imperfectly understood original, chinoiserie became a style in its own right. One example is the willow-pattern motif on English porcelain. Rooms were decorated in palaces and châteaux, like the famous Chantilly near Paris, the equally famous porcelain rooms at the Palace of Queluz near Lisbon, the Palace of Aranjuez in Spain and of Capodimonte in Naples, giving French, Portuguese, Spanish, and Italian examples of chinoiserie. French rococo painter Antoine Watteau appears to have produced the earliest chinoiserie when he decorated a royal residence in that style. François Couperin's music *Les chinois* accompanied these paintings of priest and pagodas, ornately dressed mandarins, parasols, and berouged maidens. French painter François Boucher designed chinoiserie tapestries which were woven at Beauvais around 1742, depicting a bizarre marriage ceremony, a royal breakfast, court ladies playing with parakeets, etc. Curiously, a set of these tapestries was sent by Louis XV to the Chinese emperor Kang H'si, who must have thought them very odd; however, a panel was still hanging in the Imperial Palace in Beijing when it was looted by European troops in 1860.

The heyday of chinoiserie is illustrated in Voltaire's 1755 play entitled *The Chinese Orphan*, based on a Chinese play, which caused a sensation because it supposedly dramatized the morals of Confucius and was performed in elaborate versions of supposedly Chinese costumes.

From Mutual Trade to Exploitation

At the end of the eighteenth century, the British sent a mission to Beijing to visit the Chinese court. The Chinese court was not impressed with the scientific instruments brought as presents by the British. These were dismissed as being ingenious clockwork toys. Within 50 years, European troops whose officers made great use of "ingenious clockwork toys" would humiliate the ancient Chinese civilization of great cultural achievement: Chinese archers firing bows and arrows while mounted on horseback could not prevail over sustained accurate rifle fire. Similarly, the Spaniards had used horses and firearms to defeat the ill-equipped Aztec armies in Mexico, and African warriors could not hurl their spears as far as European artillery could shoot back at them. Using their fire power and their lust for wealth, Europeans would come not only to dominate but to exploit the four corners of the world.

Between 1450 and 1750, Europeans explored virtually the whole earth, leaving their mark everywhere they went through exploitation and acculturation. Disease carried by Europeans decimated the populations of America; the transatlantic slave trade depopulated Central Africa. From the outset, Europeans had gone in search of new riches, from fur and gold to people.

Porcelain for Palaces

When Portuguese navigator Vasco da Gama rounded the Cape of Good Hope and reached the Orient in 1498, he ushered in a new age of trade between Europe and the East. Direct access by ship, rather than relying on overland traders, brought a wide array of items to the European marketplace including silk, spices, tea, and porcelain. In response to the vast, new European market for porcelain, the Japanese began making porcelain to order for the Portuguese market, and later for Europeans in general.

By the seventeenth century, such large quantities of porcelain were being imported to Europe that some have referred to the onset of "china-mania" at this time. The increasing popularity of porcelain was reflected in its progression in European homes, first out of the cabinet of curiosities onto the table and then from the table onto the walls. Porcelain as a decorative accessory reached its peak in the late seventeenth and early eighteenth centuries in "porcelain rooms" where walls were covered in Chinese and Japanese porcelain.

An example of extensive use of

—⁕—

Decorative pieces such as this porcelain clock (left) and Japanese tankard were found in many European homes.

porcelain could be seen in the Porcelain Room at Charlottenburg, Berlin. Here, gold-covered wooden brackets hold a wide variety of vases that were selected for size, shape, and colour. Chinoiserie figures wearing upturned basins as hats hold up large bowls, while tiers of bottles, cups, and saucers line the edges of mirror-plates. In designing this room, nothing was left to chance: Chinese and Japanese porcelains were carefully mixed together so that the colours and shapes achieved symmetry and harmony.

By the eighteenth century, Europeans had learned the sophisticated Oriental techniques for making porcelain. With the establishment of porcelain production at locations such as Meissen, Germany and the passing fad of Porcelain Rooms, the trade in porcelain declined. While fine china and porcelain remains popular in Europe and North America, the leading names are no longer Japanese or Chinese but rather European: Delft, Wedgewood, or Royal Doulton.

The common thread one finds when studying the age of European exploration and colonization is the primacy of profit. Whether studying the French, English, Dutch, Spanish, Portuguese, or the results of European contact in America, Africa, or Asia, one cannot help but realize the driving force behind three centuries of exploration was economic gain; and the result of three centuries of European colonization was the decimation and exploitation of millions of people from numerous societies.

Reflections

In 1500, Europeans did not know the full extent of the Americas; they had no knowledge of Australia or New Zealand and no European had ever visited Japan. Africa south of the Sahara was a mystery. It was not until 1800 that the shape of the continents and oceans was mapped and became common knowledge. Ships sailed frequently from Europe to all points of the globe; European goods were traded wherever there was a market for them; many crops from overseas were now regularly imported to Europe for consumption.

The establishment of a global economy was not a gentle or peaceful affair: Europeans fought each other for the control of markets and territory. Above all, the plantation economies of the New World had caused a demand for forced labour by African slaves. Europeans stripped millions of people of their human rights and dignity, to say nothing of their lives. The very struggle between European powers stimulated advances in military technology: nobody in the world had better weapons than the Western Europeans.

Although Europeans liked to imagine that their religion and culture were attractive or even necessary to the wider world, in fact it was their technology—especially their military power—that explained their success in establishing the capitalist world system.

The encounter with distant societies stimulated the European imagination. This chapter has stressed the idea of an island idyll in an exotic location that was described in the novel *Robinson Crusoe* and the sympathetic idea of China in the eighteenth century. There were many other influences on Europe that came from overseas. By 1800 scarcely any region of the world escaped the effects of European power and trade.

Key Concepts, Figures, and Events

Christopher Columbus	Treaty of Tordesillas	Grand Exchange
Juan Ginés de Sepúlveda	Abolitionist Movement	Abbé Guillaume-Thomas-François Raynal
Ottoman Empire	Daniel Defoe	Chinoiserie

Topics for Further Thought

1. Changes took place at the start of the sixteenth century which would have global implications. To what degree were these changes the product of the new technology and ideas generated in the preceding century?

2. For generations, students have been taught about the heroic exploits of the explorers who "discovered" new lands. Why are traditional images of heroic discoverers inadequate when studying the age of exploration? To what degree must the primacy of profit be seen as the most potent force behind European exploration and colonization?

3. Regardless of the consequences for millions of people of numerous cultures, Europeans, without question, became the dominant economic and military force in the world after the sixteenth century. How can we explain European success at dominating much of the world, including well-organized, advanced civilizations in Mexico, Peru, China, and India?

4. In Chapter 2, we discussed von Herder's idea that cultures could and should remain pure. This idea has been applied by the Nazis and by genocidal ethnic cleansing in Bosnia, for example. (In both cases, books justifying it have been published.) Considering the exchange of foods, ideas, and products brought about by a global economic system, is the existence of pure cultures possible or is it merely a philosophical fantasy with dangerous implications?

5. Despite the radical changes in thought and technology brought about by the Renaissance and the Enlightenment, unenlightened attitudes seemed to cling tenaciously to European minds. What evidence of this is there in the way non-Europeans were perceived and treated? Refer to the Las Casas-Sepúlveda debate and the views held by Spanish settlers.

6. During the eighteenth century, Europeans came to see the mistreatment of Amerindians, Asians, and Pacific Islanders as morally wrong. Why was the same view not extended to blacks? Was the continued abuse of blacks through slavery a result of racist assumptions or economic pressures?

7. The Ottoman Empire had long been considered a threat to Eastern Europeans. Why were the Ottomans viewed with such apprehension? What aspects of their military, government, and culture made them a power to be feared? What ultimately weakened the Ottoman Empire, turning it into the Sick Man of Europe?

8. During the eighteenth century many Europeans, including *philosophes* Voltaire and Diderot, were fascinated by China. What elements of Chinese culture caught the imagination of Europeans? How did this fascination with China lead to change in European culture? Is this impact still evident today in Western societies?

Topics for Further Research

1. Select one of the European powers which established overseas empires and compare the extent of their empire in 1600 and in 1800. Also, research the nature of their empire. Did they establish colonies, import slaves, intermarry with the indigenous peoples? What products were produced, exported, and imported in the colonies?

Britain	France	The Netherlands
Portugal	Spain	

2. The Grand Exchange brought about a transformation in the cuisines of many societies. Select a recipe well known in one of the countries listed below. Trace the origin of each ingredient. In the end, conclude whether or not this recipe is native to the country or is the product of the Grand Exchange.

France	Italy	Mexico
Brazil	China	Middle East
Japan		

3. When Europeans began to explore the world, they encountered civilizations previously unknown to them. Select one of the following civilizations and research their political system, religion, social structure, level of technological expertise, and economic system:

Aztecs	Maya
Inca	Iroquois
Japanese	Bantu (West Africa)
Tupinamba or Amazon group	

4. China has unquestionably had a large impact on Western culture. Research the influence of one of the following elements of Chinese culture on Europe and the West:

Chinese Food	Silk
Chinese Philosophy	Chinoiserie

Responding to Ideas

1. One of the difficulties students face when dealing with primary documents is the temptation to read them from their own twentieth-century perspective. In his book *The Fall of Natural Man: The American Indian and the Origins of Comparative Ethnology*, Anthony Pagden offers the following advice to those studying early contact between Europeans and Amerindians: "The early chroniclers... were not committed to an accurate description of the world 'out there.' They were attempting to bring within their intellectual grasp phenomena which they recognized as new and which they could only make familiar, and hence intelligible, in the terms of an anthropology made authoritative precisely by the fact that its sources ran back to the Greeks." How do Pagden's insights into the early documents help us to understand the reaction of Europeans toward the peoples they encountered? Why is it important that we understand the mindset of those who recorded past events rather than merely accepting their observations at face value?

2. In studying the relationships between European powers (metropolises) and their colonies (satellites), it is important that we realize that the foundations for First World and Third World status were laid in the seventeenth and eighteenth centuries. Running throughout the capitalist world economy are—and were—metropolis-satellite relations that allowed the metropolis to dominate and exploit the satellites. In his provocative essay "The Development of Underdevelopment," André Gunder Frank argues that most Third World nations have been intentionally underdeveloped to serve the capitalist needs of the metropolis. Gunder Frank wrote: "When we examine this metropolis-satellite structure, we find that each of the satellites... serves as an instrument to suck capital or economic surplus out of its own satellites and to channel part of this surplus to the world metropolis of which all are satellites. Moreover, each national and local metropolis serves to impose and maintain the monopolistic structure and exploitive relationship of this system... as long as it serves the interests of the metropolis...." What evidence in this chapter supports Gunder Frank's argument? Can you suggest arguments in defence of European imperialism that would refute the claims made by Gunder Frank?

5

The French Revolution and Napoleonic Europe

CHAPTER HIGHLIGHTS

- The impact of increased poverty levels on the political climate of France

- The development of a collective political will in France

- The important changes that took place in the political structure during the "year of liberty"

- The effect of the French Revolution on the political climate and popular resistance in other European nations

- The important role of women in the Revolution

- Europe after the French Revolution: the rise and fall of Napoléon Bonaparte

---

All over Europe, toward the end of the eighteenth century, there was a growing unease among the intelligentsia about absolutist governments. Reactions against the increasingly discredited older forms of monarchy were not confined to France or even Europe: the American Revolution (1775–1783) was initiated by a colonial elite dissatisfied with government from London. In the mining areas of the Portuguese colony of Brazil, the local elites conspired unsuccessfully against the royal government of Lisbon in 1789. Revolts or disturbances broke out in Holland against the Stadholder (viceroy) in Switzerland in the 1780s, as well as in the Austrian Netherlands, where urban radicals rejected—sometimes for conservative reasons—the authority of the enlightened Emperor Joseph II in Vienna.

Although events in France made the most dramatic break with the past at the end of the eighteenth century, the same atmosphere of conflict was found in much of Europe. In 1784, a supplement to the *Moscow Gazette* praised American General George Washington for founding a republic that "without doubt will be the refuge of liberty forbidden in Europe by luxury and corruption." This kind of political commentary was becoming much more frequent at the end of the eighteenth century.

Poverty and Politics

One reason for the general unease was the increase in the numbers of poor people in Europe. The birth rate exceeded that of job creation during the eighteenth

The Three Estates in France

First estate	The clergy	Main privileges
About 130 000 people	• 138 archbishops and bishops • 2 800 canons and priors • 37 000 nuns and 23 000 monks • 60 000 parish priests	• had their own law courts • exempt from certain taxes
Second estate	**The nobility**	**Main privileges**
Between 120 000 and 350 000 people	• king and queen • nobles of the sword: princes, dukes, marquises, counts, viscounts, barons, knights • nobles of the robe	• had the right to carry a sword • received special treatment in law courts • exempt from certain taxes • exempt from military service
Third estate	**Everybody else**	**Privileges**
About 27 million people	lawyers, doctors, businessmen, merchants, soldiers, craftsmen, shopkeepers, peasants, etc.	None

century. Agriculture did not employ the excess rural population and there were not enough alternative types of work. Taxation and other payments were heavy but different social categories, especially priests and nobles, had exemptions. Although local situations varied, in France on the eve of the Revolution, 6–10 percent of the land belonged to the Church; 20–25 percent to the nobility; 25–30 percent to the bourgeoisie; and 40–45 percent to the peasantry. The Church and nobility together numbered no more than 3 percent of the population. The bourgeoisie, in the sense of townspeople who did not work with their hands, constituted about 6 percent, artisans another 10 percent, and 80 percent of the population were peasants.

French peasants had to pay the royal taxes that were either levied directly on each family or in an indirect way, as in those parts of the country where a special tax was paid on salt. As well, they often had to pay the seigneur, either in cash or with a share of the crops, for the right to cultivate his land. The Catholic parish priest also expected a tenth part, or tithe, of the crop. This left little for peasant families to live on. Even in the most productive agricultural areas of Europe, in England and the Netherlands, the same kind of modest farming family was under pressure: small farmers were forced out of insufficiently profitable small holdings by richer, large-scale landowners who introduced new and more efficient methods of agriculture.

In the dry lands of Southern Portugal, Spain, and Italy there were large estates owned by absentee landowners which were worked by day labourers whose low wages did not keep pace with rising living costs. In areas with good rainfall, such as Germany and France, changes in crop patterns, like replacing of rye with wheat cultivation and the introduction of the potato, brought prosperity to some farmers but difficulties to others.

In Eastern Europe, serf labour was also affected by population growth. The miserable conditions of the peasants had caused the biggest rural rebellion in Russian history in 1773–1775. Led by Cossack soldier ***Yemelyan Ivanovich Pugachov***, it brought together Cossacks (horsemen) and peasants in a vast antifeudal movement calling for an end to serfdom. Serfs were urged to massacre noble landowners and take over their houses. The government of Catherine the Great savagely repressed this uprising and the country gentry became increasingly apprehensive about the concealed hostility of the peasantry. The situation was symptomatic of country tensions which continued among the Slavic serf populations of Eastern Europe. A Russian nobleman, Aleksandr Nikolayevich Radischev, published *Journey from Saint Petersburg to Moscow* (1790), which exposed the evils of serfdom and autocracy in Russia. He was initially sentenced to death but later exiled to Siberia.

Migration

To escape poverty, poor people began looking for opportunity in towns. Larger cities became magnets for poor migrants from areas of economic distress. Internal migration in France was at an all-time high on the eve of the French Revolution.

This surge in the number of jobless people demanding assistance was found in other zones of Western Europe. However, in the late eighteenth century, governments had little sense of responsibility for the needy. For the widow encumbered with small children, for orphans too young to support themselves, for the sick or handicapped, help was mostly left to private charity. The demand for aid in many places was beyond the capacity of private donors or institutions.

Intellectuals Versus Bureaucrats

The Enlightenment called for creative change. Above all, the elite wanted to deal with the problem of the government deficit and the perception of waste and incompetence in government procedures. Many merchants, for example, were critical of the pensions and exemptions given to nobles; the mass of the population wanted fewer financial levies and taxes.

The 1787 dissolution of an assembly of notables called to address the French financial problem was yet another demonstration that the French Government could not carry through the needed reforms to cover its deficit. The inability of the royal treasury to meet payments led to the collapse of the *ancien régime* in August 1788. Although emergency credits allowed the government to continue operating, the seriousness of

the financial crisis was evident. The idea of an Estates-General (French National Assembly), which had last convened in 1614, was in the air.

More and more commentators on public affairs came to the conclusion that the monarchy as it had evolved during the eighteenth century—without any public participation—could no longer heal itself. The combination of social unease and discontent at all levels of society was particularly strong by the late 1780s. Harvests were bad in 1787 and 1788 and urban riots against high bread prices occurred in the early months of 1789.

French Public Opinion on the Eve of the Revolution

Nobody in France in 1789 could have imagined where the nation was going. What many hoped for was a reformed constitutional monarchy. However, even before the Estates-General were recalled by Louis XVI on May 5, 1789, reactionaries were alarmed. The king's brother said in 1788:

> Sire, the state is in peril... a revolution in the principles of government is under way... the authority of the throne and the rights of the privileged order is in question. Soon property rights will be attacked.

In using the word "revolution," the prince showed how it had come to designate a wholesale upheaval in society. His outburst serves to remind us that, from the beginning of the revolutionary process, many in France opposed any basic changes to the government. Censorship of publications was relaxed and many pamphlets were printed that expressed individual opinions. The most famous of all was *What Is the Third Estate?* by the abbé (a priest in minor orders) Emmanuel Joseph Sieyès. His answer, at the expense of the first estate (the clergy) and the second estate (the nobility), was that the third estate (the middle class) was everything.

The crown, seeking to consult the French people directly, called for statements of grievance to be drawn up by various entities. These notebooks of complaints, or *cahiers de doléances*, are one of the great sources of information for historians of France at the time of the Revolution. They were not necessarily radical, as we see from the canons of the cathedral chapter of

On July 14, 1789, the people of Paris stormed the Bastille, a symbol of royal authority and oppression.

Auxerre:

> The conservation of monarchical government is the first wish of the Auxerre Chapter. This government is the only one which is suitable to the vast expanse of the kingdom, and the happiness which the nation has tasted for so many centuries makes it feel the need to belong to its kings, its only true legislators.

Others, like the inhabitants of a small village from the Pyrenees Mountains, which separate France from Spain, railed against the tax collector:

> ...one and only tyrant; the financial administration, which night and day is busy to take gold from the crown, silver from the crozier, steel from swords, ermine from robes, the copper from the counters, iron from the plows and other tools and even the bronze of the bells.

The desire to express opinion led to the establishment of discussion clubs in major French cities. Elections of deputies to the Estates-General were held in March and April of 1789.

The Year of Liberty in France: 1789

The Estates-General

The meeting of the Estates-General at Versailles soon produced a deadlock between the three orders of the National Assembly. The first and second estates (clergy and nobility) combined could outvote the third estate (middle class) despite the fact that the third estate represented the vast majority of the nation. Deputies of the third estate decided to meet and protest against this situation. Louis XVI, considering the actions of the third estate both intolerable and in defiance of his authority, had the meeting hall locked and guarded by soldiers. When the members of the third estate found themselves locked out of the palace, they feared the king was going to break up their assembly by force. With rain falling, they took cover in the nearest vacant building they could find, a tennis court a short walk away. There, on June 20, 1789, the deputies of the third estate swore an oath, known as the *Tennis Court Oath*, which stated they were the majority—hence the Nation—and that they would not dissolve until this fact was accepted.

On June 23, 1789, the king sent a courtier to tell the deputies of the third estate to disperse and for voting to continue. In response, Mirabeau, a leading elected member, announced that they would only yield to force. The courtier messenger turned to the president of the Assembly, the astronomer Sylvain Bailly, who backed Mirabeau by saying "The nation is assembled here, and receives no orders." This legalistic exchange between the king's messenger and parliamentarians has been seen as the effective end of the legal authority of the old monarchical order: national will was set above the orders of the king.

Popular Urban Violence

Several weeks after the proclamation of the National Assembly, on July 14, 1789, a crowd attacked the Bastille (the Paris state prison). It was the symbol of the oppressive nature of the *ancien régime* because it held special prisoners sent there without trial at the order of the authorities. Located in the east end of Paris, the Bastille, in fact, held only seven prisoners (one of whom was insane), who were treated much better than common criminals. However, the crowd believed it to be full of wretched prisoners kept in subhuman conditions. The Bastille did not fall to ravening, famished, lower-class attackers but to small craftsmen, journeymen, and shopkeepers representing a cross section of the Paris population, which was becoming politicized by the revolution, especially in the period between 1789 and 1794.

Although King Louis XVI wrote "Nothing" in his diary for that day (interpreted also to mean poor hunting), it henceforth became evident that political power was now in the streets of Paris: mob violence could force decisions in a different way than decisions taken by ministers in the gilded rooms of the Versailles palace or the meetings of the Assembly. Republican governments of France later decreed July 14 a national holiday as a gesture of approval of popular participation in politics.

Country Protest

During the summer of 1789, news was coming in from the countryside of peasant dissatisfaction with the payments and services exacted by landowners. Country people wanted an end to extortion based on medieval conditions of feudal landownership, with all economic rights in the hands of the seigneurs, or feudal lords. They included various kinds of quit-rents (rent paid in money rather than in services) and the need to submit to the authority of the feudal lord as a judge in all aspects of life. Peasants now started to attack castles and tried to burn records of feudal dues, rents payable, and taxation.

On the unusually hot night of August 4, 1789, the Assembly stayed in session and abolished a whole series of feudal rights. The abolition of the specific terms of feudalism in 1789 (completed in 1793) was seen as an important part of making the rural economy more efficient. However, the perception by commoners of nobles who profiteered from the work of others and as enemies of social change dominated the events of that fateful summer. In June 1790, titles of nobility were abolished, reflecting the strong desire of French citizens for equality.

Government Moved from Versailles to Paris

As long as the king, the court, and the Assembly remained in Versailles, the people of the largest city in the kingdom felt uneasy for the security of the Revolution. In October, there was a great demonstration

Demanding bread for their families, angry women stormed the Palace of Versailles in October 1789.

by Parisians motivated by fear of bread shortages. It was led by women from the central markets who trudged to Versailles to protest against high food prices. When they arrived, they burst into the royal apartments, seeking to take the good king from what they thought to be the bad company of Queen Marie-Antoinette and the courtiers. The demonstration returned to Paris in triumph, with carts carrying sacks of flour and escorting the royal family in the royal carriage back to the old and long-disused Tuileries Palace in the centre of Paris. Now the court and the Assembly were under the watchful eye of the politicized population of the French capital.

Results of the Year of Liberty

By the end of 1789, important changes had taken place in France: the Estates-General had become the National Assembly, also known as the Constituent Assembly, and was charged with writing a constitution. The king was no longer the central source of authority, although his approval of what the Assembly decided was needed to make state authority fully legal.

Many nobles were anxious about events and began to emigrate; the clergy was aware that its property and internal organization were at risk; the population at large was apprehensive of the level of violence. The liberal Marquis de Condorcet complained in a pamphlet toward the end of 1789 about what he called the

The Declaration of the Rights of Man and the Citizen

 At the outbreak of the French Revolution, *The Declaration of the Rights of Man and the Citizen* outlined the principles that were to guide the revolutionaries in their attack on the *ancien régime* and the creation of a modern republic. The *Declaration of Rights* reflected the influence of the doctrines of the Enlightenment as well as the English *Bill of Rights* (adopted a century earlier), and the principles of American *Declaration of Independence* in 1776. A careful reading of this document also reveals a male and bourgeois bias as power passed from the monarchy and aristocracy to the educated and affluent of the third estate. What evidence can you find in the following document that suggests the foundations of the new republic would favour men of wealth and talent rather than ensuring full equality for all people?

The representatives of the French people, organized in National Assembly, considering the ignorance, forgetfulness, or contempt of the rights of man are the sole causes of public misfortunes and of the corruption of governments, have resolved to set forth in a solemn declaration the natural, inalienable, and sacred rights of man, in order that such declaration, continually before all members of the social body, may be a perpetual reminder of their rights and duties....

Accordingly, the National Assembly recognizes and proclaims, in the presence and under the auspices of the Supreme Being, the following rights of man and citizen.

1. Men are born and remain free and equal in rights; social distinctions may be based only upon general usefulness.

2. The aim of every political association is the preservation of the natural and inalienable rights of man; these rights are liberty, property, security, and resistance to oppression.

3. The source of all sovereignty resides essentially in the nation; no group, no individual may exercise authority not emanating expressly therefrom.

4. Liberty consists of the power to do whatever is not injurious to others; thus the enjoyment of the natural rights of every man has for its limits only those that assure other members of society the enjoyment of those same rights; such limits may be determined only by law.

5. The law has the right to forbid only actions which are injurious to society. Whatever is not forbidden by law may not be prevented, and no one may be constrained to do what it does not prescribe.

6. Law is the expression of the general will; all citizens have the right to concur personally, or through their representatives, in its formation; it must be the same for all, whether it protects or punishes. All citizens, being equal before it, are equally admissible to all public offices, positions and employments, according to their capacity, and without other distinction than that of virtues and talents.

7. No man may be accused, arrested, or detained except in the cases determined by law, and according to the forms prescribed thereby. Whoever solicit, expedite, or execute arbitrary orders, or have them executed, must be punished; but every citizen summoned or apprehended in pursuance of the law must obey immediately; he renders himself culpable by resistance.

8. The law is to establish only penalties that are absolutely and obviously necessary; and no one may be punished except by virtue of a law established and promulgated prior to the offence and legally applied.

9. Since every man is presumed innocent until declared guilty, if arrest be deemed indispensable, all necessary severity for securing the person of the accused must be severely repressed by law.

10. No one is to be disquieted because of his opinions, even religious, provided their manifestation does not disturb the public order established by law.

11. Free communication of ideas and opinions is one of the most precious of the rights of man. Consequently, every citizen may speak, write, and print freely, subject to responsibility for the abuse of such liberty in the cases determined by law.

12. The guarantee of the rights of man and citizen necessitates a public force; such a force, therefore, is instituted for the advantage of all and not for the particular benefit of those to whom it is entrusted.

13. For the maintenance of the public force and for the expenses of administration a common tax is indispensable; it must be assessed equally on all citizens in proportion to their means.

14. Citizens have the right to ascertain, by themselves or through their representatives, the necessity of the public tax, to consent to it freely, to supervise its use, and to determine its quota, assessment, payment, and duration.

15. Society has the right to require of every public agent an accounting of his administration.

16. Every society in which the guarantee of rights is not assured or the separation of powers not determined has no constitution at all.

17. Since property is a sacred and inviolable right, no one may be deprived thereof unless a legally established public necessity obviously requires it, and upon condition of a just and previous indemnity.

false opinion that the people had taken of their rights, imagining that the "tumultuous will" of the inhabitants of a city, town, or village is a type of law that has the same authority as the will of a legal assembly.

The peasants gleefully welcomed an end to the seigneurial rule they so disliked, but found a new enemy in the revolutionary officials and townspeople who still seemed to exploit them. The peasants were also unhappy over the new religious policy, which denied the authority of the Pope over the French Catholic Church, closed monasteries and convents, and confiscated Church land and property. Peasant resistance to the Revolution would cause two major instances of civil war inside the country: the resistance of Western France in 1793, and the insurrection in the Southwest in 1799. Donald Sutherland, a Canadian historian of the French Revolution, argues that this peasant resistance constituted in itself a social revolution of the countryside, with different economic and cultural goals than those of urban politicians and intellectuals.

The Constituent Assembly: 1789–1791

Once the Assembly had made clear its authority, it turned to implementing the reforms necessary to put France back into shape. The government renewed the French legal system and wrote a constitution that would influence every subsequent constitution in France; it reorganized France into new units called departments, sold Church estates (thus releasing land to more productive management), and set up the so-called Civil Constitution of the Clergy, which provided for the election of bishops and priests by the people. Perhaps the change that caused the greatest conflict was the abolition of the obligation of the French Church to obey the papacy.

Mirabeau (1749–1791)

The pre-eminent figure of the early revolution was Honoré Gabriel Riqueti, comte de Mirabeau, known as *Mirabeau,* eldest son of a noble family from Provence. His father was a noted writer of economics and proponent of tax reforms who sided with the physiocrats and their insistence on the primacy of an agricultural economy (as opposed to the *philosophes,* who were more interested in encouraging urban manufacturing). As a young man, Mirabeau defied the authority of his father, although males in the *ancien régime* were legal minors until age 25. He was imprisoned at

the request of his father, with a warrant written by a local official. Mirabeau responded by writing the first of a series of pamphlets (1782) denouncing arbitrary arrest as well as putting forward his own views on justice and constitutional government. He was equally vehement in criticism of financial speculation.

Mirabeau's pamphlets showed his skill at making complicated issues understandable to the public. He was elected a member of the Assembly in 1789 and was in the forefront of the resistance to direction by the royal ministers, yet he made himself the spokesman for a parliamentary monarchy. He urged the royal family to accommodate the revolution. He also filled his pockets with gifts of money from the royal family. On the other hand, he hurled barbs at the left wing of the Assembly, consistently spoke against Robespierre's Terror and against those he thought were dangerous to social harmony. Mirabeau's death in April 1791 was considered a national catastrophe by those who believed in a compromise between the court and the Assembly. He received a state funeral at Notre Dame Cathedral in Paris. Significantly, just two years later he was exhumed from the Pantheon, the mausoleum for the most famous individuals of France, and his remains were put into a convicts' graveyard. This made space for the body of the assassinated Marat, the very kind of radical Mirabeau so strongly detested, who wrote after Mirabeau's funeral: "Oh people, ...your most redoubtable enemy has fallen."

Mirabeau's death marked a transition from what might be described as conservative radicalism, which failed because there was no agreement about the direction to be followed in the Revolution among the "political class" in mid-1791.

The attempt of the royal family in June 1791 to escape from France was thwarted at the small town of Varennes, where the identity of Louis XVI was recognized and the family was prevented from crossing into the Netherlands; instead, they were returned to Paris. Three months later, new deputies met in a new Legislative Assembly. Those men who had sat in the National Assembly were disqualified from seeking re-election. As a result, experienced politicians such as Robespierre sought a power base in the discussion clubs. The inexperienced newcomers to the Legislative Assembly had to face a difficult situation. In the following spring, they took France into war.

There was strong division between those deputies who supported the government ministers and those who did not. There was little willingness among leading politicians to accept the decisions taken by their political enemies. France was to pass through a great deal of stress before the political class would come to value order over freedom. As well, France was racked with disputes over the place of Catholicism in the nation. The Revolution was increasingly viewed by devout Catholics as an onslaught on their religion.

Robespierre (1758–1794) and the Jacobins

As the Revolution began to take shape, two dominant political groups emerged to direct the course of events. The Girondins, a moderate group, came largely from the Bordeaux region in Southern France, which did not support extending political rights to the working class, known as the **sans-culottes**, meaning literally "without breeches" (the knee-length garment of the well-to-do; the lower classes adopted long trousers). These urban workers found support among the more radical Jacobins. The Jacobins, who took their name from the former Jacobin convent in which they met, were a Parisian club that advocated radical reform and harsh measures to bring about the change they desired. The French Revolution in its early stage marked a legalistic desire for an end to social privilege and it was carried out with the respect for law one might expect of an Assembly primarily composed of lawyers. Increasingly, however, legalism broke down into state terrorism, in which those who disagreed with policies were forced into submission.

If Mirabeau symbolized the attempt to set up a liberal constitutional monarchy in France, he is naturally compared with a younger man, **Maximilien de Robespierre**, a leading revolutionary radical elected to the Estates-General in 1789, who aimed to establish a republic. Robespierre was a small-town lawyer from Northern France who expressed the general culture of the Enlightenment. His honesty made him immune to attempts to influence him away from his path.

Robespierre believed that eternal values were more important than specific experiences. He saw little difference between his view of reason and morality. In his own way, he was a moralist and a utilitarian who saw the useful in terms of the good. Following in Rousseau's steps he looked for good in the community rather than in the individual. In one of his speeches, he contrasted the people and the government: "In the virtue and sovereignty of the people it is necessary to find a preservative against the vices and despotism of the government."

Revolutionary Wars

During the first years of the French Revolution, the other great powers of Europe were not particularly upset by what seemed a series of major domestic reforms in France. Concern did begin to mount, however, when the Alsatians declared themselves to be French and no longer subject to historical feudal rights of German seigneurs, or when Avignon, a papal enclave in Provence, was annexed in September 1791 at the request of the inhabitants, who wanted to be part of France. Foreign governments were increasingly apprehensive that the Revolution was out of control. A declaration was made at Pillnitz in August 1791, in which the Austrian emperor and the Prussian king threatened retribution if any ill befell the French royal family. In fact, this only increased the unpopularity of the monarchy. The Austrian emperor Leopold II died in March 1792 and was replaced by the impetuous Francis II. An Austrian ultimatum to France was rejected and war was declared by France on April 20, 1792.

The declaration of war against Austria resulted from factional in-fighting among French politicians and from the provocative language used by Vienna about the feudal rights of German princes in Alsace. Some, like Brissot, favoured war and others, like Robespierre, were against it. Louis XVI had hoped for a foreign military intervention so that he would become the mediator between invaders and the Assembly. He hoped to avoid bloodshed by accepting limits on his own constitutional authority and by out-manoeuvring radicals inside France and reactionary émigrés outside.

The struggle with Austria brought about the War of the First Coalition (1792–1797). The fiercely nationalistic response it elicited can be gauged from the words of the *Marseillaise*, which Claude Rouget de Lisle modified from a popular war song for the Army of the Rhine in 1792 and which was to become the national anthem of France on July 14, 1795:

Come Children of the Fatherland
The Day of glory has arrived
Against us tyranny
Raises its bloody standards
Do you hear in the fields

The bellowing of these ferocious soldiers
Who have come to our arms
To slaughter our sons and spouses....
Let impure blood
Irrigate our ditches.

From 1792 onward, there followed a devastating series of wars. By March 1793, the French were at war with Austria, Prussia, Britain, Holland, and Spain. They revealed themselves as aggressive expansionists in search of territorial gain just like the continental monarchies. Apart from a brief pause in 1802–1803, the wars would not end until 1815, with the defeat of Napoléon in the Battle of Waterloo.

The dramatic events that unfolded in France seemed to have no direction. Paris was the epicentre of a great upheaval that would grip most of Continental Western Europe, marked by wars and invasions of Italy and the Low Countries, and which would be carried forward in another wave of expansionism by Napoléon to Warsaw and Moscow, Madrid and Lisbon—even into Egypt and the Eastern Mediterranean countries. The consequence of so much fighting in Europe was that Britain's global naval supremacy was not effectively challenged by the French navy.

The war against the Queen Marie Antoinette's brother, the Austrian king, and the suspicion which surrounded the royal family caused a steady fall in their popularity after their flight was foiled at Varennes. As a result, the Tuileries Palace was invaded by a mob of *sans-culottes* in June 1792 and the king insulted, but the intruders left. However, on August 10, 1792, there was an armed attack on the palace and the royal family was taken into custody. During the following month, there was no clear focus of political power. Authority was claimed by the municipality of Paris and the discussion clubs, especially that of the Jacobins, where Robespierre was prominent.

The Convention

A new turning point was reached on September 20 1792, when the Legislative Assembly dissolved and the Convention convened. On the same day, the Prussian invasion under the elderly Duke of Brunswick was halted at Valmy when an ill-trained citizen army stopped the Prussian regulars. Losses were light (180 Prussians and 500 French) but the invaders went back to Germany and the legendary prowess of Prussian armies was disproved.

The Convention received news of the victory on September 21 with tremendous exultation. The membership of the Convention contained 749 men, including 189 deputies from previous assemblies. They were mostly lawyers, although there were two workers, a peasant, and even 23 former nobles. There was a black deputy who lived in France but who represented the sugar colony that is today Haiti. They sat in a semicircle facing the president, with the radicals on the left and their more conservative opponents on the right, while the majority seated themselves in the middle. From this chance arrangement comes the modern terminology of the political left, right, and centre.

On September 20, 1792, the French fought the Prussians in what was mainly an artillery duel. The significance of this victory was that it was hailed as a great triumph that routed the much feared Prussian army. The French were ecstatic with the news of Valmy, which spread at the same time they heard of the proclamation of the new Republic by the Convention on the next day: September 21. Documents were henceforth to be dated "Year One of the Republic." Former king Louis XVI went on trial and was sentenced to death despite the efforts of the Girondins to save his life. He was decapitated in public on January 21, 1793 by the new "humane" killing machine called the guillotine.

The execution of the sovereign who had been anointed with holy oils in his coronation ceremony was horrifying to Catholic monarchists. It caused a sharp increase in foreign hostility to France by other European monarchies. By executing Louis rather than putting him in prison, the radicals signalled their determination to defy Europe and to break with the past.

Once the king was dead, there were struggles between groups of

This cartoon, *The Zenith of French Glory: The Pinnacle of Liberty,* was critical of the French Revolution and the execution of Louis XVI.

deputies in the Convention. Between 1793 and 1794, France was threatened by foreign armies, by political struggles in which the losers were executed, and by the threat of civil war. From 1792 onward, French foreign relations took on a highly ideological tone not unlike the twentieth-century hostility between fascist and democratic states (1933–1945) or the cold war (1945–1990) between capitalist and socialist states.

Republican slogans contained lines such as these: "War to the castles! Peace to the cottages!" Propaganda portrayed France as the homeland of revolution and political innovation. There were acts of conscious novelty, like the invention of a religion (the Supreme Being), the designation of the martyrs of liberty, a new calendar with a 10-day week, and an end of formalism in dress and conversation in favour of the dishevelled, revolutionary look, addressing people in the familiar form (*tu* instead of the formal *vous*), and calling strangers "citizens." Before the royalist Charlotte Corday stabbed him to death, doctor and journalist Jean-Paul Marat had raged against "the despotism of liberty to crush the despotism of kings." Playwright Jean-François de la Harpe criticized the famous naturalist Buffon for calling the lion "the king of beasts."

This phase of the French Revolution was characterized by violence in language and politics. The political scientist Hannah Arendt stressed: "Robespierre had substituted an irresistible and anonymous stream of violence for the free and deliberate actions of men." In his history of the French Revolution, Canadian historian John Bosher also underlined the political instability caused by the constant recourse to violence. During this period, the idealization of the lower classes became the hallmark of radical thought. The notion that the poor and exploited members of society are morally admirable and deserve to be led to triumph over the rich—who deceive and exploit them—became a new version of Christian hopes for the future. It would reappear later in European Marxism and socialism (discussed in Chapters 17–19).

Each faction in the Convention reviled their enemies as either extremists or moderates. On June 2, 1793, 29 Girondin deputies were arrested for treason. Most of them in due course were condemned to death. The fate of these Girondins showed that being a revolutionary deputy was dangerous. The Girondins opposed the excessive centralism of Paris over the rest of the country. Their elimination left the Jacobins as the ruling force in the capital.

The Constitution of 1793 is the most decentralized, democratic, and unworkable constitution that France has ever known. It was supposed to come into effect at the beginning of peace, but peace was a long way off and France soon had other constitutions.

The Reign of Terror

The leaders in Paris instituted a reign of terror, known as **_the Terror_**, against the enemies of the Revolution. A revolutionary tribunal would summarily try individuals accused of political crimes and sentence many of them to death. From March 1793 to June 1794, there were 1251 executions; at its peak from June 10 to July 27, 1794, a further 1376 were guillotined in Paris. In November, Jean Sylvain Bailly, who had presided at the Tennis Court Oath of 1789 and served as mayor of Paris, was just one more revolutionary to die on the scaffold. Some 40 000 people died a violent death during the Terror (6.5 percent were priests; 8.5 percent nobles, and the rest commoners).

The Terror was also marked by flight. The number of French émigrés was lower in proportion to the population than the number of British Loyalists who left the U.S. and settled in Canada after the American Revolution. Most of the émigrés later returned to France, especially after 1800, hoping to find the same France they had left behind.

The Terror was possible thanks to a revolutionary system of government with two powerful executive committees: the Committee for Public Safety (which fought against food shortages, foreign enemies, and political subversion) and the Committee for General Security. Both used drastic methods.

The revolutionary government dated from the proclamation that set up the Committee for Public Safety (1793), which said: "The government of France is revolutionary until the peace." A young revolutionary of the time, Louis Antoine Saint-Just, expressed: "There shall be neither rich nor poor: opulence is infamous."

In August 1793, a mass levy of men to fight was decreed. This became famous as an example of the modern concept of total war in which the whole population has a part to play. The edict defined the roles for each group in the population:

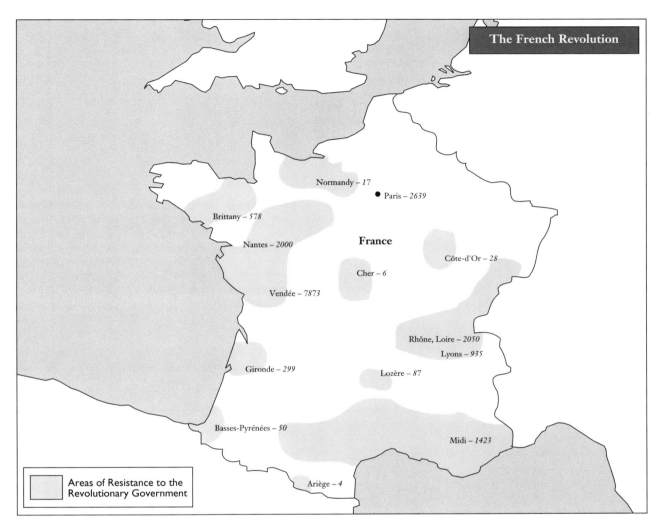

The French Revolution

Normandy – *17*

Paris – *2639*

Brittany – *578*

Nantes – *2000*

France

Côte-d'Or – *28*

Cher – *6*

Vendée – *7873*

Rhône, Loire – *2050*

Lyons – *935*

Gironde – *299*

Lozère – *87*

Basses-Pyrénées – *50*

Midi – *1423*

Ariège – *4*

Areas of Resistance to the Revolutionary Government

Young men shall go to fight; married men shall forge arms and transport food supplies; women shall make tents, clothes, and serve the hospitals; children shall make bandages from old linen; elderly men shall sit in the public squares to excite the courage of warriors, preach hatred of kings, and the unity of the Republic. Bachelors shall fight with banners inscribed: "The French people stands against tyrants!"

Robespierre's ideas on democracy did not include accommodation or compromise: he wanted no constitutional checks and balances by judiciary and second chambers. He wanted males previously excluded from voting to participate in politics: actors, Jews, and Blacks were now part of the nation. He proclaimed that "each man... should take part in public affairs." Significantly, no mention was made of "each woman."

Women in the Revolution

Women who took an interest in revolutionary politics were not approved of by many male voters. Yet Condorcet argued that women ought to vote as well as men: "Why should beings who have pregnancies and passing indispositions not be able to exercise rights which nobody has suggested taking from men with gout or who catch cold easily?" In 1788, Condorcet

The Final Thoughts of Madame Roland

As France attempted to rebuild society after the collapse of the *ancien régime*, individuals of widely divergent views clashed. Often, these clashes had deadly results. Madame Roland, the wife of an inspector of manufactures in Lyon, was an ardent supporter of the cause of liberty. In the years leading up to the Revolution, Madame Roland had surrounded herself with idealists and radical thinkers who shared her vision for the future. Herself an intelligent, energetic, and self-educated philosopher—well read in English and Italian and well versed in the theories of Rousseau—Madame Roland welcomed the French Revolution.

"Friends of humanity, lovers of liberty," she wrote, "we believed that it would regenerate the race.... We welcomed it with rapture."

As one of those who fervently welcomed the Revolution, Madame Roland was also bitterly disappointed when events took a bloody turn during the Reign of Terror. An outspoken woman and defender of freedom, Madame Roland was to be among the thousands killed by the Jacobins. Moments before she was decapitated on the guillotine, she is reported to have declared: "O Liberty, what crimes are committed in thy name!" Her enemies described Madame Roland as "a petty philosopher and small-time intellectual." They accused her of being disdainful of the people and the judges, arrogant, and opinionated. According to her enemies, her greatest crime resulted from her failure to accept the limitations of her sex. They wrote, "...and yet she was a mother but she sacrificed nature in her wish to rise above it; her desire to be an intellectual led her to forget the virtues of her sex and this forgetfulness, always dangerous, finally led her to the scaffold." When Madame Roland's husband, who was away from Paris, heard of her execution, he committed suicide.

During her final months, when she had decided to starve herself to death, Madame Roland penned these final thoughts, in which she pours out her disdain for those who had destroyed the Revolution:

Is life a blessing which is bestowed upon us? I believe it is. But I also believe that there are conditions attached which we must observe. We are born to seek happiness and to serve the happiness of our fellow mortals. The social order merely extends the range of this objective and indeed of all our faculties; it adds nothing new.

So long as we can see a course ahead in which we may do good and set a good example, it behoves us not to abandon it. We must have the courage to persist even in misfortune. But when a term has already been set to our life-span by our enemies, we are surely entitled to shorten the period ourselves, particularly when nobody on earth will gain anything from our battling on. When I was first arrested I flattered myself that I could contribute to my husband's reputation and help to enlighten the public in any trial that they might set up. But they were too clever to give me the chance. They still ran the risk of powerful opposition from those of our friends who were beyond their reach and they had to be circumspect. But now they have nothing to restrain them. The Terror triumphs; all opposition is crushed. Insolence and crime rage furiously together and the people bow down in mindless homage. A vast city, gorged with blood and rotten

———— ❧ ————

Madame Roland's outspoken manner would lead to her execution during the Reign of Terror.

with lies, wildly applauds the foul murders which are supposed to be necessary for its safety.

Two months ago, I coveted the honour of going to the scaffold. It was still possible to speak and I thought that a demonstration of vigorous courage might set a useful example. But now all is lost. The present generation, brutalised by the high priests of slaughter, treats all those who love humanity as conspirators and makes heroes of the dregs. I feel soiled and degraded to be living amongst these vile, cowardly monsters.

I know that the empire of evil never lasts long. Sooner or later the wicked get their deserts. If I was unknown, tucked away in some silent corner, I might find it possible to ignore the horrors that are tearing France apart and to wait patiently for better times, keeping virtue alive in private. But here in prison, a proclaimed victim, every hour that I remain alive gives tyranny new scope for boasting. I cannot beat them, but I can at least defraud them.

made it clear that all property owners of sufficient status should vote, irrespective of sex. Thus, a woman who paid property tax and was not a minor or mentally handicapped, should vote. It was property that should grant the right to vote. Condorcet's views were not widely shared.

A number of radical women in the French Revolution tried to make speeches and establish women's clubs. Most famous is the Belgian Théroigne de Méricourt. She was avidly interested in the debates at the Estates-General, but later became mentally ill and died in an insane asylum in the early nineteenth century. Some of her enemies claimed that her madness was a result of her unnatural, unfeminine interest in politics. There were lower-class highly politicized women in the French Revolution: a gang of Jacobin women once attacked Méricourt. Women's clubs for political discussion were closed down by the autumn of 1793 and leading women were executed.

Women's Consciousness in the Eighteenth Century

Women in France had lower literacy rates than men, as various studies of signatures on large samples of marriage contracts reveal. The female press reinforced the status of women by reporting on fashion, wigs, lace, ribbons, songs, etc. rather than public debate.

Feminine values and consciousness were upheld by Catholicism: convents were among the rare large organizations with economic resources where women could hold positions of power, albeit at the cost of being a bride of Christ and confined. In 1789, no society in Europe had a better nursing service than that of the French Sisters of Charity. In prerevolutionary France, some 2000 hospitals were run by women whose only remuneration was their keep: from peasant woman to hospital nurse, women's work was poorly rewarded.

The Revolution of 1789 ended the political supremacy of the old court culture—where women were often highly influential—and replaced it with an Assembly of middle-aged men who would discuss male rights in *The Declaration of Rights of Man and the Citizen*. Even the most radical revolutionaries could not accept the idea of women participating in politics. They also suspected country women of being too influenced by priests and counter-revolutionaries. In fact, the assumption that women were strongly influenced by Roman Catholicism was used as an excuse to deny them the vote during the nineteenth century. The following excerpt from an article in the *Moniteur* of November 19, 1793 expresses the male attitude with painful precision.

> Women, do you wish to be true Republicans? Then love, follow and teach the laws that guide your husbands and sons in the exercise of their rights... Be diligent in your housework; never attend political meetings with the intention of speaking there."

The Revolution not only brought no change to the patriarchal attitudes of traditional European society, it actually dispelled women's hopes of advance through political life.

Economic Radicals

In 1793 and 1794, there were food shortages due to a poor grain harvest. Many people complained of rising food costs and, in February 1793, a deputation in Paris called on the Convention to legislate lower bread prices. Robespierre struck at economic radicals who wanted price controls. He also turned on his former colleague Georges Jacques Danton and had him condemned to death. In the summer of 1794, Robespierre unwittingly caused his colleagues at the Convention to unite against him by announcing that another purge of enemies of the Revolution was coming—without giving names. Almost everyone in the Convention feared that he might be on the hit list. The normally docile deputies had the motion removed and voted that Robespierre and his associates be arrested. Robespierre, his brother Augustin, the young radical Saint-Just, and others were sent to the guillotine on July 27, 1794 (9 Thermidor in the revolutionary calendar).

After Thermidor

Robespierre's death on 9 Thermidor marked the end of the most radical phase of revolutionary government. Henceforth, struggles within the political class would establish a more stable regime.

Gradually, the committees of Public Safety and of Security were remodelled. The Revolutionary Tribunal, which had sentenced so many to death, now acquitted the accused. The so-called Gilded Youth of rich young people would mistreat on the streets those they suspected of being radical sympathizers. In November 1794, the Jacobin club was ordered closed. Marat's remains were removed from the Pantheon. Especially in the south of France, attacks on former

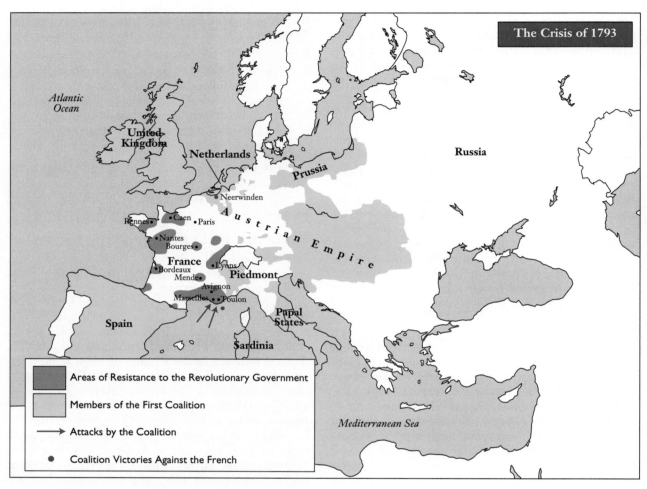

The Crisis of 1793

Legend:

- Areas of Resistance to the Revolutionary Government
- Members of the First Coalition
- → Attacks by the Coalition
- • Coalition Victories Against the French

Jacobins took revenge against those who were militants during Robespierre's Terror. This is sometimes called a "White Terror" by contrast with the radical "Red Terror" of the revolutionaries. During this period, many churches were reopened.

The winter of 1794–1795 was the coldest in 100 years and the paper money of the Revolution (called *assignats* because its value was assigned to national assets) was rapidly losing its value: sellers often refused to accept *assignats*. At the same time, food was scarce and very expensive. Generally in the aftermath of Robespierre's government, there was a relaxation of revolutionary fervor.

On April 1, 1795, revolutionary militants surged into the Convention, demanding bread and the 1793 Constitution. They held the Assembly captive for several hours. There were more violent demonstrations in Paris during May, culminating with the arrest of the leaders. These disorders, known as those of Germinal–Prairial (from the names of the months in the revolutionary calendar) were the last spontaneous popular uprisings in Paris during the Revolution. In the aftermath of the backlash against extremism, radical activists such as Gracchus Babeuf, who dreamed of an egalitarian society, were arrested and executed.

The period of Thermidor and the Directory regime (which followed the Convention) was a time of economic inflation and speculation; it also saw new political leaders coming to the fore. In general, the Directory resisted both royalists and leftist radicals but it did not govern effectively. It did, however, undertake military activities in Italy that would favour a young general who would have an immense impact on France and also on Europe.

Napoléon Bonaparte (1769–1821)

Napoléon Bonaparte was to his contemporaries as well as to posterity almost superhuman in his military and governmental achievements. He came to symbolize order after the effervescence and excesses of the revolutionary decade, with its civil strife, confiscations, and arbitrariness.

Charles Maurice de Talleyrand-Périgord, a bishop of the *ancien régime* and revolutionary politician who also served under Napoléon, observed: "He was clearly the most extraordinary man I ever saw, and I believe the most extraordinary man that has lived in our age, or in many ages."

Napoléon Bonaparte was born on Corsica in 1769, one year after the French foreign minister purchased that Mediterranean island for France from Genoa. (Corsicans spoke Italian.) Napoléon's father was a lawyer who at age 18 married Laetitia, aged 14. They had 13 children, of whom eight survived to maturity. Laetitia had a powerful personality and she instilled a keen sense of pride in her children. Napoléon had strong family ties and in due course seated three brothers on European thrones and married his sisters into established dynasties. As self-styled emperor, Napoléon fathered a son with the daughter of an Austrian emperor and proclaimed the child King of Rome.

In 1778, Napoléon arrived at Marseilles unable to speak French. He was enrolled in several military colleges and showed a special interest in artillery. As a young officer, he was given his first garrison posting in the south of France. At the outbreak of the Revolution he joined the local revolutionary club in the town of Valence. In general, Napoléon welcomed—or at least did not resist—the Revolution, unlike some of his wealthier aristocratic former companions at the military college. He no longer felt sympathy for those who wanted Corsican independence. He was grateful for the French connection that had provided him with a good education and wanted to pursue his future in France. By the time of the Terror in 1793, he was involved in the attack on the Mediterranean port of Toulon, which had gone over to royalism and the English. His success got him praise and recognition.

Opportunity presented itself in the aftermath of Jacobinism. The winter of 1794–1795 was exceptionally cold. The Thermidorians (winners of the political crisis of 9 Thermidor) did not wish to return to a monarchy; however, they were exhausted by revolutionary government and the political purges. They wanted to consolidate the internal changes in France but they were under the constant pressure of European war.

In 1795, two years after the fall of the monarchy, the royalists began to agitate. The Thermidorians were as apprehensive of vengeful royalists as they were of fanatical Jacobins. Napoléon, who had returned to Paris, showed his decisiveness when he fired on a mob of royalist demonstrators on October 5, 1795. This incident near a downtown Paris church is known as the "whiff of grapeshot." A leading Thermidorian politician, Paul de Barras, used his influence to advance Napoléon's career. At Toulon, Napoléon had shown his military skill, and in Paris he showed that he could be ruthless as well. At age 26 in 1796, he was appointed Commander-in-Chief of the French army invading Italy. It was unusual to entrust such an important position to such a young officer.

This famous painting by Jacques-Louis David shows Napoléon crossing the Alps on May 20, 1800, although the march is said to have been actually made on muleback.

Italy and Revolution

The invasion of Italy in 1796 recalled the *furia francese* (French fury) of earlier centuries when the rich cities of the peninsula were looted by invaders. The Italian intelligentsia was also drawn to the notion that these armies might purify the corrupt feudalism of the different states and perhaps even establish a unity in the form of a state. Filipo Buonorotti, described by one biographer as Europe's first professional revolutionary, wrote of Sicily:

> The people are weighed down with a feudal government and nobles but the youth among the commoners who are enlightened by philosophy earnestly desire Revolution.

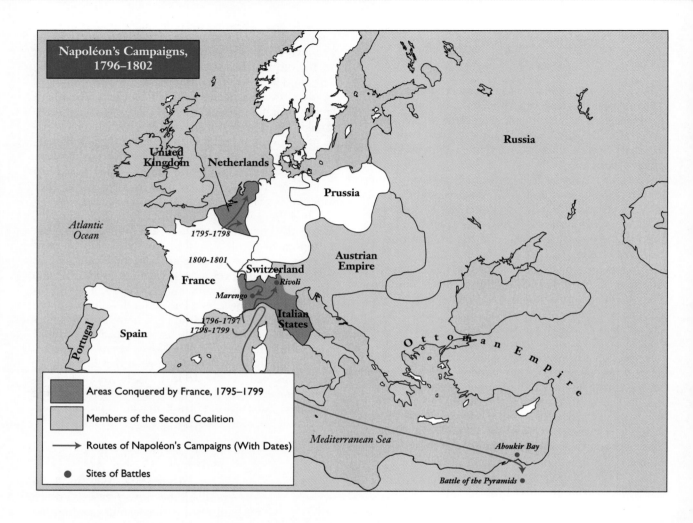

Napoléon's Campaigns, 1796–1802

Areas Conquered by France, 1795–1799

Members of the Second Coalition

Routes of Napoléon's Campaigns (With Dates)

Sites of Battles

In other parts of Italy, there were those who were sympathetic to the reforms of the Revolution and they hoped for the same changes in their own society.

Once Napoléon had had some military success, he proclaimed the Cisalpine Republic in Northern Italy, on December 27, 1796, which guaranteed freedom of the press, the right to petition, the right to education, and equality before the law. The French vigorously fought the Austrian armies and, by October 1797, the Austrians conceded a humiliating defeat in the Treaty of Campoformio. Later, the French pushed southward and captured Rome, continuing on to establish a Neapolitan Republic.

Many Italians welcomed the French as friends but more hated the pillaging foreigners. In 1799,

anti-French revolts broke out in Northern Italy; in Naples, Cardinal Ruffo stirred up peasant hatred against the collaborators. In June 1799, an Army of the Holy Faith entered Naples and massacred more than 100 Italian Republicans. In the same month the ghetto of Siena was sacked and three Jews were burnt alive with a Tree of Liberty (a symbol planted in France and elsewhere to mark the acceptance of civil equality as taught by the revolutionary codes). In Tuscany and Umbria, peasants attacked French sympathizers (mostly landowners) in the name of Catholicism. Various images of the Virgin and Christ in Italy were said to have wept to show their revulsion at the Godless French.

In Italy, Portugal, Spain, the Low Countries, and Germany, it should be stressed that the French invasion polarized the local population into friends and foes of the French. It is important to note that this focus on social and legal change was the result of military force rather than of free debate.

Napoléon's Military Genius

Napoléon said of his troops: "They are a freemasonry, and I am their Grand Master." This was a telling image at a time when reactionary writers such as Augustin Barruel explained the French Revolution as "the work of the machinations of godless freemasons." Napoléon often took time for small acts that the soldiers could repeat about him. He wrote a special warning from Poland to a brave corporal who drank too much but who had been awarded the Legion of Honour (the honorary institution that Napoléon created in 1802 to reward the prowess of his troops). He told the corporal to behave himself and drink less: "One must not take the cross away from him because he is a bit fond of wine." This human touch was appreciated by his soldiers. It personalized their commander's concern for their welfare. There was strong loyalty to Napoléon by the rank and file.

Napoléon fought best with small armies. He had a strategy of smashing the centre formation of the enemy troops and then "mopping up" the soldiers who were now separated from the main body. He was quick to take decisions on the battlefield and skillful at improvisation. He also mixed infantry and cavalry instead of keeping them in separate formations.

In 1789, the French army had 228 000 men under aristocratic officers. Proof of four noble forebears was required for admission to the officer corps of the old army. The decree of August 23, 1793 requisitioned the male inhabitants of the nation: "From this moment until the enemy shall have been ejected from the territory of the Republic, all of the French are requisitioned for the service of the armies," thus opening the army to all.

However, under the Directory, a conscription law of September 23, 1798 made all Frenchmen between the ages of 20 and 25 subject to military service. This produced an annual levy of 200 000 young who were not particularly well trained but were full of youthful impetuosity. Later, Napoléon developed a special elite force of 80 000 men, called the Imperial Guard. If they had not been killed by cold and guerrilla fighting in the disastrous retreat from Moscow in 1812, it is doubtful that he would have suffered defeat in the field. The

This famous cartoon showed England, represented by Prime Minister Pitt, and France, represented by Napoléon, carving up the globe.

French casualties of the Napoleonic wars—600 000 is a recent estimate—did not shake the loyalty of his soldiers.

Marshal André Masséna was the son of a minor Sardinian merchant, and he had served in the French army for 14 years before 1789, rising no higher than to warrant officer. He never forgot, as he said himself, what it was to be a private soldier paid five sous (cents) a day. When he had the opportunity to loot and plunder, he lined his pockets, so he ended up as a wealthy man with a palatial house. By 1814, he was a marshal of France and a prince. He fought bravely as at the Battle of Rivoli. Masséna's career illustrated well how service under Napoléon offered a ladder of promotion to the able soldier.

Napoléon defeated the Prussians at Jena in 1806, smashed the Austrian armies, and burnt Moscow in 1812. He slept as a conqueror in many of the capitals of the Continent. His military adventure following that of the revolutionary wars meant that the map of Europe was permanently redrawn. The Holy Roman Empire was much reduced, a significant step toward the unification of Germany achieved by 1870. The presence of French institutions in parts of Italy prepared the way for the later Italian unification under the house of Piedmont. The disruption that the Napoleonic invasion caused in Spain stimulated Latin American independence movements. The invasion of Portugal caused the Braganza dynasty to cross over to Brazil and introduce policies that would lead to Brazilian independence in 1822. Warfare in the Napoleonic period had major repercussions in Europe and overseas; however, Napoléon's attempt to subjugate the Continent of Europe failed in the same way that Louis XIV's bid for hegemony had failed a century earlier.

Napoleonic Government

Napoléon took power in 1799 by the coup d'état known as the 18 Brumaire (9–10 November), one month after his return to France from a military campaign in Egypt. In the Constitution of the Year VIII, published in December 1799, Napoléon strengthened the centralization of government in France: there were to be three consuls as executive, the first of whom would serve for 10 years; there were three assemblies and a complicated electoral system for men over 21. Despite the organizational formalities in practice, Napoléon dominated the government as First Consul.

In May 1804, the Tribunate asked that Napoléon be proclaimed "hereditary emperor of the French." It is striking that he did not use the traditional title of the French ruler, king, but the medieval title of emperor, like Charlemagne. There was a referendum in which 3.5 million voted yes and only 2500 voted no to the proposal that "The government of the Republic is confided to an emperor who will carry the title of the Emperor of the French." He was to swear to uphold the integrity of the territory of the Republic, respect the Concordat with the Catholic Church, freedom of religion, equality of rights, political and civil liberties, the irreversibility of the sale of confiscated properties; no tax was to be levied without a law; and he was to "govern with the sole aim of the interest, happiness, and glory of the French People."

The 1799 Constitution had set up the prefectoral system, with its parallels to the earlier system of nominees by the king (intendants) of the *ancien régime*. Napoléon also set up the State Council, described by French novelist Stendhal as "the fifty least stupid Frenchmen," which drafted legislation. It also reorganized the civil law code, which came to be known as the **Code Napoléon** (1804), on the basis of equality before the law and in taxation. Even if married in a religious ceremony, couples had to go through a civil ceremony to register their union with the state. The Criminal Code specified jury trial for major cases. Napoléon worked with the State Council on legal reforms and insisted that they derive from general principles rather than local conditions. Napoleonic laws, although revised and expanded, subsequently remained the basic law of France and have been accepted in other parts of the world, such as Quebec.

Gradually, Napoléon took a number of important initiatives to bring stability and order back to France. In 1801, he concluded a concordat with Pope Pius VII, which was intended to assuage the resentment of Catholics over the despoliation of the Church and the treatment of the clergy. The Concordat of July 1801 recognized Roman Catholicism as the religion of the majority of the French and agreed to pay the parish clergy. The Pope could refuse government nominees for the clergy.

Purchasers of Church lands were henceforth guaranteed ownership of the property. The freedom to practise other religions was upheld. Civil marriage and divorce, two major innovations of the revolutionary period, were maintained. This religious policy did not satisfy everybody but it rallied a lot of support. It aimed to end animosities on religious grounds among citizens. In 1807, Napoléon called a meeting of Jewish rabbis to discuss the relation of their congregations to the French state. His general aim in matters of faith was to remove the main causes of friction between government and believers.

Napoléon reorganized the higher educational system, setting up a system of *lycées* (secondary schools) under military discipline. There were also municipal colleges. Graduation from this system was a requirement for entry to the so-called Big Schools in Paris, which trained engineers and teachers. Other institutions reinforced an educational system based on opportunities for those with the best results in examinations.

It is fair to say that Napoléon fixed the forms of government that carried France through political difficulties during the nineteenth century. The administrative reforms were the most durable part of his legacy. Counter-revolutionary philosopher Joseph de Maistre rightly said in 1814, when the brother of Louis XVI ascended the French throne: "Louis XVIII has not been restored to the throne of his ancestors, he has simply ascended the throne of Bonaparte." Napoléon's attributes of imperial majesty derived from a new mystique of war as ennobling the common man. The

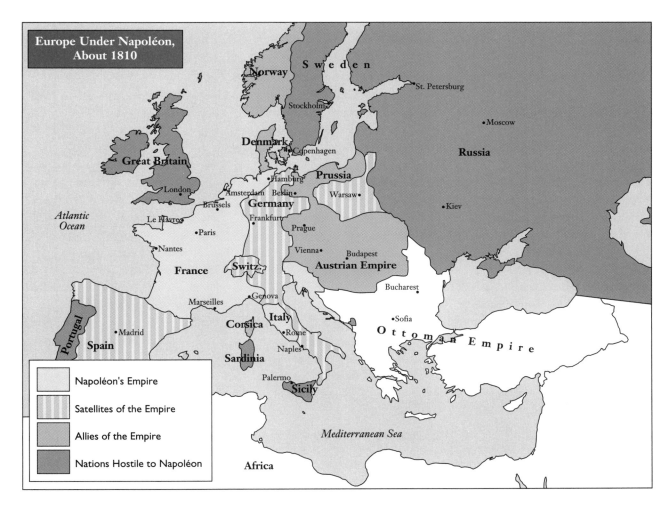

emperor and his marshals reached the highest levels of fortune and position through bravery.

End of Napoléon's Reign

Napoléon had fought wars in different areas of Europe but the Russian campaign of 1812 greatly weakened his forces. In 1813, the Russian, Prussian, and Austrian armies combined to defeat Napoléon's army at the "Battle of the Nations" in October. Allied armies invaded Southwestern France from Spain and also from Germany. By the end of March, foreign armies entered Paris. On April 11, 1814, Napoléon abdicated. He was exiled to the small island of Elba in the Mediterranean—without his empress, who had gone home to Vienna and the Habsburg court taking with her the King of Rome, Napoléon's son.

Europe in 1815 was very different from Europe in 1715. The Congress of Vienna ended the dazzling Napoleonic adventure: it assembled in September 1814 and was clearly dominated by the great powers who were victorious: Russia, Great Britain, Prussia, and Austria. The Revolution had created the idea of the *grande nation*, a European federation of different peoples linked by *The Declaration of the Rights of Man and the Citizen*. Indeed, revolutionary armies exported this viewpoint out of the mouths of their cannons. The *grand empire* was the same, with the difference that it was to have been a Europe accepting an emperor of the Revolution.

Louis XVI's brother had been recalled to the French throne for lack of a more suitable candidate. Many of his advisers were out of touch with the new

Exile in Elba

Napoléon Bonaparte, who had risen from his humble Corsican roots to be the master of Europe, finally faced defeat in 1814. Under the Treaty of Fontainebleau, Napoléon had agreed to abdicate, in exchange for which he was given the tiny kingdom of Elba. Elba, a small island in the Mediterranean, lies only 12 km from Italy. Rich in mineral deposits, Elba has been inhabited since the early Iron Age. By the eighteenth century, Elba had taken on significant strategic importance, as it was a good base for fleets patrolling the Mediterranean.

There could be few more pleasant places to be exiled. Elba's moderate temperatures year-round and its clear blue Mediterranean waters washing up on white sand beaches make this island a popular destination for European vacationers. The island has become so popular in recent years that it is virtually impossible to find summer accommodations without making advance reservations. A common sight on the Island of Elba on warm summer evenings are young people sleeping on the beach or in their cars, as even campgrounds are filled to capacity.

When Napoléon arrived on Elba on May 3, 1814, he brought with him ambitious plans to reform government and stimulate the economy. To improve communications between the island's strategic points, Napoléon encouraged road construction. He also helped to modernize agriculture and improved fishing by introducing tunny nets. He also worked hard to win the support of the island's bourgeoisie by flattering them with honorary titles and invitations to his court. Beyond these measures, however, Napoléon accomplished little on the island. His efforts to revitalize the mining industry were thwarted by his own greed as he pocketed much of the money from the mines and

---

The island of Elba, just off the coast of Italy, to which Napoléon was first exiled, is a pleasant Mediterranean island.

increased land taxes. These measures led to revolts, which were suppressed under the threat of arms.

Napoléon's main residence on Elba was the Palazzina dei Mulini, at Portoferraio. The work in remodelling the Palazzina dei Mulini and his country homes was all given to architects, decorators, tapestry workers, and cabinet makers brought in from France. In the end, an accurate assessment of Napoléon's reign on Elba is difficult, due to the brevity of his stay. What is certain is that little economic change and few of the planned governmental reforms were put in place before his departure.

On the evening of February 26, 1815, Napoléon took advantage of the temporary absence of his English custodian, Colonel Campbell. Under the cover of night, he silently slipped away from Elba, returning to the mainland, where he was joined by loyal supporters. This would begin his famous final Hundred Days ending with the Battle of Waterloo. The next time Napoléon was captured, his exile would not be to such a pleasant island but to the wind-swept island of Saint Helena, far out in the Atlantic Ocean.

France. The Restoration (of the old order) soon lost popular support. Napoléon decided to attempt a comeback. On March 1, 1815, he escaped from the Island of Elba and landed on the southern coast of France, in his so-called "Flight of the Eagle," taking a route through areas known to support him. In fact, about a half a million partisan volunteers, called *fédérés*, welcomed him throughout the country.

Europe was appalled at the ease with which Napoléon returned to power. There was a second allied invasion and Napoléon suffered defeat at Waterloo in Belgium in June 1815. Subsequently he was sent into exile on the small island of St. Helena in the South Atlantic. There he died mysteriously in 1821.

The Congress of Vienna

The Vienna political settlement, or **Congress of Vienna**, failed to deal with liberalism or nationalism in Europe. After nine months of wearisome negotiations in Vienna, the treaty was signed in Paris on June 19, 1815, the day after the final defeat of Napoleon by Arthur Wellesley, Duke of Wellington, at the Battle of Waterloo. Talleyrand called the diplomatic intrigue leading up to the 121-article treaty "vaporizing"; the Austrian representative said it enveloped his mind in "a fog of unreality."

The great powers accepted the Vienna Treaty: Britain, Austria, Prussia, Russia, and France in the name of the restored Bourbon king, Louis XVIII. Sweden, Spain, and Portugal also signed, and so did myriad smaller powers. Only the Pope and the Turkish sultan withheld assent to the new arrangements. Belgium was incorporated into the kingdom of the Netherlands (a union that broke down in 1830); Prussia was strengthened, and so was the House of Savoy in Italy. By 1870, Germany and Italy both became unified modern nations. The losers were Poland (which was once again partitioned), the Italian nationalists (whose hopes in 1815 for a country were dashed), and Saxony (which lost two fifths of its territory to Prussia).

German philosopher Friedrich Hegel, trying to encapsulate the impact of the French Revolution on Europe, wrote of the "fury of disappearance" and the "universal freedom" that resulted from an upheaval that could only destroy and not build. Napoléon's legacy has been seen as more positive because of his administrative, educational, and legal innovations, which

Marshal Ney and the rearguard of the Grand Army of France are shown in retreat from Moscow in this painting by Adolphe Ivon.

endured despite the change of dynasties and forms of government. The Congress of Vienna also established how international meetings should be conducted and defined diplomatic usage. In broad terms, it was a settlement that helped to avoid a general European war for almost a century—until the summer of 1914.

Reflections

The quarter-century between the outbreak of the French Revolution and the end of Napoléon's reign had brought drastic change to Europe. The *ancien régime* had fallen and ideas of the Enlightenment had taken root. Although there would be efforts by conservative forces in Europe to turn back the clock and restore the old order, Europe had entered a new age. No longer would the nobility be able to lay claim to the privileges it had held for centuries. Nor did the Roman Catholic Church remain the unquestionable authority it had been in previous centuries. The French Revolution had brought a new social and political order to France and the Napoleonic Wars had spread this change through much of Europe. As the nineteenth century dawned, so too did a new era.

Key Concepts, Figures, and Events

Yemelian Ivanovich Pugachov
Mirabeau
The Terror
Congress of Vienna

Estates-General
Maximilien de Robespierre
Napoléon Bonaparte

Tennis Court Oath
Sans-Culottes
Code Napoléon

Topics for Further Thought

1. The years leading up to 1789 were difficult times for the French peasantry. How did living conditions for the peasants lay the foundations for the French Revolution?

2. When the French Revolution erupted, it found its leadership among merchants and lawyers: the middle class. What aspects of the *ancien régime* did the middle class abhor? How did the changes brought about in the first few years of the Revolution reflect the dominance of the professional middle class?

3. The French Revolution is a classic example of a major event that can only be understood by examining a multiplicity of causes. Prepare a list of the causes that led to the Revolution. Be sure to consider the disenchantment of all levels of society as well as significant intellectual trends. Once you have prepared your list, indicate which of the causes were underlying factors and which were the immediate triggers.

4. Out of the chaos of revolution emerged Maximilien de Robespierre. Considering both his philosophical foundations and his actions while in power, show that he embodied both the ideals of the French Revolution and the horrors of fanatical despotism.

5. During the English Civil War in the mid-seventeenth century, Thomas Hobbes warned against revolution, claiming that it produces instability and destroys what has taken centuries to build. Do the events between 1789 and 1794 support Hobbes's belief and the criticisms levelled against France by royalists and other nations?

6. The rallying cry of the French Revolution was "Equality, Fraternity, and Liberty." Did the Revolution succeed at any point in achieving these goals in light of the rights granted to women? Why were men, so intent on ending the *ancien régime*, so reluctant to recognize women as full and equal citizens?

7. Napoléon Bonaparte, who rose through the army and earned his reputation on the battlefield, relied on the continuance of war to maintain his power. Respond to this statement by reflecting on Napoléon's effectiveness as a ruler as well as the nature and purpose of the wars he fought after 1804.

Topics for Further Research

1. During the French Revolution, several people came to dominate the political stage. Prepare a biographical sketch of one of the following:

Maximilien de Robespierre
Honoré Gabriel de Riqueti, comte de Mirabeau
Jean-Paul Marat
Georges Danton

2. Despite the efforts to restrict their participation in politics, several prominent women made important contributions during the years of the French Revolution. Prepare a biographical sketch of one of the following women including their major contributions/accomplishments.

Marie Antoinette

Madame Roland

Madame de Staël

Charlotte Corday

Josephine de Beauharnais

Olympe de Gouges

Thérèse Cabarrus

Théroigne de Méricourt

3. Napoléon Bonaparte, often best remembered for his military exploits and his love affair with Josephine, also made several important contributions to the reform of French government and society. Research one of the following areas:

1799 Constitution

Code Napoléon

Concordat with the Roman Catholic Church

Educational Reforms

Responding to Ideas

1. The French Revolution has spawned much debate over the past two centuries. One of the issues of popular discussion is the primary causes of the Revolution in 1789. Many historians have emphasized the economic factors to explain the collapse of the *ancien régime*. French historian Henri Peyre, in an article titled "The Influence of Eighteenth-Century Ideas on the French Revolution," argues that ideas, not economics, were the crucial factor in the outbreak of the Revolution. He wrote: "If there is really one almost undisputed conclusion on the origins of the Revolution reached by historical studies... it is that pure historical materialism does not explain the Revolution.... No great event in history has been due to causes chiefly economic in nature and certainly not the French Revolution. France was not happy in 1788, but she was happier than the other countries of Europe and enjoyed veritable economic prosperity.... Eighteenth-century philosophy taught the Frenchman to find his condition wretched, or in any case, unjust and illogical and made him disinclined to the patient resignation to his troubles that had long characterized his ancestors." After reading this quotation, as well as the previous two chapters, do you believe Peyre's argument can be defended? How would historians defending economic factors respond to his argument?

2. Few individuals have had as much written about them as Napoléon Bonaparte. Debate over Napoléon's role in the revolutionary period began even before his death and continues to this day. Below are statements by three historians regarding Napoléon's role in history. Note whether each historian sees Napoléon in a positive or negative light. Which of the quotes do you feel most accurately describes him? Defend your answer.

i. Geoffrey Bruun: *Europe and the French Imperium, 1799–1814*

> Napoléon lent his name to an epoch because he symbolized reason enthroned, because he was the philosopher-prince who gave to the dominant aspiration of the age its most typical, most resolute, and most triumphant expression.

ii. Alfred Cobban: *Dictatorship: Its History and Theory*

> Napoléon came to power as a dictator from the right, not, of course, as a leader of the old reactionary party, but as a dictator supported by the propertied classes, the financiers and commercial men, the upper bourgeoisie, and speculators, who had made large fortunes out of the Revolution and had bought up church or crown lands...

iii. George Rude, from Norman F. Cantor: *Perspectives on the European Past*, Vol. II:

> ...if we judge Napoléon on what he actually did and not only on those things that are usually remembered (despotism and foreign conquest), we must concede that his armies "liberalized" the constitution of many European countries.... In this sense, Napoléon was a revolutionary... Napoléon was indeed a military despot, but he did not destroy the work of the Revolution; in a sense, in a wider European context, he rounded off its work.

6

Art, Music, and Literature in the Enlightenment

CHAPTER HIGHLIGHTS

- Versailles as an influence on European art and architecture

- Art of beauty and sadness

- Bach and baroque music

- The link between the classical and romantic eras

- Restoration comedies combining social satire and ribald humour

- The eighteenth-century novel

What does it mean to be enlightened? When applied to the cultural achievements of the eighteenth century, the word "Enlightenment" connotes an abandonment of the grand—but somewhat oppressive—character of seventeenth-century art and the renewal of the ancient classical, humanistic spirit that created the Renaissance. This revival of the classical ideal, enclosed in exquisite forms of art, architecture, music, and literature, became the dominant aesthetic of the age. The key words of the eighteenth century are balance, harmony, wit, elegance, grace, charm, and scrupulous control of emotion. And yet this enlightened age did not lack feeling: underlying all the arts were the powerful ideas and emotions that would culminate in social, artistic, and political revolutions at the end of the century.

Art in the Eighteenth Century

Art trends of the eighteenth century reflect the tensions between the state and the rising middle class. The grandiose seventeenth-century *baroque*, a style characterized by elaborate ornamentation, and eighteenth-century *classicism*, a style stressing simplicity, regularity, and restraint, illustrate the desire of the absolute monarchs to hold on to their power. The extremely ornate *rococo* style and the rise of romanticism reflect the growing power of the middle class.

To fully understand the art of the eighteenth century, one must look back to the seventeenth century and consider the baroque (1600–1750) and its counterpart, classicism. Baroque art may be seen as a reaction to the art and architecture of the Italian Renaissance.

Whereas Renaissance art is characterized by its static, classical qualities that appeal to the intellect, baroque art is characterized by its dynamic qualities that appeal to the emotions. Classicism also developed in the seventeenth century; it was a reaction to the baroque, a reworking of the Renaissance style on a far grander scale. Classicists felt that the baroque was too emotional, too "real"; they strove to emulate the "ideal" world of classical Greece and Rome.

The struggle of intellect versus emotion, or of classicism versus romanticism, persists to this day. Two seventeenth-century paintings that illustrate the conflict between these two **aesthetic** philosophies are Flemish painter Peter Paul Rubens's *The Crucifixion of St. Peter* and French painter Gaspard Poussin's *The Burial of Phocion*. The Rubens painting is a dramatic, physically graphic depiction of St. Peter's execution: St. Peter's physical pain and psychological anguish assault the viewer. This is a dynamic, passionate work with a powerful interplay between light and dark enhancing the drama of the moment. Now consider the Poussin painting, which has truly captured a moment in time: there is no movement; indeed, stillness is palpable. Even though this painting illustrates a funeral, usually an event full of sorrow, Poussin has created an ideal, tranquil image. It is useful to have a sense of the work of these two extraordinary masters because European painting in the seventeenth and eighteenth centuries was divided into two camps: those who followed Rubens, or Rubenists, and those who followed Poussin, or Pousinists. Later, this conflict would be turned into romanticism versus classicism.

Art of the Early Eighteenth Century

The early eighteenth century was very much a continuation of the style and aesthetic philosophy of the seventeenth, which was strongly influenced by Louis XIV, a monarch whose rigid political control extended to the arts. Louis established the Royal Academy of Painting and Sculpture in l648, a regulatory body to ensure that all art met with the conservative standards of the state.

The standards of the state were further strengthened by the construction of the Palace of Versailles, designed to be a monument to Louis XIV's glory and power. It became the **archetype** for the building of all other European monuments in the seventeenth and eighteenth centuries. Versailles was to be a microcosm of Louis' absolute monarchy. Although there are

Nicholas Poussin: *The Burial of Phocion*

baroque features in this building, Louis favoured classicism. He felt it to be more serious, more suited to his taste for displaying his complete control. Louis believed his control was not just over his subjects, his country, and Europe but also extended to nature. Versailles is the supreme example of the eighteenth-century desire to subordinate nature to the power of the human intellect. The huge formal gardens of Versailles may be considered a work of art in themselves and are designed to manipulate the person who walks through them.

All over Europe, many royal or aristocratic families tried to emulate Louis XIV's stunning architectural achievement. Some of the resulting buildings were designed to commemorate political victories over Louis himself. In England, the Duke of Marlborough had Blenheim Palace[1] built to commemorate his victory over the French in the War of the Spanish Succession. This baroque palace has been criticized for the ponderous, theatrical design of its structure. Like Versailles, it celebrates a power which, at the time of its construction, was losing its appeal. Of course, the people who paid for these colossal monuments to a few people's glory were getting restless. Thinkers began to deplore the extravagance of the few at the expense of the many.

---

[1] Winston Churchill was born and buried in Blenheim Palace as he is a direct descendant of the Duke of Marlborough, who built it.

Antoine Watteau: *Pilgrimage to Cythera*

In reaction to buildings such as Versailles or Blenheim Palace, English architects looked to the classical archetype once more but this time they strove for simplicity and rationality rather than power and authority. The resulting style, called neoclassicism, is an illustration of the philosophy of the Enlightenment. Small, beautiful, reasonable structures reflect the new spirit of reason and sensibility. In neoclassical buildings, ordinary people could sit together and talk. In continental Europe, however, things took quite a different turn.

Rococo

When Louis XIV died in 1715, there was a period of relative calm. The rigid formality of French classicism was countered by the sensuous and ornate rococo. The word comes from the French word *rocaille*, which literally means "loose stones" and refers to the small shells that became the principal design element of rococo interiors with their flowing lines and heavily ornate decoration. Unlike the interiors of Versailles, where enormous rooms and mirrored galleries overwhelmed the occupant, rococo interiors were far smaller and made people feel at ease.

Because its beautiful spaces afforded the occupants the opportunity to converse with one another, the rococo salon became an extremely important part of eighteenth-century society. Influential women became the dominant figures in these salons. Although one may consider witty conversation, gorgeous clothing, and food rather frivolous, the salons did bring together some of the greatest minds of the age. People conversed and exchanged ideas, many of which led to the huge social upheaval at the end of the century: the French Revolution.

Outside of France, rococo manifested itself in some beautiful and unusual structures. In Munich, architect François de Cuvilliés designed the exquisite palace called Amalienburg. He gave the exterior of the building the same flowing lines as the interior decoration, creating a truly unified piece of rococo architecture. Some of the most stunning rococo buildings are the pilgrimage churches of Southern Germany. The exteriors still carry some baroque characteristics but the interiors are entirely rococo ; the spiritual love of God is illustrated by secular, even **pagan** motifs. They are full of white and gold ornamentation; sculpted cupids and nymphs pirouette up to the richly painted ceiling. The gorgeous interplay between the light and gold surface and rich painting reflect the baroque interplay of musical themes.

Painting in the early eighteenth century also took two paths that strongly reflected social and political context. ***Antoine Watteau***, a Rubenist painter, illustrates the rococo aesthetic perfectly. His works may be compared to delicate pieces of chamber music, as consciously contrived as a rococo salon. However, there is a serious note to them: they show the agony of a doomed society. The pleasure-seeking individuals in his paintings seem conscious of the fact that pleasure is fleeting, that the golden moment of European aristocracy is almost over. Watteau's *Pilgrimage to Cythera* depicts a group of visitors to the mythical island of Cythera in search of pleasure. Ironically, the visitors are having to leave almost as they arrive. What should be a carefree outing becomes tinged with sadness at the realization that such pleasures are transitory. Consider too the painting of the actor and clown Gilles. Note the intensity of sadness in his eyes in ironic contrast to his role as the clown. Those who gaze up at him in amusement or mockery seem unaware of their own short stay on the world stage.

Watteau suffered from tuberculosis and died at 35. Perhaps his dream paintings reflect the evanescence of his life and of his society.

Like Watteau, *Jean-Baptiste Chardin* gives a view of French society in the eighteenth century, but it is a completely different one. Chardin's paintings pay homage to the life led by the French middle class. His beautiful, simple interiors rejoice in the beauty of domestic life: people go about their daily duties, untouched by extravagance or wealth. Chardin's paintings portray a shift of attention away from the aristocracy and toward the middle class, reflecting the shift in power from one to the other in society.

England too produced a marvellous illustrator of eighteenth-century society and politics: *William Hogarth*. Where Watteau painted the aristocracy and Chardin painted the middle class, Hogarth painted both—but had no great love for either. He despised the vanity of the wealthy and the hypocrisy of the **nouveau riche**. He painted and etched works in narrative series of satirical nature, in which he criticized his society. Hogarth's *Marriage à la mode* shows a young couple's gradual descent into boredom and unhappiness. His many political satires point out the need for reform in England's political system.

Art of the Late Eighteenth Century

The art of the second half of the eighteenth century reflects the growth of the middle class as a power in society and politics. The new attention given to individual and feeling, rather than to the state and intellect foreshadowed what would become known as the age of romanticism. The painter whose philosophy and work exemplify the blend of the neoclassical and romantic worlds is *Jacques-Louis David*. David rejected rococo for classicism, yet he felt strongly that his art must appeal to people and teach a lesson or a moral. He was active in the French Revolution and was friendly with Marat and Robespierre. David used stories from the Roman Republic to illustrate his ideals. *Oath of the Horatii* tells the story of three brothers vowing to give their lives for Rome. Their strong patriotic stance and hard forms contrast with the soft curves of the crying women who slump in mourning away from the men. Thus, determined action and strong feelings of love for country and family are celebrated in this work. Although not meant to be revolutionary, *Oath of the Horatii* became a political statement for the Revolution.

David's *Death of Marat* is at once a political painting and a revealing psychological study of one of the heroes of the Revolution. Marat was murdered in his

Jacques-Louis David: *Oath of the Horatii*

⁂

bath by a political enemy, Charlotte Corday. David commemorated the death of his patriotic friend with a painting. *Death of Marat* depicts the murder scene in detail and also reveals the character of the dead man. In this focus on the individual, we see the seeds of romanticism.

David was such a highly successful and influential painter that his works had a great effect on the artists of the nineteenth century. He was a classicist, no doubt, but his devotion to truth, feeling, and morality are strongly romantic. The polarization of classical and romantic styles continued through the end of the eighteenth century. The two styles would continue to coexist as Europe went through the revolutionary turmoil that characterized the nineteenth century but romanticism began to dominate by the first decades of the nineteenth.

Music in the Eighteenth Century

Early Eighteenth-Century Music

Like the art and architecture of the eighteenth century, the music of the period may be divided into two styles. The first half of the century was dominated by the baroque (which had begun in the early seventeenth century) and the second half saw the emergence of classicism.

Like the painters, sculptors, and architects, musicians continued to be patronized by the rich courts of Europe. Like the monumental buildings erected to the glory of kings and aristocrats, their music, whether religious or **secular**, also reflected the wealth and power of those who commissioned it. However, musical geniuses such as *Johann Sebastian Bach* and *George Frideric Handel* were able to experiment within the jurisdiction of their masters and make stupendous achievements in music within the existing musical forms of the time.

Bach was a great religious artist. His works are intensely spiritual. Bach's greatest musical achievements were in the form of cantatas and **oratorios**, or sacred operas.

Handel was the great master of the secular opera. An opera is a drama that is sung. Because opera is a blend of instrumental and vocal music, it involves many participants: singers, chorus, actors, and even ballet dancers. It is a very complicated art form to produce successfully. The plot of the opera is carried forward by a musical narration called a recitative. The aria, perhaps the equivalent to a soliloquy or monologue in a play, is usually a long song revealing the emotions of the singer. If an opera were a film, the arias would be the theme music or song that the audience remembers. Indeed, in the eighteenth century, opera, like film today, became the most popular entertainment for aristocrats and common people alike. Oratorios, such as Bach's famous *Christmas Oratorio* and the *St. Matthew Passion*, are religious operas performed without costumes or scenery.

Handel wrote great religious operas, such as the *Messiah*. He also produced many secular operas that influenced artists such as *Wolfgang Amadeus Mozart* later in the eighteenth century. Handel was a German composer who spent most of his adult life in England, where he enjoyed being a part of the royal court and prospered as one of the directors of the Royal Academy of Music. He was incredibly prolific in his writing of opera, composing 40 in 30 years. He continued writing serious opera until it became apparent that comic opera such as John Gay's *The Beggar's Opera*, written in English, was becoming more appealing to the middle-class audience. He struggled to adapt his works but found his health failing and, like Bach, went blind from cataracts. When Handel died, all England mourned.

In the late baroque era, music shifted from the religious to the secular. Paralleling art, music also shifted from the monumental seriousness of the baroque to the lightness and sensitivity of rococo, composed to be performed in salons by few musicians.

Consistent with the neoclassical period in painting and architecture is the development of the classical style in music. The four great masters of this period were three Austrians, Franz Joseph Haydn, Wolfgang Amadeus Mozart, and Franz Peter Schubert, and one German, *Ludwig van Beethoven*.

It was during the classical period that the orchestra as we know it today was developed. Concerts were given in large halls; therefore the great composers had an opportunity to perform their works and appeal to a far greater public than ever before. The classical style, in a carryover from rococo, is noted for its recognizable melodies. The music appealed to the average ear. Classical composers also incorporated folk elements into their music which further appealed to their middle-class audience.

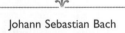

Johann Sebastian Bach

While large orchestras performed symphonies, small groups of musicians continued to perform exquisite chamber music that reflected the private conversations of salongoers in its elegance and lyricism. Opera was also still very popular. The serious classical opera was joined by the Italian comic opera. Mozart wrote some of the most beloved comic operas, such as *The Magic Flute* and *The Marriage of Figaro*.

When people are asked to name a classical composer, it is Mozart that most often comes to mind. Mozart is synonymous with genius, magic, humour, and personal tragedy.

Wolfgang Amadeus Mozart
(1756–1791)

 In 1756, the world stood still as it witnessed the birth of one of the greatest composers who ever lived. Wolfgang Amadeus Mozart can undoubtedly be called one of the most absolute geniuses in the history of music.

Born in Salzburg, Austria, Mozart was a most extraordinarily gifted child. He began to compose at the age of four and, at the age of six, he was an accomplished performer on the harpsichord, organ, and violin. His father, Leopold Mozart, a famous teacher and composer, took young Mozart on a series of triumphal tours around Europe. Mozart was greeted as a wonder child in each country. By the age of 13, Mozart had written sonatas, concertos, symphonies, religious works, an opéra bouffe, and the operetta *Bastien and Bastienne*. At the age of 17, Mozart had become a mature composer.

After rebelling against the patronage system and being dismissed at the age of 25 by the Prince Archbishop of Salzburg, Mozart became a free artist and spent the last ten years of his life in a struggle for financial security. He married Constanze Weber, a soprano, at the age of 26, against his father's wishes. It was a happy marriage, except for the fact that Constanze always seemed to need more money than her husband could provide.

Mozart reached the peak of his success with the opera *Le nozze di Figaro* (*The Marriage of Figaro*), written when he was 30 on a libretto by Lorenzo da Ponte, which was commissioned by Joseph II, Emperor of Austria. His new opera was enthusiastically received in Vienna and Prague, and the Prague opera director asked him to write a new opera. Together with da Ponte, he produced *Don Giovanni* (*Don Juan*), which has been called a "perfect opera" and was well received in Prague. The Viennese, however, thought the opera was "too heavy" because Mozart had used the orchestra to underline the drama. In this and other ways, Mozart was born 50 years ahead of his time.

Mozart was temperamental and undisciplined: during the last years of his short life, he lived in poverty, constantly borrowing money from his friends. To make ends meet, Mozart, who was now a father, threw himself into a frenzy of composing. In his final year, Mozart produced the comic opera *Die Zauberflöte* (*The Magic Flute*) on a libretto by Emmanuel Schikaneder. His work on this opera was interrupted several times by other commissions. The last opera he wrote was *La clemènza di Tito* (*The Clemency of Titus*) for the coronation of the Holy Roman Emperor Leopold II at Prague, which was hardly listened to. Sad and exhausted, Mozart returned to Vienna and *The Magic Flute*.

Mozart's final composition, commissioned by an anonymous patron, was his *Requiem*. Ill and depressed, Mozart became convinced that this requiem was for his own funeral. On December 4, 1791 he gave his pupil Sussmayr instruction for the completion of the *Requiem* and, that night, the great Mozart died. He was almost 36. His body was buried in an unmarked grave, almost unattended by friends and in silence.

In his short life, Mozart wrote an astounding number of musical works. His favourite musical form was the opera; his favourite instrument was the piano; he was able to make the piano sing, shimmer, and thunder. It has been said that Mozart "taught the instruments to sing." His handling of the human voice has never been surpassed. He usually wrote instrumental pieces with opera in mind; he knew exactly which voices were high and brilliant, somber, caressing, or capable of quick, articulate patter songs.

Although his talents were not fully recognized during his era, Mozart's soul continues to live through his music. His brilliance will no doubt shine for many years to come. Mozart was a jewel, snatched from mortal hands too soon; the beauty of his work was not fully appreciated until it was too late.

Beethoven is the composer who spans both the classical and romantic eras. Like David, he too was caught up in the French Revolution and closely followed the Napoleonic adventure. Like Michelangelo in the sixteenth century, Beethoven had struggled to achieve his artistic vision: he had to overcome family problems, as he was obliged to support his mother and sisters at an early age. His musical virtuosity made him beloved by the great aristocratic houses of Vienna. He was not attached to a court but had many people who helped him with money or gifts. In an age that was starting to celebrate the individual, he considered himself to be a nonconformist: it suited him to work on his own, not to entertain or glorify others.

In his 20s, just as his career was blossoming, he was struck by deafness. After a heroic struggle within himself, he decided to pursue his art as a way to overcome his affliction. This decision reflected a purely romantic philosophy. Beethoven's musical themes centred around humanity's triumph over despair and conflict. His music went through various stages but it is through his symphonies, nine in all, that he was able to reach all humanity then and now. One of the most notable of his symphonies is the Third, *Eroica*, which he dedicated to Napoléon—until Beethoven received the news that Napoléon had proclaimed himself emperor. It is said that Beethoven then wanted to tear it up; fortunately for us, however, he refrained. The *Fifth Symphony* is perhaps his best known for its famous opening notes, which to many symbolize the hand of fate knocking at one's door. The *Ninth Symphony* is probably the most evocative of Beethoven's ultimate triumph over his cruel illness. He ends the symphony with a gorgeous choral movement using the words of the German poet Friederich von Schiller's *Ode to Joy*. This is the archetypal romantic work of art: the romantic hero has triumphed over pain and despair to rejoice in life.

Beethoven wrote one opera, *Fidelio*, which tells the story of a group of people struggling to gain their freedom from prison. Again, this theme mirrors Beethoven's personal obsession and the obsession of the time: freedom from oppression. How ironic that he was so afflicted with deafness yet was able to rise above it and give us the joy of participating in his music, much of which he could not hear.

Beethoven's works provide the bridge between the structured, intellectual music of the eighteenth century and the dynamic, passionate music of the nineteenth. By the end of his career, the romantic movement had taken over all aspects of the arts.

Literature in the Eighteenth Century

As we have just seen, the greatest achievements in the art and music of the eighteenth century were centred in Continental Europe, mainly France, Germany, and Austria. But it can be said that England dominated the literary scene in the eighteenth century, as it had done for centuries before.

The literature of the eighteenth century belongs to a literary period that began in the mid-seventeenth century with the Restoration of the English Monarchy after the Puritan Revolution of 1649 and ended with the French Revolution in 1789. During these turbulent political times, English writers were still very much at the whim of those who financed their art. Charles II, for example, was a staunch patron of the arts. When he was established as king, he brought musicians and painters from the Continent to enliven his court. He also encouraged the theatre.

England was recovering from Puritanical austerity and the people were hungry for pleasure and luxury once more. By contrast, almost a century later, England under George II was run by the practical and powerful Prime Minister Robert Walpole. Since Walpole had no interest in literature, writers had to look to publishers (rather than the court) to obtain money. Now writers had to appeal to a broad literate public in order to support themselves. Thus, as with painting and music, literature began to focus on the needs of the

George Frideric Handel

middle class and came to protest the political and moral corruption of the ruling bodies of church and state. Satire was born and literature became a powerful social tool.

Literary Theory

The Restoration period in England, starting in 1660, signalled the start of the neoclassical movement in literature. Like neoclassical English architecture, this literature was a strong reaction to the extravagance of the European literature of the late Renaissance and early seventeenth century—and the violent politics that accompanied it. Writers of the late seventeenth century strove to express their ideas through the classical ideals of order, simplicity, and reason. Under Louis XIV, France produced a vast body of classical literature. This literature, as well as French fashions and manners imported by Charles II, had a great influence on English society. However, English writers felt that English literature should stay true to the tradition of Chaucer and Shakespeare and tried to remain wholly English in character by resisting these influences.

English writers called this period of neoclassical literature the *Augustan age* because its literature was strongly influenced by the Roman writers Virgil and Horace, who celebrated the peace and order brought to Rome when Emperor Augustus took over after the civil war that broke out when Julius Caesar died. Writers now applied classical standards to poetry, just as classical standards were applied to painting. A poet had to be a genius, endowed with an imagination; however, these attributes had to be tamed through order, form, and wit.

Nature in the neoclassical period was seen as the permanent, universal order representing universal truth. Nature became a standard by which to judge all aesthetics. Thus, eighteenth-century literature, as art, was a blend of ancient tradition and the new, enlightened ideas.

Needless to say, the poetry of the Augustan age was very strict in form. A particularly disciplined form of poetic expression was the heroic couplet. Each couplet contained a pithy or witty pronouncement on some aspect of nature, society, or humanity in general. The master of this form was *Alexander Pope*. Here is an excerpt from his *Essay on Man*:

Know then thyself, presume not God to scan
The proper study of mankind is Man.

Later, blank verse, or unrhymed iambic pentameter, became a popular form that gave slightly more leeway to poets.

Restoration and eighteenth-century literature expressed moral truth through a variety of genres. In the late seventeenth century, there was, as stated, a movement away from the extravagance of the late Renaissance style toward the neoclassical. There was also a reaction to Puritanism, which resulted in Restoration comedy. These comedies were based on the corruption in the court and the political arena. They were full of sexual intrigue and ribald humour, very much like Roman comedies, and they actually called for moral reform.

The other great achievement in this period was in the work of *John Dryden*. He developed a beautiful clear prose that became the model for all writing. In the spirit of the neoclassical age, Dryden's prose was plain and practical: everyone could read it. This was also a time of newspapers. Naturally, ideas and opinions were expressed through newspapers such as the famous *Tatler*. As eighteenth-century France created the salon in which to exchange ideas, eighteenth-century England created the coffeehouse, where people gathered to have coffee, read the paper, converse, and criticize the government.

Two masters of the social questioning that became characteristic of the eighteenth century were Alexander Pope and *Jonathan Swift*. As England was becoming a world power to rival France, so did the corruption in the court and government become more and more apparent. Alexander Pope wrote brilliant essays on social problems but his most famous work is his mock epic *The Rape of the Lock*, where he satirizes the shallow behaviour and values of the court. The plot is simple: a young dandy interferes with the coiffure of a beautiful society woman. He cuts off a lock of hair and the result is a battle of the sexes of epic proportions. Pope includes all features of the traditional epic form: invocation to the muse, epic battles, epic heroes and heroines. The poem is a brilliant satire on the hypocrisies and foibles of eighteenth-century court society; it also describes a certain charm and beauty within the shallowness.

The Eighteenth-Century Novel

The eighteenth century saw a rebirth of the novel, which appealed to a wide audience, providing novelists

Jonathan Swift's *A Modest Proposal*

Satire was one of the major genres of eighteenth-century literature. Jonathan Swift was a spirited satirist who wrote against the English oppression of the Irish. His anger was particularly directed toward Protestant absentee landlords, who ruthlessly exploited Irish Catholic peasants in their own land.

Children all over the world are familiar with *Gulliver's Travels*. In this, his most famous satire, Swift criticizes the corruption of the English court in particular and the flaws of human nature in general. Swift did not adopt Rousseau's belief in the essential goodness of humanity, which prevailed in his time; rather, he felt that humanity was essentially evil and that the social evils of his time were a product of the flaws of human nature. Yet he cared passionately for

the plight of the Irish peasants. This passion is evident in the following excerpt from his article *A Modest Proposal*, admired for its brilliant and powerful satiric prose.

It has taken almost 300 years since Swift wrote *A Modest Proposal* for the hope of peace to reach Northern Ireland after such a bitter conflict. Let us hope that there will be no more sources of inspiration for works such as *A Modest Proposal*.

A Modest Proposal for Preventing the Children of Poor People in Ireland from Being a Burden to Their Parents or Country, and for Making Them Beneficial to the Public (1730)

It is a melancholy object to those who walk through this great town or travel in the country, when they see the streets, the roads, and cabin doors, crowded with beggars of the female sex, followed by three, four, or six children, all in rags and importuning every passenger for alms. These mothers, instead of being able to work for their honest livelihood, are forced to employ all their time in strolling to beg sustenance for their helpless infants: who as they grow up either turn thieves for want of work, or leave their dear native country to fight for the pretender in Spain, or sell themselves to the Barbados.

I think it is agreed by all parties that this prodigious number of children in the arms, or on the backs, or at the heels of their mothers, and frequently of their fathers, is in the present deplorable state of the kingdom a very great additional grievance; and, therefore, whoever could find out a fair, cheap, and easy method of making these children sound, useful members of the commonwealth, would deserve so well of the public as to have his statue set up for a preserver of the nation....

I shall now therefore humbly propose my own thoughts, which I hope will not be liable to the least objection. I have been assured by a very knowing American of my acquaintance in London, that a young healthy child well nursed is at a year old a most delicious, nourishing, and wholesome

food, whether stewed, roasted, baked, or boiled; and I make no doubt that it will equally serve in a fricassee or a ragout. I do therefore humbly offer it to public consideration that of the 120 000 children already computed, 20 000 may be reserved from breed, whereof only one-fourth part to be males; which is more than we allow to sheep, black cattle, or swine; and my reason is, that these children are seldom the fruits of marriage, a circumstance not much regarded by our savages, therefore one male will be sufficient to serve four females.

Jonathan Swift

That the remaining 100 000 may, at a year old, be offered in sale to the persons of quality and fortune throughout the kingdom; always advising the mother to let them suck plentifully in the last month, so as to render them plump and fat for a good table.

A child will make two dishes at an entertainment of friends; and when the family dines alone, the fore or hind quarter will make a reasonable dish, and seasoned with a little pepper or salt will be very good boiled on the fourth day especially in winter.

I have reckoned upon a medium that a child just born will weigh 12 pounds, and in a solar year, if tolerably nursed, will increase to 28 pounds.

I grant this food will be somewhat dear, and therefore very proper for landlords, who, as they have already devoured most of the parents, seem to have the best title to the children....

I profess, in the sincerity of my heart, that I have not the least personal interest in endeavouring to promote this necessary work, having no other motive than the public good of my country, by advancing our trade, providing for infants, relieving the poor, and giving some pleasure to the rich. I have no children by which I can propose to get a single penny; the youngest being nine years old, and my wife past child-bearing.

with a means to teach a moral lesson or satirize a situation. Everyone is familiar with **Daniel Defoe**'s novel, *Robinson Crusoe*, an adventure story with serious undertones. Defoe also wrote the great comic novel *Moll Flanders*, defying convention by means of a female protagonist who enjoys many adventures. However, it is Samuel Richardson who is considered the writer who really took off with the novel form in his work *Pamela*. *Pamela* is the story of a housemaid in an aristocratic domain. Her virtue is constantly under attack by the lecherous master. The novel is a series of letters describing her situation in a serious tone. Richardson felt that he could expose the immorality of his society through such a work.

Henry Fielding took the comic novel to great extremes in *Tom Jones*. He also did a parody of Richardson's *Pamela* in his work *Joseph Andrews*, where a young man encounters problems similar to Pamela's. These works are similar in that they describe journeys and adventures. The novel opened up reading to a great number of people.

No discussion of the eighteenth century could be complete without reference to **Samuel Johnson,** an archetypal eighteenth-century man. He was a neoclassical humanist who defended the ideals of the Augustan age and deplored the rising tide of sentimentality that foreshadowed the romantic age. His *Dictionary of the English Language* gives a wonderful sense of eighteenth-century humour, wit,

Samuel Johnson

and sensibility. He gathered around him a literary circle who worshipped him and his work. His death in 1784 signals the end of the Augustan period and the beginning of the romantic age in England.

Reflections

As in every age, era, or century, one is always aware of tension between two opposing realms of thought. Born of the rigid, academic world of Louis XIV, the character of the early eighteenth century reflects the order and domination that the French king imposed on European society. When we reflect on history, we realize that human beings cannot stay under such control for long without reacting in some way. People in the eighteenth century slowly came to regard freedom of thought and spirit as something to strive for, and at the end of the century, something to die for. Thus, all the arts of the century, within the confines of order and structure, show a gradual movement toward the expression of feeling and emotion as a legitimate subject for art. We celebrate the eighteenth century for its reaffirmation of the beauty and forms of the classical period, yet we rejoice in its recognition of people from all walks of life. By the end of the eighteenth century, the romantic movement signalled the progression from a world that celebrated order and reason to a world that rejoiced in freedom and emotion.

ART
Key Concepts, Figures, and Events

Baroque   Classicism   Rococo
Antoine Watteau   Jean-Baptiste Chardin   William Hogarth
Jacques-Louis David

I. Find two paintings from the seventeenth century (other than by Poussin or Rubens), one of which appeals to your intellect and one to your emotions. Consider the Flemish school. Look for an intellectual Saenredam or Vermeer to compare to a Rembrandt. How does each convey its ideas by appealing to the mind or to the emotions?

2. Research and compare the Hall of Mirrors in Versailles to a rococo interior, such as a room in Amalienburg. Compare the effect created by these two very different spaces. What does each room say about the society for which it was created?

3. One of the most beautiful pieces of neoclassical architecture is Thomas Jefferson's home in Monticello, Virginia, which was inspired by the Roman architect Palladio. Find some pictures of this piece of architecture and read about the details of the construction. How is this building typical of the eighteenth century?

4. English art critic Kenneth Clark describes Watteau's paintings as musical. Choose one or two of his works and discuss the musical qualities. Perhaps compare them to an opera by Mozart, such as The Marriage of Figaro.

5. How would William Hogarth's political satires be excellent illustrations for Gulliver's Travels?

6. How do the paintings of David catalogue the state of French politics during the late eighteenth century?

7. Research and compare David's painting Napoléon Crossing the Alps to the painting by Ingres Napoléon as Emperor. How does Napoléon's concept of himself change?

MUSIC
Key Concepts, Figures, and Events

Johann Sabastian Bach   George Frideric Handel   Wolfgang Amadeus Mozart
Ludwig van Beethoven

I. Find a recording of Bach's Goldberg Variations (pieces for solo piano). Among the most powerful recordings are two by Glenn Gould, a Canadian pianist who has an international reputation as an interpreter of Bach. After you listen to the music several times, compare it to some of Beethoven's late piano sonatas. Or, find various solo jazz piano pieces by Keith Jarrett or Bill Evans and compare their music to that of Bach.

2. A beautiful rendition of Bach's music is done by the contemporary jazz musician Ron Carter on his acoustic bass. Find a recording and note how Bach's music achieves a timeless quality through Carter's exquisite playing. Try to find recordings of the same pieces done on baroque instruments and compare the two renditions.

3. Attend an opera. Record your impressions as you watch and listen. If you cannot attend an actual performance, listen to a recording. How is opera an assault on one's ears, eyes, and emotions?

4. Handel's music is as descriptive of life in the eighteenth-century English court as Pope's poetry. Listen to his *Water Music*. What are some of the images it evokes for you? Compare his music to the interior of a rococo church or a Watteau painting.

5. Beethoven's life is well worth exploring. Research information on his deafness. What caused it and what was the effect on his mind and consequently on his music?

6. Compare Beethoven's *Fifth Symphony* to one of Michelangelo's unfinished sculptures, known as *The Captives*. You will find the figure emerging from the unfinished piece of marble comparable to Beethoven's themes emerging from the symphony. How do both pieces convey enormous power of mind and heart?

LITERATURE
Key Concepts, Figures, and Events

Augustan Age	Alexander Pope	John Dryden
Jonathan Swift	Daniel Defoe	Samuel Johnson

1. Since Roman times, satire has become a tool for critics of institutions. Look in the newspapers and pick out some cartoons that criticize the current political situation. Compare the targets of their satire to those of Swift in *Gulliver's Travels*.

2. One of the great eighteenth-century satires is Voltaire's novel, *Candide*. Read the novel and discover its satiric implications.

3. Alexander Pope's *The Rape of the Lock* is a brilliant satire. It also furnishes us with an excellent description of eighteenth-century life in the English court. How do Hogarth's satiric paintings and etchings illustrate Pope's satire?

4. Three French playwrights who skillfully depicted French eighteenth-century society were Molière, Corneille, and Racine. Read a work by one of these authors and compare it to any of the English Restoration comedies.

5. Choose one of the many eighteenth-century novels which are rich in character, setting, and plot. Consider works by Sterne, Fielding, or Richardson. How do these works reveal an eighteenth-century consciousness?

6. Jane Austen's novels create a world in which intriguing characters live very ordered, but very interesting lives. Choose one: *Mansfield Park*, *Emma*, or *Pride and Prejudice*. How do they reveal the lives of middle-class women in the eighteenth century?

7. David Hume was one of the most influential and powerful philosophers in Western thinking. Research his life and philosophy. How do his ideas fit into the age of reason and the Enlightenment? Why is he still considered such a relevant thinker today?

UNIT I

Skills Focus

Developing Historical Skills

All too often, history is seen as a subject which requires memorizing countless dates and names. In fact, students of history must develop the skills to carefully analyze information from primary or secondary sources. In lower grades, much emphasis is often placed on gathering and organizing information. Senior students begin to pay closer attention to the information they gather and must be critical of the sources they draw on in researching an essay. Understanding the nature of historiography and developing sound historical skills will be crucial to success in history courses at the senior high school or university level.

In the prologue, the nature of historiography was discussed. It was noted that history is shaped as much by those who write it as by those who have lived it. Consequently, it is crucial that all sources of information are carefully scrutinized. Primary documents, which are based on eyewitness accounts, can be of invaluable assistance in understanding both concrete and abstract elements of a civilization. However, students using primary documents must be aware of potential problems that can accompany such documents. For example, John Lok, on a voyage to Guinea in 1554, recorded this observation: "The elephant (which some call an oliphant) is the biggest of all fourfooted beasts.... They love rivers, and will often go into them up to the snout, wherewith they blow and snuff and play in the water. They have continual war against dragons, which desire their blood because it is very cold; and therefore the dragon lieth in wait as the elephant passeth by."

Given that Lok's quotation above is based on an eyewitness account, how do we explain the presence of dragons? We can make sense of Lok's entry only by understanding the mindset of the audience for which this passage was intended. He was recording observations of the voyage with an eye to the investors who had sponsored it. Given their limited knowledge of the world, these investors fully expected to hear of mythological beasts in the faraway lands the ships visited. In fact, they were more likely to believe in dragons than in anteaters, of which they had never heard. Obviously, understanding something about the author, his or her audience, and the purpose of the document can help a great deal in making effective use of primary documents. The following questions can serve as a good guide when reading primary documents:

1. Can you detect a slant or bias in the document, e.g. ethnocentric bias?
2. Is there evidence of that bias?
3. Is the information presented factual or is it the opinion of an observer?
4. If factual evidence is presented, can it be verified by other sources?
   Upon verification, has the author exaggerated facts and figures?
   If so, can the document still be considered useful?
5. Is this a first-hand account or is it based on second-hand knowledge of a contemporary event?

Secondary accounts, such as those written by historians, also require careful scrutiny. All historians bring a particular point of view to their work: it is impossible to do otherwise. Their perspective may be shaped by political or economic bias, the age in which they lived, religious beliefs, or a number of other factors. For example, in the Responding to Ideas section of Chapter 5, you were given three different views of Napoléon Bonaparte. Another view of Napoléon as a dictator, for example, was published in 1939 by Alfred Coban, at a time when fascist and communist dictators were threatening the security of Europe. Did the age in which he lived shape Coban's view of Napoléon? When carrying out research you may want to use the following questions as a historiographical guide to secondary sources:

1. Who is the author and what is his or her background?
2. What was the author's intent in writing the piece? Did this shape his or her perception of the events? Was the writing intended as propaganda?
3. Who is the intended audience? How might this have influenced the writing of the document?
4. How might the period in which the author was writing have affected his or her view of the events discussed?
5. Does the author subscribe to a particular view of history? Has this view shaped the way in which the author interprets events in the past?

Practising Your Historiographical Skills

From a list of sources you have prepared for a major essay, (a) select three or four secondary sources that deal with similar issues; (b) read the preface and/or introduction of each book carefully for the author's slant or viewpoint; (c) try to determine the author's purpose: virtually all writers have a purpose in mind when they set out to write a book; (d) read the section of each book pertaining to the particular issue you are focusing on. As you read the relevant sections, keep the five questions for secondary sources (outlined above) in mind. Once you have a clear understanding of each author's point of view and of the ways in which he or she has addressed the issue, write a 500-to-700-word historiographical essay. This essay should discuss the various points of view presented, the value of each of the sources, and the inherent problems of each source. Be sure to include a clear, effective introduction and conclusion and to document your essay properly.

Suggested Sources for Further Research

Anderson, Bonnie and Zinsser, Judith, *A History of Their Own, Vol. II* (Harper and Row, 1988).

Black, Jeremy, *Eighteenth Century Europe* (Macmillan Education Ltd., 1990).

Bluche, François, *Louis XIV* (Franklin Watts, 1990).

Braudel, Fernand, *The Perspective of the World* (Harper and Row, 1979).

Chartier, Roger, *A History of Private Life: Passions of the Renaissance* (The Belknap Press, 1989).

Connelly, Owen, *The French Revolution and the Napoleonic Era* (Holt, Rinehart and Winston, 1982).

Davis, Natalie Zeman and Farge, Arlette, *A History of Women in the West, Vol. III* (Belknap Press, 1993).

Dickson, Olive, *The Myth of the Savage and the Beginnings of French Colonialism in the Americas* (University of Alberta Press, 1984).

Grendler, Paul, *The Roman Inquisition and the Venetian Press* (Princeton University Press, 1977).

Hughes, Robert, *The Fatal Shore* (Alfred A. Knopf, 1987).

Jones, Colin, *The Longman Companion to the French Revolution* (Longman, 1988).

Kelly, Linda, *Women of the French Revolution* (Hamish Hamilton, 1987).

Maland, D., *Europe in the Seventeenth Century* (Macmillan, 1967).

Pagden, Anthony, *The Fall of Natural Man* (Cambridge University Press, 1982).

Riasanovsky, Nicholas, *A History of Russia* (Oxford University Press, 1984).

Zipes, Jack, *The Complete Fairy Tales of the Brothers Grimm* (Bantam Books, 1992).

The Emergence of a New Europe

Myriad forces came together in the nineteenth century to bring about radical changes in nearly every facet of life in Europe. In the decades following the French Revolution, Europeans struggled to find their way through a maze of political reform, while the Industrial Revolution brought about profound changes in economics and society. The advent of mass production transformed the societies of Europe as well as Europe's relationship with overseas colonies. At the same time, the rise of a mass electorate, an expanded press, and a growing middle class radically changed the nature of European politics and society.

The nineteenth century was also a period of revolutionary change in scientific discovery and intellectual thought. Whether discussing the political ideology of communism, the new scientific belief in Darwinism, the provocative ideas of Nietzsche or Freud, or viewing the art of the Impressionists, no aspect of life in the nineteenth century remained untouched by the winds of change. By the end of the century, imperialism, nationalism, and racism had extended the arm of Europeans around the world and laid the foundations for global warfare that would be the hallmark of the first half of the twentieth century.

Political/Military	INTELLECTUAL	Cultural
1810		Frédéric Chopin born
1814		Francisco de Goya: *The Third of May, 1808*
1815 Congress of Vienna		
1817	David Ricardo: *The Principles of Political Economy*	
1819		Jean-Auguste Ingres : *La Grande Odalisque*
1821		John Keats dies
1830 Fall of Bourbon Monarchy in France		Eugène Delacroix: *Liberty Leading the People*
1831 Jamaican Slave Revolt		
1832 Reform Bill extends the vote in England		
1833 Factory Act passed in England		Claude Monet moves to Giverny
1834 New Poor Law passed in England Slavery abolished in British Empire		
1837		Charles Dickens: *Oliver Twist*
1839 Opium Wars in China (start)		
1840		Pyotr Ilich Tchaikovsky born
1842 Opium Wars in China (end)		
1844	Freidrich Engels: *The Condition of the Working Classes in England*	
1847		Charlotte Brontë: *Jane Eyre* Emily Brontë: *Wuthering Heights*
1848 Revolution sweeps through Europe	Karl Marx: *The Communist Manifesto*	
1850		Alfred, Lord Tennyson: *In Memoriam* Elizabeth Barrett Browning: *Sonnets from the Portuguese*
1852 Louis Napoléon Bonaparte establishes Second Empire in France		
1853		Giuseppe Verdi: *Il trovatore; La traviata*
1854 Crimean War (start)		Oscar Wilde born
1856 Crimean War (end)		George Bernard Shaw born
1857 Indian Mutiny		
1859	Karl Marx: *Das Kapital* Charles Darwin: *On the Origin of Species*	
1861 American Civil War (start)		
1862		Victor Hugo: *Les Misérables*
1863		Edouard Manet: *Le Déjeuner sur L'Herbe*
1864	Pope Pius IX: *Syllabus of Errors*	
1865 American Civil War (end)		
1869	John Stuart Mill: *The Subjection of Women*	Richard Wagner: *The Ring Cycle*
1883		Claude Monet moves to Giverny
1886	Friederich Nietzsche: *Beyond Good and Evil*	
1890		Vincent van Gogh commits suicide near Paris
1897		Auguste Rodin: *Balzac*
1898 Spanish-American War		
1899 Boer War	Sigmund Freud: *The Interpretation of Dreams*	
1902 Russo-Japanese War	V. I. Lenin: *What Is to Be Done?*	
1903	Marie Skelodwska Curie, Pierre Curie, and Henri Becquerel receive Nobel Prize for work on radioactivity	
1904	Max Weber: *The Protestant Ethic and the Spirit of Capitalism* Albert Einstein: Theory of Relativity	Giacomo Puccini: *Madama Butterfly*

CHAPTER
7
Europe, 1815–1850: The Industrial Revolution and the Birth of Modern Politics and Society

Europe in 1815

In 1815, following the turmoil of the French Revolution and Napoleonic Wars, Europe entered into a new period not of stability but of further dramatic change. The victors over Napoléon at Waterloo reached a new understanding about relations between states, but domestically those same aristocratic rulers confronted unprecedented economic change and ongoing social and political unrest. Consequently, the period from 1815 to 1850 is characterized by peace between states and by conflict within states, and revolution rather than war was the engine of historical change.

These forces of change came in the form of what contemporary British economic historian E. J. Hobsbawm has aptly called a "dual revolution." On the one hand, there was the political revolution, which tried to turn the ideas and hopes of the French Revolution into a living reality. On the other hand, remarkable economic and social changes had commenced in England, where the *Industrial Revolution* would in turn transform the economies and societies of Western Europe. More than two separate revolutions, there was "dual" or two-track revolution. Economic changes and social conflict undermined customary authority and demanded new political solutions. Conservative forces tried to preserve tradition and find sources of stability in the midst of unprecedented change; reformers and radicals found church and state tied to outmoded aristocratic privilege and sought emancipation by political and social reform. Transformations and conflicts of such magnitude forced men and women to reconsider the received wisdom of tradition, and to re-examine the intellectual foundations of their government, society, and culture.

Consequently, the dual revolution became a period of intellectual and artistic creativity and innovation. The industrial and political revolutions also secured Europe's dominance over the rest of the world.

In this chapter, we will look at the Industrial Revolution and then at the political transformations effected between 1815 and 1850. Subsequent chapters will deal with cultural developments and with the global impact of Europe's dual revolution.

The Industrial Revolution

Some forms of manufacturing (milling, brewing and distilling, for example) existed prior to the nineteenth century. Nonetheless, with the Industrial Revolution, the production of goods by machines took on an altogether new dimension. In fact, the word "manufacture" itself acquired a new meaning. Formerly, manufacture had meant "to make by hand"; with industrialization, it began to mean "to make by machine." Earlier forms of production had been limited by the sources of power: human and animal muscles, wind, and water.

The First Industrial Revolution harnessed a new source of inanimate power: steam. The application of this new power source involved much more than boiling water; it involved harnessing the expansive power of steam to run a wide range of machinery. Today, we tend to associate steam power with railway locomotives or ships but, in fact, these uses came relatively late. Early innovation used steam power to move stationary engines: steam pumps in mines, steam bellows and hammers in iron foundries, steam engines for spinning and weaving machines in textile mills, and steam-threshing machines to harvest the grain in the fields. All these applications, and countless others, involved technological innovation of considerable ingenuity, yet the history of the Industrial Revolution is more than the history of mechanical invention.

Industrialization also involved an economic revolution. In the course of two or three decades, industrial innovations significantly increased the production of goods, the scope of domestic and international trade, and the wealth generated as a result. This increase in production came from the new steam technology and, just as importantly, from new ways of organizing production and human labour. In his economic classic, *The Wealth of Nations* (1776), Adam Smith said little about new machines, but he elaborated on how more specialized forms of production and labour, together with more efficient systems of trade, greatly enhance productivity. The Industrial Revolution effected changes in the form and supply of money, the provision of credit, and in forms of investment; it changed financial institutions such as banks and stock exchanges; it altered the role of the state in relation to the economy; and it brought about a new understanding of economics. Yet the Industrial Revolution was more than a technological and economic revolution.

Because it transformed the way human beings went about making a living, the Industrial Revolution was also a social and cultural revolution. The Industrial Revolution created a new middle class as well as a new working class living under new urban conditions and new patterns of work, family life, and leisure. Cities became new centres of both wealth and poverty.

Industrial entrepreneurs became municipal leaders setting the tone for the conspicuous consumption of the new middle class, which began to include industrialists, clergy, doctors, lawyers, bankers, and merchants. The new industries created new forms of labour, most notably at factories, where new machinery and new concentrations of workers were brought together. These changes were so dramatic that people began to think of themselves as living in a new era. The term *Industrial Revolution* came into use in England in the 1830s to express how extensively society had changed within the living memories of that generation.

It is not surprising that the term "Industrial Revolution" first came into use in England. The "First Industrial Revolution" began there in the 1780s and progressed rapidly during the French Revolution and Napoleonic Wars, from the 1790s to 1815, transforming Great Britain into the "workshop of the world." Industrialization in Continental Europe followed the British lead. What is now Belgium led the way beginning around 1810. In France, industrial innovations began to have a noticeable influence in the 1830s and, in Germany, in the 1840s and 1850s. Other countries experienced their own industrial revolutions in the second half of the nineteenth century; for example, Italy and Spain in the 1870s and Russia after 1890. Some historians see the timing of the industrial revolutions as having had profound consequences for the twentieth century: countries with later industrialization proved to be more prone to totalitarianism after 1914. We need to keep this chronological difference in mind, for it affects not only the character of political movements and social conflict, but also their resolution in different countries in the period from 1815 to 1850.

The First Industrial Revolution: England, 1780–1851

Preconditions

With no earlier models to follow—and no blueprint or plan—the First Industrial Revolution was an instance of "spontaneous combustion." Between 1800 and 1850, the national income rose by 125 percent, while the share of national income derived from industrial production rose by 230 percent. This "take-off" of the economy occurred around 1780, and was due to a number of preconditions peculiar to Great Britain. There already existed a capitalist system in agriculture, in which land was privately owned and income was derived chiefly from marketing produce instead of simply from collecting rent. Although 80 percent of the land was owned by the aristocracy and gentry, they—unlike the European nobility—were not a feudal landlord class collecting dues from dependent peasants; instead the cultivators of the soil were independent landowners, tenants, or landless wage-earning labourers. It should be remembered that, in the eighteenth century overall, the weather was warm, the harvests were reliable, and farming was prosperous.

Aside from farming, the landed aristocracy developed other sources of income from their land: they financed the mining of coal and iron, and they built roads, charging a toll on what came to be known as "turnpikes." They also constructed an elaborate network of canals. Heavy or bulky cargoes such as coal, iron, grain, raw wool, or cotton could not be hauled in horse-drawn wagons over rough roads. The solution lay in building canals to float the heavy cargoes on barges. These canals served as a transportation network for the first 50 years of the Industrial Revolution, until the new railroads began replacing them in the 1830s and 1840s.

The prosperity of market agriculture and the building of a transportation network of canals were evidence of a thriving national economy. In fact, unlike in France or Germany, there were no internal tariff barriers restricting the flow of goods within Great Britain. Furthermore, there were well-established financial institutions, such as banks and stock exchanges, both in London and in leading provincial towns. This well-established and thriving commercial sector, trading in agricultural produce and in handicraft products such as woolen textiles, also had an important international dimension reaching out not simply across the English Channel to Europe, but across the oceans to Africa, Asia, and the Americas.

By the end of the eighteenth century, Britain had established itself as the world's leading maritime nation: it had ousted France from Canada and India. British ships were the main carriers of the profitable trade in slaves from Africa to the Americas, and the West Indies were the jewels of the British Empire supplying slave-grown sugar to the British Isles and Europe. Despite the setback of the American Revolution, trade with the newly independent United States continued to grow. Moreover, expanding trade with Asia created a demand for new products. It was no accident that the development of a national taste for an exotic drink from the East, tea, sweetened by West Indian sugar, should be consumed in cups and saucers called *china*. In addition to fine porcelain from Japan and China, cotton textiles were imported from India. Soon, pottery and cotton textiles became important new industries in England. Raw cotton was first imported from India and Egypt but, by the 1790s, the main supply came from the slave plantations of the United States. British foreign trade grew steadily, expanding by over 70 percent between 1700 and 1750; it then underwent an upsurge just at the beginning of the Industrial Revolution, increasing by 80 percent between 1750 and 1770.

All these signs of economic vitality meant that England had the best-fed and best-housed population in Europe. Furthermore, a relatively high proportion of the population, roughly 30 percent, was no longer directly dependent on agriculture for its livelihood. England was also exceptional in the size of its "middling sort" of bankers, merchants, professionals, traders, shopkeepers, and self-employed artisans. Below the tiny elite of landowners, they constituted some 40 percent of the population and were only outnumbered by the labouring poor, who accounted for just over half of the population. This cluster of economic and social peculiarities came together in the 1780s to ignite the Industrial Revolution. The spark that set off this spontaneous combustion was consumer demand.

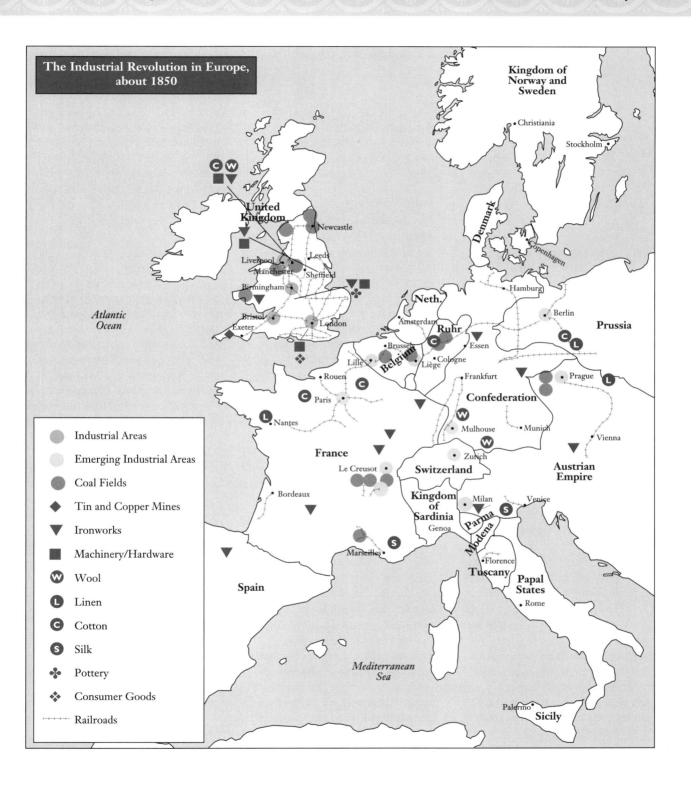

The Industrial Revolution in Europe, about 1850

Legend:
- Industrial Areas
- Emerging Industrial Areas
- Coal Fields
- Tin and Copper Mines
- Ironworks
- Machinery/Hardware
- W Wool
- L Linen
- C Cotton
- S Silk
- Pottery
- Consumer Goods
- Railroads

Railroad Stations and

No other technological development of the nineteenth century so profoundly affected the development of European towns as the railroad. The railroad station became one of the principal forces in society for order and discipline; at the same time it became a new focus for crime and violence.

Time

For a railway system to function, it was crucial that trains leave on time and that there be a standard national time. Prior to the age of trains, people's daily lives were regulated by "God's time" or the movement of the sun through the sky. The advent of railroads revealed that even over relatively short distances of a few hundred miles there were differences in time of up to 15 minutes. These discrepancies in time made an efficient and effective railway system impossible and led to the adoption of Greenwich mean time (GMT), often referred to as "railway time," as the national time for England in 1880.

The issue of time was an even greater problem in nations that were more expansive than England. This concern led Canada's Sir Sandford Fleming, a railway engineer, to turn his attention to time zones in Canada and prompted him to organize an international conference in 1884. At this conference, international standard time was adopted, paving the way for efficient global communications in the twentieth century.

Town Planning

The development of railway systems was one of the greatest factors influencing town planning in the nineteenth and early twentieth centuries. Prior to the development of steam power, towns were often centred around the marketplace or a major cathedral. Station-building decisively redesigned the contours of cities, shifting and promoting the flow of traffic and population, and acting as a prime determinant for commercial and residential building. Cities such as Chicago owed their growth to the meeting place of 27 different railway lines. Even in older cities such as London, railways tried to get their stations as close to the city centre as possible and splendid new structures such as Victoria Station were built to proclaim the railroad's arrival. In cities such as Coventry, England, where the railway remained on the periphery, failing to penetrate to the city centre, the railroad acted as a magnet drawing the town and any new development out of the centre toward the station. S. H. Beaver described the ultimate railway plan for a city as follows: "The ideal railway plan for a large city thus somewhat resembles a wheel: the city is the hub, the main lines are the spokes, and the circumference is the belt line." Travel to virtually any European town or city today and you will still notice the dominant role played by the railroad station. It is a hub of activity carrying people and goods to and from the city.

Crime

Just as the railroad station served as a major source for order and city-planning, it also became a haven for social outcasts and a magnet for crime. Drifters, drug addicts, beggars, and the homeless have also found the station to be open 24 hours a day, and a convenient source of light, warmth, and shelter. Mingling with the transient crowds passing through the station on their way home or to work have always been members of society's dark underside: pickpockets, prostitutes, and pimps who lie in wait for innocent youngsters who have run away from home and found their way to the big city lured by prospects of fame and fortune. T. Norman Chamberlain described the "station loungers" who could be found in every station: "Every degree of tidiness and cleanliness, of dirt and disreputability is represented. Their ages vary from 14 to 23, the most common age being 16 to 19.... Except when cadging off a passer-by, they seem a sociable, happy-go-lucky set of lads with many opportunities of seeing life...."

Nineteenth-Century Towns

The most common crime occurring at the railway stations was theft. The most common items stolen were food, clothing, wine, spirits, and tobacco. In 1853 David Stevens, Goods Manager of the LNWR wrote: "Thieves are pilfering the goods from our wagons here to an impudent extent. We are at our wits' end.... Not a night passes without wine hampers, silk parcels, drapers' boxes or provisions being robbed." Although murder was less frequent, there were horrific incidents, such as the acts committed by Fritz Haarman. Haarman prowled around Hanover Station picking up teenage boys. He then sexually abused and murdered them, selling their clothes and disposing of their bodies. When he was eventually caught in 1924, he confessed to 40 murders and was beheaded. Today, railroad stations remain a magnet for young people, some seeking a place of refuge, others passing through on their travels through Europe. And today, railroad stations retain their reputation as being potentially dangerous. Travellers young and old are well advised to keep their valuables hidden and not to linger unnecessarily in stations.

The Goderich Railway Station, in Goderich, Ontario, quickly became a central feature of the town following its opening in the late nineteenth century.

Consumer Demand and the Multiplier Effect

The existing system of domestic manufacture under the cottage system could not keep pace with the demand for goods. More consumers had sufficient income to afford new exotic groceries, such as tea and sugar, and manufactured goods such as cotton cloth and china. Those who benefited the most from this new situation were the middlemen. These traders purchased raw materials, such as cotton or wool, let it out to the craftworkers in their homes to finish into cloth for piecework payment, and sold the finished product. In the last half of the eighteenth century, middlemen realized that if they could produce goods in greater quantity at a cheaper price, they could find more consumers, and thus make a higher profit.

It was out of the limitations of the domestic system and the demands of consumers that the industrial entrepreneurs were born. The middlemen, with limited funds and credit from existing trade, invested small amounts of capital in new properties and machines. Innovations were not without risk and not all were successful, but those entrepreneurs who increased their profits would reinvest in further innovations. Consequently, once set in motion, the process of industrialization gained its own momentum.

Self-sustained growth was intensified by the impact of new technologies. Mechanical inventions, which had parallels in many industries, stimulated the quest for new machines to solve technological bottlenecks. This pattern, called the *multiplier effect*, explains why once industrial innovation started, it became an ongoing process.

The introduction of new machines solved problems but also created new ones. For example, James Kay's flying shuttle (1733) greatly increased the capacity of handloom weavers to produce cloth, but it put great pressure on the spinners who made thread from raw wool or cotton. Consequently, the spinning process was the first to be industrialized, thanks to James Hargreaves's spinning jenny (1764) and to the introduction of water power into factories and spinning mills. The productivity of spinning mills was further increased with the application of steam in place of water power. These innovations created pressure on the weaving process. The mechanization of spinning introduced factory labour and, ironically, increased employment for handloom weavers working under the old domestic system. But weaving was a far more difficult process to mechanize than spinning, and even Samuel Compton's power loom (1779), a cumbersome machine, required many modifications to be effective. Consequently, there was as much as a 30- or 40-year gap between the industrialization of spinning and that of weaving. Textile factories with steam-powered looms did not become common until the second decade of the nineteenth century.

The cotton industry used to be considered the industry with the greatest multiplier effect during the First Industrial Revolution. It was one of the first to mechanize and use steam power; its pioneering use of factory labour transformed Manchester and the surrounding boom town of Lancashire; it became the largest single employer of industrial labour; and cotton cloth became the most valued commodity in Britain's export trade. However, more recent historians stress that developments in coal mining, iron production, and machine design had a more significant impact on the economy. Consequently, both in the realm of technical innovation and in the numbers of people employed, the combination of coal, iron, and steam had a greater multiplier effect than the cotton industry. This impact would become most visible in the 1830s and 1840s with the introduction of steam locomotion and the boom in railroad construction.

The railroad was also key to the later industrialization of Continental Europe after 1830. By that time, Britain had established itself as the world's leading industrial power. With a population of 21 million—less than 10 percent of the total population of Europe in 1850—Britain was producing two thirds of the world's coal, one half of its iron, and one half of its cotton cloth.

Industrialization on the Continent: 1815–1850

Industrial change began to have an effect on the European continent two or three generations after its commencement in Great Britain. This delay was a reflection of differences between British and European society, and it had important consequences for the disparities in the patterns of Continental industrialization. The social conflicts and political movements of Continental Europe in the first half of the nineteenth century also stemmed from these differences.

The key to industrial change was the emergence of consumer demand for manufactured goods. Britain and Continental Europe both experienced a population boom in this period. The European population grew from 188 million in 1800 to 266 million in 1850. The British population grew at an even faster pace: from about 10 million in 1800 to 21 million in 1850, but, during the same period, the growth of the British economy surpassed that of the population. In contrast, population growth in Europe in the early nineteenth century outstripped the growth of the economy. Consequently, labour was abundant and cheap, but peasants and workers experienced a decline in living standards and often could not afford manufactured goods.

The lengthy period of warfare with the French Republic and with Napoléon disrupted trade and commerce, absorbed the resources of European states, and led to conscription of potential workers into military service. Political divisions, especially in the numerous small states and principalities of Germany, hampered trade. The Zollverein, a customs union formed by several German states in 1834, facilitated the flow of goods, which opened up the Rhine River as a major transportation artery. Transport over land remained difficult, though, and in many areas coal and iron resources could not be readily exploited.

In Western Europe, revolution and war loosened the grip of the landed nobility. The breakup of some noble estates into ownership by small peasant communities did not advance the modernization of agriculture. In England, tenant farmers and landless wage labourers worked for large gentry-owned estates, whereas in Continental Europe, small peasant landholders dominated rural society. In France and Western Europe, creditors of governments as well as bankers and bondholders from the wealthy bourgeoisie benefited from the demands of war. War also created career opportunities for middle-class professionals in government bureaucracies and the military. Thus, while the turmoil of the French Revolution and Napoleonic Wars disrupted economic activity, a fresh start began after 1815.

Even by the time of Napoléon's defeat at Waterloo in 1815, early industrial initiatives in textiles, coal mining, and iron production had begun in Northern France and what is now Belgium. These initiatives copied British techniques and inventions. Anxious to protect its industrial lead and to prevent industrial espionage, the British government prohibited the export of machinery and the emigration of engineers and machine operatives. Nonetheless, British entrepreneurs took their capital, their inventions, and their knowledge across the Channel. Continental manufacturers also sent their agents to observe developments in Britain. It is well known that Friedrich Engels, one of the fathers of communism, was sent to live in Manchester by his father, a German textile manufacturer. There, Engels had a vision of the new industrial future, and his classic, *The Condition of the Working Classes in England* (1844), had a profound influence on Karl Marx and other socialist thinkers. On the Continent, the new industries—with their steam engines and factories—did not take hold as quickly as British entrepreneurs or Friedrich Engels had imagined.

The real boom in the Continental Industrial Revolution occurred with the construction of railroads. Here the Continent followed quickly on Britain's introduction of steam locomotion in 1830. In France, railway construction led industrial development in the 1830s and 1840s; in Germany, railways, which were essential for the transport of raw materials and finished goods, were built in the 1840s and 1850s. Railway construction acted as a "multiplier effect" because it required increased production of coal, iron, steam locomotives, railway carriages, and a host of related machines and mechanical devices. The railway boom laid the foundations for Continental heavy industries, and as a labour-intensive industry, railroads created whole new categories of industrial employment.

The Social Impact of the Industrial Revolution

The early years of the Industrial Revolution, from 1780 to 1850, were a period of intense social unrest. Despite these signs of dramatic social change, the pace of the impact of the new industries should not be exaggerated. For example, new industrial conditions, such as factory labour, were still exceptional rather than typical. Even in Great Britain in 1850, more people were employed in agriculture than in

The Crystal Palace, completed in 1851, stood as a symbol of industrial Britain.

manufacturing. Cotton textile mills employed 272 000 women, whereas 905 000 worked as domestic servants. The new demands of industry stimulated not only new forms of employment, but also traditional handicraft production. For example, construction materials, such as bricks and iron nails, were still hand-produced by women and children doing piecework. Women and children, rather than factory operatives, had the most exploitive work conditions and the lowest rates of pay.

Conservative moralists, such as Thomas Carlyle, and political radicals such as Friederich Engels, were shocked by conditions in the expanding industrial cities and dismayed by the new social relationships between employers and their workers. On the other hand, economists and engineers stressed the unprecedented growth of wealth, the labour-saving efficiency of the new machines, and the improvement of the living standards of both factory owners and factory operatives. These contradictory observations set in motion a long-standing debate over the impact of the Industrial Revolution. The "optimists" argue that conditions improved; the "pessimists" claim that conditions got worse.

The Standard of Living

By today's standards, 1850s work conditions and urban environment were appalling, but extreme poverty and city squalor were no innovation of the Industrial Revolution. It is more appropriate to assess the situation by nineteenth-century standards to understand the limits of the optimist-vs.-pessimist debate. No one disputes that the landed aristocracy and the new middle class (industrial entrepreneurs, merchants, professionals) benefited as owners, investors, and consumers. The debate is over the living standard of the labouring population dependent on wages, who, in Britain, constituted over two thirds of the population. No one disputes that after 1850, the Industrial Revolution in Britain created greater material abundance for all social ranks in the long term. The debate is over the short-term impact of the Industrial Revolution.

Conditions of Urban Life

If one looks at the entire nineteenth century, two striking developments are apparent: (a) a remarkable increase in the total European population (from 188 million in 1800 to 401 million in 1900) and (b), an increase in urban population as the century advanced. With the exception of Great Britain, most people continued to live under rural conditions even in the second half of the nineteenth century, but larger cities came to dominate the social and political landscape. This was particularly true of large capital cities, which became the enormous metropolitan centres that they are today.

With industrialization, small centres of handicraft manufacture and commerce also became large modern cities. In fact, not only did more people live in cities, but a larger proportion lived in cities of more than 100 000 inhabitants. In 1800, Europe had 22 cities of more than 100 000 people; by 1895, there were 120 cities of more than 100 000 and their residents comprised 10 percent of the population. At the beginning of the nineteenth century, only two German cities (Berlin and Hamburg) had more than 60 000 people; by 1871, there were eight German cities with more than 100 000.

The growth of cities was remarkable in the sense that, until the 1860s, cities did not grow by natural increase but depended upon migration from the countryside. Overcrowding, poor housing, scarcity of fresh water, and poor or non-existent sanitation made cities an ideal environment for the spread of disease, and the death rate exceeded the birth rate.

In the period from 1780 to 1850, the most outstanding examples of urban growth were in the industrial areas of the British Isles. Signs of such urban growth were evident in Belgium and France from the 1830s, but the pace of urbanization intensified there and in the German states from the 1840s onward. British municipalities were symbolic of a new and frightening age, with unplanned and unregulated explosion from the 1820s onward. In 1800, 17 percent of the British population lived in towns of more than 20 000 people; by 1851, about 35 percent; and by 1891, more than 50 percent. In the crisis decades of the 1830s and 1840s, the leading industrial cities grew at a phenomenal pace: Manchester from 182 000 to 300 000; Leeds from 123 000 to 172 000; Birmingham from 144 000 to 233 000; and Bradford from 13 000 in 1800 to 104 000 in 1851, or by 800 percent.

People flooded into cities from the countryside in search of jobs in the new industries. Beyond employment, their first need was housing. Workers needed to live close to their place of work since there was no public transit, and rural customs persisted. People were used to work and home being in the same place, and it was normal for parents and children to work together. They also ate at home—the main meal was at noon—and so needed to walk to and from work several times during the course of a working day, which extended from 12 to 16 hours. Employers and builders constructed housing cheaply and quickly with a mind to profit rather than to living requirements.

It was common for families to have two rooms, one for cooking and sitting, and the other for sleeping, with all family members sharing a common bed. In the worst conditions of overcrowding, in which as many as eight or 10 people shared one room, families and single people of both sexes would sleep together, much to the dismay of contemporary moralists. Houses were built in rows or in squares with a common courtyard in which there might be a water tap and a common privy. In these crowded conditions, there was little access to fresh air and little provision for clean water or the removal of refuse, including human excrement. In a Parliamentary Report for 1845, James Smith reported on conditions in Leeds:

But by far the most unhealthy localities of Leeds are close squares of houses, or yards, as they are called, which have been erected for the accommodation of working people. Some of these, though situated in comparatively high ground, are airless from the enclosed structure, and being wholly unprovided with any form of underdrainage, or convenience, or arrangements for cleansing, are one mass of damp and filth.... The ashes, garbage, and filth of all kinds are thrown from the doors and windows of the houses upon the surface of streets and courts.... The privies are few in proportion to the number of inhabitants. They are open to view both in front and rear, are invariably in a filthy condition, and often remain without the removal of any portion of the filth for six months. The feelings of the people are blunted to all seeming decency, and from the constantly contaminated state of the atmosphere, a vast amount of ill health prevails, leading to listlessness, and inducing a desire for spirits and opiates; the combined influence of the whole condition causing much loss of time, increasing poverty, and terminating the existence of many in premature death.

Skilled artisans and other more highly paid mechanics lived in better conditions, but many operatives in the textile mills of Leeds and elsewhere lived in the crowded and unhealthy conditions depicted by James Smith.

Conditions of Work

Next to the new urban environment, labourers faced new conditions of work. Under the preindustrial handicraft or domestic system, the family worked as a unit and had some measure of control over the pace of work. When their product was in demand, they worked extremely hard for long hours; at other times, especially when the market was slow, they worked at a more leisurely pace. Under the mechanized and specialized system of production in the factory, the pace of work was set by the steady and uninterrupted motion of the machine. In addition, since the workplace was the factory, not the home, the employer could dictate the work time and leisure time.

With work now determined by the machine, it became important for the workforce to arrive to work on time. Early factories had clocks above the entrance, so workers would arrive at a specified time. Employers had a great deal of difficulty imposing this new time-related discipline. Labourers persisted in the preindustrial habit of "Saint Monday" in which they took a day off to recuperate from the excesses of Saturday night and Sunday. Employers imposed fines and penalties for lateness, for interruptions in work, and for absenteeism. In fact, many of the disciplinary features associated with strict nineteenth-century schools—penalties for lateness, permission to leave the room, quietness in corridors, and corporal punishment for misdemeanours—were originally factory practices.

Beyond the new intensity of machine-paced work and time-related discipline, there was the simple question of the hours of work. The workweek followed Biblical **precept** of six full working days and one day of rest on Sunday. Saturday was payday, and Saturday evening was a time for dressing up, shopping, and partying. Some of the longest hours were put in by shop assistants, a respectable but poorly paid job for girls and young women, who worked up to 90 hours a week. The factory day began at 5 or 6 in the morning, with a breakfast break at 8. Although actual working time was from 12 to 14 hours, the working day lasted 14 to 16 hours when meal times were included, and concluded at 8 or 9 in the evening. Not surprisingly, labour disputes were often not only about wages but over hours of work.

Work and Family Life

One of the most contentious issues in the Industrial Revolution was child labour. In the early 1830s, at the height of the abolitionist movement against West Indian slavery, industrial reformer and moralist Richard Oastler led an effective campaign against what he termed "Yorkshire slavery." Oastler argued the child labour in woolen textile mills was comparable to the chattel slavery of Africans on the plantations in the Americas.

The Industrial Revolution did not invent child labour. Children in the preindustrial domestic system had been expected to contribute to the family income,

Working conditions in factories and mines were particularly harsh for women and children.

and commonly boys and girls of 9 or 10 were sent to live and work with a farmer, master craftsman, or merchant. The first generation of factory operatives attempted to preserve the practice of working as a unit, and whole families were employed to tend spinning machines. As machines grew larger, employers had less need for adult males and employed larger numbers of women and children.

Child abuse and sexual harassment were not invented at this time either, but abuse of children—both long hours and corporal discipline—and sexual harassment of young female operatives occurred when male supervisors were no longer husbands, fathers, or other kin, but strangers. The division of occupations by gender perpetuated the distinction that the primary breadwinner was the male, and consequently, females, secondary breadwinners, were paid lower wages.

If the division of space between work and home and between work and leisure had created stress, the division of family members by age and gender made family life chaotic. Patterns of employment divided the working class by gender. Males became work-centred, and even leisure time was spent with workmates at pubs or fraternal lodges. Women divided their time between work and home, and the neighbourhood court or street was often a female domain. The preferred practice was for married women, especially with the arrival of the first child, to leave paid employment. For many women, widowed or abandoned with young children, or with husbands unemployed or in poor health, paid work was a necessity. Many women now faced the double shift of paid employment and domestic chores. Nonetheless, middle-class reformers blamed them for neglecting their domestic and maternal duties; and they also blamed their husbands for failing to provide sufficient income, attributing to them an inveterate laziness and excessive alcohol consumption.

The urban environment, the nature of work, and the stress on the family obviously influenced the standard of living. So did spending patterns according to an individual's age. Both male and female factory operatives in their teens and early twenties had a reputation for spending freely. They were also known for having a rather independent, even insolent, manner that went with a reasonable income and few responsibilities. On the other hand, young married couples with small unemployed children experienced very trying circumstances. Conditions improved in middle age, until advancing years would sap physical vigour and increase vulnerability to disease. Without the provision of state or private pensions and, with the expectation that one worked until death, old age brought the years of greatest poverty. Of course, at any age, ill health, an industrial accident, or unemployment could mean economic disaster.

Class and Ideology

Class and the "Cash Nexus"

Changes in living standards, patterns of work, family life, and experience according to age created stress and required significant adaptation by individuals and by the community. As people lived through these changes, they learned from their experience and developed strategies for exerting greater control over their lives. Quite independently of the individual's age, the cycles of expansion and contraction in the economy had a direct bearing on the individual's and the community's sense of well-being. In its early stages, the Industrial Revolution was subject to a series of radical booms and slumps. In boom times with fuller employment, living conditions were better, but during economic depressions, widespread unemployment among large urban populations posed much more than a serious social problem. In 1842, one of the worst years of the nineteenth century, there were 50 000 unemployed people in Manchester. They were not simply an impoverished mass but a social menace and a threat to the established order.

Fluctuations between times of prosperity and times of hardship changed people's expectations. Having experienced improvement in good times, they were less tolerant of hard times, and demanded action by employers and politicians. The experience of industrialization created a sense of common identity among working people, and this class consciousness expressed itself through political demands for the vote and for social change.

Working-class political activists, middle-class radicals, and conservative moralists interpreted the misery of the urban environment and the harshness of industrial-work conditions as a new state of human relations. Thomas Carlyle, who believed in the need for leaders (such as captains of industry) and in the duty of workers to labour, thought that human relations had been reduced to what he called a "cash nexus": the employer's interest was solely in profit, and labourers were no longer human beings, but simply a cost factor in production. Resisting the logic of the cash nexus, trade unionists and other working-class activists asserted the values of community and cooperation, and sought a remedy in an egalitarian democracy. Thomas Carlyle and other conservative moralists, such as the young Benjamin Disraeli and Charles Dickens, defended the social hierarchy. They hoped to restore a kind of paternalism in which employers and the state had a moral obligation toward their less fortunate social inferiors.

Laissez Faire

Manufacturers thought they had a good understanding of how economies functioned free from old-fashioned morality. After all, the new science of political economy advised that freedom from government or other restrictions optimized economic growth. In the early nineteenth century, these advocates of *laissez faire*—or of a free market—held a very pessimistic view of the possibilities for improvement in the living standards of the poor.

Thomas Malthus, an Anglican clergyman and pioneer of demography (the science dealing with the dynamics of population growth), studied the growth of population and increases in poverty in rural England. In his *Essay on Population* (1798), he concluded that the population grew more quickly than the food supply. Even if living standards improved, the poor would simply have more children, and breed themselves back into poverty. British economist David Ricardo, in *The Principles of Political Economy* (1817), linked Adam Smith's ideas about the free pursuit of individual self-interest with Malthus's theory of population. Ricardo concluded that population growth and diminishing levels of profit created an iron-bound law limiting the level of wages. Consequently, little could be done to raise living standards.

The ideas expressed above gave powerful support to the liberal policy of laissez faire and of resistance to regulation of trade and industry. They also confirmed the entrepreneurs' vision of their own success through the virtuous practice of self-discipline, diligence, thrift, and independence. The difficulty was that liberal theory and social reality were in conflict.

Christian moralists, shocked by conditions in the new industries and the expanding cities, felt compelled to intervene. Tory **paternalists**, tired of liberal criticism of the status quo, readily pointed to the human suffering in the manufacturers' domain. An even greater urgency was created by the riots, strikes, and political protests of farm labourers and industrial workers who demanded redress of their social and economic grievances. Following a policy of laissez faire, the government did nothing while social realities called for political action.

Jeremy Bentham and Utilitarianism

Jeremy Bentham, an original and influential liberal philosopher and moralist, pointed a way out of the social impasse of the early nineteenth century. He accepted Adam Smith's argument that it was best to free individuals to pursue their own self-interest. Smith had argued that in the competition between individuals conflicts were reconciled by an "unseen hand." Bentham, more realistically, accepted that conflicts were real and that there could be clear winners and losers. Believing that all human responses were either pleasurable or painful, Bentham thought that the impact of legislation could be calculated by a simple formula called the "principle of utility." This principle stated that laws should be designed to create "the greatest happiness of the greatest number." If real conflicts arose, the government could intervene and create an artificial measure of societal utility. In Bentham's thinking, Adam Smith's principle of free competition served to eliminate the need for such a measure — usually applied during conflict— making interventions unnecessary or exceptional. Nonetheless, his utilitarian philosophy made government action more acceptable. After his death in 1832, his influence manifested itself through his followers, who investigated social conditions and had a hand in shaping the new social legislation of

Jeremy Bentham's preserved body and head are still displayed in the boardroom of University College, London.

the 1830s and 1840s. Ironically, partly due to the influence of Bentham, this age of laissez faire saw an expansion of the role of the state and the creation of a modern civil service.

Social Legislation

The social legislation of the times addressed issues such as the provision of relief for the poor, conditions in factories and mines, and the regulation of public health. A growing and more impoverished rural population and the abuse of parish relief led taxpayers to protest against the Old Poor Law (which was promulgated under Queen Elizabeth I in 1597). In drafting a revised law, the government for the first time conducted a survey of the existing system, and from this survey, members of the Royal Commission, some of whom were Benthamites, drafted the *New Poor Law* of 1834, which was based upon a pleasure–pain calculation called the "less eligibility principle." In order to receive poor relief, an individual had to enter a workhouse and, in order to discourage people from going on relief, conditions in the workhouse were designed to be worse than conditions outside. The new law also introduced the Benthamite idea of a central board overseeing local administration.

The New Poor Law was successful in addressing abuses in rural areas, but was unsuited to industrial areas subject to periods of mass unemployment. Consequently, there were extensive protests against the new law. The protesters saw workhouses as prisons and named them "Bastilles." Nonetheless, the Poor Law of 1834 remained the basic provision of social welfare until 1909, and during its 75-year history, about 5 percent of the population was dependent on its provisions.

Bentham's ideas also influenced other pieces of social legislation. Evangelicals such as Richard Oastler and Michael Sadler, shocked by conditions in textile factories, demanded regulation of the employment of women and children. The Factory Act of 1833 thus prohibited the employment of children under 9 and placed limits on the working hours of those between the ages of 9 and 18. Unlike its predecessors, this act proved effective because it adopted the Benthamite principle of a central authority with an inspectorate. Out of the experience of these inspectors and further pressure from evangelical reformers and trade unionists, the new Factory Act of 1847 limited children to a 10-hour day. This limit became the standard working day for adults in textile mills.

Another royal commission investigating conditions in coal mines revealed shocking underground conditions of work for women, girls, and boys. In mining communities, children were stunted in growth and reached puberty at an older age; adults aged prematurely. Women, who worked underground hauling coal wagons to the surface even while pregnant, suffered miscarriages and internal injuries. The Mines Act of 1842 prohibited the employment of women, girls under 10, and boys under 10 in underground mines.

In the 1840s, Edwin Chadwick, a physician who had been Bentham's secretary as well as commissioner for the Poor Laws and Mines Act, reported on the high rates of mortality in cities. With public pressure mounting, an outbreak of cholera—a killer disease with a nasty tendency to spread from inner cities to middle-class suburbs—prompted the government to act. Once more, Edwin Chadwick, serving on an investigative commission, helped draft the Public Health Act of 1848, which included a General Board of Health to oversee conditions.

Taken as a whole, the social legislation passed in the age of laissez faire redefined the government's role in social policy. It established new ways of investigating social problems and created a body of professional civil servants who would become a new source of influence on future legislation.

Europe Restored: 1815

By 1815, the steam engine had begun its revolutionary changes in British society and its reverberations had begun to be heard on the Continent. As monarchs and princes gathered to determine the shape of Europe after Napoleon, the ascendant forces appeared to be those not of reform but of reaction. Apart from France with its legacy of the Revolution, the old social order of the landed nobility and its dependent peasantry still dominated the social landscape of Europe.

With Napoléon and his revolutionary legions defeated, Europe's statesmen undertook the task of restoration. Its political leaders dreamed of turning the clock back but, try as they might, they could not return to 1789: the French Revolution had created new political visions and it had unleashed the forces of popular insurrection. Whether moderate or radical, political reform was to have only one certain outcome: the weakening of the authority and privileges of kings and nobles.

The Napoleonic Wars had exposed another danger: in a restored Europe, no single power could be allowed to dominate the Continent. Diplomats were moderately successful at drawing up a peace settlement. In fact, no single power became dominant and there would be no general European war for almost a century, until 1914.

The task of restoration within states proved far more difficult. Population growth and economic change undermined the basis of the restored order, and social discontent gave new meaning to the famous French revolutionary call for "liberty, equality, and fraternity." The forces of conservative reaction were no match for the demands for change articulated in the competing claims of liberalism, democracy, nationalism, and socialism.

Prince Klemens von Metternich of Austria emerged as the most important political figure of the post-Napoleonic era.

Metternich and the Congress of Vienna

With Austrian and Prussian soldiers occupying Paris and Napoléon temporarily exiled on the Italian island of Elba, the victorious Allied Powers restored the French monarchy under the legitimate Bourbon claimant, Louis XVIII. The terms of this First Treaty of Paris, concluded in May 1814, generously and realistically recognized France's continued status as one of the great powers.

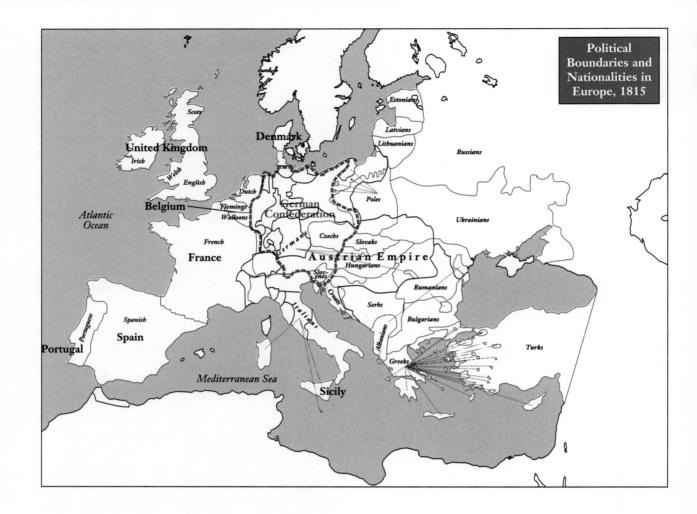

Political Boundaries and Nationalities in Europe, 1815

When they reconvened in Vienna in October 1814, the crowned heads of Europe brought with them their aristocratic courtiers and retainers. As host, the Austrian Emperor had to provide accommodation, lavish banquets, and entertainment for 14 000 visitors. Much to the annoyance of the princes of lesser states, the real work of the **Congress of Vienna** was accomplished by the private meetings of representatives of the principal powers: Austria, Russia, Prussia, Great Britain, and France. These proceedings were unexpectedly interrupted in March of 1815 with news of Napoléon's triumphant return from Elba. The ensuing 100 days ended with Napoléon's defeat at Waterloo (in what is now Belgium) and his safer exile to the British island of St. Helena, weakened the negotiating position of Prince Talleyrand, the French delegate, but did little to alter the objectives of the Congress.

Prince Klemens von Metternich (1773–1859), the Austrian foreign secretary, was the leading figure at the Congress. An aristocrat, self-confident to the point of vanity about his appearance and intelligence, Metternich sought to preserve and protect the position of Austria in the redrafted European order. Less of a visionary than a political realist, he recognized that Austria's interests were best served by the preservation of the conservative principles and institutions he cherished and by the establishment of stable diplomatic relations.

The Concert of Europe

In addition to the territorial settlement, the Congress initiated the practice of leading statesmen consulting with one another in order to resolve potential disputes. This idea of a "concert" of Europe worked best with respect to France. The four victorious powers, Russia, Prussia, Austria, and Great Britain, formed the Quadruple Alliance, in which they agreed to act in concert should France show signs of expansionist revival.

A far more contentious idea was proposed by Czar Alexander I of Russia, who was fervently attached to absolutism and wished to unite his diplomacy with his personal Christian mysticism. The czar believed that harmony in Europe depended upon states adopting the divinely sanctioned order of rule by legitimate monarchs. The principle of legitimacy asserted that rulers were chosen by God through hereditary succession, not by representative assemblies or elections. The Congress had followed this principle in restoring the legitimate Bourbon monarchs to the thrones of France, Spain, and Naples. To protect such legitimate rulers, the czar proposed that, under the Holy Alliance, member states would agree to intervene in the internal affairs of other states should their monarchs be challenged by the twin evils of the French Revolution: liberalism and popular insurrection. Fearful of the forces of reform and anxious not to offend the czar, Austria and Prussia joined the Holy Alliance.

Metternich had little time for the czar's mysticism, but he fiercely opposed any form of liberalism. Until the Revolution of 1848 proved his undoing, Metternich resisted the destabilizing tide of liberal reform. Consequently, he was prepared to use the Austrian army and support the actions of his partners in the Holy Alliance to intervene in the internal politics of lesser states. Castlereagh, the British foreign secretary who had supported Metternich in the construction of a new balance of power, forthrightly refused to join this alliance. In Great Britain, a constitutional monarch ruled through a powerful and elected parliament. Castlereagh rejected the idea that a Holy Alliance of powerful states could intervene in the internal affairs of other states in order to impose some divinely inspired political order.

In 1820, in view of the Spanish and Italian uprisings, Austria, Prussia, and Russia signed the Troppau Protocol, agreeing to intervene against any sign of revolutionary upheaval. Castlereagh refused to sign the Protocol: he thought that such interventions simply created greater conflict. But Britain also had its own self-interested motives for not signing: the Spanish-American colonies were in revolt, and their independence would offer Britain new commercial prospects, so Castlereagh wanted no part in a European alliance seeking to reimpose Spanish legitimacy in South America.

The divisions over the Holy Alliance were indicative of troubles to come. The restoration had established a new equilibrium among the great powers, but it had done so at a price: the lands and peoples of lesser states were placed under the authority of larger states. In the restoration of governments, restoring the authority of legitimate monarchs had been the primary objective; little attention had been given to the rights of their subjects. Wishing to undo the impact of the French Revolution, Metternich and his allies inadvertently helped to revive the revolutionary forces they had sought to overcome.

Reaction and Reform: 1815–1830

Napoléon and his armies claimed to be liberating Europe from royal absolutism and aristocratic privilege. Conquered peoples often saw these claims as French propaganda, but nonetheless there was a germ of truth that with Napoléon came constitutions and laws bearing the stamp of the Enlightenment and the Revolution. In the Low Countries, the Rhineland, Spain, and Italy, segments of the middle class had benefited from the Napoleonic reforms so they did not necessarily welcome the restoration of absolutism in 1815. On the other hand, in Central and Eastern Europe—with the notable exception of Poland—these reforms made little headway, and absolutism remained secure in Russia, Prussia, and the Austrian Empire. For self-interested reasons, the two great powers, Britain and France, cooperated in the restoration of legitimate rule and, together, paved the way for future conflicts. When those conflicts materialized shortly after 1815, reasons of state would continue to dictate the strategies of the great powers, and they would have a decisive role in determining the success or failure of movements for reform.

Chartism

Chartism, although unsuccessful in achieving its political objectives, was a significant working-class movement in the development of democratic and socialist politics in Britain and Europe. In 1836, William Lovett, a printer and founder of the London Workingmen's Association, proposed a national campaign to draw up a People's Charter. The idea of a charter appealed to the concept of parliamentary liberties granted by Magna Carta, which was forced on King John in 1215. In the form of a national petition to be presented to Parliament, the People's Charter similarly set forth the people's grievances and demands.

The campaign for the Charter took place in the most severe economic depression of the nineteenth century, in the midst of the crisis provoked by the stresses of industrialization and rapid urbanization. The Chartist campaign involved the holding of mass meetings at which people signed the petition and elected representatives to an alternate People's Parliament or National Convention. To property owners, the idea of universal suffrage, promoted by a national campaign of mass meetings and petitions, was a threat of revolution.

When Chartists presented the first National Petition, with 1 250 000 signatures, Parliament rejected it out of hand. The Chartists then split over tactics. The "moral force" Chartists argued in favour of a campaign to gather more support while the "physical force" Chartists argued in favour of revolution. The Chartist movement reached its peak in 1842, the worst year of the depression, although, even at its highest point, the Chartists were more revolutionary in their rhetoric than in their actions. After 1842, with divisions in the movement and an improving economy, the Chartist movement declined.

Despite its evident failures, Chartism shaped the political traditions and culture of the British working class and influenced radical views of popular political movements in the new urban industrial age. For the remainder of the nineteenth century, the democratic goals of the Chartists set the political agenda of radical reformers and labour advocates. At right is the national petition drawn up and presented to Parliament by the Chartists.

The Six Points of the People's Charter

1.
A Vote for every man twenty-one years of age, of sound mind, and not undergoing punishment for crime.

2.
The Ballot—To protect the elector in the exercise of his vote.

3.
No Property Qualification for Members of Parliament—thus enabling the constituencies to return the man of their choice, be he rich or poor.

4.
Payment of Members, thus enabling an honest tradesman, workingman, or other person, to serve a constituency, when taken from his business to attend to the interests of the Country.

5.
Equal Constituencies, securing the same amount of representation for the same number of electors, instead of allowing small constituencies to swamp the votes of large ones.

6.
Annual Parliaments, thus presenting the most effectual check to bribery and intimidation, since through a constituency might be bought once in seven years (even with the ballot), no purse could buy a constituency (under a system of universal suffrage) in each ensuing twelve-month; and since members, when elected for a year only, would not be able to defy and betray their constituents as now.

Liberalism, Democracy, and Nationalism

Until 1848, liberalism challenged the authority of absolute monarchy while rejecting the claims of popular democracy. The reinvigorated conservatism, defending the restored order of 1815, rejected the claims of liberalism and radical democracy. Consequently, liberals and radicals were often political allies against absolutism, but their differences quickly became apparent when the reforming alliance proved victorious. Inevitably they fell out over the key questions of who had the vote and were full citizens, and whose economic interests should the state protect and advance. A growing population and a developing economy pressed these issues to the forefront of the political agenda.

As the forces of reform advanced against the tide of conservative reaction, the main struggle was the one between liberalism and democracy. With the rise of the urban population and the growth of industry, advocates of democracy among middle-class radicals, artisans, and wage labourers redefined their political and social objectives by the new ideology of *socialism*.

Another legacy of the French Revolution, linked to the competing claims of liberalism and democracy, was the idea of *nationalism*. The new sense of identity derived from one's citizenship of a nation-state rested upon the idea of popular sovereignty. This idea that the state belonged to the "people" and that the government derived its authority from the people was given particular intensity by the experience of the French Revolution and Napoleonic armies. Soldiers saw themselves as armed citizens first defending and advancing the cause of popular liberation against the forces of aristocratic reaction. The French conquest of other peoples created the opposite reaction as peoples defined themselves in opposition to the occupying forces of France.

Nationalism may have originated at this time but there were few, if any, examples of mass nationalism prior to 1848. Older forms of identity with the locality, of deference to local notables, and of a vague allegiance to the distant figure of the monarch persisted. Nationalism, with its sense of citizenship and popular sovereignty, was both new and radical. The post-1815 settlement imposed by the Congress of Vienna created conditions for a fusion of the more limited demands of liberalism with the first stirrings of nationalism. The Congress had restored absolute monarchs in place of Napoléon's appointees. When liberals protested against this restored absolutism, the great powers, led by Metternich and the czar, intervened to halt the progress of liberal reform. Consequently, in the minds of their liberal opponents, the restored monarchs were guilty of absolutism and treason against the nation.

Liberal and Nationalist Revolts, 1815–1830

From 1815 to 1830, the great powers faced a series of political crises caused by uprisings in several of the less powerful states. Within the loose confederation of German states, university students protested against the restraints imposed by the restoration of absolutist rule.

The Defence of Absolutism

In 1819, Metternich, the Austrian foreign secretary, wary of any sign of reforming liberalism, persuaded the leading German states to issue the Carlsbad Decrees, which curtailed political meetings, censored the press and universities, and further limited the powers of legislative assemblies. This intervention was a significant setback for the development of liberalism in the German states: it spread police surveillance as established in Austria and strengthened the aristocratic authority of the Prussian state.

In 1820–1821, Metternich also faced liberal and nationalist upheavals in several Italian states (which were not under Austrian domination). He used the Austrian army in a quick intervention to quell the revolts. The ensuing protests in Naples and Piedmont, inspired by a small revolutionary organization, the Carbonnari, laid the foundation of the Italian nationalist movement.

In Spain, an uprising against the restored Bourbon monarchy of Ferdinand VII had greater, if only temporary, success. The Spanish Constitution of 1812, proclaimed during Napoléon's invasion, included the radical principle of universal male suffrage, but the Bourbon restoration abolished this democratic measure. In 1820, a faction of the middle class, led by officers in the army, successfully overthrew the monarchy and restored the Constitution of 1812. In 1823, France, with the backing of its allies, intervened with 100 000 troops to restore the monarchy and absolutism.

Also during the Polish revolt of 1830–1831 and other instances, intervention by a great power

Romantic artist Eugène Delacroix depicts the massacre of thousands of innocent Greeks by the Turks on the island of Chios.

successfully crushed liberal and nationalist protests that were symptomatic of an emerging political consciousness, but had not yet grown into mass movements. Some comparable liberal and nationalist movements in the period up to the 1830s were more successful. In these instances, the protesters met not with the resistance but with the support of foreign powers.

Greek Independence: 1821–1830

The Greek struggle for independence from the Ottoman Empire in 1821–1830 aroused the greatest sympathy in Europe. An evocative mix of history, culture, and religion gave the Greek struggle the mythic proportions of a battle between David and Goliath. From the biased perspective of Europe, the Ottoman Turks represented the decadent, exotic, and infidel culture of the Islamic Orient. The struggle, in which both sides committed savage atrocities, took place in the mountainous terrain and Aegean islands made familiar by the tales of Homer and the history of Classical Greece. The Greek struggle aroused the political passions and imaginative fancy of leading poets and writers of the Romantic Movement. In Athens, the ancient Acropolis and its Parthenon provided a dramatic setting for the struggle between Greek and Turkish battalions. Lord Byron, as romantic in his life as in his poetry, sped to Greece to assist in the cause, and there met an early death, not in battle but—less romantically—from an infection.

The outcome of the Greek struggle was determined by more prosaic influences. The great powers had conflicting interests in the decline of the Ottoman Empire. In jockeying for influence in the Balkans, Austria feared a Russian appeal to the Greeks and other peoples on the basis of their common religion, Orthodox Christianity. With its vital trade to India, which still travelled from the Eastern Mediterranean to the Persian Gulf, Britain also had a strategic interest in the area. These conflicting interests arising from the decline of the Ottoman Empire led to a long diplomatic struggle known as the Eastern Question, a source of tension and conflict right down to 1914. The one asset of the Ottoman Turks was the superiority of their navy. The European powers joined their naval forces and defeated the Turks at the Greek port of Navarino in 1827. This intervention turned the struggle in favour of the Greeks, whose independence was recognized in 1830.

Reform and Conflict: France and England, 1815–1848

France

In France, the unrealized dreams and fearful memories of the Revolution continued to shape political struggles. At the same time, a growing population and the beginnings of industrial change created new demands on the state and its political masters. These tensions led to revolutionary crises in 1830 and 1848.

The Restored Monarchy: 1815–1830

When the Bourbon monarchy was restored after the defeat of Napoleon, Louis XVIII took power as a constitutional and not as an absolute monarch. The king still claimed rule by divine right, but a Constitutional Charter, which remained in effect until 1848, placed limits on royal powers, thus securing some of the reforms effected by the Revolution. The Charter provided for equality before the law, including the right to due process. Unlike in the pre-1789 *ancien régime*, important state offices were not reserved for the nobility; careers were instead "open to the talents." Freedom of conscience, religion, and expression was guaranteed, but the place of the Catholic Church in the restored order remained uncertain. To prevent returning aristocrats from claiming ancient lands and to secure the revolutionary gains of landowners from the middle class and wealthy peasantry, security of private property was also guaranteed. In addition to these Charter guarantees, there would be a legislature, with a hereditary upper house or Chamber of Peers and an elected Chamber of Deputies. This elected assembly had a very small electorate of wealthy property owners numbering about 100 000 voters in a population of 28 million.

Although he retained the pomp and ritual of an absolute monarch, Louis XVIII was a pragmatic politician who accepted many of the rationalizing and centralizing administrative reforms installed by Napoléon. He also recognized that under Napoléon, wealthier segments of the bourgeoisie had acquired more wealth, social status, and positions in the state, and that he was best advised to accept these new sources of influence and power rather than attempt a full restoration of 1789 conditions. Unfortunately, many of Louis XVIII's relations, friends, and advisors were not so pragmatic. Full of romantic and conservative fantasies of their years in exile, the ultraroyalists pressed the king to restore absolutism.

Opportunity for the Ultras came with Louis XVIII's death in 1824. At age 62, Charles X, his brother, more conservative and less astute, came to the throne. The new king favoured his aristocratic friends among the ultraroyalists and, eventually, his extreme measures alienated influential members of the bourgeoisie who had originally supported him.

After the election of 1830, Charles X refused to convene the legislature and imposed more restrictive controls on the press. He called for a new election with a revised and limited electorate sure to exclude opposition deputies. In effect, the king had staged a coup d'état on his own state. A ruler with a better sense of history could have predicted the result. In July 1830, students, workers, and liberal politicians called for a popular uprising. Revolutionary barricades 15 m or more in height appeared on the streets of Paris, and the troops proved ineffective during three days of riots and demonstrations. Charles X, without the means to enforce his authority, fled the country. Louis Philippe, his cousin, upon invitation of moderate liberal monarchists in the Chamber of Deputies and supported by the army, assumed the throne.

The July Monarchy: 1830–1848

The coronation installing this new *July Monarchy* displayed a liberal constitutional character. Louis Philippe was not proclaimed "King of France" but "King of the French People." More ominously, the Revolution's tricolour, with its red, white, and blue symbolizing liberty, equality, and fraternity, was restored as the national flag.

The constitutional reforms that followed also reflected the liberalism of the new regime. Reforms on age and property qualifications to vote enlarged the electorate to 200 000 in a population of 32 million. In addition, laws providing for censorship of the press were abolished, and church and state were declared separate.

The July Monarchy was neither a republic nor a democracy, but a liberal oligarchy of property owners. It removed the political influence of clerical and ultraroyalist factions, but failed to satisfy the political aspirations of radicals and democrats. In 1832, republican students and workers, in an episode made memorable by Victor Hugo's *Les Misérables*, took to the streets and reconstructed their revolutionary barricades. The insurrection was effectively, if bloodily, crushed.

Faced with growing discontent and challenges to rule by property owners, the July Monarchy, despite its liberal foundations, grew more repressive. The turning point occurred in 1835, in the aftermath of a failed attempt to assassinate Louis Philippe. Fearing a widespread conspiracy, the government passed the September Laws, which restricted radical political organizations and censored the press. Ever mindful of the precedents of 1789 and 1830, the radicals looked to revolution as the means out of this political impasse. There was a severe depression in 1845–1847. Bad harvests and high food prices intensified discontent in rural and urban areas. In 1848, revolution went from radical fantasy to political possibility.

Pierre-Joseph Proudhon and French Anarchism

By the 1830s, socialist ideas began to influence the political demands of radical democrats who hoped to win the vote and then bring about socialist reforms. Pierre-Joseph Proudhon (1809–1865), an influential French radical, addressed the question of the source of violence and repression in society. Contrary to the common view, he claimed that the responsibility for violence and crime lay not with individuals but with governments. The state, through its laws and police force, compelled humans to live in an unnatural condition of inequality and oppression, and the grossest inequality of all was in the ownership of property. His famous pamphlet of 1840 asked the question "What is Property?" and he answered "All property is theft." A popular revolutionary insurrection, in his mind, should do away with private property and create conditions of social equality. Having removed the source of oppression and violence, the state itself was no longer needed. Unlike most other radical thinkers of his age, Proudhon deeply distrusted the state, and his view of the repressive character of government made him one of the founders of anarchism. The extract that follows is taken from Proudhon's *What is Property?*

Method followed in this work. Idea of a revolution.

If I had to answer the following question, "What is slavery?" and if I should respond in one word: "It is murder," my meaning would be understood at once. I should not need a long explanation to show that the power to deprive a man of his thought, his will, and his personality is the power of life and death. So why to this other question, "What is property?", should I not answer in the same way, "It is theft," without fearing to be misunderstood, since the second proposition is only a transformation of the first?

One author teaches that property is a civil right, based on occupation and sanctioned by law; another holds that it is a natural right, arising from labour; and these doctrines, though they seem opposed, are both encouraged and applauded. I contend that neither occupation nor labour nor law can create property, which is rather an effect without a cause.

One day I asked myself: Why is there so much sorrow and poverty in the world? Must people always be unhappy? I am not satisfied with the various explanations given by reformers, some blaming the general distress on the cowardice and incompetence of those in power, some on conspirators and troublemakers, and others on ignorance and general corruption; and weary of the endless quarrels of the politicians and the press, I have wanted to investigate the matter for myself. I have consulted the masters of science, and I have read a hundred of volumes of philosophy, law, political economy, and history: would to God that I lived in an age when so much reading was unnecessary. I have made every effort to obtain exact information, comparing doctrines, responding to objections, incessantly making equations and deductions, and weighing thousands of syllogisms on the scales of the most rigorous logic. In the course of this laborious effort I have collected many interesting facts, which I shall share with my friends and the public as soon as I have the leisure. But I must say, I recognised from the first that we have never understood the meaning of these common as well as sacred words: justice, equality, liberty; that in each case our ideas have been deeply obscure; and that this ignorance has been the sole cause both of the poverty that devours us and of all the calamities that have afflicted the human race.

England

Protest and Reaction: 1815–1821

After ending the war with France in 1815, England experienced a lengthy depression until 1821. Historians of differing political persuasions have argued that, during these years of intense social conflict, two new classes, a middle class and a working class, came into being. Economic hardship provoked protests, and government repression in turn confirmed the need for reform.

Pressure for parliamentary reform had been gaining strength since the 1760s. Population growth and industrial development exacerbated the problem of representation. The rural south was overrepresented, whereas the industrial areas of the Midlands and the North were underrepresented. Some of the new industrial cities had no members in Parliament and, given the local peculiarities of the franchise, many middle-class residents as well as members of the working class were without the vote.

In 1811–1812, an extensive campaign of machine wrecking occurred in the knitting-frame areas of the Midlands and in textile areas in the English North. The machine wreckers claimed to be followers of General Ned Ludd, a mythical folk hero and redresser of the wrongs of the poor, fashioned after Robin Hood. The Luddites (the term is still used to describe those who resist technological innovation) attempted to protect jobs and wages being undercut by the new machinery. Claiming to be enforcing existing laws, they justified a campaign of threats and violence against the persons, property, and machines of the owners of the new industries.

Following the suppression of the Luddites, widespread political disruptions recommenced during the depression of 1815–1818. These protests took on a new threatening character. Large numbers of people—20 000 to 50 000 or more—followed a parade of bands and banners to assemble in open spaces near large urban centres and hear speeches by popular orators. On August 16, 1819, 60 000 gathered at St. Peter's Field, near Manchester, to hear Orator Hunt, when the Yeomen of the Guard, a local mounted militia, charged into the crowd, killing 11 and wounding over 400. In mockery of Wellington's victory at Waterloo, the radicals named this episode the Peterloo Massacre. It became a symbol of the government's tyranny over popular rights.

The Reform of Parliament: 1830–1832

In 1830, the accession of a new king, William IV, necessitated an election. In the rural south, riots had aroused fears of an agrarian insurrection, and in July news arrived that a revolution in Paris had toppled Charles X. Hopeful that the time was ripe, middle-class and working-class reformers revived their campaign for parliamentary reform. Among the parliamentarians, the aristocratic Whigs (later, Liberals), who had been out of office for 40 years, also saw a need for reform.

The reform bill introduced by Lord John Russell tried to bring some order to the archaic mix of constituencies and voter qualifications. The bill proposed an extensive redistribution of seats in which small boroughs with few or no voters, called *pocket boroughs* and *rotten boroughs*, would lose their seats to the new industrial cities. The bill also reformed the **franchise**, making a net worth of £10 per household mandatory for borough constituencies, and making only modest changes to voter eligibility in rural or county seats.

In Parliament, the bill took from 1830 to 1832 to be passed. These years were a period of economic downturn, and the combination of social unrest and a political crisis strengthened the possibility of revolution. The redistribution of seats to the new industrial centres had more immediate significance than the attempt to make the franchise more fair. Despite these changes, rural constituencies still predominated, and over two thirds of MPs came from the landed interest. Nonetheless, industrial areas at least had a voice in Parliament and the number of voters increased by 50 percent to 652 000, or 18 percent of the adult male population.

The question of whom the bill enfranchised and the process of its passage had longer-term consequences. Opponents of reform warned that once the old system was altered, there would be no way to halt further reforms. This fear of the thin edge of the wedge, or of modest reform in 1832 opening the way for democracy, proved accurate. Sir Robert Peel warned that, in making the House of Commons more representative, the ***Reform Act*** made the monarch and the House of Lords less important, and provided no principled reason for stopping further extension of the vote until Britain was made an "unmitigated democracy." This process was not completed until the twentieth century: women over the age of 30 got the vote in 1918; women over the age of 21 got the vote in

1928, achieving equal voting rights with men. (Middle-class men got the vote in 1832.)

The Origins of Socialism

Liberalism, Democracy, and Socialism

Liberalism, democracy, and socialism were part of the legacy of the French Revolution and its rallying cry for "liberty, equality, and fraternity." Liberalism, a political philosophy attuned to the interests of the middle class, stressed the liberty of the individual both in relation to the state and in the pursuit of economic self-interest. Liberals feared that, under democracy, the will of the majority might predominate over the interests of the individual; consequently, they tied the full rights of citizenship, including the vote, to the possession of property. Radical democrats, who included middle-class, lesser property owners (such as shopkeepers, salary-earning professionals, and small peasant landholders) as well as working-class artisans and wage labourers, sought equality of citizenship with universal suffrage.

During the French Revolution, some observers began to ask whether universal suffrage was sufficient to give real meaning to the ideals of liberty, equality, and fraternity. In this view, the emancipation of all members of society required much more than new constitutions, laws, and ballots. In the first half of the nineteenth century, the growth in population, the impact of industrial change, and the evidence of a growing disparity and conflict between the rich and the poor confirmed the belief of radical thinkers that, beyond democracy, a genuine liberation required a new kind of society.

The Utopian Socialists

Count Henri de Saint-Simon (1760–1825)

Count Henri de Saint-Simon was a French aristocrat and an eccentric visionary. He doubted whether changes in constitutions, even the extension of the vote, would make much difference in the material and spiritual well-being of the entire population. Saint-Simon had a keen interest in scientific discoveries and was confident that technological innovations would bring about greater material abundance. The difficulty was to find a way in which wealth would not be possessed by the few but would serve the needs of everyone. He defined this goal according to the principle "From each according to his ability, to each according to his work."

Saint-Simon thought that society would have to be reorganized. As an aristocrat, he still thought of society as hierarchical, but he believed that social planning could produce a new, more prosperous and harmonious social order. He created a following among intellectuals and reformers, many of whom were engineers, and they would have a hand in industrial development and urban planning under the Second Empire of Napoléon III. Saint-Simon's contribution lay in the realization that a political liberation was incomplete without social change, and in his vision that technological innovation and social planning would make life more equitable and fulfilling.

Robert Owen (1771–1858)

In England, Robert Owen shared Saint-Simon's optimism about the social potential of industrial technology, but his direct experience as a cotton manufacturer made him extremely pessimistic about the consequences of unrestrained industrial capitalism. He thought that the emphasis of industrial entrepreneurs on individualism and competition, including the effort to maximize profit by demanding optimum productivity for the lowest possible wage, was harmful to the individual and destructive of the fabric of society. He feared the degradation of working people and the rise of sharp class antagonisms, which could result in destructive class warfare.

In place of individualism and competition, Owen emphasized community and cooperation. In an early instance of what later would be called industrial psychology, he argued that workers with better living conditions, better pay, and shorter hours would be more efficient and productive. To test his ideas, he built model communities in New Lanark, Scotland, and in New Harmony, Indiana. The experiment failed but it did introduce innovations: community self-government and profit-sharing.

Charles Fourier (1772–1837)

Like Robert Owen, Charles Fourier was another eccentric French theorist who experimented with model communities. He thought that capitalism, especially the system of industrial wage labour, destroyed the essential goodness of human nature, so he sought to create model communities to liberate the human spirit. His ideal community (tried several times in the United States) was a small self-sufficient unit of 1560 people. Living communally on 2025 ha (5000 acres), the whole community shared both the labour and produce of agricultural and industrial pursuits.

Like Saint-Simon, Fourier was an early advocate of the emancipation of women. He thought that conventional marriage was little more than a form of prostitution in which families sold their daughters into an oppressive dependency on their future husbands. In his ideal communities, Fourier abolished marriage and called for sexual freedom with partnerships based on love. Within the puritanical sexual morality of the nineteenth century, Fourier's ideas, and the fact that some socialist men and women put them into practice, made socialists dangerous on moral as well as political grounds.

Karl Marx (1818–1883) and *The Communist Manifesto*

A severe economic depression and widespread unemployment in 1845–1847 brought this ferment of socialist proposals to the boiling point in 1848, the year of revolutions. Anticipating that the deepening economic depression would build into a political confrontation, the Communist League, a small society of exiled German radicals, commissioned one of their members to write a pamphlet advising German workers on how to respond to the impending crisis. By February 1848, in just six weeks, Marx, with assistance from Engels, produced *The Communist Manifesto*, one of the most influential pamphlets in modern history. The word "communist" in the title was chosen deliberately to set it apart from other socialist tracts. Those "utopian socialist" works were largely the product of middle-class intellectuals who criticized the capitalist system of private ownership and advocated common ownership of land and industry, but had little idea of how to put their ideas into practice. Communism also advocated common ownership of the means of production but, in contrast, it embraced the power of

Karl Marx proposed radical changes that would lead to revolutions in twentieth-century Europe.

the new working class, and preached that neither reason nor votes but only revolution would bring about the new socialist order.

Karl Marx, the son of a Jewish lawyer who had converted to Christianity, studied philosophy at the University of Berlin. A rather impractical and sometimes difficult person, he worked as a journalist and political activist organizing small groups of exiled radicals, moving from one European capital to another one step ahead of the police. *The Communist Manifesto* brought together the three main intellectual influences of his day: the political lessons of the French Revolution, the economic lessons of the Industrial Revolution in England, and the **dialectical** lessons of the German philosophical revolution.

The Lessons of History

Marx asked the tough political question, If the existing social and political order was oppressive, how did a new liberating social order come into being? For an answer he looked to history, and the answer he found was optimistic, but neither simple nor superficial.

The Communist Manifesto begins with the famous sentence, "The history of all hitherto existing societies is the history of class struggles." Looking to the French Revolution of 1789, Marx argued that the old order of aristocratic feudalism had reached a point of revolutionary crisis, and had been overthrown by the new capitalist order of the bourgeoisie. This new order, most advanced by the Industrial Revolution in England, operated by a competitive spirit in which the rich got richer and the poor got poorer. Furthermore, wealth accumulated in fewer and fewer hands and producers, growing in number and poverty, were reduced to living solely by selling their labour. The labour of these wage-earning proletarians was actually the source of wealth, so that the bourgeoisie (factory owners, bankers, and merchants) made its profits by the theft of other people's labour.

Applying the concept of the **dialectic** (a process of change through thesis and antithesis being resolved in truth, or synthesis) drawn from Hegel's philosophy, Marx claimed that each stage of history gave rise to the antagonistic forces which were the source of its destruction. Just as the feudalism of the aristocracy (thesis) gave rise to its antithesis in the capitalism of the bourgeoisie, he predicted that capitalism in turn would result in the communism of the proletariat (synthesis). These historical contradictions were a product of profound changes working over time, and in the struggle between classes they reached a climax in revolution. Using a metaphor from the age of steam, Marx called revolutions the "locomotives of history": they were the great engines that drove the historical process forward.

The first part of *The Communist Manifesto* set out Marx's scheme of history with its emphasis on class struggle and the inevitable outbreak of revolution. Marx claimed that his theory, called *dialectic materialism*, unlike that of earlier socialists, was not utopian or idealistic but scientific, because it rested on the laws of historical change. In this view, one did not have a choice about political strategy, for revolution was inevitable. The only choice was how one could advance the course of the revolution.

Preparing for the Revolution of 1848

In light of his historical understanding, Marx offered advice about the particular circumstances of 1848. The second part of his manifesto set out the program of the German communists. Part of the platform restated well-established radical proposals that went back to the time of the French Revolution: the unification of Germany, universal suffrage, and a progressive tax against the wealthy. Newer socialist objectives included state ownership of banks, mines, and railroads, and a more original proposal involved the creation of large-scale, scientific, collectivized agriculture. *The Communist Manifesto* concluded with his advice to radicals and workers: "Workers of the world, unite."

His advice to German workers was more specific. He observed that Germany had not advanced as far as England in industrial development, nor as far as France in liberal political development. In fact, Germany still needed its bourgeois revolution, so he advised German workers to support middle-class liberals in pressing for constitutional reform.

In 1848, Marx had an opportunity to observe several revolutions at first hand. To a certain degree, this year of revolutions confirmed Marx's analysis.

Clearly, revolutionary outbreaks were possible, and even common. It was equally evident that historical conditions did not yet exist for the success of a workers' revolution and, in Central Europe, even bourgeois revolutions achieved temporary but not lasting victories.

The Revolutions of 1848

Revolution brought down the July Monarchy in Paris in February 1848. In the next few months, an epidemic of revolutions spread from one European capital to another and, like an epidemic, the revolutions were short-lived. Again, Paris led the way. In June, the revolutionaries remounted the barricades, but this time met defeat at the hands of a reconstituted government and its armed force. Thereafter, the tide turned. During the following year, monarchs and generals restored authority and order throughout Europe.

The Revolutionary Crisis

The peculiar pattern of sudden revolutionary upheaval followed swiftly by the defeat of the revolutionaries raises a number of important, yet tricky, historical questions. The revolutionary outbreaks occurred in response to a serious economic crisis. Over the longer term, a rising population had put pressure on the food supply and resulted in a decline in living standards. In the short term, poor harvests and the potato blight in 1845–1847 created a sudden increase in the price of food. In some rural areas of Germany, Central Europe, and Italy, peasants struggled to avoid starvation. At the same time, a financial crisis disrupted commerce and industry, and created widespread unemployment among both handicraft and industrial workers in the cities. In France, over a million people were unemployed. The economic distress spilled out into the streets, as people joined in protests seeking a political remedy for their plight.

The Spring of Revolutions: February–June 1848

Liberal and nationalist demands for a new constitutional order, combined with popular discontent in the countryside and in the cities, created the revolutionary crisis of 1848. Facing riots and barricades in the streets of Paris, and with a National Guard unwilling and unable to reimpose order, Louis Philippe abdicated on February 24. During the first six months of 1848,

Revolutions in Europe, 1848–1849

◆ Locations of Revolts
.... German Confederation

similar revolutionary outbreaks occurred in Vienna, Budapest, Berlin, Piedmont, Prague, and various Italian cities.

The Counteroffensive: June 1848–August 1849

France: From the June Days to Louis Napoléon Bonaparte

In France, a Second Republic was proclaimed following the February Revolution. Its provisional government, dominated by moderate republicans and liberal reformers, reluctantly bowed to the popular demand for universal suffrage but resisted the inclusion of radical social and economic reforms. Louis Blanc, one of the two representatives of the Paris working class, managed to gain support for a form of national workshops, a relief program of public works for the unemployed. The April elections confirmed the moderate direction of the Republic as the radicals elected about 100 delegates out of a total of 800 members of the Constituent Assembly. In the countryside, small landholders, fearful for their property, grew ever

more suspicious of the Parisian radicals, while, by June, 120 000 workers, many committed to radical reform, had enrolled in the national workshops.

With the support of rural France and middle-class property owners, the government decided to dissolve the workshops. The working class took to the barricades once more and, between June 22 and 26, a bloody class war was fought on the streets of Paris. During these terrible "June Days," the government and the army prevailed, and over 10 000 people were killed or injured. This bloodshed had a lasting effect on class relations and class politics in the second half of the nineteenth century. The immediate benefactor was not a person but a name from the past. In the presidential elections of December 1848, Louis Napoléon Bonaparte, Emperor Napoléon's nephew, won a landslide victory that pointed to a new pattern of politics. Universal suffrage had not opened the door to revolution but to dictatorship.

The Austrian Empire

In the Austrian Empire, aristocratic officials and military leaders felt more confident when the ineffectual emperor abdicated in favour of Franz Joseph, his 18-year-old nephew. There had been one gain from the reforms of March: the peasantry had been freed of serfdom, with its forced labour and feudal dues. Having achieved their principal objective, the rural population became passive observers of the struggles in the cities. Rural sons, who made up the rank and file of the Austrian army, also had a new reason for defending the Empire.

In pitched battles with civilians on city streets, the military were limited both by the reluctance of the soldiers to engage in this dangerous combat against fellow subjects and by an unwillingness to use artillery (because of its power to destroy not only lives but property). With new determination, on June 17, the Austrian commanders used their cannon to bombard Prague and crushed the revolt of Czech students and radicals. By the end of July, the Austrian forces had a similar success against liberals and nationalists in Northern Italy. In October, the army, at a cost of 4000 lives, repossessed Vienna from the control of radicals and students. Italian radicals held out until July 1849, when the French army intervened. Hungarian nationalists, having established their own state and army, were the last to fall. The Austrian forces received support from rival ethnic minorities such as the

Rumanians and Croats, but it took 130 000 Russian troops to bring an end to Hungarian independence in the summer of 1849.

1848 and the Birth of Modern Politics

Such a catalogue of failure has tempted some observers to conclude that the Revolutions of 1848 made no lasting historical imprint. But 1848 brought the age of revolution to a close. After the spring of 1848, modern states would never again be so fragile in the face of popular insurrection. If absolutism was not dead, its days were numbered. Serfdom had been abolished in the Austrian Empire. Monarchs with absolutist pretensions survived in Prussia, Austria, and Russia, but in defending against revolution, these states had redefined the basis of their authority.

France, the mother of revolution and modern political ideologies, gave birth to the first modern politician, Louis Napoléon Bonaparte, who became president by promising a democratic electorate that he would restore order in society and government. The peasantry and the middle class responded to his appeal, and he continued to cultivate their backing as emperor. A democratic electorate transformed the foundation for political legitimacy, and proved the secret to stability in modern states.

Reflections

After 1848, the states most successful at unifying territory and consolidating authority, Germany and Italy, shook off the remnants of absolutism and redefined the basis of the state's authority by joining elitist rule with electoral approval by a democratic majority.

Regimes that clung to absolutism and failed to incorporate a means to win legitimacy from a popular electorate suffered the consequences: eventually, the Austrian Empire would be dismembered and czarist Russia would face revolution.

The losers of 1848 would appear to be the real revolutionaries: the socialist radicals and the working class. Yet 1848 confirmed their belief that universal suffrage by itself would not achieve a liberation from social and economic oppression. The experience of 1848 also destroyed the romantic myth that popular insurrections invariably captured the imagination of the people and led to the overthrow of governments. The people were divided by social class and, by and large, the middle classes, rural landholders, and even the poor had a stake in stability rather than change. After 1850, the growth of industry would extend some of its benefits to workers as well as owners, and improvements in living standards dampened political volatility. If the politics of mass democracy made revolution more difficult, it also allowed for the possibility of reform. Contrary to the theory of Marx and Engels, the most advanced industrial society, Great Britain, proved the most impervious to revolution, whereas the least developed, Russia, proved the most vulnerable.

The observation that the Revolution of 1848 was "the revolution that failed to turn" needs to be reconsidered. It would be more accurate to say that the Revolution of 1848 failed to turn in the direction anticipated by the revolutionaries. Nonetheless, it brought a period of revolutionary change and upheaval to a close, and pointed the way toward a new age characterized by industrial growth, nationalist rivalry, democratic politics, and mass culture.

Key Concepts, Figures, and Events

Multiplier Effect	Jeremy Bentham	Prince Klemens von Metternich
Karl Marx	New Poor Law	July Monarchy
Laissez Faire	Congress of Vienna	Reform Act

Topics for Further Thought

1. The period between 1780 and 1850 was one of revolutionary change. Why is it more accurate to refer to one "dual revolution" rather than to two separate revolutions: political and industrial?

2. The Industrial Revolution radically altered many facets of life in Europe. Describe the impact of the Industrial Revolution in terms of the technological, economic, social, and cultural changes that occurred.

3. What features of England's social, political, and economic structure paved the way for the world's First Industrial Revolution? Why was it less likely that an industrial revolution would first happen in other European countries?

4. The net result of the Industrial Revolution in the nineteenth century has long been debated by historians. While some offer an optimistic view, others present a more pessimistic one. Explain this historiographical debate by summarizing the two opposing points of view.

5. The Congress of Vienna attempted to restore order to Europe after a quarter century of revolution and war. Briefly outline the specific objectives of the Congress and assess to what degree these objectives were successfully met.

6. The forces of change brought about by the dual revolution of the early nineteenth century made political change a necessity in England. Outline the major political reforms that came about and comment on their success at adapting England's political system to the new realities of the nineteenth century.

Topics for Further Research

1. The Industrial Revolution was driven by numerous innovations in technology. Research one of the following technological developments of the nineteenth century and assess its impact on the economy and society:

Cotton Gin   Flying Shuttle
Power Loom   Steam Engine
Internal Combustion Engine   Railway

2. In the period between 1820 and 1850, there were several attempts by various groups to throw off the rule of dominant powers and to establish national independence. Research one of the following independence movements and account for the foundations of the movement as well as its success or failure:

Greece   Poland
Belgium

3. The foundations for many of the changes that reshaped European nations in the nineteenth and twentieth centuries were laid by intellectuals who had visions of a new society. Research and prepare a biographical sketch of one of the following individuals:

Pierre-Joseph Proudhon
Count Henri de Saint-Simon
Robert Owen
Charles Fourier
Friedrich Engels

4. Europe was shaken by a series of revolutions in 1848. Research the underlying causes, events, and outcome in one of the following revolutions:

France   Austria
Budapest   Prussia
Piedmont

Responding to Ideas

1. In his book *The Birth of the Modern World Society, 1815–1830,* Paul Johnson defends his choice of this 15-year span as the beginning of the modern age when he writes: "The actual birth of the modern world, delayed by the long, destructive gestation period formed by the Napoleonic Wars, could begin in full measure only when peace came and the immense new resources in finance, management, science, and technology that were now available could be put to constructive purposes." Given what you have learned about the eighteenth century and the first half of the nineteenth century, do you agree with Johnson's hypothesis? Defend your answer.

2. In his famous *The Communist Manifesto,* Karl Marx outlined a view of history which suggested that European society had progressed to the point where a revolution that would bring about a classless society was imminent. He stated: "The history of all hitherto existing societies is the history of class struggles.... Our epoch, the epoch of the bourgeoisie, possesses, however, this distinctive feature: it has simplified class antagonisms. Society as a whole is more and more splitting up into two great hostile camps, into two great classes directly facing each other: bourgeoisie and proletariat." Either defend or refute Marx's view of history, drawing on your knowledge of the sixteenth to nineteenth centuries as well as on events since *The Communist Manifesto* was published. Be sure to address to what degree you believe the study of history is the study of class struggles.

CHAPTER

8

Europe, 1850–1914:
Nation, Society, and Culture
in Upheaval

❧
CHAPTER HIGHLIGHTS

- The unification movements in Germany and Italy
- The development of democracy and a mass electorate in Europe
- The rise of Germany as a dominant European power
- The impact of Darwin's theory of evolution on European society
- Growing tensions in Europe on the eve of World War I

Nation, Society, and Culture

In contrast to the idealism of the preceding period of revolutionary struggle (1789–1848) the second half of the nineteenth century was an age of realism. After 1848, the hope of a conservative restoration turning the clock back to 1789—or even to 1815—was dead and in 1848, the year of revolutions, liberal, radical, and nationalist movements had equally failed to advance their competing visions of a better future. After 1850, visions of an idealized past or of a utopian future took second place to the realistic possibilities of the present.

Nation

In the political realm, the focus was on the power of the nation-state. The desire for power and international standing led political leaders to attempt to consolidate smaller states into larger nation-states. By 1871, this process of unification had created modern

Germany and modern Italy, altering the balance of power. Although general European war did not break out until 1914, a state of peace did not exist. The unification of Italy and Germany involved limited wars. After 1871, the major powers were rivals in a contest for power. The power of a state was initially measured by its territory, population, and military capacity; the size and international scope of its economy became increasingly important. Thus, the struggle for land and wealth between states occurred primarily outside Europe, in the form of imperialism. Imperialism, fuelled by nationalism, would eventually erupt in world war in 1914.

Even though all European countries except France and Switzerland were monarchies, the authority of the state rested on some recognition of the sovereignty of the people. Nationalism, the dominant ideology of the age, expressed the individual citizen's identity with the state and became a powerful means to mobilize populations in support of governments or movements for the foundation of new nation-states.

The power of nationalistic ideology rested upon new historical conditions, a new form of economy, and an increasingly urban society, all of which emerged in the second half of the nineteenth century. Deep and sincere national sentiment also intervened but, as the historical examples below suggest, the success of nationalism would not depend upon national sentiment, but rather on the capacity of political leaders to harness the power of the state in pursuit of national objectives.

France: Napoléon III and the Second Empire

A political adventurer led the way in cultivating popular support for the authority of the state. *Louis Napoléon Bonaparte* (1808–1873) also showed that such popularity depended upon success. He ruled as president (1848–1852) and then emperor (Napoléon III, 1852–1870) of France during years of prosperity in

which Paris was restored as the diplomatic and cultural capital of Europe. But it all ended in disaster. Prussia's overwhelming victory over France in 1870 brought Napoléon III and his Second Empire to a humiliating end, and marked the ascendancy of modern Germany as the dominant power in Central Europe.

Louis Napoléon Bonaparte's election as president of the Second Republic in December of 1848 unexpectedly elevated him from political obscurity. Following the terrible bloodshed of the June Days of the same year, the French electorate was still split between monarchists and republicans. To the monarchists, the name of Napoléon offered order in place of republican anarchy; to the republicans, it offered republican virtue in place of aristocratic corruption. Together, they voted for Louis Napoléon, giving him a lead of almost 4 million votes over his nearest rival.

For Louis Napoléon, the constitution of the Second Republic had one serious limitation: the president's term was limited to four years, without the possibility of re-election. The National Assembly, dominated by a monarchist majority, created the possibility of a presidential appeal directly to the people. Still fearful of popular radicalism in Paris, the Assembly censored the press, revised the franchise (or right of vote), by reintroducing a property qualification, and arrested leading radical deputies. In a campaign of public speeches, Louis Napoléon linked the memory of his uncle to the principle of popular sovereignty and his own leadership. In October of 1849, he announced: "The name of Napoléon is in itself a whole program. It means order, authority, religion, popular welfare at home, national dignity abroad."

On December 1–2, 1851, the army occupied Paris and the police arrested 78 National Assembly deputies. Parisians awoke to the news that the president had dissolved the National Assembly and restored universal male suffrage. (Women would not receive the vote until well into the twentieth century.) Although Louis Napoléon and his advisors desired a peaceful coup d'état, on December 4, the army killed 200 rioters in suppressing a left-wing uprising in Paris. In engineering this coup, Louis Napoléon claimed to be restoring democratic rights, and in fulfillment of this claim he introduced a new form of election by direct vote, the **plebiscite**. On two occasions, in December 1851 and December 1852, the French electorate supported Louis Napoléon and the Second Empire in a plebiscite.

Under Napoléon III's Second Empire, the French populace seemed content with the symbols rather than the substance of democracy. The economy was prosperous as the boom in railroad construction had a multiplier effect that stimulated French industries and generated employment. Napoléon III had sound advisors, knowledgeable about the functioning of the economy and interested—partly due to Saint-Simon's influence—in government assistance and planning. Legislative reform facilitated the development of joint-stock and limited-liability companies. The Second Empire created Crédit Mobilier, an

investment trust in which citizens deposited savings, which in turn financed industrial development.

The most visible sign of planning during the Second Empire was the transformation of Paris. Baron Haussmann, prefect of the Seine region, directed the work of redesigning the centre of Paris by removing crowded tenements and widening narrow streets into broad boulevards. Paris would become one of the splendours not only of Europe but of the world.

Prosperity maintained political peace for a few years. By 1860, financial scandals, dissent over foreign policy, and discontent with a censored press reawakened political criticism. Napoléon III responded by a series of liberalizing reforms that relaxed controls on the press, allowed freer debates in the legislative assembly, made ministers more responsible to elected representatives, reduced the influence of the Church on education, made schools more accessible to females, and legalized trade unions and the right to strike. These reforms came into place gradually between 1860 and 1869 and, even though they provoked criticism, Napoléon III remained popular. A plebiscite in 1870 revealed that 7.3 million approved of the emperor's policies and 1.5 million dissented.

Napoléon III aspired to emulate his uncle in restoring French prestige among nations. In 1854, he challenged the Russian claim to be the protector of all Christians in the Ottoman Empire. The ensuing Crimean War of 1854–1856 was really fought to resist Russian expansion beyond the Black Sea into the Balkans and the Eastern Mediterranean. None of the major armies (French, British, or Russian) distinguished itself in battle. More soldiers died from disease than from gunfire. The horrific conditions were brought to light by the English nursing pioneer Florence Nightingale and by reports from the battlefront from a new breed of journalist, the war correspondent. Politically, the Russians were the great losers in the war and, symbolically, Napoléon III was the victor. The Peace Congress held in Paris in 1856 accepted the Russian concessions and restored Paris as the diplomatic centre of Europe.

Louis Napoléon Bonaparte poses with his wife and son in a family portrait.

The Unification of Italy

Legend:
- Territories Annexed in 1859
- Territories Annexed in 1860
- Territories Ceded to France in 1860
- Territories Annexed in 1866
- Territories Annexed in 1870
- Boundary in 1871

who sought to create a new nation. Unification had to overcome the opposition of Austria and the Papacy, as well as the entrenched interests of political leaders attached to the existing fragmented structure.

The Risorgimento, or movement for Italian unification, originated during the French occupation of Northern Italy by the Revolutionary and Napoléonic armies. After 1815, small groups of intellectuals, students, and radicals organized secret societies, the Carbonari, and planned insurrectionary outbreaks against Austrian rule in the north, against administrative corruption in the Papal States, and against the restored Bourbon monarchy in Naples. In 1820–1821, and again in 1831, such uprisings proved to be isolated and largely futile attacks on entrenched authorities.

Out of the failed uprisings of 1831, *Giuseppe Mazzini* (1805–1872), who had himself been arrested as a conspirator, founded the Young Italy Society in Marseilles, France. Born in Genoa and the son of a doctor, Mazzini came to personify a romantic revolutionary nationalism not only for Italians but for all Europeans. Through Young Italy, he publicized the goals of Italian nationalism which aimed to bring together the principles of nationalism and liberalism. Mazzini's new Italy would be both a democracy and a republic; he aimed to achieve that goal through popular insurrection.

In quick succession, members of Young Italy joined popular insurrections in the principal cities, including Palermo, Naples, Rome, Turin, Milan, and Venice. An uprising in Rome established Mazzini as president of a radical, democratic republic. Since Rome was also the seat of the Vatican and the Papacy, its status was not just an Italian but an international question.

In a combined action to restore the Pope to Rome, 30 000 troops from Naples, Austria, and France intervened against the Republic. The defence of the city was led by *Giuseppe Garibaldi* (1807–1882), a romantic revolutionary and leading nineteenth-century exponent of guerrilla war by irregular forces. Garibaldi led his 10 000 irregulars, known as Red Shirts, in a heroic defence of the Roman Republic, but eventually they were forced to abandon the city and fled to the hills. Shortly thereafter, the last holdout of the 1848 revolutions, the Republic of Venice, surrendered to the Austrians in August of 1849.

The defeat of the Roman and Venetian republics also defeated Mazzini's vision of the Risorgimento. The task of unification needed a more centralized direction

The Unification of Italy

The struggle for the unification of Italy (1848–1871) involved an idealistic nationalism seeking liberation through popular insurrection, and an exercise in *realpolitik*, in which politicians used the power of the state to create a new unified nation. Although Italian unification would not have been possible without the idealism of the nationalists and the realism of the politicians, these two factors often acted in conflict rather than in harmony.

The making of an Italian nationality was not a "natural" or inevitable product of geography or of history, but the result of the struggle of Italian nationalists and a more expert use of political power. This task was taken up by **Count Camillo Cavour** (1810–1861), a moderate liberal aristocrat from Piedmont.

As Prime Minister of Piedmont in 1852, Cavour showed that he was not an idealist, but a realist in politics. He secured his political support through astute, even fraudulent, electoral management, and in his foreign policy, he used diplomatic cunning and threats of war to pursue his objectives. Cavour realized that he needed the assistance of powers outside Italy. He joined forces with France, first against Russia in the Crimean War and later against Austria. As a result of his diplomatic manoeuvres Cavour managed to have the Italian question discussed at the Paris Peace Congress in 1856 and to bring about the unification of Northern Italy, except for Venice, by 1860.

The initiative then passed from Cavour to Garibaldi. His irregular Red Shirts had been involved in the campaign in Lombardy, and rather than disband his private army, the guerrilla leader took 1000 soldiers to Sicily. There, his Red Shirts and peasant brigands defeated the army of the Bourbon king. The guerrilla army then invaded the mainland and quickly captured Naples.

Garibaldi's success presented a problem to Cavour. The conquering forces of radical republicanism and popular insurrection gave every indication of continuing their northward march. Cavour dispatched the Sardinian army through the Papal States, and met Garibaldi south of Rome. Garibaldi, who was more of a soldier than a politician, agreed to the union of north and south on Cavour's terms. In March 1861, the new Kingdom of Italy came into being with Victor Emmanuel II as its constitutional monarch, with an assembly elected on a limited property franchise, and with its capital at Turin in Piedmont. Cavour died only 11 weeks after the creation of his Kingdom of Italy.

As it stood in 1861, Italy was still incomplete. Venice remained in Austrian hands, and the Pope still held the remaining Papal States and the city of Rome. Once again diplomacy and war completed the task of unification. In 1866, Italy supported Prussia in its short, victorious war against Austria, and received Venice as its reward. In 1870, Napoléon III, facing war with Prussia, pulled French soldiers out of Rome. Italian troops occupied the city, the Pope retreated to the Vatican, and Rome became capital of a fully united Italy in 1871.

Guiseppe Garibaldi and his men depart Genoa in 1860 en route to Sicily during their campaign to unify Italy.

Bismarck and the Creation of Modern Germany

The unification of Germany, even more clearly than that of Italy, came not from a popular nationalist movement but from the exercise of *realpolitik*. Out of the experience of the occupation of German lands by Napoléon, and from the Romantic Movement's interest in folk traditions and history, there emerged a sense of a common culture and tradition of German-speaking peoples.

From 1815 to 1848, liberal nationalists dreamed of the creation of a unified Germany under a liberal constitution. There were, however, significant political obstacles to the realization of this vision. The German Confederation of 1815 brought together 38 states, including two larger and more powerful ones, Prussia and Austria. The purpose of this confederation was not to bring German states together, but to preserve the existing political structure of small states ruled by absolutist princes. Prussia and Austria were potential leaders of the confederation, and the lesser states were divided in their loyalty to the two rival powers. Social and economic development had begun to break down some of these divisions. In 1834, the Zollverein, or customs union, brought the northern German states, including Prussia but excluding Austria, into closer economic association. The extension of railroads and urbanization in the 1840s and 1850s also weakened the parochialism of regions, and fostered a sense that economic growth and the exercise of diplomatic influence required a larger, more unified nation-state.

The liberal nationalists had an opportunity to give substance to their dream in 1848 but, like their contemporaries' in Italy, their efforts ended in failure. As they met in the Frankfurt Assembly, they could not agree on the definition of the new German state. The "Greater Germans," who favoured the inclusion of Austria, were drawn largely from southern Catholic regions. The "Lesser Germans," who favoured the exclusion of Austria and looked to Prussian leadership, were drawn largely from northern Protestant areas. The failure of the Frankfurt Assembly and the reassertion of royal autocracy in Berlin and Vienna in 1848–1849 brought an end to the fusion of liberalism and nationalism in German unification.

Count Otto von Bismarck (1815–1898), a conservative aristocrat and ardent supporter of the Prussian monarchy against the liberal nationalists of 1848, was the unexpected agent of German unification. A man of exceptional physical strength and vitality, who as a student and as an adult had a well-deserved reputation for his consumption of food and drink, Bismarck was equally exceptional for his astute intellect. Although his memoirs suggest that he followed long-range plans, his real skill was in adroitly adapting to situations in pursuit of the broadly conceived objective of enhancing the power of his beloved Prussia. His flexibility in action also gave him a reputation for paying only lip service to long-term commitments, and for cunning—even deceit—in his pursuit of immediate goals. Bismarck's contempt for liberalism and his belief in the central role of power in politics and diplomacy were encapsulated in his famous speech to the Finance Committee of the Prussian Diet on September 29, 1862:

> Germany is not looking at Prussia's liberalism but at her power.... Prussia must preserve her power for the favourable moment, which has already several times passed. Prussia's frontiers are not suited to a healthy national life. The great questions of our times will not be decided by speeches and majority decisions—that was the mistake of 1848–1949—but by Blood and Iron.

In time, even German liberals came to accept the views of the "Iron Chancellor."

In 1864, Denmark resurrected its claim to Schleswig and Holstein, two neighbouring principalities with German-speaking populations. Infuriated by this claim, German nationalists called for action. Bismarck took the initiative by arranging for joint Austrian and Prussian military intervention. The short war demonstrated the superiority of the Prussian army over Denmark, but the victors could not agree over the future of the two conquered duchies.

In an endeavour to appeal to German public opinion, Bismarck took the unexpected step of proposing a reorganization of the German Confederation, including the creation of a national assembly elected by universal male suffrage. He knew that this proposal, in apparent contradiction to his own well-established conservative principles, would be rejected out of hand in Austria. Liberal opinion was still distrustful of Bismarck and Prussian militarism, but this initiative now raised the possibility that a long-debated and much-needed reform had a better friend in Berlin than in Vienna.

In the Austrian capital, Emperor Franz Joseph and his ministers thought that war was inevitable and they, along with informed opinion in general, thought that Austria would win any military contest. Within just seven weeks, from June to August 1866, the Austro-Prussian War was over. Prussia defeated Austria in the field and Bismarck reformed the German Confederation.

The Prussian generals, under the leadership of Helmuth von Moltke, had deployed new industrial technology to achieve victory, and pointed the way to modern warfare. Prussian soldiers had the advantage of a new needle gun or breech-loading rifle. The troops were amassed in greater numbers with greater speed by the use of the railroad, and the speed of communications was greatly enhanced by the electric telegraph. Buoyed by their success, the Prussian generals were set to march on Vienna; Bismarck, mindful of political objectives, negotiated a lenient peace.

The Peace of Prague of 1866 brought an end to the tussle between Austria and Prussia within the German Confederation. In keeping with the Italian involvement in the war, Venice joined the kingdom of Italy. A newly constituted North German Confederation excluded Austria and included an enlarged Prussia, which annexed formerly independent states by adding some 3300 square kilometres and 4.5 million in population.

The new association incorporated two thirds of the former Confederation, except for the southern German states. King William I of Prussia headed the government, which had an assembly elected by universal male suffrage. Bismarck was confident that rural voters would elect conservative landholders and not middle-class liberals. Military and foreign affairs were under the direction of the ministers of the Confederation, appointed by the king, and under Prussian control.

The four South German states, Bavaria, Württemburg, Baden, and Hesse-Darmstadt, remained outside the North German Confederation, but had signed a military alliance with Prussia. With Austria out of the picture, they also had no other option than to develop closer economic and political relations with the Prussian-dominated North German Confederation. Bismarck kept a watchful eye on France, realizing that Paris deeply distrusted the new Germany, and would try to exploit the remaining divisions among the German states. When in May 1870, Napoléon III had a resounding victory in a plebiscite, Bismarck, perceiving danger in inactivity, prepared for confrontation with France.

The Franco-Prussian War originated in a diplomatic dispute over the succession to the Spanish throne. The war's origins were petty, whereas its consequences were profound. In 1868, a revolution in Spain had resulted in the abdication of Queen Isabella II, and Madrid offered the Spanish crown to Prince Leopold of the Hohenzollern house, a distant relative of William I of Prussia. The possibility of an ally in Spain had great appeal to Bismarck but it terrified the French, who feared the prospect of a Spanish-Prussian alliance and a two-front war. Newspapers in France and Germany, encouraged by political leaders such as Bismarck, inflamed public opinion by warning that the issue at stake was nothing less than national dignity and prestige.

Meeting with King William I in Ems, Germany, the French ambassador succeeded in getting a withdrawal of the Hohenzollern candidate but, in addition, he demanded a commitment that the proposal would not be revived. The king refused this second demand, and telegraphed the results of the meeting to Bismarck. Upon receipt of the telegram, Bismarck shortened the text, making the king's refusal seem far more brusque, and released the Ems Dispatch to the press. The press release inflamed French opinion and, on the call to defend the nation's honour, Napoléon III took the

The Unification of Germany

(light)	Territories Annexed by Prussia as of 1866
(diagonal)	Territories Ceded by France, 1871
(dark)	Territories Joining Prussia to form North German Confederation, 1867
——	Boundary of the German Confederation, 1815
- - - -	Boundary of the North German Confederation, 1867

foolhardy step of declaring war against Prussia on July 19, 1870.

Using the modern methods which had proven so successful against Austria, including the rapid movement of 500 000 troops to the front by railroad, the Prussians achieved a stunning victory in the Franco-Prussian War. The capture of Napoléon III and 100 000 French soldiers at Sedan in September 1870 led to the collapse of the Second Empire. The war continued for another four months. Paris lay under siege, and the population had to resort to eating their pets and rodents to avoid starvation. The Treaty of Frankfurt, May 1871, imposed harsh terms: the provinces of Alsace and Lorraine were ceded to Germany; France had to pay 5 billion francs and endure German occupation for the three years it would take to complete the payment. To add insult to injury, King William I was proclaimed German Emperor over a unified nation, now including the four southern states, at the Hall of Mirrors in Versailles, formerly the seat of Louis XIV, the Sun King and the glory of France.

The Austrian Empire

In contrast to the consolidation of the new nations of Italy and Germany, the great autocratic Austrian Empire was weakened rather than strengthened by the forces of nationalism. In the aftermath of the revolutions of 1848–1849, the Habsburg monarchy appeared victorious over the forces of nationalism and liberalism. In an age of nationalism, however, the Austrian Empire was increasingly becoming an anachronism. It was a dynastic state, not a nation-state. Its territories and peoples were thrown together as part of the hereditary lands of the Habsburg dynasty. Under Franz Joseph, the young king who gave new resolve to the forces of reaction in 1848 and who would survive until 1916, the purpose of Habsburg rule was to preserve that territorial inheritance and, if possible, to extend its boundaries. For this task, the monarchy had the support of the landed aristocracy, the Catholic Church, and an extensive bureaucracy and army largely under the direction of German-speaking officials.

For the national minorities, Habsburg rule, in spite of its oppressive qualities, was at least a known quantity. National separation, even if an attainable political objective, presented the prospect of replacing Habsburg control by the external influence of either the Hohenzollerns from Bismarck's new German Empire, or the Romanovs from czarist Russia. This balance of contending nationalist and dynastic interests became even more complex with the decline of the Ottoman Empire in the Balkans. Here Slavic nationalism created new possibilities for Russian influence, whereas in Vienna, Francis Joseph and his advisors wished to fend off Russian intrigue and at the same time exploit the weakness of the Ottoman Turks. The explosive mix of nationalist ambition and great power rivalry made the Austro-Hungarian Empire and the Balkans the powder keg that would ignite a much larger conflict in 1914.

Czarist Russia

Russia, the other great autocratic monarchy, was caught between the desire to preserve a conservative aristocratic order and the need for economic and industrial reform. Russia's defeat in the Crimean War, 1854–1856, demonstrated the need for industrialization of the economy and modernization of the army. Under Alexander II, a cautious but moderate reformer who ruled between 1855 and 1881, the difficult task of reform commenced.

The most significant change was the **emancipation** of 22.5 million serfs in 1861. This reform had to accommodate the powerful influence of the Russian gentry who feared the loss of their income from land, their control over the peasantry, and their legal privileges. The peasantry paid the price of reform: while legally free and in possession of limited plots of land, the peasants had to pay an indemnity to the state for their emancipation.

The gentry and the reformers had feared that emancipation would create a landless and rootless rural population. Consequently, traditional peasant communes continued to control land usage under the customary open-field system and to restrict the movement of peasants away from communal villages. The peasantry were still trapped in a poverty made worse by an increase in population. Russian export of grain grew rapidly with the extension of the railroads but, at the same time, grain prices fell sharply. Peasants found themselves having to produce more grain for less income while having to feed larger families and work under a system of land use which discouraged innovation. Under these conditions, the additional hardship of a bad harvest readily transformed discontent into violent protest.

A typical Russian village around 1870.
(The Granger Collection, New York)

With the encouragement of the government, the first wave of industrialization occurred in the 1860s. Railroad construction and associated industrial development led to the growth of cities and to the creation of a new working class. Like the first generation of industrial workers elsewhere, these wage earners experienced exploitive conditions with low pay and no protection by state legislation. Some working-class leaders began to look favourably on Marx's analysis of industrial capitalism and to a revolutionary solution to their oppression.

Czar Alexander II, his bureaucracy, and the aristocracy had only cautiously introduced reform. When faced with criticism and discontent, and in reaction to a nationalist uprising in Poland in 1863 (which was partly under Russian domination), the czar reverted to a policy of repression. The small but nonetheless growing ranks of the intelligentsia remained troubled by the backward conditions of their homeland. The populists looked to the peasantry as a source of popular insurrection rehabilitating Russian traditions rather than simply imitating Western practices. Faced with increased state repression, others were attracted to the ideas of the anarchists, and others still saw no hope for change except by violence.

In 1881, one such terrorist's bomb succeeded in assassinating Alexander II. Contrary to the assassin's expectations, the death of the czar did not provoke a general uprising, but rather introduced a new and prolonged period of repression under the new czar, Alexander III. After 1881, Russia seemed to move in a direction contrary to trends in Western Europe. In Russia, the forces of autocracy grew in strength; in Western Europe, the period after 1870 marked the advent of the new politics of democracy.

The Advent of Democracy

The Creation of a Mass Electorate

Between 1850 and 1914, most countries implemented a broad franchise, if not universal male suffrage. In 1871, both the new German Empire and the new Third Republic in France had elections based on "democratic" suffrage of adult male citizens. In Great Britain, after 1867, urban male householders could vote in parliamentary elections. By 1914, even conservative Russia and Austria had introduced universal male suffrage.

Between 1815 and 1848, the prospect of a mass electorate had terrified conservatives and liberals, yet when democratic politics arrived, the predicted disaster did not occur. In fact, conservative politicians, Otto von Bismarck in Germany and Benjamin Disraeli in Great Britain, granted the vote to the working class. When the widened electorate went to the polls, the winners were conventional politicians drawn largely from the landholders or upper middle class, who espoused conservative to moderate liberal beliefs. The most potent expression of popular feeling was not for radical reform, but for militant nationalism. On the other hand, radicals and socialists, who claimed to be the politicians of the people, did not immediately win the support of voters; when they did win, they did not remake their societies into more egalitarian social democracies either.

This result was not simply a historical accident; it was an outcome of the new politics of modern states and mass electorates. A politician once remarked that war was too important a matter to be left to the generals; similarly, elections were too important to be left to the voters. Even though popular franchise and regular elections were instituted, the power of elected representatives to control state finances and to hold ministers responsible for their acts varied widely between states. Given the entrenched political influence of the landed interest and the pace of rapid urbanization, rural and more conservative communities tended to be overrepresented and urban populations underrepresented in legislative assemblies. Within cities themselves, the drawing of constituency boundaries had become an exact science. Various strategies were used to enhance the weight of moderate, property-owning, middle-class suburbs in comparison to that of working-class neighbourhoods.

France: The Third Republic

The Third Republic was born out of the humiliating defeat dealt by Prussia in 1870, and the savage class war of the *Paris Commune* in 1871. After the collapse of Napoléon III's Second Empire, the new government of the Third Republic was elected on the basis of universal male suffrage. Paris, whose population had been under siege for four months, once again found itself out of step with the provinces. The elections returned a monarchist majority prepared to accept the German terms of peace. To the people of Paris, the politicians were traitors. To make matters worse, the government approved the landlords' claim for back rent accrued during the siege of the city.

The people of Paris took to the streets to oppose the newly elected government. Modelling themselves on the revolutionary government of 1793–1794, they created the Paris Commune under the leadership of radical democrats, with the backing of the socialists. After six weeks, the army of the Third Republic suppressed the insurrection with unprecedented savagery. In its final days, the Commune killed about 100 hostages, including the Archbishop of Paris. Estimates vary, but at least 20 000 Communards were executed as political prisoners in the week following the end of the street fighting, and many of those fatalities came as summary executions without benefit of trial. The experience of the Commune decimated the French left for more than a decade, and it embittered and weakened the radical cause throughout Europe. The Commune became a symbol of Parisian and republican valour, and its memory persisted in the mutual fears and hatreds of the respectable bourgeoisie and the radical working class.

The monarchist majority of the first government of the Third Republic hoped to establish order with a restored monarchy, but it overlooked the political lesson of the Second Empire. Napoléon III had shown that **universal suffrage** and authoritarian government were quite compatible, as long as the economy was prosperous and the populace, through the symbols of democracy, was made to feel part of national life. Here the monarchists were an absolute failure. They had trouble finding a potential king, and the Bourbon candidate was unwilling to accept the tricolour, the national flag and symbol of the Republic. Without a king, the monarchists were left with the task of recreating the republic.

The monarchists, never comfortable with a republican constitution, made several attempts to reform the constitution. In 1879, General Patrice MacMahon (1808–1893), president and formerly marshal of France, failed in his attempt to protect the royalist cause by dismissing the government and influencing the election. A second coup from the right also failed in 1889, when General Georges Boulanger (1837–1891) plotted without success to restore a Bonapartist empire. The right wing attracted royalists and Bonapartists— who defended the Catholic Church against republican secularism—as well as defenders of the army— who included nationalists seeking revenge against Germany for the humiliation of 1871. These groups, all of whom associated republicanism with national weakness and dishonour, also espoused a virulent anti-Semitism which identified the Jews as a common scapegoat for the alleged weaknesses of the Republic.

Anti-Semitism split French society during the Dreyfus affair, which lasted from 1894 to 1906, after having reached explosive proportions in 1898–1899. In 1894, Captain Alfred Dreyfus (1859–1935), a Jewish officer on the French General Staff, was court-martialled for allegedly passing secrets to Germany. The espionage continued after Dreyfus's imprisonment, and charges were then laid against another member of the General Staff. In court proceedings, army officers attempted a cover-up, even forging evidence against Dreyfus. When these matters came to light, French society was polarized into two hostile camps. On the one side, the patriots of the right defended the charges against Dreyfus; on the other side, the defenders of the Republic on the left exonerated Dreyfus and charged that the conduct of the General Staff brought dishonour to France. Eventually, Dreyfus was acquitted and readmitted into the army, but the case had radically polarized French society, and left long-lasting wounds. Deep divisions in French society would persist through World War I, and be exposed even more dramatically in the politics of the Vichy government and France's collaboration with Nazi Germany during World War II.

The French left, decimated by the suppression of the Paris Commune in 1871, only began to revive in the 1880s. The socialists were the heirs of the revolutionary tradition and, from memories of the Commune, were reluctant to collaborate with the bourgeois politicians of the Republic. Nonetheless, with the Republic in danger from the right, with Boulanger's failed plot in 1889, and more particularly with the Dreyfus Affair in the 1890s, the socialists came to support republican institutions.

Between 1789 and 1871, France had a history of political upheavals leading to the contrasting alternatives of authoritarian and republican governments. By 1914, the Third Republic had established a continuity in its institutions. This resolution of a history of political conflict did not arrive overnight, but was a result of working out a political settlement reflecting the character of French society. A minority on the right, still entrenched in the powerful enclaves of landholders, the army, and the Church, failed to dismantle the Republic.

The strength of the Republic lay in its electoral support among the urban middle class and among the small landowners, independent businessmen, and shopkeepers of provincial France. Industrial development lagged behind that of its competitors; consequently, the French working class was smaller. This mix of political ideology and electoral support created the broad consensus that emerged in support of the Republic.

Bismarck's Germany, 1871–1890

Of the leading conservative politicians of the late nineteenth century, Bismarck was among the most adventuresome in appealing for popular support. His efforts to manage the electorate came not from any constitutional necessity, but from his own sense of how his political power could be enhanced by popular backing.

The constitution of the German Empire of 1871 provided a symbolic rather than substantive measure of democracy. The democratic element, the parliament or Reichstag, was elected by universal male suffrage, but had very limited powers. As a talking shop, it could not initiate legislation but it could obstruct its passage. On financial matters, the Reichstag had the power to approve budgets, but it mysteriously failed to do so. Ministers were not responsible to the elected representatives, but were appointed and dismissed by the Kaiser, who by hereditary succession was the king of Prussia.

German constitutional structure did have one liability in that the potential existed for resentment against Prussian dominance, and to avoid this potential for fragmentation, Bismarck worked to secure support for his policies. During the 1870s, his main source of opposition lay in the Catholic or Centre Party, strongest in the Rhineland and the South German states. To counter its influence, Bismarck adopted a national secular policy of *Kulturkampf*. He endeavoured to restrict church influence on education and on matters such as marriage and divorce. He appealed to the secular views of the National Liberals, who had supported him in the policy of unification in the 1860s. The policy of *Kulturkampf* proved unsuccessful, for not only did the Catholic or Centre Party continue to grow stronger, but Prussian conservatives, including Lutheran pastors, feared the reduced influence of the different churches on the state.

In 1878, Bismarck shifted course by abandoning the policy of *Kulturkampf* and turned his attention to the new enemies, the socialists. In 1875, the Social Democratic Party (SPD) was formed out of a union of Marxists and followers of the German economist Ferdinand Lassalle, who in the 1860s had argued for political action to secure political and social reforms. The SPD quickly built support in urban working-class constituencies. Bismarck, who once called the socialists and their working-class supporters "the menacing band of robbers with whom we share our largest towns," decided to nip the movement in its youth. In 1878, he passed an antisocialist law which declared socialism to be an enemy of the state; it also restricted newspapers as well as meetings and other activities of the social democrats and their allies, the trade unions. Bismarck recognized that, in dealing with the SPD, a policy of suppression would be insufficient, so, between 1881 and 1888, he passed the most advanced social legislation in Europe. The legislation introduced sickness and accident insurance, and most innovatively, old age pensions.

As a consummate politician, Bismarck recognized that, even with the authoritarian structure of the German Empire, electoral politics mattered. Through various strategies, the introduction of universal male suffrage in the 1860s, the *Kulturkampf* policy of the 1870s, the antisocialist law, and the social legislation in the 1880s, he tried to cultivate popular support to weaken the appeal of his opponents. Even this policy had its limits. With rapid industrialization and urbanization in the late nineteenth century, the appeal of the SPD grew until it became the most popular political party in the Empire. Aware of this danger, Bismarck contemplated introducing restrictions on the franchise. The young Kaiser Wilhelm II, wanting to be popular, and anxious to be free of Bismarck's domineering influence in foreign affairs, dismissed his aged chancellor in 1890. With SPD strength growing, the weakness of the Reichstag in relation to the Kaiser's ministers was exposed. The German state, its Kaiser, and his ministers needed a source of popular appeal beyond the domestic politics of social reform. In a climate of intensified international rivalry from 1890 onward, militant nationalism provided the means to unite the German state and the German people without meaningful democratic reform.

Britain in the Age of Disraeli and Gladstone: 1867–1894

Great Britain had had a long history of peaceful government through king and Parliament. This tradition of parliamentary rule had shown a capacity for reform. By the mid-1860s, the issue of the vote had been resurrected and the question was not so much whether a further extension of the vote would take place, but when and by whom. The extension of the vote proceeded by measured stages. In 1867, **Benjamin Disraeli** and the Conservatives passed a Second Reform Act, which granted the vote to male urban working-class householders. In 1884, **William Gladstone** and the

Liberals extended the vote on the same terms to male householders in rural constituencies.

Unlike many in his party, Benjamin Disraeli (1804–1881) was an optimist and knew how to seize opportunity. His optimism rested on his belief that a natural alliance existed between a paternalistic landed interest and a deferential working class, whereas a natural animosity existed between workers and the middle-class manufacturers who supported Gladstone's Liberals. In a famous speech at the Crystal Palace in 1872, Disraeli redefined the appeal of conservatism across class lines by calling on tradition, on patriotism, and on paternalism, embodied in three key words: "Monarchy, Empire, and Social Reform."

When Disraeli became prime minister, 1874–1880, he based his policies on these three principles. He persuaded Queen Victoria to come out of her reclusive widowhood after the death of her husband Prince Albert in 1861. From Disraeli's influence, the modern monarchy and the modern royal family came into existence as a symbol of tradition closely attached to the values of the Conservative Party.

Disraeli also appealed to pride in empire. He made Victoria Empress of India and purchased shares in the Suez Canal. He pursued an aggressive colonial policy, engaging in wars in Afghanistan and Southern Africa. His ministry also passed the most innovative social reforms of the second half of the nineteenth century, improving the legal status of trade unions and introducing legislation on consumer protection, industrial safety, and the first legal measure for public housing. On this basis, Disraeli helped build the modern Conservative Party by identifying it with traditional institutions such as the monarchy, by making it the party of imperialism, and by linking it to a program of social reform.

Under the leadership of William Gladstone (1809–1898), the Liberals' rallying cry was "Peace, Retrenchment, and Reform." By peace, they advocated free trade and opposed costly foreign and colonial adventures. By retrenchment, the Liberals espoused a laissez faire policy in

Benjamin Disraeli was a prominent British politician and personal friend of Queen Victoria.

which the role of government was strictly limited, and costs and taxes were reduced as far as possible. By reform, they had in mind doing away with outmoded laws that benefited the privileged. Accordingly, the Liberals reformed the army and the civil service to eliminate patronage, enabled students who were not Anglicans to graduate from Oxford and Cambridge Universities, and, in 1870, introduced national primary education.

Ultimately, it was their own slogan of peace that proved to be the Liberals' undoing. Over 12 000 Bulgarian Christians had been killed by Turkish forces in 1876, yet Disraeli, for strategic reasons, backed the Ottoman Empire in its war with Russia, 1877–1878. The enormous public interest in these moral and strategic questions was given a renewed charge by William Gladstone in 1879–1880. For the first time in British and European history, a politician embarked on a modern political campaign. In his Scottish campaign of 1879, Gladstone travelled by train from Liverpool to Edinburgh, stopping at towns on the way, and delivered speeches condemning the immorality and costs of Disraeli's imperial policy. After a second Scottish campaign in 1880, the electorate tossed out the Conservatives, and gave Gladstone and his Liberals a majority.

Gladstone, who had supported the cause of national liberation in Europe, wrestled with the imperial conflicts in Africa and nationalism in Ireland. When he introduced his Irish Home Rule Bill in 1886, he split the Liberal Party. As a result, the conservatives—the party of patriotism and empire—became the dominant party in British politics for the next two decades.

The difficulties which the Liberals experienced with imperialism in Africa and with Home Rule for Ireland were symptomatic of more fundamental changes at work. After 1885, the Conservative Party was not simply a party of the landed interest, for it won a majority of urban middle-class constituencies. These voters were interested in stability rather than reform, and were attracted to the Conservatives' appeal to the patriotic symbols of monarchy and empire. On the other hand, the Liberals' reluctance to take up social reform led radical reformers and trade unionists to look to socialist alternatives, and to the formation of a working-class political party. Middle-class support of the Conservatives and the divisions within the ranks of the Liberals increased. Thus, the advent of democracy in Great Britain had the paradoxical result of strengthening not the forces of reform but the forces of tradition.

Europe in the Age of the Masses

The political transformations examined so far—the consolidation of nation-states, the appeal of nationalism, and the advent of democracy—occurred within a novel social and cultural context. While many of the features of this new urban and industrial society originated in the period prior to 1850, the process of industrialization was greatly accelerated in the second half of the nineteenth century. These changes—the growth in population, the expansion of commerce and industry, and the rapid pace of urbanization—restructured European society. Some social commentators thought that they were living in a new "age of the masses."

Despite the remarkable growth in population (from 266 million to 401 million from 1850 to 1900), the economy, whether measured by volume of trade or by value of industrial output, grew at an accelerated rate. Consequently, the standard of living of the majority, including landowning peasants and industrial wage earners, improved in the period from 1850 to 1914. The most dramatic increase in living standards occurred between 1873 and 1896, the so-called great depression years. In this period, prices fell, partly due to transportation improvements and increased production. Consequently, as the cost of goods declined, persons with a steady income experienced a remarkable improvement in living standards. Regularly employed, skilled wage earners in Britain saw their real income increase by 70–100 percent. From the mid-1890s to 1914, however, the trend was reversed: rising prices and business profits increased; middle-class investors benefited, whereas working-class consumers faced higher prices and greater employment insecurity.

The two decades prior to the outbreak of war in 1914 witnessed increased labour unrest and social strife, but the new pattern of middle-class affluence and of a more prosperous life for most of the working class continued during this time of stress.

The Second Industrial Revolution

Like the first one, the so-called Second Industrial Revolution (1880–1939) was characterized by a number of significant technological breakthroughs and new principles in the organization of production and labour. Some developments which we associate with the early twentieth century originated prior to 1900. It is easy to focus on the new telephone, electric lights, phonograph, motion pictures, and automobile, but we should not forget the less striking but equally significant developments of the late nineteenth century. Inventors were still finding new uses for steam power, and railroad construction proceeded at a faster pace than in the 1840s and 1850s. Between 1850 and 1870, world steam power increased 4.5 times and the length of railway track 8 times.

Although the development of the internal-combustion engine and the automobile can be traced back to the nineteenth century, in the beginning, motor cars were only a luxury replacement of the horse and carriage for the very rich. The most significant innovations in personal transport in the 1880s and 1890s were the humble but pervasive bicycle, and the electric streetcar. Electric streetcars, including subway systems in London and Paris, served as the daily form of transport for millions of riders by the beginning of the twentieth century.

The Second Industrial Revolution involved the use of new sources of energy comparable to the role of steam in the First Industrial Revolution. This time, scientific research played a more significant role. New discoveries in physics and chemistry led to multiple applications of electricity. The development of the internal-combustion engine was dependent on a new fuel: refined petroleum. Germany and the United States took the lead in the new science-based technologies of chemicals and electrical engineering. With larger domestic markets, Germany (with a population of 68 million) and the United States (92 million) surpassed Great Britain (45 million) in industrial productivity and technological innovation. London remained the world's financial centre and Britain the dominant player in global shipping, commerce, and investment. Japan also experienced its industrial revolution in this period and became the first non-European state to join the industrial nations.

The new technologies required larger amounts of capital than the pioneering family enterprises of the First Industrial Revolution. Though the small firm employing fewer than 50 people still was more common, the new industries, most evident in Germany and the United States, were larger. Krupp, the German steel, engineering, and munitions giant of the Ruhr Valley, employed 72 people in 1848, and 12 000 in 1873. Larger establishments, financed and owned as joint-stock enterprises, began to develop control of various stages of production in what was termed "vertical integration." Corporations owned firms involved in extracting and processing raw materials, in manufacturing the finished goods, and in the transport and retailing of products. This concentration of ownership had not yet become common, but the trend was now evident. In the United States and Germany, the steel, chemical, electrical, and petroleum industries, large corporations, such as cartels and trusts, dominated whole sectors of the economy, were interrelated with financial institutions, and their chief executives had close links with political leaders.

New machines also facilitated the ongoing transition from craft production to factory manufacture. In the 1870s, American-designed machines converted shoe and boot making by hand into factory production, and cobblers, who practised an ancient and prestigious craft, were reduced to shoe repairers. Similarly, another American invention, the Singer sewing machine, allowed factories and small workshops, largely employing women at piece rates, to replace tailors and seamstresses. The production of machine-produced clothing went hand in hand with a revolution in retailing. Until the 1870s, clothes were made to measure, or the less well-to-do purchased second-hand clothing. Now new department stores and retail chain stores sold ready-to-wear garments produced by the operatives of sewing machines.

The spread of retail stores also created new forms of employment that were part of the larger expansion of the service sector using "white-collar" labour. This expansion was particularly evident in office work, both in private business and in government. Again technological innovations had an impact, especially with the introduction of the typewriter and the telephone, which brought about an increase in the number of women employed in office work. Men, nonetheless, still greatly outnumbered women in offices up to 1914; the rapid feminization of this work force occurred during World War I.

Religion, Science, and Darwinism

Church and Society

The new urban environment was secular, and the churches were losing the battle for the allegiance of the masses. In England, a religious census in 1851 shocked contemporaries: only 50 percent of the population attended church and, in some working-class areas, fewer than 10 percent. In Catholic countries, the Church, led by the Pope, pronounced itself the determined opponent of the forces of secularism and modernization. In the *Syllabus of Errors* in 1864, Pope Pius IX rejected any idea that "the Roman Pontiff can, and ought to, reconcile himself and come to terms with progress, liberalism, and modern civilization." The identification of the Church with conservatism made anticlericalism, in countries such as France and Italy, a owerful part of the creed of reason and progress among liberal reformers and working-class radicals.

In the 1880s and 1890s, advocates of social Catholicism in France and Germany criticized the impact of industrial capitalism, and developed programs of social reform addressing the needs of the working class. Similarly, in Protestant countries, churches began to see the need to address questions of social reform. This social gospel, strongest in Britain among Baptists, Methodists, some elements within the Church of England, and new religious organizations, such as the Salvation Army, created a climate more accepting of social legislation and even of democratic socialism. Nonetheless, these agencies of various churches largely failed to halt the growing indifference toward religion among working and middle-class city dwellers.

Darwin and Darwinism

A more fundamental challenge to religious orthodoxy came from studies in natural science resulting in the theory of evolution of Darwin and Wallace. When **Charles Darwin** published his *On the Origin of Species* in 1859, religious controversy already existed over the biblical account of human origins from Adam and Eve. Discoveries of fossils of early humans in Europe extended the biological history of human beings far beyond the chronology of the Bible. In addition, new historians studied the Scriptures as historical documents and questioned their veracity. There existed indeed an atmosphere of intellectual and religious controversy. The idea of evolution was also not new in 1859 (in France, Jean-Baptiste de Lamarck had pioneered the idea of animal evolution in the early nineteenth century). What Darwin provided was a new range of biological evidence presented in a careful, coherent, and persuasive manner.

Darwin's originality lay in a new explanation for the development of biological species over time. Darwin borrowed from Thomas Malthus the idea that nature was extremely fertile. Darwin postulated that species changed by the elimination of their less-adapted individuals through evolutionary time (the fittest surviving by leaving more offspring). This idea of natural selection was summed up in social philosopher Herbert Spencer's phrase, "the survival of the fittest." Darwin's theory on the mechanism of evolution by natural selection was immediately extrapolated to humans. For moralists and theologians, Darwin had thus transformed the understanding of the biological and the moral universe as well. Instead of being a moral example, nature, as the poet Alfred Lord Tennyson described it, was "red in tooth and claw."

Darwin's theory of evolution was applied to support views about human society. Often these views, referred to as "social Darwinism," were quite at odds with Darwin's theory, but they reflected the strong influence of the concept of evolution by natural selection. Herbert Spencer advanced the case that individualism and the competitive nature of capitalism were simply the expression of natural laws. In contrast, some followers of Marx, for example Friedrich Engels, claimed that Marx had reached an understanding of the laws of historical development just as Darwin had perceived the laws governing biological development. Both theories emphasized the process of progressive change, and both stressed that such changes were a product of conflict and were determined by forces beyond human control.

Late-nineteenth-century commentators applied Darwin's

Darwin's controversial *On the Origin of Species* drew much criticism, such as this cartoon depicting him as an ape.

ideas to conflicts between nations and between human groups identified as races. These theorists stressed that struggle was an inherent part of the human condition, and that success went inevitably to the most powerful. Social Darwinism was most influential in two countries: Germany, a new country concerned with its national stature and with the ethnic minorities of Central Europe, and the United States, which was warring with Native Americans, inventing new ways to segregate African Americans after emancipation, and seeking to justify a subordinate status for new immigrants.

In Britain, Victorian society portrayed itself as the pinnacle of human achievement and other peoples were classified as unprogressive barbarians, or as childlike primitives of the human family. These ideas were usefully applied during the new age of imperialism, when European colonial powers were intervening in Asia, Africa, and the Pacific and reducing once autonomous cultures and peoples to a subordinate status.

European Civilization Reassessed

While confidence in reason, science, and progress continued as a commonplace assumption until World War I, a significant minority of creative artists, scientists, and intellectuals of the age began to question this certainty. This pre-1914 generation established the intellectual and cultural framework for the more troubled, sceptical, and disordered world of the twentieth century.

Friedrich Nietzsche (1844–1900)

Among those who challenged the belief in progress and human reason, **Friedrich Nietzsche**, an original and deeply troubled German philosopher, exerted an unsettling influence on his contemporaries. Even a century later, he continues to cast a probing light on the shallow presumptions of our culture. Nietzsche questioned the emphasis on reason in Western civilization and asserted that creativity rested upon the human will. In his famous phrase, "God is dead," he not only challenged the received wisdom of Christianity, but argued

Class, Gender, and the Edwardians

The late nineteenth century was a period of rapid social change spurred by economic pressures, feminism, socialism, patriotism, and war. Well known to most students of history are the major political movements, the breakthroughs in technology, and the diplomatic manoeuvring of nation-states. Less well known is the experience of ordinary people who lived during this time of rapid and profound change. Below are brief descriptions of the lives of two people: Lady Violet Brandon from England's upper class and Fred Mills, a semiskilled worker.

Lady Violet Brandon

Lady Violet Brandon was born into an upper-class family that perceived itself in a national rather than a local sense, and it followed seasonal migrations. Her father's ancestral home in Norfolk was so large that she could not remember the number of rooms it contained; although Lady Violet did remember that there were two grand halls, a large and a small dining room, a library, parlors, numerous bedrooms, a nursery, a china room, a schoolroom, and many other rooms. The house was well staffed by a wide assortment of servants ranging from butlers, footmen, and valets to a governess, nurse, cook, and numerous maids. These servants looked after the Norfolk home only. As well, the family had a home in London, a country estate in Ireland, and a villa on the Mediterranean where they spent the winter.

Lady Violet was one of five children who, although she enjoyed a luxurious lifestyle, was very restricted in her childhood. The four girls in the family received their entire education at home from a governess and private instructors. Their education included foreign languages, art, literature, and music. At mealtime, the younger children ate their meals separate from their parents, usually in the schoolroom or nursery.

As a child, Lady Violet and her siblings saw little of their parents. On rare occasions, they "went down scrubbed up after tea" or may have seen their mother in the garden; Lady Violet noted: "We were frightened of her, quite frightened of her I think. But we did adore her." The children saw their father even less as he was often away speaking in elections or attending social functions. As a result of the limited time spent with their mother and father the role of parent and playmate was often filled by servants with the children's nurse playing a particularly important role.

As the children grew older, they were more often invited to share time with their parents, reading from great works of literature, playing tennis, or just sitting and talking. The highlight of young Lady Violet's life came when she was introduced to the London social scene. "It was something I looked forward to tremendously..." commented Lady Violet. "There was a great sort of excitement spread about coming out, and you thought you were going to be free. We knew very few young men in our ordinary life till we came out." Even "coming out" did not remove the restrictions placed on a young woman's life.

At dinner parties, Lady Violet's position as a daughter of a marquis required that she often be seated next to an elderly host; at dances her mother insisted that she follow social conventions by continually changing partners, and even walks in the park required a chaperone. This sheltered life came suddenly to a halt in 1914 when the necessities of war thrust Lady Violet into the role of nurse with less leisure but with the full freedom of an adult for the first time in her life.

Fred Mills

Fred Mills was one of 12 children born over a 20-year span to a farm labourer and his wife. Although Fred never remembered there being any more than seven children in the home together, a family of this size meant certain poverty on the meager wages of a farm labourer. At school, Fred was continually reminded of the superiority of other children, such as the farmers' daughters who rode bicycles to school or the children of craftspeople.

The elegance of the lawn party (right) of the upper class contrasts sharply with the rustic nature of an English farm-family home (below).

At the worst of times, the Mills family was forced to turn to the church for support in the form of parish relief and, even during the best of times, the family was partly dependent on charity. Fred often received bread and jam after school from a neighbour who would give it to him with the stern warning: "If you don't stop swearing I shan't give you no more." The children also begged strangers for money or for old clothes. The homes Fred lived in throughout his life were always small with at most three bedrooms, a living room, and a lean-to.

Even with charity and begging, the family barely had enough to survive. The boys wore no underclothing; they went barefoot in the summer and were always underfed. Two meals a day consisted of tea and bread, sometimes with homemade jam, and the main meal served at midday consisted of some sort of batter or suet pudding; they never had milk to drink. Fred Mills was not a strong child, small from birth and undernourished much of his life. Nonetheless, by the age of seven he was already earning money for the family by running errands or delivering eggs before and after school. Unlike Lady Violet Brandon, restrictions created by social conventions were the least of his worries; survival was what preoccupied Fred for much of his life.

that the individual could only find meaning and purpose through exertion of the human spirit. He saw that the prevailing trends of the age, the rise of mass culture, the emergence of democratic politics, and the reforming energy of socialism, were all sources of delusion and weakness. He was equally critical of the pretences of bourgeois culture, and thought that only exceptional individuals could fulfil their creative potential through superior force of character.

Nietzsche's reputation has been adversely affected by his personal association with Richard Wagner, the musical genius who dedicated his art to German nationalism, and by the subsequent use of some of Nietzche's ideas to justify atrocities committed by Hitler and the Third Reich. Nietzsche was critical of the militarism, nationalism, and anti-Semitism of his own time. His insight into the limitations of human reason, his perception that science was more of a human creation than an objective description of nature, and his effort to come to terms with the sources of human creativity struck a responsive chord in the thinking of other philosophers, artists, and scientists of his age.

The New Physics

The most revolutionary challenge to the certainties of science came from scientists themselves. In physics, for example, Isaac Newton's synthesis of the laws of motion in the late seventeenth century provided a vision of an ordered universe and a model of scientific truth resting on the precision of mathematics. This Newtonian universe now came under scrutiny, as scientists explored those features of the structure of matter and the dimensions of space for which existing explanations were inadequate. From the work of Marie Curie (1867–1934) on radium and radioactivity, and from other scientists' work on the atom, the old view of matter as solid was challenged. The subatomic world did not behave as a mini-universe according to Newton's laws. The mysterious properties of these particles could only be explained by the new theory of quantum physics formulated by German physicist Max Planck (1858–1947). Probabilities rather than fixed laws provide a better explanation for the behaviour of matter and energy than do Newton's laws.

The new work at the subatomic level also had implications for the grander dimension of the cosmos. For Albert Einstein (1879–1955), a German Jewish mathematical genius, the assumption that matter and energy,

or time and space, were fixed absolutes failed to explain natural phenomena in relation to the speed of energy or light. In his theory of relativity (1905), Einstein put forward the revolutionary hypothesis that time and space were dependent on the frame of reference of the observer. In his famous equation, $e = mc^2$, he demonstrated that, the equivalence of matter and energy.

The new quantum physics and the theory of relativity required a grasp of advanced mathematics, which widened the gap that existed between the understanding of the scientists and the common-sense view of the educated public. The new physics also challenged the idea of an objective, value-free science independent of the observer. In both scientific and humanistic learning, in the study of natural phenomena and human thought, the observer now had a greater role in making the subject intelligible.

Sigmund Freud and the Subconscious

The new uncertainty was also evident in the new science of psychology, which studied the human mind and personality. In the course of the nineteenth century, medical scientists had come to a better understanding of how the brain functions, and early psychologists had attempted to draw conclusions about human and animal behaviour through controlled experiments. *Sigmund Freud* (1856–1939), a Jewish Viennese doctor who treated people suffering from hysteria and other mental disorders, formulated the psychoanalytical theory of the human personality.

In his research, Freud used both the meticulous observation of the scientist and the intuitive insight of the therapist. In fact, many of Freud's ideas arose from intensive introspection of his own psychological make-up and childhood experiences. From his studies, he became convinced that the existing presumptions of human rationality neglected the submerged, subconscious roots of human behaviour. In Freud's view, the psychic life of the individual was characterized by conflict between subconscious desires and the restraints imposed by society through the conscious level of thought and morality. He identified dreams as a window on this internal civil war and, as a therapist, sought to free individuals from anxieties and neuroses by bringing subconscious desires and repressed childhood experiences to the level of consciousness.

Freud's ideas were controversial in his own time and have continued to be the subject of intense debate. According to some observers, his theories of human

"Classes and Masses":
ELITE AND MASS CULTURE

 During the latter half of the nineteenth century, the diversification and enrichment of cultural and leisure pursuits affected the lives and values both of the affluent middle class and the financially more restrained but numerically much larger lower-middle and working classes. Differences in disposable income and in taste produced two cultures. One appealed to the affluent elite, or what the English called the "classes," and another served popular audiences, or what somewhat derisively were called the "masses." By the end of the century, the clear lines that divided the classes were beginning to blur in the fields of sports and entertainment, much to the chagrin of the upper and affluent middle classes.

The great public cultural institutions associated with nineteenth-century cities—art galleries, museums, libraries, theatres, opera houses, concert halls, and symphony orchestras — reflected a middle-class quest for cultural enrichment. In addition, technical innovations in printing and publishing made books much cheaper, and created a modern reading public anxious for the latest works of the great novelists of the nineteenth century. In addition to these cultural pursuits, the middle class developed new ways to spend its increased leisure time. The railroad created the possibility of short excursions to the picturesque countryside and seaside resorts. Travel agencies, led by English travel agent and missionary Thomas Cook, provided more elaborate holidays to the Mediterranean Riviera, the Alps, or, for the more adventuresome, to Palestine and Egypt.

Closer to home, a whole new range of organized sports and pastimes developed for the amusement of the young and more physically active. On the large lawns of their suburban villas, the middle classes played lawn tennis and croquet, while the schools promoted team sports and individual competitions such as athletics. These sports were thought to train youth in the bourgeois virtues of discipline and self-reliance. Some sports faced competition from working-class athletes. Boxing, running, and cycling attracted paid athletes from the working class, especially since promoters and gamblers had a monetary as well as sporting interest in winning. Both pay and gambling were unsuited to the athletic endeavours of "gentlemen" as distinct from "players." Consequently, the cult of amateurism developed to separate middle from working-class athletes and led to the revival of the Olympic Games in Athens in 1896.

Despite the efforts to keep leisure and associated pastimes segregated by class, the popular culture that emerged in the late nineteenth century crossed class lines, drawing its participants from the working and lower-middle classes, as well as from elements of the more affluent bourgeoisie. Entrepreneurs readily cultivated the new consumer demand for entertainment. Travelling amusement shows and circuses put on spectacular displays for audiences enthralled by exotic animals, superhuman feats of strength, and death-defying acrobatics. In addition to these spectacles, professional sports, led by soccer in Great Britain and cycling on the Continent, attracted mainly male working-class spectators, who, by the 1890s, attended in the same numbers as sporting events a century later. Similarly, the modern music industry grew out of the late-nineteenth-century music hall and other forms of popular theatre. Leading music hall entertainers were identified as "stars," and received high earnings and popular adoration in the tabloid dailies.

These new forms of popular entertainment, combined with the growth of mass-circulation tabloid newspapers and cheap sensational pulp fiction, led moralists to bemoan the degeneration of taste in this new age of democracy and popular culture. To these pessimistic social commentators, the centres of this degeneration were the large cities within which the old deference from the poor to the rich no longer functioned, and traditional values enshrined in religion and custom no longer prevailed.

sexuality and childhood development were a product of his own personal history and of the constraints of bourgeois society in pre-1914 Vienna. From his work as a therapist dealing with psychic injuries inflicted by repression, Freud has mistakenly been interpreted as an exponent of sexual liberation. His premise was that the history of cultures parallels the development of the individual, including a past of repressed sexual violence. In *Totem and Taboo* (1912–1913) and later in *Civilization and Its Discontents* (1930), he argued that the free expression of instinctive drives was as destructive of society as it was to the individual. Repression of sexual desire was the source of creativity in religion, art, music, and other aspects of culture. Freud viewed human beings as forever struggling between reason and desire. Repression was necessary for social stability and civilization; it was also the source of aggression, violence, and war.

New Directions in Social Thought

Freud's focus was on the individual, and from these studies he extended his analysis to cultures. Other contemporary thinkers began with society rather than the individual but, like Freud, they explored non-rational sources of human conduct. Emile Durkheim (1858–1917), a French Jewish social scientist and one of the founders of the new discipline of sociology, explored the sources of collective consciousness. His interest grew out of studies of individual loneliness and alienation, most dramatically revealed in incidents of suicide. Contrary to conventional liberal assumptions, Durkheim concluded that modern urban, industrial society threatened to create an excessive individualism dangerous to mental health and social well-being. Max Weber (1864–1920), a German liberal economist whose thought had a profound influence on the social sciences in the twentieth century, shared with Durkheim the concern for the individual within an impersonal and secular environment. In his influential work *The Protestant Ethic and the Spirit of Capitalism* (1904–1905), he challenged the economic ideas of Marx and argued that religious beliefs and values shape economic organization and behaviour.

Weber was particularly concerned with the basis of political and social action in modern capitalist societies organized on a rational and secular basis. The price of this new, more rational order was the disillusionment of the individual and the growth of bureaucracy. To overcome the rules and regulations of these entrenched bureaucratic structures, Weber looked to the possibility of a dynamic or charismatic leader. He did not predict or advocate the rise of totalitarian dictators but, in looking for some scope for individual action within impersonal social institutions, Weber thought that such leadership offered the individual a greater purposefulness in modern secular society.

In the early years of the twentieth century, a varied range of social theorists and observers questioned the assumptions about human reason built into democratic ideology. They contributed to the climate of social conflict which existed prior to 1914 and, in the longer term, created an intellectual legacy conducive to the totalitarian regimes that followed World War I.

Tension and Unrest in the Capitals of Europe, 1900–1914

The horrors of the first half of the twentieth century—two world wars, the economic depression of the 1930s, and the excesses of totalitarian states—shape our perception of European civilization immediately preceding 1914. We are subject to two contrary feelings. On the one hand, after the horrors that followed, we look back nostalgically at the beginning of the twentieth century, when the sumptuous ease and cultural refinement of the wealthy encouraged creativity in the arts and sciences. On the other hand, we realize that the seeds of the oppression and violence that characterized European civilization after World War I were planted prior to 1914.

Vienna, the seat of the Habsburg monarchy and in many ways the cultural capital of pre-1914 Europe, exemplified these contrary perceptions. Vienna was already a traditional centre of music and the arts; it now experienced a cultural renaissance attracting Europe's leading composers and musicians to its concert halls and theatres. It was also a centre of profound intellectual developments, including the psychoanalytical movement of Sigmund Freud and his circle. At the same time, the Austro-Hungarian monarchy festered in political immobility, and Vienna itself had become the anti-Semitic capital of Europe. This environment of political futility and ethnic hatred fostered the politics of an obscure young commercial artist called Adolf Hitler.

Despite the optimism bred by prosperity, and despite the elegance and civility of the affluent elites during the first decade or so of the twentieth century, the diplomats drawn from those elites seemed unwilling to settle differences between nation-states. Domestically, these same states were unable to accommodate the demands for reform made by women and labour; thus, these states were more subject to the divisions and violence generated by aggressive nationalism.

Women

Gender and Inequality

The lower status of women had significant repercussions in the public sphere (politics and employment) as well as the private sphere (marriage and the family). The emergence of a feminist movement in the second half of the nineteenth century grew out of dissatisfaction with the subordinate status of women rooted in tradition and enforced by law. This dissatisfaction grew more acute as adult males gained equality before the law and the right to vote. Inequality on the basis of gender became an obvious contradiction to the newly established principles of equality.

Steps toward the emancipation of women were taken thanks to both the efforts of feminists to change the law and significant innovations that came with economic and social change. The expansion of the middle classes, especially new forms of female employment, the spread of state education, and the increase in leisure, eased some of the restrictions which had constrained the lives of women both inside and outside the home. This informal emancipation also brought women face to face with the formal restraints of their unequal legal and political status.

The Feminist Movement and the Vote

Feminist movements in different countries confronted differing obstacles in accordance with the particular features of their national culture and political system. In Germany, feminists faced the combined obstacles of a conservative middle-class culture in which women's subordination was sanctioned by both Protestant and Catholic churches, and a political structure which made legislative reforms extremely difficult. Consequently, the German feminist movement was small in size and moderate in its goals until the

beginning of the twentieth century. Then a radical group of feminists emerged who, in addition to demanding legal equality and the vote, demanded access to birth control, the right to abortion, equal pay for equal work, and state provision of day-care.

In France, the polarized politics of the Third Republic placed the feminists, whose ideology of emancipation had roots in the Revolution, on the left among the defenders of republicanism. The feminists' opposition on the right came mainly from the Catholic Church, which defended the subordinate status of women and the traditional family. Although their anti-clericalism may have isolated the feminists from many French women, the belated achievement of reforms in France reflected the immense resistance reformers faced. French feminists began calling for a reform of marriage law in the 1880s, but married women only became legal persons able to possess property in 1938. Women in France did not gain the vote until 1945.

In Great Britain, the feminist movement originated earlier in the nineteenth century and, by the beginning of the twentieth century, suffrage societies were able to conduct a more sustained political campaign than their sisters on the Continent. In 1857, divorce courts were created; by 1882, married women secured the same rights as single women to own property.

The rallying cry of the suffragists, "votes for women," had both political and psychological significance. The vote offered female electors the possibility to select politicians who would be more responsive to women's issues. Not having the vote was also the most obvious symbol of women's inequality.

Measures for female voting had been introduced in Parliament at regular intervals for 30 years since 1867, but they were never passed. The frustration of those expectations fuelled a vigorous campaign involving new tactics of both civil disobedience and violence.

In 1903, Emmeline Pankhurst and her daughter Christabel launched a new suffrage society, the Women's Social and Political Union (W.S.P.U.), dedicated to winning the franchise for women on the same limited terms as then existed for men. The members of the W.S.P.U., who became known as "suffragettes," differed not so much in their aims as in their methods. The Pankhursts decided on a campaign of vigorous direct action. The campaign began with the questioning of politicians on public occasions and continued with disruptions of political meetings and mass rallies before Parliament. These demonstrations led to confrontations with the police, arrests, and further demonstrations. The suffragettes began to engage in passive disobedience, chaining themselves to lampposts, going on hunger strikes in prison, and refusing to pay taxes. These measures escalated to violence against property: smashing windows, destroying male turf such as golf greens, setting fire to public buildings, slashing paintings in art galleries, and, most dramatically, the political suicide of Emily Davison, who threw herself before the king's horse at the Epson Derby in 1913. But, despite the extent of the feminist campaign and its militancy, the Liberal government remained unmoved.

The outbreak of World War I in August 1914 temporarily resolved the issue. Christabel Pankhurst and the W.S.P.U. called on men and women to support the war effort. Prior to 1914, with the exception of Finland and Norway, the political systems of Great Britain and the major European powers had proven unable—and their political leaders unwilling—to accommodate the demand of women for equality of citizenship.

Labour

Trade Unionism

Throughout Europe, the law and its administration were biased not only on the basis of gender but also on the basis of social class. Working people had two options by which to attempt to redress the hardship and inequity of their economic and legal position: they could engage in direct action at their place of employment to attempt to improve wages and working conditions or they could become active politically to try to change the law.

With the advance of industrialization, working people attempted to make improvements by creating trade unions. Early unions had historical links with preindustrial crafts and usually included highly skilled trades attempting to protect their craft and wages against competition from newer industrial processes. As more people were hired by industry, especially at larger firms employing more people doing similar tasks, trade unionism spread among the semi-skilled. In place of the older craft unions organized by each separate trade, industrial unionism, from the 1880s onward, joined all workers employed in a particular industry, for example in coal mining or on the railways.

The extent of unionization varied in accordance with the level of industrialization. By the early twentieth century, over 2 million workers were organized in Great Britain, over 3 million in Germany, and over 1 million in France. The new industrial unions were very militant. The trade unionists' capacity to organize and put pressure on employers through strikes and picketing depended upon the law, which in most states still restricted the actions of trade unions. Consequently, labour organizations, especially where the law was punitive and where qualifications for the franchise still excluded many working people, had to press for political change.

Socialism: Revolution and Revisionism

Socialism addressed the political needs of trade unionists and working people directly. Apart from the British labour movement, European labour advocates and socialists were strongly influenced by Karl Marx's analysis of industrial capitalism. Marx accurately predicted that industrial capitalism would continue to expand and draw increasing numbers of people to a system of wage labour. Furthermore, his description of the conflict between employers and employees—more generally, between the bourgeoisie and the working class—conformed to the daily experience of many late-nineteenth-century industrial wage earners.

Aside from interpreting capitalism and advocating a proletarian revolution, Marx worked as a political organizer helping to create the First International Workingmen's Association in 1864. This first attempt to build an international socialist political organization was one of the many failures of the Paris Commune in 1871. With its defeat and the collapse of the French left, the First International disbanded in 1876.

The idea of an international organization of socialists was revived with the foundation of the Second International in 1889. By this time, industrialization had extended in Germany, France, and elsewhere on the Continent; working people were now more widely organized in trade unions and in their own national political parties. This situation offered the possibility that the workers might gain at the ballot box what Marx had said could only be achieved by revolution. In 1899, German socialist theorist Eduard Bernstein proposed that socialism could be won gradually by elected governments implementing socialist measures over time. The debate over Bernstein's so-called revisionist strategy deeply divided the Second International as

Victorian Feminism
and the
Contagious Disease Acts

 Prostitution was seen as one of the great social evils of the nineteenth century. Attempts to control and regulate prostitution reflected a belief on the part of the dominant middle class that the state should intervene in the lives of the "unrespectable poor." Throughout the nineteenth century, most prostitutes remained the "unskilled daughters of the unskilled classes." A study of London prostitutes showed that 90 percent held in the Millbank prison were the daughters of unskilled and semiskilled workers. Of these women, over 50 percent had been servants and most of the rest had worked in equally poorly paid jobs. These young women had left home for economic reasons, forced to survive on their own resources. When asked why she didn't tell her mother of her plight, one prostitute replied, "Oh, what could she have done for me? Father couldn't afford to keep me at home; and I was ashamed for my mother to know I was so bad off."

"Swindling Sal," a London prostitute, provides us with a sense of what motivated poor young women to turn to prostitution: "I was a servant gal away down Birmingham. I got tired of workin' and slavin' to make a living...I'd sooner starve. After a bit I went to Coventry...and took up with soldiers.... Soldiers is good...but they don't pay; cos why they ain't got no money; so I says to myself, I'll go to Lunnon [London] and I did."

By the 1850s, prostitution had become a great social evil in England, seen by the middle class as an infectious disease attacking respectable society. In an attempt to control prostitution, the government chose to oversee the social lives of the unrespectable poor through the Contagious Disease Acts. These acts sought to curtail prostitution by placing controls on the female body rather than the male clients of prostitutes. Under the Contagious Disease Acts, a woman could be identified as a "common prostitute" by a special plainclothes policeman and then required to submit to a biweekly examination. If the woman was found to have either syphilis or gonorrhea, she was placed in a special hospital for up to nine months. The definition of a common prostitute was vague, giving police officers wide discretionary powers. If a woman refused to submit to an examination, she was brought before a magistrate, and the burden of proof that she was virtuous fell on her.

The feminist movement of the nineteenth century is most often associated with the crusade to win women the vote. In addition to pressing for the vote, mid-Victorian feminists, from the 1860s to the 1880s, engaged in a campaign for the repeal of the Contagious Disease Acts. Under the leadership of Josephine Butler, feminists and moral reformers demanded that the laws be repealed as an intolerable invasion of a woman's privacy. The reformers insisted on a single standard for men and women: chastity before wedlock and fidelity within marriage. Josephine Butler's crusade was successful in having the Acts repealed in 1886 and had an impact on similar campaigns in France, Germany, and the United States, where moral reform and feminism became one.

well as various national movements, including the social democrats in Germany and the socialists in Russia. Those still committed to Marx's ideas argued that a socialist restructuring of the economy and society could only be achieved by revolution.

Bernstein and his revisionists lost the debate within the Second International; however, the political conditions within which socialist parties functioned meant that they were often revolutionary in ideology but revisionist in practice. The Social Democratic Party in Germany, the most successful socialist party in Europe, attracting 4.5 million votes and becoming the largest party in the Reichstag (German parliament) in 1912, remained committed to revolution in theory, but focused their energies on conventional electioneering.

The French left remained divided between those nominally committed to revolution but ready to enter electoral politics, and those who looked to direct action in the revolutionary tradition. Radical trade unionists and syndicalists favoured the politics of direct action through strikes and industrial sabotage over electioneering. Moderates favoured the open and humanistic socialism of Jean Jaurès (1859–1914), a philosopher and journalist of middle-class background who became the leading French socialist and orator of the late nineteenth and early twentieth centuries. He built a popular working-class following but refused to join coalitions with non-socialist parties. In 1914, he campaigned against the dangers of militant nationalism only to be assassinated by a nationalist fanatic that same year.

The British labour movement, the least influenced by Marx and his revolutionary doctrine, was the most revisionist in its political strategy. Out of the growth of the trade-union movement, the Independent Labour Party, and other working-class and socialist groups, the Labour Party was created in 1900, and fought the 1906 election as a lobby attempting to secure changes in labour law and social reform. There were also middle-class groups, such as the Fabian Society, whose members engaged in research and made proposals for social legislation. They believed in gradual reforms and sought to permeate the established Conservative and Liberal parties. The leading Fabians, for example Sidney and Beatrice Webb and George Bernard Shaw, were sceptical about an independent working-class party, and before 1918 had only a limited influence on the Labour Party.

Syndicalism

Despite the success of labour advocates in organizing trade unions, and of socialists in creating their own political parties and making gains at elections, they had limited influence on governments or on legislative reforms. At the same time, rising prices and increased unemployment led some workers to demand more tangible results. Putting more faith in direct action than in political process, labour advocates argued that industrial unions could use their power to achieve both economic and political gains.

Under the influence of French sociologist Georges Sorel's theories on violence and direct action, radical trade unionists—called *syndicalists*—advocated the use of general strikes to force concessions from employers and politicians. In countries where the rights of trade unions and the right to vote were still restricted, for example Italy and Spain, syndicalist tactics of direct action pitted working people against the army and police who defended employers and the state. An uprising in Barcelona was savagely repressed in 1909; in France, the authorities repeatedly used the police and the army to crush industrial and political strikes. Syndicalist ideas also influenced the British trade union movement. After two years of widespread strikes, in 1913, three of the largest industrial unions, the coal miners, transport workers, and railway workers, formed a triple alliance. They pledged to disrupt the national economy by a general strike to achieve their industrial and political goals.

In several European states on the eve of World War I, the revolutionary rhetoric of the socialists and the militancy of trade unions created a sense that both the economy and the state were potential hostages to direct action by an organized working class. In Western Europe, this perception of an industrial and political crisis was more apparent than real. In Eastern Europe, under more repressive political regimes and less advanced economies, this sense of crisis, even of revolution, had more serious foundations.

Russia: The Revolution of 1905

In the early 1890s, under Czar Alexander III and from 1894 until 1917 under Czar Nicholas II (the last czar), the contradictory policies of rapid industrial development and continued political repression created the potential for a revolutionary explosion. Under the guidance of the first constitutional prime minister of czarist Russia, Sergey Witte (1849–1915), Russia experienced a second wave of rapid industrial development relying on financing by foreign capital. With industrialization, the working class grew in size and engaged in clandestine revolutionary activity under the scrutiny of the czar's secret police.

The leading Marxist party, the Russian Social Democratic Party, operated out of exile in Switzerland. Along with other socialist parties, it engaged in the debate on revisionism, and in 1902, one of its leading militants, Vladimir Ilich Ulyanov, known as Lenin (1870–1924), published an influential pamphlet under the title *What Is to Be Done*. In defending the necessity of revolution, Lenin argued that it was not sufficient to wait for a spontaneous insurrection of the masses. He advanced the idea that a dedicated core of professional revolutionaries, the vanguard of the party, could take a political crisis and lead the working class into full-scale revolution. In subsequent debates, Lenin and his more militant faction won a small majority and became known as the Bolsheviks, whereas his more moderate social democratic or revisionist opponents constituted a minority that became known as the Mensheviks.

For the Russian socialists, these debates had more than theoretical significance, for in 1905 they found themselves in a real revolution. Added to an economic slump which had created extensive hardship among the peasantry and industrial workers, the defeat of Russian naval and military forces by Japan in 1904–1905 created a political crisis. This crisis escalated into revolution when, on Bloody Sunday (January 22, 1905) troops killed several hundred peaceful and unarmed demonstrators who sought to petition the czar to grant political reforms and economic relief. A prolonged constitutional crisis—coupled with extensive rural unrest, recurrent general strikes, a mutiny in the navy, and incidents of political violence—finally forced Nicholas II to create a Duma, or parliament.

Even though the new Duma, like the German Reichstag, had limited powers, the reform was sufficient to split the forces pressing for change. The social revolutionaries attempted to continue their campaign of strikes, but were crushed by the army at the end of 1905. A regressive reform of the electoral law weighted the Duma even more favourably toward conservative property owners. Nicholas II, never fully reconciled to even this moderate degree of constitutional rule, governed in an increasingly autocratic manner. Eventually,

a much more severe crisis brought on by the stresses of war launched a full-scale revolution in 1917.

Prior to 1914, Russia had been the state most repressive of political dissent and most prone to revolutionary upheaval. Political regimes elsewhere in Europe were not in danger of popular insurrection, despite the signs of labour unrest and the protests for female emancipation. A more serious source of political conflict lay in nationalism, which not only excited popular enthusiasm and violence, but also enticed political and military leaders to seek national glory through war.

Nationalism

Aggressive Nationalism and Political Conflict

With the spread of industrialization and the mounting economic competition between European states, national rivalry and imperial ambition led to an arms race and to the formation of diplomatic alliances in anticipation of the possibility of war. Nationalism aroused not only loyalty toward an individual's own state and people, but also antagonism toward those states and peoples perceived as an alien threat. John A. Hobson, a liberal British economist and critic of imperialism, observed the jingoistic response of the British populace during the Boer War in South Africa (1899–1902). In *The Psychology of Jingoism* (1901), he commented that aggressive nationalism became:

> "an inverted patriotism whereby the love of one's own nation is transformed into the hatred of another nation and fierce craving to destroy the individual members of that other nation."

In Europe, between 1900 and 1914, the populace as well as the political and military leaders were conditioned by various forms of aggressive nationalism. This sentiment, deliberately inculcated, led to an anticipation of war as a celebration of national valour and as a way to destroy the nation's enemies.

Nationalism and the State

National and imperial rivalry put new pressures on domestic politics within states. The Prussian aristocracy, which dominated the offices of state and the army, identified its own power with the pre-eminence of the

German nation. With the backing of industrialists anxious to profit from the arms race, politicians and generals wrestled with the problem of Germany's encirclement within Central Europe. They began to see the need for—and the inevitability of—a great war as the means for Germany to assume its rightful and dominant place on the Continent. Consequently, in the critical weeks of crisis diplomacy in July 1914, there was a willingness to think that the time had come for a lasting peace through a victorious war.

In Britain, rivalry with Germany, especially the naval arms race to build modern warships, or dreadnoughts, fostered a constitutional crisis. The Liberal government needed to finance the dreadnoughts and new social measures, such as old-age pensions. Prime Minister David Lloyd George's People's Budget of 1909 introduced taxes on inherited wealth. In response, the landed aristocracy in the House of Lords defeated the budget and brought down the government. This constitutional crisis, whereby a hereditary peerage brought down a popularly elected government, reflected a new willingness of conservative, traditional interests to challenge the authority of the state.

The Liberal government was pledged to a policy of Home Rule for Ireland and, after the constitutional crisis of 1909–1910, became dependent on Irish nationalist support in the House of Commons. In Ulster, Protestants, with close ties to the Conservative Party and to officers in the army, feared the prospect of Home Rule. Some Conservative politicians and army officers, claiming to be patriots for "king and country," demonstrated their willingness to fight by advocating mutiny against the elected government and its Irish policy.

Reflections

Nationalism and the Origins of World War I

The expression of aggressive nationalism and the polarization of domestic politics in a number of states do not provide a satisfactory explanation of why the European nations were ready to go to war in August of 1914. Such an explanation requires a study of diplomacy and military planning. At most, this aggressive nationalism and its popular appeal can explain why domestic political considerations did not inhibit the politicians and the generals from going to war. It also explains why, when war was declared, recruits readily signed up to fight and die for their country, and why the populace welcomed the military test of national valour.

In a more specific way, nationalism accounts for the more immediate origins of the war. Nationalism presented the gravest threat in the Balkans where a complex mix of cultural and linguistic groups, and two archaic empires—the Ottoman Empire and the Austro-Hungarian monarchy—failed, not surprisingly, to resolve the competing claims of various nationalities. These nationalities—Rumanians, Bulgarians, Serbs, Bosnians, Croats, and others—were residents not only of the Austro-Hungarian Empire, but also of its Ottoman neighbour. After two local Balkan Wars in 1912–1913, the rival ambitions of the nationalists and of great powers such as Austria-Hungary and Russia remained unresolved. The Balkan Wars hardened the resolve of rival nationalists to a point at which no participant was ready to make any concessions to the demands of its opponents.

In this climate, an isolated spark set off an engulfing fire: the assassination of the Austrian Archduke Francis Ferdinand and his wife by a Serbian nationalist at Sarajevo on June 28, 1914. The incident quickly escalated from a Serbian-Austrian confrontation into a full-blown European and world war. The assassin's bullet marked a new beginning for European civilization. Never again would there be a confident belief in human reason and progress. In the new twentieth century, the engine of historical change would not be liberation through revolution, but destruction through total war.

Key Concepts, Figures, and Events

Louis Napoléon Bonaparte
Giuseppe Mazzini
Giuseppe Gariboldi
Count Camillo Cavour
Count Otto von Bismarck

Paris Commune
Dreyfus Affair
Benjamin Disraeli
William Gladstone
Charles Darwin

Friedrich Nietzsche
Sigmund Freud
Socialism
Syndicalism

Topics for Further Thought

1. One of the dominant political figures of the mid-nineteenth century was Louis Napoléon Bonaparte of France. How did his style of politics reflect the nature of change that had taken place in Europe by 1850?

2. Nationalism was one of the great forces that shaped the history of the second half of the nineteenth century. Explain how nationalism helped shape the history of Germany and Italy. Explain why nationalism did not have the same effect in the Austrian Empire. Do you believe that the nation-states created during the nineteenth century will survive the twenty-first century given the nature of change presently under way in Europe?

3. The nineteenth century was an era of tremendous democratic reform, during which the right to vote was granted to a wide range of men. How did the extension of the vote alter the nature of politics in the late nineteenth century?

4. The two men who dominated British politics during the second half of the nineteenth century were Benjamin Disraeli and William Gladstone. Compare and contrast the philosophies and policies of each and explain their successes and failures in politics. Given the current nature of politics, do you believe either of these men would be successful today? Explain your answer.

5. The impact of the Industrial Revolution extended well beyond the factories. Explain the impact of the Industrial Revolution by commenting on the rise of white-collar work, shopping habits and the retail industry, and changes to daily life.

6. Explain the nature of change that took place in scientific thought during the latter half of the nineteenth century. How did these changes present challenges to the foundations of European society?

7. Many would argue that the foundations of World War I lay in the late nineteenth century. In fact it could be argued that, to truly understand the origins of World War I, one must look to the last few decades of the 1800s. Explain this statement and support your explanation.

Topics for Further Research

1. The period 1850–1900 was an era often dominated by colourful, if not inspirational, figures. Research and write a biographical sketch on one of the following individuals:

Giuseppe Garibaldi   Giuseppe Mazzini
Count Camillo Cavour   Count Otto von Bismarck

2. Although women would not receive the vote until the twentieth century, strong women's movements sprang up in several European countries as well as in North America during the nineteenth century. Research the women's movement in one of the countries listed below. Be sure to explore their aims and objectives, methods, and degree of success.

Britain   France   Germany
Italy   Canada

3. The Industrial Revolution, which transformed Britain during the first half of the nineteenth century, swept over the rest of Europe and North America by the end of the century. Research the impact of industrialization on one of the following countries:

Russia   United States   Canada
Italy   Germany   France

4. The publication of Darwin's controversial work, *On the Origin of Species*, had a profound impact on Western society well beyond the realm of science. Research the impact of Darwinism on one of the following areas:

Religion
Economics
Racism and Imperialism
Social Policy (i.e. Poor Laws)

Responding to Ideas

1. One of the great writers of the late nineteenth and twentieth centuries, George Bernard Shaw, once wrote: "Men with empty phrases in their mouths and foolish fables in their heads have seen each other, not as fellow creatures, but as dragons and devils, and have slaughtered each other accordingly." Although written in the twentieth century, do you believe this statement to be relevant to the nineteenth century? How appropriate is this phrase for the world today?

2. In the Introduction to his book *Darwin, Marx, Wagner: Critique of a Heritage*, Jacques Barzun explains why he wrote about this threesome: "To name Darwin, Marx, and Wagner as the three great prophets of our destinies is but to recognize a state of fact." Barzun claims that Marx was *the* sociologist and Darwin *the* scientist of the nineteenth century. He goes on to state that, should you open any book dealing with the problems of our time, "you will find Darwin and Marx repeatedly coupled as the great pair whose conceptions revolutionized the modern world." Do you agree with the importance Barzun attaches to the ideas of Karl Marx and Charles Darwin, not only to the age they lived in but to ours as well? Explain your answer.

Europe and the Wider World: Colonialism and Resistance in the Nineteenth Century

---

CHAPTER HIGHLIGHTS

- An understanding of different types of imperialism
- An understanding of the factors leading to the first wave of emancipation and decolonization

- How industrialization shaped the new world order of the nineteenth century

- How the French Revolution and Napoleonic Wars shaped Latin America's struggle for independence
- The nature of resistance in colonial empires

The Modern World System, 1815–1914

Economic globalization is an ongoing process over the past 500 years. The history of colonial conquest, settlement, and trade created a **metropolis** or centre of the modern world in Western Europe, and a dependent **periphery** in Eastern Europe and in the wider world of Australasia, Asia, Africa, and the Americas. This long-term process was greatly accelerated in the nineteenth century, as European economies, societies, and nation-states were transformed by industrialization. The new industrial and military technology gave Europeans the capacity to overrun peoples and territories in the periphery, and the political organization and ideologies associated with the modern nation-state gave Europeans the power to exercise unprecedented control.

In 1815, there was a striking contrast between the modern world on the one hand and the conquered lands of the Americas and the dependent lands of Asia and Africa on the other hand. In the Americas, conquest and disease had decimated the Amerindian population. The demographic structure was altered by voluntary migration of European settlers and by forced migration of African slaves. By 1815, the trend was clear. Growth in European settlement and capitalist forms of production pushed native Americans farther into the hinterland. Conflicts over land led to bloody localized wars, and natives were forced into a dependent economic and political status.

Prior to 1815, there were no comparable examples of conquered territories in Asia or Africa. In these continents, Europeans had established commercial relations, usually through strategic coastal enclaves, where indigenous merchants traded local products for European goods. Formal political conquest of territories and populations was limited. In Asia, exceptions were the Dutch in the East Indies, coveted for their spices and other tropical crops, and the British in India, where the East India Company engaged in trade, administered the law, and collected taxes in conquered provinces. Africa's interior was still an undiscovered mystery to Europeans, who had only established slave-trading posts in West Africa and a small settlement at the Cape of Good Hope. In the South Pacific, although trading links existed, British settlement commenced in Australia only in 1788.

The relationship of European states with the peoples of the non-European world took two forms. One was the *informal imperialism* of commercial and political relationships with indigenous elites, which did not involve military conquest or land occupation. The other was *formal imperialism*, or colonization, where European powers, by force of arms and by the occupying presence of settlers, conquered territories, bringing land and people under their political authority. During the nineteenth century, both types of European imperialism instituted unequal economic and political relationships between the colonizing powers and the colonized.

The colonized peoples were not simply passive victims, but engaged in a variety of forms of resistance to foreign European intervention and control. This history of resistance laid the foundations for colonial nationalist movements in Asia and Africa. The history of colonization in the nineteenth century encompasses the ways in which the imperialism of European states and the resistance of colonized peoples transformed the modern world system.

The Expansion of European Empires, 1815–1914

European colonization did not occur at an even pace throughout the nineteenth century. In fact, from the American Revolution in 1776, until 1870, informed political opinion expressed opposition to formal acquisition of colonies, preferring informal trade relationships. In 1800, Europe and its overseas possessions constituted 55 percent of the world land mass, and by 1878, that proportion had risen to 67 percent. European colonization intensified very markedly in the last two decades of the nineteenth century so that, by 1914, Europe and its possessions accounted for 84 percent of the world's land mass.

Effective occupation of colonial territories depended upon a European military and administrative presence and transformation of land and population by white immigrants. From 1871 to 1914, Europe's population grew by about 200 million and an additional 30 million migrated overseas. The United States attracted about two thirds of these immigrants, just under 2 million came to Canada, and the remainder settled in Australia, New Zealand, South America (principally Argentina and Brazil), Algeria, and South Africa. There was also an extensive migration of European Russians to Asiatic Russia.

European imperialism and the migration of white populations are usually linked, but the colonial empires were also great agents for forced and voluntary migration of non-European peoples. Although Britain and the United States ceased to trade in African slaves in the first decade of the nineteenth century, the transatlantic slave trade continued, chiefly to Brazil and Cuba. From 1811 until the virtual end of the slave trade by 1870, almost 2 million Africans were brought to the Americas as slaves. The mid-century gold rush in California, Australia, and British Columbia attracted voluntary immigrants not only from Europe but from China. The demand for labour in mining, railway construction, and agriculture prompted various schemes of voluntary and indentured labour.

The workers were mainly Chinese and South Asians from the Indian subcontinent. This migration was global. Indian immigrants went to Fiji and Queensland, to Southeast Asia, to Mauritius and the Seychelles in the Indian Ocean, to East and South Africa, to the Caribbean (principally Trinidad and Guyana), and to British Columbia. Chinese immigrants went to similar destinations, including Australia, Southeast Asia, South Africa, the Caribbean and, on the west coast of the Americas, to British Columbia, California, Peru, and Chile. There were also more localized migrations of South Sea Islanders to work plantations in Queensland, of African West Indians within the Caribbean and Central America, and within Africa an extensive trade in slaves destined for America and the Middle East. Later in the century, African migrant labourers worked on plantations, on railway construction, and in mines in West, Central, and South Africa.

Global migration created new kinds of multiracial and multiethnic societies. Besides throwing peoples of diverse origins and cultures together, imperialism constructed societies in which peoples were unequal in wealth and power, and it fostered racial and ethnic divisions to maintain European authority. Probably the most enduring and painful legacy of nineteenth-

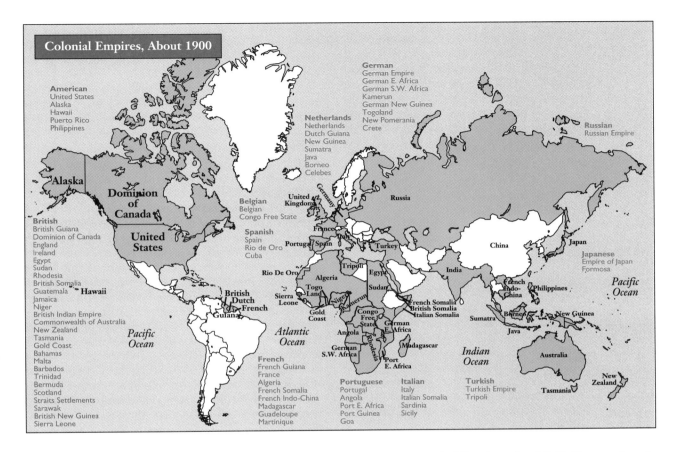

Colonial Empires, About 1900

American
United States
Alaska
Hawaii
Puerto Rico
Philippines

British
British Guiana
Dominion of Canada
England
Ireland
Egypt
Sudan
Rhodesia
British Somalia
Guatemala
Jamaica
Niger
Commonwealth of Australia
New Zealand
Tasmania
Gold Coast
Bahamas
Malta
Barbados
Trinidad
Bermuda
Scotland
Straits Settlements
Sarawak
British New Guinea
Sierra Leone

Netherlands
Netherlands
Dutch Guiana
New Guinea
Sumatra
Java
Borneo
Celebes

Belgian
Belgian
Congo Free State

Spanish
Spain
Rio de Oro
Cuba

French
French Guiana
France
Algeria
French Somalia
French Indo-China
Madagascar
Guadeloupe
Martinique

German
German Empire
German E. Africa
German S.W. Africa
Kamerun
German New Guinea
Togoland
New Pomerania
Crete

Portuguese
Portugal
Angola
Port E. Africa
Port Guinea
Goa

Italian
Italy
Italian Somalia
Sardinia
Sicily

Turkish
Turkish Empire
Tripoli

Russian
Russian Empire

Japanese
Empire of Japan
Formosa

century imperialism is the ideology of racial superiority, known as *racism*, and the establishment of multiracial societies based on racial inequality.

Migration of white settlers and of non-European peoples went hand in glove with colonial economic development. As the nineteenth century advanced, European nations began to rely less on informal empire and more on formal political control of the periphery. In Asia, the British extended their possessions from India into neighbouring Burma, the Malay Peninsula, and Singapore. Similarly, the Dutch enlarged their formal political jurisdiction in the East Indies, and the French colonized Indochina from the 1850s to the 1880s.

The Manchu dynasty in China was pressured by rival European and American interests, and internally by warring factions, until it fell in the Revolution of 1911. Japan was the great exception in Asia. Militarily vulnerable to Western naval superiority, the arrival of the Americans in 1853 exposed the weakness of the

Shogunate, and following the Meiji Restoration in 1868, the Japanese initiated a program of industrial development and political reform on their own terms. In this way the Japanese not only managed to preserve their autonomy but, by the 1890s, had become an imperial power in their own right.

The rush for colonies in the late nineteenth century was a global phenomenon, but the focus of imperial activity was in Africa. Beyond the trading outposts and forts established on the west coast, the two principal areas of European settlement in Africa were the Dutch colony at the southern Cape of Good Hope, and French settlement in Algeria, which had begun in the 1830s. During the Napoleonic wars, the British took the Cape from the Dutch and, until the 1880s, fought a series of local wars to establish a secure frontier against the independent Dutch settlers who pushed north and the southward-moving Bantu-speaking Africans led by the formidable military force of the Zulus.

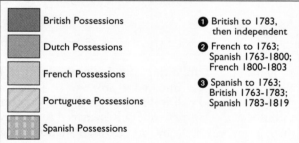

Latin America Before Independence

British Possessions

Dutch Possessions

French Possessions

Portuguese Possessions

Spanish Possessions

❶ British to 1783, then independent

❷ French to 1763; Spanish 1763-1800; French 1800-1803

❸ Spanish to 1763; British 1763-1783; Spanish 1783-1819

made it important strategically and economically, and the ongoing conflict between the British and the Boers (the descendants of the Dutch living in South Africa) led to the Boer War, 1899–1902.

Developments in mining and agriculture led to a variety of experiments with forced and migratory labour, involving not only Africans but labourers from India and China. These experiments created new forms of labour exploitation and of social and political segregation, which were institutionalized in the oppressive system of apartheid in the new Union of South Africa, founded in 1910.

The extraordinary expansion of the European empires in the course of the nineteenth century, especially from 1870 onward, did far more than alter the political map of the world. Imperialism involved a social and economic as well as a political transformation. This intrusion of the Western powers in the non-Western world imposed change on formerly autonomous peoples and cultures. At first, the peoples affected by this juggernaut tried to restore their traditional ways, but as the transformation to a modern world system took hold, colonized peoples began to develop their own forms of nationalism as they sought new ways to assert their freedom. By 1914, those nationalist movements had only recently been founded but, prior to World War I, the signs were already evident that the nineteenth-century age of empire was entering a new phase of crisis and conflict.

The Modern World System in the Age of Democratic Revolutions

Colonialism in the Age of Democratic Revolutions, 1776–1867

The Age of Revolutions in Europe, 1789–1848, had a corresponding revolutionary impact on Europe's relationship with the wider world. In this broader global perspective, some historians have stretched this period back to the American Revolution (1776), and labelled it the *Age of Democratic Revolutions*. The first wave of decolonization and emancipation grew out of the new political principles proclaimed by the American and French Revolutions and with the new forms of economic and social organization that began with the First Industrial Revolution in Britain, 1780–1850. This

From the 1880s onward, the European powers engaged in a frantic competition for colonies in Africa. The colonizing powers moved outward from their established centres in West and South Africa and from the strategically sensitive area of the eastern Mediterranean, Suez, Egypt, and the Sudan. Once the European powers established their military and political presence, white traders and settlers followed in the late nineteenth and early twentieth centuries in East and Central Africa (principally in Kenya, Rhodesia, and Mozambique) and in the west and south in the Congo, Angola, and South African colonies. The discovery of diamond and gold deposits in South Africa birth of the modern world from the dual revolution in politics and in industrialization transformed the relationship of the metropolis to its periphery.

The first movement for colonial independence began with the revolution that made the United States independent from Britain. The American Revolution inspired the movement for the liberation of Mexico and the South American republics from Spain (1808–1825). In British North America, this decolonization occurred at a later date and in a peaceful way. The evolution of principles of representative and responsible government within British colonies eventually led to the establishment of the Dominion of Canada in 1867.

During the Age of Democratic Revolutions, another form of liberation transformed social and economic rather than political relationships. The first wave of emancipation of African American slaves was initiated by the slaves' own revolution in Haiti in 1791. Toussaint L'Ouverture led the slaves in a revolution that not only established their freedom and independence in Haiti, but inspired slave revolts elsewhere and fuelled an international debate on slavery.

Great Britain and the United States ended their involvement in the slave trade (1807–1808), and slavery itself was abolished in the British Empire in 1834. The new Latin American republics, in keeping with their liberal founding principles, abolished slavery. France ended slavery in its empire with the Second Republic founded by the Revolution of 1848. Thereafter, the principal slave powers were Cuba, which remained a Spanish colony, Brazil, under the Portuguese Empire, and the United States, ironically the world's foremost liberal democracy.

White Metropolis and Coloured Periphery

A closer look at the first wave of emancipation reveals a troubling pattern: in North America, where European settlers were predominant within a capitalist economic order, the United States and Canada became part of the industrialized and metropolitan sector of the modern world. Haiti and the Latin American republics were liberated from colonialism, yet remained part of the economically dependent periphery or the Third World. The colonies of the British and French Empires in the Caribbean, where slavery had been abolished, remained under the control of London and Paris as part of the dependent, colonized periphery. Similarly, imperial possessions in mainland Asia, the Dutch East Indies, and British India were not part of this first wave of emancipation and, like the former slave colonies in the West Indies, did not achieve independence until after 1945.

The first emancipation in the Age of Democratic Revolutions was thus only a partial liberation. In fact, after 1870, in apparent contradiction to the ideals of colonial independence and freedom that characterized the Age of Democratic Revolutions, the imperial powers imposed a more comprehensive colonialism on the peoples of Asia and Africa.

The rise of industrial economies increased the contrast in wealth between the metropolitan centres and the periphery. The partial implementation of new principles of individual liberty and representative government also increased the contrast between free citizens and mere subjects. In some cases, the law threatened rather than protected liberty, and specifically denied particular groups, such as black slaves and other non-whites, equality of status, and the right to due process. The contrast between the metropolitan areas of North America and Western Europe and the colonized periphery created a world more starkly divided by race.

The economic and political inequalities in the world fostered the illusion that the modern, civilized order belonged to whites and the servile, colonized order belonged to non-whites. To defend this illusionary racial order and its denial of the universality of human rights proclaimed by the American and French Revolutions, scientific racism preached that the privileged status of white males, particularly the middle class, was reflective of a natural rather than a human order. Racist scientists attempted to demonstrate that the inequalities within particular societies were reflective of the differing biological inheritance of human groups. Their science was constructed on false premises, since the evident inequalities in wealth, political power, and status between peoples were not products of biology but of history: global inequalities were the result of past human actions. Racial inequalities in the Americas were the result of the military conquest and enslavement of Amerindians and Africans, and the political power of white elites who constructed a social and legal order that perpetuated their privileged status.

Industrialization and a New World Order

The ways in which human beings constructed the inequalities that existed within societies and within the larger world order changed over time. The Age of Democratic Revolutions marked a period of momentous change involving partial liberation and reconstruction of the economic and political basis of unequal relations. In economic terms, the industrial revolution brought about a transformation in productive capacity and distribution of wealth. Colonies formerly served simply as sources of commodities, such as furs, fish, sugar, tobacco, coffee, spices, tea, and precious metals; now they began to represent potential markets for manufactured goods. This shift from commercial capitalism to industrial capitalism created greater differences in wealth and it transformed relations between the metropolis and the periphery.

Under industrial capitalism and its doctrine of laissez faire, the restraints of the colonial empires came under attack and the new idea of free trade became the orthodox economic doctrine. During the globalization phase of the world economy, the policy of free trade took time to be introduced; not surprisingly, its main champion was Great Britain, the leading industrial power possessing the largest empire.

In the eighteenth century, Britain imported cotton cloth produced by handloom weavers in India. When the cotton textile industry was established in new factories in England, the trade was reversed. In the early nineteenth century, under imposed conditions of free trade, Indian handloom weavers could not compete in price with British manufacturers of cotton cloth, so India became an importer of cotton textiles and an exporter of raw cotton. Under free trade, a form of informal imperialism, industrial societies became economically predominant and colonies in Asia, Africa, and the Americas became dependent sources of raw materials as well as markets for the manufactured goods of the metropolis.

African Slaves and Their Emancipation

Slavery on the Defensive

The new industrial order stressed both the individualism of the entrepreneur and the value of labour in a modern economy. These values were in direct conflict with the dependence of the older colonialism on the coerced labour of African slaves. During the Age of Democratic Revolutions, the practice of chattel slavery, in which human beings were regarded as merchandise and forced to labour for their owner's benefit, came under attack. In one of the most significant advances in

human freedom, slavery, an institution as old as recorded history, came to an end under the combined assault of changing economic circumstances, the rise of an international anti-slavery movement, and the slaves' resistance to their oppression.

These three factors first became evident in the Caribbean Islands, where the institution of slavery was the most vulnerable to attack: the prime crop of the West Indian plantations was cane sugar, which made extreme demands on the soil and on slave labour (for harvesting and refining cane into sugar). Some historians have argued that both the slave trade and West Indian slavery were already in economic decline by the beginning of the nineteenth century, but recent historians stress the economic viability of both the trade and the system. Consequently, more emphasis has been placed on the political dynamics of emancipation.

Politically, the West Indian colonies were particularly vulnerable. Unlike the United States with its institution of slavery, the West Indies were not politically independent, but were colonies subject to political decisions in London, and to events in revolutionary Paris. In those capitals, the antislavery movement pressed first for the abolition of the slave trade and then for the end of slavery itself. The abolitionists, whose campaign began in the 1770s, and continued as a vigorous movement for almost a century, declared slavery to be a violation of human rights as defined by the Enlightenment and as put into constitutional form by the American and French Revolutions. British and American abolitionists organized the largest and most effective movements, combining an appeal to human rights and to evangelical Christianity, which declared slavery to be both immoral and unchristian.

The Slaves' Revolution in Haiti, 1791

The balance between the vested colonial interests defending slavery and the humanitarianism of the abolitionists was tilted by the actions of the slaves. The slave revolution in Haiti sent shock waves through the plantation communities throughout the West Indies, South America, and the southern United States. In Haiti, a tiny minority of French planters ruled 800 000 slaves, many of whom were newly arrived from Africa. Aware of their African families and communities, these slaves were especially hostile to the oppression of New World slavery and struggled to retain their language, religion, and culture. The slaves' opportunity came with the French Revolution. Under the leadership of François

Dominique Toussaint L'Ouverture, a slave about the age of 50, who was literate and had served as an estate manager, the Haitians defeated French, British, and Spanish attempts to suppress their revolution. Toussaint L'Ouverture helped the French abolish slavery in 1794 and he was made a general. But Napoléon had him imprisoned in France when he declared Haiti a black republic. He died in prison in 1803.

The British West Indies

In the British West Indies, similar situations existed, as tiny white planter elites faced the potential of mass insurrection of their slaves. The example of Haiti, and the demand for ships and seamen during the Napoleonic Wars, gave the abolitionists new practical as well as moral arguments, which led Britain to abolish the slave trade in 1807.

Ending the importation of African slaves did not decrease the number of slave insurrections. In the British West Indies, slave uprisings occurred in Barbados in 1816, in Demerara (Guyana) in 1823, and in Jamaica in 1831–1832. The uprising in Jamaica was decisive for the abolition of slavery in the entire British Empire. Rumours had spread among the slaves that Parliament had ended slavery, but that the planters had refused to emancipate them. In the ensuing riots, the authorities dealt savagely with the rebels, killing over 200 and executing another 540. Back in England, news of the Jamaica uprisings enabled the abolitionists to demonstrate that the slaves themselves found their conditions intolerable, and that the planters' only answer was brutal repression. Even the planters recognized that in the long term they faced continued slave resistance, perhaps another Haiti, and consequently they consented to the abolition of slavery at a price. When slavery was abolished in 1834, the British Parliament compensated the slave owners with 20 million pounds and a scheme of apprenticeship or gradual emancipation that lasted until 1838.

The Haitian Revolution, the ending of British and American involvement in the slave trade, and the abolition of slavery in the British Empire constituted a first wave of emancipation. There remained the more entrenched slave regimes in the United States, Cuba, and Brazil, which were economically productive and less vulnerable to slave insurrection or abolitionist political influence. Eventually, each of these slave regimes faced an internal crisis and, as in Haiti and the British Empire, that crisis emerged from the antislavery crusade and the slaves' resistance.

The United States

In the United States, the manifest contradictions between slavery and the founding principles of the democratic republic eventually provoked a civil war, 1861–1865. Though often seen as a conflict within white America between a pro-slave South and a free North, African Americans, both slave and free, helped generate the crisis that led to the Civil War and then they exploited the circumstances of the war to turn the crisis into a struggle for emancipation. Even in the pro-slave South, African Americans were usually a minority and faced much larger white populations than did the revolutionaries in Haiti or the rebels in Jamaica. Consequently, slave revolts were less frequent in the United States, though some, such as Nat Turner's rising in Virginia in 1831, were inspired by the example of Toussaint L'Ouverture. Turner's rebellion and others were savagely repressed, as Southern authorities organized a reign of legal terror to deter any sign of slave resistance.

Consequently, American slaves sought liberation through escape rather than through rebellion. The brave and the lucky escaped north to freedom and to the refuge of free blacks and abolitionist sympathizers. Some fled the country altogether. The secret flight to the northern U.S. and Canada, set up by abolitionist sympathizers, is called the Underground Railroad. To put a stop to the escape of fugitive slaves, Southern politicians had Congress pass the Fugitive Slave Act (1850) which made it illegal to protect fugitive slaves, and in effect extended the authority of the slave

Toussaint L'Overture, a former slave, led the 1791 Haitian Revolution.

states into the free states of the North. This intervention of the slavemasters' authority began to threaten not only the life and liberty of blacks but the rights of whites as well. Consequently, the institution of slavery was seen to be corrupting the whole country. When it became clear that the country could not be half slave and half free, a southern secessionist movement provoked a civil war.

At the beginning of the Civil War in 1861, President Abraham Lincoln and the northern forces claimed to be fighting to restore the Union and not to end slavery. In the first two years, the war went badly for the North, and the flight of slaves into areas under Union control made it difficult to reimpose slavery on the fugitives. Furthermore, black regiments had joined the Union army, and there was no doubt that they were fighting for emancipation. African Americans, abolitionists, and many recruits in the army redefined the struggle as a war against slavery. In January 1863, Lincoln issued his Emancipation Proclamation, which freed the slaves, authorized the creation of black military units, and changed the war into a struggle against slavery.

Slaves in Cuba and Brazil had a similar role in their own emancipation. The struggle to end race slavery took over a century, and although often overlooked by white historians, the resistance of the slaves themselves was essential to their liberation. Out of this history of resistance, as we shall see, black peoples of the African diaspora to the New World founded a tradition that would both challenge new forms of racist oppression and build an alliance with their African brothers and sisters to mount a nationalist movement against colonialism.

Decolonization and Informal Empire in Latin America

The Age of Democratic Revolutions gave rise to not only the first wave of emancipation against slavery, but also the first movement for colonial independence. The new liberal principles of individual liberty and representative government and the new economic doctrines of laissez faire and free trade challenged the established practices of colonial rule. The old colonialism of conquest was best exemplified by Spain's empire in Latin America. Between 1808 and 1825, political upheaval and armed struggle liberated most of Spain's American colonies.

Class and Race in the Spanish American Empire

In the Spanish Empire in the eighteenth century, there were three sources of authority—the administrative bureaucracy of the Spanish monarchy, the Catholic Church, and the white creole elite, a landed aristocracy descended from the conquistadors. Together, these authorities ruled over an impoverished Amerindian and mestizo majority. Thus, under a variety of forms of coerced labour, the impoverished majority provided rent and services to the creole (born in America of Spanish descent) landowners and the Church, and tribute or taxes to the royal officials. In return, the peasantry preserved a measure of cultural autonomy and a protected legal status under the supervision of the Spanish crown and the Church. In areas where plantation agriculture existed, African slaves endured a similar oppressed and subordinate condition. In an ambiguous intermediate status, there existed a mestizo and mulatto population, product of the union of white males and Amerindian and African women.

The creole elite desired greater autonomy from the Spanish crown as well as greater access to the expanding trade of the Western Hemisphere, chiefly with the newly founded United States and with Great Britain. Political reforms granting more autonomy and freedom to the creoles carried the risk of liberating the subordinate majority of Amerindian peasants and African slaves. The danger of an insurrection from below was made evident by a peasant movement in 1780 led by the Inca Tupac Amaru to restore the ancient rule of the native Incas in Peru, and by the slaves' revolution in Haiti in 1791. Caught between a desire for reform and the need to preserve their authority, the creoles were split between the majority that still supported the Spanish monarchy and the Church, and a minority that sought reform in the light of the new ideas of the Enlightenment and the liberating example of the American Revolution.

The Impact of the French Revolution and Napoleonic Wars

This situation was unexpectedly changed by the French Revolution and Napoleonic Wars. The British defeat of the Spanish Armada (1588) and the effective British blockade of transatlantic trade caused a break in commercial relations between Spain and its huge American empire. In 1808, Napoléon invaded Spain and put his brother, Joseph Bonaparte, on the Spanish throne. These events created a crisis of legitimacy within the creole elite, who were divided between those still loyal to Spain and those seeking independence under a liberal constitution. The resultant Civil Wars (1808–1820) proved inconclusive until both the royalists and the liberals recognized that the Spanish government was unwilling to extend greater autonomy to its colonies and that appealing to the crown as a source of political legitimacy was no longer a viable option. The only course was independence, the terms of which would be decided by further armed struggle.

The Struggle for Colonial Independence

In Mexico, the elite chose independence for conservative reasons. Faced with protracted civil strife that began with an uprising of peasants and slaves in 1810, the Mexican landholders, led by Catholic priest Miguel Hidalgo, declared themselves independent from Spain in 1821. They feared reforms from a liberal republican government in Spain and opted for independence to preserve the existing social hierarchy.

In South America, the forces of liberalism were at the vanguard of the movement for independence. In the Andes Mountains, José de San Martín (1788–1850) led the armed struggle for the liberation of what is now Argentina, Chile, and Peru. Inspired by the American and French Revolutions, San Martín, an Argentine son of a Spanish army officer, hoped to establish independent constitutional monarchies in South America, but failed.

Simón Bolívar (1783–1830) led the armed struggle to the north and became known as the Liberator. Bolívar was born into a prominent creole Venezuelan family and dreamed of establishing independence under republican governments inspired in part by the United States and Revolutionary France. His grander vision was to found a great Pan-American federation similar to the United States, but that vision foundered on the political divisions within South America and the opposition of the United States and Great Britain. Despite his republican sympathies, Bolívar, like many of his liberal European contemporaries, was suspicious of democracy, and his experience in the early struggles for independence led him to rely on a more centralized political authority. After initial failures, Bolívar and his armed supporters established the independent states of Venezuela, Colombia, Ecuador, and Bolivia. Despite his achievements, he became disillusioned with his

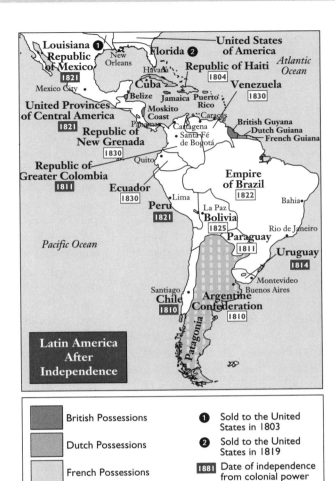

failure to unite into a federation the republics he had helped create. He said: "Those who have served the revolution have ploughed the sea." Bolívar died in 1830 at 47 on his way to self-exile in Europe.

The Aftermath of Independence: Rule by the Caudillos

The newly founded republics developed liberal constitutions, but failed to develop a political culture which could sustain that liberalism. Furthermore, civilian governments were subject to interventions by the army and to periods of authoritarian military rule. The wars of independence were really civil wars within the creole

Simón Bolívar:
"The Great Liberator"

 Travel to any Hispanic American nation and you will find the name Simón Bolívar prominently displayed in town squares or taught in the schools. Bolivia was named after him. Known to many as "The Great Liberator," Simón Bolívar was a man of heroic proportions who embraced the ideals of the Enlightenment in his struggle to free Latin Americans from the colonial chains that bound them.

Born in 1783 in Venezuela to a family of the elite, Simón was orphaned by the young age of nine. As a teenager, he was sent to Spain to further his education and to polish his social graces. Upon his return to Venezuela in 1802, Bolívar married the beautiful María Teresa Rodríguez del Toro, only to lose her to tropical fever within eight months. Following this tragic loss, Bolívar returned to Europe in 1803 to complete a grand tour taking him to Paris, Geneva, and Rome. His grand tour happened to coincide with the heady days of Napoléon Bonaparte, during which the armies of France were rearranging Europe into a "continental system."

Bolívar's tour through Europe did much to shape his political ideas and to strengthen his resolve to lead the people of Latin America to freedom. While in Europe, Bolívar was introduced to the ideas of Voltaire and Rousseau and met with Jeremy Bentham, from whom he seems to have developed a utilitarian philosophy of life. The driving force behind Bolívar's politics was that he never saw freedom as an end in itself; rather, he believed that government existed to maximize human happiness and its function was to make policy as well as to satisfy interests.

The period 1776–1848 in Europe was characterized by a vicious attack on the ancien régime. This struggle between monarchy and republic, conservatism and liberalism, and aristocracy and democracy was carried to Latin America by Simón Bolívar, who had embraced the Enlightenment ideals of sovereignty of the people, natural rights, and equality. In describing the Spanish American Revolution, Bolívar once said: "A republican government, that is what Venezuela had, has, and should have. Its principles should be the sovereignty of the people, division of powers, civil liberty, prohibition of slavery, and the abolition of monarchy and privileges. We need equality to recast, so to speak, into a single whole, the classes of men, political opinions, and public custom."

When Bolívar returned from Europe in 1807, he joined a secret organization committed to winning independence from Spain. Bolívar's dream was to unite the Spanish colonial empire, which stretched from California to the southern tip of South America, in an alliance of free and independent states. In 1819, after years of frustration, defeats, and exile, Bolívar addressed a revolutionary council in the Venezuelan town of Angostura (today Ciudad Bolívar). Here he outlined his proposal for a nation which would unite what we know today as Venezuela, Colombia, Ecuador, and Panama in a single independent state. This new state would form the cornerstone of the alliance of Latin American states of which he had dreamed. Over the next six years, Bolívar spearheaded a revolution which led to the liberation of Venezuela, Colombia, Ecuador, Peru, and Bolivia. Ultimately, his dream of a united Hispanic America failed to materialize due to internal divisions.

Simón Bolívar died in Colombia in 1830, his body destroyed by tuberculosis, his spirit destroyed by bitterness. Today, over a century and a half after his death, Bolívar's dream of a united Latin America remains alive.

elite. Beyond the quest for autonomy from Spanish authority, the creoles wished to avoid any political participation of the mestizo majority. There was no real middle class or working class to sustain pressure for reform based on liberal individualism or egalitarian democracy. In the republics, founded by the liberating armies led by Catholic priest José María Morelos in Mexico and by Bolívar and others in South America, military leaders were drawn from the landed elite. They championed the interests of rural society over the cities, and headed their own private armies. Appealing to the historical precedents of founding liberators such as Hidalgo, Bolívar, and San Martin, they claimed to be saviours of the nation in crisis. After 1825, military leaders called caudillos took over and made dictatorship a part of the political tradition of Latin America.

Latin America and Informal Empire

In the confused aftermath of their foundation, the new republics were vulnerable to a restoration of Spanish colonialism, had it not been for the protection of Great Britain and the United States. The British controlled the sea routes between Europe and South America, and worked in diplomatic councils to resist any threatened restoration of colonial rule. In 1823, James Monroe, the president of the United States, declared the Western hemisphere a sphere of influence of his government, and his Monroe Doctrine committed Washington to resist any European intervention.

British and American protection of the new republics preserved their political independence without hindering new, dependent, economic relationships. Free from the colonial connections with Spain, Latin American republics forged new trade and investment links with the world's predominant maritime and industrial power. Great Britain obtained raw materials and agricultural produce largely from Argentina, Chile, Peru, and Brazil, the largest South American republics. In return, these republics imported British manufactured goods, and from the 1850s, British firms and technology were used to build railroads and other engineering projects. The British negotiated trade agreements on the basis of free trade, which had the effect of opening Latin American markets to British manufacturers but also slowed Latin American industrial development because British industries could produce goods more cheaply. In contrast, the United States was using protective tariffs to allow its own industries to become established.

In the second half of the nineteenth century, the expansion of American economy led the United States to overtake Great Britain as the leading foreign economic interest in Latin America. Under the imperialism of free trade, the South American republics, having established their political autonomy, forged new forms of economic dependency. Eventually, this dependency created U.S. interest in the domestic politics of South America, and from the 1890s, especially in the Caribbean and in Central America, the United States displayed an increased willingness to intervene both politically and militarily.

The Age of Empire, 1850–1914

New Patterns of Imperialism: From Informal to Formal Empire

Within the evolving world system of Western dominance, a significant shift occurred in the second half of the nineteenth century. After 1870, and even more dramatically after 1885, there was a remarkable increase in European acquisition of colonial territories in the South Pacific, Asia, and Africa. In 1870, about 10 percent of Africa had been colonized, whereas by 1895, 90 percent had come under European colonial control. As noted above, earlier in the nineteenth century, imperial powers preferred the techniques of informal empire, in which commercial and political relations were established with indigenous elites but formal military conquest and colonization were thought unnecessary. After 1870, European powers began to rely more upon colonization or formal empire than on informal economic ties.

The explanation for this "new imperialism" has generated an enormous historical literature, partly because the topic remains central to the relationship of the wealthier Western industrial world to the poorer, non-Western, non-industrial periphery. At the centre of this political debate is the question of whether the new imperialism is considered a political phenomenon involving the extension of the power of Western nation-states or whether it is considered an economic phenomenon creating new forms of dependency and exploitation in the Third World.

Eurocentric Explanations of Imperialism

An initial *Eurocentric* approach, which concentrated on the political and economic motives for imperialism,

Sugarcane was one of the main assets acquired during the era of colonial possessions in Africa.

looked at events from the standpoint of London, Paris, Brussels, Berlin, or Washington. For example, the key political event in the race for colonization in Africa was the Berlin Conference of 1884–1885. Bismarck called together representatives of 15 nations to deal with rival colonial claims in Africa, especially with the creation of the Congo Free State by King Leopold II of Belgium.

Ignoring the rights of existing African kingdoms and peoples altogether, European powers claimed the right to acquire inland territories by expansion from existing coastal possessions. To avoid dominance by a single state or war between rival colonial powers, the Conference agreed that possession involved more than a "paper partition" based on claims made over a map; they agreed that possession should involve effective occupation of the land and control over the people. After 1885, Africa was swiftly partitioned among the European rival powers.

According to this Eurocentric view, the primary motive for colonization was political: governments, encouraged by the chauvinism of a mass electorate, enhanced their power and prestige by possessing colonies. But the actual defence of colonial acquisitions was rarely a matter of politics alone. Proponents of empire claimed that the superiority of industrial civilization gave Europeans the right to take over territories. In *The Control of the Tropics* (1898), British popular writer on imperialism Benjamin Kidd stressed that Europe was under the obligation to develop the tropics as "a trust for civilization." He claimed that "If our civilization has any right there at all, it is because it represents higher ideals of humanity, a higher type of social order." Kidd and other advocates of empire made the assumption that Western industrial civilization was superior, and that a kind of trusteeship existed in which colonies would be developed for the benefit of the colonizing power and for the subordinate colonized peoples—a condescending and racist assumption shared by many at the time.

The rival Eurocentric view of the new imperialism, the theory of ***economic imperialism***, challenged the claims of Kidd and other advocates of empire. This theory, proposed by liberal English economist J. A. Hobson in 1902, and later used by Russian statesman Lenin, argued that the primary motive for empire was economic. The main benefactors of imperialism were not the colonized peoples or the white populations of Europe or North America. According to Hobson and Lenin, colonies were acquired as fields for investment at the urging of capitalists with surplus wealth. These investors, some of whom owned popular newspapers and had an influence on politicians, promoted imperialism to get the state to acquire territories and protect their overseas investments. Lenin identified this form of imperialism with an advanced or monopoly stage of capitalism, and predicted that competition for colonies would eventually lead to war and revolution. Like the political explanations of imperialism, which stressed the role of European diplomacy, this economic theory of imperialism is Eurocentric in the sense that it focuses on the economies of advanced industrial nations and pays little attention to the economies in the non-Western world.

Peripheral Explanations of Imperialism

Contemporary explanations of imperialism have shifted the focus away from metropolitan centres in Europe and North America onto events in the periphery: Australasia, Asia, and Africa. According to this view,

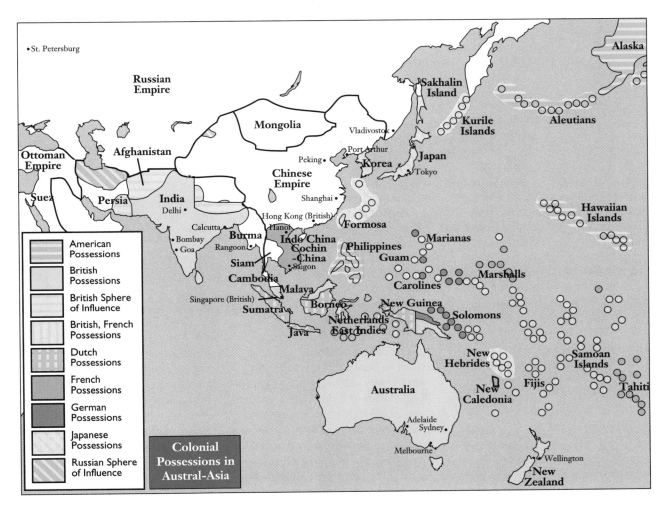

Colonial Possessions in Austral-Asia

American Possessions
British Possessions
British Sphere of Influence
British, French Possessions
Dutch Possessions
French Possessions
German Possessions
Japanese Possessions
Russian Sphere of Influence

the informal free-trade imperialism of the early nine-teenth century relied upon creating relations with collaborators drawn from merchant and political elites within the indigenous populations. As these economic relationship developed, Western influences began to effect a transformation of traditional European society and culture; movements to resist this transformation began to develop and networks of collaboration broke down. In order to restore the now necessary economic and political relations, Western colonial powers resort-ed to force, and imposed formal colonial rule by military conquest.

Superficially, it might be assumed that free trade was within the natural order, without the need for gov-ernment regulation but, in fact, free trade was a form of commercial relationship created, sometimes by

force, by the European powers, chiefly Great Britain. For example, although Western countries wanted access to the enormous market of China, the Chinese were relatively self-sufficient and the Manchu dynasty discouraged Western trade. Opium, a drug traded by the British from India and Southeast Asia to China, was one commodity for which the British created a demand in China, where opium was unknown until the British introduced it. When the Chinese government sought to control this pernicious trade, the British intervened militarily to defend it as free trade.

Through the **Opium Wars**, 1839–1842, the British succeeded in securing their demands for trade and took control of the important trading centre of Hong Kong. In response to increased Western influence and trade—and to the internal anarchy of Chinese politics—the

The Indian Mutiny of 1857

In the middle of the nineteenth century, European nations were not only experiencing a great deal of turmoil within their own borders but also facing resistance and revolt in the various nations which they ruled. In India, the British had been slowly increasing their influence and control since the early 1600s, when they established their first trading post. The function of the British firm John Company (later called the East India Company) was initially only trade but gradually, over the course of some 200 years, the Company forged alliances with local rulers who were involved in political disputes and wars of succession. The British established a number of puppet governments by militarily and financially supporting a local contender for power who would then rule according to their wishes and directly appoint them to various positions of power. By means of their overwhelming influence, they were changing the face of India in a number of ways: the agrarian structure was completely reformed; railways were introduced and transformed the movement of people and goods; the first telegraph lines were laid; and a national postal system was developed, creating new and far more efficient methods of communication.

Along with these progressive reforms, however, British influence also intruded upon many areas of Indian life that were resistant to change. The missionaries, preachers,

and lay reformers who had followed the merchants into India succeeded in their attempt to introduce English-language education and, as a result, opened the doors to Western culture and Western ideas about religion, politics, and so on. The advent of English education sparked an ongoing internal debate between those who believed that it would pose a threat to the preservation of indigenous culture and those who supported the idea and who, eventually, were able to use their knowledge of English and Western philosophy to speak to the British on their own terms during later movements toward independence.

The concern that the British were slowly making inroads into the local culture and threatening the survival of age-old traditions and social systems escalated as they implemented new social laws and introduced changes in the army. They had formally abolished the Hindu practice of *sati*, whereby widows may choose or be required by their families and communities to take their own lives by throwing themselves upon their husband's funeral pyre (cremation fire). In 1856, they passed a law which allowed Hindu widows to remarry—a practice that was unheard of.

Regarding the army, the General Service Enlistment Act forced Indian soldiers to accept service anywhere within the vast British Empire. This threatened to cause chaos within the society since social behaviour among Hindus was, and to a lesser degree still is, governed by a rigid social system of castes. The caste system is a

complex, hereditary system of social hierarchy, which dictates everything from a person's marital prospects to occupation and eating habits. It establishes one's status in society—a status which must be forfeited by those who deviate from accepted behaviour. One of these deviations was the act of "crossing the black waters," or leaving the Indian subcontinent to travel abroad. Thus, when the British required soldiers to accept service anywhere within the empire, they were undermining a basic part of the social structure.

The last straw was the introduction into the army of the new Enfield rifle. Soldiers had to bite the tip off the cartridges of the rifles when loading and unloading. A rumour spread that the cartridges had been smeared with animal fat and if the soldiers, who were, according to their religions, forbidden from eating specific types of meat, were to put the cartridges in their mouth, they would be violating one of their most sacred customs.

What would be recorded by historians as the Mutiny of 1857 began with an army brigade refusing to load their rifles. The British had the defiant soldiers imprisoned. The next day, three regiments rose in revolt while British officers were in church. They freed the prisoners, killed several officers, and marched upon the capital, Delhi. In Delhi, Indian soldiers opened the gates for the mutineers and allowed them to bring in and restore upon the throne a displaced Mogul ruler. News of the revolt spread and triggered revolts across the country. It is important to note, however, that there was little organization and no common thrust to the rebellions as some consisted of armies in revolt, some of peasants showing resentment toward losing their land during the agrarian reform, and still others complaining against excessive taxation. No leadership emerged, no unity was evident, and there was certainly no real concerted effort made toward driving the British out of India. Therefore, while some historians insist that the Mutiny of 1857 was the first organized show of resistance to the British in India and the forerunner to the later Independence movements, others suggest that it was little more than sporadic disobedience.

The British retaliated with vengeance: mutineers were put to death. Delhi was recaptured by British and Sikh troops and battles continued in northern and central India until late 1858. The most important result of the mutiny was the Government of India Act passed by the British Parliament in 1858, which transferred all rights of the East India Company directly to the crown. The British government formalized the control they had hitherto exerted through a trading company and, from then on, all decisions regarding the fate of the Indian people would be made in the British Parliament.

Indian Mutiny in Delhi

antimonarchist Taiping Rebellion erupted from 1850 to 1864. European military forces intervened in support of the Manchu dynasty and helped crush the rebellion, thus winning further privileges for Western traders. In this way, the policy of free trade imposed by Western military force brought China within the informal imperialism of Western power, and provoked Chinese resistance to the alien influences on their society.

In other instances, the breakdown of collaborative relationships led to the imposition of formal imperial authority. The British East India Company had secured an effective, if informal, economic control of the Indian subcontinent by the 1780s. The cumulative impact of Westernizing reforms in the economy, in administration, in the law, in education, and in religion made Indians fearful of the loss of their rich, varied, and ancient traditions and values. In 1857, in Northern India, a mutiny among the sepoys (native Indian troops serving in the British army in India) led to widespread unrest and to the perpetration of atrocities against Europeans. British forces retaliated in kind. In 1858, the British government disbanded the East India Company and created the Government of India under a Viceroy directly responsible to the British Parliament. Thus, the breakdown of existing forms of collaboration and the outbreak of resistance in the form of the Sepoy Mutiny led the British to impose formal imperial control.

Developments in Jamaica show a similar process at work. In 1865, conflict between black peasants and white landowners over vacant land led to a riot in Morant Bay, in which 18 people died. In response, Governor Edward John Eyre imposed martial law for six weeks, during which 439 people were killed or executed, another 650 were flogged, and over 1000 peasants' homes were burned. The brutality of the repression raised a public outcry in Britain, but the political repercussions of the rebellion were longer-lasting. In order to preserve Britain's imperial control and to defend the privileged status of white planters against the rising demands of the non-white middle class and peasantry, the elected legislative assembly was disbanded and Jamaica returned to crown colony status. It would be ruled from London until 1884. At the same time, the remaining colony of British North America renegotiated its relationship with the British Parliament, and became the self-governing Dominion of Canada in 1867.

Technology and Empire

European imposition of formal colonial rule in response to the breakdown of collaboration was made possible by advances in Western technology. In earlier times, tropical regions had presented a powerful natural barrier to white settlement: disease. With advances in medicine, especially with the use of the antimalarial drug quinine, white soldiers, administrators, traders, and missionaries could now live in regions once considered inhospitable to Europeans. These agents of white empire were now equipped with a new technological capacity enabling them to control territories and peoples in a fashion that was not possible even in the first half of the nineteenth century: the breech-loading rifle and the machine gun. These technological innovations gave even small brigades of European soldiers a decided advantage over much larger armies of natives equipped only with spears and muskets. Arms, supplies, and soldiers could also be transported quickly and efficiently on steam launches navigating interior lakes and rivers; the railroad facilitated far more extensive control over large tracts of densely populated land.

In addition to advances in transportation, the world-wide network of postal services and the telegraph, though slow by today's standards, revolutionized communications, enabling officials to communicate quickly with metropolitan authorities. Technological advances gave Westerners the capacity to exercise power in a new way, but the will to put that capacity to use stemmed from the political and economic imperatives behind colonial expansion.

The Partition of Africa

The partition of Africa is a classic case of late nineteenth century imperialism. The events that brought political and economic imperatives into action occurred not in the metropolitan centre of Europe but in the periphery: in Africa itself. From a British perspective, Africa represented a strategic rather than an economic interest in that the continent's shoreline was part of the route to India. There were areas of vital concern along this important trade route: the Suez Canal, Egypt, the Red Sea, the Horn of Africa, and the Cape of Good Hope, which was a naval and fuelling station.

Britain had the largest established empire and dominated the route to India by defending strategic outposts, arousing rivalry with other European powers.

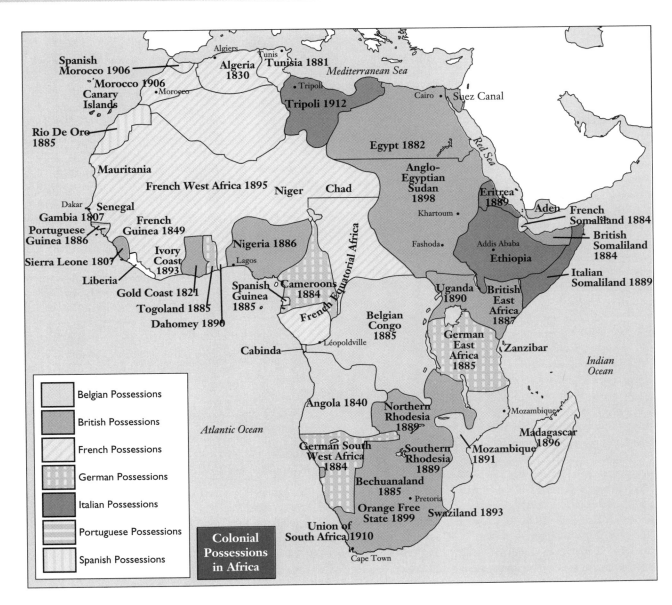

Colonial Possessions in Africa

Legend:
- Belgian Possessions
- British Possessions
- French Possessions
- German Possessions
- Italian Possessions
- Portuguese Possessions
- Spanish Possessions

France had its own interest in Suez, Egypt, North Africa, and West Africa. In Southern Africa and in East Africa, the Germans also sought to establish colonies. King Leopold II of Belgium sought recognition for his Congo Free State. In addition, colonial interests and settlers, including private companies with private armies in West Africa, French colonists in Algeria, and British and Boer settlers in Southern Africa, encroached upon African and Arab territory, sparking wars of resistance. These competing interests put strategically sensitive areas of Africa in turmoil. Trying to contend with this unrest, the colonial powers were drawn deeper and deeper into Africa, partitioning the continent at first, and later formally making colonies out of areas of influence.

The turmoil in the periphery was itself a product of the informal influence of the Western economic presence, and the political and economic needs of the

The Jamaican Slave Revolt of 1831

The abolition of slavery in much of the Western world during the nineteenth century was the result of many forces. The ideals of the Enlightenment, which stressed individual freedom and tolerance, are often cited as a primary force in the European decision to end slavery. But one must not overlook the role of the slaves themselves in bringing about their own emancipation. The Jamaican slave experience provides a valuable look at their determination to be free.

Throughout the eighteenth century, violent protests against slavery in the form of riots or rebellions were a common occurrence. Uprisings to end slavery, such as the Maroon wars of 1738 and 1795, occurred on average every five years and met with limited success, especially in the mountain districts. Revolts such as these played a significant role in the British government's ultimate decision to abolish the slave trade in 1808. After this date, there was little agitation until the 1820s when, under the influence of the anti-slavery movement in England, further disturbances began to break out in Jamaica.

The condition of slavery in Jamaica was similar to many other countries where slavery existed: a white minority ruled over a slave population nearly ten times as large; the exclusion of slaves as witnesses in courts was indicative of the assumption that they were creatures of inferior intelligence; family life was discouraged to demonstrate the intrinsically animal nature of the African slaves; and the use of the whip as an instrument of punishment symbolized the use of terror to maintain slavery.

In 1831 word reached the slaves in Jamaica that the British government had passed legislation to end slavery. This rumour was spread by Sam Sharpe, a domestic slave who worked in Montego Bay. Sharpe was intellgent,

---

In 1831, rebels attacked the Monpelier Old Works Estate during the Jamaican Slave Revolt.

literate, and ambitious. Although he was himself aware that no such legislation had been passed, he used the rumour to fuel a slave rebellion. Beginning in August 1831, Sharpe and his associates started to organize for a Christmas rebellion. By December 1831 the agitation for revolt was reaching a peak. On December 27, 1831, missionary minister William Knibb tried to warn the African slaves: "I learn that some wicked persons have persuaded you that the King has made you free. Hear me, I love your souls—I would not tell you a lie for the world. What you have been told is false—false as Hell can make it. I entreat you not to believe it, but to go to your work as usual."

Knibb's warning served only to disappoint and anger the slaves, who felt missionaries were concerned with law and order but not with their freedom. On the same day as Knibb's warning, a fire on the Kensington estate in St. James, one of the most important sugar-growing parishes, marked the beginning of a slave rebellion that would engulf the western part of the island of Jamaica. The rebellion would last a few weeks but ultimately proved unsuccessful. Lack of unification between various groups, a shortage of weapons, and poor military training all contributed to the ultimate defeat of the rebel slaves.

Despite the failure of the revolt, its significance should not be overlooked. The organization of the rebellion demonstrated some degree of political maturity as they sought to bring about reform to Jamaican society rather than create a utopian world. The rebellion did contribute indirectly to the abolition of slavery. Following the rebellion, white slave owners blamed missionaries for the rebellion and, in retaliation, chapels were destroyed. This led the missionaries to conclude that the only way they could carry on their work was if slavery was abolished. They therefore sent delegates to England, where they became invaluable propagandists in the fight to end slavery. Slavery was completely abolished in the British empire on January 1, 1835.

colonial powers drew them further into these conflicts. In the frantic rush to obtain colonies in the last two decades of the nineteenth century, European powers intervened in Africa, Asia, and the Pacific, not so much in quest of immediate gain as out of fear that a rival power might gain future strategic or economic benefit. Having premised the acquisition of colonies on the prospect of gain, the colonial powers, once they had secured effective occupation, made every effort to make the colony pay back. At this point in the process, the lives of the peoples of Australasia, Asia, Africa, and the Americas began to be transformed in new and more substantial ways, and often those changes were imposed by force.

Colonial Labour and European Racism

Colonial Development and Labour

In the view of the European powers, colonies were not to be a drain on the treasury of the metropolitan state but rather the cost of maintaining economic dominance over the colony was to be borne by the colony itself. The costs of colonial administration and military presence were obtained through local taxes. For example, the Indian Army, paid for by taxes imposed on the people of India, served the British Empire not only in India, but in Southeast Asia, Hong Kong, Persia, Egypt, and East Africa. Taxes usually involved payment in cash, thus serving the additional purpose of forcing non-Western populations into a cash economy. Taxation created a need for colonial people to become wage earners engaged in growing agricultural produce or mining minerals for export. In this way, as wage earners with a cash income to pay taxes, workers in Asia and Africa became part of the larger world economy and were converted into consumers of manufactured goods produced by the industrialized nations.

The conversion of peoples into wage labourers and consumers had to overcome a number of substantial obstacles. In some cases, there was not a sufficient number of suitable labourers. For example, in Queensland, Australia, the local aboriginal population and the white settlers could not meet the needs of the sugar planters. Labour contractors recruited—or captured—over 62 000 "blackbirds," or South Sea Islanders, and brought them to work on the Queensland plantations. Beyond the question of labour supply, self-sufficient peasant cultivators did not respond immediately to the lure of a wage income and a market economy stressing production for export. Labour on plantations or in mines involved more arduous work for longer hours at a lower living standard than could be achieved in a traditional farming or hunting economy.

Facing these obstacles to the supply of labour, colonial developers often resorted to various forms of compulsory labour. The moral prestige of the anti-slavery movement meant that slavery, the traditional form of coerced labour, could not be reinstituted. Furthermore, in the metropolitan industrial world, the principle of free labour and democratic political rights, such as the vote, had been established by the late nineteenth century. The colonial world moved in the opposite direction. Colonial development relied on new forms of compulsory labour and, apart from white-settler communities, the "natives" or "coloured races," to use the language of colonialism, were subject to discriminatory laws and denied the rights of citizens. These blatant contradictions between Western principle and practice were reconciled by the pervasive racist ideology of the time: racism gave freedom as a right to the whites but denied it to non-whites.

The Legacy of Emancipation

The British West Indies

New forms of compulsory labour developed out of the legacy of race slavery. In the British West Indies, former slaves worked as wage labourers on plantations or as small independent cultivators on their own tracts of land. From the 1830s onward, the West Indian sugar industry was in decline from the competition of European sugar beets and Cuban sugar. Still attached to their slave-owning past, the planters held the former slaves responsible for the economic decline. Claiming that the native blacks were unproductive, costly labourers, estate owners sought alternative cheap labour by importing indentured workers from India. The former defenders of the black population, the abolitionists, believed that once slavery had ended and individual freedom existed under the law, progress and prosperity would follow. Even though the abolitionists denounced race prejudice, their assault on slavery did not lead to a movement against racism. With the decline in the West Indian sugar economy, many abolitionists began to view emancipation as a failure and became tolerant toward the planters' demands for cheap migrant labour.

The American South and Segregation

British and American observers applied the lessons of the apparent failure of emancipation in the West Indies to policies in the southern United States after the Civil War and to British policies in Africa. From 1865 to 1876, the policy of Reconstruction, including some land redistribution to former slaves and the extension of political and civil rights to African Americans, was imposed on the South by the victorious North. As northern reform energy weakened, white southerners reasserted their political power, and dismantled the reforms of Reconstruction. White control of land perpetuated the former slaves' dependency. The system of sharecropping met the former slaves' desire to be independent cultivators, but kept them in chronic debt to white landowners. The southern elite, backed by poor whites seeking privileges from their racial status, also reasserted their political predominance and excluded blacks from the political process. Under the Jim Crow legislation of the 1890s, the practice of racial segregation was incorporated into law and enforced within communities by vigilante attacks on blacks, including widespread lynchings, by the Ku Klux Klan and other white racist gangs.

The experience of the American South influenced developments elsewhere. Some observers saw that the South and its innovative policy of segregation provided a model for other multiracial societies and applied the American example to Southern Africa and other colonial societies.

Indentured and Migrant Labour

Indentured Labour

Plantations had been most fully developed in the slave societies of the New World, but in the course of the nineteenth century, colonists adopted the use of gang labour for the production of crops to be exported to Asia, the Pacific, and Africa. Plantation workers produced tea in Ceylon, rubber in Malaya, sugar in Queensland (Australia) and Fiji Islands, sugar in Natal (South Africa), cloves in Zanzibar, cocoa in the Congo and Angola, rubber in the Congo, and palm oil in West Africa. Like the plantations, the mining industry and large construction projects, such as railroads, also used gang labour. By the end of the nineteenth century, extensive internal migration existed in Africa, especially to the gold mines in South Africa and to the copper belt in the Congo and Rhodesia.

The most extensively organized system of migrant labour was the trade in indentured labourers from India and China. Between 1830 and 1870, at least 1 million—possibly as many as 2 million—indentured labourers were sent from India to various British colonies. This trade continued into the 1920s, with most immigrants going to Ceylon (today Sri Lanka), Burma (today Myanmar), and Malaya (today Malaysia), but significant numbers worked on plantations in Fiji, Mauritius, and Natal. The longest and most hazardous journey was to the British West Indies. Between 1838 and 1900, 200 000 Indian labourers were settled in British Guiana; another 150 000 were taken to Trinidad. The indenture schemes assumed that the cost of the journey would be borne by the employer, but in the British West Indies, it was paid by the colonial governments out of taxes on consumer goods. Thus black consumers paid for the indentured labourers who competed with them for employment on the plantations.

Chinese migrants more commonly worked in mining and construction than on plantations. In the mid-nineteenth century, there were 42 000 Chinese miners in the Australian gold fields, and a total of 200 000 Chinese went to California to work in the gold mines and railroad construction, and in the growing and processing of fruit. After disease and exhaustion decimated Hawaiian migrants employed in the extraction of nitrate from the guano (bird excrement) beds in Peru, 90 000 Chinese indentured labourers were recruited for this dangerous work (workers experienced lung damage from toxic fine particles). In Peru and the United States, Chinese labourers also worked on railroad construction: 15 000 were recruited from Hong Kong alone to complete the Canadian Pacific Railway. Chinese labourers were most extensively recruited to work in Southeast Asia, where they would work in the tin mines and on spice plantations in Malaya and Singapore. For a brief period in the aftermath of the Boer War, gold mining companies in the Transvaal recruited over 50 000 indentured Chinese miners as an alternative to African miners who were in short supply, demanded higher wages, and posed a political threat.

The indenture was a contract to work for a specified period of time, usually five years. The contract provided for transportation to the colony, lodging, and wages. The aim of indentured labourers, who were predominantly males, was to work to send monies back to their families in India or China. Although technically a voluntary contract labour system, the indenture system was considered by many to be a new system of slavery. Contractors in India and China recruited the labourers from the most impoverished classes. When offered the inducement of a small advance, many recruits, already facing punishment for debt, were entrapped into contracts they did not understand. At the end of their lengthy sea voyage, the labourers faced demanding physical work, lived in crowded barracks, received inadequate food and no health care, and lacked a normal family life. When they had a conflict with their employers, they faced a legal system and a police force ready to enforce their employers' conditions. Indentured labourers often had to earn money to buy their return passage. In the West Indies, the return could cost an additional five years of labour. Consequently, indenture, though intended to be temporary, often became a permanent migration to a new home.

Immigration and the White Dominions

Concomitantly with the system of compulsory migrant labour, voluntary migration of non-whites to the so-called "white" dominions of the British Crown and the United States was closed off by exclusionary immigration policies. After an initial period in which Chinese, South Asians, and other non-white immigrants entered these self-governing colonies, Australia, New Zealand, South Africa, and Canada instituted "whites only" immigration policies. These discriminatory restrictions were an embarrassment to the British government, as they contradicted the imperial claim that all persons, regardless of skin colour, were equal subjects of the Queen.

Faced with the protests of the governments of India, China, and Japan, the dominions found non-racial ways to exclude non-white immigrants. Australia, New Zealand, and South Africa imposed a literacy test in a European language, and allowed wide discretion on the part of immigration officers. For example, when a South Asian or Chinese immigrant with literacy in English applied, Australian officials demanded literacy in another European language. Canada adopted a similar strategy by insisting that immigrants travel directly from their home port to a port of entry into Canada. Since most ships from India

and China went via Hawaii, immigrants could not readily pass this entry requirement.

When taken together, exclusionary immigration policies and compulsory migrant labour constitute one of the clearest signs of Eurocentric racism that characterized the age of imperialism. Racism also constitutes one of the most painful and enduring legacies of colonialism. In areas of European settlement, it created the myth that in the past and in the future, these lands were by right "a white man's country." In areas of forced mass migration like Fiji, Malaya, South Africa, and Guyana, colonialism left a legacy of communities divided by race and ethnicity.

In order to overcome this racist legacy, we need to understand that such conflicts are not a reflection of human nature but the result of the past actions of humans seeking their own immediate gain. We must also realize that prejudice and conflict are readily transmitted to future generations through the education of our children rather than through heredity.

Wage Labour and the African Peasantry

Wage Labour and the Cash Economy

In Africa, colonial developers made extensive use of migrant labour, and used a variety of strategies to compel Africans into a cash, wage-labour economy. Even though such imposed change was often defended as bringing the benefits of civilization or modernization to "backward" peoples and cultures, the supposed benefits were not readily apparent to those peoples directly affected. In some instances, Africans not only found their lives changed against their will, but also came to endure working and living conditions inferior to those they experienced prior to Western intervention.

Between 1890 and 1914, colonial developers faced the problem of changing African populations from traditional pastoral and agrarian economies to wage labour geared for agricultural export, in industrial enterprises such as mines, and in large infrastructure projects such as the building of railways. For the colonial government or investor, the task was to bring the resources of the colony—land, natural resources, and labour—into production to gain a profit. Indigenous African societies had their own systems of production and trade that were relatively self-sufficient, and thus they did not necessarily respond to opportunities for trading with European entrepreneurs or for working as wage earners for colonial employers.

When diamonds were discovered in 1871, thousands of European fortune hunters flocked to South Africa. The African workers in the mines were exploited and treated harshly.

The Congo Free State and "Red Rubber"

The process of converting Africans into labourers in a cash economy exhibited its most brutal features in the Congo Free State (today Republic of Zaire), between 1885 and 1908. King Leopold II of Belgium took about half the land into his private ownership or gave it to companies granted concessions in return for railroad development. The Congolese now had more restricted use of land for their own agriculture, while Leopold and the concessionaires compelled the local population to harvest natural rubber.

To satisfy the demand of the industrial world for rubber for pneumatic tires on bicycles and automobiles, Congolese workers had to find and tap the rubber trees in the tropical rain forest. They often had to work far from their home villages, and brutal retaliations were inflicted upon them for failure to meet the required quotas. Adolescent boys were punished by mutilation including cutting off ears or hands. Failure of particular villagers to meet quotas resulted in raids on their home villages, where women were raped, children and the elderly beaten, and houses destroyed. In 1908, an international crusade of humanitarian agencies finally pressured Leopold II to turn his private domain in the Congo over to the Belgian government. By that time,

the production of rubber on plantations in Malaya had replaced the brutal harvest of "red rubber" (referring to the blood of Africans) in the Congo.

The Origins of Apartheid in South Africa

The Belgian Congo was the most notorious case of brute force to compel Africans into wage labour and a cash economy. South Africa had a system of migrant African labour in the gold mines, which laid the foundation for **apartheid** and which had long-term consequences. In 1867, rich diamond deposits were discovered at Kimberley. Mine owners recruited migrant African labour to work the deposits on short-term contracts. In order to prevent the theft of diamonds, they placed labourers in compounds separating men from their families. This compound system was later adapted in Witwatersrand in the Transvaal, where extensive gold ores were discovered in 1886. Miners from Europe would handle the technology for working underground and African labourers shifted the ore to the surface. In order to recruit workers, poll taxes were levied on Africans to create a need for cash income. Men migrated to the mines, while their families remained in homelands engaged in traditional pastoral and agricultural pursuits. This system enabled employers to pay Africans less than an economic wage for, unlike that of European workers, the pay did not have to provide for wives and families.

These economic and social changes revived the long-standing conflict between the descendants of the Dutch settlers, the Boers, and the British. The gold mines were financed and administered by British companies, and attracted British settlers, but the gold fields were located in the three republics created by the Boers (Natal, Transvaal, and Orange Free State). Conflicts over control of the gold fields and treatment of British settlers led to the Boer War, 1899–1902, which ended with the surrender of the Boers.

In the negotiations for the Union of South Africa, the rights and interests of Africans were largely ignored, despite British claims to the contrary. With the exception of the "Cape coloured" who already had the vote, the constitution of the new Union of South Africa denied Africans all political rights, including the vote. The new Union also passed laws to institutionalize the practice of a segregated, migrant African labour force. Although Africans constituted about 80 percent of the population, the 1913 Lands Act allocated 13 percent of the land for

African homelands. Africans also were restricted in their freedom to settle in the cities, and laws required them to carry passes for travel and residence outside of designated areas. From these beginnings, the system of apartheid made racial segregation the overriding reality of South African society.

In examining various forms of migratory and compulsory labour, we have focused on those peoples most dramatically affected by late nineteenth century colonialism. Even in 1900, many hunter-and-gatherer and agriculturalist societies in the Third World had only begun to feel the impact of a global market economy. Nonetheless, by 1900 the directions of change were clear. The transition to modern capitalist forms of production often required force; consequently, this modernizing process produced instability and conflict. Colonialism fundamentally altered economic and political relationships as well as the whole fabric of the social and cultural life of communities. Colonized peoples developed their own strategies of resistance in response to Western intervention.

Nationalism and Resistance in the Colonial Empires, 1850–1914

Colonialism and Resistance

Apart from colonies of white settlement, the winning of national independence in Asia, Africa, and the Caribbean occurred after World War II. It would be a mistake, though, to think that colonial nationalist movements were so recent in origin. In fact, the resistance of the peoples of Asia and Africa to colonialism was contemporaneous with the new imperialism of the nineteenth century. Out of this long struggle, there emerged a sense that all colonized peoples shared elements of a common history and identity. Consequently, unlike the nation-state nationalism of Europe, the colonial nationalist movements developed a sense of being part of a larger international movement of colonized peoples seeking liberation from colonialism and racial oppression.

As noted earlier in the discussion of peripheral explanations of imperialism, the creation of formal colonies by European states often occurred in response to the breakdown of earlier forms of collaboration, which in turn were occasioned by the outbreak of popular protests. These anti-Western protests, sometimes called primary resistance movements, aimed to kick the foreigners out and restore the culture to its original state. This effort at restoration through popular violence often took on a religious form that opposed the decadence and corruption associated with Western influences.

The resistance of peoples under threat of colonization accounted for the frequent colonial wars during the age of imperialism. In resisting the encroachment of white settlers, aboriginal peoples engaged in a series of unsuccessful wars in the American West; similarly, in the 1840s and again in the 1860s, the Maoris of New Zealand fought to preserve their land and culture. As noted earlier, the Indian Mutiny led by sepoy troops in 1857 attempted to put a halt to the Western reforms that British rule had imposed on India. The next generation of Indian nationalists looked back to the Sepoy Mutiny as the origin of the movement for independence from British rule. In China, as noted before, the Taiping Rebellion of the 1850s and 1860s was a reform movement inspired by religious and political ideals in opposition to Western influence.

In the partition of Africa, the contending forces of indigenous resistance and Western encroachment were also at work. In what today is South Africa, Bantu-speaking peoples, most notably the Zulus, organized by their great chief, Shaka (1787–1828), into a military caste, conducted a long struggle against both Boer settlers and British authorities from the 1830s to the end of the nineteenth century. Years later, under the leadership of Catewayo, the Zulus inflicted a defeat on the British army at Islandhlwana in 1879, but the British army received a quick supply of reinforcements and took its revenge a year later.

In West Africa, where trading relationships between local coastal states and Europeans had existed for 400 years, British and French intrusion in the interior in search of gold, palm oil, and other tropical products brought the British and the French into conflict with large and powerful African states. After a series of wars commencing in the 1870s and ending at the beginning of the twentieth century, Britain and France established the colonies of West Africa.

The French advance from Senegal into the interior brought them into conflict with Islamic states; in the

Sudan, the British also confronted Islamic forces attempting to preserve their autonomy from Western influences. In 1885, the Islamic leader, or Mahdi, and his followers succeeded in capturing Khartoum and killing its British commander, General Gordon. They secured control of the area for more than a decade. In 1898, a British force at Omdurman, equipped with machine guns, killed 11 000 Sudanese and lost 28 British soldiers, putting an end to this Islamic revolt. British success antagonized the French, and the two countries came near to war in a confrontation at Fashoda (today Kodok, in the Sudan) in 1898.

In this fashion, African resistance and European colonization were antagonistic participants in a common historical process. In the short term, the global phenomena of resistance to Western imperialism in Asia and Africa may have failed, but in the longer term, this resistance laid the foundations for the modern nationalist movements for liberation from colonial rule.

The Origins of Colonial Nationalism

Once military force had established political control, the task of colonial administration and economic development depended upon recruits drawn from the indigenous population. In the early twentieth century, the Raj, or British rule in India, relied on a staff of about 1000 British civil servants, and a total resident European population of about 150 000, including British army officers, soldiers, and their wives and dependants, to administer 300 million Indians. Obviously, in the army, in government, and in private businesses like banking, commerce, and the railways, Indians were employed in a host of jobs that required a knowledge of English and some familiarity with Western legal, administrative, and business practices. At considerable expense, Indian families had their sons educated at colleges in India or, when possible, in Britain, to make them qualified for employment in these occupations.

Mohandas Gandhi (1869–1948), the future leader of the Indian nationalist movement, went to London to train as a barrister. In West Africa, a similar class of Western-educated Africans received their training at mission schools and colleges and, in some cases, went on to study law or medicine at British and European universities.

These Western-educated, highly qualified professionals became disenchanted with European rule and founded nationalist political parties seeking first reform and eventually independence. In the late nineteenth century, European racism intensified and colonial administrators began exercising an authoritarian form of governance. They had little tolerance for democracy within Europe—let alone within colonial empires. Consequently, white officials restricted African and Asian professionals to subordinate positions and also denied that equality before the law and the right to political representation were suited to colonial societies or to non-European peoples. As victims of the racism practised by foreign intruders, Western-educated elites developed a legitimate sense of grievance and a desire to be masters in their own lands.

The Indian National Congress

Founded in 1885, the **Indian National Congress** was one of the earliest of colonial nationalist political parties, and one of the most influential examples followed by nationalists elsewhere. In its origins, the Congress was moderate in its proposals for reform, seeking a larger role for Indians within the councils and administrative structure of the British Raj, but not seeking full political independence. From the outset, though, leaders of the Congress questioned the direction of economic developments in India. The modernization of agriculture and the extension of railroads had changed patterns of landholding and had converted some areas into the production of export crops. These reforms had also increased the peasants' indebtedness and their vulnerability to famines that struck in the 1870s and 1880s. Some Indian nationalists charged that the British connection acted as an economic drain on the resources of India. Although the leaders of the Congress were moderate and constitutional in their demands, British officials viewed them as unrepresentative troublemakers, until more radical voices and popular protests began to change the face of Indian nationalism.

The supporters of the Congress were largely high-caste Hindus with a Western education and representative of urban interests. Their foremost spokesperson was G. K. Gokhale (1866–1915), a constitutional moderate who challenged the conduct of the British administration. A rival and more militant nationalism, associated with the revival of the Hindu religion and with support from rural communities, developed under the leadership of B. G. Tilak (1856–1920). At the cost of his own imprisonment, he championed the freedom of the press and demanded independence from British rule. Popular violence and protests, some involving conflicts between Hindus and Moslems, led the British to propose a partition of the province of Bengal in 1905. This provoked widespread rioting and a boycott of British goods and British institutions. The British proposal to partition Bengal, militant Indian nationalism, and the potential for an independent mass movement radicalized the Indian Congress and, in 1905, the party committed itself to the goal of Indian self-government.

Origins of the Pan-African Movement

The Indian National Congress became a model for other colonial nationalist parties in its creation of a broad-based coalition with the common goal of national independence. In fact, colonial nationalist movements often had an international dimension. In July 1900, a group of men and women from Africa or of African descent held the first **Pan-African Conference** in London, the capital of the world's largest empire. The Conference was organized by Henry Sylvester Williams, a Trinidadian schoolteacher who had studied law at Dalhousie University in Halifax and King's College in London. Williams brought together representatives from the independent black states of Abyssinia, Liberia, and Haiti, as well as lawyers, clergymen, and journalists from South and West Africa. About 50 people attended the conference, and those from the Americas outnumbered those from Africa. The Rev. Henry B. Brown, an African-Canadian clergyman from Ontario, served as vice-president. The President of the Conference and leading speaker was Bishop Alexander Walters of the African Methodist Episcopal Zion Church of New York and chairman of the Afro-American National Council. From the U. S., young W. E. B. DuBois, who would have a long and distinguished career as a scholar, civil rights activist, and champion of Pan-Africanism, assisted with the preparation of the Conference's "Address to the Nations of the World."

This gathering of intellectuals, lawyers, clergymen, journalists, and students gave early expression to the solidarity of African peoples. The participants understood that in the struggle against colonialism and racism, the peoples of Africa and the descendants of slaves transported to the Americas were joined in a common battle. Their liberation could only come with the liberation of all peoples from racial oppression. Although the address itself attempted to appeal to liberal and humanitarian opinion in Britain and elsewhere in the Western world, it forthrightly set out the demands of African peoples, and of colonized peoples in Asia and elsewhere, for equal and universal rights as human beings and as democratic citizens. In a phrase later made famous by W. E. B. DuBois, the address identified:

> The problem of the twentieth century is the problem of the colour line, the question as to how far differences of race—which show themselves chiefly in the colour of the skin and texture of the hair—will hereafter be made the basis of denying to over half the world the right of sharing to their utmost ability the opportunities and privileges of modern civilization.

A small group of black activists meeting in London in 1900 had little immediate impact beyond articulating an alternative vision to the predominant imperial and racist conception of the world's peoples. Within the course of six or seven decades, through heroic struggle and many painful setbacks, the visionary idealists of 1900 helped transform the world.

Colonial Nationalism and Resistance Prior to 1914

The Pan-African Conference was unusual in its global vision of how racism and colonialism affected peoples of African descent in particular and colonized peoples in general. Prior to 1914, the more usual pattern had been the outbreak of localized and apparently unrelated uprisings, wars, and revolutions. The causes of these outbreaks might well have been local, but knowledge of these conflicts became widespread. The revolution in communications not only enabled the metropolitan powers to impose their authority more effectively, it also enabled colonized peoples to understand the global dimension of colonial conflict and racial oppression. In Japan, China, India, the Middle East, South and West Africa, the West Indies, and among the African American community in the United States, daily newspapers reported these events from a non-Western perspective. From this point of view and that of some Western observers, these localized outbreaks fit into a larger pattern indicating that the face of imperialism and global power would be fundamentally altered in the new twentieth century.

A quick survey of some of these conflicts in the two decades prior to 1914 provides a measure of this emerging sense of a global crisis. In 1898, Spain faced nationalist uprisings in the last strongholds of its mighty empire: Cuba and the Philippines. Cuban and Filipino nationalists challenged the authority of Madrid, only to be faced with the intervention of a former colony that had become an imperialist power: the United States of America. In both instances, the United States intervened, ostensibly to protect American lives and property, and ended Spanish colonial rule in their last two colonies. Filipino and Cuban nationalists now found themselves living in client states of the new American power.

In 1899, a secret martial-arts society in China, known as the Society of Harmonious Fists, or Boxers, conducted a campaign of murder and assault against Westerners in China. Intervention by the Western powers only intensified anti-foreign feelings and weakened support for the Manchu dynasty. From 1906 to 1910, Japan, the new Asian imperial power, faced protests and riots from Koreans resisting Japanese rule. In India, especially in the province of Bengal, the British faced hostile demonstrations and boycotts. In Egypt in 1906, *fellaheen* (peasants, in Arabic) attacked a British hunting party; in retaliation, an innocent Egyptian was beaten to death, and another four were executed. This event profoundly alienated nationalist opinion and, in order to control dissent, the British imposed press censorship and detention without trial.

Similar events in Africa laid the foundation for the subsequent development of nationalist agitation both within the continent and outside. In 1896, Emperor Menelik of Ethiopia and his army

of 100 000 defeated Italian forces at Adowa and preserved the kingdom's ancient autonomy. Ethiopia had a special significance in African culture: it had links with the civilization of ancient Egypt; in the Bible, Ethiopia was synonymous with all of Africa; and it was also the home of Coptic Christianity. Influenced in part by African American missionaries, South African Christians founded the Ethiopian movement, which appealed to African converts throughout the continent, to found an autonomous church independent of European missions corrupted by imperialism.

If the Union of South Africa was innovative in the development of racial segregation, its oppressed peoples were equally innovative in developing strategies to resist oppression. In the aftermath of the Boer War, there were protests against the importation of 50 000 indentured Chinese labourers to work in the gold mines. In Natal, in 1906, Zulus rose in insurrection against efforts to compel them into wage-labour mining. The Indian community of Natal and the Transvaal faced racial discrimination in the denial of the vote, in restrictions on their businesses, in the obligation to carry identity passes, and in the government's refusal to recognize the legality of both Hindu and Moslem marriages. Mohandas Gandhi, a barrister who went to South Africa to be an advocate for the Indian community, having exhausted conventional legal avenues, launched a campaign on a new set of principles: passive resistance and civil disobedience. When he returned to India, he was already a well-known champion of Indian rights—the Indian press had followed his career—and had protested against the mistreatment of South Asians in South Africa, British Columbia, and elsewhere in the British Empire. In 1912, Africans, frustrated by the omission of their rights in the constitution of the Union of South Africa, formed the South African Natives National Congress, the forerunner of the African National Congress.

In Latin America, the forces of nationalist and popular protest had to contend with the authority of

Sun Yat-sen, who despised the corrupt Manchu dynasty, led the 1911 Revolution that brought down the world's oldest empire.

the caudillos and the landed elite. They also had to deal with American economic and political influence which had become more visible with the readiness of Washington to intervene in the domestic politics of the Caribbean and Central America. In addition to American intervention in Cuba and Puerto Rico in the Spanish-American War (1898), Washington promoted a secessionist movement in Colombia, and intervened in 1903 to establish the client state of Panama to secure lands for the future Panama Canal. American troops also occupied Nicaragua in 1912 to support the United Fruit Company, and invaded the Dominican Republic in 1914, and Haiti in 1915.

The most significant upheaval occurred in Mexico, where Washington also tried to influence events, but where a revolutionary crisis, 1910–1920, created a social upheaval too large for the simple machinations of an external power. In the north, under the leadership of Pancho Villa, and in the south under the leadership of Emiliano Zapata, the peasantry struggled to reclaim control of the land. In the course of this revolutionary war, over a million peasants died. In the South, where there was a large Amerindian population, the Zapatistas fought for land and for the preservation of Amerindian culture. The Zapatista movement inspired a new nationalism among Amerindian communities elsewhere in Latin America.

The Russo-Japanese War, 1904–1905

The upheavals in the world's periphery signified nothing more than a series of localized bush fires set alight by the conflict between metropolitan forces of modernization and indigenous sources of resistance. One such event, though, did capture the global imagination and proclaimed to the world—both Western and non-Western—that a new age had arrived.

The victory of Japan over Russia in the Russo-Japanese War of 1904–1905 was remarkable in two ways. Firstly, not only had a non-Western power defeated a major European power in war, but the war had been fought using the full arsenal of modern military technology. 300 000 troops were engaged on either side, and Japan defeated the modern Russian navy. Here was proof that a non-European power could claim equal standing with a large and powerful nation.

The Russo-Japanese War had important consequences for the direction of world history. Russian interests were deflected from Asia to Europe and added to the buildup of diplomatic tensions that led to the Russian Revolution in 1905 and to World War I in 1914. The Russian Revolution served as an inspiration for revolutions elsewhere. The news of the Japanese victory was widely celebrated in the nationalist press of China, India, the Middle East, and Africa. In the European press, journalists worried about the blow inflicted upon the perceived imperial majesty of all Europeans; fanatical racists feared a new Yellow, Brown, and Black Peril sweeping the globe. In Persia, an insurrection in 1905 led to a constitutional revolution that created an elected assembly under the Shah. In 1908, a coup by young army officers, the Young Turks, introduced modernizing reforms to the Ottoman Empire. Popular disorder and mounting nationalist pressure led the Dutch to create a People's Council with Indonesian representatives for the East Indies. In India, liberal reforms placed Indian representatives on the Viceroy's Council.

The most stunning change occurred in China: the Revolution of 1911 brought down the Manchu dynasty and proclaimed a new republic based on the principles of nationalism, socialism, and democracy. The first president of the Republic was Dr. Sun Yat-sen, the son of a peasant family, who converted to Christianity as a teenager and later became a doctor. Sun Yat-sen had spent many years abroad, living for a time in Vancouver, and received support from the expatriate Chinese communities around the world. As recently as 1907, Vancouver's Asian community had been the target of a white race riot. They, like other peoples who experienced racial discrimination and colonial oppression, knew at first hand the cost and the necessity of the struggle for liberation.

Reflections

It is important to recognize the global dimension of revolutionary conflicts engendered by Western imperialism and to appreciate the deep historical roots of movements seeking liberation from colonial and racial oppression. It is equally important not to underestimate the power of the colonial empires. On the eve of World War I, they were at the zenith of their power. One must also recognize the unprecedented difference between the capacity of people to resist and their capacity to achieve their liberation. The transformation of the modern world system in the course of the nineteenth century involved an enormous expansion of the colonial empires and an equally unprecedented increase in their military might and economic power. In the twentieth century, it would take two world wars to shake the foundations of the world powers.

The peoples of the Third World played an important role in their liberation from colonial domination and racism. We need to remember the experience of those such as Toussaint L'Ouverture, Simón Bolívar, Sun Yat-sen, and Gandhi. People with intelligence, courage, and determination, even if from obscure backgrounds without access to the power of the state, have risen in times of crisis and conflict to advance the common cause of liberation.

Key Concepts, Figures, and Events

Informal/Formal Imperialism

Racism

Age of Democratic Revolution

Simón Bolívar

Eurocentric

Economic Imperialism

Opium Wars

Partition of Africa

Congo Free State

Indian National Congress

Pan-African Movement

Topics for Further Thought

1. Some historians have referred to the period 1776–1848 as the Age of Democratic Revolutions. What impact did these revolutions have on the slave trade and overseas empires? Why was the process of liberation reversed after 1870?

2. By the late nineteenth century, the process of industrialization and imperialism had radically altered the relationships between various parts of the world. Explain how and why the world had become divided along racial lines. How was science used to support the new world order of the late nineteenth century?

3. Briefly explain the differences between commercial and industrial capitalism. How did the advent of industrial capitalism alter relations between the metropolis and the periphery?

4. Throughout the nineteenth century, various factors combined to bring an end to slavery. Briefly explain these factors and comment on the comparative roles played by enlightened thinkers in Europe and North America and rebellious, politically active slaves.

5. A vision of a liberated and united Latin America was shared by many. Explain in further detail the nature of the dream for Latin America and comment on why those leading the independence movements in Latin America were unable to realize their vision fully.

6. Create an organizer which allows you to compare and contrast the Eurocentric, Economic, and Peripheral explanations for imperialism. Why is this understanding of historiography important in the study of the nineteenth century?

7. Although slavery came to an end in the nineteenth century, racism continued. Explain how patterns of labour helped to continue racism despite the emancipation of slaves.

8. The struggle for political and economic independence continues in many parts of the world today. The foundations for these movements, however, were laid down in the nineteenth century. How did colonial resistance at the turn of the twentieth century help shape the world we presently live in?

Topics for Further Research

1. European imperialism underlay many important political and economic events around the world in the nineteenth century. Research one of the following events, focusing on the causes and significance of the event:

Opium Drug Wars
Indian Mutiny of 1857
Jamaica Slave Revolt
Origins of Apartheid in South Africa

2. During the late eighteenth and nineteenth centuries, slave rebellions occurred in several British and Latin American colonies. Research the slave rebellion in one of the following colonies, focusing on the underlying causes and the outcome of the revolt:

Haiti
Barbados
Jamaica
Guyana

3. During the nineteenth century, the end of slavery came about as a result of a wide variety of factors. Research the factors that brought about the end of slavery in one of the following countries:

Cuba
Brazil
United States

4. Throughout the two decades prior to World War I, conflicts resulting from colonial nationalism occurred in several parts of the world. These conflicts, when viewed together, suggest an emerging global crisis. Research the nationalist uprising in one of the following countries:

Cuba
Philippines
China (Boxer Rebellion)
Egypt
Ethiopia

Responding to Ideas

1. Immanuel Wallerstein concludes his book *The Modern World System* by stating: "The mark of the modern world is the imagination of its profiteers and the counter-assertiveness of the oppressed. Exploitation and the refusal to accept it as either inevitable or just constitute the continuing antinomy [contradiction] of the modern era, joined together in a dialectic which has far from reached its climax in the twentieth century." What evidence from this chapter supports Wallerstein's position? Do you agree with his warning for the twentieth century and beyond?

2. In an essay entitled "The Development of Underdevelopment," André Gunder Frank suggests that many Third World countries have been intentionally underdeveloped to serve the capitalist needs of the metropolis. He argues that Europeans seldom set out to explore the world without the desire to exploit it. The result of this relationship between metropolis and periphery has been the enrichment of Europe and North America, often at the expense of countries which served as sources of cheap labour, raw materials, and a market for cheap manufactured goods. To what degree does the history of imperialism and colonialism support the view put forward by Gunder Frank?

Changing Patterns: Life in Nineteenth-Century Europe

CHAPTER HIGHLIGHTS

- The impact of the rise of a dominant middle class in Europe

- Changes in town and country life during the nineteenth century

- The evolving nature of the family

- Growing up in the nineteenth century

The nineteenth century was an age of rapid and profound change. The effects of industrialization, nationalism, and new intellectual developments—such as Darwinism—have been well documented. What of the change in the daily life of Europeans: their fashions, their homes, their diet, and their family relationships? Just as the nineteenth century brought significant change to the workplace, so it also witnessed momentous change in the private lives of the people earning a living from the new factories in the growing industrial centres of Europe. What about the peasantry? The often forgotten class of the nineteenth century, the peasants who continued to eke out an existence from their small landholdings, experienced far less rapid change than their urban cousins. The effects of industrialization were slow to be felt in the European countryside. So too were the benefits that new and improved technology eventually brought to the urban working class. By the end of the nineteenth century, the majority of European peasants still lived as meagerly as in the previous century.

This chapter is devoted largely to the significant changes that affected Europe during the nineteenth century. Since the Industrial Revolution occurred first in England, the greatest effect on nineteenth-century society can be seen in this European country. Consequently, much of this chapter focuses on the English experience. Keep in mind, as you read, that the changes discussed were also occurring at different paces and with varying consequences in other parts of Europe during the nineteenth and early twentieth century.

A key ingredient to the growth of industrialization and to the overall improvement in the standard of living for all Europeans was the harnessing of energy. As long as Europe relied on the toil of humans and beasts of burden, poverty would continue to afflict the vast majority of the population. Even damming the rivers and streams could not provide the energy necessary for Europeans to make significant advances. Only after they had harnessed new sources of energy, such as coal, steam engines at the beginning of the century, and hydro-electric power at the end of the century, would Europeans make the major breakthrough that would allow most people to improve their standard of living.

With new sources of energy available, people were able to work more efficiently, produce more, and live better. Over time, working hours would be reduced, labour-saving devices would make life easier, and wages would rise. By the early twentieth century, the invention of the refrigerator would allow more varied foods to reach the dinner tables; improvements in medicine would save lives and alleviate suffering; and rapid changes in transportation would allow people to travel more quickly and comfortably. These advancements came over time, but not before a century of change and turmoil.

The Rise of a Dominant Middle Class

The most distinctive feature of the nineteenth century is the dominant role that the middle class came to play. As a result of the Industrial Revolution, Europeans experienced a shift from an elitist society (in which the aristocracy held sway) to a mass culture (in which the middle class defined the morality, customs, fashions, and trends). The middle class did not achieve its desired transformation of working-class men and women into model citizens, but it did exert considerable influence on the working class. As the dominant group of the nineteenth century, the middle class enjoyed a role in society that it had not played since the Renaissance in Florence.

The increase in economic power was accompanied by an increase in political power, enabling merchants, industrialists, bankers, and other professionals to assume a much greater role in defining the society in which they lived. Thus, the ascension of the middle class led to profound changes in many aspects of society.

In 1887, historian Sir Walter Besant wrote a vivid portrayal of the place of the middle class in English society prior to the advent of the Industrial Revolution. He noted:

Men in professions of any kind could only belong to society by right of birth and family connections; men in trade—bankers were still accounted tradesmen—could not possibly belong to society. The middle class knew its own place, respected itself, made its own society for itself, and cheerfully accorded to rank the deference due.

As the size and influence of the middle class grew in the nineteenth century, so too did its own sense of self-importance. Members of the middle class became increasingly critical of certain aspects of aristocratic society. As well, their sense of moral responsibility led to more concern for the poor and a strong emphasis on the middle-class values of sobriety, thrift, hard work, piety, and respectability as a means of providing guidance to the lower classes. Although there were minor variations in what was considered respectable, there were universally condemned behaviours, such as wild and drunken activity, godlessness, self-indulgence, flamboyant dress, and overt expression of sexuality or behaviour deemed to be promiscuous. From a very early age, middle-class children were thus instructed in the behaviour and appearance of the idealized, perfect lady or gentleman.

George Bernard Shaw's famous play *Pygmalion* is a satirical view of the self-importance of the middle class in nineteenth-century England. In this comedy, Professor Higgins attempts to imbue a woman of low social standing with the grace and manners of the upper middle class. Through this light comedy, we get a sense of the social order of the late nineteenth century and the dominance of middle-class values.

With the rapid decline in importance of titles and land, a vacuum was created with regard to the morals and values of European society. The emerging middle class was able to make sense of this new world and give meaning to their lives by basing their values on the capacity to live a spiritual life outside the formal and hereditary trappings of the nobility. A true Christian, it was felt, had to live a spiritual life every minute of every day. All actions and thoughts had to be judged within the eternal scheme. Self-knowledge was the essence of salvation. William Cowper, a middle-class poet, wrote:

My boast is not that I deduce my birth
From loins enthroned or rulers of the earth
But higher far my proud pretensions rise
The son of parents passed into the skies.

The Evolution of Fashion in Europe

When we talk of the significance of the French Revolution, we often speak of the dramatic break with the ancien régime in terms of political and religious changes. The impact of the French Revolution went far beyond the political and religious realm, reaching into many areas of daily life, such as the style of clothes worn by Europeans. Prior to the nineteenth century, fashions for men and women were similar: note in the illustration at left that both the man and the woman have long hair and are wearing clothes with many ruffles and fine lace. Today, the man's costume would be considered quite feminine but, in the eighteenth century, such dress suggested culture and refinement.

With the attack on the favoured position of the nobility during the French Revolution, male attire like that shown in at left fell out of favour and was replaced by the conventional suit we are familiar with today. This change was caused in part by the popularity of army dress during Napoleon's reign. Notice in the illustration at right, however, that women's dress has undergone some change, but certainly less drastic than that of men. What changes have men's and women's fashion undergone over the past 150 years? Can you suggest reasons for these changes?

Many among the middle class believed society to be rotten to the core and blamed this decay on religious emptiness. The aristocracy came under harsh fire for its acceptance of male infidelity and for politically arranged marriages that belittled the care and companionship that the middle class considered an essential part of the marriage sacrament. This strict sense of morally acceptable and respectable behaviour would become a hallmark of the Victorian Age.

The rise of the middle class did little to end the snobbery of European societies. In England, children flaunted their social position from a very young age. It was common for sons of professional men to point at other boys and comment "Sons of merchants, don't you know." The sons of merchants would, in turn, look at other boys and remark "Sons of clerks, you know" and the sons of clerks would look contemptuously at sons of shopkeepers and say "Tradespeople's sons, I believe!" In fact, to be considered middle class required more than a minimum level of income, it required a certain lifestyle and a certain type of employment, preferably a profession. Even among the middle class, there existed a clear hierarchy, with three professions ranked as superior: law, the church, and medicine. As the nineteenth century progressed, other professions gained acceptance as respectable careers. Architects, engineers, actuaries, senior civil servants, accountants, and teachers were highly regarded—the latter, provided they taught in well-respected schools.

Hush! The Concert, by James Tissot, captures the elaborate manner in which the bourgeoisie socialized in their homes.

Changes in Town and Country Life

In the eighteenth-century preindustrial economy of Europe, prior to the advent of widespread capitalism, certain features of society helped to ensure the well-being of people. For example, common land, a holdover from feudalism, was often vital to the poor in earning a living. Common land was land owned by no one, and was used by the general population for necessities such as gathering wood or peat, or cattle grazing. By the nineteenth century, common land had largely been taken over by private landowners.

Another facet of preindustrial economy which addressed the needs of the community was the *moral economy*, which refers to the belief that the first fruits of the soil belong to the community. The moral economy meant that farmers were expected to bring their produce to the village market and sell it at a fair price. If there was a surplus after the market, the farmer could sell his produce out of the area. The concept of the moral economy prevented farmers from profiting from the hunger of the community. When a farmer attempted to sell at inflated prices or to ship goods out of the area, riots would ensue, often led by the women of the community. The goods would be seized and brought to market, where they would be sold at a fair market price.

In the nineteenth century, the traditional market economy, like common land, had disappeared due to capitalism, which placed the profit motive and the well-being of the individual ahead of the community's. As Europe became increasingly urbanized and industrialized, the features of the rural economy and society which had offered support to the poor were often lost in a competitive capitalist society. Middle-class attempts at reform to help the poor would often be aimed at the burgeoning masses that began crowding the major cities.

The Evolving Nature of Private Space

Prior to the French Revolution, buildings that housed both rich and poor on different floors were common in European cities. The nineteenth century, with its dominant middle class and expanding proletariat, saw

This bourgeois home displays the family's wealth by showing the silver dishes.

⚓

an end to such social intermingling. In every European city of the nineteenth century, exclusive neighbourhoods were built for the wealthy bourgeois, whereas the proletariat was relegated to ghettos in which the bourgeois were sure never to set foot.

Nineteenth-century Europe experienced other changes in the home: the home became a family affair, a private place away from the prying eyes of the community. Unlike in previous centuries, when young couples took up residence with their parents, the home became a symbol of independence. Homes became castles in which individuals were not governed by the rules of the workplace or the government. In fact, the working-class poor often preferred the less spacious but independent apartments they rented on their own: workhouses provided by employers had many rules and limitations on private life.

As with most other aspects of nineteenth century life, the middle-class home set the pattern of conduct. Despite national and regional variations, it is possible to discern a pan-European, nineteenth-century bourgeois style, which English social historian Michelle Perrot has described as "a subtle mixture of functional rationality, still modest comfort, and nostalgia for the age of aristocracy."

Homes of the Bourgeois

During the nineteenth century, the homes of the bourgeois were almost universally laid out according to a rational scheme: there were rooms for public show, rooms for private family gatherings, and purely functional rooms. Inside the front door was an impressive foyer that welcomed guests but beyond which guests

did not venture unless invited. The dining room was used for the family's daily private meals as well as for entertaining guests. When entertaining, the family wealth would be put on display in the dining room: silverware, china, crystal, and of course a centrepiece commissioned from a goldsmith. The meal itself was a testimony to the family's wealth and good taste; consequently, formal dinner menus were planned down to the last detail. In some instances, families even carried out a dress rehearsal before the guests arrived.

Another room of great social importance was the salon. Even the pettiest of the petty bourgeois would sacrifice a great deal to have a salon where the lady of the house could receive and entertain guests. In many homes, the salon went virtually unused but its symbolic importance should not be underestimated: it signified membership in a class. By symbolizing urbanity and sociability—two essential characteristics of the bourgeoisie—the salon was the room that defined the family's class.

In the nineteenth century, sexuality became a topic increasingly shrouded in silence. Middle-class religious values had made a taboo of sexual pleasures. The master bedroom, because it had the marriage bed, became a private place where it was no longer acceptable to receive guests. The bedroom became a sacred temple dedicated to procreation, and it was to remain private.

Considering the rational ordering of bourgeois homes, it could be expected that the kitchen and bathroom would have received some attention. Surprisingly, this would not be the case until the late nineteenth and early twentieth centuries: the kitchen was hidden from sight at the back of the home, with little attention to cleanliness; bathrooms, if any, were placed far from the bedrooms, at the back of the home. Although the English had begun using flush toilets in the early nineteenth century, and had passed legislation in 1855 requiring all waste to be disposed of through sewers, in France, many considered sewers to be a terrible waste of water and of human excrement (which farmers still used to fertilize their fields). It was the work of Louis Pasteur on germs that finally convinced Europeans of the need for better hygiene; for example, washing hands after using the toilet, building sewers, installing flush toilets, sterilizing kitchen utensils, and keeping the kitchen clean.

A common feature of middle-class homes in the late nineteenth century was the accumulation of

Dining
IN THE NINETEENTH CENTURY

 The nineteenth century brought some rather significant changes to the diet of the English. Increasing overseas trade brought an abundance of new and exotic foods to the tables of the upper and middle classes. For the poor, the change was of a different sort. Prior to the Industrial Revolution, most people lived in rural areas, where they were able to grow small amounts of food. The changes brought by industrialization served to drive people from the land into the cities, where they were compelled to buy food. One of the cruelties of the Industrial Revolution is that it made money a necessity of life: in order to obtain food, money was now required. Some may wonder why people who left the land to move to the city would not return to the land if conditions were so bad in the urban environment. The answer to this question lies in the fact that the country is like a door that slams shut once you leave. Land sold or left untended for any period of time becomes unproductive. To return to the land requires the patience to wait for it to become productive once again after a crop has been sowed, allowed to ripen, and harvested. This was a luxury many of the poor did not have. Rather, once in the city, they struggled the best they could to eke out a meager existence on the poor wages they were paid. Below are two recipes common to the nineteenth century. The first, The English Royal Family's Christmas Pudding, was a dessert typically enjoyed by the middle and upper classes. The second recipe, Toad-in-the-Hole, would have more commonly been eaten by farmers or reasonably well-off skilled workers who could afford meat in the diet.

The English Royal Family's Christmas Pudding

600 g suet (fat)
500 g Demerara sugar
500 g raisins
500 g sultanas
125 g orange peel
125 g candied peel
1 teaspoonful mixed spice
1/2 teaspoonful nutmeg
500 g bread crumbs
250 g flour
500 g eggs (weighed in their shells)
250 mL milk

Prepare all ingredients, whip the eggs well, add to the milk, and thoroughly mix. Let stand for 12 hours in a cool place. Place in a well-greased pot and boil 8 hours or longer. Feeds 20–28 people.

Toad-in-the-Hole

4 eggs
250 mL milk
250 g flour
Salt and pepper to taste
4 sausages

Beat the yolks of 4 eggs with milk and then beat in the flour until creamy. Add salt and pepper. Let the mixture stand until needed. Meanwhile, whip the egg whites until stiff peaks form and fold them into the batter. Boil for one hour in a buttered pudding mould. Pour batter over hot (previously fried) sausages.

trinkets and objects from around the world. Bourgeois homes often displayed a diversity of antiques ranging from the Renaissance to the Enlightenment, as well as fabrics from India and the Orient, furs from North America, brass and pottery from the Middle East, and wood carvings from Africa. To our eye, the Victorian home might appear cluttered and eccentric; to the bourgeois of the nineteenth century it was cosmopolitan and reflected their knowledge of the world.

Homes of the Urban Poor

The homes of the urban poor were quite different from those of the middle class. Best described as living in filthy hovels, the poor were forced to tolerate indiscriminate mingling even at the most intimate times. The apartments of the urban poor were barren except for mattresses, kitchen utensils, a table, a few chairs, and occasionally a family chest. Rarely could one find a symbol of pleasure, such as a bird in a cage, or of privacy, such as a curtain. Sometimes the apartment walls were decorated with a colour print cut from a weekly magazine. The floors were poorly tiled and the ceiling was supported by roughly hewn black wooden beams. As cities grew, housing shortages became acute and overcrowding in filthy apartments increased dramatically, making privacy virtually impossible for even the most intimate moments.

Rural Homes

Along with the advent of the Industrial Revolution came the rise of the rural myth. This myth, which persists to this day, purports that life in the country is more wholesome; that fresh air abounds and children live a happier, healthier life. The homes of the rural poor of the nineteenth century certainly do not suggest an easy or healthy life. One description of the small farms which predominated throughout France noted that a home consisted of a room that served as kitchen, dining room, and bedroom for the whole family as well as sometimes serving as stable and barnyard. This description went on to say: "Occasionally a smoky oil lamp is used for light, but usually the only light comes from the fire. The floor is of rough, damp earth, with puddles here and there. One steps in them, and young children wade in the mud." Another description, found in a medical thesis of the mid-nineteenth century, provides vivid details of life in the homes of the rural poor:

> The same hovel is used for preparing food, storing leftovers used for feeding the animals, and storing small farm implements. The sink is in one corner and beds are in another. Clothes are hung on one side, salted meats on the other. Milk is made into cheese and dough into bread. Even pets share the same room, in which they eat their meals and satisfy their physical needs. The chimney, which is too short and too large in diameter, allows a cold wind to enter, forcing the smoke back into this wretched dwelling, which is home to the farmer and his family.

With our attention turned to the growing cities and the effects of industrialization, we often ignore the lives of the rural poor. Liberal French economist Adolphe Blanqui described the rural poor in the 1850s as follows: "There are entire cantons in which some items of clothing are still passed on from father to son, where the only kitchen utensils are a few miserable wooden spoons, and where the only furniture is a bench and a rickety table. Hundreds of thousands of men still have no notion of bed sheets. Hundreds of thousands have never worn shoes, and millions have never drunk anything but water and seldom or never eat meat or even white bread." Obviously, the plight of the rural poor matched that of the industrial proletariat regardless of the inattention they received.

The Family

1994 was declared International Year of the Family. During this year we were encouraged to work to keep our families strong. What exactly is meant by the term "family"? In the late twentieth century, many people believe that the

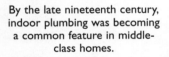

By the late nineteenth century, indoor plumbing was becoming a common feature in middle-class homes.

foundation of our society is the nuclear family. We think of the "traditional family" as the nuclear family, but this view is at best short-sighted, since the nuclear family has only been the norm of the Western world for the past 150 years. The concept of family is not static but dynamic and ever-changing, which makes it difficult—if not dangerous—for moralists to focus on one recent type of family, the nuclear family, as the structure that needs to be saved in order to preserve the integrity of our society.

Prior to the Industrial Revolution, when the nuclear family emerged as the dominant family structure, systems of kinship that varied from region to region were the norm throughout Europe. Today, as societies continue to evolve, the family is being redefined to include gay spouses and parents, single parents, and situations where children have two homes (one with their mother and one with their father). The family circle has grown to encompass step-parents, step-siblings, and step-grandparents. Consequently, when we study the history of the family, we must not be caught in the trap of seeing it as having some sort of immutable, final form but, instead, we must pay attention to the forces that have moulded and reshaped the family unit. In the nineteenth century, these forces were those already quite familiar to you: industrialization, urbanization, individualism, and a growing desire for privacy.

Photographs and Correspondence

One of the products of nineteenth-century industrialization was increased mobility of the people. Sons and daughters went away to school or moved to other cities to find work. The railroad helped to make the 1800s the great century of paper as families attempted to keep in touch with each other by writing letters. Children who were away at school were expected to write daily letters to their parents; husbands and wives who were separated for any period of time would write to each other every two or three days. Even distant relatives maintained a fairly regular correspondence, keeping their kinship informed of health matters, births, deaths, and marriages.

By the end of the nineteenth century postcards had become a very popular way to carry on a regular correspondence. One family of five from France (a mother, a father, and three working daughters) exchanged over one thousand postcards between 1904 and 1914. Aside from regular family correspondence, regular formal family gatherings became an important demonstration of family unity. With the invention of the camera, family photographs became a central feature of every home. By the end of the nineteenth century, many families kept neatly arranged albums filled with photographs commemorating family events.

Marriage and Divorce

Despite the efforts of the middle class to encourage respectable behaviour, change came slowly in Europe. During the first three decades of the nineteenth century, the traditional pattern of males marrying late and of fairly widespread celibacy among women was replaced with more and earlier marriages, leading to a significant increase in birth rate. By the latter half of the century, declining infant mortality and other factors led women to have significantly fewer children in many Western European countries. Increased sexual activity among the unmarried produced high illegitimacy rates. In many areas, local parish priests and vicars often attempted to arrange marriages in order to avoid illegitimate births. Despite these efforts, it was estimated that up to 50 percent of the population of Paris in the early nineteenth century was illegitimate.

Another challenge to the emerging nineteenth-century sense of morality was the number of people who opted not to bother with the formality of marriage, choosing instead to live together out of wedlock. This practice was so widespread in the England of the eighteenth century that the Marriage Act of 1753 was passed in an attempt to end irregular unions by making legal marriages easier. Still, in the early nineteenth century, it was quite common in rural areas for couples to evade formal weddings. For those who did choose to marry, elopement was fairly common. Most often, couples eloped when their parents would not consent to the union or when they wished to leave an existing marriage without the enormous trouble and the unlikely success of obtaining a legal divorce. Although living together was considered bigamous, colonies such as South Africa and Australia did not enforce England's marriage laws.

Adultery, although fairly widespread, seldom led to divorce. Often marriages were dead from the start as they were based on political arrangements rather than a sense of love and commitment. Among the upper class, adultery was so widespread and accepted that it was not uncommon for a husband and wife to openly carry on affairs, living in the same house as

The first automobile, or motor carriage as it was often called, appeared on the roads as early as 1898.

---

their spouse but occupying different rooms. The Earl of Oxford's wife even bore several children by different lovers once she had produced an undoubted heir. In his book *The Birth of the Modern World Society 1815–1830*, Paul Johnson relates an interesting story of Mr. Penton and his mistress.

> Mr. Penton, who seduced his wife's pretty maid; deserted the family home; took the girl to Italy, where she learned to sing professionally and became a leading diva; then brought her back to England where she sat at the head of his table. Stuffy people like Sir John Truern and Lord Thomond dined with them to hear her sing afterwards, but they did not take their wives.

When marriages did break down, the consequences varied for people of different classes. Until the Marriage Act was revised in England in 1857, only the wealthy and influential could afford to pursue a legal parliamentary divorce. Among the lower classes, divorces, albeit illegal, did take place. A woman who was deserted or beaten often would "return the ring" in front of witnesses, signalling the end of the marriage. A man who remarried while his first wife was still alive was said to be "on a lease," while a woman who was allowed by her husband to remarry was said to be "leased out." Among

the working class, a traditional form of divorce in the early nineteenth century was referred to as the "wife sale." The ceremony involved the husband, wife, and the wife's lover, who would take over responsibility for her upkeep. On the day of the sale, the husband led his wife to the location with a halter around her neck. There she was handed over to her now "owner." This exchange most often took place in the market square, always with the approval of parish authorities. By the 1820s, the "new morality" of the Industrial Revolution was making the justices of the peace feel increasingly uncomfortable. In time, most poor couples did not bother with the ceremony. If the marriage broke down, they simply moved apart and perhaps remarried in the future, despite the absence of a formal divorce.

Violence in the Family

The nature and level of family violence varied according to class. Among working-class people, wife-beating was a male prerogative. Husbands, perhaps drunk or frustrated by a long day at work, often vented their anger by beating their wives. One man's excuse for beating his wife to death was "Dinner wasn't ready and the fire had gone out." Although children also faced the wrath of their fathers, women were the primary victims of family violence in the nineteenth century. Bourgeois families rarely turned to physical violence to deal with their marital problems. Poisoning seemed to be a preferred solution for many, especially after the development of arsenic and phosphorus. Doctor Cornevin wrote in 1840: "There is a crime which lurks in the shadows, which creeps into the family home, which frightens society, which seems, owing to the artifices of its employment and the subtlety of its effects, to defy the apparatus and the analysis of science... and which is proliferating at a frightening rate year after year: that crime is poisoning." Between 1825 and 1885, 2169 cases of poisoning were reported, which led to 831 deaths. Of those charged, 53 percent were women. Family violence became a favourite theme for crime stories appearing in major newspapers. These stories vividly illustrate the problems of private life in the nineteenth century.

The Role of the Father

European society throughout the nineteenth century remained male-dominated. Without question, the father ruled the household as men ruled society. Despite his frequent absence from the home, the husband's presence always dominated. Several rooms in a typical middle-class home were the exclusive preserve of the father: the billiard parlor and smoking room where men withdrew after a formal dinner; the library filled with books read primarily by the husband; and the office.

From law to philosophy to politics, the structure of European society was such that the father's legitimate authority would go unquestioned in the home. Napoléon's Civil Code, which laid the foundation for laws throughout much of Europe, granted the husband absolute superiority in the family. Wives and mothers were legally stripped of all legal capacity by Article 213 of the Civil Code, which stated: "The husband is obliged to protect his wife, the wife to obey her husband." Because married women had no legal rights, they could not be part of family councils where key decisions might be made nor were they allowed to serve as the guardian for an underage child: this role would fall to a male relative. Furthermore, adulterous men faced no risks, whereas adulterous women could face a penalty as severe as death because their crime struck at the very root of the family: the legitimate birth of a male heir to carry on the family name. Finally, men had complete control of all family property, including any wages earned by the wife. Only in wealthy marriages, where the women's property was protected by a marriage contract, could an equitable settlement be expected in case of divorce. A common practice in the nineteenth century was for the wife's wages to be paid directly to the husband, who then granted her an allowance to buy food and other necessities. Husbands' control over the spending of a couple's wages remained the norm in France until a change in the laws in 1907.

The father also had absolute authority over his children. Any decisions regarding education or marriage were made by the father. It was believed that mothers would be guided by emotions rather than reason and logic in making decisions concerning the children. Until 1896, children under the age of 26 could not marry without parental consent. In cases where the children proved to be disobedient or obstinate, the father could request that the child be arrested and held in a state prison. Until the age of 16, children could be held in prison for up to one month; those between 16 and the age of majority could be held for up to six months. If, at the end of the sentence, the father refused to take back the child, the child could be held in prison until he or she reached the age of major-

ity. Such was the power and dominance of the father in the household of the nineteenth century.

Women in the Nineteenth Century

While women had begun to agitate for the type of changes that would significantly alter their participation in society, their domestic lives during the nineteenth century remained at best restricted and at worst harsh and brutal. During the 1820s, the well-known philosopher and economist *John Stuart Mill* began his campaign against wife-beating and the failure of the courts to take appropriate action. His long struggle culminated in 1869 with the publishing of the powerful and influential book *The Subjection of Women*. Mill argued beyond the need to bring an end to the physical abuse of women, insisting that women as well as men required freedom to achieve happiness. Mill was not alone in his crusade for the rights of women. William Thompson wrote an interestingly titled tract: *An Appeal of One Half of the Human Race, Women, Against the Pretensions of the Other Half, Men, to Retain them in Political, and Thence in Civil and Domestic Slavery*. In this publication, Thompson claimed that the home was not "the abode of calm bliss," but "the eternal prison-house of the wife…. The house is *his* house, with everything in it; and of all the fixtures the most abjectly *his* is his breeding-machine, the wife."

The nineteenth century would be a transitional period for European women: a time of continued exploitation and yet a time when female literacy improved rapidly and women began the crusade that would eventually win them full rights in the twentieth century.

These gains belonged, however, to the future. During the nineteenth century, women continued to find themselves restricted and exploited in a paternalistic male-dominated society. During the first half of the century, bourgeois women were commonly involved in the family business by taking on such tasks as keeping the books. By the 1850s and 1860s, business had grown and the bourgeoisie had ceased to live near the family business, choosing the expensive new neighbourhoods instead. Women, consequently, retreated into the home, where they raised the children and tended to household duties, such as looking after the large staff of servants, and hosted social teas.

Women of the urban working class, however, were largely homemakers, which is not to suggest they had nearly the leisure time their middle-class counterparts enjoyed. The list of responsibilities attached to a homemaker of the nineteenth century is staggering. Firstly, she was responsible for the care and supervision of the children. Everywhere a woman went, she took her children in tow. Her second function was to care for the family by performing countless household chores. These would include shopping for the best price on food, often bartering and gathering what free items she could find in the city; preparing meals, gathering fuel, and fetching water; washing, tailoring, mending, and patching the family's clothes. Beyond carrying out household chores, working-class women were often counted on to earn a supplementary income for the family by cleaning the houses of others, taking in laundry, making deliveries, or selling items at the street corner. During the last 30 years of the nineteenth century, the garment industry began to exploit this pool of labour by having women sew garments in their homes. In time, factory work won out over the unsupervised sweatshops in which women toiled.

Childhood in the Nineteenth Century

Children became the centre of the European family during the nineteenth century; greater interest was placed on child-rearing practices and on how best to educate children. In fact, by the end of the century, a new science of child-rearing had emerged. Among the middle class, breast-feeding by the mother became much more common and the practice of swaddling, whereby children's movements were restricted by being tightly wrapped, came to an end. By the mid-nineteenth century, the first pieces of social legislation aimed at the welfare of children were being passed. In France, a law was passed in 1841 limiting the hours of factory work for children. Despite being a relatively ineffective piece of legislation, it was a symbolic move toward recognizing the need to protect children's rights.

Birth remained a home event during the nineteenth century, although increasingly the well-to-do were employing the help of a male doctor for the delivery rather than the traditional midwife. Giving birth in a hospital was still considered a sign of poverty or of illegitimacy. The hospital was where unwed country girls went to give birth before abandoning their babies. Following the birth of the baby, the father announced the arrival of the child at the town hall, thus welcoming the child to the family as well as society.

Prior to the 1800s, childhood was seen as a long stretch of ill-defined time that differed little for boys or girls. By the nineteenth century, childhood was divided into three distinct phases: early childhood (up to age eight), childhood proper, and adolescence. In the child's early years, the task of raising and nurturing was left solely to the mother since early childhood was seen as feminine. Children of both sexes under the age of four wore dresses and long hair and played with dolls that tended to be androgynous. The early education of children was left to the mother.

By the time children reached the age of eight, they were believed to have reached the age of reason. At this point in their lives, young boys could expect their fathers to begin playing a more active role, sometimes acting as tutors. Daughters could seldom expect their fathers to play a significant role in their education. By the age of 15, most middle-class daughters were sent away to boarding schools to complete their moral education and to be prepared for social life.

This Plaster-of-Paris jacket and tripod were among the new experimental methods being used in the 1800s to cure ailments such as ataxia (defective muscular co-ordination).

Boys were often sent to boarding schools at an even earlier age. There they endured barrack-like conditions as they prepared to pass the baccalaureate, the distinguishing mark of the bourgeoisie.

Reflections

The nineteenth century was a period of revolutionary change in European society. The effects of industrialization and urbanization transformed the workplace and the home. Change was far less rapid and revolutionary in the rural areas of Europe. Although industrialization and urbanization were changing the urban landscape, the often forgotten peasantry of Europe witnessed slow change and little improvement in their standard of living. While great political theorists such as Karl Marx and scientists such as Charles Darwin were reshaping the political and intellectual landscape of Europe, a more subtle yet equally profound change was occurring in the home. Family relationships were being redefined, the way in which children were viewed was changing, and a new sense of Christian morality was reshaping values and mores.

By the end of the nineteenth century, the middle class had established a clear predominance in European culture and women were beginning to press their demand for equal participation in society.

Meanwhile, the effects of the Industrial Revolution were beginning to bear fruit for the working class as well as for the middle and upper classes. Europe was on the verge of seeing an end to the perpetual poverty that had afflicted the vast majority of its population in previous centuries. Soon most homes would be properly heated and ventilated, and an increased awareness of the importance of good hygiene would help to dramatically reduce the threat of disease. The nineteenth century had brought European society into a modern industrial age. The century that followed would witness change at an even more rapid pace, bringing with it its own unique problems.

Key Concepts, Figures, and Events

Mass Culture
Pygmalion

Moral Economy
Marriage Act of 1753

John Stuart Mill

Topics for Further Thought

1. The effect of the dual revolution that swept across Europe in the late eighteenth and early nineteenth centuries was to give rise to a dominant middle class. How did the rise of the middle class alter the nature of European culture and society?

2. Despite the rise of the middle class, European societies remained divided along class lines. To what degree does the "class snobbery" evident in the nineteenth century remain in our society? How do we presently define the terms class, wealth, occupation, and lifestyle? Defend your answer.

3. Homes in the nineteenth century were an indicator of social standing. Describe the differences in homes between the various classes and explain how these differences reflected class distinctions.

4. During the nineteenth century, it was common for people to communicate frequently through letters. Today letter writing has become virtually a lost art. How do the differences in the societies of the late nineteenth and late twentieth centuries account for this? Be sure to consider technological as well as cultural changes.

5. To what degree did people's responses to marriage and divorce in the nineteenth century reflect widespread reaction against outdated marriage laws and expectations? Is there evidence today of a similar rejection of the formal institution of marriage? Explain your answer.

6. Describe the family structure of the nineteenth century by commenting on the role of the mother, father, and children. Looking back to the nineteenth century, do you believe the family structure was a positive or negative feature of society? Defend your answer.

Topics for Further Research

1. This chapter has focused largely on daily life in Britain. Using the structure of this chapter as your guide, research society and class structure in one of the following countries:

France   Spain   Italy
Russia   Canada

2. Research the structure of society in a non-European country. Use your research to compare and contrast the nature of society in Europe with a non-Western culture in the nineteenth century.

3. The nineteenth century abounded with new inventions. Research one of the following innovations that had a direct impact on the daily lives of Europeans. Focus on the development of the item and its impact on society.

Bicycle   Telegraph   Photography
Phonograph   Pasteurization

Responding to Ideas

1. In *The Subjection of Women*, published in 1869, John Stuart Mill called for the complete legal equality of the sexes. Mill contended that the origins of women's subordination to men lie deep in the past, when physical power determined the nature of relationships. Further, he argued, the inequality of the sexes had no sound moral basis; in fact, it hindered the progress of society. With regard to marriage, Mill wrote: "The equality of married persons before the law is not only the sole mode in which that particular relation can be made consistent with justice to both sides, but is the only means of rendering the daily life of mankind, in any high sense, a school of moral cultivation..." Do you agree with Mills's belief in the origins of the subjection of women? Do you agree that inequality between the sexes hindered progress in the nineteenth century? Have we achieved legal equality within marriages? Do you believe most marriages today are based on a true sense of equality and mutual respect between the spouses?

2. Former Canadian Prime Minister Pierre Trudeau once said that the government has no place in the bedrooms of the nation. The debate over the balance between the public and private sphere has existed for centuries. Jean Jacques Rousseau, the Enlightenment philosopher, wrote: "If I had to choose my place of birth, I would have chosen a state in which everyone knew everyone else, so that neither the obscure tactics of vice nor the modesty of virtue could have escaped public scrutiny and judgment." By contrast, French political writer Alexis de Tocqueville wrote in 1850: "Individualism is a feeling of comfort which allows each citizen to withdraw from the mass of his fellow men in order to keep company with his family and friends in such a way that, having created a small society that suits him, he willingly leaves the larger society to its own devices." What evidence is there that the nineteenth century strove to establish a boundary between the public and the private, using the family as the anchor, and with the father at the head? What changes would you make in our society to help stabilize the boundary between public and private life?

Introduction

The late eighteenth and early nineteenth centuries in Western Europe have been called the romantic period; the second half of the nineteenth century in England has been called the Victorian age. However, as useful as these labels may be, they are a bit limiting. Both ages contain elements of the eras from which they sprang. Both are vitally connected by ideas and historical events. Both are full of incredible achievements in every branch of the arts.

The nineteenth century may be described as the time that gave birth to the modern world. Thus, it was a century of painful change and joyous achievement as, slowly, the future overtook the past as the focus of all thought and art. The age of progress had arrived; however, the belief in progress was questioned by people who felt that the new mechanized, industrial society was alienating and dehumanizing the common people. These people began to question established authority.

Through the study of history, we have learned that a large variety of ideologies and beliefs grew out of the challenge of industrial progress. Liberalism, radicalism and socialism, to name a few, were matched by an equal number of "isms" in the world of the arts. *Romanticism*, *realism*, *naturalism*, and *expressionism* were all offspring of the restless, questioning intellectual climate that pervaded European society in the nineteenth century. Artists abandoned tradition and convention and, perhaps overwhelmed by the number of ideologies (questions) confronting them, looked to their personal visions of life and art to find answers.

When romanticism is used in an artistic context, the words freedom, emotion, nature, and individual come to mind. The romantic movement, characterized by a highly imaginative and emotional treatment of life, began in the late eighteenth century and continued until the mid-nineteenth century. However, in the arts, there have always been painters, musicians, and writers whose works are infused with romanticism. There has always been tension between the emotional, romantic approach to art and the formal or classical approach. The early nineteenth century was a time when the romantic aesthetic held sway: artists explored the subconscious of society as a whole through their art.

Francisco de Goya: *The Third of May, 1808*

Consider the name given to the eighteenth century: the Age of Reason. In a reaction to that symmetrical, formalized classical world, the artists of the late eighteenth and early nineteenth centuries strove to break away from the confines and restrictions they felt had been imposed upon them by the academic world. They began an artistic revolt to match the political and social revolutions that ended the eighteenth century. It was a revolt that touched all the arts of Europe.

Art of the Nineteenth Century

The Early Nineteenth Century

As the eighteenth century turned into the nineteenth, France became the focus of Europe due to the Revolution of l789 and Napoléon's subsequent domination of Europe. The art of Napoléon's official painter, Jacques-Louis David, provided a connection between the neoclassical and romantic periods. His blend of formality and strong feeling had a strong influence on the art of early nineteenth-century France and Europe. The four great artists of this time were **Ingres**, **Géricault**, and **Delacroix** from France and **Goya** from Spain. Each of these outstanding painters gives a valuable perspective of the political and social climate of the time and, as romantic artists, their works reveal their personal vision of life.

Jean-Auguste Ingres (1780–1867)

Ingres was heavily influenced by classicism and is far closer to David in style and technique than the others. In fact, at one time he rejected David's art as straying too far from the classical ideal. He became leader of the academics, who disapproved of the art of Delacroix and Géricault. Ingres, for our purposes, is important because of his portraits of the influential people of his time. His portrait of Napoléon as Emperor is an interesting counterpart to David's portrait of Napoléon as conqueror. Both artists capture Napoléon's view of himself at different times in his life. David portrays the romantic, heroic aspects of young Napoléon that captured Beethoven's imagination. Ingres portrays the subsequent emperor as static, self-satisfied, and possibly contemptuous of the spirit of the great freedom-loving romantics.

Perhaps Ingres's most famous and beloved work is *La Grande Odalisque*, which depicts a reclining nude in a style which shows his affinity to the Renaissance, particularly Raphael. However, the subject, a harem girl, shows the romantic penchant for the exotic, even erotic elements of romantic thought. The painting, in one sense, may be considered a beautiful piece of sculpture, yet her elongated body puts her in the realm of the abstract. Although the art of Ingres provokes an immediate intellectual reaction, a further look provides a glimpse into a purely romantic world.

Francisco de Goya (1746–1828)

In violent contrast to Ingres's ideal classical world is the artistic vision of the great Spanish painter Goya. Where Ingres flirted with romanticism, Goya lived it. Goya is so original that he really belongs to no particular school or style of painting. However, he was truly a romantic hero in his defiance of the strong, authoritarian regime that ruled Spain at that time. It is ironic then, that he spent several years as court painter to the Spanish king Charles IV.

Goya portrayed the royal family as a rather grotesque crew. The royal family seems to have been too ignorant to realize that it was the object of Goya's savage satire of an institution that he despised.

Goya also hated the institution of war. He was witness to the brutality of the Napoleonic regime in his country. His series of engravings, *The Disasters of War,* is a collection of etchings that depict the horrific cruelties inflicted upon Spain by Napoléon. Goya's most powerful indictment is his painting *The Third of May,*

1808 (shown on the previous page), which depicts a firing squad executing a group of Spanish citizens in retaliation for a shooting incident. Note how Goya has deliberately compressed the space between the firing squad and its victims, emphasizing the contrast between the dehumanized, mechanical line of soldiers and the chaotic mass of townspeople awaiting death. Central to the painting is the man in the white shirt, who, like a crucified Christ, flings his arms open in a gesture that is as full of defiance as it is full of despair. Goya's *The Third of May, 1808* has become a universal symbol of the horror and dehumanization of war. Goya's dark vision rejected the eighteenth-century view of humanity as reasonable and the nineteenth-century view of humanity as naturally good.

Théodore Géricault (1791–1824)

Another painter who was fascinated by the darkness of the human spirit and death was Théodore Géricault. However, where Goya deliberately distorted his human forms, Géricault painted them in classical style. He depicted the events of his time on huge epic canvasses. Whereas Goya the Spaniard vilified Napoléon, Géricault the Frenchman glorified him. He celebrated the brutality and horror of war as part of a glorious experience. Géricault's works are powerful in the same way as epic films. They appealed to people because they provided an escape from reality and yet depicted real events.

Géricault's most celebrated work is *Raft of the Medusa*, a gruesome depiction of a famous incident at sea. The crew of a slave ship, which was foundering in heavy seas, built a raft on which to tow excess human baggage and thus lighten the ship's load. The crew cut the ropes holding the raft and the slaves were left to drift and die. However, there were survivors of the ordeal who lived to tell their horrifying experience, which included cannibalism. Géricault decided to record the event as graphically as possible. He actually had the original carpenter reconstruct the raft. He spent time in morgues drawing dead bodies and severed limbs. The result is a masterpiece of epic proportions. His dying slaves are beautiful in the classical manner of David's heroes. They are hardly depicted as the dying men, maddened with thirst and hunger, that they really were.

Géricault excels when he remains true to his subject. His studies of the criminally insane are brilliant portraits of a side of humanity that the public would rather not see. Géricault painted them with disturbing

Eugène Delacroix: *The Death of Sardanapalus*

realism: perhaps he saw his own madness in their faces. True to his wild personality and his obsession with death, he fell from a horse and died prematurely at the age of 32.

Eugène Delacroix (1798–1863)

Delacroix admired the work of Géricault, but he is generally considered to have moved beyond Géricault in his vision of human nature, death, and suffering. He too depicted epic scenes of human suffering, whether real, imagined, or inspired by literature. However, his work is infused with his personal belief that the savage, instinctive, and primitive aspects of humanity are what aligns us to nature. Where the still monumentality of Géricault's epic and narrative works mirrors David's classicism, Delacroix's masterpieces are dynamic and full of movement. For him, the story was secondary to the emotional intensity of a moment. Like so many of the romantics, he wanted to shock and thrill his viewers in order to capture their imagination and inspire them with passion and fear.

Two of Delacroix's great narrative works, one that inspires and one that shocks, are *Liberty Leading the People* and *The Death of Sardanapalus*. *Liberty* is an allegory commemorating the Parisian revolution of 1830. The picture tells a story, although it records no actual incident. Liberty is symbolized by a semiclad woman reminiscent of the Venus of Milo. She is holding the flag of the revolution and is surrounded by the

Joseph Turner: *The Fighting Téméraire*

different types of people who become revolutionaries—a young street boy, a rich dandy, a poor old man. There are echoes of Géricault's *Raft of the Medusa* here as Liberty moves through the dead and dying. The composition is also familiar: Liberty's strong arm, which bears the flag, is reminiscent of the gesticulating arm of the dying sailor on the raft. Both figures are strong symbols of hope in the face of impending death. Delacroix's picture reveals the political atmosphere of the early nineteenth century as one of tension and revolt in all aspects of society.

The Death of Sardanapalus also deals with the overthrow of tyrants but gives a wholly different point of view. Delacroix often chose literary subjects for his paintings: this one was inspired by Byron's poem about a Turkish king who, in defeat, commands all his possessions, including his wives and horses, to be destroyed while he watches. Where *Liberty* celebrates the nobility and courage of humanity, *Sardanapalus* reveals its savagery and ruthlessness. The king, in a relaxed pose, watches the senseless carnage he has inflicted. He is the cause of the destruction, yet he is placed off centre. He is secondary to the action but he controls it by his brooding presence. His relaxed demeanour makes the murders even more horrifying.

These two paintings represent the two poles of Delacroix's vision of human nature: on one hand, he immortalizes human bravery in the midst of suffering; on the other, he offers a similar, if not more realistic, view of the human capacity for cruelty. Delacroix's

paintings are disturbing even today, when we often feel immune to the extremes of human passions that we witness each day on television. This is testimony indeed to the power of his art.

The Romantic Movement in English Painting

There is a big difference between English and French romantic painting: English romantic painting is much more akin to the works of the of the German romantic painters. Where the French depicted emotion and action through narrative paintings, English and German painters conveyed their feelings through natural landscapes. This is, of course, allied to the powerful romantic movement in literature—specifically the nature poetry of Wordsworth and Coleridge. The two great English landscape painters for us to consider are John Constable and Joseph Turner.

Constable's painting may be aligned with the poetry of William Wordsworth: he too expresses his deep love of nature through his art. Constable was searching for the truth of nature by recording every detail he observed, yet he was not trying to express a completely realistic vision. His approach was at once scientific and poetic. He wanted to record the moods and shifts of the natural processes around him. For example, he painted hundreds of cloud studies to record the movement of mist and atmosphere across the sky. Constable's most famous painting is *The Hay-Wain*. This deceptively simple work records the passage of a hay cart across a stream. The simple subject of the painting allows the observer to move into the landscape. Constable paintings are comfortable in their beauty; they are, ultimately, the most approachable, most accessible paintings to the average viewer. Thus, they are beloved.

Turner, on the other hand, was not interested in providing comfort or ease for his audience. In fact, an audience did not interest him at all. Turner was a renegade, a rebel. His personal vision of nature, specifically the seas and skies with which he surrounded himself, is somewhat akin to that of Delacroix. Turner too was fascinated by the powerful, often destructive forces of nature. However, he had a passion for the science of light and colour: he performed endless experiments trying to achieve exact renditions of light in his paintings. Turner's philosophy of life, which is also evident in his poetry, reveals a pessimistic view of the fate of humanity. All these facets of Turner's aesthetic and personal philosophies reveal that the man who created some of the most powerful paintings in the history of English art had a diversified mind and a huge heart.

Like many of the great romantics, Turner began painting in the classical tradition; however, his aforementioned fascination with light and colour caused him to move away from tradition into a world of his own peculiar creation. He saw colour as a way to convey deep emotion: his canvases boil with deep reds and oranges to convey war and destruction. Others are filled with dark, sombre shadows of black, purple, and blue to portray sadness and death. *The Fighting Téméraire* is a narrative in which he exploits his colour symbolism to its fullest. The red-and-orange sunset spanning the sky behind the old vessel symbolizes its days as a warship. The gorgeous blue-black hollow beneath it symbolizes its death and the death of the old world of sailing vessels in the face of the new technology of the industrial age.

Turner's later works became more and more experimental and abstract, composed around a vortex, which ties into his personal philosophy regarding the fate of humanity. He saw humanity as being doomed to destroy itself in a whirlpool of fate. These late, visionary works were incomprehensible to the public and critics; only John Ruskin appreciated and supported and defended the incredible power of Turner's poetic and artistic vision. Turner spent his last years living secretly by the ocean so he could immerse himself in the two elements he loved most: the sea and the sky.

Later painters, most notably the Impressionists, were indebted to Turner for the breakthrough he made in the use of colour and light and his technique. He underwent such hardship in order to pursue his goals that we may consider Turner to be the ultimate romantic hero.

Late Nineteenth-Century Art

Realism

In striking contrast to the romantic qualities of art during the first half of the nineteenth century, which attempted to transcend reality, the art of the second half of the nineteenth century attempted to portray life as realistically as possible. Interest in science and technology replaced interest in spirituality. Thus, art now searched for truth through the recording of factual rather than personal experience. Yet artists seemed unable to remove themselves completely from romantic subject matter; their imaginations still predominated. Even the most scientifically based experiments of the Impressionists produced impressions of reality, not reality itself.

The tradition of landscape painting continued in France in the work of Jean-Baptiste Camille Corot and Jean-François Millet. Both belonged to the Barbizon school of painters, who concentrated on simple, realistic landscapes and human figures. Although still romantic in subject matter, the art of these men signals a move away from the early romantics' concern with the visionary and symbolic aspects of nature and art. Corot was interested in the achievements of the new science of photography, which he tried to emulate in his work. Corot is famous for his gorgeous portrayal of light and dark elements: he captures the quality of sunlight and shadow almost to perfection. We are able to walk into his works and feel the warmth of the sun and the cool of the shade. Millet is known for his depiction of the dignity and nobility of humble people. Just as English romantic poet William Wordsworth emphasized the importance of the working class in poems such as "The Solitary Reaper" or "The Leech Gatherer," so does Millet convey this sense of worth through his monumental, almost sculptural figures. His work also reflects the current trend toward socialism.

Concern with the social situation of the time is reflected in the work of Honoré Daumier who, like William Hogarth in the preceding century, used satire to point out the social ills of the time. Daumier made no attempt to glorify the lower classes; rather, he depicted them as he saw them: victims of the industrial society which was slowly dehumanizing the mass of the population.

Art has thus become more concerned with concrete problems rather than abstract ideas. Two of the great realists who tackled some of these social and aesthetic problems were ***Gustave Courbet*** and ***Edouard Manet.*** Courbet represented French society exactly as he saw it. His stark, sombre canvases make no attempt to beautify the French landscape or the French people. He was vilified by the traditional tastes of both public and critics, who felt his work was too ordinary, too crude in subject matter and technique. The lower and middle classes were becoming a political factor and there were those who felt that artists such as Courbet were vehicles for their cause. Possibly his work struck too close a chord with the novels of Balzac, Zola, and Dickens and the politics of Marx and Engels. All these writers empathized with the working class and criticized the prosperous moneyed classes.

Courbet's masterpiece *Burial at Ornans* best exemplifies his vigorous style. He makes no concession to the viewer. He does not seek to astonish or entertain; he simply depicts a small-town funeral and, in his simplicity of form and content, he achieves a monumental, universal work of art.

Courbet's defiance of popular demands led the way for the art movement known as Impressionism. Manet is one of the founders of this movement. Manet's art also shocked and disturbed the public. He achieved a new perspective on life: he was able, through the use of bright, heavy planes of light, to achieve an objective, distanced view of humanity and nature. His realism is directly related to photography. He makes no conscious concessions to beauty, yet his works are strikingly beautiful for their unusual composition and subject matter.

Manet's subjects were often taken from traditional pieces. He took a Renaissance work, *Fête Champêtre*, by the Venetian painter Giorgione, and depicted the same figures, not in a pastoral setting, but in a Parisian park. Viewers somehow felt brutalized by this work and, ironically, they considered it pornography. Manet merely referred them to its predecessor in the Louvre. Manet's bold experimentation with subject and form, and his movement away from the traditional toward the abstract, laid the foundation for what we may consider modern art. Thus, he helped smooth the way for the Impressionists, the next outstanding movement to appear in the art of the late nineteenth century.

The Impressionists

The Impressionists were a group of artists who tried to depict true contemporary life through artistic impressions that reflected an interest in science and the study of light. Like the romantic poets, Impressionists felt themselves to be innovators in their art. Indeed, each Impressionist painter is unique in style, yet has many qualities in common with other Impressionists. Some of the great Impressionists were Auguste Renoir, Edgar Dégas, Camille Pissarro, Mary Cassatt, and Claude Monet. We shall concentrate on the work of *Claude Monet*.

Monet's work combines an obsessive intellectual interest in the scientific properties of light with an emotional interest in the sensations created by those properties. Thus, even his most scientific observations of the qualities and passage of light are infused with deep feeling. In an attempt to record an accurate picture of light, Monet painted his subjects, such as the Rouen Cathedral or haystacks in a field, over 40 times! Each time he would paint from the same point of view but he would record the changing conditions of light and atmosphere. Monet also experimented with colour by placing complementary colours together using thick, textured brush strokes to create the effect of shadows. Like Turner, he would use flat white to complement an object's colour.

Monet spent the last years of his life painting hundreds of pictures of the garden at his house in Giverny. By placing his own stream of consciousness on canvas, he achieved what writers such as Virginia Woolf and James Joyce did in the early twentieth century. The huge canvases of his water lily garden are records of pure sensation, the culmination and refinement of Monet's aesthetic vision: he lovingly records the colour, light, and texture of the lake in his garden and the trees, plants, and skies reflected therein. These works reflect the character of Impressionism but, like the art of other Impressionists, Monet's work is completely his own.

Post-Impressionist Art Movements

The Impressionist movement in its pure form was short-lived; however, many artists responded to Impressionist art and broke new ground. *Georges Seurat* took a strictly intellectual approach to painting. He created pointillism, a style in which the artist uses small dots of colour to create form, resulting in a disciplined, ordered, rational work of art.

Paul Cézanne was also concerned with conveying the underlying order of nature through his art. His is a classical approach, as he uses geometrical forms to create solid, monumental, indeed classical forms. His favourite subject for his experiments with colour and light is the still-life genre, where colour does not move and shift. Rather, Cézanne painted in solid colour to enhance the solidity of his shapes. He, like Monet, painted scenes familiar to him such as Mt. Ste.-Victoire, a mountain near his home. Cézanne began painting in a realistic manner and ended by removing all incidental detail in order to reveal the elemental shape and mass of the scene before him.

In contrast to Cézanne's intellectual approach is the art of **Vincent van Gogh.** A veritable mythology has grown around this artist, most of it debatable, if not completely untrue. What we must look at are his highly expressive and riveting paintings. Do they express a tormented artistic consciousness? Perhaps, but surely they are of value for their highly expressive qualities of colour and texture alone. The added joy is that we, through his art, experience a highly personal vision of a complex, interesting human being. Indeed, van Gogh's art may offer us the ultimate expression of the stream-of-consciousness technique.

The subjective experience, perhaps in conjunction with the emergence of psychology as a new field of study, became the focus of late nineteenth-century and early twentieth-century art. Paul Gauguin painted his personal experiences in the South Seas, blending the elements of Eastern and Western art in his vivid studies of the people and landscapes of Tahiti. Artists such as Odilon Redon or Henri Rousseau pursued the inner world of dream and fantasy. The art of Norwegian painter Edvard Munch plunges us into a world of nightmare. His work *The Scream* has become a metaphor for the "Age of Anxiety" in twentieth-century Europe.

Although painting was the dominant artistic expression of the late nineteenth century, we cannot overlook sculpture. For this we need to look to the works of **Auguste Rodin.** As did Balzac and Zola in literature and Manet and Turner in painting, Rodin rejected the traditional, classical style in sculpture. Rodin was a rebel, defying the staid French artistic community in order to pursue his romantic vision. His powerful symbolic figures, seen in pieces such as *The Burghers of Calais* or *Balzac*, typify the romantic hero struggling against all odds to maintain his truth and not be beaten by convention. Rodin's art takes sculpture into the realm of Impressionist and Expressionist painting. His figures reveal the inner joys and torments of the artist and the viewer alike. Look at the sheer beauty of his *Danaid* and compare it to the tormented souls who people his *Gates of Hell*. From here on, sculpture would never be quite the same.

Auguste Rodin: *Balzac*

The nineteenth century began with a monumental struggle to free the individual and ended with the individual locked in a struggle to come to terms with him- or herself. As we can see, the twentieth century was born into a world filled with a multitude of conflicting artistic ideologies and styles, all of which contributed to form what we may call the Modern Age.

Music in the Nineteenth Century

The French Revolution signaled a new era of cultural freedom in art, literature, and music. As in the fields of art and literature, in the nineteenth century, music became part of the culture of all people. Music, by its very nature, appeals first to the emotions of the listener. Thus, the romantic age, with its focus on the emotions of the individual, was the perfect time for musicians to break free of restrictions and explore their personal artistic visions. Advances in technology, the economic shift from aristocracy to middle class, and the philosophy of the age, all inspired musicians to make enormous achievements.

The Industrial Revolution had a strong influence on the development of music. New technologies produced better and less-expensive instruments. For example, the improvements made to wind instruments allowed horns to play melodies. The creation of the tuba and the saxophone enriched the sound and possibilities of an orchestra. The piano was improved to give a deeper, more ringing tone; therefore, a different type of piano concerto was developed.

With the new emphasis on the middle class and the expansion of education came the creation of music schools. Musicians began to receive better training. The composers of the nineteenth century now had excellent performers at their disposal. Their music began to be performed in public concert halls rather than churches, and orchestras grew in size and number, as did audiences.

Larger orchestras allowed for a far greater variety of musical compositions. They also had an influence on the type of sound produced. In the eighteenth century the composer's range had been limited to soft or loud. With the addition of so many instruments to the orchestra, the composer could play with his audience's moods through contrasts between soft, gentle harmonies, and huge towering crescendoes. These violent contrasts mirror the art of Turner and the poetry of Byron. Thus, orchestration became a new art form. As artists used colour and contrasts in light and dark to portray mood, so did composers. A whole new vocabulary was developed to convey these mood swings.

The new freedom to play with form and content was due also to the fact that nineteenth-century musicians no longer had to work for an aristocratic patron. They were now supported by the middle class; their appeal, therefore, was to a far greater audience. Solo performers became stars and were welcomed into fashionable society but were no longer the glorified servants of the rich.

Musicians soon became educators and founded conservatories. *Felix Mendelssohn* founded the great Conservatory of Music at Leipzig, where Johann Sebastian Bach had spent so many years. *Franz Liszt*, the greatest pianist of the age, influenced countless musicians by teaching them his brilliant technique. *Richard Wagner* opened his own theatrical school in which he taught his revolutionary kind of *opera*, called "musical drama." Now people, through the printing of musical scores and musical journals, could enjoy music in their own homes.

As the opportunities for musical education increased, so did the number of women performers. Many women became accomplished pianists, as society found it socially acceptable for women to play the piano to entertain guests. Women also found musical careers in the opera as singers, although they were not known as composers. Women continued to be patrons of the arts through their role as society hostesses, affording the public a further venue in which to enjoy music.

In the spirit of the new age of rising nationalism, musicians incorporated folklore and national idioms in their work. And, because music is so easily able to cross ethnic and cultural boundaries, people were able to enjoy the rhythms and flavours of all areas of Europe. Hungarian, Polish, Bohemian, and Russian folk music was incorporated into music that was heard everywhere. Musicians sometimes went outside their personal national identity. Northern musicians were fascinated by the folk music of Spain and Italy, whereas Russian composers looked to Asia as inspiration for their work. This was the beginning of the huge influence Asian and Oriental music was to have on the composers of the early twentieth century.

Musical Styles

For all the reasons already given—new instruments, larger orchestras, greater freedom, and larger audiences—composers were able to perfect their art through many types of music. Songs, operas, and instrumental pieces appealed to every listener through the use of popular and memorable melodies that were easy to remember. The *symphony* became the most important musical form of the age and has been compared to the novel in literature. Through its (usually) three movements, the symphony tells a musical story. The first movement usually contains the main melody or theme, which recurs throughout the work. The second movement is often slower and softer. The third reiterates the first movement's themes and brings the work to a dynamic conclusion.

In the eighteenth century, symphonies were often of short duration, lasting 20 minutes or so. Mozart composed 41 and Haydn composed 104. Romantic composers were not as prolific, considering they had to compete with Beethoven's virtuosity. Some composers only produced three to five works since they took a great deal of time in composing. Composers felt that their music, like the compelling art and literature of the romantic age, put them in touch with humanity as a whole and with the individual listener in particular. Thus, they felt their works should contain a vision to elevate and enlighten the mind and spirit of their audience.

Richard Wagner

Literature of the Nineteenth Century

The Romantic Age

The romantic movement in literature had its roots in eighteenth-century France and Germany. The writings of the French philosophers Rousseau and Voltaire inspired not only the intellectuals who engineered the French Revolution but also the poets and philosophers of the British Isles. It is amazing to think that a small group of men and women could initiate such an enormous change in the thinking and feeling of an entire continent and start a literary movement which still influences the literature of our time.

It is difficult to characterize the literature of the early nineteenth century because the poets and writers who started the romantic movement strove to be unique in their art. They would not appreciate being lumped together as a group of artists whose works all had the same characteristics. However, it is useful to describe a few that will help direct an exploration of romantic literature. Think about the bywords that have already been mentioned: emotion, revolution, freedom, nature, the common person. These concepts are present in some form in all aspects of the literature of the early nineteenth century.

As in the world of art, romantic poets and writers reacted against the formalized poetry and literature of the Enlightenment. As eighteenth-century writers sought to express pure truth through the intellect, romantic writers sought to express pure truth through emotion. One of the most famous statements on the literary philosophy of the romantic period is by William Wordsworth, who described poetry as "emotion, recollected in tranquillity." This desire to express feeling was not new to the nineteenth century. Remember that the artists and musicians of the late eighteenth century tried to convey powerful emotions too. However, they used classical forms that intellectualized feelings. The poets of the romantic age abandoned those forms and experimented with poetry. They developed the lyric style, combining rhyme schemes and line length. Some of the lyrics are very close to the abstract free-verse form of what we call modern poetry.

Clara Schumann

We talk today of "superwomen": women who are in the forefront of scientific research, women who fight for independence and freedom in countries that allow them none, women who hold down demanding careers and run successful families. One such nineteenth-century woman would have fit well into the late twentieth century. Clara Schumann was a very supportive wife to composer Robert Schumann. She also took the young Johannes Brahms, 14 years her junior, into her home to support him in his art and dealt with his romantic passion for her. She was herself a composer and a renowned concert pianist. She had eight children, one of whom died. After Robert Schumann's death, she had to support her children through her music.

Clara Schumann was an outstanding person because she *knew* she had talent; she did not have to prove it. She faced opposition at an early age, when her father tried to prevent her marriage to Robert Schumann. At a time when most women obeyed their parents rather than their feelings, she defied her father and married Schumann. Now another problem confronted her: she was far more famous than Robert, due to her success as a concert pianist. She compensated for this by dedicating her musical career to furthering his. She gave performances of all his music, supported him through bouts of depression, and bore their eight children.

Clara apparently resigned herself to the fact that she would never find success as a composer. Perhaps she realized that her choice of lifestyle did not allow her to explore her creative talents fully. Even Robert did not support her endeavours. Like the famous author of children's books, Beatrix Potter, she managed to live a full life. One wonders whether her life and career would have been very different if she had had the freedom of choice that her husband had. She must have been an exceptional woman because, long after the passion Brahms had felt for her as a young man had subsided into friendship, he could still tell her: "I love you more than myself and more than anybody and anything on earth."

Romantic writers sought to convey intense emotional experience through their works. This intense experience was usually a result of some communication or connection with the natural world. Nature took on a whole new appearance in the romantic period. In the eighteenth century, humanity had enjoyed exercising power over nature. An example of this are the manicured gardens of the Versailles Palace. Nature had not really been the subject of writers. Only Swiss-born philosopher Jean-Jacques Rousseau had described a communion with nature when he lived on an island in the Swiss lake of Bienne. Nature, in the eighteenth century, was subordinate to the greater belief in reason, but nature is not reasonable, it is highly volatile, moody, irrational, even cruel and often dangerous. This is what delighted the romantics about the natural world. Like intense feelings, nature was tempestuous and appealed to the senses.

France and Germany had their own romantic movements. The founder of the French movement was François-René de Chateaubriand, who rejected eighteenth-century society and morality. In his poetry, he explored the worlds of the mysterious and the irrational. He was very much like Byron: restless and moody and despairing of life. Later French romantics included Victor Hugo, author of *Les Misérables*, Honoré de Balzac, author of countless novels that decried the hypocrisy of postrevolutionary Paris, and Alexandre Dumas, author of *The Three Musketeers* and *The Count of Monte Cristo*. The romantic movement in Germany was not limited to one circle of writers but extended to different circles in different cities. Most German and French writers recognized the influence of Wolfgang von Goethe, the eighteenth-century philosopher and writer, as the impetus for the romantic movement on the continent. Goethe's attitude toward nature and freedom certainly prefigured the romantic movement everywhere.

However, it was the British romantics who had the most impact on the literature of the nineteenth century. English romantic poets lived in remote parts of the British Isles, deploring the cities, which they felt had been ruined by the Industrial Revolution. They also deplored the state of civilization. They rejoiced in Rousseau's idea of the "noble savage." They felt that to truly know oneself, one should move away from the distractions of the city and discover inner truth by surrounding oneself with beautiful landscapes. Nature was now an inspiration rather than a nuisance, and this attitude to nature is still an influence on our thinking today.

The major historical impetus for the romantic revolution in literature and the arts was, of course, the French Revolution. Romantic poets, many of whom were actually involved in the revolutionary movement, celebrated the French people's struggle against the aristocracy. They also championed the individual who they felt had been lost in the vast industrial and social changes that had so affected Britain. Thus, their literature glorified the poor, working-class people who laboured around them. Fifty years before, the great poetic works and writings had dealt solely with the aristocracy; only novels had considered common people as worthy of mention. Now the poorest labourer became the subject of long dissertations on the plight of the everyday person. Here poetry changes from an observation to a new philosophy; again, one that still influences the literature of our time.

The above-mentioned changes in content and form constituted a literary revolution. As in any revolution, there are incidents which foreshadow the upheaval to come. In the mid-eighteenth century, there emerged several poets who, although writing in the eighteenth century, expressed romantic inclinations. Thomas Gray and William Collins, through their sentimental poems, "Elegy in a Country Churchyard" and "Ode to Evening," foreshadow the romantic spirit of the nineteenth century. Gray's "Elegy" celebrates the lives of the English peasants who, but for their station in the rigid social structure of their country, might easily have been geniuses in any field of endeavour. Collins's "Ode" addresses the beauty of nature, albeit in a sentimental vein. In Scotland, Robert Burns's earthy yet profound lyrics were adored by all classes of people. His "To a Mouse" and "A Man's a Man for A' That" expressed concern for the less fortunate, just as Gray's poetry did.

William Blake, perhaps the most mystical of the early romantic poets, expressed his extraordinary vision in esoteric lyrics whose subject matter ranged from child slavery in the mills of industrial Britain to the power of nature. Blake's powerful and unusual poetry and painting were completely different from the works of his contemporaries. He was a true revolutionary and perhaps may be seen as the transition-maker from the Age of Reason to the age of romanticism.

Whenever anyone thinks about the romantic period in English literature, two very special names come to mind as the two most powerful forces in the early romantic movement: *William Wordsworth* and *Samuel Taylor Coleridge*. Their anthology, *Lyrical Ballads*, published in 1798, is considered the definitive collection of romantic poetry. And its famous Preface is considered the definitive philosophy of the poets who wrote it.

Wordsworth had also felt the appeal of the revolutionary spirit that pervaded the Continent prior to 1789. He was in France during the early years of the Revolution. During the reign of terror that followed, the situation became too dangerous for him to stay, so he returned to England where, living with his beloved sister Dorothy, he started to write the poetry for which he is so famous. It was during this time that Wordsworth met Samuel Taylor Coleridge and teamed with him to publish *Lyrical Ballads*. They prefaced their anthology with a treatise on the nature of poetry; they felt poetry should express "the spontaneous overflow of powerful feelings" and "emotion recollected in tranquillity." Yet both poets had a different vision of the natural world and their place in it.

Wordsworth saw nature as a moral guide. He was a religious man who hoped to come to a sense of God through emotional communion with nature. He believed that it is through an intense experience with nature that we recapture the innocence, for Wordsworth the godliness, of our early childhood. His "Ode on the Intimations of Immortality" exemplifies this philosophy, which pervades all his works and is often echoed in the works of other poets of his century.

I

There was a time when meadow, grove, and stream,
The earth, and every common sight,
To me did seem
Apparelled in celestial light,
The glory and the freshness of a dream,
It is not now as it hath been of yore;—
Turn whereso'er I may,
By night or day,
The things which I have seen I now can
 see no more.

II

The Rainbow comes and goes,
And lovely is the Rose,
The Moon doth with delight
Look round her when the heavens are bare,

Waters on a starry night
Are beautiful and fair;
The sunshine is a glorious birth;
But yet I know, where'er I go,
That there hath past away a glory from the earth.

Wordsworth saw nature, then, as a way of recapturing a spiritual connection with God. As a youth he enjoyed a powerful emotional connection with nature. However, Wordsworth found that these moments of rapture seemed to lessen in intensity as he grew older. He became frustrated and unhappy until he suddenly refound his youthful passions through experiences such as those he describes in his other short poem "Tintern Abbey" and, of course, his "Ode" quoted above.

Coleridge, on the other hand, viewed nature as an inspiration to look deeper into one's self, not in a religious sense, as did Wordsworth, but in a psychological sense. His works are concerned with the metaphysical supernatural realm, which one reaches through a connection with the physical, natural realm. Coleridge is best known for his work *The Rime of the Ancient Mariner*.

This long narrative poem, written in the style of a medieval ballad, is a myth for our time. The mariner may be seen as a modern Ulysses in a quest for his spiritual identity and his connection to the universe. The ship's voyage takes the mariner and his crew around the tip of South America. As they sail near the South Pole, they are followed by an albatross who becomes a mascot of good luck for the sailors as they struggle with the ice and snow. One day, for no apparent reason, the mariner shoots the albatross with his crossbow. As the ship becomes trapped in the ice, the other sailors curse him and hang the dead bird around his neck as a penance. The ship, however, sails free of the ice and the superstitious sailors cheer the mariner for his action. Unfortunately the ship quickly moves into the doldrums and all the sailors, save the mariner, die of thirst. His is a living hell: the mariner is overcome with guilt over his stupid, senseless actions. However, one night, perhaps in a delirium of thirst, he watches the beautiful watersnakes swimming by the side of the boat and unconsciously blesses them. All at once, the albatross falls off his neck. The crew, as ghosts, revive and steer the ship out of the doldrums. When the mariner reaches his home port, he is indeed a "sadder and a wiser man." His penance is to retell his tale again and again to warn others of the folly of human nature. *The Rime of the Ancient Mariner* explores the oddities of human nature. It poses the existential questions: Why are we here? What is our function in the universe? Why do we commit unspeakable acts? How do we pay for those acts? All these questions are explored again and again in the late-nineteenth and early-twentieth-century works of Conrad and Sartre, and the philosophies of Nietzsche.

Wordsworth and Coleridge led the way for the next generation of romantic poets, such as Byron, Shelley, and Keats. These later poets actually lived the romantic adventure and all three met an untimely death. Their work shares many of the same general characteristics of early-nineteenth-century verse, yet each poet was an individual in theme and style.

George Gordon, **Lord Byron**, is known more for his bohemian life style and romantic adventures than his poetry. He took it upon himself to live out the role of a romantic hero. He was notorious for his many love affairs and scandals with members of the aristocracy. Like Géricault, he too courted death and eventually died in his 30s while on a military campaign in Greece to help free the Greeks from the Turks.

Byron's poetry belongs more to the eighteenth century than to the nineteenth. His greatest work, *Don Juan*, is a satire against his modern world, written in an epic style. His love poems are similar to the works of the seventeenth-century lyrics of chivalry. Byron's work is important for his exploration of the satanic hero, who is perhaps an extension of his own persona as rebel prince.

Another romantic rebel was **Percy Bysshe Shelley**. He was the son of a wealthy father, yet he was determined to dedicate his life to correct the evils of social injustice and tyranny everywhere. Due to his unorthodox activities at Oxford and subsequent expulsion, he was vilified by London society as an atheist and revolutionary. He had also left his young wife and two children and formed a relationship with the 17-year-old Mary Godwin, daughter of a political activist. When his wife killed herself out of grief and Shelley lost custody of his two children, he and Mary married and moved to Italy.

Shelley's life on the Continent was marred by constant struggle with money and the death of his two children. Mary, as a result, went into deep depression. However, it was under these harsh circumstances that he wrote his most interesting and beautiful poetry. In poems such as "The Cloud," Shelley developed a new three-line verse form to emulate the movement of clouds. His greatest poem, *Prometheus Unbound*, is a symbolic drama which explores the nature of evil within mankind and celebrates a rebel hero who defies the gods. Shelley felt that the control of evil is the moral responsibility of humanity and, until that control is established, people will be unable to fully realize their creative potential.

Of all the romantics, **John Keats**, in a much more subtle yet more powerful way than Byron and Shelley, is a true hero in a romantic sense. He was not of aristocratic origin, not a scholar at one of the large universities; he gave up his career in medicine to become a poet. It is so unfortunate that Keats only lived to age 26 since, even in this short lifetime, his poetic achievement was prodigious. Poems such as "The Eve of St. Agnes" and *"La Belle Dame Sans Merci"* show the romantic interest in medieval legend. His odes "To Autumn" and "To a Nightingale" are insightful explorations into nature and our existence within it. Keats's poetry appeals to all the senses and gives a full appreciation of the poetic experience, yet there is a sense of power or control over the language, which is conveyed through the incredible craftmanship of his poems. Sonnets such as "When I have Fears" immerse the reader into a sensuous dream world of love and regret. One is caught in the gentle whirlpool of emotion in which Keats himself is trapped, yet all this feeling is conveyed within the strict boundary of the sonnet form.

Often Keats's poetry is simply the exploration of a beautiful object—a work of art or a piece of nature. Keats is able to lose himself, and his readers too, in contemplation of beauty. However, something that affords him exquisite pleasure may also afford him exquisite pain. Like Watteau, Keats was ever conscious of his approaching death from tuberculosis. Every lovely work that deals with the transitoriness of beauty and happiness is tinged with melancholy. For him,

Lord Byron

love and death both offered escapes from the cruel reality of his desperate situation.

Novels and drama provide us with some of the richest works of art in the early nineteenth century. Sisters **Emily** and **Charlotte Brontë** gave us *Wuthering Heights* and *Jane Eyre*, respectively, and thereby became two of the greatest writers of the time. *Jane Eyre* is marvellous for its depiction of controlled passion and the wonderful character portrayal of the first-person narrator. In contrast, *Wuthering Heights* depicts passions out of control. Using a complex narrative frame, the tale of lovers Cathy and Heathcliff has become legendary as one of the greatest love stories in literature.

The Victorian Age

Romantic adventure subsided as England moved into the Victorian Age. As England grew in prosperity, idealism changed to practicality. Just as we saw a shift in the art of the late nineteenth century from romance to reality, we now see a similar shift in the literature of the same period. The literature of the Victorian Age reflects a deep desire to solve the serious problems facing the new, prosperous industrial age.

The literature also explored the conflict between religion, science, and the negative effects of the new age of prosperity and territorial expansion. Essayists such as Thomas Carlyle, Thomas Macaulay, John Henry Newman, and Thomas Huxley examined history, science, and education in their works. Theirs were not romantic, ideal explorations into the philosophy of these disciplines; rather, they tackled concrete, practical problems.

Victorian poetry was also concerned with difficult social and moral realities; however, Victorian poets expressed these concerns artistically. Their poetic structures often reflected the structures of arguments or discussions, yet Victorian poets could also magically transport the reader to other worlds to explore again the age-old problems of love.

The poet whose work perhaps most exemplifies the Victorian era is *Alfred, Lord Tennyson*. He is best known for his long poem *In Memoriam*, which encapsulates, in form and content, the general tenor of Victorian literature. The work is an extended elegy that records his reaction to the death of his close friend Arthur Hallam. In this series of poems, Tennyson works through his grief, expresses his acceptance of the answers he finds through spiritual questioning, and comes to a renewed sense of faith. The subject of untimely death recurs frequently in Tennyson's poetry. "Tears, Idle Tears" and "Break, Break, Break" are further lamentations over lost friendship, lost youth, and lost life.

Tennyson was also interested in myth: "The Lady of Shalott" tells one of the Arthurian legends from a psychological perspective. "Ulysses," a dramatic monologue and one of Tennyson's greatest works, looks to Greek mythology for its inspiration. The narrator is the old Ulysses, who mourns the loss of his past, adventurous life and wants to go forth again and risk all he has to undertake new adventures. These lines from the poem symbolize the credo of the Victorian age:

> One equal temper of heroic hearts,
> Made weak by time and fate, but strong in will
> To strive, to seek to find, and not to yield.

Tennyson's great contemporaries were the Brownings: Elizabeth Barrett and Robert. Elizabeth is best known for her *Sonnets from the Portuguese*, a collection of 44 beautiful sonnets written to Robert during their courtship. Robert Browning's poetry reflects typical Victorian concerns but he is perhaps the liveliest of the poets. He perfected a style of poem known as "dramatic monologue." "My Last Duchess" and "The Bishop Orders His Tomb" are among the most celebrated of this genre. These monologues are far more than clever poetic speeches. They are fascinating character revelations of the self-conscious, first-person narrator who uses the monologue to tell his particular story.

The novels of **Charles Dickens** provide us with one of the greatest series of social commentaries of all time. Dickens, through his wonderful plots and powerful characterization, harshly criticized the social injustices to which the poor and working classes were subjected in industrial England. Dickens's novels took place primarily in urban settings

Emily Brontë

Mary Shelley's *Frankenstein*

The word Frankenstein conjures up images of a horrific monster complete with hulking form, green skin, and bolts emerging from a huge, unsightly neck. This is not the true image of Frankenstein; it is a Hollywood rendition of a creature for whom we should feel the utmost compassion and understanding. The real monster is Dr. Frankenstein, who creates a monster to gain fame and fortune, but ends up destroying the life of everyone around him.

To get an absolutely true picture of the Frankenstein story, one must read the powerful novel *Frankenstein*, written by the 18-year-old Mary Shelley, wife of the poet Percy Bysshe Shelley. Mary Shelley wrote *Frankenstein* as part of a contest devised by her husband and Lord Byron to see who could write the best horror story. She was the only one who managed to complete a real work of art. *Frankenstein* is far more than a horror story; it is not particularly frightening in a physical, suspenseful sense. The fear surrounding the myth of the monster has been cultivated by Hollywood films. The fearful part of *Frankenstein* exists in the character of Dr. Frankenstein, who cold-bloodedly creates living flesh from the dead and then, only because his creation does not fulfil his expectation of beauty and perfection, abandons it to a cruel, unsympathetic world.

If Frankenstein were the parent of a child, he would be condemned for the most horrible sort of child abuse. He takes upon himself the incredible responsibility of creating life and then does not fulfil his obligation of nurturing it. As a result, the creature has to fend for himself. As he starts his life, he is full of love and compassion. Where Frankenstein is a cold, selfish individual, the creature is desperate to give love and receive it.

However, due to his horrible appearance, he is met with constant abuse and thus resorts to violence to gain the attention of his creator by murdering Frankenstein's younger brother, William. William's adopted cousin is accused of the murder and Dr. Frankenstein, knowing full well who the killer is, allows her to be hung for a crime she did not commit.

Finally, the creature and he confront each other and Frankenstein is forced to listen to the story that his creation has to tell. The creature desperately wants a mate so he can find some outlet for his love. Frankenstein reluctantly agrees and travels to the nether reaches of Scotland to make her. Just as he is about to give life to the creature's companion, he spots the grinning face of the creature through the window and in an irrational rage, tears the body of the desired mate to pieces. The creature vows revenge and kills Frankenstein's new wife, Elizabeth, on their wedding night. Frankenstein then pursues the creature up to the North Pole. Nearly dead with fatigue and illness, he is found by the captain of a ship which is trapped in the ice floes, and he tells him his story. He dies, never having learned the lesson that it is better to have compassion

---

Mary Shelley

for one's fellow creatures than to recklessly pursue one's selfish goals in order to gain fame. The monster appears at his deathbed and weeps with love for his creator. He then swims off into the night vowing to burn himself to death at the North Pole.

The plot, however, is secondary to the real importance of this novel. *Frankenstein* is full of amazing imagery and Mary Shelley's narrative technique is highly complex. The whole novel is devised in a framed narration. The story is actually told to us by the ship's captain, who finds Frankenstein on the ice. He hears Frankenstein tell his story and then the creature's story. Thus, we have three levels of narration. The more distanced we are from the story, the more into the realm of myth we are plunged. Also, the whole story takes place on the ship trapped in the ice floes. This takes us back to the setting of *The Rime of the Ancient Mariner*. Once Frankenstein's story is told, the ship's captain learns from it by allowing his men to return home rather than pursue the dangerous goal of finding the Northwest Passage. Once he—unlike Frankenstein—shows compassion for his men, the ship is freed from the ice. The last image in the novel is the huge figure of the monster, swimming off through the dark seas to find his death. But does he actually carry out his threat?

Mary Shelley was an extraordinary young woman. She went through dreadful catastrophes in her personal life with the death of her children and later of her husband, yet she survived to become one of the leading champions of women's rights in the nineteenth century. What began as a simple horror story has become a very serious novel that stresses our moral responsibility to our fellow humans, to our children, and ultimately to ourselves. Maybe one day, a film will emerge that omits the horror and deals with the truly important aspects of the novel.

such as London. The novels of Thomas Hardy focused on life in rural England, usually Wessex County in the South. Hardy explored humanity's passions and problems, often through the idea of a hero or heroine struggling helplessly against an almost Shakespearean hand of fate. Hardy was one of the first novelists to explore human sexuality, specifically female, as a theme.

The great French novelists were also exploring similar issues in their works. Emile Zola and Honoré de Balzac deplored the hypocrisy and degeneracy of the upper middle class and aristocracy of the nineteenth century. Their works are scathing condemnations of the abuse of wealth and power at the expense of the common people. Like the painters Courbet and Manet, they sought to express truth through realism. They not only portrayed social evils, but also presented deep psychological insights into the human condition.

Drama also became a venue for social commentary. Two prolific and powerful playwrights were **George Bernard Shaw** of Ireland and **Henrik Ibsen** of Norway. Shaw satirized society through his comedies, many of which were quite black in humour. Ibsen was the serious counterpart to Shaw. Like Balzac's novels, his plays explored the negative aspects of human nature. Norwegian artist Edvard Munch's painting, *The Scream*, is an apt illustration of Ibsen's tormented vision of late nineteenth-century life on the Continent.

When the nineteenth century came to a close, there was a period of stagnation in literature. Perhaps this was due to the effect of the political problems facing Europe. Perhaps the Victorian writers dominated the literary scene too powerfully to allow any new creative ideas to emerge until the advent of T. S. Eliot and Virginia Woolf in the early twentieth century. Nonetheless, the nineteenth century produced some of the greatest works in the English language, which are still studied and loved, and which remain a source of inspiration to this day.

Reflections

It has been almost one hundred years since the nineteenth century came to a close. It was a century of incredible turmoil and change for all people as the middle and lower classes struggled to change the oppressive regimes of the eighteenth century. We have seen how that struggle was reflected in all branches of the arts as the romantic movement swept across Europe and developed into the many styles and aesthetic philosophies that we have just studied. As we leave our study of the nineteenth century behind, consider whether people felt the same way then as we do now. Did they feel any nostalgia or pain at leaving the 1800s behind or were they happy to begin a new century? We know that the problems that faced all aspects of society at the end of the nineteenth century continued into the twentieth century, culminating in the horror of World Wars I and II. Perhaps this knowledge will help us to be more cautious and more realistic as we move into the twenty-first century.

ART
Key Concepts, Figures, and Events

Romanticism	Expressionism	Eugéne Delacroix	Edouard Manet	Paul Cézanne
Realism	Jean-Auguste Ingres	Francisco de Goya	Claude Monet	Vincent van Gogh
Naturalism	Théodore Géricault	Gustave Courbet	Georges Seurat	Auguste Rodin

1. Goya's *The Disasters of War* and his *Portraits of the Spanish Royal Family* reveal a sordid underpinning of nineteenth-century politics in Spain. Carefully study some of the etchings from *Disasters*, and a few portraits. Research why Goya was so unhappy with the Spanish monarchy and show how these powerful works of art reveal that rage and despair.

2. Eugène Delacroix was a good friend and strong supporter of Frédéric Chopin. They formed part of a larger circle of artists who lived and worked together. Research this relationship. What does it tell you about the nature of these artists and their art? You will often find that many great artists did not work in isolation.

3. The art of John Constable is not as dramatic as that of Turner, but just as important for the breakthroughs he made in technique and subject matter. Study a few of his landscapes and find some realistic ones to compare to his more impressionistic views. How does he prefigure the Impressionists? Compare some of his landscapes to those of Gainsborough before him or Turner.

4. Although Turner could barely write a grammatical sentence himself, he undertook the study of Goethe's book *The Theory of Colour* to gain an understanding of the physical properties of light and their effect on colour. Attempt to discover a simple explanation of Goethe's theory. Then, show how Turner tried to put it into effect in paintings such as *Angel Standing in the Sun* or *The Morning after the Deluge*.

5. Choose one of the following great Impressionist painters: Renoir, Pissarro, Dégas, or Sisley. Look at several of his paintings and discuss why he has been labelled an Impressionist and how his works differ from all of the others.

6. One of the greatest Impressionist painters was Mary Cassatt, a student of Dégas. Her paintings of mothers and children are very simple yet very moving studies. Discuss her art in relation to that of the others.

7. Try to find several of Cézanne's studies of Mont Ste.-Victoire. See if you can chart a progression in style, subject matter, and composition as you study them.

8. Van Gogh's life is one of the most mythologized. Study one or two of his works while ignoring his personal life story. Discuss the nature of his paintings. Why are they considered so powerful?

MUSIC
Key Concepts, Figures, and Events

Felix Mendelssohn   Franz Liszt   Richard Wagner   Opera   Symphony

1. Felix Mendelssohn is famous for the *Wedding March*. However, he was a prolific composer whose works include a wonderful violin concerto and a marvellous piece of incidental music composed for Shakespeare's *A Midsummer Night's Dream*. Find a recording of this Mendelssohn piece and compare its movements to the acts in the play.

2. Franz Liszt was renowned for his virtuosity on the piano as well as his compositions for this instrument. One intriguing piece is the *Mephisto Waltz* which recreates a man making a pact with the devil. Listen to this piece of music and show how Liszt conveys a sense of the demonic in his work. His music and Byron's poetry also make an interesting comparison.

3. Richard Wagner's *Ring Cycle* is based on German mythology. Some of the music from the *Ring* has become very well known. Find a recording of famous pieces from these musical dramas. If you listen to a few of these you will get a sense of Wagner's musical vision. How does his music create a sense of power? Once you have enjoyed his operatic compositions in an orchestral form, perhaps you will be inclined to listen to or even attend one of his operas.

4. Another favourite opera composer is Puccini. His works have been used in films such as *A Room with a View* and *Fatal Attraction*. Try to find a recording of some of the famous arias from his operas. You will probably recognize them. Compare his type of opera to that of Wagner.

5. There were a number of Russian composers in the late nineteenth century. Pyotr Ilich Tchaikovsky is the most celebrated and prolific. He is famous for his ballets *Swan Lake* and *The Nutcracker Suite*. He wrote a number of beautiful symphonies and his *Piano Concerto Number 1* is thrilling. Listen to any of these works. What makes Tchaikovsky the archetypal romantic composer?

6. Russian composers such as Borodin or Rimsky-Korsakov are definitely romantic in style, but there are distinct Russian themes in their works. Listen to *Scheherazade* by Rimsky-Korsakov and try to pick out particularly Russian and Oriental themes in the music. How does this piece of music reflect the story of the brave princess who kept her life by telling her bloodthirsty husband a different story for 1001 nights?

7. The piano concerto became a common genre for romantic composers. Brahms's *Piano Concerto Number 1* is known as the king of concertos. Listen to his first and second piano concertos and try to make comparisons. Even if you are not a musician, you will be able to sense a great difference in the musical narratives and the moods each piece conveys.

LITERATURE
Key Concepts, Figures, and Events

William Blake
William Wordsworth
Samuel Taylor Coleridge
Lord Byron

Percy Bysshe Shelley
John Keats
Emily Brontë
Charlotte Brontë

Alfred Lord Tennyson
Charles Dickens
George Bernard Shaw
Henrik Ibsen

1. Research the life and philosophy of Jean-Jacques Rousseau. Discuss how one contradicts the other. Discuss why Rousseau had such an influence on the romantic movement.

2. Research the poem by William Blake entitled "Preface to Milton," sometimes known as Jerusalem." How does the poem make reference to the Industrial Revolution?

3. In his book *Civilization*, Kenneth Clark states that in the nineteenth century, nature became an object of worship. After reading "Tintern Abbey" by Wordsworth, show how nature became a moral teacher for some romantics.

4. Coleridge's poem "Kubla Khan" was the actual recording of a poem that came to him in a dream. The poem is unfinished because he was woken from his sleep by a visitor and, when he went to write down the poem, he could only remember a fragment of it. Study the lines carefully but do not try to make sense of the imagery. Rather, discuss how the language of the poem creates a particular rhythm. A close study of the language will help the reader discover a "meaning."

5. Read a biography of the Brontë sisters. Living as they did, in a tiny village in Haworth in northern England, how did they come to have such an extraordinary understanding of human nature and relationships?

6. The essays of Thomas Carlyle are worth reading to give you an idea of how to write arguments in an interesting and creative manner. Read one or two essays and comment on how Carlyle makes his arguments persuasive.

7. Elizabeth Barrett Browning's book *Sonnets from the Portuguese* is a beautiful testament to the great love she and Robert shared as husband and wife. Read a number of these sonnets and discuss Elizabeth's ideas about love and life. Compare these sonnets to several of Shakespeare's. How do they differ in style? How are they similar in their expression of great love?

8. Read Charles Dickens's *David Copperfield* or *Great Expectations* and discuss your favourite characters. How do these people make the novel?

9. Thomas Hardy was the great Victorian pessimist. Compare his vision of human fate in *Tess of the d'Ubervilles* to that of Shakespeare in *Hamlet*.

UNIT 2

Skills Focus

Causation in History

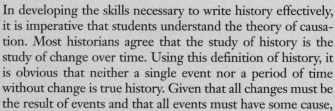

In developing the skills necessary to write history effectively, it is imperative that students understand the theory of causation. Most historians agree that the study of history is the study of change over time. Using this definition of history, it is obvious that neither a single event nor a period of time without change is true history. Given that all changes must be the result of events and that all events must have some cause, rational or irrational, the historian is continually asking the question "Why?"

A historian is never satisfied with only preserving the memory of people or events, but rather searches for a deeper understanding of the past. Furthermore, historians can never be satisfied with dealing with single causes of events but must explore a multiplicity of causes. For example, a historian who wrote about the Revolutions of 1848 as being the product of poor harvests in 1847 would produce a work of little value, for a true understanding of these uprisings involved numerous factors. To ensure that history has some relevance for today, it is essential that we develop an understanding of the interrelation of the various causes so that we can begin to discern trends and recognize patterns that may assist us in dealing with future events.

In any area of historical study, the historian will come across a multitude of causes so great that it would be not only too time-consuming but also misleading to place the same emphasis on all causes of an event. Therefore, a historian cannot simply list the causes of an event but must establish a hierarchy of causes and sometimes must decide which cause or category of causes is the ultimate cause. In establishing a hierarchy of causes, the historian not only decides on which cause(s) to place the most emphasis, but also which causes are of too little importance to include at all. By rejecting some causes and developing a hierarchy of others, the historian is able to introduce some order and unity into the apparent chaos of events.

Applying the Concept of Causation

Throughout this unit, we have examined many of the major forces that reshaped Europe as well as much of the wider world during the nineteenth century. We have considered political, economic, technological, intellectual, and sociological factors. Select one of the following events or trends from the nineteenth century. Randomly prepare a list of 10 causes with brief explanations. Once your list is complete, establish a hierarchy of causes. You may chose to delete some of the causes in your first list if you do not consider them significant. Explain and justify your decisions. Finally, using the ground work you have prepared, write a short essay that explains the origins or causes of the event on which you have focused. Note: Some of these topics may require some additional research beyond the information presented in the textbook.

Events/Trends

The Revolutions of 1848

The Process of Unification in Italy or Germany

The Struggle for Independence in Latin America

The Abolition of Slavery

Colonial Resistance

The Spread of Democracy and Political Reform

The Shift from Informal to Formal Imperialism

The Rise of Labour Unions

The Development of the Women's Movement

The Development of Socialism

The Industrial Revolution in England

The Foundations of World War I

Changing Morals and Values in the Nineteenth Century

Suggested Sources for Further Research

Anderson, B. and Zinsser, J., *A History of Their Own: Women in Europe Vol. II* (Harper and Row, 1988).

Barzun, J., *Darwin, Marx, and Wagner: Critique of a Heritage* (The University of Chicago Press, 1981).

Breunig, C., *The Age of Revolution and Reaction, 1789–1850* (Norton, 1970).

Davidson, B., *The Black Man's Burden: Africa and the Curse of the Nation State* (Random House, 1992).

Edwards, M., *Last Years of British India* (World Pub. Co., 1964).

Fieldhouse, D. K., *The Colonial Empires: A Comparative Survey from the Eighteenth Century* (Delacorte Press, 1967).

Freund, B., *The Making of Contemporary Africa* (Indiana University Press, 1984).

Gardner, L., *Art Through the Ages* (Harcourt Brace Jovanovich Inc., 1986).

Hobsbawm, E. J., *The Age of Capital: 1848–1875* (Abacus, 1989).

Hourani, A. H., *A History of the Arab People* (The Belknap Press, 1991).

Johnson, P., *The Birth of the Modern World Society 1815–1830* (Harper Collins, 1991).

Perrot, M. ed., *A History of Private Life: From the Fires of Revolution to the Great War* (The Belknap Press, 1990).

Rich, N., *The Age of Nationalism and Reform, 1850-1890* (Norton, 1977).

Stromberg, R., *European Intellectual Heritage Since 1789* (Prentice Hall, 1990).

Webb, R. K., *Modern England* (Harper and Row, 1980).

Wolf, E., *Europe and the People Without History* (University of California Press, 1982).

UNIT
3
Europe and the World Wars

World War I (1914–1918) marked the beginning of the modern world. In 1914 the so-called "Hundred Years Peace," the period of industrial and scientific progress from 1815–1914, ended in a war made more terrible by industry and science. People of the time called it the Great War, greater in death and destruction than any war known to history. However, this "war to end war" was followed by an even greater war. Some historians describe a "continuum" of violence in modern history, running from the mass slaughter of soldiers in World War I to the genocide of World War II. Each episode of violence appeared to drive the destruction of humans to greater extremes. The following chapters trace the course of this destruction. They describe the most violent half-century in European history. The story begins in 1914 with Europe at the peak of power in the world. It ends in 1945 with the Continent in ruins.

Political/Military	INTELLECTUAL	Cultural
1902	Lenin: *What Is to Be Done*	Joseph Conrad: *Heart of Darkness*
1905		Debussy: *La Mer*
1907		Picasso: *Demoiselles d'Avignon*
1908		Matisse: *Red Room*
1911	Marie Curie awarded a second Nobel Prize, for the discovery of radium and polonium	
1912		Marcel Duchamp: *Nude Descending a Staircase*
1913		Stravinsky: *The Rite of Spring* Benjamin Britten born
1914	World War I begins	
1915	Battle of the Somme fought	
1917	United States enters World War I	
1918	End of World War I	
1919	Versailles Treaty signed	John Maynard Keynes: *The Economic Consequences of the Peace*	
1920			Yeats: "The Second Coming"
1921	Beginning of Lenin's New Economic Policy in the Soviet Union	Ludwig Wittgenstein: *Tractatus Logico - Philosophicus*	
1922	Benito Mussolini comes to power in Italy		James Joyce: *Ulysses* T. S. Eliot: *The Waste Land*
1925	Locarno Pact signed	Adolf Hitler: *Mein Kampf*, Part 1	Erik Satie dies
1927	Joseph Stalin consolidates power in the Soviet Union	Adolf Hitler: *Mein Kampf*, Part 2	
1929	Great Depression begins in Europe and North America First of Stalin's Five Year Plans begins Roman Catholic Church signs Lateran Accords with Mussolini government		
1930			Maurice Ravel: *Concerto for Left Hand*
1931	Japanese invade Manchuria (China)		Salvador Dali: *The Persistence of Memory*
1932	Franklin D. Roosevel elected President of the United States		
1933	Great Terror begins in Soviet Union Rome-Berlin Axis signed		
1934			Ralph Vaughn Williams: *Greensleeves*
1935		John Maynard Keynes: *The General Theory of Employment, Interest and Money*	
1936	Spanish Civil War begins		
1937			Pablo Picasso: *Guernica*
1938	Munich Agreement signed		
1939	World War II begins	Frank Lloyd Wright: *An Organic Architecture*	
1940	Nazi Germany invades and conquers France		
1941	Nazi invasion of Soviet Union (Operation Barbarossa) begins		
1943		Jean-Paul Sartre: *Being and Nothingness*	
1944	Allied forces launch D-Day invasion and establish a beach-head at Normandy		
1945	World's first nuclear bombs dropped on Hiroshima and Nagasaki, Japan World War II ends		

12

Into the Age of the State: Europe and World War I

CHAPTER HIGHLIGHTS

- The underlying causes leading to the outbreak of war in 1914

- The outbreak of the revolution in Russia

- Changes in the nature of leadership during World War I

- The controversy over the War Guilt Clause in the Treaty of Versailles

World War I

June 28, 1914 marked the beginning of a crisis in Europe: in Sarajevo, capital of Bosnia, a young Serb terrorist fired the shots that killed Archduke Franz Ferdinand, heir to the Austro-Hungarian Empire. These were truly shots that were heard around the world, causing the whole European order to tremble. What followed was "the dance of death": the whirl of negotiations between political leaders who were half-determined to save peace and half-determined to make war. Within little more than a month, the "guns of August" fired the first shots of World War I. To understand how an assassination in the Balkans resulted in a world war is to understand the passions and politics of a whole era in European history.

Background of the War

The causes of the European catastrophe of 1914 must be studied within a historical framework going back to the German victory in the Franco-Prussian War of 1870–1871. The new German Empire was the house that Bismarck built, and the old Iron Chancellor spent his last years in politics trying to preserve it. France, bitter in defeat and bent on revenge, was looking for allies to match German might. With diplomatic genius, Bismarck kept the French alone and isolated by tying the major powers into alliances with Germany. He brought his country together with Austria (1879) and Italy (1882) to form the *Triple Alliance*. Finally, in 1887, he joined with Russia in the Reinsurance Treaty. Bismarck, who made his way into history by winning wars, ended by building an alliance system for peace. In fact, his binding together of powerful nations by permanent military commitments started Europe on the road to 1914.

An event in 1890 changed the game of great power relations: Bismarck was dismissed from office. Young new Kaiser Wilhelm II, breathing ambition, forced the aging chancellor into retirement and put himself at the centre of German affairs. Advisers convinced him that Bismarck's alliance system was too complicated, and that Austria and Russia had too many quarrels between them to be common allies with Germany. As a result, Berlin stayed with its Germanic partner, Austria, in the older Triple Alliance and let the Reinsurance Treaty with Russia expire. Russia and France, two societies so different from each other, now had something in common: both were out in the cold. What followed was a revolution in European affairs. In 1894, France and Russia signed a mutual-defence pact. Soon after, Britain was having second thoughts about its "splendid isolation" from European neighbours. In need of better relations, the British joined with France (1904) and Russia (1907) in a loose agreement described as an *entente cordiale*, a "friendly understanding," a vow of closer association. Now it was Germany's turn to feel surrounded by enemies.

In the face-off between the Triple Alliance and the **Triple Entente**, Germany had the weaker allies. Austria-Hungary was a power in decline. Italy was likely to jump to the other side at the first chance. Germany, however, made up the difference. It was the power-house of the continent, the new superpower whose size and muscle challenged the whole European order. Leading everyone in industry and output, Germany had the best technology, scientists, and universities in the world. Its army was the finest, coming out of three smashing victories in the wars of unification. Its population, 65 million in 1914, was the largest in Europe outside Russia. Its steel production was greater than that of Britain, France, and Russia put together. Germany was a new nation, a latecomer, but already its

strength was out of proportion to the other powers. The Old World had a "German problem," the problem of a nation too big and too powerful for any other to face alone.

Under Wilhelm II, German power was enhanced by a driven and blustering ruler. In love with dashing uniforms and dramatic poses, the Kaiser brought to foreign relations a roughhouse style that set nerves on edge. At times he wanted to make peace; at times he threatened to make war; at times he wanted to make peace by threatening to make war. His policies were as bristling as his personality. To him, the twentieth century was to be "Germany's century." Where Bismarck saw Germany as a contented nation, at peace with its place in the world, Wilhelm saw a nation still rising to greatness. Where Bismarck believed that Germany's greatness was in its army, Wilhelm wanted to make it a sea power too. Where Bismarck wanted to keep out of competition with France and England for colonies around the world, Wilhelm wanted Germany to have "a place in the sun." The result in Europe was a cold war, an armed peace, and one war scare after another.

Germany and France appeared close to the brink of war in 1905 and again in 1911, when the Kaiser threatened to resist French designs on Morocco. His bullying, however, always made things worse. This time he rankled the British, and brought them more closely to the side of France. At this point, German-British relations were already tense over Wilhelm's dream of sea power. As an island nation with a lifeline to the sea, Britain was determined to rule the waves. German naval planners, however, convinced the Kaiser that sea power was essential to great nation status, and that battleships were essential to sea power. So, Germany built battleships. Britain's plan was to match them two to one. In 1905, the British began work on the *Dreadnought*, the first of a new class of battleship—larger, faster, deadlier, and far more expensive than anything afloat—that made all other battleships obsolete. Both nations went back to the starting line and the naval race between Britain and Germany began all

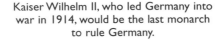

Kaiser Wilhelm II, who led Germany into war in 1914, would be the last monarch to rule Germany.

over again. Larger ships and larger armies were driving military spending, and military spending was straining nerves and budgets.

The more governments faced the threat of war, the more they placed their hopes in military men. These men, in turn, placed their hopes in war plans for victory. The German plan in 1905 was the work of army chief **General Alfred von Schlieffen**, who designed it to overcome the danger that Germans feared the most: a two-front war against Russia and France. His scheme was to beat them one at a time. Schlieffen thought that Russia, always slow to move, could be held off for a time by Austria-Hungary. A German attack on France was to be first, fast, and fatal, winding up in six weeks. German armies, bursting through Belgium, were to roll past Paris in a vast wheeling movement, driving the French armies to defeat against the Alps. The Schlieffen Plan was war by timetable. "Do not build forts," said Schlieffen, "build railroads." Trains would speed the mass invasion of France. After victory, trains would again speed the mass transfer of troops to Russia. The Schlieffen Plan, like the war plans of other powers, inspired hope and courted disaster. It was geared to quick success based on a dangerous idea: victory goes to the one who attacks first.

Europe was on a hair trigger. The powers were ready for war—but not for the kind of war that was coming. Europe was ready for nineteenth-century wars: wars lasting several months to a year, with victory or defeat stemming from a few decisive battles. Wars were a custom of the system of nation-states on the continent. They were a way in which countries could defend their honour and interests after diplomacy had failed. The great Prussian military theorist Karl von Clausewitz expressed this idea around 1830 in a famous phrase: "War is the continuation of foreign policy by other means."

The nature of war was changing for the worst. The 600 000 dead of the American Civil War (1861–1865) could have been a warning that modern weapons could turn war into mass slaughter going on year after year. Unfortunately, this warning overseas was too distant to be heard. Now the danger signals were up in Europe. The alliance system, created by Bismarck to keep the peace, instead had set the stage for great power warfare on a continental scale. There were dreadnought navies and million-man armies; there was an arms race, naval race, and war plans.

There were the high emotions that went with international crises, emotions rising and falling with every war scare. And there was "jingoism," the rowdy, flag-waving patriotism that took its name from a popular British song of the day:

> We don't want to fight
> But by jingo if we do
> We've got the ships
> We've got the men
> We've got the money too

Importantly, every such description of the background to war in 1914 must include as well the story of men and women in all countries who were alarmed by the dangers of these weapons and emotions. Movements for peace and disarmament were as much a part of the history of this period as preparations for war. From them came peace ideas of all kinds, ideas for world law, a league of nations, arbitration of international disputes, education for peace, and arms control.

As governments increased military spending, some men of wealth spent their own fortunes on projects for peace. When he died in 1896, Swedish industrialist and inventor of dynamite Alfred Nobel, for example, bequeathed large sums in the form of yearly peace prizes to support outstanding contributors to world order. American steel millionaire Andrew Carnegie established in 1910 the Carnegie Endowment for International Peace to promote better understanding between nations. The strength of peace came as well from the bottom of the social pyramid. Millions of working-class members of Europe's socialist movements identified the cause of socialism with the cause of peace. To them, militarism stirred hatred, turned nation against nation, and defeated the common purpose of working people everywhere to create a better life together. In parliaments, the socialist parties, following this anti-war line of the Second International Workingmen's Association, voted year after year against conscription and military budgets.

As Europe moved toward war, it was full of illusions about the power of peace. In 1900 a great International Exhibit in Paris (held to celebrate the high civilization of the West at the beginning of the new century), drew over 50 million visitors to a vast display of scientific and industrial inventions. Such wonders, and a generation of peace since 1871, encouraged some Europeans to believe that they had advanced too far to return to war again. The structure of peace was too strong. Commerce connected nation to nation. In most capitals, government was still in the hands of aristocrats, men of culture and conservatism with a common interest in the international order. Ruling families shared blood ties. The crowned heads of England, Russia, and Germany were cousins, related through Queen Victoria of England, whose many descendants connected the grand families of the Continent. The strength of peace, some Europeans believed, was that too many had too much to lose by war.

In 1898, **Czar Nicholas II**, unable to keep pace in military spending with the Western powers, called for an international conference to limit armaments. The results were the **Hague Peace Conferences** of 1899 and 1907, the first meetings nations had ever had on the issue of arms control. Delegates debated the same hard questions that such meetings have debated ever since: Do fewer weapons keep peace or does peace come through strength? Do weapons cause or deter war? Finally, the conference left everything important about weapons to national governments to decide on their own. The ideal of international cooperation for arms control was no match for the reality of nations bent on defending themselves by arming to the teeth. The ancient world handed down an old saying: "If you want peace, prepare for war." Thus, longing for peace, Europeans prepared for war.

In the end, the peace movements were overwhelmed by the outburst of popular enthusiasm that greeted the coming of war in 1914. In every capital, as governments read out declarations of war, crowds cheered and sang patriotic songs; socialists embraced their nation's cause; labour unions promised to end strikes. World War I began as a people's war. And, at the start, Europeans of all classes were in it together.

The Causes of the War

Early in the century, great power rivalries in Europe were centred in two areas. One was in the west, where France and England confronted the growing might of Germany. The other was in the Balkans, where three empires, Russia, Austria-Hungary, and Ottoman Turkey, struggled for mastery. Long before 1914, observers described the Balkans as the real trouble spot, the place where catastrophe was waiting to happen. Bismarck himself said it plainly: "The next war will come as a result of some damned foolishness in the Balkans." When the crisis came over Sarajevo, the

When hostilities erupted in 1914, the French, like many others, expected a short and glorious war.

powers in the Balkans indeed were ready to risk war. When Austria-Hungary appealed to its German ally and France sided with Russia, the two conflict areas—the Balkans and the West—merged into one, and Sarajevo became a major crisis involving all of Europe.

Historically speaking, the trouble in the Balkans began when the Ottoman Empire, after centuries of control over the region, began to weaken and became "the sick man of Europe." In decline, the Turks were making concessions during the struggle of Balkan peoples for national liberation. The Serbs, a South Slavic people, broke free of the Ottomans and received recognition from the European powers as an independent nation in 1878. Serbs dreamt of a "Greater Serbia," with borders expanded to the Western Balkans to include all the South Slavs. In the fulfilment of this dream, Serbia crossed paths with Austria-Hungary moving into the area to take the place of the Ottoman Empire in resisting the liberation of the South Slavs.

The Austro-Hungarian Hapsburgs, struggling against the odds to preserve a multinational empire in an age of nationalism, lived in fear of national movements and came to fear expansionist Serbia. Austrian officials saw Serb efforts to arouse the nationalism of South Slavs as a menace that could spread to other peoples under their control. Each nation saw danger in the eyes of the other: Serbia believed that Austria threatened the dream of Greater Serbia and Austria believed that Serbia threatened the future of the Empire. Thus the mighty Hapsburgs, rulers of over 50 million people, became the enemy of little Serbia, with a population of about 3 million.

The real danger came when Serbia turned for help to another mighty empire: Russia. The Russians had their own dream about the Balkans: they longed to possess strategic Constantinople (now Istanbul) and the Dardanelle Straits connecting the Black Sea to the Mediterranean. In coming to protect Serbia against Austria, however, Slavic Russia was responding as well to Pan-Slavism, the idea of a brotherhood of all Slavic peoples, and to its historic role in protecting them against foreign oppressors.

In 1908, the Russian and Austro-Hungarian Empires came to the brink of war after Austria **annexed** Bosnia and Herzegovina. These provinces were the home of South Slavs, peoples that Serbia longed to include in the Greater Serbia of the future. After months of crisis, Russia, weak after defeat in the Russo-Japanese War of 1904–1905, decided not to fight. Instead, it issued a warning: next time, there would be war. "Next time" came on June 28, 1914, when Franz Ferdinand and his wife were murdered at Sarajevo. Within weeks, Europe was in a death spiral and, on August 4, Germany invaded Belgium and began World War I.

Few periods in history have been more closely studied than these last days of peace. Much of the later debate among historians in the war guilt controversy dwelt on the words and deeds of political leaders during this so-called July Crisis. Austrian leaders were certain—but had no proof—that Serbia was behind the assassin of Austria's Archduke in Sarajevo. Their intent was to punish Serbia in a brief and overpowering war, and get out before Russia had time to come to its rescue. As insurance against misfortune, Austrian Foreign Minister Leopold von Berchtold obtained from his German ally on July 6 a promise of full support in dealing with Serbia. This was the famous "blank cheque," the binding commitment from Germany to back Austria in the case of a Balkans showdown. So armed, on July 23 Berchtold sent Serbia an ultimatum: a list of ten demands so harsh that rejection was expected. Serbia replied cleverly with a display of reasonableness that impressed all observers—but rejected two of the demands.

To Berchtold, no meant no. Austria declared war against Serbia on July 28 and began the bombardment of Belgrade the next day. After years of stress, Austria had a saying about the need to roll the dice against Serbia: "Better a fearful end than an endless fear." Looking back, a historian said simply, "Austria committed suicide out of fear of being murdered."

Called to the defence of Serbia, Russia now set the stage for disaster. Despite last-minute telegrams from Kaiser Wilhelm pleading with him to negotiate with Austria, on July 30 czar Nicholas ordered his army to mobilize for war. The czar's advisers had convinced him that Russia had to keep its word to protect Serbia. With this, the clock started running against Germany because the Schlieffen Plan timetable had an essential condition: Germany had to strike first, driving into France while Russia was still going through the motions of preparing for war. The situation was clear: Germany either had to stop Russian mobilization or start the war itself. In an ultimatum on July 31, Germany ordered Russia to halt mobilization within 12 hours. In the tradition of great nations, Russia did not surrender to threats. Receiving no reply, Germany declared war against Russia on August 1, and against France two days later. The next day, August 4, German troops were advancing through Belgium.

Next came the turn of the most uncertain player of all: Britain. Other nations were bound to their partners by written treaties, although secret clauses in the agreements kept enemies in the dark about important commitments. Britain, however, had only a "friendly understanding" with France and Russia, nothing written and nothing signed. As a result, Germany reasoned that the British, having no stake in the war, would remain neutral. Wishful thinking: condemning the German invasion of Belgium as the violation of a treaty signed back in 1839 pledging to respect the neutrality of the Belgian nation, Britain declared war on Germany, placing the full weight of the Triple Entente on Germany. Jolted, German officials denounced this decision to go to war over "a scrap of paper" from the last century. Had London first warned Berlin of its intention to fight for Belgium, they asserted, there would have been no German attack and no war. Thus, as battle started, all nations had the idea that they were being forced to fight, that their cause was just, and that the other side was to blame.

The War Guilt Controversy

Who was guilty of causing World War I? After their victory, the winners said it was the losers, and tried to make the point stick by writing the responsibility of Germany and its allies into the Versailles Treaty itself (article 231): "The Allied and Associated Governments affirm that Germany accepts the responsibility of Germany and its allies for causing all the loss and damage to which the Allied and Associated Governments and their nationals have been subjected as a consequence of the war imposed upon them by the aggression of Germany and its allies." This so-called "*guilt clause*" did not end disagreement over the causes of the war; instead, it started a quarrel between nations and historians that continued for most of the century.

As emotions cooled, the early verdict against Germany gave way in Western countries to a more balanced judgment. Most historians agree that every power had some responsibility for the catastrophe of 1914. Serbian officials should have had no part in the Sarajevo assassination. Austria should not have so recklessly risked war over it. Germany should not have given its ally a "blank cheque." Russia should not have suddenly raised the stakes by ordering mobilization for war. France should not have written a "blank cheque" of its own, promising full support to Russia in opposing Germany. Britain should not have kept Germany in the dark about its intention to make war over Belgium. Nations miscalculated their enemies; failed to restrain their allies; became captive to rigid war plans. Recent scholarship supports the old argument that Germany was most at fault. Few, however, wish to oversimplify in terms of guilty nations and innocent nations. There was little innocence and enough guilt to go around in 1914.

The Beginning of the War

"The lamps are going out all over Europe," said British Foreign Secretary Sir Edward Grey on the eve of the war, "and we shall not see them lit again in our lifetime." The event that truly turned out the lights was the Battle of the Marne on September 6–9, 1914, when the German assault on France was stopped in its tracks. After marching through Belgium and sending the French reeling in retreat, Germany had over a million men advancing across northern France when one of its armies attempted a manoeuvre that caused it to veer away from the line of attack. The result was the "Marne gap," an opening in the German lines at the Marne River northeast of Paris. In a savage counterattack, French commander-in-chief Joseph Joffre threw into the opening all the reserves at hand, halting the German assault and ending the German illusion of a lightning victory.

Germany now faced a hard reality: the need to fight a two-front war. When the battle began in the west, the feared Russian army, the largest but worst equipped of the great powers, struck from the east, driving a small German force back into Germany. There, however, at Tannenberg, the Russian "steamroller" fell into a trap. In the first great victory of the war, the Germans destroyed the advancing army with a blow so crushing that the Russian commander committed suicide on the battlefield. In the fall and into the winter, the two sides battled back and forth across Russian land until a loose line of defence came to form the eastern front. Here, movement and manoeuvre remained possible for most of the war. In the west, in contrast, the front was solid in the first months.

After the "miracle of the Marne," the two sides were lined up at close range along a front stretching over 725 km from the sea in Belgium to the Alps mountains at the Swiss frontier. It was a front without flanks, gaps, or room to move. Shut in, the soldiers dug trenches and strung barbed wire. And there they stayed, separated from the enemy by a "no-man's-land". These trench lines of 1914 moved little in either direction until the last year of the war (1918). Instead of *Blitzkrieg*, or lightning war, fighting in the west was a *Sitzkrieg*, a sitting war or **stalemate**.

In past wars, lightning came from the cavalry. The charge of men on horseback would break through the enemy line and roll up the flank. War was the art of movement, with all advantage on the side of the offence. As a result, most military men held the same opinion on the best way to make war: attack, attack, attack! In the first battles of 1914, however, the cavalry rode into the muzzle of machine guns and rapid-fire artillery: men and horses were mowed down like grass. Developments in firepower had taken the lightning out of war and shifted the advantage to the defence. Early on, however, the generals held to the old idea of "offence to the limit," using infantry attacks where the cavalry charge had failed. The infantry paid the price in blood.

In 1915, Britain tried to get around this slaughter in France by landing an invasion force on the Gallipoli peninsula in the Dardanelles of Turkey. The plan was to open a front in the Balkans against Ottoman Turkey, which had joined forces with the so-called Central

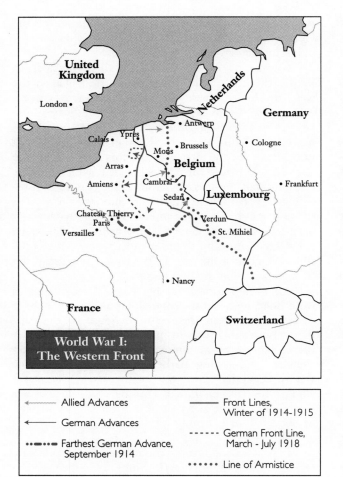

World War I: The Western Front

⟵— Allied Advances	—— Front Lines, Winter of 1914-1915
⟵— German Advances	- - - German Front Line, March - July 1918
•••◆•••◆ Farthest German Advance, September 1914	•••••• Line of Armistice

The effect was to change the war from a fight between European alliances into a world-scale war.

This war fed on men, material, and nations. As many as 6 million men went to war in 1914, and the number increased to over 65 million before the fighting ended in 1918. To keep the men coming, military conscription became sweeping. Germany drafted all able males from ages 16 to 50. France made soldiers out of the people in its African and Asian colonies. England called in the Empire, bringing troops from Canada, Australia, New Zealand, India, and South Africa. In fact, only industrialized nations could keep up with the demands of the war for supplies and munitions. Nonetheless, both sides worked to win over nations and peoples of every description. Bribes and promises became the stuff of wartime diplomacy.

Italy, having deserted the Triple Alliance in 1914, joined the Triple Entente (called the Allies) after receiving promises in the secret Treaty of London in 1915 of territory to be taken from Austria-Hungary after the war. Germany used the same ploy to bring Bulgaria to the Central Powers. Britain coaxed Arab leaders into rebellion by promising to liberate their lands from the Ottomans. Then London made a bid for Jewish opinion by promising "a national home for the Jewish people" in Palestine. Before the war was over, 38 nations, some as far away as Japan and Brazil, were involved in a war caused by the death of an archduke in a corner of the Balkans.

When the Canadian officer John McCrae wrote his poem "In Flanders Fields" in 1915, the idealism of duty and sacrifice was still strong. Over time, however, the daily slaughter took its toll on the fighting men. Worst were the days of the big offensives, always beginning and ending in the same way: first massive artillery fire to "soften up" the enemy. Such was the roar of weapons that on a still day the sound could be heard in London and Paris. Then came the massacre, the mad rush of men going "over the top" and into the machine guns and barbed wire. What was left of the romance of war vanished after 1916, when the idea of "offence to the limit" finally was buried under dead bodies.

That year started with the German assault on Verdun. The fortress of Verdun was a symbol of French military glory, and the German commander believed that the proud French would defend it to the last man. There, he said, he could "bleed them white." In reality, the two sides bled each other. For four months, German metal fell on Verdun like snow: over a million

Powers, Germany and Austria-Hungary, in 1914. The failure of this operation, however, made it plain that there was no easy way out. The war would be decided by a fight to the finish on the western front, in which the chances of success depended on bringing more force to bear against the enemy: more men, more material, more allies, more science, more propaganda. In a word, to make total war. By way of definition, total war can be described as a war in which the total resources of society are committed to the fighting effort. Conditions for a war of this nature probably were long present in Europe, but total war first "happened" at this point in World War I because of the determination of both sides to break the stalemate.

Art: A Window to Our Past

Unit 1: Colour Plates

Much can be learned about a society through its art. Artistic expression is often a mirror of the values and aspirations of a people as well as a reflection of the intellectual milieu. Throughout the ages, humans have sought to express their innermost thoughts, desires, and fears and to record their triumphs and defeats through art. Such attempts at visually expressing significant aspects of a culture have provided us with a fascinating window to the past.

As the seventeenth century gave way to the eighteenth, the forces that were reshaping Europe and the world came to be reflected in art. The eighteenth century, the Age of Enlightenment, was a time during which faith in science was supplanting faith in God, a time when human intellect came to be the unifying force of Western civilization. One art historian described the art of the eighteenth century as "more refined, more delicate, more sensuous, more intellectual, more emotional, and more secular." This was a century during which notions of civilization, education, and the pursuit of pleasure were alternately challenged and promoted. Further shaping the intellectual and artistic milieu of the eighteenth century was a revival of neoclassicism, in part generated by the uncovering of the ancient Roman towns of Pompeii and Herculaneum in 1738 and 1748.

To consider the art of eighteenth-century Europe in isolation from the wider world would be pure folly. Just as a global economy was beginning to emerge and the exchange of foodstuffs and other goods was altering cultures worldwide, so too could the impact of the world be seen on the art of Europeans. Europe was no longer an insular society whose history unfolded in isolation from other parts of the world. The ideals of the Enlightenment and the increasingly profound impact of the wider world on European culture and society are reflected in its art.

Antoine Watteau
Gilles (1717)

Watteau's paintings recreate the world of eighteenth-century French theatre in their musicality and deliberate artifice. However, his tuberculosis made him aware of the fragility of such a world. The face and figure of Gilles, the clown, reveals the sad reality of life. Gilles is there to provoke humour, yet there is no laughter in his eyes. Watteau's stage, like Shakespeare's, may ultimately be a tragic one.

Tea and Chocolate Service (c.1740–1745)

This tea-and-chocolate service, with a fitted leather case for travelling, was made about 1740. The larger cups and saucers along the top were for hot chocolate, whereas the smaller cups and saucers were for tea. Services such as these reflect the increasingly global nature of European society. The set was made at Meissen, Germany, following designs learned from Japanese porcelain makers. The tea that accompanied the service would come from India or China, and the chocolate was brought from the Americas.

Courtesy of the George R. Gardiner Museum of Ceramic Art, Toronto

Antonio Canova
Cupid and Psyche
(1783–1793)

This beautiful sculpture by Italian painter Antonio Canova reflects the neo-classicism of the age and the eighteenth-century fascination with the mind; it made the theme of Cupid falling in love with the maiden Psyche popular.

◁ Benjamin West
The Death of General Wolfe (1770)

In this famous painting depicting the death of General Wolfe on the Plains of Abraham, Benjamin West carefully placed his subjects, many of whom had never even been to North America. Notice the Amerindian depicted in a stereotypical crouch.

⬩ Jacques Louis David
Coronation of Napoléon and Josephine (1805–1807)

David's early training was in the studio of Joseph-Marie Vien, a history painter. David was imprisoned for a short period, but rose to prominence once again and glorified the exploits of Napoléon with this painting.

Scala/Art Resource, New York

⬩ John Constable
The Hay Wain (1812)

As Chardin created warm and familiar interiors, Constable created an approachable and inviting world in his landscapes. *The Hay Wain* depicts a scene familiar to Constable: that of a friend's farm. One of the most important paintings in the English Romantic school, it had a profound influence on both English and French painters in the nineteenth century.

Art Resource, New York

Unit 2: Colour Plates

By the time of Napoléon's defeat at Waterloo, the forces that would reshape European society and culture were already in place. The ideals of the French Revolution, exported by Napoléon's armies to the Netherlands, Austria, Germany, and Italy, had planted the seeds for national self-determination. Meanwhile, in Britain, the foundations of industrialization had firmly taken root and would sweep over the continent and the world during the next century. A quarter century of revolution and war had left Europeans sceptical of the Enlightenment's emphasis on reason and logic. In their place, the romantics of the early nineteenth century stressed emotions, as feelings became both the subject and object of art.

The second half of the nineteenth century was a period during which the foundations of Western culture were challenged by intellectuals and artists. It was between the years of 1848 and 1900 that such great minds as Marx, Darwin, and Nietszche were challenging long-accepted axioms regarding politics, religion, and society. At the same time, artists were challenging the long-held belief that art should be beautiful as well as functional. Artists were beginning to promote art for art's sake and to challenge the aesthetic principles that had for centuries been the foundation of art. Consequently, the art that dominated the late nineteenth century was as revolutionary as the ideas that pervaded society.

J. M. Belisario
Koo, Koo, or Actor-Boy (c. 1810)

This colourful painting by J. M. Belisario was one of a set of five. The paintings reflect the lively and vibrant culture of African Jamaicans, which developed despite years of slavery and oppression.

Courtesy of the National Library of Jamaica

⇪ **Théodore Géricault**

The Raft of the Medusa (1818–1819)

This painting is considered Géricault's masterpiece. It depicts the fate of a group of
people from a slave ship, left to survive on a raft in the ocean. It is the epitome of
French romantic painting as it has a grandiose subject and explores human suffering
at the hands of man and nature.

Giraudon/Art Resource, New York

◁ **Barnum and Bailey
Circus Poster (c. 1850)**

Colourful posters such as this one
attracted large crowds to circuses in the
nineteenth century. Promising death-
defying acts, exotic animals, and the
"Greatest Show on Earth," travelling circuses were a popular form of entertainment for mass audiences in the days
before radio and television.

Use of Ringling Bros. Poster courtesy of
Ringling Bros. and Barnum & Bailey.

Eugène Delacroix
Liberty on the Barricades (1830)

Among the most famous of the Romantic artists was Eugène Delacroix. In this well-known work, the woman carrying the tricolour flag and musket represents Liberty. She is shown leading revolutionaries over a barricade in a Paris street during the Revolution of 1830.

Eyre Crowe
After the Sale: Slaves Being Sent South from Richmond, Virginia (1853)

Slavery, which came under fire during the Enlightenment, lost support in virtually all parts of the Western world during the nineteenth century. By the 1830s, it had been abolished in the British Empire but remained a controversial practice in the United States until after the Civil War. *After the Sale* shows African Americans being loaded in wagons after being sold at a slave auction.

Courtesy Chicago Historical Society. Painting;
1957.27; *After the Sale: Slaves Being Sent South From
Richmond, Virginia*. Richmond (Va.); 1853;
Artist: Eyre Crowe.

Vincent van Gogh
Starry Night (1889)

Van Gogh's brand of expressionism involves the use of colour and texture to reveal his disturbing, claustrophobic vision of nature and humanity. His paintings enclose the viewer in heavy swirls of bright-coloured paint as we are caught in an often nightmarish world of a reality that belonged only to Van Gogh.

Oil on canvas, 29" x 36¼" (73.7 cm x 92.1 cm)
The Museum of Modern Art. Acquired through the
Lillie P. Bliss Bequest. Photograph © 1995
The Museum of Modern Art, New York.

Mary Cassatt
In the Omnibus (1891)

After moving from Philadelphia to Paris, Mary Cassatt joined a group of artists known as the Impressionists. Like her fellow Impressionists, Cassatt commonly used contemporary life as her theme, although for her, a particular emphasis was placed on women and children. As can be seen in this painting, Cassatt liked to juxtapose near and far, light and dark, and large and small.

In the Omnibus, drypoint, soft-ground and aquatint colours, 1891, 37.9 cm x 26.7 cm. Mary Cassatt, American, 1845–1926. © The Cleveland Museum of Art, 1995. Bequest of Charles T. Brooks, 41.71.

Henri Matisse
Red Room (1908–1909)

Matisse led a group of artists known as the Fauves or Wild Beasts. They sought to break free from academic restraints and express the painter's deepest feelings. Matisse intellectualized these feelings through his use of simple, clear forms and figures; however, he also loved nature and colour as seen in this painting.

Scala/Art Resource, New York

Unit 3: Colour Plates

By the end of the nineteenth century, the forces of industrialization and urbanization had transformed the Western world. The dramatic nature of change could clearly be seen in the art of the early twentieth century. For the first time since the collapse of the Roman Empire, humanity and human form ceased to be the primary focus of art. As artists sought meaning in an increasingly mechanized world, machines, speed, motion, and flight became favourite themes. Those who continued to depict the human figure and human condition increasingly reflected the despair and isolation felt by many in a highly urbanized and technological society. As a result, much of the art of the early twentieth century is filled with despair and anguish, with subjects who are tortured from without and within.

The rise of dictators and the experience of destructive World Wars in 1914–1918 and 1939–1945 would serve only to heighten and confirm the despair reflected in the art of the early twentieth century. In fact, despite the loss of many of Europe's finest writers and artists, the period between the Wars was one of the most fertile in Western art. Artists, searching to understand the madness that had descended upon Europe, began to question the values of Western culture and civilization.

Marc Chagall
I and the Village (1911)

Marc Chagall painted in Paris and New York, but he grew up in a Russian village. He never forgot his Russian heritage and painted scenes from his childhood over and over again. As well as reflecting his — for the most part—joyous vision of human nature, Chagall combined Biblical images with scenes of modern Jewish life to create very moving depictions of the plight of the Jews in twentieth-century Europe.

Oil on canvas, 6'3⅝" x 59⅝"(192.1 cm x 151.4 cm). The Museum of Modern Art. Mrs. Simon Guggenheim Fund. Photograph ©1995 The Museum of Modern Art, New York.

Pablo Picasso
Olga Picasso in an Armchair (1917)

Through most of Picasso's long career, he produced works that did not look anything like the "real world." However, in this rare example, Picasso demonstrates that indeed he had the ability to draw lifelike images, but usually chose not to.

Joan Miró
Carnival of Harlequin (1924–1925)

During the 1920s, a group referred to as surrealists emerge, led by André Breton. The surrealists rejected a rational and ordered view of the world, choosing instead the intuitive realm of the human mind. Artists like Joan Miró attempted to penetrate the world of dreams and the unconscious in paintings such as *Carnival of Harlequin*.

Oil on canvas, 26" x 36⅝" (66.04 cm x 93.04 cm)
Albright-Knox Art Gallery, Buffalo, New York,
Room of Contemporary Art Fund, 1940

Diego Rivera
Detroit Industry, North Wall (1932–33)

Diego Rivera's enormous murals in many public buildings in Mexico and the United States typify this style. *Detroit Industry* is an ambitious four-wall panorama conceived as a tribute to the city and the worker. The detail shown here portrays the manufacture of the 1932 Ford V-8 automobile. The mural treatment bestows a grandeur on the everyday operations of the assembly line.

W. B. Deschamps ◊
Surrendering (1944)

During both World War I and World War II, Canadian war artists were employed to record visually the events of war. A priceless collection of war art, demonstrating their efforts, is stored in a vault in Ottawa. This painting shows Canadians capturing a lightly armed German scouting in a small French village.

⬦ **William P. Roberts**

Women Railway Porters in Wartime (1936–1944)

The demands of war weighed heavily on all during the World War II. In this painting, on exhibit in the Imperial War Museum in London, British women are shown working on railroad jobs formerly held only by men.

Unit 4: Colour Plates

At the conclusion of World War II, Europe lay in ruins and America emerged as the leading power economically, politically, militarily, and culturally. As Europe attempted to rebuild itself, it would find the leadership of Western civilization had slipped from its grasp and passed to the Americans, who through the Marshall Plan, would ensure a strong presence throughout Europe. The United States assumed the mantle of leader of the Western world, not only in economic terms, but also in artistic terms. Between 1945 and 1970, New York would become the leading artistic capital of the West. In the post-war years, artists attempted to redefine art. Abstract Expressionism and pop art were a part of the economic boom that followed the war and spawned an American culture, which was bold, materialistic, and youthful.

◁ Andy Warhol
100 Cans (1962)

The age of consumerism and dominance of American culture were reflected in the pop art of the 1960s. Andy Warhol was one of the best-known pop artists. He first established a reputation for using images of commercial art, such as Campbell's soup cans, for his work. He used universally recognized images to emphasize the mass reproduction of cultural icons.

Oil on canvas, 72" x 52" (182 cm x 132 cm),
Albright-Knox Art Gallery, Buffalo, New York,
Gift of Seymour H. Knox, 1963

▷ David Hockney
A Bigger Splash (1967)

Unlike many contemporary realists, David Hockney's witty interpretations of American life create a positive imagery. In *A Bigger Splash,* Hockney captures the key elements of California life: palm trees, a modern home, and the ever-present swimming pool. This painting manages to suggest at once both an eerie stillness and motion.

Acrylic on canvas 96" x 96" (243 cm x 243 cm) © David Hockney

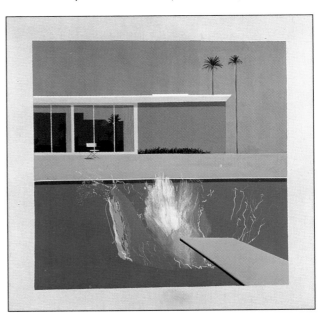

◁ Jackson Pollock
Convergence (1952)

When one thinks of modern art, in particular, abstract expressionism, the name Jackson Pollock often comes to mind. His approach to painting has made him at once a respected and controversial figure in the art world. Pollock is known for pouring paint on his canvas and then walking through it. His particular mood at the moment of creativity dictates the form and aspect of his painting. He feels that nothing is accidental but everything is the result of inner forces at work upon the artist. The result is a dynamic, exciting portrayal of the mental and physical forces at work in the artist.

Oil on canvas, 93½" x 155" (237 cm x 393.7 cm),
Albright-Knox Art Gallery, Buffalo, New York,
Gift of Seymour H. Knox, 1956

Julian Schnabel
Rebirth I (1986)

Schnabel frequently paints on unconventional surfaces with unconventional materials. In this painting, the blossoming trees are from the theatre backdrop, turned upside down; Schnabel has painted the eyes and the horizontal lines.

shells, the greatest bombardment in the history of warfare, blasting to pieces fortress, earth, and already dead bodies. The Germans suffered 280 000 casualties, the French 315 000. The Germans gained 7 km.

In July came the British offensive at the Somme River, an all-out attack on the Germans, who were entrenched on high ground. There were 60 000 British casualties on the first day. For this, British General Douglas Haig would be remembered as the man of the "meatgrinder war." When the fighting ended in November, the Germans counted 450 000 casualties, Britain 420 000, and France 200 000. All told, a million men were dead or wounded. The British gained 10 km. In the trenches, the soldiers sang a song: "If you want to find the old battalion, I know where they are. They're hanging on the old barbed wire." From these disasters came the vision of World War I as a scene of utter destruction, with blasted landscapes, blundering generals, and senseless deaths.

The Rise of New Leaders

The butchery of 1916 indicated that military deadlock was total. It indicated also that the fighting spirit of the men was being lost. After another bungled attack early in 1917, mutinies spread in the French trenches. This was not a rebellion but an outcry by foot soldiers asking their leaders to make war in a different way. In response came a new commander and a different strategy. Marshal Philippe Pétain was a champion of defensive warfare, "lavish with steel and stingy with men," a soldier's general who promised to end suicidal attacks. Pétain was the first of the new leaders who believed that the way to victory was not mass offensive but firm endurance. The winning side would be the one to hold out the longest. Thus, the greater reserves of the Allies in men and industry would mean victory in the end.

In Britain, the idea of making war "to the bitter end" found its leader in David Lloyd George, a fiery Welshman who became prime minister in 1916. In France, it was Georges Clemenceau, "the tiger," a fiercely patriotic man who was appointed premier the following

year. When the war broke out in 1914, most people said that "the boys will be home by Christmas." By 1917, with no end in sight, some were calling for protests and peace talks. The role of Lloyd George and Clemenceau was to fight against every sign of defeatism in the population. When a high public figure, who had been premier of France, appealed for a compromise peace with Germany to save what was left of Western civilization, Clemenceau had him arrested for treason. "You ask me for my policy," said Clemenceau, "it is to make war. Home policy? I make war. Foreign policy? I make war. Always, everywhere, I make war."

Most military leaders in France and Britain were generals without victories, so these countries put power in the hands of civilians. In contrast, two German generals who won battles and fame in Russia in 1916 were called to control affairs in Berlin. General Paul von Hindenburg was an old and wooden Prussian officer who had been called out of retirement at the start of the war. On the eastern front, he joined with General Erich Ludendorff, the rising star of the officer corps, a man of cold character and high talent who became the dominant voice in the capital, Berlin. Together, the two men established a near-military dictatorship in Germany.

Time was not on their side. From 1914, war strategists in Berlin were aware that the greater resources of their enemies endangered Germany in a war that went on "to the bitter end." For victory, Germany needed a breakthrough, a wonder weapon, a gamble that would pay off in quick results. In 1915, Germany's leaders were the first to use poison gas in hope of a dramatic advance in Flanders. But this new and horrific weapon failed, so they looked to another: the submarine.

Through the war, the German high-seas fleet was kept safe in harbour, away from the superior might of the Royal British Navy. Only once, in 1916, did the two fleets meet head on in the **Battle of Jutland** in the North Sea. After this encounter, a draw at best, Germany decided not to engage in

Paul von Hindenburg and Erich Ludendorff were both prominent generals and politicians at the time of World War I.

a second round. Britain then used its sea power to blockade German ports, choking off military and civilian supplies alike. As a result, hunger took hold in the country in the "turnip winter" of 1916, when root vegetables became the main diet of the population. To turn the tables, Germany threw its own "hunger blockade" around Britain, making use of a shocking new strategy: unlimited submarine warfare. Berlin declared British waters to be a war zone and threatened to torpedo on sight any ship in the area, enemy or neutral. This provoked a distant country that was making good profits from sailing supply ships into British ports: the United States.

As neutrals, Americans protested from the start against German violation of "the freedom of the seas." Their indignation increased with the sinking of the British passenger liner *Lusitania* in 1915, which caused the death of over 100 Americans on board, mostly women and children. Wary, Germany decided for a time to call off attacks on neutral vessels. In 1917, desperate to break the stalemate on land, Ludendorff decided to roll the dice in the sea war. Naval officers convinced him that six months more of unlimited submarine warfare would cause the British to starve, the Allies to collapse, and the war to be over before America could arm. "I give Your Majesty my word as an officer," the navy chief told a nervous Kaiser, "that not one American will land on the continent."

Responding to new submarine attacks, the United States declared war against Germany on April 6, 1917. Now ammunition from the "arsenal of democracy" began landing in Europe by the boatload. Meanwhile, the Allied invention of the *convoy system*, merchant vessels sailing in tight formation with warship escorts, soon reduced the German submarine menace. When American troops finally began landing in France in 1918 at a rate of 300 000 per month, the strength of the Allies broadly surpassed the resources of the Central Powers.

German gambles turned out better on the eastern front. The **Russian Revolution** of March 1917 overturned the czar and raised hope in Berlin for victory and an end to the two-front war. The new leaders in Petrograd (now St. Petersburg), however, wanted to continue the fighting. In response, Germany decided to make use of a Russian revolutionary who talked of leading a more radical upheaval in that country, one that would take Russia out of the war once and for all. Vladimir Ilich Ulianov, a hard-line Marxist intellectual known by his underground name, Lenin, was living in exile in Switzerland when the Germans arranged to transport him by train into the revolutionary events in Russia. In Lenin, the Germans had discovered a real wonder-weapon. Without knowing it, they were setting loose one of the greatest revolutionaries of modern history.

War and Revolution in Russia

Czar Nicholas II was a weak personality trying to rule with a strong hand. He never really recovered from the twin shocks of 1905, from defeat in the Russo-Japanese War, or from the revolution at home that followed it. In panic, he granted his subjects a constitution and the right to elect a parliament, called the Duma. But thereafter, he tried year after year to undo his own reforms. In this, he was encouraged by his German-born wife, Alexandra, and the strange, religious man who was her favourite in the royal court. Rasputin, a sordid character accused of every sexual vice, was despised by court and country alike. The czar and empress adored him, mostly for his mystical power to stop the internal bleeding of their hemophilic son, the Czarevitch Alexis. All told, the ruling family was one of the most unpopular in Europe.

Even in Russia, public discontent was overcome by the patriotic emotions of 1914, when it entered the war. But when discontent returned upon news of defeats, Nicholas II took personal command of his armies. At court, loyal supporters, wishing to rid the czar of a pernicious influence, murdered the sinister Rasputin. This did not, however, save Nicholas from war. An Allied summer offensive against Austria-Hungary in 1916 began with smashing success and ended in disaster and a million casualties on both sides. Austria, near exhaustion, asked for German support to stay on its feet. The Russian collapse came in the following spring, beginning in the cities at the rearguard.

Russian cities in 1917 were places of bread lines, labour strikes, and peace demonstrations. The streets had large numbers of factory women, working long shifts in war industries in place of men. There were army deserters by the thousands as well—men in uniform living outside the law and on the run from authorities. On March 8, women in Petrograd marched in an International Women's Day demonstration for "Peace and Bread." The march turned into a riot, the riot into a revolt. Military units, ordered to put down the crowds, lost control. Worse, some soldiers switched over to the side of the revolt. Without power to restore order, Nicholas abdicated his throne on March 15. This was the March Revolution of 1917, a political surprise, swift and unplanned, in which the Romanov dynasty, after ruling over Russia for three centuries, was brought down in one week.

Power now passed to two very different organizations. One was the Provisional Government, a group of mostly middle-class politicians from the last Duma who wanted to introduce liberal reforms. The other was the Soviets (councils), large assemblies of delegates elected by workers, peasants, and soldiers, and inspired by socialist ideas. Despite their differences, both organizations wanted to continue the war. To lose it now, most believed, was to lose everything won in the March Revolution. Thus, the new leaders wanted to fight; by contrast, the soldiers had had enough. "The army," concluded military headquarters, "is simply a

huge, weary, shabby, and ill-fed mob of angry men united by their common thirst for peace and by common disappointment."

If not for this hunger for peace, Lenin might have passed unnoticed in history. When he arrived in Petrograd in April 1917, his political party had little more than 20 000 members—the Bolsheviks (majority). This small band of intellectuals liked to think of itself as "the vanguard of the proletariat." In reality, it was the minority wing of the small party of Russian Marxism, the Social Democrats. Known for their dogmatism and ironclad organization, the Bolsheviks had appeared out of date in the previous period of democratic socialism in Europe. Now, in the crisis conditions of the war, Lenin's methods turned out to be an advantage. The provisional government wanted to concentrate on fighting the Germans and put off the hard questions facing the nation until the election of a

The Use of Poison Gas: 1915

The use of asphyxiating gases in warfare was banned by international agreement at the Hague Peace Conference in 1907. Determined to find a breakthrough weapon, the Germans in 1915 transported 6000 cylinders of chlorine gas to the front near Ypres in Flanders. Late in the afternoon of April 22, a bright, clear day with a gentle west breeze, Algerian troops in a French Colonial unit saw a yellowish green cloud rise from the German side and roll across the battlefield toward their position in the Allied line. Choking, blinded, noses and throats burning, the troops fled in panic, opening a 6 km front to attack. German commanders, however, failed to exploit their success in this first use of poison gas on the western front (an earlier attempt in

Russia failed due to wind and cold), and the Allies soon rushed in Canadian reserves to close the gap.

Allied nations reacted with rage at this use of chemical warfare. Voices denounced the violation of honoured traditions of war. Five months later, however, on September 25, Britain used gas for the first time, and chemical weapons soon became a

common feature of attacks by both sides. Effective gas masks were quickly developed, and soldiers learned that the danger of gas could be overcome by training and equipment. Ordinary explosives were harder to escape. Thus, despite the horror caused by the new use of gas warfare, conventional weapons remained a greater threat to the fighting men.

| Farthest German Advance | ••••• Brest-Litovsk Boundary, 1918 |
| ------ Farthest Russian Advance, 1914-1916 | ◆ Battle Sites |

World War I: The Eastern Front

constituent assembly in the coming months. Lenin, however, had immediate answers. His slogan was "Land, peace, bread": immediate distribution of land to the peasants, immediate peace with the Germans, immediate Marxist revolution in Russia, and "All power to the Soviets."

The Bolsheviks, now 200 000 and growing, took control of the Soviets in the fall. On November 7, in a swift coup organized by Lenin's brilliant lieutenant Leon Trotsky, the Bolsheviks seized power from the provisional government. Its last leader, Alexander Kerensky, final hope of the democratic ideals of the March Revolution, escaped into exile. The March Revolution against the czar had been the spontaneous uprising of a suffering people. In contrast, this November Revolution—called "Red October" in accord with the old Julian calendar then in use—was a planned operation in which a revolutionary minority grabbed power from a more democratic government that had lost the support of a people weary of defeat. This was the "Red Miracle" of 1917, the birth of communism in one of the most unlikely nations according to the predictions of Marx. (Russia was an agrarian rather than an industrialized country.)

Significantly, this new regime was born fighting: immediately, its enemies fell upon it from all sides, beginning the Russian Civil War that was to last four years (1918–1921). The war with Germany, however, was over and done. On March 15, 1918, Lenin signed the Treaty of Brest-Litovsk, taking Russia out of the war in defeat and humiliation. The terms were brutal, stripping away Finland, Poland, Ukraine, and the Baltic provinces from the old Romanov Empire. At last, one of Germany's gambles seemed to have paid off.

Lenin wanted the new communist state to be a turning point in history. To that end, the Bolsheviks changed its very name from Russia into Union of Soviet Socialist Republics. They wanted their U.S.S.R. to be a new star in the East, a sign to exhausted peoples in the West to rise against the war. On the day after coming to power, Lenin issued his *Decree on Peace*, calling for immediate peace without victory or defeat for either side. To stir anger, he published documents found in czarist files, revealing the secret treaties between the Allies to divide the spoils of war. For some Europeans, exhausted by war and senseless death, this message went deep. One response was the rising number of strikes and protests in the last year of the war. In effect, communist peace propaganda was the first Soviet challenge to the Western world.

The propaganda war between the Allies and Central Powers had been fought as hard as the war at the front. The difference was that governments aimed most propaganda not at the enemy but at their own people. Citizens wanted to know what they were fighting for, what this war over the death of Franz Ferdinand was all about. Hard question. British soldiers had a song to explain why they were in the trenches: "We're here because we're here, because we're here, because we're here." Hard put to answer, their government said the reason was German war crimes and atrocities. A British report in 1915 accused the enemy of "murder, lust and pillage... on a scale unparalleled in any war between civilized nations during the last three centuries." In contrast, Lenin's propaganda explained the war in terms of a broader, Marxist version of European history.

On January 8, 1918 United States President Woodrow Wilson announced the famous **Fourteen Points** or conditions for a peace settlement on American terms. In part, this was a reply to the challenge of Lenin's propaganda: where Lenin denounced the war as a struggle between capitalist powers for markets and profits, Wilson defended it as "a war to make the world safe for democracy." Lenin called for a communist society; Wilson called for free nations. Both demanded an end to secret treaties made by aristocrats behind closed doors. Both called for more open and democratic world diplomacy, for government under the eyes of the citizens. The debate between Lenin and Wilson on communism and freedom was the first battle of modern propaganda war, a protracted war between the Soviet Union and the United States that was to continue through most of the century.

The War Experience: Soldiers and Civilians

Writers said that every nation in the war became two nations: front and rear. English poet Rupert Brooke at first described the war as "a magnificent escape from a civilian world grown old and cold and weary." Some veterans spoke not of hating the enemy but of hating modern war. Bravery counted little; what counted was industry, science, and steel. The result was horrible to see and hear. Soldiers described a "symphony of hell," the sound and fury of modern weapons: machine guns, powerful explosives, heavy artillery, and—loudest of all—the German 20-tonne cannons, the "Big Berthas," that fired shells weighing over a tonne. French war writer Henri Barbusse said that even the dead could not sleep. He remembered watching enemy fire rip and tear at already dead bodies: under this storm of metal, dead men stirred as if coming back to life.

Terrible weapons caused terrible losses. In 1913, 161 students graduated from the Ecole Normale Supérieure, France's celebrated institution of higher learning. By 1918, 145 of them were casualties of war. Observers said that Europe was destroying the flower of its youth, those whose talents would have enriched the life and culture of the Continent. Men who survived described the misery, mud, rats, and lice of the trenches. Through all this, however, most armies fought well and followed orders. Most were loyal to their country and leaders. Thus, when the fighting was over, the unanswered question for historians was not why some soldiers rebelled against such an awful war, but why so many fought and obeyed.

The war experience influenced different men in different ways. To some, it was civilization gone mad; to others it was men at their most manly. German-born American novelist Erich Maria Remarque, several times wounded, said that the war was the ruin of his life.

Literature and the Reality of War:
All Quiet on the Western Front

Erich Maria Remarque's *All Quiet on the Western Front*, first published in 1928, has been described as the greatest of all war novels. In simple but moving prose, it tells the story of German youths coming of age in the trenches. The main character of the novel, wounded in battle, describes the scene in a war hospital behind the lines:

Day after day goes by with pain and fear, groans and death-gurgles....

On the next floor below are the abdominal and spine cases, head wounds and double amputations. On the right side of the wing are the jaw wounds, gas cases, nose, ear, and neck wounds. On the left the blind and the lung wounds, pelvis wounds, wounds in the joints, wounds in the testicles, wounds in the intestines. Here a man realizes for the first time in how many places a man can get hit....

A man cannot realize that above such shattered bodies there are still human faces in which life goes its daily round. And this is only one hospital, one single station; there are hundreds of thousands in Germany, hundreds of thousands in France, hundreds of thousands in Russia. How senseless is everything that can ever be written, done, or thought, when such things are possible. It must all be lies and of no account when the culture of a thousand years could not prevent this stream of blood being poured out, these torture chambers in their hundreds of thousands. A hospital alone shows what war is.

Future German Nazi dictator Adolf Hitler, several times wounded and gassed, said it was "the greatest and most unforgettable time of my earthly experience." Some feared that the individual's sense of identity and worth would be crushed under the sheer weight of mass armies and mass death. Others, in contrast, recognized that the fighting created proud new identities.

Canadian soldiers entered the war as part of the British army and distinguished themselves fighting for king and empire. In April 1917, in a striking victory at Vimy in northwestern France, they swept the enemy from Vimy Ridge, a strongpoint on high ground where German defenders had held off every other attacking force for two years. Wrote a historian, "Canadians then and later knew that they had done a great thing and that on such deeds nations are built."

Overall, both "front" and "rear" nations were changed by the war. As leaders came to see that the conflict would be long and hard, they realized that war production at home was as important as sending soldiers to the trenches. This was a war of industrial peoples. Those least advanced, Austria-Hungary, Russia, and Italy, were the first to show strain. No nation, however, could continue "business as usual." People, resources, and production, all had to be organized, managed, and driven as never before. The result was an increase in government controls over the life of society, over wages, prices, profits, opinions, and news.

Thus, as the war became more total, so did the powers of the state. Germany, landlocked by the British naval blockade, became a fortress under siege. The home front was mobilized like the war front, with the economy under military command and all males between ages 16 and 60 bound by the Support Services Law to accept work in war industries. But if Germany came closest to the later totalitarian vision of the state-as-war-machine, its enemies were showing some of the same signs.

Important in this total war was the role of women. Some, of course, opposed the conflict. Most women, however, stood with their men under the flag of their country. In Britain, in the period before the 1916 conscription law, the government looked to women to persuade their menfolk to get into uniform. Patriotic organizations told women to keep their distance from men in civilian clothes, and to disgrace them on the street by giving them a white feather, symbol of cowardice and dishonour. Governments needed women to replace their men at work.

The war economy opened opportunities to women as never before. In Britain, about 1.5 million new female workers entered the labour force. Many found jobs in war production. The munitions arsenal at Woolwich, for example, which employed 125 women in 1914, employed 25 000 by 1917. Numbers of female workers increased in every sector of the economy. Women replaced men as plumbers, labourers, truck drivers, and police officers. As well, over 100 000 British women joined the military units for females established by the armed services. With this change in women's lives came changes in their lifestyle and dress. Many wore pants, shorter skirts, and cosmetics; some took to drinking, smoking, and night life. With the men at war, the other half of the human race entered the "man's world" of work and leisure.

Still, female workers were kept in their "place": women's wages were lower than those of men. When women demanded "equal pay for equal work," men argued that this would keep females from returning after the war to their "true roles" as mothers and wives. Men also worried that cheap female labour would threaten their own pay scale. In any case, when peace came in 1918, governments, employers, and labour unions banded together in wanting to return men to work and women to their "proper place" somewhere else. The working-women of World War I had been merely substitutes for workingmen. When the fighting stopped, it was time for them to go back home and return the world to normal.

Both sides in the war, however, wanted to reward women for doing their patriotic duty. Before 1914,

Posters such as this were used in Canada to gain public support for the war effort.

the suffragette struggle for the right to vote had met hard resistance. That right came virtually as a gift from men. Beginning in Russia in 1917, the great powers, except France, extended the franchise to women. All told, the war was a force for change in women's history, but it was proof of the strength of tradition in gender relations as well. In the voting booth, women became first-class citizens. In the world of work, they remained the second sex.

The End of the War: 1918

In April 1917, the Americans declared war on Germany. In December of the same year, they declared war on Austria-Hungary. This turned the course of the war in favour of the Allies because it brought fresh troops and resources into the equation. The German spring offensive in the west in 1918 heightened war activity. Strengthened by troops returning from victory in Russia, Ludendorff's "all-or-nothing" assault brought his armies close to Paris. They bled all the way, taking heavy casualties for every mile of advance. This time there were no replacements. After four years of magnificent effort, the great German superpower was out of men and low in endurance. The Allies struck back in July, beginning a grinding offensive that continued to the last day of the war. By this time, the generals had new ideas and new weapons for offensive warfare. The British had high hopes for the tank, but these iron "motor-monsters" were too slow and trouble-prone to make much difference in this war. The difference now was that the Allies had more of everything and their enemies had less. The Germans did not crack: they simply fell back. When the fighting ended, they were still on French soil. Behind them, their own country remained largely untouched by the war.

In Germany, however, the events of these last weeks of the war poisoned the future of the nation. His nerves broken, Ludendorff told Kaiser Wilhelm II on September 29, 1917 that the war was lost. Before leaving the stage, the general advised the Kaiser to seek an armistice and appoint a new government of democratic leaders to open negotiations for peace on the terms of President Wilson's Fourteen Points. Later, critics would say that Ludendorff had a dark motive in mind: he wanted to shift responsibility for defeat from the military leaders to the democratic politicians. The most important of these politicians were moderate socialists of the Social Democratic Party. First, in 1914, they supported the war. Later, they turned away, and warned

Cradling shells, not babies. Women in Italy, as in many countries, did their part for the war.

that the nation's leaders would be made to account for the suffering of the people. "Now," said Ludendorff, "they will eat the soup that they cooked for us."

The new leaders were handed a nation on the edge of revolt and ruin. Sailors had broken into mutiny; revolutionaries were fighting in the streets. The Social Democrats picked up the pieces—and made enemies on every side. On November 9, they proclaimed their nation a republic, ending the German Empire and the Hohenzollern dynasty. Bitterly, Wilhelm II abdicated and left the country that his ancestors had created in the last century. He died in exile in Holland. Two days later, November 11, 1918, representatives of the new German Republic met Allied officers in France and, in a simple railway car, signed the armistice that ended World War I. For this, angry voices on the right would accuse them of a crime against the nation: the surrender of a German army that was still fighting on foreign soil. Here is where the myth of "the stab in the back" arose, the claim of unforgiving right-wing patriots that the German army, undefeated at the front, was struck down from behind by democrats, socialists, and traitors.

Soon enough, the new republic had unforgiving enemies on the left as well. Involved, in particular, were radical Social Democrats who had rebelled against the "treason" of the party's decision in 1914 to support the war. Some of them, inspired by the Bolshevik Revolution, now became the first members of the new Communist Party of Germany. In Berlin, they were led

By 1917, the battlefields of France and Belgium had become muddy quagmires in which tanks and troops became bogged down.

by two militants who soon became cult figures in the history of modern communism: Rosa Luxemburg and Karl Liebknecht. In January 1919, these radicals struck for power. Against this revolution from the left, the new government turned for support to army leaders and the volunteer bands of armed veterans known as the Free Corps. These tough street fighters crushed the uprising, murdered Luxemburg and Liebknecht, and moved quickly to restore order throughout Germany. This the German communists would remember as more treason by the Social Democrats against the working class. Thus, as it was being born, the new Germany created enemies on the left and right who would hound its political life to the end.

When Germany signed the armistice, the defeat of the Central Powers was complete. Bulgaria and Turkey had given up the fight. The Austro-Hungarian Empire, or what was left of it, signed an armistice on November 4, 1918. Already the Czechs, Poles, and South Slavs were creating their own nations in the old Hapsburg lands. Thus, even before the peacemakers met at Paris in January 1919 to remake the map of Europe, the peoples already were remaking it themselves.

The Treaty of Versailles: 1919

Twenty-seven Allied nations participated in drawing up the *Treaty of Versailles*, named for the magnificent old palace outside Paris where the final document was signed on June 28, 1919. In reality, most decisions at the Paris Peace Conference were made by the so-called Big Four: Britain, France, the United States, and Italy. However, Italian Premier Vittorio Orlando soon complained of being slighted by his powerful partners, and Italy came away disappointed, carrying its resentment against the Paris peace into the post-war world. The achievement of the conference was to bring together different views: the hard-line demands of Clemenceau to dismember Germany, the more moderate aim of Lloyd George to keep Germany and France in balance, and the idealistic plan of Woodrow Wilson to contain Germany by bringing it into a new world order of democratic and independent nations. Observers called the result a compromise peace. The compromise, however, was only between the victors. The defeated nations were given no place and no voice at the peace table. To Germany, therefore, the treaty was a *Diktat*, a peace dictated by the Allies. Germany itself, of course, had dictated a much harder peace to the Bolsheviks at Brest-Litovsk in 1918.

Critics said that the Versailles settlement, in contrast, was hard and soft at the same time. The reason was perhaps that Europe itself was of two minds. Many people were moved by Wilson's ideal of a just peace but they were also out to punish Germany. The Allies were going to "squeeze Germany like a lemon," said a British leader, "and keep squeezing until you can hear the pips squeak." The Versailles Treaty reflected both the toughness and the moderation of these public moods. The victors slashed Germany's military strength to ribbons, reducing its army to 100 000 troops. Germany lost Alsace and Lorraine to France. It lost eastern territory to the revived state of Poland, which was also granted a land corridor to the Baltic Sea. This corridor separated East Prussia from the rest of Germany. Germany lost its colonies around the world but the country was not dismembered: its population of 60 million remained larger than any of its neighbours; its factories and mines—some temporarily under French control—remained capable of returning the nation to the status of an industrial power. The German giant had been defeated but it was still a giant.

Austria paid a higher price in the Treaty of Saint-Germain. (Separate treaties were signed with each of the defeated powers.) Western liberals had viewed Austria-Hungary as a land of repressed minorities, peoples longing for nationhood. In Woodrow Wilson's mind, this repressed nationalism was the cause of war, of the Sarajevo assassination, and of European discontent. The way to peace, he believed, was to complete the revolution of nationalism in European history, to give the right of self-determination to all national peoples. The result was the dismemberment of the old Hapsburg Empire and the emergence of the new nations of Hungary, Czechoslovakia, Poland, and Yugoslavia. When the Big Four were finished, the empire of Austria-Hungary had disappeared from the map. What remained was Austria itself, now a little republic of less than 7 million.

The time was up for the Ottoman Empire as well. Despite Allied promises to recognize the independence of Arab lands after the war, most of these lands were taken over by Britain and France as mandates from the new League of Nations. The mandate system, designed to do away with old-style imperialism, included a provision for the great powers to govern particular regions during a period of development. Britain, given a mandate over Palestine, kept its wartime promise to provide for a Jewish national home in the Holy Land, setting the legal foundation for the future state of Israel. Arab peoples, for their part, saw little difference between old-style imperialism and new-style mandates. To them, the right of self-determination appeared to be for Europeans only.

The peacemakers were more interested in an old empire closer to home, where communism had replaced czarism in the largest country on earth. Already, in 1917, Allied troops had been sent to Russia to try to keep that country in the war against Germany. Afterward, with fears rising that communism could spread to the West, they stayed on through most of the Russian Civil War. Mostly, these troops of Britain, France, the United States, and Japan—about 100 000 in all—were warriors in the dark, half involved in supporting the fight of the so-called White armies against the Red forces, half involved in trying to stay out of it. However, with the Bolsheviks thus tied down in a fight for survival, new nations were able to emerge in the old Romanov lands in the west: Finland, Estonia, Latvia, Lithuania, and Poland. As the old empires broke into pieces, the result was the most immense shuffling of borders in the history of the state system on the Continent.

The Europe of kings and emperors gave way to the sovereignty of the people. France and Portugal were the only republics in Europe before the war; after, there were more republics than monarchies. Many, however, were weak and defenceless. Most had troubles with minorities within their borders. The different peoples of the continent simply lived too entangled to make it possible for different peoples to have their own states. Despite Wilson's ideal of self-determination, large national minorities, such as Germans living in Czechoslovakia, continued to live unhappily outside the country of their choice. With the fall of the old empires, therefore, the middle of Europe was made up of small and inexperienced states, with revolutionary Bolshevism to one side and a discontented Germany on the other. Critics of the Versailles Treaty argued that this new Europe was more unstable than the old one. The settlement of World War I, they concluded, planted the seeds for World War II.

The American President was aware of the problems of the peace. His faith was that they could be set right in coming years by the **League of Nations**. The League was Wilson's idea, a way to bring international cooperation to a jumbled world of more and more nations. He first included his idea in his Fourteen Points and, in Paris, he worked successfully to establish the League as part of the Versailles settlement. After a history of American isolation from Europe, Wilson led his country into the affairs of the Continent. Many Americans did not want to stay. When the United States Senate refused to ratify the peace treaty or join the League, the United States returned to its original isolation and left the problems of European security to the Europeans. Britain, in turn, decided to go back to its own isolation and left the problems to France. The real trouble with the Versailles peace, some historians have concluded, was that the peacemakers did not stay around to enforce it.

The result was that the German problem came back to challenge Europe all over again. The "war to make the world safe for democracy" made Germany a difficult place for democrats. Leaders of the new **Weimar Republic** (so named because of its beginnings in the city of Weimar) wanted to show the world a Germany of culture and peace. The defeat, however, left behind too much resentment. The Versailles *Diktat* and the guilt clause added more. In 1921, Allied experts set the cost of reparations at 33 billion dollars. Some economists, even in Allied countries, warned that the sum was too high and ruinous for all concerned. In Germany, anger over the reparations was added to the anger of a defeated and humiliated nation. The Weimar Republic was heading for self-destruction.

Militarism or Pacifism:
The Moral Dilemma of World War I

 When war broke out in 1914, it brought with it much controversy. Norman Angell's *Grand Illusion* had argued that when two or more major powers went to war, there were no winners. Despite widespread enthusiasm for the war among many Europeans, a committed body of pacifists remained stalwart in their opposition. On both sides of the controversy, issues of morality figured prominently. The following two extracts address the morality of war. The first was written by a Russian socialist who usually sided with the pacifist. The second, written after the war, is by Britain's leading pacifist Bertrand Russell. Which of the arguments do you find more convincing? Given the arguments presented by these two writers, how was the experience of World War I a psychologically shattering experience? In which situations would you support the pacifist cause today? In which situations would you consider pacifists detrimental to the well-being of a nation or its people?

Sir

May I be allowed to say a few words in connection with the excellent letter by my compatriot, Professor Vinogradov, which appeared in your paper today. Professor Vinogradov is absolutely right when he says that not only is it desirable that complete unity of feeling should exist in Russian political circles, but that this unity is already an accomplished fact.

The representatives of all political parties and of all nationalities in Russia are now at one with the Government, and this war with Germany and Austria, both guided by the Kaiser, has already become a national war for Russia.

Even we, the adherents of the parties of the Exteme Left, and hitherto ardent ant-militarist and pacifists, even we believe in the necessity of this war. This war is a war to protect justice and civilization. It will, we hope, be a decisive factor in our united war against war, and we hope that after it will at last be possible to consider seriously the question of disarmament and universal peace. There can be no doubt that victory, and decisive victory at that (personally I await this in the immediate future), will be on the side of the Allied nations — England, France, Belgium, Servia, and Russia.

The German peril, the curse which has hung over the whole world for so many decades, will be crushed, and crushed so that it will never again become a danger to the peace of the world. The peoples of the world desire peace.

To Russia this war will bring regeneration.

We are convinced that after this war there will be no longer any room for political reaction, and Russia will be associated with the existing group of cultured and civilized countries.

Professor Vinagradov is right when he says that in Russia not one of the political Left parties has at the present time modified its program in any way in view of the war. The word on all lips in Russia now is "Freedom". All are hungrily awaiting a general amnesty, freedom of the Press and of national life.

All the parties, without any exception, have supported the Government without even waiting for it to make any definite announcement about these crying needs. This is the measure of the belief of the people in the inevitableness of liberal reforms. The Government, unfortunately, still seems irresolute and has up till now only done the minimum to justify the popular belief in it, but we are convinced that circumstances will develop in such a way that the Government will not be able to delay for long that which has become for Russia a historical necessity. And the sooner this happens the better.

To ensure the complete success of Russia in this war against Germany and Austria, and also for the time when the terms of peace will be discussed, the strongest and most firm national unity is necessary. And this unity of all nationalities and all parties will be possible only when the Russian Government will frankly and resolutely inaugurate a new and free era in the political life of the country.

We are convinced that we have supporting us both the public opinion of England and that of its Allies — France and Belgium.

Yours truly,

V. Bourtzeff

The most difficult period in which to keep one's head was the very beginning, before that battle of the Marne. The rapid advance of the Germans was terrifying; the newspapers, and still more private conversations, were full of apparently well-authenticated atrocity stories; the stream of Belgian refugees seemed to strengthen the case for defending Belgium. One by one, the people with whom one had been in the habit of agreeing politically went over to the side of the war, and as yet the exceptional people, who stood out, had not found each other. But the greatest difficulty was the purely psychological one of resisting mass suggestion, of which the force becomes terrific when the whole nation is in a state of violent collective excitement. As much effort was required to avoid sharing this excitement as would have been needed to stand out against the extreme of hunger or sexual passion, and there was the same feeling of going against instinct.

It must be remembered that we had not then the experience which we gradually acquired during the war. We did not know the wiles of herd-instinct, from which, in quiet times, we had been fairly free. We did not realise that it is stimulated by the cognate emotions of fear and rage and bloodlust, and we were not on the look-out for the whole system of irrational beliefs which war-fever, like every other strong passion, brings in its train. In the case of passions which our neighbours do not share, their arguments make us see reason; but in war-time our neighbours encourage irrationality, and shrink in horror from the slightest attempt to throw doubt upon prevailing myths.

The great stimulant to herd-instinct is fear; in patriots, the instinct was stimulated by fear of the Germans, but in pacifists fear of the patriots produced a similar result. I can remember sitting in a bus thinking: "These people would tear me to pieces if they knew what I think about war." The feeling was uncomfortable, and led one to prefer the company of pacifists. Gradually a pacifist herd was formed. When we were all together we felt warm and cosy, and forgot that an insignificant minority had become a majority. We did not know that one of us was to become prime minister, but if we had known we should have supposed that it would be a good thing when he did.

In times of excitement, simple views find a hearing more readily than those that are sufficiently complex to have a chance of being true. Nine people out of ten in England during the war never got beyond the view that the Germans were wicked and the Allies were virtuous (crude moral categories, such as "virtuous" and "wicked," revived in people who, at most times, been ashamed to think in such terms). The easiest theory to maintain in opposition to the usual one was the Quaker view, that all men are good at heart and that the way to bring out the good in them is to love them. We had been taught that we ought to love our enemies, and few people cared to say straight out that it was a mistake. Those who genuinely held the Quaker view were respected, and the Government disliked having to send them to prison.

The class-war opinion, that capitalist wars are wicked but proletarian wars are laudable, could be preached with success to working-class audiences; it had the advantage of giving an outlet for hatred, of which many persecuted pacifists felt the need. Frequently, in meetings nominally opposed to all war, the threat of violent revolution was applauded to the echo. This view was, of course, the one of all others most hated by the authorities, but it was psychologically capable of being held by a majority.

The view which I took, and still take, was that while some wars have been justified (for instance the American Civil War), the Great War was not justified, because it was about nothing impersonal and raised no important issue. This view required too much argument to be effective in such a violent time; it could be put forward in books but not at meetings. It was also impossible to get a hearing for the view that a war cannot be justified by its causes but only, if at all, by its effects. A "righteous" war was supposed to be one which had the correct diplomatic preliminaries, not one in which victory would bring some benefit to mankind. One of the most surprising things about the war, to me, was its power of producing intellectual degradation in previously intelligent people and the way in which intellectual degradation always clothed itself in the language of a lofty but primitive morality.

To stand out against a war, when it comes, a man must have within himself some passion so strong and so indestructable that mass hysteria cannot touch it.

Bertrand Russell

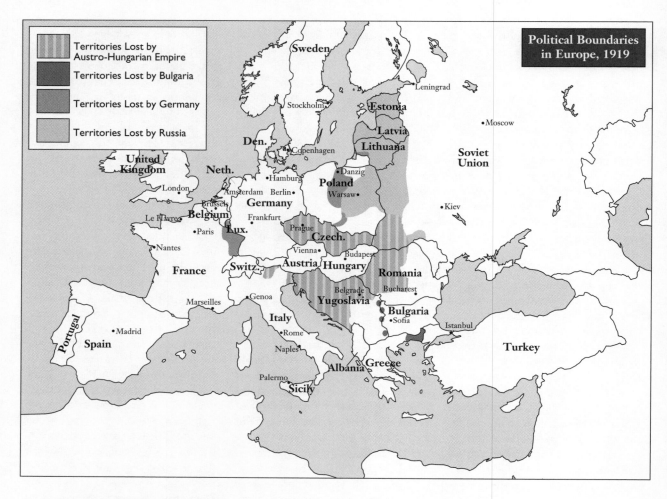

Political Boundaries in Europe, 1919

Legend:
- Territories Lost by Austro-Hungarian Empire
- Territories Lost by Bulgaria
- Territories Lost by Germany
- Territories Lost by Russia

The famous guilt clause of the Versailles Treaty was not included merely to humiliate Germany but to give a legal basis to Allied claims for reparations. The cost of the war had been immense. It had been financed on the Allied side by loans, especially from the United States, turning the countries involved into debtor nations. The logic of the guilt clause was plain: Germany was guilty of starting a war of aggression, thus Germany was responsible for the damages. Twelve years earlier, nations at the Hague Peace Conference had considered war to be an accepted instrument of state policy.

This war was different. The new level of violence, the horror of gas weapons, the attacks on civilians by submarines and aircraft, made war on this scale appear to be a threat to civilization itself. A war of this kind could not be accounted for as "the continuation of foreign policy by other means." The guilt clause represented a different principle for the twentieth century: to wage an aggressive war was in violation of international law. Thus, World War I changed the way in which the West viewed war and peace in modern times.

The Results of the War

World War I was a great divide in history. It ended a period of relative peace and began a period of total war and totalitarian movements. The events of 1914–1918 were a war and a revolution, which in turn unleashed other wars and revolutions. Most important were the four revolutions that shaped the rest of the century: (1) the communist revolution, (2) the fascist revolution, (3) the revolution in military technology, and (4) the anti-Western revolution. It is important to point out that these revolutions all arose from the death experience of World War I.

The most outstanding characteristic of this war is that it was a death experience, a human massacre of enormous proportions. In all, some 10 million were killed, including roughly 2 million Russians, 2 million Germans, 1.5 million French, and nearly a million British. Perhaps 30 million were wounded, though the number is uncertain. From all this destruction came forces and moods that no peace settlement could overcome. Although the war appeared to be a victory for democracy, it gave rise to two radical movements that would carry state power over the individual to new limits in Western history. Both communism and fascism, of course, had their origins in the last century, but the war gave them new form and passion. After the Allied victory of 1918, therefore, the real challenge to democracy was still to come.

Some historians use the term "the Second Thirty Years War" to refer to this period of "the German problem" and the challenge to Western democracy between 1914 and 1945. They mean that only a brief peace separated World War I (1914–1918) from World War II (1939–1945). The enemies were the same; what changed was the scale of destruction. From 1914 onward, a momentum toward greater destruction became obvious as military leaders, with the western front in deadlock, extended the war to the civilian population by the use of submarines and aircraft. To military strategists, new weapons and easier targets appeared to be the way out of the stalemate.

The result was a revolution in military technology, brought about in particular by the development of air power. The first flight of an airplane came only 11 years before 1914—by the Wright brothers in the United States in 1903—but airplane design advanced rapidly during the war. From simple reconnaissance work, pilots moved on to strafing and bombing behind the lines. In his memoirs, the American ace Billy Mitchell recalls flying over the trenches and into open airspace over Germany, looking down on undefended towns and factories. Here, he wrote, was the place to strike the enemy in the heart:

> To gain a lasting factor in war, the hostile nation's power to make war must be destroyed. This means manufacturing, communications, food products, and even places where people live and carry on their lives.

Armed Forces and Casualties in World War I

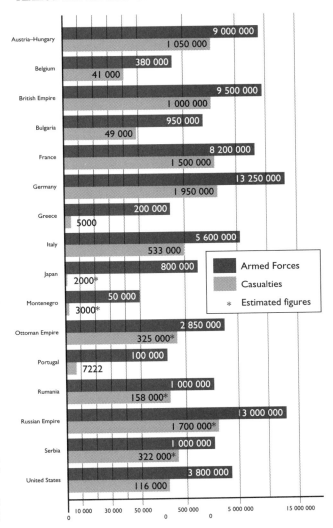

In effect, Mitchell was redefining total war by blurring the distinction between military and civilian targets. If total war was war in which the total resources of a nation were engaged, then these total resources—military and civilian—must now become targets for war. Conclusions such as these, drawn from the total war of 1914, made possible the "more total" war of 1939–1945.

Reflections

In the wake of World War I, an epidemic of influenza, the worst on record, circled the earth in 1918–1919. The toll was 20 million dead, twice as many as those killed in the war. Yet the influence of this much greater human loss simply could not match the influence of the Great War on history. It was said that the most important casualty of the war had been the Western mind.

Wounded was the pride and confidence of Europeans in themselves and their values. Now Western thought was overtaken by pessimism, by concern with violence and the irrational in human behaviour. As Europe appeared to lose mastery, the other peoples of the globe began to stir, making ready for the revolt against Western control over their lives. In the results of the war were the conditions which, over time, would bring the end of the European Age in world history.

Key Concepts, Figures, and Events

Triple Alliance/Triple Entente
General Alfred von Schlieffen
Czar Nicholas II
Hague Peace Conference

Guilt Clause
Battle of Jutland
Russian Revolution
Fourteen Points

Versailles Treaty
League of Nations
Weimar Republic

Topics for Further Thought

1. There are generally said to be four main causes of World War I: nationalism, imperialism, militarism, and the alliance system. Briefly explain how each contributed to the outbreak of war. Given the situation in the decades leading up to the World War I, do you believe war could have been avoided? Explain your answer.

2. Reflecting on the events leading to the outbreak of war in 1914, do you feel the guilt clause in the Versailles Treaty was justified? How should victors treat the vanquished if their primary objective is to ensure a lasting peace?

3. During the course of the war there were several significant battles, although few managed to end the stalemate in the trenches. Why was the Battle of the Marne considered the event that "turned out the lights"?

4. The late nineteenth century was an era of technological innovation. Unfortunately for the millions who died between 1914 and 1918, much of this technology was used to improve the killing efficiency of war machines. How did technological developments alter the nature of warfare and make World War I the first modern war?

5. During the course of the war, there was a noticeable change in the style of leadership in many European countries. How did this change in leadership reflect the changes in the nature of war and society during this period?

6. Briefly explain the events surrounding the entry of the United States and the exit of Russia from the war. Assess the significance of these new developments on the eventual outcome of the war.

7. In many ways, World War I helped put an end to the myth that war is a heroic adventure filled with glory for young men. How did the experiences of the soldiers in the war help to destroy this false image of war?

8. The Versailles Treaty is an example of a flawed peace imposed on the vanquished by the victors. There should be little surprise that peace was so short-lived since the Treaty failed to establish a balance of power in Europe. Respond to this statement.

Topics for Further Research

1. Prior to the outbreak of war, there were several people who made efforts to help secure peace. Research the efforts made by one of the following:

Alfred Nobel
Andrew Carnegie
Norman Angell (*The Grand Illusion*)

2. The nature of warfare was changed drastically in World War I by the application of new technology. Research the impact of one of the following on warfare during 1914–1918:

Dreadnoughts   Submarines   Airplanes
Machine Guns   Gas   Tanks
Trucks   Railways

3. Research one of the major battles of World War I, focusing on the major events of the battle, the outcome, and the significance of the battle on the outcome of the war. Select from the following list:

Battle of Jutland   Battle of the Somme
Battle of Ypres   Battle of Passchendaele
Battle of Vimy Ridge

4. The first two decades of the twentieth century were years of radical change in Russia. Research the role played by one of the following individuals from the period:

Czar Nicholas II   Rasputin
Leon Trotsky   Lenin

Responding to Ideas

1. In reviewing the book *War and Human Progress*, English historian Hugh Trevor-Roper wrote: "Is war or is it not a means of progress? Does it—quite apart from the cost of fighting or the spoils of victory—hasten commercial and industrial development?" In these questions lies the subject of debate which has raged among historians for generations. While some maintain that the demands created by war inevitably lead to economic growth, others contend that there are no winners in war; that, in fact, even the victors suffer economically as a result of war. Given the experience of World War I, which position seems to be more tenable?

2. Many would argue that the twentieth century arrived amid the bloodshed of total war during the years 1914–1918. Historian Roland Stromberg wrote: "During the war, propaganda took over and truth suffered as never before, and out of the war there emerged a new kind of cynicism, a loss of faith in humanity and values...." To what degree can World War I be seen as a microcosm of the major themes that would come to dominate the twentieth century?

13

The Russian Revolution and the Rise of Fascism in Europe

CHAPTER HIGHLIGHTS

- The process of rebuilding a war-torn Europe
- The rise of totalitarian regimes in Europe

- The effects of the Great Depression and attempted solutions

- The effects of Stalin's Great Famine, Great Terror, and Five Year plans on the Soviet Union
- Germany's rise under Hitler and the Nazi Party

World War I brought the rule of democracy to Europe. In the years after the war, all the Western powers were democracies with liberal constitutions and free markets. A revolt against this democratic order, however, was not long in coming. It came most clearly in 1922 with the rise of fascism in Italy. Italy's leader **Benito Mussolini** used the word "totalitarian" to describe a form of state power in stark contrast to liberal and democratic ideals. Gone was the difference between public and private life. "For the fascist," said Mussolini, "the state is all-embracing; outside it no human or spiritual values exist."

After the Great Depression of 1929, the real challenge to democratic belief came from totalitarian regimes in the Soviet Union and Germany. In these countries, the evolution side by side of the dictatorships of *Joseph Stalin* and *Adolf Hitler* was one of the most important events of the twentieth century. Together,

these regimes carried out the greatest crimes in world history. The rule of Stalin and Hitler opened a window on the nightmare world of George Orwell's novel *1984* and the possibilities of total power over society. Against them in the 1930s, democratic peoples were forced onto the defensive and feared for the survival of free institutions. "Do you want to know what the future looks like?" asked a character in Orwell's *1984*. "Imagine a boot being ground in your face, forever."

From War to Peace: France and Germany, 1919–1923

European history after 1914 can be simply described: Western democracies won the war and lost the peace. The defeat of Germany in 1918 was not final and the apparent victory of democracy was not apparent for long. In 1919, France in particular was filled with illusions of victory. With Germany beaten and disarmed, France appeared once again to be the greatest power in Europe. In reality, the nation was weaker than before. With the lowest birth rate of the great powers, France was seriously affected by the human losses of the war. Once a creditor nation, it was left with a war debt of over 7 billion dollars. Its currency, one of the most solid in Europe before 1914, was losing value year by year. Also, Germany and Britain were virtually untouched by destruction, whereas France had been a battlefield. Now, after the Versailles Treaty, this great but wounded nation was left by its allies to enforce the peace with Germany.

As a result, relations between France and Germany were the centre of European events in the post-war years. And at the centre of these relations was the issue of the day: war reparations. France was determined to make Germany pay for the war. Moreover, the French needed to feel secure against a possible revival of German power. For this, they wanted to keep their enemy poor, weak, and disarmed. Clemenceau said, "Peace is the continuation of war by other means." Just as France was determined to enforce the Versailles Treaty to the letter, so Germany was determined to defy it at every opportunity. French fears increased in 1922, when Germany signed the Rapallo Agreement with the Soviet Union. In this accord, the two defeated and outcast nations exchanged promises of support. Involved in this new relationship, the French believed, were secret arrangements to permit Germany to conceal weapons and train soldiers behind the scenes in Soviet territory.

A showdown between France and Germany occurred the following year. After Germany failed to deliver shipments of coal as part of a reparations payment, French Premier Raymond Poincaré decided on a tough response: French troops would go into the German mining area in the Ruhr valley, occupy it, and bring out the coal themselves. Thus, on January 11, 1923, French and Belgian troops entered the Ruhr to begin a long

Benito Mussolini, in his characteristic pose, addresses his troops.

and hard military occupation. In response, German leaders called for passive resistance and a strike by Ruhr workers. Defiantly, they printed piles of paper money to support the resistance and pay the strikers. What followed brought despair to both sides.

The cost of the war had already set off galloping inflation in Germany. Rising prices and bloated currency were bringing misery to families living on savings, pensions, and fixed incomes. The massive release of new money into the economy brought on a ruinous inflationary spiral. The great inflation of 1923 left a scar in the mind of the nation. In November of that year, the German mark, fallen in value to 4 trillion to the American dollar, became virtually worthless. Germany was in torment. Radical movements were rising left and right. In the Ruhr, French troops faced riots, sabotage, and a sense of a failed mission.

The experience of the Ruhr occupation was the turning point in relations between France and Germany. The French had second thoughts about using strong-arm methods to force reparations out of Germany. These methods had already brought criticism from the United States and Britain. As wartime emotions cooled in these countries, more citizens were having doubts about the Versailles settlement. They criticized the idea of blaming Germany for the war and all the damages. They criticized France for keeping Germany out of the League of Nations and for using the League to enforce strict obedience to the Versailles Treaty. After a "war to end war," they condemned France as well for disarming Germany without disarming itself. France had said that it would disarm when Germany backed down and paid up. The trouble in the Ruhr, however, brought home a hard lesson: Germany would not pay at the point of a gun—and could not pay so long as it was poor and miserable.

An idea was becoming fixed in Western opinion: reparations had been set too high for Germany to bear. Important in this was the influence of the British economist *John Maynard Keynes*, whose 1919 book *The Economic Consequences of the Peace* warned that reparations would impoverish Germany and other nations alike. A prosperous Europe, said Keynes, needed a prosperous Germany. In 1923, a new leader appeared in Berlin who recognized the need for Germany to come to terms with the Versailles Treaty. Gustav Stresemann, made chancellor in 1923, called for an end to resistance in the Ruhr and began work to restore order to German life. With him, a new "politics of understanding" began between Germany and France. By agreement, a committee of experts in international finance, led by the American banker Charles Dawes, put together a plan to end the Ruhr occupation and restore the German economy. The Dawes Plan, by stretching out reparations payments and arranging foreign loans for the reconstruction of German industry, set the stage for economic recovery. With it, Europe turned from the protest and rage of the post-war years to a period of peace and order.

The Rise and Fall of Post-War Protest

In a sense, the radical protest between 1919 and 1923 was a form of vengeance against the war itself: the fighting had not brought a better world. Some Europeans said that millions of young men had died for nothing. Writers spoke of a spirit of pessimism, a "disenchantment," spreading in Western culture. At the same time, two new radical movements were gaining strength. One, on the left, was modern communism, born in Moscow in 1919, when the Bolsheviks formed the Communist International (Comintern), an organization of communist parties that were taking shape in different countries. The other, on the right, was *fascism*, the name given to extreme nationalist movements after 1922, and best known in the context of Mussolini's Fascist Party in Italy.

In communism and fascism, the Continent had two antidemocratic forces rising at opposite extremes. Outwardly, the communists claimed to be struggling for the "real democracy" that would come with human equality in a communist future. In contrast, the first fascists presented themselves as enemies of democracy, equality, and the tradition from which they came. In this period of new "isms," fascism was the one that broke most radically with the nineteenth-century heritage of liberty. Fascists attacked the entire Enlightenment ideology of humanism and rational thought. Fascism, said Mussolini, was not about thinking; it was about acting. It had no ideology; it simply wanted to take power.

In truth, there was little to no fascist thought at the time of fascism's origins in Italy. The movement was largely a display of patriotic emotions: it celebrated the nation, war, and hardness; it held weakness and humane feeling in contempt. Fascism placed the state above the individual, passion above reason, man above woman, and the will of the leader above the rule of law. It was more style than substance, a show of marching men, flags, uniforms, and ceremonies. Fascists did not try to win over their enemies, they beat them up. In brief, early fascism had about it the violence and smell of World War I. Fascism emerged during Mussolini's political transition (1914–1919) from hard left to hard right.

Born in 1883, the son of a village blacksmith, Mussolini left a failing career as a schoolteacher to start a promising one in the Italian Socialist Party. The war turned his life around. Between 1914 and 1919, Mussolini changed from a socialist against the war to a nationalist in support of it, and from wounded soldier to angry war veteran. After the fighting, the country was full of discharged soldiers like himself. Some on the left wanted to bring Bolshevism to Italy. Some on the right wanted to take revenge against the Versailles Treaty for cheating Italians out of their victory in the war.

From his beginnings on the radical left, Mussolini now joined veterans on the radical right. Together, they combined socialist jargon and nationalist passions into a hot mix of war cries that passed for the ideology of a new movement: fascism. Some in the ranks wore the black uniforms of the *Arditi*, the Italian elite shock troops of World War I, and soon the black shirt became the symbolic dress of the Italian Fascist Party. During the "red years" of 1919–1920 (years of strikes and left-wing protest), the Black Shirts organized themselves in fighting squads to take on the socialists and labour unions. Region by region, they beat down the "Reds" with fists, clubs, knives, and revolvers. Fascism thus came into existence in the curious guise of a radical movement in defence of law and order.

Fascists received support from those who lived in fear of revolution in Italy. Money came from business and landholding interests; political protection came from important military and government figures. The left said that the fascists were doing the dirty work of capitalism. The fascists said that they were saving Italy from communism—and had earned the right to power as a result. By 1922, certain leaders in government were ready to agree. When Mussolini ordered his followers, about 200 000, to begin "the march on Rome," the country's political elite simply stepped aside. King Victor Emmanuel III made this fascist "revolution" legal by appointing Mussolini as the new prime minister. Thus, without resistance, the Black Shirts paraded in triumph upon the capital city. This was the major event of the period of post-war radicalism. The play revolution of fascism was the first successful response of the European right to the Bolshevik Revolution in Russia.

After three years in power, Mussolini closed down what was left of democracy in Italy. By this time the fascists—a small minority when taking power in 1922—had won an impressive election victory (65 percent of the vote) in 1924. This election, full of Black Shirt brutality and fraud, demonstrated nonetheless that Mussolini was swinging the country to his side. Suddenly, in 1925, opinion turned on the fascists after the murder of Giacomo Matteotti, a popular socialist who was "taken for a ride" by Black Shirt killers after speaking out against Mussolini. Defiantly, Mussolini now declared himself dictator and, with state power in hand, began to build his version of the fascist state. The Fascist Party was merged with the Italian state. Police powers were increased across the board. Public propaganda made a cult of Mussolini as *Il Duce*: the leader of the Italian people. On the street, uniforms, parades, and the raised-arm salute infused pageantry into everyday life. In public schools, instruction was aimed at developing "the new fascist man" of the future, and the young were organized into movements to carry fascism to the next generation.

Italian fascists had a simple saying: "Mussolini is always right." In fact, Mussolini ruled by consent. His government rested on the support of the traditional institutions and elites of the country. In this connection, his most popular move was to sign the Lateran Accords with the Catholic Church in 1929, bringing fascism to terms with the Papacy and the religion of the Italian people. Mussolini now recognized the independence of Vatican City; the Pope, in turn, called on the Italian people to support fascist rule. The effect was to end a quarrel that had divided church and state in Italy since 1870.

Mussolini had most success, therefore, when he held to the traditions of the Italian people. He had less when he tried to change them. His experiment with the "corporate state," for example, made few converts.

Corporatism was meant to give fascism an economic system of its own. The idea was to get representatives of business, labour, and government to sit together in councils to plan and coordinate production and workplace relations. In effect, the project made for little progress and a lot of propaganda. On the whole, fascism had support high and low in the population, but its ideology did not go deep into the nation: under Mussolini, Italian society stayed much the same as before. Italian fascism, in this sense, was no match for the dynamism, power, and passion that Hitler and the National Socialists—called the Nazis—would release from German society.

In the protest years of 1919–1923, however, the German movement was running far behind the Italian fascists. Hitler, in fact, had tried in the year after Mussolini's "March on Rome" to lead a revolutionary march of his own followers in Munich. He ended up in a jail cell. After this event, called the Beer Hall *Putsch* (revolt), he told the story of his young life in a book he entitled *Mein Kampf* (My Struggle). In looking back upon his youth, Hitler in reality was describing his preparations for the radicalism of the time. In fact, however, his book was written just as the years of this radicalism were coming to an end. The Ruhr occupation, sometimes described as "the last battle of the First World War," turned out to be the last battle of post-war extremism as well. As the public mood softened, the radical movements started to decline. Left in the cold, fascists and communists alike turned inward and began to organize themselves for survival and the battles to come.

The Success of the Democratic Order

The period of peace and order between 1924 and 1929 was the high point of Western democracy in the years between the two World Wars. Underlying it was a prosperity which, for a time, overcame the anger left by the Great War. From near disaster, the German economy took off after the weight of reparations was lightened. In France, Poincaré became "the saviour of the franc" and victor over inflation. In England, the final rumble of social unrest came in 1926, when millions of workers tried to shut down the country in a massive general strike. Called to support miners suffering through the decline of the coal industry, the strike

The signing of the Locarno Pact in October 1925 brought a new, although temporary, spirit of conciliation and hope to Europe.

instead rallied the public behind the Conservative government. When the strikers caved in, the Labour Party decided to give up on revolutionary protests altogether. After years of strikes and struggles, social peace settled over Western democracies.

With peace at home came the opportunity to make peace abroad. The result can be described as the first period of **appeasement** in the relations of France, Britain, and Germany. In a conciliatory gesture, France and Britain responded to Germany's need to rise from defeat; in turn, Germany responded to the need of France and Britain for guarantees of peace and security. Involved were three men who made "appeasement" a word of honour in foreign relations. One was Gustav Stresemann, who now had moved to the post of Foreign Minister at Berlin. In Paris, Aristide Briand, Foreign Minister in a new middle-of-the-road government, convinced French leaders that Germany could not be held down forever as a second-rate power. The way to keep the Germans at peace, he believed, was to make a peace that was worth keeping. In London, British Foreign Secretary Austen Chamberlain was working on his own project to reconcile France and Germany. Today, historians explain

that the three men had hidden designs to advance the interests of their own nations. At the time, however, these were the "good Europeans," the three statesmen honoured in the press for bringing a new era of peace to the Continent.

Their greatest achievement was the Locarno Pact of 1925. In this non-aggression agreement, Germany promised to accept its new boundaries in the west and to respect the demilitarization of the Rhineland. England, for its part, agreed to act against all violation of these arrangements. The Versailles settlement, it appeared, was secure in the west. Observers noted with unease that Germany made no commitment to accept its eastern borders with Poland and Czechoslovakia. Stresemann promised, however, that any changes there would be by peaceful means. Finally, it seemed that Europeans had put World War I behind them. In London, the *Times* reported on the Locarno Pact under a banner headline: "Peace at Last."

What was most important about the Locarno Pact was the spirit of friendship in which it was made. Later, "appeasement" and "collaboration" would become dirty words in the relations between England, France, and Germany. Between 1925 and 1929, they were part of "the spirit of Locarno." For their work, Chamberlain, Briand, and Stresemann received the Nobel Peace Prize, and the spirit of Locarno became the spirit of the time. France withdrew more occupation troops from German soil. In 1926, Germany was admitted to the League of Nations. Two years later, Briand and American Secretary of State Frank B. Kellogg drafted an international agreement, called the Kellogg-Briand Pact, outlawing wars of aggression. Some 60 nations agreed to its terms. Finally, in 1929, came the Young Plan, a schedule for a softer settlement of the reparations problem. Drawn up by American lawyer Owen D. Young and a panel of experts, the plan tried through "wise business sense" to take the heat out of the reparations debate by reducing the total amount and extending payments far into the future—all the way to 1988! The Great Depression came first.

The Great Depression and the Rise of the Welfare State

Five months after the Young Plan came "Black Tuesday," October 29, 1929, the day the New York stock market crashed and the "roaring '20s" came to a close in the United States. It was the beginning of the end for the economic recovery that had sustained "the spirit of Locarno." Pessimists already had warned that this recovery was on shaky ground: large amounts of American capital had been invested overseas, chasing after high interest rates in Europe. As a result, industry on the continent was propped up by American money. In fact, some of this money simply went around in a circle. The dollars invested in Germany were used to pay reparations to France and Britain, and these nations, in turn, used them to pay war debts to the United States. Thus, when Americans in the 1929 Wall Street crash withdrew their investments from the continent, the circle was broken and European nations started to slide toward crisis.

Economists described 1931 as "the terrible year," the year in which the depression came to the continent and changed the direction of events. It started with the collapse of Austria's largest bank, and spread outward in a ripple effect across Europe. The impact was uneven. France, with a large sector of small-scale enterprises sheltered behind tariff walls, took longer to get into the depression and longer to get out of it. The British were harder hit. A world empire of free trade, it was driven to raise tariffs against foreign goods and close doors to foreign immigrants. The British pound sterling, the proudest currency in Europe, backed to the penny by hard metal, was taken off the gold standard and reduced in value when the nation was forced to sell off its gold reserves. Worse was the case of Germany, where the depression went deeper and was more devastating than anywhere else in Europe. However, every country except the Soviet Union showed the same signs of the worst depression on record: falling production, falling prices, falling profits, and falling wages.

What went up was unemployment. This was the black plague of the depression years. The number of jobless hit a peak at the same time that the depression hit bottom in 1932. The count was 30 000 unemployed in France, three million in Britain, six million in Germany, and close to 14 million in the United States. Behind all the extraordinary events of the period were these facts and figures of the Great Depression. With them came all the miseries of the "dirty thirties": homelessness, bread lines, soup kitchens, and millions of destitute men and women living "on the dole."

What was wrong? Most Western leaders thought that the downturn was part of the normal bust-and-

Unemployed workers from Glasgow set out for London on a "famine march" in 1934.

boom cycle of a laissez-faire economy. This time, however, the old remedies of tariffs and spending cuts did not work. To ease the debt burden on Europe, American President Herbert Hoover in 1931 called for a temporary moratorium on reparations payments and war debts. What was "temporary" became permanent. When Germany stopped paying reparations to the other powers, they stopped paying war debts to the United States. In sum, the result of the moratorium was a massive default on reparations and war debts alike—leaving the Americans holding the bill. So ended the tug-of-war over the financial settlement of the Versailles peace—with resentment all around.

Capitalism was not working. This was the common opinion of the depression years. It made the 1930s a time of new experiments and new movements: some wanted to save the capitalist system; others wanted to end it. In the United States, the new president, Franklin Delano Roosevelt, elected in 1932 as a safe and sane free-enterprise candidate, instead set the country on a course of reform. He called it the *New Deal*. The idea was to get citizens working and buying again. The method was to use government to "prime the pump." Roosevelt plunged into deficit spending, pouring dollars into public works, government loans, farm subsidies, and a system of welfare payments for the aged, disabled, and unemployed. The result was economic recovery, along with bigger government, regulation, debt, and taxes. Some Americans never forgave Roosevelt; however, he was re-elected president three times. (He died during World War II, near the start of his fourth term in office.)

In Europe, neither France nor Britain would go so far. The new Popular Front government in Paris, a coalition of centre and left-wing parties elected in 1936 to resist fascism, passed laws to improve labour conditions and control the banking industry. In Britain, Parliament mostly fought the depression in the old-fashioned way: less spending and more tariffs. The rise of the Labour Party, however, which had passed the Liberals in 1922 to become the official opposition party, indicated that many British too were looking to government to take a larger role in social welfare. In general, the effect of the Great Depression was to bring back to government some of the control over the economy that it held during World War I.

In the making was the modern welfare state. In 1936, John Maynard Keynes provided it with "the new economics," the ideas for public management of a private-enterprise economy. In his prescription, government bureaucrats took the place of the "free forces" of the marketplace. The way out of the depression, Keynes argued in his book *The General Theory of Employment, Interest and Money*, was for government to put money into the economy to drive up spending and demand. More demand would bring more supply; more supply would mean more production, investment, and employment. In the new economics, the role of the state, said Keynes, was to keep a steady course between inflation and depression, to take money out of the economy when the economy heated up, and to put money in when it cooled down. Some economists said Keynes saved capitalism from death and disgrace in the depression. In their eyes, he had explained the way to make private enterprise work again. His theory would end the capitalism of bust and boom, a system always roaring out of control, piling up private wealth and spreading public misery. In contrast, critics said his theory was the road to ruin. Keynes's ideas would spread the "dead hand of government" over economic life. They would increase the size, cost, and power of government, and replace the good old values of saving and thrift with an easygoing philosophy of tax-and-spend.

In fact, as a result of the depression, governments had caught on to the new economics before Keynes wrote about it. His ideas came mainly to provide the supporting theory for the rising welfare state. In any case, the real increase in state spending that brought the West out of the depression in the 1930s was not the result of new economic ideas. It was the result of a new political danger: the rise of dictatorships. The new spending went to support an old habit: armaments.

The Great Depression and the New Dictatorships

The depression brought an end to the belief that the death of old empires and the birth of new nations would secure democracy, peace, and disarmament. This was an American illusion, impressed upon Europe by President Woodrow Wilson at the Paris Peace Conference in 1919. The challenge to it came first in Eastern Europe. One by one, the nations of that region, beset by weak economies, minority problems, and border disputes, turned from democracies into dictatorships. Most dictatorships were of the right-wing variety, in which the military took power with a claim to be saving the nation from communism and enemies within. The first "man on horseback" appeared in Hungary, where the navy leader Admiral Miklós Horthy took charge of the country as early as 1920. Next, after Mussolini ended democracy in Italy, came Marshal Joseph Pilsudski in Poland in 1926, the royal dictator King Alexander in Yugoslavia in 1928, and King Carol in Rumania in 1930. Others appeared in Bulgaria, Greece, and eventually in the three Baltic states: Estonia, Latvia, and Lithuania. The result was a clean sweep for dictatorship in Eastern Europe, with strongmen ruling the whole area from the Baltic Sea to the Mediterranean.

Dictatorship was brought to Central Europe by the depression. There, only Czechoslovakia, under its admired liberal leaders Thomas Masaryk and Edvard Beneš, stood against the tide. In Germany, Hitler ended Weimar democracy in 1933. Austria fell to its own fascist leader, Engelbert Dollfuss, the following year. As dictators strutted abroad, democrats at home quarrelled with each other. Democracy, once in style across the continent, had been pushed back into the West. There, weak and divided, it was in for the fight of its life. Within the democratic nations, communist and fascist parties found new life in the depression. Writers lamented that the best of democratic youth

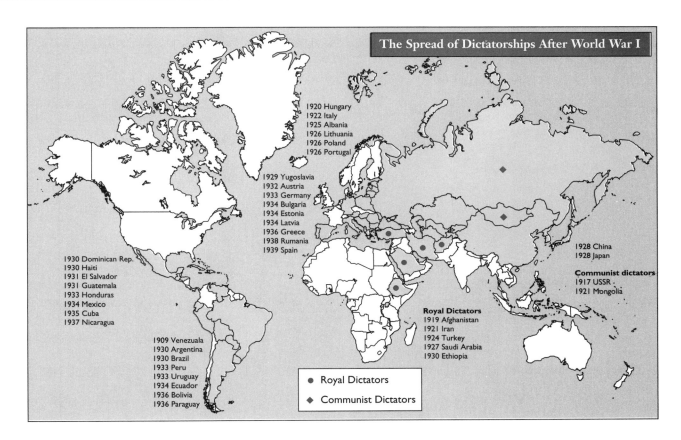

The Spread of Dictatorships After World War I

1920 Hungary
1922 Italy
1925 Albania
1926 Lithuania
1926 Poland
1926 Portugal

1929 Yugoslavia
1932 Austria
1933 Germany
1934 Bulgaria
1934 Estonia
1934 Latvia
1936 Greece
1938 Rumania
1939 Spain

1930 Dominican Rep.
1930 Haiti
1931 El Salvador
1931 Guatemala
1933 Honduras
1934 Mexico
1935 Cuba
1937 Nicaragua

1909 Venezuala
1930 Argentina
1930 Brazil
1933 Peru
1933 Uruguay
1934 Ecuador
1936 Bolivia
1936 Paraguay

1928 China
1928 Japan

Communist dictators
1917 USSR
1921 Mongolia

Royal Dictators
1919 Afghanistan
1921 Iran
1924 Turkey
1927 Saudi Arabia
1930 Ethiopia

● Royal Dictators
◆ Communist Dictators

was moving left and right. Years earlier, in 1921, the Irish poet William Butler Yeats warned in his poem "The Second Coming" (quoted below) of an approaching catastrophe. Now, as power increased at the political extremes and weakness spread at the centre, his prophecy, it seemed, was coming true.

> Things fall apart; the centre cannot hold;
> Mere anarchy is loosed upon the world,
> The blood-dimmed tide is loosed, and everywhere
> The ceremony of innocence is drowned;
> The best lack all conviction, while the worst
> Are full of passionate intensity.

In summary, the effect of the depression was to strengthen a trend in modern history: the increase of state power. The most extreme expression of this trend came with the rise of so called "totalitarian" regimes in the Soviet Union and Nazi Germany. These two nations, the weakest of the powers in the 1920s, appeared to become the strongest in the 1930s. The losers of World War I were becoming the winners.

More than the radical movements within the democratic nations, the regimes in Moscow and Berlin became the real challenge to what was left of the Versailles order in the West.

The Origins of Communist Rule in Russia

The nature of communist rule in Russia was determined by the history of a long revolutionary struggle against the old czarist state. The Russian empire in the nineteenth century was big and sprawling, with a vast mix of peoples, languages, cultures, and religions. To keep order in such an unruly land, the czars believed that all authority had to come from above. As a result, Russian revolutionaries faced a large and stubborn enemy. Their movement had been a story of failure, of small numbers of radicals fighting against overwhelming odds. The state was too strong to overturn, the population too ponderous to move, and the weight of

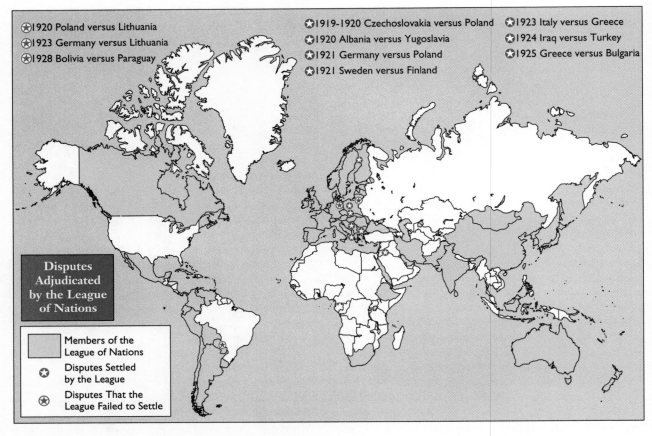

★ 1920 Poland versus Lithuania
★ 1923 Germany versus Lithuania
★ 1928 Bolivia versus Paraguay

☆ 1919-1920 Czechoslovakia versus Poland
☆ 1920 Albania versus Yugoslavia
☆ 1921 Germany versus Poland
☆ 1921 Sweden versus Finland

☆ 1923 Italy versus Greece
☆ 1924 Iraq versus Turkey
☆ 1925 Greece versus Bulgaria

Disputes Adjudicated by the League of Nations

☐ Members of the League of Nations

☆ Disputes Settled by the League

★ Disputes That the League Failed to Settle

the past too heavy on czar and people alike. These conditions left the revolutionaries with a central question: What is to be done? How was revolution to come to Russia?

Some radicals said that the way was to "go to the people," to change their way of thinking and bring them to revolt. The result was the Populist Movement of the 1870s, when thousands of Russian youth went to live and work with peasants to educate them for revolution. The peasants scorned them and reported them to the police. This failure of youth idealism caused other revolutionaries to turn away from all shining ideas about the peasants and the people. The revolution, they believed, had to be made by the revolutionaries themselves.

These were the men and women of the Russian terrorist movement. Their ideal was the fully committed individual, a revolutionary devoid of softness, ready to kill for the cause and ready to die for it. One of these young revolutionaries, Alexander Ilich Ulyanov, eldest

brother of Lenin, was hanged in 1887 for plotting to assassinate the czar. Lenin himself decided to make revolution in a different way. He started by embracing a set of ideas that was just beginning to make the rounds in Russia: Marxism.

As a Western philosophy based on the idea that communism would come first in the most advanced capitalist nations, Marxism would seem to have had little appeal for Russian intellectuals. Their country was still a peasant land, with a small capitalist class and only the beginnings of industrial development. Stated plainly, Russia was backward. Marx had said, however, that capitalist development was a way out of backwardness and toward communism. Thus, when George Plekhanov, the father of Russian Marxism, founded what was to become the Russian Social Democratic Party in 1883, this was the idea at the core of the movement, the idea that the rise and fall of capitalism was the route by which backward Russia could move toward communism. In sum, Russian Marxism was born with the idea that the destiny of Russia depended on becoming a modern state.

The same idea was driving the czarist government—but for very different reasons. After defeat in the Crimean War against France and England in 1856, the czars recognized that backwardness was putting their nation at risk. To continue as a great power, Russia had to catch up with the industrialized countries in the West. Thereafter, the czars rushed toward modern development at one moment and backed away from it at the next. Count Sergei Witte, Minister of Finance from 1892 to 1903, borrowed heavily from abroad to finance a program of industrial growth. However, when protests and strikes occurred, Czar Nicholas II dismissed Witte and called for more time. Two years later, the Russo-Japanese War, with its astonishing defeat of a European power by an Asian nation, proved that time does not wait. After this, Peter Stolypin, Minister of the Interior, started another push for development and reform. But time ran out for czarism: World War I broke out in 1914. If there is a theme to modern Russian history, it can be described as follows: when the czars could not bring about industrialization in the country, the communists did it in their place; when the czars could not industrialize by autocracy, the communists did it by totalitarianism.

This story, from the communist side, begins with **Lenin**. Born in 1870 into the family of a minor civil servant in rural Simbirsk on the Volga River, Lenin trained for the law before devoting his life to revolutionary politics. After this activity landed him in a Siberian prison colony between 1895 and 1900, he fled to exile in Western Europe. There he lived the life of that subclass of intellectuals and professional people that Russians call the intelligentsia. His best years were spent in cranky debates with other Marxists before World War I, and he was already 47 at the time of Red October in 1917. His whole life had been a preparation for that moment. "There is not another man who for 24 hours of the day is taken up with the revolution," a companion wrote of Lenin in exile, "who has no thoughts but thoughts of revolution, and who even in his sleep, dreams of nothing but revolution."

What made this "compulsive revolutionary" different from most other Russian Marxists was his idea that the revolution would be led not by the working class but by Marxist intellectuals. In a masterpiece tract in 1902 called *What Is to Be Done*, Lenin said that the workers, left to themselves, could think only of better pay and small improvements in the conditions of labour under capitalism. It was the intellectuals, he claimed, who could see beyond the capitalist system and lead the workers to overthrow it. At issue was a struggle for the soul of Russian Marxism. Plekhanov had created the movement to advance the democratic development of the labouring people of the nation. Lenin said simply that democratic methods would not work in the Russian police state. Against czarism, success could come only from an organization of the best revolutionaries, a party of a single truth, small, secret, directed from above, and closed to opposition groups within. "Give us an organization of revolutionaries," he wrote "and we will turn Russia upside down."

He was describing a "party of a new type," a body of "professional revolutionaries" bound together by iron discipline and total commitment to the "truth" of Marxism and the cause of revolution. In effect, he was describing a party in his own image, one reflecting the two sides of his own intellectual development: Lenin was a Westerner, bringing Marxist ideas into Russian context; he was also intensely Russian, a Slavophile bringing to Marxism the spirit of the revolutionaries of his brother's generation, true believers determined to overcome the greater power of the enemy by the strength of their own willpower.

Meeting in exile in 1903, the Russian Social Democrats split over the issue of party organization. Lenin came away with a majority in one of the votes and took the name *Bolsheviki* (majority) for his followers. After this, the movement of this "organization man" of Russian Marxism began its own history.

Lenin's ideas were made for the needs of revolution in Russia. There, public affection for the czar was destroyed on Bloody Sunday in 1905, when troops slaughtered an unarmed crowd of 200 carrying a peaceful petition to the imperial palace. The 1905 Revolution, crushed by loyal regiments, revealed the weakness of the Russian government, behind its police and prisons; but it revealed as well the weakness of the forces that had attempted to overthrow it. Lenin now decided that the Bolsheviks would have to do the work themselves.

As described in the last chapter, what made possible the Bolshevik victory in 1917 was World War I. Lenin ordered an assault upon a government that had lost the support of an army and a people exhausted by war. The significance of this event was not long in coming. The previous government had simply put off the great questions of the day. The leaders of the March Revolution wanted these questions to be answered by a future Constituent Assembly. This was to be Russia's first experiment in democracy, a body chosen in a free election by a free people. In fact, the election took place on November 25, 1917, three weeks after the Bolshevik coup. The vote confirmed that Lenin's party, with 25 percent of the ballots, remained a minority in the country. Lenin insisted, however, that Bolshevik rule, called "the rule of the working class," was "a higher form of democracy" than that of an elected majority. No sooner had the Constituent Assembly met on January 18, 1918, than he ordered armed guards to close its doors for good. This assembly, elected to begin a Russian democratic republic, sat for only a single day. As before, Russia's great questions would be answered from above.

Lenin knew that the task of holding power would be enormous. Bolshevism would need the advantages of unlimited force, terror, and dictatorship. To support this, he fell back upon an idea found in Marx's writing: the dictatorship of the proletariat. Involved was the concept of a temporary dictatorship coming after the Revolution, when the communists would use the power of the state to crush the remaining opposition. Writing in 1917, Lenin made the mission of this dictatorship vast and enduring. Now he gave his party the role of "leading the whole people to socialism, of directing and organizing the new system, of being the teacher, the guide, the leader of all the working and exploited people in organizing their social life...." The party leads, the people follow. In building the Bolshevik party, Lenin had created a power machine greater than anything in the hands of the czars. In this

How Bolshevism Got Its Name

The debate at the Second Congress of the Russian Social Democratic Party in 1903 caused a rupture in the organization that never healed. For about a year, Russian Marxists had argued over the ideas in Lenin's *What Is to Be Done?* on party organization and the role of intellectuals as bearers of revolutionary consciousness. In these ideas, critics saw evidence of Lenin's intellectual elitism and authoritarian attitudes. His views, they said, were at once an attack on Marx's own conception of the workers as a revolutionary class and a design for the rule of intellectuals over the socialist movement. Meeting in Brussels in July 1903, the 56 delegates at the Second Congress soon divided in sharp

disagreement on the question of party organization and membership. Lenin and his supporters lost the vote on the issue when a narrow majority (28–23) passed a motion

❧

Lenin , the organization man of Russian Marxism, addresses troops at a celebration.

calling for a more open party structure. Later, after a number of delegates left the meeting, he won a vote on a separate matter. On the strength of his majority, Lenin—without much justification—took the name *Bolsheviki* (majority) for his followers. Unwisely, his opponents accepted his sneering and inaccurate description of them as *Mensheviki* (minority). After the congress, one of them made a remarkably accurate prediction of the end result of Lenin's ideas on party organization. Said Leon Trotsky (later a Bolshevik himself), "As we shall see, these methods lead to this: the party organization is substituted for the party, the Central Committee is substituted for the party organization, and finally the dictator is substituted for the Central Committee."

idea of its "leading role" in society, he gave the party the myth which was to support its long rule over the nation. After this, Lenin's ideas could no longer be described by the term Marxism alone. They were different enough to need a new name of their own: Marxism-Leninism.

What Lenin had invented was the kind of leader-centred, mission-driven, vanguard party that became a feature of many one-party dictatorships in the twentieth century. This type of organization, he said in the beginning, was needed to make revolution in Russia in the first place. Now he said it was needed to lead the people to socialism. Thus the historic mission of the party had become in part the same task that czarist reformers set for themselves in the past: the economic development of the country.

The Rise of Stalin

Communist rule in Russia was marked by the hard conditions of its birth. War, civil war, and famine resulted in the loss of perhaps 15 million people between 1914 and 1921. At the same time, the fall of the Romanov dynasty, after three centuries of rule, raised hope in the people for freedom and democracy. In these circumstances, resistance to the rising communist dictatorship was wide and deep in the nation. In 1918, an assassination attempt against Lenin himself, for example, left the communist leader severely wounded. In the end, the Bolsheviks overwhelmed the opposition by greater violence and terror. The result, however, was a separation between state and people that remained a lasting feature of Soviet history.

Czarist Russia, the most conservative state in Europe, had become Bolshevik Russia, the most revolutionary. As a result, the consolidation of this first Marxist state on earth caused a separation as well between Bolshevism and the outside world. It began, in particular, in the Civil War between 1918 and 1921, when one army of Russians lined up against another, Reds against Whites. In the conflict, the communists found themselves fighting alone against all their enemies together, from old czarists to left-wing radicals. Their sense of being threatened and isolated increased when foreign troops from France, Britain, the United States, and Japan entered the country in 1918. As described in the previous chapter, the Western Allies sent these soldiers in an attempt to bring Russia back into the war against Germany and to keep arms stockpiles out of hands of the communists. The Bolsheviks

believed instead that they had been sent to kill communism in its cradle. In fact, these troops did aid the White forces, though not enough to make much difference. Bolsheviks and Western leaders, however, both saw treachery in the eyes of the other. The effect of this Allied intervention in the Civil War, therefore, was to raise a wall of separation between communism and the West, setting them apart in suspicion and distrust that lasted for most of the twentieth century.

The Civil War gave Lenin's regime a bloody beginning in history. Led brilliantly by **Leon Trotsky**, named Commissar of War, the Red Army fought a savage war against a savage enemy. Numbering as many as a million men, the Reds conquered piece by piece most of the country that the Bolsheviks were to govern. Their victory, however, meant defeat for the Ukrainians, Georgians, and other non-Russian peoples who once had hopes for homelands of their own. In the sheer brutality of the fighting, repression became Bolshevik style. Behind the lines, the Cheka, the new Bolshevik political police, spread the Red Terror, shooting opponents and suspects in droves. Included was the whole family and all household attendants of the fallen Czar Nicholas. Cheka gunmen said that they shot the "class enemies" of the revolution. In fact, they shot enemies of every class and kind, and many who were not enemies at all.

Bolshevik repression soon spread to their allies as well. As the communists tightened their hold on power, the reality of one-party rule became more open to the eyes of those who had fought to free the country of czarism. Revolutionaries who struggled beside Lenin in 1917 now struggled against him. Men and women once locked up in czarist jails were now locked up in communist ones. As these jails filled, prisoners were transported to forced labour camps in remote areas. Such, in effect, was the beginning of what the Russian novelist Aleksandr Solzhenitsyn has called the Gulag Archipelago, the chain of concentration camps for political dissenters that soon spread across the country. In 1921, an event shook the morale of the party: the Kronstadt revolt, the rising of the Petrograd naval base against the communist dictatorship. The Kronstadt sailors had been heroes of the Bolshevik revolution in 1917. Now Leon Trotsky used the Red Army to crush their resistance. After this, Lenin was ready for a "breathing spell."

The country was a wreck: the ruin caused by the civil war came on top of the ruin caused by the

Bolshevik economic plan known as "War Communism." In this headlong leap into communism, the party in 1918 had taken command of the whole economy. The result was a catastrophe of falling production and human suffering. Armed squads of communists from the cities seized "surplus" crops from starving peasants. Between 1920 and 1922, a famine in the countryside took an estimated 5 million lives. Resistance was everywhere, and in 1920 alone, nearly half of the Red Army was needed to hold down peasant protest in the villages. The Bolsheviks, Lenin admitted, were "barely holding on." At this stage, the Russian peasantry, over 120 million people, were too much for the party to handle.

In 1921, Lenin announced the New Economic Policy (NEP), a return to more free market methods. The government kept control of what it called the "commanding heights" of the economy: large industry, banking, and foreign trade, but other activity was opened to private buying and selling. The result was an economic recovery at a time when the party needed it most. Within seven years, production was returning to pre-1914 levels. More importantly, the peasants were at peace with the regime. In their hands at last was the soil of Russia. This "breathing spell," however, would not last forever. With the work of building communism still unfinished, too many party members were not at peace with the NEP.

First they needed a new leader. From the moment that Lenin suffered a paralytic stroke in 1922, a fight for leadership began among the top personalities in the party. Everyone looked to the intellectuals, men like Lenin himself, educated, skilled in Marxist theory, and familiar with European culture. Best and brightest was Leon Trotsky, brilliant in revolution, victorious in command of the Red Army, and the favourite of

From Czarist Autocracy to Soviet Dictatorship

On Lenin's order, on July 17, 1918 a Cheka execution squad murdered Czar Nicholas II, his family, and the household staff in the distant city of Ekaterinburg (now Swerdlovsk) in the Ural region. This act by the new revolutionary government was meant to break continuity with the authoritarian traditions of the czarist past. In fact, these traditions prepared the Russian mind for the Soviet dictatorship to come.

The bodies of the imperial family were buried in an unmarked location and all details of the event became state secrets. In 1920 a young woman recovering from amnesia in a Berlin hospital identified herself as Anastasia, youngest of the czar's daughters. The woman's resemblance to Anastasia and her intimate knowledge of Romanov family life (though she did not speak Russian) led a small following to

believe her story. The legend of Anastasia's survival continued from that time.

The burial place of the Romanovs was discovered in 1991. Russian experts reported in 1994 that Anastasia's remains were present, but that those of her brother Alexey and sister Maria were not found. Today, this location has become a place of pilgrimage for admirers of Russian czarism.

The Russian imperial family.

left-wing circles in the West. Other Bolshevik leaders, however, remembered him as an old Menshevik who came late to Leninism. Moreover, the arrogance of this clever Jewish loner set them on edge. Nor was Trotsky a man of patience for bureaucratic battles. Instead, this was the strength of his rival, Joseph Djugashwili, known as Stalin, the man of steel.

This long-time Bolshevik had come up the hard way. Born in Georgia in 1879 to a poor family, Stalin was studying to be a priest before turning to revolutionary activity. Before 1917, while other Bolshevik personalities lived in exile abroad, he worked in the party underground in Russia, and was arrested seven times as a result. After the Revolution, he advanced on his talent for paperwork and in 1922 became the General Secretary of the party, the man at the top of the organization's growing administrative structure. Here, in his control over the machinery of the Party (called the "apparatus"), was the secret to his coming success.

What made Stalin was the change in the party from a small, radical movement to a large ruling officialdom. In the process, the organization became bureaucratized. The prime need was no longer for revolutionary intellectuals but for day-to-day organizers. At this work, the plain and plodding Stalin had true genius. Before his death in 1924, Lenin warned in his "last testament" that Stalin was taking too much power into his hands and should be removed from the post of General Secretary. However, the bright lights in the leadership race had more fear of each other than of this ordinary man who kept the books. As they fed on each other, Stalin quietly took the party in hand. Some historians have said, in fact, that Stalin came to rule the Soviet Union before most people even knew his name.

At a time when Mussolini in Italy set the style for fascist dictators with shiny uniforms, dramatic poses, and speeches full of bluster, Stalin gave communist leadership an entirely different image. He was an "office dictator," simple in dress and lifestyle, a ruler poor at public speaking and without charisma of any kind. As indicated, his power was in the *apparatchiki*, the men (there were few women) of the apparatus, the full-time bureaucrats who did the everyday work of the party, who knew the organization inside out, and who made it run. For this work, Stalin chose personalities like himself, individuals without formal learning, without experience in the world outside Russia, and without interest in anything beyond politics. Together, they

Leon Trotsky (second from left) provided crucial military leadership to the early Bolsheviks, but was later driven from the USSR by Joseph Stalin and assassinated.

made the party the greatest power machine in the history of Russian government. Its grassroots organizations, called "cells," were located in every institution and area of life, in all the neighbourhoods, villages, factories, military units, police detachments, and youth groups. The dictator sat in the Kremlin, the centre of government in the communist capital of Moscow, but his eyes and ears were everywhere.

Essential to Stalin's success in the leadership struggle was the lesson that Lenin had taught every Bolshevik: the duty of absolute loyalty to the party. Now, in a way of speaking, the party had become Stalin. To lay claim to the Bolshevik legacy, he made a cult of the dead Lenin. The body of the first Bolshevik leader was embalmed and displayed like a sacred relic in a tomb in Kremlin Square. As well, party propagandists made clear the connection between the old leader and the new. "Stalin is the Lenin of today," they said. Thus an atheist state, which repressed religious activities and persecuted priests, began to create gods of its own.

The struggle for leadership in the party between 1924 and 1928 was hidden behind a debate on the New Economic Policy. Trotsky pressed the hard Marxist line that communism could not be made from scratch in a peasant society. What was needed, he insisted, was

Joseph Stalin (second from right), who Lenin felt was untrustworthy, would dominate life and politics in the Soviet Union for three decades.

industry at home and revolution abroad, an immediate crash program to industrialize the Soviet Union and an immediate push in the Comintern to carry revolution to the capitalist countries in the West. Arguing against this was Nikolay Bukharin, the champion of NEP. Peace with the peasants, he said, was the safest way to advance the country. Trying to start revolutions abroad—certain to bring retaliation from the great powers—was the sure way to ruin it. During this debate, Stalin acted as he had acted during most other loud quarrels between his rivals: he remained silent and smoked his pipe.

When he spoke, it was of "socialism in one country," of keeping a moderate course and making the most of Russian conditions. Stalin's mastery was in playing off rivals against each other. First he sided with two of Lenin's old companions, Grigori Zinoviev and Lev Kamenev, to defeat Trotsky and expel him from the party. Then he sided with Bukharin to defeat Zinoviev and Kamenev. Finally, when power was his, he ended the debate on NEP by ending NEP itself. The Soviet Union, Stalin announced in 1928, was starting upon a *Five Year Plan* to modernize the whole nation. "We shall see then," he said, "which countries can be labelled as backward and which are advanced." As it turned out, therefore, Stalin's idea of "socialism in

one country" was Trotsky's idea of crash industrialization—but without Trotsky.

More than the Revolution of 1917, this first Five Year Plan in 1928–1932 was the true dividing line between the old Russia and the new. After defeating his rivals, Stalin put at risk all that he had gained by plunging into a vast economic transformation of Russian society. With speed and brutality, he forced the country through an agricultural, industrial, and social revolution all in one. However, by concentrating on building "socialism in one country," Stalin at the same time brought into Soviet communism a spirit of nationalism that changed the nature of the movement. Thus he described to party members in a speech in 1931 how, throughout Russian history, backwardness had brought military defeat, and how, without success in the Five Year Plan, their new "socialist fatherland" would be defeated again. "We are 50 or 100 years behind the advanced countries," he said. "We must make good this lag in ten years. Either we accomplish this or we will be crushed."

The Five Year Plan and the Terror Famine, 1929–1932

With the start of the Five Year Plan on December 27, 1929, a sweeping process of "collectivization" brought all industry, commerce, and agriculture under state control. The result was a "command economy" in which production was regulated by a central plan and the labour force driven by production quotas. The quotas, set high and beyond the capacity of most workers and managers, set the economy racing at breakneck speed. Electrical power plants, for example, were ordered to increase output by 400 percent, heavy industry by 300 percent, and agriculture by 200 percent. Consumer goods had low priority, and the goods themselves were often shoddy and unfinished. Resources were directed instead to megaprojects: hydroelectric plants, tractor factories, and new industrial cities built up out of the wilderness.

Party leaders later criticized the first Five Year Plan for "gigantomania," for too many boundless goals and massive projects. In truth, the goals could not be met. Yet at a time when capitalism in the West was paralyzed in the Great Depression and millions of workers were idle, communism in the Soviet Union made remarkable advances in industry—and there was no unemployment. Iron production increased almost 100 percent, coal 80 percent, and steel nearly 50 percent.

Said a British visitor at the time, "I have seen the future, and it works." This was the Soviet Union's Industrial Revolution, its "iron age" of material progress. On the surface it was a dynamic social experiment; underneath it was a human tragedy.

Stalin mobilized his people for industrialization in the way a nation mobilized for war. State propaganda urged the population to work hard and sacrifice to the "production front." In factories, medals were given to "the heroes of Soviet labour," the workers who exceeded their production quotas. Those who were late, lazy, or absent met with punishments and police measures. Long hours, low wages, poor housing — this was the lot of Soviet labour as the state made the exploitation of its people the method of financing the Five Year Plan. No Western banks in this day would make loans to a communist government, especially one which had refused to repay the czar's state debts to foreign creditors. Thus, to get money for industry, Stalin had to skin his own people.

In particular, Stalin fell upon those in the countryside, where close to 80 percent of the population lived and worked the land. Here the state took everything: land, livestock, and farm equipment. According to plan, the nation's 25 million peasant farms were collectivized into large common farms where the peasants worked as field hands under a party manager. Their task was to meet production quotas dictated from above. At harvest, the state carried off the quota, sold it at steep prices in the cities, and poured the money into more industrial growth. Those on the collective farms lived or died on what was left in the field.

Against this, the peasants reacted with fury: they burned crops and slaughtered their own livestock. Thus, between 1929 and 1932, the Soviet Union lost 50 percent of its horses and cattle and 60 percent of its sheep and goats. The party responded with still greater fury: the Five Year Plan in the countryside was declared to be a form of class war against the *kulaks*. Said Stalin: "We have switched to a policy of liquidating the *kulaks* as a class." The *kulaks* generally were described as rich peasants, a class living off the rural poor and profiteering on the harvest. In fact, the word *kulak* had a loose and slippery meaning, and came to be used by the communists to describe virtually any peasant who opposed them. Army and police units raided villages, forced peasants off their lands, and shot them in droves. In the process, some 2 to 3 million people were packed off to forced labour in the gulags of Siberia. Famine was the greater killer. Left without food when the party confiscated entire harvests, an estimated 7 million rural people starved to death between 1931 and 1933. The death toll was especially high in Ukraine, where Stalin wanted to crush peasant resistance and Ukrainian nationalism at the same time. Some historians have called this the *terror famine*. According to them, Stalin's policy against peasant opposition was simply to starve people to death. The result, in any case, was one of the greatest mass deaths in modern history.

The Great Terror, 1935–1938

The first Five Year Plan was celebrated as a success when Stalin called it to an early end in 1932. In fact, the Kremlin was left with production problems in agriculture that would last as long as the Soviet Union itself. In industry, however, the changes brought by the modernization drive shifted great power relationships in Europe. Now the Soviet Union entered the industrial age and, by 1939, had surpassed England in overall production. However, the years of crisis had put the Soviet system under severe strain. It appears, in fact, that reports of suffering in the countryside brought tension into Stalin's own household, leading his second wife to commit suicide in 1932. As opposition and discontent threatened to spread disorder, Stalin took measures to put Soviet society into a strait-jacket of controls. His method was to bring the state into more and more areas of public and private life. The Five Year Plan transformed the Soviet Union into a totalitarian society.

The process of repression soon was carried into the party itself. A key event was the assassination on December 1, 1934 of Sergei Kirov, a rising star in the communist leadership. Caught red-handed, the assassin confessed on the spot to acting for opposition elements in the party. The following year, the secret police, now called the NKVD (the name of the secret police often changed; the existence of the organization was permanent), reported the discovery of a "terrorist centre" in the party, bent on murdering Soviet leaders and "wrecking" the new Five Year Plan. In reality, the truth of this whole episode remains uncertain to the present day. Stalin said the murder of Kirov was proof of a secret conspiracy within the party that had to be destroyed root and branch. Most historians have said since that time that Stalin himself was behind the killing. His plan, they claim, was to use the report of a "terrorist centre" behind the assassination as a cover story to justify a massive purge of so-called "opposition" elements in the party.

What followed was a wave of arrests, murders, and executions that swept over party members and the Soviet elite. Arrest followed arrest, and confessions came one after the other, each one naming more suspects, more crimes, more conspiracies at every level of the party. New laws ordered the death penalty for citizens who failed to inform on the guilt of others. Punishment was decreed for children over 12 who failed to report the crimes of their parents. This was the *Great Terror* of 1935–1938. Before it was over, an estimated 1 million victims were dead and another 4 to 6 million were in forced-labour camps, most of them never to return.

The most sensational drama of the Great Terror was the show trials of party leaders. Most were tough old Bolsheviks who had lived for the Revolution and once stood at Lenin's side. Now they confessed in open courtrooms to the blackest crimes against the Soviet Union: terrorism, sabotage, and spying for capitalist countries. Worse, they confessed links to the "traitor" Trotsky. This once great revolutionary—now in exile—had become Stalin's own devil figure. In the show trials, horror stories on the evils of Trotskyism made up the most bizarre part of courtroom testimony. Thus, Bukharin confessed at his trial in 1938 to membership in something called the Bloc of Anti-Soviet Rightwingers and Trotskyites, described as a wicked conspiracy of fascist agents in the pay of Germany and Japan. Western writers pondered why such innocent men confessed to such vile crimes. Much later, after Stalin's death in 1953, one of his successors gave an explanation from the inside. Soviet leader Nikita Khrushchev told party members in 1956 that Stalin had a simple method to get confessions out of his enemies: "beat, beat, and once again beat."

From Khrushchev came details on the path of destruction throughout party ranks. Out of the nearly 2000 members who attended the XVIIth Party Congress in 1934, he reported, 1108 ended up in the hands of the secret police. Out of the 139 individuals elected at that time to sit on the Central Committee of the party, 98 were arrested and shot. Behind it all, Khrushchev claimed, was the twisted personality of one man: Stalin. Said Khrushchev:

Stalin was a very distrustful man, sickly suspicious; we knew this from our work with him. He could look at a man and say: "Why are your eyes so shifty today?" or "Why are you turning so much today and avoiding to look me directly in the eyes?" The sickly suspicion created in him a general distrust even toward eminent Party workers whom he had known for years. Everywhere and in everything he saw "enemies," "two-facers" and "spies."

Some Western observers concluded, however, that such massive terror could not be caused by one personality alone. Stalin needed the secret police, the party organization, the powers concentrated in the Kremlin, and the support of an ideology that appeared to justify the use of such extreme force. Thus the cause of the Great Terror, they believed, was not the dictator alone but a broader system of power and ideas. They called it totalitarianism. By 1938, in any case, fear, conformity, and silence had become the way of life in the Soviet Union. In the gulags, there were as many as 8 million prisoners, many from important elements of the population. The regime, for example, had turned on its own military leaders, arresting or killing about half of its high officer corps, including 90 percent of its generals. Now, however, with the rise of fascism in Europe, the Soviet Union had to bring an end to the Great Terror and this reckless waste of its own people.

Already the Nazi rise to power in Germany in 1933 had spread panic among communist leaders. Communism had met a force more radical than itself. As fascist movements increased in strength in Western countries as well, communist parties in the democracies were suddenly on the defensive. What followed in 1935 was a dramatic shift in Comintern strategy. Now communist parties everywhere called on all democratic parties to join them in a Popular Front against fascism. Formerly enemies of "bourgeois democracy," the communists now became its most determined fighters. New recruits, men and women who hated fascism the most, came to communism in mass numbers. Intellectuals joined in a literature of "engagement," committing themselves and their works to the cause of the radical left. In 1936, the new Popular Front strategy had its greatest success when an antifascist front of left and centre parties won a sweeping electoral victory in France. None of this, however, turned back the march of fascism. More and more, the march of fascism came to mean the march of Hitler and National Socialism in Germany.

The Rise of National Socialism

In the Weimar Republic, the peace and prosperity of the boom years 1924–1929 ended in the Great Depression. As anger returned, politics turned radical, and *National Socialism* began its rise to power. Some history books have described Nazism wrongly as a movement that responded to the deepest longings of the German people, that told them what they wanted to hear, and that swept the nation from start to finish. In truth, the Nazi party in the early years lived on the margins of Weimar society. Its numbers were small and its ideas too racist and vile for decent opinion. In the 1928 elections, the party took less than 3 percent of the total vote. Then, with the depression, came an astonishing explosion in Nazi popularity.

As the economic crisis deepened, the Nazi vote went up and up. It soared to 18 percent in the election of September 1930 and 37 percent in the depths of the depression in July 1932. When the first signs of economic recovery came in the fall of that year, the Nazi vote in the November elections slipped to 33 percent. Already, however, the Nazis were the largest party in the Reichstag. Still short of a ruling majority, they were long enough on votes to cause the ruling circles in the nation to give them a chance to govern. One chance was all that Hitler needed. On January 30, 1933, he became Chancellor of Germany. In summary, the Nazis came to power without a clear majority of the people behind them. More importantly, however, Hitler, the enemy of democracy, took on the democratic parties of Germany at their own game, and beat them at the polls. If the socialists and communists had formed a coalition, they would have defeated Hitler, but they refused to join forces.

Hitler called his victory "the triumph of the will," the victory of a party of iron determination over an opposition weak in backbone and spirit. After the failure of the Beer Hall Putsch in 1923, he had decided that revolution was hopeless against the armed strength of a modern state. Power must be won by legal means, and the way to win it was to win the people. Thereafter, Hitler built his party into a propaganda machine. Historians have agreed that Hitler's most clever ideas, and the best pages of *Mein Kampf*, were on the art of mass propaganda. These ideas revealed his contempt for the intelligence of the common people, and his opinion that the best propaganda was that directed at the least intelligent among them. The message, he said, must be simple, emotional, and totally one-sided; especially, it must be repeated and repeated. Hitler believed, above all, in the influence of the spoken word. "The power which has always started the greatest religious and political avalanches in history...," he wrote in *Mein Kampf*, "has been the magic power of the spoken word, and that alone." His hypnotic powers, his "finger-tip feeling" for the mood of the crowd, and his raging and brutal language have become notorious. Of all the European dictators of the period, he was the master spellbinder. Hitler, one historian has said simply, was "the greatest demagogue in history."

Hitler said that the "granite foundation" of all his thinking was formed during his years as a young man in Vienna before World War I. Born on April 20, 1889, in an Austrian village near the German border, he was the son of a minor Austrian customs officer, a man of peasant stock who had made his way into the lower middle class. Later, there would be rumours of a Jewish grandfather in Hitler's family tree, but no hard evidence was ever found. Dreaming of becoming an artist, Hitler was crushed by his failure to gain admission to the Vienna Academy of Fine Arts in 1907. An angry youth, he stayed on in Vienna and became steeped in the national hatreds that divided the peoples of the Hapsburg Empire. In particular, he watched the losing struggle of his own German minority there against the rising influence of the Slavic populations. Here, in this conflict of peoples, Hitler picked up the ideas that became the passion of his life.

His ideas were not new. Mostly they were a jumble of Central European hatreds: hatred of Marxists, Slavs, and Jews. Other thinkers in the nineteenth century had already dressed these hatreds in the language of Darwinism and the "science" of race. They had described history as a "struggle for existence" of race against race, of blond Aryans against dark Semites, and of the German master race against Slavic subhumans, Jewish parasites, and faceless socialist hordes. What Hitler brought to these ideas was a depth of hatred that would drive him to greater extremes than any other racist in history. He brought to them, as well, a way with words and propaganda that somehow released the same hatreds in the mind of the crowd. Someone said that what Hitler did was to bring out the Hitler in other people.

In 1913, Hitler left Vienna for the German city of Munich. The next year, as a common soldier in the German army, Hitler proved his courage on the western front, where he was one of the few enlisted men to be awarded the Iron Cross, first class, for bravery under fire. He described his ordeal in World War I as the supreme experience of his life. Word of the German defeat came as he was being treated for temporary blindness as the result of an Allied gas attack. The news was a shock. Full of anger, he set himself upon a path of revenge against those politicians at home who he believed had betrayed the Germany army. To him, this "stab in the back" was the work of the same enemies of his people that he had discovered in Vienna: the Marxists and Jews, especially the Jews. To fight them, he said, had become a sacred duty. "By defending myself against the Jew," he wrote in *Mein Kampf*, "I am fighting for the work of the Lord."

In 1919, in a Munich beer hall, he attended a meeting of the German Workers' Party, a small group—scarcely 50 people—who talked of combining nationalism and socialism into a movement to defend the German workingman against Jews, Marxists, and foreigners. Within a year, Hitler made the organization his own. He changed its name to the National Socialist German Workers' Party (in German, NSDAP) and developed it into a leader-centred movement with himself as its *Führer* (leader). From him came Nazism's black symbols and menacing features. He introduced the wearing of uniforms, the swastika emblem, the "*Sieg Heil*" salute, and the display of flags, standards, and marching men. In 1921, he added a paramilitary squad, the *Sturmabteilung* (SA), or storm troopers, also known as Brown Shirts. These tough veterans in brown shirts and jackboots stood guard at party meetings and fought brawls with Hitler's enemies. Soon they became the terror of Weimar streets, beating up bystanders, trashing Jewish shops, and marching into socialist neighbourhoods. To Hitler, this violence was a form of propaganda in itself, an expression of the brute strength of his movement.

At this early stage, however, the Nazis were not much different from the many other small, right-wing parties of post-war radicalism. A change came after the Beer Hall Putsch in 1923. In a show of force, Hitler had led about 2000 followers on a protest march through the streets of Munich. When police fired upon the march, the Nazis broke and ran. With this failure, Hitler gave up on thoughts of seizing power by revolutionary means. At his trial for treason after the Putsch, he turned failure into success. His defiant speeches in the courtroom made front-page news and gained him national attention for the first time. Now he decided that the road to Nazi dictatorship led through Weimar democracy. After his release from prison in 1924 (Hitler served but one year of a five-year sentence), he started the Nazis on a new strategy to win power by winning the people away from the Weimar Republic.

The Republic, child of the 1918 defeat, was not loved by most of its citizens. Its freedom and openness brought a brilliant flowering in the arts and culture, but its democratic life and easy morals were too far removed from the world that most Germans had grown up in before the war, the world of Kaiser, family, and church. Weimar, it was said, was "a democracy without democrats and a republic without republicans." However, German society in 1924 was easing into the good years of jobs and profits that took the anger out of the public mood. Hitler, therefore, had to wait. His new strategy had little success until the coming of the Great Depression in 1929, when a mass of new members and new votes suddenly made the Nazis the largest political force in Germany.

In part, these new supporters came to Nazism in response to the electioneering genius of Joseph Goebbels. Named by Hitler in 1929 to be the new Nazi propaganda chief, Goebbels took over just in time to exploit the resentments caused by the depression. Far from the Nazi ideal of the tall, blond, Nordic man, Goebbels was small, dark, and wiry, with a clubfoot that seemed to leave him bitter at life. Most brilliant of the Nazi leaders, he had a wicked talent for exciting human emotions, and believed with Hitler that the role of propaganda was not to stimulate thought but to stop it. Goebbels had a trick for making Nazi ideas sound nationalist,

The storefront sign declaring "Germans! Defend Yourselves! Don't Buy in Jewish Shops!" was typical of the demonstrations throughout Germany on the anti-Semitic boycott day held on April 1, 1933.

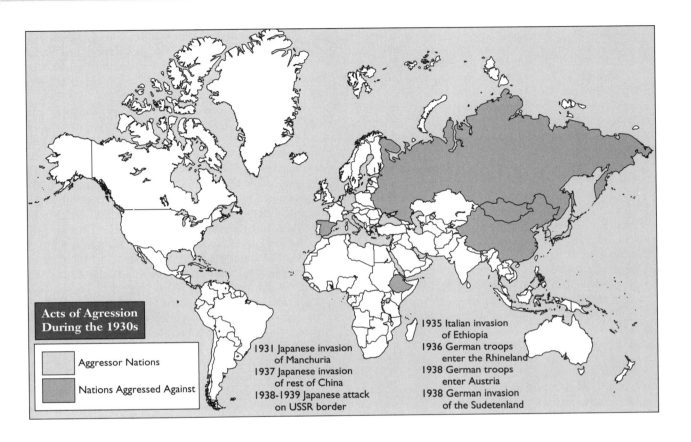

Acts of Agression During the 1930s

☐ Aggressor Nations

☐ Nations Aggressed Against

1931 Japanese invasion
of Manchuria
1937 Japanese invasion
of rest of China
1938-1939 Japanese attack
on USSR border

1935 Italian invasion
of Ethiopia
1936 German troops
enter the Rhineland
1938 German troops
enter Austria
1938 German invasion
of the Sudetenland

socialist, capitalist, or anti-Semitic, according to crowd demand. Thus farmers were told that Jewish capitalists were driving them to bankruptcy; shopkeepers were told that Jewish communists were out to destroy them. Where attacks on Jews were not popular with the crowd, the Nazis simply attacked someone else. Briefly put, National Socialism became a mass movement by being all things to all people.

Scholars once concluded that Nazi votes came mostly from the lower middle class, but recent research has revealed that the party had appeal to all levels of the population. By the end of 1932, however, Goebbels's propaganda had reached its limits. The Nazis then had 450 000 party members and 400 000 SA Brown Shirts, a paramilitary force four times the size of the German army. In the November election of that year, they received 12 million votes. This, however, was almost two million less than they received four months earlier. The movement had peaked. The plan to win power by winning elections had fallen short.

The Nazis never received more than 37 percent of the German vote. Now, however, with his party losing momentum, Hitler got the break of his life: he was handed power in a political deal.

Conservative politicians around Reich President Paul von Hindenburg had tried for some time to convince this grand old World War I general to come to terms with the idea of a Hitler government. One of them in particular, the crafty Prussian aristocrat Franz von Papen, argued that Hitler could be "used." The Nazis had the masses. Thus, only a deal with Hitler, Papen concluded, could bring this mass support to the side of the conservative forces in the country. Hindenburg, however, wanted no part of the vulgar Hitler. Only when the Nazis started to decline at the polls—and Hitler became easier to handle—did Papen wear down the resistance of the old soldier-President. Papen promised Hindenburg—now nearly senile at age 84—that a Hitler government would be surrounded and controlled by conservative politicians. To this

Hitler agreed, promising to appoint a majority of conservative ministers to his cabinet—and only three Nazis. In return, President Hindenburg appointed the Nazi leader as Chancellor of Germany on January 30, 1933. Said von Papen, "Within two months, we will have pushed Hitler so far into a corner that he will squeak." Historians have said that Hitler had an advantage over his opponents: they always underestimated him.

The Making of the Third Reich

The compromise with the conservatives that brought Hitler to power was important in shaping the history of the Third Reich, the name given to Nazi rule in Germany from 1933 to 1945. Like the fascists in Italy, the Nazis had to live with their conservative allies. Therefore, as Hitler's followers moved into position as a new political class in Germany, the old elites held their place in society. The same bureaucrats ran the state machinery, the same industrialists ran the economy, the same Prussian generals ran the army, and the same judges and professors (those who did not emigrate out of fear of Nazism) ran the courts and universities. Nazi Germany, therefore, was not the model of a streamlined totalitarian society. Importantly, however, the internal history of the Third Reich was the story of National Socialism's driving passion for domination and control. Over time, state regulation increased, police powers grew, the opposition was beaten into submission, and the conservative elites came one by one to their knees before Hitler. By 1938, Germany had become "the Hitler state," a form of dictatorship far more totalitarian than the fascist regime in Italy.

The push toward total power began in the first months of Nazi rule. When fire gutted the Reichstag building in Berlin on February 27, 1933, and a deranged communist youth was arrested on the spot, Goebbels screamed about communist plots against the state. In the uproar, Hindenburg gave Hitler emergency powers to suspend civil liberties and maintain order in the country. With this, the SA began arresting communists and socialists. At the same time, Nazi organizations at the grassroots used the new police powers of the party to take over local government in cities and towns. In this atmosphere, with a new Germany in the making, an election on March 5— which Hitler made sure would be the last—again left the Nazis short of a majority at 44 percent. However, the support of Hitler's conservative allies gave the government a majority in the Reichstag. Hitler now forced through the Enabling Act, legislation which, in giving him power to rule without parliament, completed the "legal revolution" that brought dictatorship out of a democratic system.

With power in hand, the Nazis began the process of *Gleichshaltung* (coordination), the action of bringing the organized life of the country under political rule. Institutions, labour unions, professional societies, womens' movements and sports, youth, and volunteer groups of all kinds now became National Socialist organizations, or were closed down altogether as private bodies existing apart from the state. Hitler's purpose was not only to spread Nazi control but to carry the ideas of his movement into the group life of the nation. One result, for example, was the dramatic night ceremony called "the Burning of the Books." On May 10, 1933 youths of the new student organization threw into huge bonfires the great books of Western culture, including the works of Jewish writers and master thinkers of freedom and democracy. The effect of these developments was the politicization of German society: the entry of the state into the once private associations of everyday life. The only thing that would remain private in Germany, said a Nazi official, was sleep. Part of this "coordination" process was the elimination of all political parties except the Nazis themselves. The result was a one-party state and the beginnings of a totalitarian society.

The transition of Nazism from a radical movement to a ruling party had the same result as the transition of the Bolsheviks from revolutionaries to government officials: the decline in influence of extremist elements and the rise of bureaucrats and technicians of power. From the start, Hitler's conservative allies called on him to restore order in the nation. Hitler responded by naming his second-in-command, Hermann Göring, to the police post of Minister of the Interior for Prussia. Göring lost no time in making the secret state police, known as the Gestapo, the most feared organization in Europe. However, much of the disorder in the country came from the wild ones of Nazism itself: the Brown Shirts. Their leader, in particular, was a bully who always urged Hitler to take more radical action. Ernst Röhm wanted National Socialism to be more socialist and revolutionary. More directly, he wanted his storm troopers to challenge the role of the regular army. Hitler, however, now had more need for a professional army than for Röhm's street fighters. Early on June 30, 1934, in a bloody purge known as "the Night of the Long Knives," Nazi detachments fell upon the SA leaders, murdered Röhm and his lieutenants, and ended the power of the Brown Shirts within the Nazi state. Thus, like the Bolsheviks, the Nazis consolidated their seizure of power by destroying their own offspring.

In putting down the storm troopers, Hitler improved his relations with "official" Germany and the law-and-order elites of the country. With their SA rivals out of the way, Germany's military leaders now came closer to the Nazi regime. Thus, on Hindenburg's death on August 2, 1934, the army command did not resist Hitler's decision to take the powers of both Chancellor and President to himself. In solemn ceremonies, officers and soldiers swore an oath of personal loyalty to Hitler as the new "Führer of the German Reich and People." The Night of the Long Knives, in this sense, marked the end of the Nazi revolution and the beginning of the cult of Hitler as Führer.

Those who did the dirty work of purging the SA were the *Schutzstaffel* (SS), or security section, an elite branch of the SA set off by sleek black uniforms and iron rules of discipline. In contrast to the emotionalism and random violence of the SA, the SS was taught to be passionless, hard, and obedient. After 1934, as the SA was withdrawn from the streets, the SS took over the work of political police. With this, the use of terror became organized. As the role of this black army increased, the power of its leader, Heinrich Himmler, increased along with it. Himmler, a Nazi fanatic behind thick eyeglasses and bland features, was at once a racist and a supreme organizer. Named by Hitler as Reich Leader of the SS and Chief of German Police, he came to control the entire police apparatus of party and state alike. Included was control over a concentration camp system that became in the end a Nazi version of the Gulag Archipelago.

The first concentration camp was opened at **Dachau**, near Munich, in March, 1933, and became a model for the many camps to follow. As many as 6000 prisoners went through these camps in the early years. Most of them were political opponents of Nazism, largely communists, socialists, and intellectuals. By 1935, Himmler's men had broken the last organized resistance to Hitler's destruction of Weimar democracy, and the number of arrests actually declined. With his real enemies out of the way, Hitler now turned on his imaginary one: the Jews. Some measures against Jews had been taken in the early months of power, when "non-Aryans" were removed from jobs in government service. However, with the announcement in September 1935 of the so-called Nuremberg Racial Laws, the Jews of Germany were separated by law from the rest of the nation. Lost were many of their rights as citizens. Marriages and sexual relations between Jews and citizens "of German blood" were forbidden. In this way, Hitler left the Jews isolated and defenceless before the more violent assaults that were to come.

In retrospect, it is important to recognize that the history of Nazism in these years was a success story. The great majority of Germans were not a people living in slavery under a hated government. While the true measure of public consent to Nazism is uncertain, it appears that the regime had wide popularity. In a state *plebiscite* (opinion poll) in 1934, 85 percent of the population gave approval to Hitler as Führer of the nation. Some historians have said that this popularity was based on "fear and the fair grounds," that is, on the terror system and the spectacle of patriotic rallies, flags, and uniforms. Each year, for example, enormous crowds of some 400 000 people joined in the "Party Days" at Nuremberg to celebrate Germany's unity and strength under Hitler. The popularity of Nazism, however, was based on more than police and parades. There were also jobs, profits, and prosperity. Hitler's programs for rearmament and public works, including the construction of superhighways (the *Autobahnen*), brought the country out of the depression and into a period of economic recovery and high employment.

Resistance was a losing game. Some churches opposed the "coordination" process and struggled with Nazism for the mind of the nation. Most eventually found something to like in Hitler's anticommunism and conservative family values. German Catholics warmed to the regime after Hitler signed a *concordat* (a church-state agreement) with Pope Pius XI in July 1933. A Papal encyclical in 1937, condemning the evils of racism, made little difference. Once Hitler had started upon his foreign policy victories in 1936, the ecstasy of patriotism overcame what was left of the resistance of the churches.

Nazism had restored the nation from its defeat in World War I. Germany was one: *Ein Reich, ein Führer, ein Volk* (one state, one leader, one people). Now it was the democracies that appeared weak and divided.

The Era of Fascism

Europe appeared to be moving toward the fulfilment of Mussolini's prophecy that the twentieth century would be the era of fascism. What was fascism? In the beginning, Mussolini had said that it was strictly an Italian creation not for export to other countries. Nevertheless, the word fascism was soon used to describe nationalist movements in other countries that appeared to resemble the Black Shirts in Rome. With the rise of Nazism in Germany, however, there appeared a form of fascism very different from the Italian model. Hitler's hatred of Jews, in particular, found no echo in Mussolini's party. Italian fascists—until 1938—opposed racism as alien to the Catholic traditions of their country.

As nationalist movements, fascist parties everywhere identified themselves with the histories, traditions, and symbols of their own peoples. In this way, all fascisms were different. At the same time, all shared some common aspects: hypernationalism, anti-Marxism, antiliberalism, anticonservatism (though some had working relationships with conservative elites), a Führer concept, a cult of youth and male dominance, a paramilitary group, and a fixation on flag rituals, Roman salutes, and coloured shirts. In brief, fascist movements were at once different and alike. As a result, the concept of fascism has remained difficult for scholars to define, and a debate on the nature of this puzzling "ism" has continued to the present day.

In general, European fascism was a tale of two cities: Rome and Berlin. Elsewhere, fascists were loud and maddening, but their parties were struggling and popular support was low. Some, in fact, were on life support, surviving on secret payments from Hitler or Mussolini. In themselves, these two dictators were

Fascism and Women

Fascism was a man's movement. In fascist thought, the difference between male and female was determined by biology. Men by nature were said to be dominant, productive, and strong; they were warriors, providers, and authority figures in family relations. Women were for reproduction and caring; they were homemakers, wives, childbearers, and mothers. What war was to men, said Mussolini, childbirth was to women. In their proper sex roles, women were as vital to the nation as men. The sexual politics of fascism, therefore, was involved in plans to roll back the rights and opportunities for women which were bringing them out of the home: employment, voting rights, education (except for homecraft instruction), and feminist organizations. Hitler disbanded all women's movements in Germany in 1933 and replaced them with a single organization under Nazi control. Its leader, Gertrud Scholz-Klink, was a model of Nazi womanhood: blond, blue-eyed, mother of four, and ready to obey the men in command. Named Reich leader of women by Hitler in 1934, she was given no voice in policy on female issues.

Fascists in Rome and Berlin had a common conception of females as essentially reproductive beings. From women came the future generations of the nation. Family welfare programs, therefore, were sometimes more advanced in the fascist states than in the Western democracies. In Germany, for example, measures to protect the health of mother and child included food subsidies, maternity clinics, and housing for single mothers. Abortion was a criminal offence, permitted only to women of Jewish birth or to those with hereditary health defects.

The level of female support for fascism is unknown. Some historians have estimated, however, that women voted for the Nazis in greater numbers than men in the last democratic elections in Germany in 1932. As well, it was a woman, Leni Riefenstahl, who produced the major propaganda films of the Third Reich, including the masterpiece of Führer worship, *The Triumph of the Will*.

In the end, the Nazi ideal of returning women from the workplace to the home was overcome by the labour needs of the rearmament program. After 1936, as the military draft reduced the male work force, women entered the economy in larger numbers than before.

different men from different movements: Mussolini's fascism was full of swagger and fanfare; Hitler's had a dark and demonic quality that stirred horror in his enemies. Europe probably could have lived with Italian fascism. Mussolini wanted colonies in Africa and more power in the Mediterranean. What Hitler wanted was limitless. In *Mein Kampf*, he spoke of Germany's need for *Lebensraum*, living space, in the east. As a German of Austrian birth, he cherished the Pan-German dream of bringing all Germans "home to the Reich," of annexing Austria and "liberating" German minorities in border areas. As well, he wanted to settle the score with France for his nation's defeat in World War I. He wanted to tear up the Versailles Treaty and change the boundary lines in Europe. More grimly, he wanted to do something about the Jews. Soon enough, Hitler's objectives became Europe's challenge. As a result, the main history of the era of fascism became the story of Germany's revival, rearmament, and return to the struggle for mastery on the continent. In the end, fascism would win or lose on the strength of Hitler's armies.

In his first week of power in 1933, Hitler told his generals in secret of his plans for rearmament. "For the next four or five years," he said, "the main principle must be: everything for the armed forces." Before the year was out, Germany had withdrawn from the Geneva Disarmament Conference and the League of Nations. The reason, Hitler explained, was that other nations had not kept their promise in the Versailles Treaty to reduce their arms. In March 1935, he was ready to bring his own violation of this treaty into the open. Germany, he announced, was rearming, and would no longer be bound by the military restrictions of the Versailles settlement. With this, a new period began in European diplomacy, a series of crises leading to World War II.

Reflections

In "the gathering storm," Hitler revealed a cunning for manoeuvre and timing that left the diplomats of Britain and France breathless. His talent was to mix words of peace and threats of war, sounding reasonable at one moment and reckless at the next. Hitler told the world that Germany was a victim nation, disarmed and dishonoured by the Versailles *Diktat*. Now it wanted simply to be equal in arms to the other powers, and to recover its fair place in Europe. In response, the leaders in London and Paris tried to learn from the history of their time. To them, the real enemy was not Hitler; it was war. They looked back to the causes of World War I in 1914, when hard and inflexible politicians led Europe to destruction. And they looked to the period of appeasement between 1924 and 1928, when the give-and-take diplomacy of Stresemann, Briand, and Chamberlain brought Germany back to peace with Europe. Here, they believed, was the way to keep the peace again. In this, a historian has said, Hitler had the advantage over his opponents in the democracies. He knew what he wanted. They knew only what they did not want: they did not want war.

Key Concepts, Figures, and Events

Benito Mussolini	John Maynard Keynes	Roosevelt's	Leon Trotsky	Great Terror
Joseph Stalin	Fascism	New Deal	Five Year Plan	National Socialism
Adolf Hitler	*Mein Kampf*	V. I. Lenin	Terror Famine	Dachau

Topics for Further Thought

1. How should history judge the regimes of Mussolini, Hitler, and Stalin? Construct a matrix to assist you in analyzing these regimes. Your matrix should include: Economic Prosperity; Technological Advances; Protection of Human Rights and Freedoms; Stength of the State; and Standard of Living for the average citizen. Once your matrix is complete, write a one-paragraph summary of your conclusions.

2. World War II has been described as simply a continuation of the European civil war which began in 1914. Assess this statement by considering the events between 1919 and the eve of war in 1939.

3. How did the ideologies of fascism and communism respond to the pessimism and disenchantment many felt towards democratic-capitalist systems? Why did both systems ultimately fail despite making considerable material progress?

4. There were many who worked very hard to ensure peace in the decades following the First World War. Why did the peace sought by Stresemann, Briand, and Chamberlain not survive the 1930s? Was their attempt at peace flawed from the outset? If so, explain the flaws. If not, what explanation can you provide?

5. Following a decade of prosperity, the Great Depression shattered the faith of many in the free-enterprise system. What can we learn from the experience of the Great Depression? Could it have been avoided? Did it expose inherent weaknesses in capitalism? Is the welfare state the ideal compromise? Be sure to explain your answers.

6. Karl Marx had predicted that a communist revolution would occur first in an industrialized nation. He also believed that capitalist development was a way out of backwardness and therefore would prepare a nation for communism. Explain the application of this idea to the Russian situation.

7. The success of the communist revolution in Russia was in part due to the adaptation Lenin made to Marxist theory. Explain the nature of this adaptation. Was Leninism a further evolution in communist ideology, or was it an adaptation suited specifically to the Russian condition?

8. Totalitarianism often relies on a cult of the leader. Assess this statement as it relates to Lenin, Stalin, Hitler, or Mussolini. Can this phenomenon be used in democratic politics? Explain your answer.

9. By tracing the rise of the Nazi Party, explain which of the following you believe to be the most important factor in their success: economics, nationalism, or racism.

10. There continues to be much debate among historians as to where the origins of the Holocaust lie. At what point did the Nazis begin considering the mass extermination of the Jewish race? What evidence suggests that the planning for the Holocaust began as early as 1933, if not earlier, and built throughout the 1930s?

Topics for Further Research

1. During the years between the wars there were several important books published addressing the main political and economic issues of the day. Select one of the following books and prepare a summary of the major ideas it addresses:

Hitler's *Mein Kampf*
Keynes's *The General Theory of Employment, Interest and Money*
Lenin's *What Is to Be Done?*

2. A common theme during the inter-war years was the redefining of the role of government. Select one of the following countries and research how the role of government changed in the years between 1919 and 1939.

Germany   Italy   Spain
Russia   United States

3. Often, when dealing with the period 1919 to 1939, we focus our attention on the dictatorships in Germany, Italy, and the Soviet Union. Dictators, however, also came to power in several other European nations. Select one of the following countries and research the nature of the dictatorship. Consider issues such as how they came to power, the ideologies they espoused, and how successful was their regime.

Poland
Bulgaria
Estonia

Yugoslavia
Greece
Latvia

Rumania
Lithuania

4. After the Communist Revolution, Russia made tremendous strides, becoming an industrial and military superpower by 1945. These advances came at a great price. Research one of the following issues related to Stalin's rise to power and the industrialization of the Soviet Union. Be sure to consider the methods by which goals were achieved, and the costs and benefits to the citizens of the Soviet Union.

New Economic Policy
Murder of Trotsky
Five Year Plans
Terror Famine
Great Terror

Responding to Ideas

1. The period between the two World Wars was a time when democracy faced severe challenges and dictators came to rule much of Europe. The "Great Man" theory of history suggests that the path of history is directed by the actions of powerful individuals. Conversely, some feel that the individuals who dominate an era are a product of history. The nineteenth century German philosopher G. F. W. Hegel wrote: "The great man of the age is the one who can put into words the will of his age, tell his age what its will is, and accomplish it. What he does is the heart and essence of his age; he actualizes his age." Considering the conditions in Europe following World War I, do you believe the "Great Man" theory is applicable to Mussolini, Hitler, and/or Stalin or that they represented the will of their age? Explain your answer.

2. Borrowing a phrase from German military theorist Karl von Clausewitz, Mao Zedong wrote in 1938: "War is the continuation of politics by other... means. When politics develops to a certain stage beyond which it cannot proceed by the usual means, war breaks out to sweep the obstacles from the way... When the obstacle is removed and our political aim attained, the war will end." Do you agree with Mao's assessment of the causes of war? If we are to accept this hypothesis, does it suggest that attempts at appeasement prior to the outbreak of war in 1939 were doomed to failure from the beginning?

14

Rebuilding a Shattered World: Life in Europe Between the Wars

---

CHAPTER HIGHLIGHTS

- The birth of consumerism in North America and Europe

- The revolution in leisure between the wars

- Changes in the nature of private life and privacy

- Life under totalitarian regimes

- The effects of the Great Depression on the family

The twentieth century arrived amidst much anticipation and optimism. Many believed that human ingenuity knew no bounds; that the application of technology and human reasoning could help to eradicate disease, build unsinkable ships, yield unprecedented wealth, and bring an end to wars. The horror of World War I and the accompanying Russian Revolution brought an abrupt end to the optimism that had prevailed in the first decade of the twentieth century. In the years following 1918, Western nations had contrasting experiences. While countries such as Canada, Britain, and the United States experienced an economic boom in the 1920s followed by a devastating depression in the 1930s, Germany, saddled with heavy war reparations, found itself mired in a severe depression for the first half of the 1920s. The rise of fascism in Germany and Italy and the birth of communism in the Soviet Union also led to a dramatically different lifestyle for the citizens of these countries than for those living in democratic countries such as France, England, and the United States.

Throughout this chapter, we will examine aspects of daily life in Europe and North America in those tumultuous years between 1918 and 1945. In so doing, we will consider the continuing evolution of the family structure, including trends in marriage and divorce, the birth of suburbs, increases in privacy as a result of improved standards of living, and the way in which technology sparked the revolution in how we spend our spare time. As well, we will take a look at how the economic collapse in the Western world in the 1930s impacted on aspects of daily life. The chapter will conclude with a contrasting look at life under the Third Reich and Stalin's Soviet Union. The issues discussed in this chapter attempt to examine life in Europe and North America under three distinct conditions: a communist regime, a fascist regime, and a free-enterprise democracy. Beyond these distinctions, space does not permit a more detailed look at the variations between countries. The decades of the 1920s and 1930s were indeed trying times: war, revolution, economic depression all took their toll on the people of Europe. Yet, in spite of the adversity they faced, people persevered and families adapted. This chapter is an examination of the daily lives of the people who experienced the highs and lows of these very difficult decades.

The Roaring Twenties in North America

While much of Europe attempted to rebuild itself after the devastation of the Great War, North Americans enjoyed the fruits of an economic boom often referred to as the *Roaring Twenties*. Many industries in Canada and the United States benefited from Europe's rebuilding process by supplying many of the materials they needed to reconstruct their cities. Although prosperity returned following the war, the innocence and optimism which had characterized the turn of the century became a casualty of war, along with the thousands of young soldiers who had died on the battlefields of Europe. The result was a decade of rampant materialism during which new fads, new fashions, and new trends in music suggested a carefree attitude as North Americans attempted to forget the horrors of war and live life with reckless abandon.

The New Age of Consumerism

The late nineteenth and early twentieth centuries had witnessed the rapid development of technological innovations. Thomas Edison had invented the light bulb, the phonograph, and other devices, Guglielmo Marconi had sent the first radio message from Signal Hill in Newfoundland, Alexander Graham Bell had developed the telephone, and Canada's Reginald Fessenden had developed sonar. In the years between 1790 and 1860 the United States Patent Office issued 36 000 patents. By comparison, in the 40 years from 1860 to 1900, there were 676 000 patents granted. By the 1920s hydroelectric power had reached most areas of Canada and the United States, revolutionizing factories and providing the electricity to homes necessary to power the numerous gadgets and labour-saving devices being churned out by North American industries. Refrigeration allowed North Americans to eat fresh fruits and vegetables year round and improved packaging produced a wider variety of packaged foods including the revolutionary new sliced bread. Consumers all over North America were purchasing electric irons, vacuum cleaners, washing machines,

This comfortable parlour was typical of bourgeois homes at the beginning of the twentieth century.

toasters, and refrigerators. Even leisure time was being radically changed by the widespread purchasing of radios and phonographs.

The *consumer revolution* that occurred in the 1920s was not merely the result of a rapid increase in the number of products available, it was also the result of a sudden growth in advertising. For the first time, advertising was being used by retailers to create consumer demand rather than just to inform the public about products and prices. American President Calvin Coolidge described advertising as "the most potent influence in adapting and changing the habits and modes of life, affecting what we eat, what we wear, and the work and play of the whole nation." This revolution in advertising was aided by the emerging mass media: newspapers, radio stations, billboards, and national magazines. In fact, critics of the consumerism of the 1920s noted that for every dollar spent by advertisers to attract buyers of their products, the government spent only 70 cents on schools.

Another radical change that helped drive the consumer revolution was the practice of buying on credit. For the first time, consumers were able to put down a deposit and pay the balance on installments. The opportunity to buy a new phonograph for "$5 down and $5 dollars a month" was irresistible to many Americans. In 1928, 85 percent of furniture, 80 percent of phonographs, 75 percent of washing machines and radios, and 70 percent of refrigerators were bought on credit. Buying on credit also brought automobile ownership within reach of ordinary North Americans.

The automobile brought about some of the most profound changes in North American culture. The earliest automobiles had been expensive luxury items restricted to the well-to-do. This changed with Henry Ford's introduction of the assembly line in automobile production in 1908. By the 1920s a Ford Model T could be purchased for $300, well within the budget of the average family. The car changed North American culture in many ways: dating habits of young people, family vacations, Sunday outings, and even where people lived, were affected by the car. North Americans could now visit far-off places and could even go on short day trips on weekends. Their increased mobility allowed people to move away from the industrial centres of cities to houses in the suburbs. The increased affluence of the 1920s and the opportunity to buy on credit began North Americans' love affair with the automobile, which has continued unabated to this day.

Suburbia and the American Family

Modern modes of transportation, including the train and most notably the automobile, played a central role in the evolution of North American cities. Already in the nineteenth century, suburbs were beginning to emerge around several Canadian and American cities as new methods of transportation allowed people to live away from their place of work. By the early twentieth century, suburbs had become more than just a place to live; they had become a new way of life. Confined to white-collar workers of the middle class and to more affluent members of the working class, suburbs became a symbol of the ideal life for the modern family. In 1903, *Cosmopolitan* magazine described the suburbs as a "compromise for those who temper an inherent or cultivated taste for green fields... with an unwillingness to entirely forego the delights of urban gaiety."

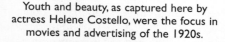

Youth and beauty, as captured here by actress Helene Costello, were the focus in movies and advertising of the 1920s.

A Revolution in Leisure

The decade of the 1920s also saw a revolution in how North Americans spent their leisure time. Movie theatres provided the opportunity to escape the real world, radios kept North Americans in touch with major events, spectator sports provided much sought after heroes, and blues and jazz music caught the ear of the rebellious youth. Movies became a national pastime attracting people from all backgrounds and all ages. In the years following the death and destruction of World War I, the movie theatre offered a place where people could go to escape. An ad in the *Saturday Evening Post* urged Americans to "Go to a movie... and let yourself go." Movie stars became cultural icons for the America of the 1920s. When the silver screen's leading heart throb, Rudolph Valentino, died suddenly at the age of 31, nearly 30 000 tearful fans attended his funeral. Movies came to be so important in American culture that the Hollywood stars became the major trend setters, transforming tastes and behaviours. A new hair style sported by Gloria Swanson, or a new dress style worn by Mary Pickford would become the rage, and thousands of women demanded the same look.

Spectator sports also experienced tremendous growth during the 1920s. Baseball, football, boxing, and hockey all produced heroes of epic proportions such as Red Grange or Babe Ruth. North Americans were able to follow the triumphs and defeats of their heroes by attending sporting events, listening to their new radio, or by reading about exploits in newspaper and magazine articles. Historian George Mowry explains North Americans' fascination with sports heroes in the following way: "The sporting field was one of the few remaining areas of pure individual expression where success or failure depended precisely upon individual physical and intellectual prowess. And if the masses themselves could not or would not participate directly they could at least, by process of identification, salute the old virtues."

Women in Early American Cinema

At the turn of the twentieth century, the silent-film industry was a new and exciting industry that was beginning to emerge. In the early years of film, the traditionally male-dominated unions and the stereotypical roles of men and women that existed in other industries had not yet been established. Consequently, the early film industry was wide open to women. Also important in establishing women as a dominant force in the silent-film era was the industry's need to bring respectability to this new form of entertainment. Many people had reservations about allowing their children to enter the new nickelodeons where the silent films were shown. Women as theatre managers and often owners, seemed to offer a sense of respectability and security to the film industry.

In her 1923 article for *The Business Woman*, Myrtle Gebhart noted:

Excluding acting, considering solely the business possibilities, the positions are held by women in the Hollywood studios as... telephone operators, hair dressers, seamstresses, costume designers, milliners, readers... set designers, and set dressers, librarians, artists, title writers, publicity writers, plaster moulders, casting directors, musicians, film editors, executives, and department managers, directors, and producers.

Obviously, the new film industry had opened up numerous career opportunities for women and, as a result, women came to play a prominent role in the early American film industry. In fact, aside from comedies and westerns, women dominated the screen in the silent era of film.

Among the important women of the early screen was Olga Petrova, film's first blatantly feminist actor. Born Muriel Harding in England, she adopted a European name and accent when she arrived in the United States. In all 26 of her feature films, Petrova portrayed women of strong mind, strong character, and strong abilities. During an interview conducted in 1918, Petrova declared, "I do want to bring a message to women—a message of encouragement. The only women I want to play are women who do things. I want to encourage women to do things—to take their rightful place in life." When she retired from acting she wrote a play entitled *Hurricane*, in which she

---

Toronto-born Mary Pickford became one of the leading women of early cinema and was popularly known as America's Sweetheart.

advocated birth control; and in her autobiography, *Butter with My Bread*, Petrova reflected: "I did achieve what I set out as a child to get, my own bread, my own butter, my own house in which to enjoy it. That—to me—is the height of what I will accept and acknowledge as greatness."

Another of the great women of the early cinema was Canada's Mary Pickford. Born Gladys Smith in Ontario in 1893, Pickford went on to become "America's Sweetheart" and by 1917 was recognized as the most famous woman in the world. Aside from showing herself to be one of the greatest actors of the silent-film era, Pickford showed herself to be a tough and ferocious businessperson "with an intelligence and negotiating skill equal to those of any of her male counterparts."

When Pickford's salary became too high for a producer to earn a return on investment, she simply became her own producer. In 1919, Mary Pickford, along with D. W. Griffith, Douglas Fairbanks, and Charlie Chaplin, created United Artists. Pickford's true importance to the film industry is reflected by the fact that she was the only woman to control her own production company, her own studio, and her own distribution set-up.

Mary Pickford and Olga Petrova are only two of the hundreds of women involved in the early film industry in America. The pioneering work of these women helped to bring women's issues to the silver screen and left an indelible mark on the films of the early twentieth century.

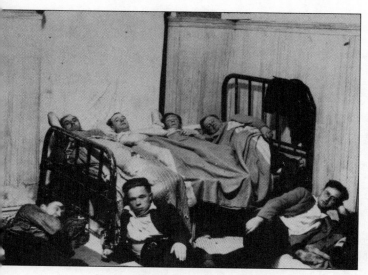

Sharing a room during the depression allowed little opportunity for individual privacy.

Daily Life in Europe, 1900–1939

Private Life and Privacy

Prior to the twentieth century, privacy was a privilege of the middle and upper classes. Workers, whether in Italy, France, or Germany, could hardly avoid the intermingling of private life with community life. Much of their lives were lived either on the job site or in public places such as taverns. Even at home, the crowded conditions allowed for little individual privacy. During the twentieth century, an increase in affluence has allowed a far greater portion of European society to enjoy private live away from the prying eyes of the community, and to have enough room at home to enjoy some opportunity for individual privacy. Because of this increase in privacy, one historian has suggested that the history of private life is the history of democratization. This trend towards increased privacy has developed slowly, however, with the most significant changes coming after 1950. Between the wars change was evident, but for many of the working class, houses remained cramped and privacy-elusive.

Homes of the Working Class

Throughout the first half of the twentieth century, the basic design of the homes of the middle and upper classes was markedly different from the homes of the working class or rural farm homes. Both workers and peasants lived in crowded homes usually consisting of one or two rooms. Often rural homes had only a single room in which both cooking and sleeping took place. While investigating health conditions in rural France in 1900, physicians Morbihan and Yonne found it typical for farm homes to have as many as four beds in a single room each occupied by two people. In the cities, many workers lived in one-room apartments that had neither electricity nor running water. In general, it could be said that overcrowding was the norm in most areas of Europe prior to 1950. According to a 1906 census, 26 percent of those living in cities larger than 5000 lived more than two to a room, while a further 36 percent lived more than one to a room. Furthermore, between 1900 and 1950 there were few improvements in home comfort and appliances other than electricity being introduced to most homes. Until 1950, many homes remained without running water, baths, or indoor plumbing, causing hygiene to be rudimentary at best.

With overcrowding, the norm for the majority of Europeans prior to 1950, individuals could enjoy little privacy within the home. Members of a family lived in close proximity to each other at all times. They had to dress in front of family members, bathe in a wooden tub in the common room, and no one had the luxury of sleeping alone. In many homes, there would be only one bed shared by as many as five people. Living conditions such as these made it difficult to keep private belongings or to harbour secrets. Also, sexual intimacy was virtually impossible, leading sexual activity to take place either in secluded public spaces or discreetly in the homes in the presence of members of the family. A specialist in rural housing observed at the turn of the century: "Morality does not suffer from the fact that nearly everyone sleeps in one room. On the contrary, a sort of mutual surveillance develops.... Only decency suffers, but this hindrance is less serious than one accustomed only to private rooms might imagine." Thus, during the first half of the twentieth century, the private lives of the European peasantry and working class was indistinguishable from family life.

Children

Among all classes in Europe during the first half of the twentieth century, children had no right to a private life: all aspects of their lives were closely monitored and controlled by their parents. Spare time after school was most often taken up by the numerous tasks assigned to children by their parents. When they did find the leisure time to spend with friends, families were very selective over which children would make suitable playmates. The opportunity to make new friends in public places, something very common among young children today, was not allowed. If a child was to show the slightest inclination towards speaking or playing with another child in a park, he or she was given a stern reprimand.

The supervision of children extended beyond monitoring their friends. Parents routinely opened their chidren's mail, seeing it as their duty to scrutinize their letters. Even letters sent to children in boarding schools had to be signed on the outside so that the school could be sure that the person sending the letter had been authorized by the child's parents.

Parents also took it upon themselves to plan their children's future by selecting which university they would attend or in which trade they would apprentice. In 1938, 30 percent of the respondents to a survey said yes to the following question: "Should parents choose a career for their children and steer them toward it from an early age?" Among the middle and upper classes, where considerable wealth was at stake, marriage was also a family concern in which parents exercised considerable influence. When planning a marriage, protecting the family fortune and status carried more weight than the emotional bond between the prospective bride and groom.

Marriage and Divorce

The changes in attitudes towards marriage and divorce during the twentieth century reveal a great deal about the evolution of the family in Europe. During the first half of the century, the purpose of marriage was still to establish a household and to have children to carry on the family name and inherit the family wealth. Hence, in selecting a marriage partner, professional prospects, wealth, and moral qualities were seen as more important than appearance or love. In fact, many couples considered a successful marriage

These American children were among the more fortunate, as they were sent to private schools in the 1920s. Others attended less well-equipped public schools.

one in which a man and woman were able to understand, appreciate, and respect each other. While love was not considered a prerequisite for marriage, many entered the union hoping that over time they would grow to love their spouse.

Given this attitude toward marriage, divorce was quite rare in Europe. Marriage was considered a permanent contract that could only be broken in very severe cases where the husband or wife was deemed to be guilty of grave misconduct. At the turn of the century, there were fewer than 15 000 divorces in France; in 1940, there were still fewer than 30 000. When granted, divorces usually resulted from an abusive alcoholic husband who had not only been unfaithful to his wife but had also become a financial burden to the family. Incompatibility was simply not sufficient grounds for divorce; even mental or physical cruelty or adultery was often not substantial enough reason to terminate a marriage.

By the 1930s and 1940s, attitudes towards both marriage and divorce in Europe were beginning to change. More rapid change, however, had already begun in North America. In the United States, the tradition of parental control over children's plans to marry was far less prevalent. The prevailing attitude among American youth was that of "romantic love as the only valid basis for marriage." As a result of the new emphasis on romance and excitement in marriage, Americans, in the first few decades of the twentieth century, were marrying younger and more often. By the turn of the century, Americans were also witnessing a rapid rise in the divorce rate. During the 62 years between 1867 and 1929, the population of the United States increased by 300 percent, the number of marriages increased by 400 percent, and the number of divorces skyrocketed by 2000 percent. By 1929, one in six marriages in the United States were ending in divorce, earning Americans the dubious distinction of the country with the world's highest divorce rate.

Effects of the Great Depression on the Family

The social consequences of the *Great Depression* are legendary: families struggling to survive against drought and massive unemployment, packing up their belongings and moving relentlessly in search of employment; young people riding the tops of trains from coast to coast in Canada and the United States hoping to find work; hobo jungles springing up along river banks and rail lines; long lines of unemployed hoping to get a bowl of soup and a warm place to sleep. What effect did these lean years have on the family?

Like the economic systems of the Western world, the family systems would survive the depression years by changing and adapting. One result of the crisis created by the Great Depression was the beginning of a new type of family based on two wage earners and a greater equality of the sexes. Prior to the depression, the family unit that had emerged in the early twentieth century was one in which the father was the breadwinner while the mother was a homemaker and cared for the children. Economic realities forced men to accept contributions from women to the family income and encouraged women to find jobs or pursue

careers. As a result, more women began to move outside the home although they seldom found their workload at home significantly reduced.

The Great Depression also had an impact on marriage and divorce rates. During the 1930s, the marriage rate in the United States plummeted as many young men chose to remain single, fearing they would not be able to support a family. The sharp decline in marriages became a grave concern to many educators and church officials because they feared delayed marriages would lead to more liberal sexual attitudes outside of marriage. To prevent young people from becoming sexually active prior to marriage, governments were encouraged to provide subsidies to young couples wishing to marry. The decline in the marriage rate was accompanied by a decline in the birthrate and a further increase in the divorce rate as marriages collapsed under the strain of the depression.

Life Under Totalitarian Regimes

In the previous chapter, it was noted that in the totalitarian states the difference between public and private life disappears and, as Mussolini stated, "the state is all embracing...." Living under a totalitarian regime, one comes to understand that the government opens mail to keep tabs on the citizens, police may be at your door at any time of day or night, and even family members are encouraged by the state to be informants on one another. And yet, even within the totalitarian regimes of the twentieth century, private life has continued to exist. Paradoxically, in fact, private life may reach its zenith under such regimes as individuals learn to lead a double life: that of law-abiding citizen, and that of a secret deviant who cautiously flaunts the laws in order to fulfill individual needs, whether spiritual, intellectual, or sexual. *Totalitarianism*, in spite of its attempt to place private life under public control, creates a secretive society. Jean-Paul Sartre wrote: "We were never so free as

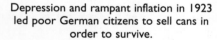

Depression and rampant inflation in 1923 led poor German citizens to sell cans in order to survive.

under the German occupation." To attempt to glimpse the private lives of individuals who lived under totalitarianism during the first half of the twentieth century, we will examine life in the Soviet Union under Stalin and life in Hitler's Third Reich.

Life Under Stalinism

The need for secrecy within a totalitarian regime is clearly borne out by the events which occurred in the Soviet Union during the 1930s, when the brutal, unrestrained terrorism of the police was most evident. People lived in constant fear of being arrested and imprisoned or killed for the slightest comment against the government. No one was safe from such persecution. Even Stalin's wife, who made the mistake of complaining of the plight of the Russian people in November 1932, committed suicide after a vulgar and abusive verbal assault in front of friends by her husband. Another aspect which people had to learn to live with under Stalinism was the constant propaganda and indoctrination. People were continually inundated—in the press, at work, and on the radio—with messages about the achievements of socialism and the perils of capitalism. Even art and literature were conscripted by Stalin to become "engineers of the human mind" as leading members of the artistic and intellectual community were rewarded for their ability to use their creative abilities to glorify the communist regime. Those who chose to use their talents to criticize or discredit Stalinism were arrested and placed in forced labour camps from which few returned.

Life in the Soviet Union prior to World War II was difficult, as people experienced a decline in their standard of living from the previous decade. People lived on little food as there were constant shortages, and wore old shabby clothing. A shortage of housing resulted in four people per room in every urban dwelling by 1940, from 2.7 in 1926. Those who were not fortunate enough to find an apartment built themselves scrap-lumber shacks or dug underground shelters in the shantytowns around the cities. There were some gains for the workers under Stalinism, though: unemployment was virtually unheard of and important social benefits such as free health care, education, and day-care, as well as old-age pensions were available to all Soviet citizens.

There were also important gains for women under the communist regime. Immediately following the Revolution, equality of rights for women was proclaimed. During the 1920s, divorce and abortions became easy to obtain and women were encouraged to work outside the home. Implicit in the newfound freedom for women was an increase in sexual freedom. Women also found numerous career and educational opportunities open to them as they began to attend university and acquire jobs in fields that had been restricted to men. In fact, by 1950 75 percent of all doctors in the Soviet Union were women.

These new gains for women had their unfortunate downside. In many cases women did not have the choice to work or stay at home. Wages were so low that a family required two incomes to be able to survive. After toiling at their jobs all day, women still carried the heavy burden of maintaining the home and caring for the children as this was still considered a woman's responsibility despite the supposed equality which was to have accompanied the Revolution. Finally, liberalized divorce laws and rapid change amid economic hardship resulted in many broken families and increased stress and burdens for women.

The Ovsey family, now living in Thornhill, Ontario, Canada experienced life under Stalinism. Zinovey Ovsey was a Jewish doctor who lived in Vilnius, Lithuania, during the years of Stalin's reign. His earnings of 125 rubles a month were enough to buy an adequate amount of food but little else. After he married, Zinovey and his wife lived in a scantily furnished one-room apartment. After a few years, the Ovsey family was able to move into a larger four-room apartment. To obtain food and other essential items, the Ovseys had to wait in long line-ups, often not knowing what would be available once they reached the front of the line. One thing they could be quite sure of was that the food they would purchase would be of poor quality. Although the family was constantly aware of the presence of the **KGB** and the threat of persecution, they were fortunate never to have to deal with the secret police. The Ovseys were also fortunate not to have experienced the strong anti-Semitism of the Soviet Union.

Life in the Third Reich

There has been much written about the rise of Nazism and Hitler's ascension to power. Only recently, however, have historians begun to pay attention to aspects of the daily lives of those who lived in the cities and towns during the period of the Third Reich. When examining the social history of this period, it is crucial that we not lose sight of the fact that Nazi Germany existed in a state of perpetual emergency and people's everyday lives unfolded amidst the killing of millions of people. Historian Richard Bessel reminds us: "The day-to-day reality of the Third Reich involved a complex mixture of fear and bribery, of terror and concessions, of barbarism and appeals to conventional moral values, which were employed in order to gain and maintain a grip on German society." At the same time, we must remember that while many under Nazi rule feared the Gestapo, did not want to go to war, and despised Nazi party bosses, they were grateful for the economic recovery and the resurgence of German power which accompanied the rise to power of Adolf Hitler. For example, prior to the outbreak of war, the Nazi government waged a successful campaign against crime, prostitution, and pornography. It is still common in Germany to hear comments about the safety of the streets and the decency in public life under the Nazis.

Nature of the Nazi State

To truly understand the nature of social change that took place in Germany during the period of the Third Reich, it is imperative that the nature of National Socialism be clearly understood. Reduced to its bare essentials, the Nazi state was based upon competition between individuals and institutions for the power to dominate and exploit others. Nazi society and the Nazi economic system were not based around methods of production but rather on preying on people. Historian Ian Kershaw summarized the nature of the Nazi regime as follows:

> Of all its vices, the ability of the National Socialist regime to separate and set human beings against one another in competition over plunder was the worst. By destroying bonds of solidarity, by fostering the egotism of both individuals and institutions, and by applauding as strong those 'who have no sympathy for any but themselves,' the National Socialist regime proceeded to create a

State and a society which 'placed men side by side, unconnected by any common ties.' This competition did not centre around production or markets, but around terror and force, the capacity to impose one's will on others by means of physical coercion.

Social Outcasts and the Third Reich

Although racism and annihilation were the least publicized aspects of Nazism, they formed the core of Third Reich politics. Those who failed to live up to the competitive criteria of National Socialism became the first targets of the Nazi regime. These people can be broken into three main groups: ideological enemies such as communists; asocials or those who went against social norms such as homosexuals; and biological outsiders who were considered a threat to the continuation of the German race. The third category included two main groups: those who were non-Aryan and therefore were considered undesirable because of their race, and those who carried hereditary defects. Of the persecution of the Jews, gypsies, and other peoples much is known. Less is written about those who were exterminated by the Nazis because of their "bad genes."

The theory of *eugenics*, which promotes the strengthening of a race through selective breeding, had become popular in many European countries during the 1920s and 1930s. In the 1920s, some German doctors encouraged "negative selection" as a means to improve or protect the gene pool. By sterilizing those with hereditary defects, they believed they could eventually weed out defective genes among the Germans. This suggestion was put into place by the Nazis within six months of their coming to power in 1933. From 1934 to 1945, nearly 350 000 men and women were sterilized under the law.

The Nazis carried their program of negative selection further by exterminating thousands of people who were considered unfit. Between 1939 and 1945,

Hitler Youth in Berchtesgaden, Bavaria, gather for Hitler's birthday on April 20, 1935.

The "Swing Kids"

The Hitler Youth movement receives much attention in studies regarding adolescents during the Third Reich. And yet, the more the Hitler Youth drew young people into its organization, and the more conformity to state-prescribed activities that was enforced, the more obvious the deviant behaviour among adolescents became. By the end of the 1930s, increasing numbers of teenagers were turning away from the organized activities of the Hitler Youth and finding their own unregimented style in independent gatherings. In 1942, the Reich Youth Leadership made the following observation: "The formation of cliques, i.e. groupings of young people outside the Hitler Youth, has been on the increase before and, particularly, during the war to such a degree that one must speak of a serious risk of the political, moral and criminal subversion of youth." One such group of teenagers was nicknamed the "swing kids."

The swing kids were teenagers from the German upper middle class. Although they rejected the Hitler Youth, they were not antifascist, they were simply indifferent. The actions and interests of these teenagers showed them to be apolitical—in other words, they supported no political factions. Rather, they sought their counter-identity in the "slovenly" cultures of Germany's wartime enemies, England and the United States. The swing kids, who could most often be found in bourgeois night clubs or in homes that were large enough to accommodate their dancing, came from families where there was enough money for them to be able to buy the latest jazz records or fashions from England and North America.

While they avoided traditional German music and culture, they eagerly embraced jazz and swing music, which was popular in England and America. An internal Hitler Youth report about a swing festival in Hamburg in February, 1940 provides a vivid description of both the actions of the swing kids and the reactions of the Third Reich to such "deviant" behaviour.

"The dance music was all English and American. Only swing dancing and jitterbugging took place. At the entrance to the hall stood a notice on which the words "Swing prohibited" had been altered to "Swing requested." Without exception, the participants accompanied the dances and songs by singing the English lyrics. Indeed, throughout the evening, they attempted to speak only English, and some times even French.

The dancers made an appalling sight. None of the couples danced normally; there was only swing of the worst sort. Sometimes two boys danced with one girl; sometimes several couples formed a circle, linking arms and jumping, slapping hands, even rubbing the backs of their heads together; and then, bent double, with the top half of the body hanging loosely down, long hair flopping into the face, they dragged themselves around practically on their knees. When the band played a rumba, the dancers went into wild ecstasy. They all leaped around and mumbled the chorus in English. The band played wilder and wilder numbers; none of the players was sitting any longer, they all "jitterbugged" on the stage like wild animals. Frequently, boys could be observed dancing together, without exception with two cigarettes in the mouth, one in each corner..."

The so-called deviant behaviour of the swing kids so bothered some leaders of the Third Reich that they urged the leaders to be placed in concentration camps for at least two years of beatings, punitive drills, and forced labour. Despite the concerns of the Nazi regime, teens throughout the reign of Adolf Hitler found ways to express themselves and to shape a counter-identity.

approximately 5000 children were murdered either by lethal injection or by malnutrition because they suffered severe handicaps. Between 30 000 and 50 000 people were murdered on the grounds of mental illness. In fact, the first gas chambers, later used to exterminate the Jews, were developed in six mental hospitals to handle the large number of mental patients who were to be killed.

Village Life

The tumultuous years of the Weimar Republic, 1918–1933, began to change the life of the traditional German village. Most homes, while remaining part of the traditional village economy, required a second income, often earned by one member of the family seeking employment in an office or factory. These households came to rely primarily on the money earned in the factory or office, yet continued to strive for self-sufficiency in food. Despite the obvious move towards an industrial economy, village life and status within the village continued to be centred around land ownership.

One of the most profound and obvious changes to village life brought about by the Nazi regime was that the political power structure within the village began to lose its paternalistic, land-based nature. Young people could no longer see a relevant connection in their lives to inheriting land (nor the wealth and power which formerly accompanied land ownership) and instead became attracted to Nazism. The older generation, meanwhile, remained skeptical of the Nazis' bravado, leading to conflict with most households. These divisions within the homes and villages deepened as the Third Reich increasingly insisted on loyalty to the Party and State above all else.

The Nazi state also came to replace the role of the nuclear family in rearing and training children. Schools became the ideal vehicle to promote racial propaganda, and to train young minds to be receptive to the militarism of the Third Reich. Over time, children were involved in paramilitary exercises and practising survival techniques rather than working on the land in the villages. There was little open hostility to the increasing role of the state in the lives of children or regulating village life. Most people had been indoctrinated with the belief that "everyone's welfare was at stake" and to show concern for individual needs was to be socially irresponsible.

Reflections

The years between 1918 and 1945 were trying times for families in both North America and Europe. The economic roller coaster that took people from the boom of the 1920s to the Great Depression first created a demand for consumer goods and then forced people to search for drastic solutions to survive. In Europe, the totalitarian regimes in Italy, Germany, and the Soviet Union attempted to make all aspects of life public, only to find the resilience of the family too great to destroy. Depression, warfare, and totalitarianism all posed great threat to the traditional family just as the Industrial Revolution in the previous century. And again, the family changed and adapted. Following World War II, further restructuring of the family would occur as society moved forward into a new age. Altered and perhaps a little shaken by the traumatic events of the first half of the twentieth century, the family would persevere to face new challenges and undergo further change.

Key Concepts, Figures, and Events

Roaring Twenties   Consumer Revolution   Great Depression   Totalitarianism   Eugenics

Topics for Further Thought

1. One of the major features of Western society between the wars was the growth of consumerism. Describe the factors that brought about the consumer revolution. What were the long-term consequences, both economically and socially, of the rise of consumerism?

2. In studying aspects of daily life, a discernible change in the twentieth century has been the increase in privacy enjoyed by all classes of society. Is the history of private life synonymous with the history of democratization? Does it reflect an increase in the standard of living for the general population? Explain your answer.

3. The lives of children today are significantly different from their counterparts' earlier in this century. Compare the lives of children in the first half of the twentieth century to the childhood you experienced. Do you believe tighter control over children produces more stability in society?

4. During the depression years of the 1930s, the family unit underwent significant change. Explain the factors responsible for bringing about this change. Was the family unit strengthened or weakened by these changes?

5. The ideologies of fascism and communism lie at opposite ends of the political spectrum. Despite ideological differences, the lives of the common people were strikingly similar under Stalin and Hitler. Compare and contrast life under a fascist and communist regime. How can you account for the ideological difference and yet similar situations in people's daily lives?

Topics for Further Research

1. This chapter has focused largely on daily life in North America, Britain, Germany, and the Soviet Union. Using the structure of this chapter as your guide, research daily life between the wars in one of the following countries:

France   Spain   Italy
Netherlands   Poland

2. The entertainment industry enjoyed considerable growth in the early twentieth century as part of the consumer revolution. Research one of the following types of entertainment, focusing on its origins and how it reflected the times:

Walt Disney Cartoon Films
Spectator Sports (Baseball, Football, Hockey, etc.)
Radio
Cinema

3. Women made significant strides during the first half of the twentieth century. Research one of the following topics (focusing on a specific country) related to the history of women in the Western world:

Women and the Third Reich
Women and Stalinism
Women in Cinema
Women in Politics
Women in the Workplace

Responding to Ideas

1. On the 25th anniversary of King George V's reign in England, British historian Sir Ernest Barker offered this reflection on the changes sweeping Western society in the twentieth century: "A gust of mechanical changes has produced a revolution in our material way of life... The pace of life has been quickened by the motor-car, the aeroplane, the telephone, the wireless [radio]." He then went on to surmise: "Perhaps some of the social and political movements of our time on the Continent of Europe are connected with the physical revolution through which we are going. They tend towards an idolization of the group—the race, the nation, the class. They use the new physical means of mass propaganda... to produce the temper and feeling of the group."

Do you agree or disagree with Barker's assessment of the impact of physical change on European society and politics? Explain your answer.

2. In *The Technological Society*, Jacques Ellul, a French sociologist, wrote: "Modern society is moving toward a mass society, but the human being is still not fully adapted to this new form. The purpose of human techniques is to defend man, and the first line of defense is that he be able to live.... Human techniques must therefore act to adapt man to the mass.... They must contribute to making man a mass man and help put an end to what has hitherto been considered the normal type of humanity." To what degree do you believe that the events in Europe between 1919 and 1939, including the changing nature of society, support or refute Ellul's hypothesis? Explain your answer.

CHAPTER 15

The Failure of Appeasement and World War II

CHAPTER HIGHLIGHTS

- Chamberlain's efforts to preserve peace
- Hitler's stunning victories over Western Europe
- The entry of the United States into the war and the Allied forces' reversal of fortune
- Diplomacy and the war effort
- The persecution of European Jews

A Tenuous Peace Shattered

When war returned to Europe in 1939, a mere two decades had passed since the "War to end all wars" had concluded. The peace established in 1919 by the Treaty of Versailles did little to restore prosperity and stability to Europe. In fact, so little had been accomplished by four years of war and the ensuing peace that some historians view World War II, not as a second world war, but as a continuation of a European civil war with global consequences. The punitive measures imposed on Germany by the Treaty of Versailles plunged the German people into a deep depression, causing them to look for radical solutions and scapegoats for their problems. Despite the severe restrictions imposed by the Treaty of Versailles, Hitler had managed to rejuvenate the German economy by building up the military of the Third Reich. By the time German tanks rumbled across the Polish border in September 1939, Hitler had amassed such strength as to be nearly unstoppable. Only after six years and over 40 million lives would the Allied forces be able to stop Nazi aggression and begin to rebuild a peace that had been so tenuous.

Appeasement in the Face of Aggression

Students studying the history of World War II often ask why Hitler was allowed to rearm despite the glaring violations of the Treaty of Versailles. In hindsight it is easy to be critical of the leaders of France and England for their failure to enforce the treaty early in the reign of Adolf Hitler. Yet, understanding historical causation is never quite so simple. To understand the roots of ***appeasement*** requires an understanding of both Hitler's actions and contemporary events in Britain, France, and the United States.

Appeasement is a term used to describe the type of diplomacy used in the 1930s between the Western

Women and children get ready to march through London
in an anti-war demonstration in 1931.

powers of Europe (those who signed the Treaty of Versailles) and the Third Reich. Simply stated, appeasement is an attempt to avoid conflict through compromise. By allowing some violations to the Treaty of Versailles, it was hoped Germany would be calmed and conflict could be avoided. It was through such diplomacy that Hitler was able to reintroduce conscription in 1935, while at the same time rapidly begin to rearm Germany. In the same year Hitler and Mussolini established an alliance of fascist states known as the Rome-Berlin Axis and a similar pact with expansionist Japan known as the Anti-Comintern Pact. In 1936, Hitler reoccupied the Rhineland (an area bordering France), which had been demilitarized under the Treaty of Versailles without considerable reaction from either Britain or France. Hitler proved to be a master of deception and a risk taker with an uncanny ability to read his opposition. By early 1938, he had concluded that his opposition was neither united nor prepared at that time to stand up against an aggressive Germany.

At a meeting of top military officials in November 1937, Hitler made it clear that he believed the increase in food production necessary to support the growing German population could not be achieved on the available arable land. Hence, Hitler concluded that "...the only remedy, and one which might appear to us visionary, lay in the acquisition of greater living space..." To

acquire greater living space, an idea referred to in German as *Lebensraum*, Hitler pointed out that "Germany's problem could only be solved by means of force and this was never without attendant risk." Throughout this meeting Hitler stressed the need to aggressively seize land no later than 1945. In making his case for the need for war in the near future Hitler argued, "while the rest of the world was still preparing its defences, we were obliged to take the offensive."

Correctly sensing that he would face little opposition, Hitler planned for the annexation of Austria and Czechoslovakia. In February 1938, Hitler met with Kurt von Schuschnigg, chancellor of Austria, at his private retreat in the Bavarian Alps. At this meeting Hitler demanded that Austrian Nazis be given better treatment and coerced von Schuschnigg to take Arthur Seyss-Inquart, an Austrian Nazi, into his cabinet. Shortly after their meeting, Austrian Nazis began to make demands for union with Germany prompting von Schuschnigg to call a national plebiscite. As a show of force and intimidation, Hitler delivered an ultimatum and amassed troops along the Austrian border. On March 11, 1938, von Schuschnigg resigned and was replaced as chancellor by Seyss-Inquart who promptly declared union with Germany. On March 14, the union complete, Hitler rode triumphantly through the streets of Vienna. During the month that followed violence was unleashed against Jews and all those who opposed the Nazis. When a plebiscite was held a short time later, 99.7 percent of Austrians gave their approval of the union with Germany. Britain and France, while lodging ineffective formal protests with the League of Nations, took no real actions against the now openly aggressive Germany.

Appeasement Policy Among the Western Powers

Why did the Western powers remain virtually silent while Hitler rearmed and openly prepared for war? Public opinion had much to do with the decisions made by the United States, Britain, and France. Immediately following the end of World War I, the United States had reverted to its isolationist policies of the prewar years. Events in Europe, it was argued, were of no concern to Americans. Leaders in Britain and France also sensed there was little support among the public for a war against Germany. Many believed that Germany had been treated unfairly by the Treaty of Versailles and that the Germans were justified in reclaiming former German lands. Also, it must be remembered that public opinion is usually a complex mix of ideas springing from a wide variety of experiences and prejudices. Some supported appeasement with Nazi Germany out of a fear of communism, while others held the belief that Germany as a fascist threat "could be killed by kindness." Many others supported appeasement for varying reasons, including a simple fear and abhorrence of war. To some degree support for the policy of appeasement in the 1930s was built on ignorance. The limited bits of information provided to the public by newspapers such as *The Times* of London about the injustices being committed in Germany were reported with incredible indifference. As a result of such reporting on Germany many people were led to believe that the Nazis desired only to regain self-respect for Germany and to redress grievances contained in the unjust Treaty of Versailles. Even Canada's prime minister, William Lyon Mackenzie King, recorded in his diary following a meeting with Hitler on June 29, 1937, the following sentiments: "I spoke then of what I had seen of the constructive work of his regime, and said that I hoped that work might continue. That nothing would be permitted to destroy that work. That it was bound to be followed in other countries to the great advantage of mankind." Obviously there was limited support for actions that might lead to bloody conflict with Germany. Instead, public opinion, while divided, seemed to favour appeasement.

Even in France, where hostility toward Germany was much higher, there was a reluctance to take actions that would prompt war. Instead, France adopted a defensive mentality in the 1930s, hoping to avert any future wars being fought on French soil. During the 1930s France committed virtually all of its defence budget to the building of the Maginot Line. The Maginot Line, which spanned the length of the France-German border, consisted of 23 artillery forts, 35 smaller infantry forts, 295 interval casemates and blockhouses, and numerous minor defences. These huge concrete structures were designed to withstand bombardment by guns such as the giant Krupp 420 mm and were heavily armed to guard against German attack. While the Maginot Line would have been an effective defence against advancing troops in 1918, it would prove futile against the German *Blitzkrieg* that Hitler would unleash against France. With the vast majority of the defence budget committed to the Maginot Line, the French had left themselves

The power of the Nazi army is displayed at the Nuremberg Rally of 1936.

vulnerable should a German attack get behind the line. With a defensive mentality France had little desire to take action against Germany for injustices occurring within its own borders. Besides, the Treaty of Westphalia in 1648 had established the legal rights for nation-states to do as they please with their own citizens. Many were unwilling to stand against Germany so long as the injustices were committed within the boundaries of German lands. For this very reason, the Western powers stood idle while civil war in Spain pitted fascism against democracy.

The Spanish Civil War: 1936–1939

By 1936 the young Spanish Republic, at the time only five years old, was in jeopardy. The democratically elected Popular Front Government had failed to live up to its promises and many people in Spain, especially in the countryside were growing restless. In 1936, General Francisco Franco led a coup d'état. Rather than topple the government the fascist forces under Franco initially met stiff resistance from the government. The result was a three year civil war in Spain. Spain was a microcosm of Europe in the 1930s and the

Spanish Civil War should have forewarned the Western world of the impending crisis. Instead, the Western powers chose to remain on the sidelines, despite the support in soldiers and air force units Franco received from Hitler and Mussolini. Only the Soviet Union sent aid to the Popular Front to assist in their struggle against fascism. Many British, Canadian, American, and even anti-Nazi Germans fought against Franco on a volunteer basis. Lacking the support of their governments, these men fought out of idealism and formed the famous International Brigades against fascism. To many, the Spanish Civil War was the "Last Great Cause." However, the governments of countries that would face the fascists on the battlefields of Europe only a few years later would not assist in democracy's struggle in Spain.

The significance of the Spanish Civil War goes beyond it being a clash of ideologies; Spain became the testing ground for Nazi weaponry and tactics that would later be used with tremendous success against other European nations. In the Basque city of Guernica, on Spain's north shore, the German Luftwaffe (air force) introduced the world to total war. On April 26, 1937, Guernica became the target of the Luftwaffe's first strategic bombing. The world was shocked by this bombing not only because of the carnage, but because Guernica was an undefended civilian city with no strategic importance. Despite atrocities, such as Guernica, and the support the fascists received from Germany and Italy, both Britain and France avoided being drawn into a conflict, still convinced the policies of appeasement could maintain peace.

The Munich Agreement

The policy of appeasement, pursued in Britain throughout the 1930s, reached its climax with the signing of the *Munich Agreement* on September 29, 1938. In the days immediately following, British prime minister, *Neville Chamberlain*, who was a strong supporter of the appeasement policy and an architect of the Munich Agreement, was widely applauded as a man of fortitude and diplomatic skill for his dedication to securing peace. The gratitude and praise heaped upon Chamberlain was short-lived. In less than a year after Munich, Europe was once again plunged into war; Chamberlain's negotiations with Adolf Hitler appeared naive and short-sighted.

Czechoslovakia, considered to be the most viable democratic state in Central Europe, was an ethnically diverse nation. A large population of German-speaking Czechs lived in an area known as the Sudetenland, which bordered Germany. In March 1938, Hitler demanded a solution to the problem of ethnic Germans in Czechoslovakia, raising the spectre of a possible German aggression. When asked by France, which had a formal treaty with Czechoslovakia, to guard against foreign aggression, Chamberlain made it clear that Britain would not go to war in defence of a far-off land. Instead, Czechoslovakians and their leader Edvard Beneš were expected to agree to Hitler's demands.

When Hitler met with Chamberlain on September 15, 1938, he made it clear that he was prepared to risk war over the issue of the Sudeten Germans, but that this would be the "last major problem to be solved." Convinced that an agreement to sign over the Sudetenland to Germany was the only way to ensure peace, Chamberlain, with the support of the French prime minister Eduoard Daladier, managed to persuade the Czech prime minister to hand over the territory in return for some compensation and an international guarantee of Czechoslovakia's defences. When Hitler increased his demands a week later, by insisting that Czechoslovakia sign over the territory by October 10 and agree to Polish and Hungarian demands on Czech territory, Chamberlain was shocked and dismayed. These new demands essentially amounted to the dismantling of Czechoslovakia. Rather than attempt to extract further concessions from the Czechs, Chamberlain and Daladier decided to leave Beneš out of any further negotiations arising from Hitler's new demands. In an attempt to resolve the crisis without conflict, Chamberlain and Daladier with the support of United States president Franklin Roosevelt requested that Hitler attend a final conference.

At the resulting Munich Conference on September 29, 1938, Chamberlain, Daladier, Mussolini, and Hitler formally agreed to transfer the Sudetenland to Germany by October 10 and to deal with Polish and Hungarian claims at a later date. Czechoslovakian prime minister Beneš, who was not invited to the conference, was left with the option of accepting the agreement or fighting the Germans alone. He chose to sign the agreement and shortly thereafter resigned a crushed man. Chamberlain, desperate to put a positive face on the Munich Conference, issued a joint declaration with Hitler, guaranteeing that Britain and Germany would never "go to war with one another again." This declaration allowed Chamberlain to return home jubilant, declaring "I believe it is peace in our time."

Any relief from impending war felt as a result of the Munich Conference was short-lived. Less than a month later, following the assassination of a Nazi diplomat in Paris by a Polish Jew, Hitler unleashed a reign of terror against German Jews. Known as *Krystallnacht* (crystal glass) or "the night of broken glass," November 9, 1938, is forever etched in history as the night Nazi thugs plundered Jewish homes and stores. Synagogues were burned and thousands of Jewish people were brutally beaten, shot, or dragged off to concentration camps. By the time the terror was over hundreds were dead or injured and thousands imprisoned. A few months later, on March 16, 1939, the Third Reich swallowed up what was left of Czechoslovakia by announcing the German Protectorate of Bohemia and Moravia. There was no longer any doubt in Britain and France that war with Germany was imminent.

Nazi-Soviet Non-Aggression Pact: The Death of Ideologies or Machiavellian Diplomacy?

With the conclusion of World War I came the dismemberment of the Hapsburg Empire and the creation of several new nations such as Yugoslavia, Latvia, and Poland. Poland's rebirth as a nation in the early twentieth century came at the expense of both Russian and German territory and consequently Poland found itself in 1939 caught between two disgruntled nations. Shortly after swallowing Czechoslovakia, Hitler turned his attention to Poland to right a wrong that he believed was committed against Germany in the Treaty of Versailles. During the spring of 1939, Hitler brought much pressure to bear on the Polish government demanding territorial concessions that the Poles repeatedly rejected. Having been stung by Hitler's lack of integrity, both Britain and France had by now abandoned appeasement and were guaranteeing Polish borders.

By the summer of 1939 it appeared the outbreak of war was merely a matter of time. Poland's poorly equipped army of about 1 million soldiers would be no match for the efficient and modern German army, leaving any hope of resistance dependent on help from Britain and France. Germany, meanwhile, hoped to avoid a two-front war such as World War I facing pressure in the west from Britain and France and from the

Soviet Union in the East. In a move that stunned the Western world, Germany signed a non-aggression pact with its enemy, the Soviet Union, on August 23, 1939. The Nazi-Soviet Non-Aggression Pact laid the basis for a division of Poland following a joint Nazi-Soviet invasion. As well, it gave the Soviet Union a free hand in Finland, Estonia, Latvia, and Lithuania in return for Stalin's assurance he would not oppose Germany's aggression in Western Europe.

Why would avowed enemies agree to assist each other? Did this agreement spell the end of ideological beliefs given that fascists and communists were now working together? In fact, an argument can be made to show that the Nazi-Soviet Pact, although Machiavellian in nature, was consistent with both the ideologies of the right and the left. Hitler's ultimate goal was to conquer Europe. Fighting a two-front war would lessen his chance for success. By negotiating a pact with Stalin, Hitler could turn his attention to Western Europe, then throw the might of the German army, combined with the resources of the conquered nations. against the Soviet Union. Stalin, meanwhile, may have seen the pact as an opportunity to prepare for communism's ultimate spread worldwide. By avoiding conflict with Germany, Stalin not only bought more time to build up the Soviet Union's military strength, but he also pitted the Nazis against the capitalist West. After years of war the West would be exhausted and the way would be paved for the spread of communism throughout Western Europe. Perhaps the Nazi-Soviet Pact was a strategic move that served the needs of both the fascists and the communists despite their mutual hatred.

Regardless of the rationale used by Stalin and Hitler, the pact left Western Europe reeling. There was no longer any option but to support Poland against Nazi aggression. When the German army rolled across the Polish border in the early hours of September 1, 1939, Chamberlain briefly wavered in his support for the Poles. Facing near rebellion in the House of Commons, the British government sent Germany an ultimatum that expired at 9:00 a.m. on September 3. Receiving no reply, Britain declared war on Germany the same day. They were joined by France, Australia, New Zealand, and, on September 6, South Africa. Canada would declare war seven days later after a brief debate in the House of Commons and a nearly unanimous vote. One member who voted against Canada's declaration of war was J.S. Woodsworth, the pacifist

The Invasion of Northern and Central Europe, 1939–1940

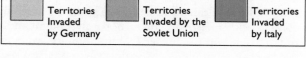

Territories Invaded by Germany	Territories Invaded by the Soviet Union	Territories Invaded by Italy

leader of the C.C.F. His opposition to the war would cost him the leadership of his party. Despite declared support by these countries, Poland quickly fell and was carved up by the Soviets and the Nazis. It would be another six months before war would reach Western Europe.

The Outbreak of World War II

The Fall of Poland

The world was stunned by the Nazi invasion of Poland not so much for the aggression as for the speed with which Hitler's armies were able to secure victory. Trench warfare, in World War I, resulted in agonizingly slow movements of troops; while few believed Poland could win a war against Germany, no one could have anticipated the invasion lasting fewer than four weeks. Utilizing a new kind of mechanized warfare called *Blitzkrieg* (lightning warfare) the German military had quickly destroyed Poland's small and largely obsolete air force and rolled over their ill-equipped

army. *Blitzkrieg* is a co-ordinated attack using *Panzer* (armoured tank) divisions supported by ground troops and an umbrella of air support. By using fighter-bombers such as Stukas and Heinkel planes, the German Luftwaffe was able to create chaos on the ground. Targeting civilians, the psychological effects of "terror bombing" were to implant defeatism into the general population and to ensure disarray among the opposing armies as they attempted to defend against advancing land troops while being bombed from above. The essential key to the success of *Blitzkrieg* was that the attack be lightning-quick and that the enemies' weak points be exploited. Surrender needed to come early or the advantage gained by catching the enemy off guard would be lost. The early and stunning success of *Blitzkrieg* was, in part, due to the lack of preparedness of its victims. It would take nearly three years for the Allied forces to come to grips with the new type of warfare and prepare successful defences against it.

On September 25, the Soviets and Nazis signed an agreement that divided the spoils of war by dismantling the Polish state. Hitler immediately began eliminating Polish intellectuals and any others who might oppose Nazi control and started the process of turning Poland into a worker state focused on supplying the needs of the Third Reich.

The Phony War

Despite declaring war in September 1939, neither the British nor the French would be actively involved in the war until the spring of 1940. They immediately began their preparations for war, including rationing and moving children to the countryside to be safe from possible aerial raids; however, the absence of active fighting earned the period between the fall of 1939 and the spring of 1940 the name the "*phony war*."

The term phony war is somewhat misleading as it applies only to Western Europe. Throughout the winter of 1939–1940 both Germany and the Soviet Union continued to aggressively seize more territory. After a failed attempt at bullying Finland into allowing naval-basing rights and surrendering a strip of land along the Finnish-Soviet border near Leningrad, Stalin had a border incident staged giving him the pretence to order an invasion. Despite committing a million troops to the invasion of Finland, the Soviet army faced stiff resistance and numerous setbacks at the hands of the 175 000 skilled and determined Finnish soldiers. By the spring of 1940, Finland could no longer hold out and agreed on March 12 to a peace treaty, accepting the demands made earlier. By the fall of 1940 the Baltic states of Estonia, Latvia, and Lithuania would also be swallowed by the Soviet Union.

During the winter of 1939–1940, Germany also prepared for further invasions. Ironically, April 9, 1940, the day of Germany's planned full-scale invasion of Denmark and Norway was also the day planned by the British and French to tighten a blockade around Germany by seizing the Norwegian port of Narvik and laying mines in the Norwegian channels that separated the offshore islands from the mainland. The outcome of the ensuing conflict was that Denmark fell in one day, and Norway, despite a determined effort from its army, was defeated by early May, though not before members of the government and the royal family had escaped to Britain. Hitler established a puppet government headed by the Norwegian Nazi leader Vidkun Quisling, whose name has become synonymous with treason and treachery. The victory over Norway was not without its costs to Germany. The loss of a heavy cruiser, two light cruisers, and ten destroyers shifted the naval balance in favour of the Allies.

The defeat of Norway would also have political consequences, prompting the resignation of British prime minister Neville Chamberlain. Seen by the public and his own Conservative party as indecisive, Chamberlain would hand over the reigns of power to Winston Churchill on May 10, 1940. Churchill had long been an ardent opponent of the policy of appeasement. He would now emerge as one of the greatest wartime leaders in British history and one of the dominant figures of the twentieth century. At the same time Churchill was forming a new national government comprised of members of the Conservative, Liberal, and Labour parties, Hitler had turned his armies to the Netherlands. By May 15, the German *Blitzkrieg* had smashed the Netherlands and Belgium and was poised to invade France. Western Europe was facing its darkest hour.

The Fall of France

The collapse of the French army came with surprising speed. By June 1940, France had fallen to the Nazis and the Allied armies had been pushed to the English Channel. Few people expected the Germans to win so quickly. In the aftermath of the war many historians have tried to determine the causes behind the stunning Nazi victory over the apparently ill-prepared Allied forces.

After quickly demolishing the Polish army, German troops wander through what remains of a small town.

The long, hard winter of 1939–1940 and the drawn out period of the Phony War, during which soldiers waited in anticipation, appear to have created boredom among the French troops, resulting in low morale. Evidence could be seen in the failure of men to salute officers, men abandoning their posts, widespread pillaging of evacuated areas, alcoholism, and a general lack of discipline. Indeed, this malaise seems to have permeated French society. Many French citizens believed it was their government's duty to avoid war. French communists also played a role in denying the French government the full support of the people. By opposing the war on the grounds that it was an imperialist war, serving only the needs of the bourgeoisie, the communists were able to undercut government efforts to arouse support for the war. The lack of conviction extended even to the leaders of the French nation, resulting in confusion. It appears that much of the French leadership wanted to pick up where they had left off in 1918, relying heavily on the Maginot Line, rather than adapting to the new realities of war.

An accurate understanding of the forces that led to the collapse of France in 1940 requires an examination of the German army. Robert Wernick, in his book *Blitzkrieg* suggests that the German troops who crossed the Meuse River in 1940, at the onset of the invasion of France, did so "in an atmosphere of almost carefree enthusiasm" and that German soldiers were reported to have jokingly said to their officers, "Pleasure-boating on the Meuse is forbidden." It would appear that in assessing the factors that led to the fall of France some weight must be attached to the positive frame of mind of the German troops.

While there is little doubt that the French entered the war a divided nation and that some of the soldiers lacked the determination to withstand the German onslaught, close examination of some of the key battles reveals that the French army initially fought with great persistence. Thus in some cases, it is possible to suggest that the collapse of French determination was the result of a highly successful German attack rather than German victory being the result of low French morale.

In the end, it would appear that several factors contributed to Germany's stunning victory over France in May 1940. The effectiveness of the German attack, the greater familiarity of the Germans with the new style of warfare, and the lack of committed Allied support seem to have contributed to the decline in French morale and the ultimate defeat of France. Poor leadership from both the French government and French generals as well as inadequate preparation further contributed to the lack of resolve displayed by the French soldiers. Many other factors including effective German propaganda and a defensive mentality created by the Maginot Line also contributed to the collapse of the French army in the face of the German attack.

The French were forced to sign the terms of the surrender in the same railway coach in which German delegates signed the armistice in 1918. France was humiliated in defeat. All of northern France would be occupied by the Germans, while a small part of the south was left in the hands of Marshall Pétain. This area came to be known as Vichy France, after the small spa town that became its capital. Pétain would blame the collapse of France, in part, on the moral decay brought about by democracy.

By June 1940, Hitler and his fascist allies controlled all of Western Europe, while the Soviet Union reigned supreme in Eastern Europe. Until the entry of the United States into the war in December 1941, Britain and the Commonwealth countries stood alone in the west valiantly attempting to withstand the fascist tide.

The Miracle of Dunkirk

Sensing the inevitability of defeat in France, the British government began planning the evacuation of the British Expeditionary Force (BEF). Admiral Bertram Ramsey and his chief of staff, Captain Day, would be responsible for the evacuation of the BEF and Operation Dynamo, the code name given to the plan. The most optimistic estimates suggested that no more than 45 000 troops could be expected to be saved from the French coast. In the end, 338 226 were plucked from the beaches of Dunkirk by an array of boats ranging from destroyers to sightseeing boats, fishing vessels, and pleasure craft. The outstanding success of the evacuation earned Operation Dynamo the more familiar nickname of the *Miracle of Dunkirk.*

There seems to be at least three explanations for this surprising turn of events. The ever dangerous Luftwaffe, which was to have prevented any evacuation from Dunkirk, seems to have been hampered by a heavy fog, which covered the English Channel, and by the efforts of Britain's Royal Air Force (RAF). At the same time, the often difficult English Channel was relatively calm, allowing for the incredible success of the vast array of boats in carrying out their rescue mission. Finally, a surprise "stop order" given by the German commander of Army Group A, Marshal Karl von Rundstedt, and supported by Hitler, to the *Panzers* on May 23, gave the British the opportunity to reach safety behind the Canal Line. Although Hitler was correct to fear the *Panzers* getting bogged down in the canals and rivers around Dunkirk, the result of his stop order, which was revoked two days later, was to allow the part of the British army that Germany needed to destroy, to escape to safety. This decision would return to haunt Hitler and the German

British prime minister Winston Churchill symbolizes England's heroic struggle against fascism.

army later in the war. These factors allowed for the success of perhaps the greatest military evacuation in history and gave the Allied forces a morale boost after a disastrous campaign.

Winston Churchill seized on the success of Operation Dynamo to provide inspiration and incentive to the remaining Allied forces. As Operation Dynamo drew to a close, Churchill declared to the House of Commons: "We shall go on to the end. We shall fight in France, we shall fight in the seas and oceans, we shall fight with growing confidence and growing strength in the air; we shall defend our Island whatever the cost may be."

The Battle of Britain

Hitler's last remaining enemy in the west was the island of Great Britain. It would appear that Hitler hoped to work co-operatively with the British rather than humiliate them as he had the French. Following the Dunkirk evacuation, Germany waited nearly a month for the British to sue for peace. In fact, until May 1940, Hitler had never contemplated an invasion of Britain, and when he did so it was with some misgivings. Even when the order to plan for an invasion of Britain was issued on July 2 and the preliminary directive was signed on July 16, Hitler still held out hope that an air assault backed by the threat of a full-scale invasion might be enough to prompt the overthrow of the Churchill government by a peace party. A month after the Battle of Britain had begun, Hitler continued to cling to the illusion that the Third Reich could co-exist and co-operate with the British empire. Confiding in Vidkun Quisling, Hitler mused "after making one proposal after another to the British on the reorganization of Europe, I now find myself forced against my will to fight this war against Britain." Perhaps this lack of commitment to the invasion of England was partially responsible for the German's bungled efforts in carrying out Operation Sea Lion, the code name for the invasion of England.

The key to success for Operation Sea Lion would be gaining command of the skies. Without the Luftwaffe in control, Germany could not launch an invasion of Britain with any hopes of success. In this regard the Battle of Britain would mark a revolutionary turning point in the history of warfare. Unlike the Battle of France, which, despite the stunning success of *Blitzkrieg*, was essentially a conventional military operation, the Battle of Britain marked the first time

aircraft were to be used as the primary instrument to destroy the enemy's will and capacity to resist. When Hitler issued Führer Directive (No. 16) on "Preparations for a landing operation against England" officials within the Luftwaffe were alarmed at the scope of the task set out before them. The Luftwaffe was to establish the preconditions for victory before the army or navy were ever involved. By early August German naval authorities were claiming that Göring was not directing air attacks with the aim of facilitating an invasion but rather was fighting a total war in the air.

Britain's successful defence against Operation Sea Lion was largely the result of the resilience of the British people and the heroic defence provided by the RAF. In the final days of the Battle of France, Churchill had wanted to send six squadrons to France. He was opposed by the commander–in–chief of Fighter Command for the RAF Sir Hugh Dowding. Dowding correctly guessed that the RAF would be essential to Britain's defence and argued that committing the six squadrons to France would be merely a vain attempt to help an ally. Eventually, the British Cabinet agreed with Dowding, which has been described as one of the best strategic decisions of history.

When the Battle of Britain began on July 10, 1940, Britain held a few important advantages. Whereas the German Luftwaffe used airfields they had recently captured and quickly adapted for their use, the British squadrons were operating from home bases they had occupied for some time. Furthermore, being on the defensive, British pilots who were forced to crash-land or bale out of damaged aircraft did so over friendly soil, while German pilots were taken prisoner or drowned in the English Channel. Although the German planes outnumbered British planes 930 to 650 when the battle began, the British overcame this problem under the brilliant leadership of Canadian-born Lord Beaverbrook. By July 1940, Beaverbrook, the minister of Aircraft Production, had geared up factories to produce 500 Spitfires and Hurricanes a month as compared with only 140 Me 109s and 90 Me 110s produced by the German factories. Lastly, the British had developed a radar system that enabled them to read coded messages sent by the Germans, thereby revealing their moves in advance. This radar system was crucial not only in the defence of Britain but in the final outcome of the war.

The first phase of the Battle of Britain, beginning July 10, was known as *Kanalkampf* (Channel Battle).

Atlantic
Ocean

United
Kingdom

• London

Le Havre •

• Nantes

Portugal

Spain

• Madrid

France

• Vichy

Marseille •

Netherlands

Amsterdam •

Brussels •
Belgium

• Paris

Switz.

Denmark

• Copenhagen

• Hamburg

Berlin •

Greater
Germany

Frankfurt •

Luxembourg

Prague •

Vienna •

Genova •

Italy

• Rome

Naples •

Palermo •

Sicily

Stockholm

St. Petersburg

Soviet
Union

• Kiev

Slovakia

• Bratislava

• Budapest

Hungary

Rumania

Bucharest •

Belgrade •

Yugoslavia

Bulgaria

• Sofia

Istanbul

Albania

Greece

Turkey

French West Africa

Libya

Mediterranean Sea

Egypt

Territories Invaded by Germany

Territories Invaded by Italy

The Invasion of the Mediterranean Region, 1940

This phase focused on the English towns of Plymouth, Weymouth, Falmouth, Portsmouth, and Dover as well as on convoys when they were intercepted. Hitler became impatient with the apparent aerial stalemate that had developed and ordered a change in strategy. Based on the assumption that the British were already defeated but refused to admit it, Hitler issued Führer Directive No. 17, which ordered the Luftwaffe to "overpower the English air force with all the forces at its command in the shortest possible time." This phase of the battle, known as Operation Eagle, began on August 13, 1940, and focused on the airfields of Britain in an effort to knock out the RAF. Any success of the Luftwaffe came at a high price but by early September the Luftwaffe had begun to win the upper hand. Apparently the victory was too slow in coming for both Hitler and the commander of the German Luftwaffe Hermann Göring.

It is widely believed that the bombing of London began accidentally when a German bomber squadron lost its way. In fact, the bombing of London, like the bombing of Guernica before it, was a calculated decision on the part of the Nazis designed to break the will of the people. Fearing that the opportunity for a land invasion may be lost to autumn winds, the focus of the Luftwaffe's efforts shifted from the airfields of Britain to London on September 7, 1940. An order dated August 24, 1940, stated: "Attacks against the London area and terror attacks are reserved for the Führer's decision." Hitler delayed giving this order still hoping to get Churchill to the negotiating table and trying to avert retaliation against German cities. Finally, in early September, Hitler could wait no longer. The order was given to bomb London and the Battle of Britain entered a new phase.

Hitler's decision to shift the Luftwaffe to the densely populated area in and around London took the pressure off the airfields. Although over 30 000 Londoners would die during the Blitz, the courage of the British people remained steadfast. Rather than breaking the will of the people, Hitler's attack on London strengthened their resolve and allowed the RAF to rebuild. Furthermore, in retaliation, Churchill ordered the bombing of Berlin, leading to the first civilian deaths in Germany as a result of enemy bombing.

On September 17, 1940, Hitler announced the postponement of Operation Sea Lion until further notice. Assuming Britain was already defeated Hitler turned his interests eastward. This did not mean the end of bombing raids on Britain by the Luftwaffe, as Hitler wanted to keep the pressure on Churchill. These raids would continue, with nighttime raids becoming the norm by October. However, there is no doubt the resilience of the British people and the heroics of the British pilots had handed the Nazis their first defeat. The full impact of that defeat would not be realized immediately, but without doubt the survival of an independent Britain was the event that brought about the collapse of Nazi Germany.

The Tripartite Pact

With Western Europe defeated, and believing that Britain was all but defeated, Hitler realized that only the United States, should they choose to enter the war, could offer serious opposition to his aggression. Meanwhile, Japan was continuing its aggressive moves in the Pacific and shared a similar concern about American opposition. In an effort to guard against such future challenges, the fascist states of Germany and Italy along with Japan signed a Tripartite Pact in September 1940, guaranteeing support from each country in the event of an attack from any new enemy. To the small countries of Eastern Europe, Soviet aggression posed a greater threat than the expansion of the German empire. Consequently, Romania, Hungary, and Slovakia all sought and were granted admission to the Tripartite Pact by November 1940.

The first concrete evidence of the Tripartite Pact came in October 1940, when Mussolini's forces invaded Greece. Unlike Hitler's peaceful takeover of the rest of Eastern Europe, the Italian campaign was a disaster, requiring help from Germany to subdue the defiant Greek forces. When Britain sent ground troops and aircraft to aid the Greeks, Hitler feared the crucial oil production in Romania could be cut off by Allied support in the Balkans. To ensure the Third Reich was not denied the critical flow of oil, Hitler ordered the invasion of Yugoslavia enroute to lend support to the Italians in the Greek campaign. Although the Germans were ultimately successful at driving out the British and occupying both Greece and Yugoslavia, Hitler's armies were never able to put down the resistance movements in the Balkans. For the duration of the war the Balkans witnessed a bitter guerrilla war, which tied down 500 000 of Germany's best soldiers, committing Hitler to the Mediterranean theatre of war he had not contemplated. These troops would be sorely missed by the Third Reich for the duration of the war.

Operation Barbarossa

Regardless of the Nazi-Soviet Pact signed in 1939, Hitler's grand design had always included the conquest of the Soviet Union. Discussions in *Mein Kampf* regarding *Lebensraum* (living space) clearly indicate Hitler's belief that the Third Reich would eventually control large tracts of land in Eastern Europe as far as the Ural Mountains where it was fabled there was untold wealth on the farms and in the mines. With the fall of France Hitler believed the war in the west to be over. Assuming Britain always preferred to have others fight for them, he could not understand why the British fought on after the defeat of France. Hitler rationalized Britain's resolve to continue fighting by believing the British continued to expect support to come from elsewhere, most likely the United States or the Soviet Union. Consequently, *Operation Barbarossa*, the code name given to the Nazi invasion of the Soviet Union, was to be a strategic move, which would fulfil Hitler's vision of *Lebensraum*; strike a blow at his most hated rivals, the communists; and deny the British support from the Soviets, thereby convincing them to follow France's lead and agree to peace terms with Germany. Furthermore, by launching a massive invasion of the Soviet Union, Stalin would need to deploy his military strength in Europe, giving Japan a freer hand to expand in the Pacific. Japanese aggression in the Pacific would ensure the United States would be preoccupied and therefore less likely to become involved in a European war.

The German attack on the Soviet Union was also prompted by racist fervour, which would make Operation Barbarossa like no other military action in modern history. Barbarossa was more than just a war between states. From the outset it was "total war" with the aim of exterminating "undesirables" such as commissars, communists, Jews, and those people with Mongoloid features. Many were to be killed on the spot, others would face mass execution, while still others would be resettled. Hitler's intent was not just to defeat the Soviet state but to annihilate large parts of the Soviet population. This was not to be a war fought according to accepted rules of modern warfare. Rather, Hitler planned to ignore accepted conventions of war, changing in the process the nature, purpose, and outcome of wars between states. As the war became a total war, involving civilians as well as the military, the nature of modern warfare also changed. The Soviets would follow the Nazi lead, imitating their savage cruelty. As well partisans (resistance forces) came to play a prominent role in the outcome of the war. For the first time since the Treaty of Westphalia in 1648, war involved interest groups that fought in their own defence rather than leaving the fighting up to the state. What first began in World War II as total war waged by the Nazis on their victims has continued to be a common feature of the postwar world. Operation Barbarossa would mark the high point of interest warfare and be the beginning of the end for this kind of warfare. It would also mark the beginning of warfare that involved governments, armies, and partisan organizations seizing the state's exclusive right to wage war or use violence to achieve their objectives.

Planning for the invasion of Russia had been under way as early as 1934 when Germany had begun photographing the Soviet Union. By 1940 the Luftwaffe was gathering photographs two or three times a day. These photos provided the Germans with vital information for target bombing, about factories, and about defensive works. Despite relatively widespread intelligence gathering, racist preconceptions prevented the Nazis from asking the key question, Can we win a war against the Soviet Union? The German belief in Slavic inferiority superseded the intelligence gathered and therefore inadequate preparations were made for the invasion. In short, German racism prevented effective use of the information gathered, ultimately resulting in the failure of Operation Barbarossa.

The scale of Operation Barbarossa was overwhelming. On June 22, 1941, armies of 3 million troops on either side, with air and naval support, spanned the length of the German-Russian border, covering half of Europe. Hitler had expected the Russian campaign to last no longer than six weeks and had not considered the consequences of the first strike not defeating the Red Army and toppling the Soviet government of Joseph Stalin. Given the success of the German army in rolling over Western Europe and the initial success in Eastern Europe, these expectations were not unreasonable, although several of Hitler's top advisors urged a continued focus on England, fearing an attack on the Soviet Union at this point would expose Germany to a two-front war.

Initially, the success enjoyed by the German army in Western Europe seemed to be duplicated in the east. During the summer and fall campaigns, Germany opened gaping holes in the Soviet defences sending the apparently ill-prepared Red Army reeling backward. The critical first-strike success of *Blitzkrieg*, however, eluded Hitler as the Soviet army was able to retreat over the vast expanse of Russia. In retreating, the Red Army followed a strategy that had been used in Russia for centuries, the "scorched earth" policy. The practice of destroying everything of any value while pulling back would prove particularly effective against the German *Blitzkrieg*. The success of *Blitzkrieg* relied on immediate collapse of the enemy, making victory less likely as time dragged on. The strategy of *Blitzkrieg*, well suited to the more compact Western Europe, was wrought with difficulties in the vast expanse of the Soviet Union. The further the German army pursued the retreating Red Army the more difficult it became to supply the army service the *Panzer* divisions.

In late August 1941, Hitler made what many historians agree to be a critical mistake. The drive toward Moscow was to be halted while the German army headed south. Hitler explained his decision to his commanders by emphasizing the economic aspects of war and the need to capture the Soviet Union's crucial economic zone from Kiev to Kharkov. The Germans would be highly successful in their drive south, destroying five Soviet armies and 50 divisions; but the attack on Moscow now faced a critical delay.

Despite the difficulties faced by the German army, by December 1941, they had made considerable progress. They had advanced beyond the Sea of Azov in the south, surrounded the city of Leningrad in the north, and had reached the western suburbs of Moscow. As well, nearly 3 million Soviet soldiers had been captured, of which half a million would die from lack of food or shelter in the first three months of winter. Victory still seemed possible, but it would not be the easy campaign Hitler had imagined. German arrogance had led them to make no preparations for a winter campaign. Delayed by the diversion south, the German army that reached the suburbs of Moscow by early December was greeted by the icy grips of an early winter. Without proper clothing and no cold-weather grease for the *Panzers* the German army ground to a halt. Emerging from the Kremlin after a month in seclusion, Stalin ordered the transfer of six Siberian divisions from Asia to head a massive counterattack. Led by General Georgy Zhukov, the Soviets were able to stop the Nazi advance, winning a great psychological victory and handing Germany their first major setback of the war. The tide was about to turn.

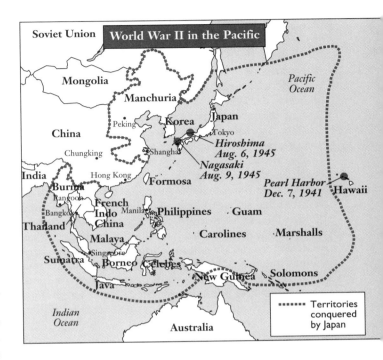

War in the Pacific: The Bombing of Pearl Harbor

Japan's entry into World War II has often been misinterpreted as fascist aggression. Although allied with both Italy and Germany, neither Emperor Hirohito nor the minister of War, General Hideki Tojo, was fascist or pro-Nazi. The Japanese, while strongly anticommunist, were not racist and had no plans to exterminate the Chinese or any other enemies. They were, however, avowedly anti-Western and determined to defeat Western nations and establish a Japanese sphere of influence in the Pacific. Japan's decision to join the Tripartite Pact was for purely practical reasons. An alliance with the Axis powers in Europe worked to Japan's advantage as the dominant Western powers in the Pacific were the French, the British, and the United States.

The defeat of France in 1940, coupled with captured British war cabinet reports passed along by the Germans indicated that the British could neither oppose the Japanese in Indo-China nor send a fleet to the Far East. This gave Japan the opportunity to secure Southeast Asia and with it the resources necessary to maintain itself as a great power. By 1941, however, Japan's occupation of Indo-China had prompted the

United States to impose a trade ban between the two nations. Furthermore, the *Two Ocean Naval Expansion Act*, passed by the United States Congress in July 1940, served notice to the world that the Americans intended to build a fleet that would rival any of the world's naval powers. By 1944, the United States navy would out-match the Japanese navy by a ratio of 3:10. According to Japanese calculations, a minimum ratio of 5:10 was necessary for them to fight a successful defensive cam-paign in the western Pacific. Tojo, as minister of War, harboured no illusions that the Japanese could defeat the United States in a full-scale war, but if war with the United States was to be inevitable for Japan to achieve its national objectives, it would need to happen soon.

The Japanese realized that their best hope for suc-cess was to quickly conquer Southeast Asia and there-after establish a defensive perimeter around their gains on which they would fight the Americans to a stand-still. By striking at the United States naval base in Pearl Harbor, Hawaii, it was hoped enough damage could be inflicted on the American navy to discourage the United States from continuing a costly war.

Japan's surprise attack on Pearl Harbor came early on a Sunday morning, December 7, 1941. It lasted only a little more than two hours but succeeded in inflicting heavy losses to the American navy. Of the eight battle-ships in the harbour four were sunk and four severely damaged. As well 10 other warships were sunk or destroyed; 188 were planes destroyed and a further 159 were damaged; 2403 American citizens were killed and 1178 were wounded. To the disappointment of the Japanese, none of the American aircraft carriers were at Pear Harbor. This prompted the architect of the sur-prise attack, Japanese commander, Admiral Isoroku Yamamoto to remark: "We have succeeded only in awakening a sleeping bear." The war, which had begun as a European conflict, now took on global proportions. Britain, in support of the United States declared war against Japan, while Italy and Germany, honouring the Tripartite Pact, declared war against the United States.

The Dieppe Raid

One of the most con-troversial military deci-sions of World War II was the ill-fated raid on the small French town of Dieppe situated on the northwest coast of France. After weeks of delay, the assault was finally launched in the early morning hours of August 19, 1942. After nine hours of fierce fighting, the Battle of Dieppe ended in disaster. It was to be the bloodiest nine hours in Canadian military history. Of the 6086 troops sent to Dieppe, nearly 5000 were Canadian. Of these over 900 were killed, 500 were wounded, and 1874 were taken prisoner. As well the Allies lost 106 aircraft and 81 pilots of which 13 planes and 10 pilots were Canadian. German losses, by comparison were quite light. Why had things gone so terribly wrong?

Dieppe was a strongly fortified defensive town held by the Germans. Aside from the high cliffs overlooking the beaches it was protected by concrete pill-boxes and artillery positions and barbed wire. In addition, the Germans had nearly 50 field and coastal guns and howitzers, three anti-aircraft batteries, and a few anti-tank guns. Against this strong position the Allies sent troops with no battle experi-ence, supported by only eight destroyers but no battleships and no heavy aerial bombardment. When the attack began the German defence forces fired down on the landing craft from the high cliffs above the beaches. Many of the soldiers were killed before they even made it to the beaches, while scores of others died as they raced for cover. The soldiers who did manage to get ashore faced overwhelming odds against the well-fortified German troops. Why was an assault against such odds launched? Why were untried Canadian troops given such a difficult assignment? These and several others questions con-tinue to swirl around the debate over Dieppe. One reason for the Dieppe raid was to appease Stalin's demand for a sec-ond front. By carrying out the attack on Dieppe, the Soviet Union, at that point in a desperate struggle against the Nazis, would get some relief as Germans troops would be drawn from the Russian front to defend in the west. As well, the Dieppe raid was to act as a trial run to assist in the preparation of the full-scale invasion that was to occur later. As one historian put it, Dieppe was a costly battle "to learn how not to invade Europe." Finally, the decision to use untried Canadian troops seems to have been made for two rea-sons. Firstly, the Canadian troops were among the best trained troops in the world despite their lack of battlefield experience. Secondly, the Canadians, who had been training in England for nearly two and half years were eager to see active duty. In the end we are left with sev-eral unanswered questions. Could any degree of success be expected with untried Canadian troops against the strongly fortified Dieppe? Were the Canadian troops sacrificial lambs sent to be slaughtered to appease Stalin? Or was Dieppe a necessary disaster for the later D-Day assault to be successful? Was expe-rience gained on that bloody day critical to success in 1944?

Following the attack on Pearl Harbor the Japanese moved quickly conquering almost all of the Western Pacific and Southeast Asia, including the Philippines, Hong Kong, and Singapore in the first six months of 1942. Using its navy to both spearhead the attack and to transport the army, Japan was able to establish a vast Pacific empire they referred to as the Greater Asia Co-Prosperity Sphere. The stage was now set for a long and bitter war in the Pacific.

Diplomacy And Coalition Warfare

America's Entry Into War

Germany's invasion of the Soviet Union and Japan's surprise attack on Pearl Harbor had brought much needed aid to the British. A short time later the three Allied powers, Britain, the Soviet Union, and the United States, would refer to themselves as the United Nations. Given the economic resources and military strength of the United States, the tide had certainly shifted in favour of the Allied forces. The great challenge that lie ahead for the Allied powers was making the diplomacy work. By 1941, Britain was economically exhausted and would rely on support from Canada and the United States to survive the balance of the war. It was therefore in their interests that the war be as short as possible. The United States, meanwhile, looked to the postwar world in which they hoped to have access to world markets; a world they hoped would be comprised of bourgeois democracies like their own. Consequently, their primary aim was to ensure not only the defeat of Nazi Germany, but the survival and spread of democracy in the postwar years. Aid to the Soviet Union, American Air Chief General Henry Arnold pointed out in 1943, was "based upon the necessity of hurting Germany, and not any desire to help Russia." General Thomas Handy agreed, suggesting aid to the Soviet Union be decreased so as not to hurt America's postwar interests. Handy argued: "Victory in this war will be meaningless unless we also win the peace." The beleaguered Soviet Union placed their own survival at the forefront. Only after the German army was being driven from their land did they begin to plan for the postwar. These conflicting objectives would present Roosevelt, Churchill, and Stalin with diplomatic hurdles to overcome if their alliance against fascist aggression was to be successful.

Ironically, although it was the Japanese attack on Pearl Harbor that brought the United States into the war, Roosevelt believed the defeat of Nazi Germany was America's most pressing task. Although he faced opposition in Congress, Roosevelt seemed to realize that Japan posed no immediate threat to the United States nor Western democracy. He therefore committed the United States to what became known as the Europe First Policy. Roosevelt's decision not only helped to assure the survival of Britain but also helped seal the fate of the Third Reich. Roosevelt, Churchill, and Stalin would meet several times over the next few years as they plotted to defeat Hitler and planned a new world order at the end of the war. Coalition warfare would require a good deal of compromise and a careful balancing act as each leader attempted to pursue political and ideological goals without losing sight of their primary objective, the defeat of Nazi Germany.

Despite their close military co-operation during the years 1941–1944, a major strategic dispute dominated the relationship between the Americans and the British. Whereas the British favoured an indirect or peripheral approach to victory in Europe, the Americans favoured a direct approach through a massive invasion of northwestern France. Although several American strategists agreed with Stalin's belief that a large-scale invasion in the west was the best strategy to defeat Germany, the earliest the United States could launch such an attack would be the spring of 1943. Needing to solidify his support at home for the Europe First Policy, Roosevelt decided a show of force somewhere in Europe would be necessary in 1942. The details of a combined British-American counter-offensive in the Mediterranean for 1942 were worked out in Washington at a meeting known as the Arcadia Conference. This meeting between Churchill, Roosevelt, and their respective war planners would be the first of several.

Stalin realized 1942 would be a critical year for the Soviet Union. Following the spring thaw, the Russian winter could no longer be counted on to impede the progress of the German army. In meetings with Churchill and Roosevelt, Stalin demanded a second front in Western Europe be opened to help draw pressure off his besieged nation. This request would not be met for over two years. Meanwhile, in May 1942, Hitler made a surprise change in direction. Rather than attempt to finish the drive to Moscow, he suddenly diverted the German army south to the Crimea and the oil fields. Hitler's rationale was that by seizing

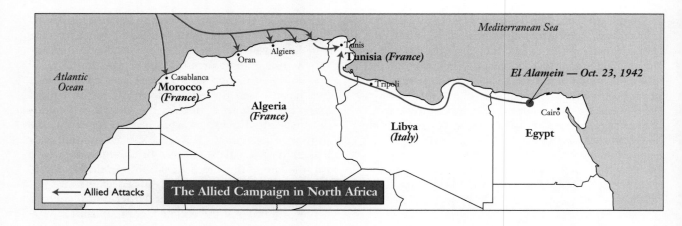

The Allied Campaign in North Africa

control of the critical oil reserves, the Soviet Union's life line would be severed, forcing them to surrender.

Despite the heavy losses inflicted by the German army on the Soviet Union, *Blitzkrieg* failed to provide the quick victory essential to the long-term success of Hitler's master plan. By the spring of 1942, the Soviet Union had managed to regroup, bolster its troops and artillery, and launch a defence with a ferocity not seen in the previous fall campaign. There are several reasons sighted for the renewed vigour of the Red Army. During the winter of 1941–1942 Stalin began to appeal to Russian nationalist sense by urging the fight for the motherland rather than urging the people to fight an ideological war. As part of this appeal to the Russian people, and to assure his new allies in the west, churches, closed since the revolution, were allowed to reopen. Another recent explanation for the dramatic turn of events in 1942 is that the suspected victims of the purges in the 1930s had in fact not been killed, but had been imprisoned in remote gulags. By releasing these highly trained soldiers and appealing to Russian nationalism, Stalin may have given the boost to the Red Army necessary to stem the tide. By October 1942, the German advances had been halted. The Soviet Union had withstood devastating attacks on major cities such as Stalingrad and Leningrad and were now beginning to hand Hitler his first setbacks of the war. When winter set in the German army was cut off from all supplies. This time they would not survive the winter. By the end of January 1943, the German Sixth Army, which had laid siege to Stalingrad, was forced to surrender. An army of 650 000 was reduced to 90 000, of which only 5000 would ever return to Germany.

The German army, which only two years earlier had seemed invincible, had been dealt a stunning defeat.

By the fall of 1942, the Allies had reached the turning point in their war against Germany by successfully counterattacking on three fronts, Egypt, North Africa, and Russia. On October 23, the British launched a successful offensive in Egypt against the overextended Afrika Korps. Two weeks later a combined British and American attack in North Africa soon closed in on Erwin Rommel's armies. While these victories signalled a significant turning point in the war, they also presented the Allied nations with a paradox. Soviet victories and assurances to Stalin that a second front in the west would be opened put pressure on Britain and the United States to launch an assault in northern France. Yet, the success in the Mediterranean prompted Roosevelt and Churchill to consider further Mediterranean offensives rather than opening the second front in Europe.

The Casablanca Conference

Early in 1943 Churchill and Roosevelt met in Casablanca, which had recently been liberated by American troops under the command of General Eisenhower. During the Casablanca Conference the two leaders mapped out the future directions for their combined war efforts. Despite mounting pressure from Stalin to open a second front in Europe, Churchill continued to press for an indirect strategy designed to weaken the German army to the point at which a cross-Channel invasion of France would be guaranteed success with minimal losses. The British delegation at Casablanca demonstrated more experience than their

American counterparts, dominating the planning sessions. In the end, the only concession the Americans were able to achieve was a joint declaration, which stated that the Western Allies would accept only an unconditional surrender from the Axis powers. This declaration was intended to appease Stalin by offering some reassurance that the West would not sign a separate peace pact with Germany and leave the Soviet Union on its own.

Other than the joint declaration, Churchill was successful at achieving his demands of the continuance of peripheral warfare. Arguing that the Germans were still not driven out of North Africa, and that time and shipping constraints made an attempted cross-Channel invasion unlikely in 1943, the British suggested the Allied forces continue to fight the Germans in North Africa, Sicily, and possibly the Italian mainland. If successful, they would be able to gain control of vital shipping lanes between Europe and the Middle East while at the same time tying down a large portion of the German army.

Operation Husky: The Invasion of Sicily

By May 1943, the Germans and Italians had been driven out of Tunisia, their last hold on North Africa. Within a few months a combined force of American, British, and Canadian troops had launched Operation Husky, the invasion of Sicily. The invasion caught Hitler somewhat off guard in part due to a brilliant plan of deception. A corpse carrying fabricated top-secret papers was planted for the Nazis to find. These papers convinced Hitler that any Allied invasion fleet detected in the Mediterranean would be heading for Greece. After six weeks of fighting, the island of Sicily fell and the Allied forces began their preparations for the invasions of mainland Italy.

The successful Allied invasion of Sicily left Italy in turmoil. Italians who had followed Mussolini into war had never expected it to be fought on their soil. This turn of events led the Fascist Grand Council to withdraw their support of Mussolini. On July 25, he was asked to resign as prime minister. Upon being summoned to the royal palace by the king, Mussolini was imprisoned and King Victor Emmanuel assumed direct command of the armed forces, while Marshal Pietro Badoglio became prime minister of Italy. Immediately the new government secretly began negotiations with the Allies for a surrender, despite publicly announcing continued support for Hitler. When the Badoglio real-ized the Allies were demanding an unconditional surrender, he stumbled in his negotiations. Meanwhile, the Germans sent additional troops to the south of Italy to intercept the Allied forces that had begun crossing the Straits of Messina on September 3. The Germans arrived in Italy prepared to fight a defensive war, while the Allied forces committed minimal troops and resources to the Italian campaign; they were now planning for the cross-Channel invasion code-named Operation Overlord. The result was that the Italian campaign became a long, indecisive affair that cost the Allied forces 250 000 casualties and would not end until the collapse of the German army 18 months later.

With Italy in disarray, the communist partisans in Yugoslavia, led by Joseph Broz (alias Tito), were able to disarm the Italian troops who occupied their country. Organized under the Revolutionary Army of National Liberation and receiving support from Churchill, Tito's forces were able to keep the eight German divisions sent to Yugoslavia occupied by their guerrilla activity.

Total War and Strategic Bombing

What had begun in Guernica as a heartless atrocity had become the norm by 1943. Total war, in which civilians became legitimate targets, was a strategy employed by both sides. Beginning in 1942, the Allies had put a great deal of faith and money into a strategic bombing offensive. Strategic bombing involved nightly raids by the RAF intended to destroy German factories, thereby destroying the productive capacity of the Third Reich. As well, German cities became the target of these nightly raids as the Allies attempted to break the spirit of the German people. In many ways, the nightly reign of terror provided by strategic bombing provided the second front Stalin wanted. Operating out of Britain, the RAF, later supported by the American Flying Fortresses, dropped 48 000 tonnes of bombs on Germany in 1942 and 207 000 tonnes in 1943.

The chief proponent of the strategic bombing offensive was British Air Marshal Arthur Harris. He believed that by maintaining nightly terror bombings of German cities the Allies could bomb Germany out of the war either by knocking out their industrial capacity or by pressuring German civilians into demanding their government surrender. Several German cities such as Cologne, Dresden, and Hamburg were virtually obliterated by the bombing raids during which incendiary bombs were used, killing several hundred thousand civilians.

Churchill's Peripheral War in the Mediterranean

Prior to the outbreak of World War II the British had a long history of involvement in the Mediterranean. There is little doubt that protecting their interests in the Mediterranean was a large factor in shaping Churchill's demand that the Allies support his Mediterranean strategy. Calling Italy "the soft underbelly of Europe" and encouraging support for the Greeks in their struggle against the Nazis as well as Tito's guerrilla war with the Germans in Yugoslavia, Churchill would maintain throughout the war that the strategy of a peripheral war would be most effective in defeating the Third Reich. Shaping Churchill's strategy was the fact that the British still retained important economic and imperial interests throughout the Mediterranean including Palestine, Egypt, Greece, and Gibraltar. Also of critical strategic significance was the Suez Canal, which had been built as a joint venture between the British, French, and Egyptians. The Suez Canal provided a crucial link to Asia and India; consequently, it was with great trepidation that the British observed Italy's attack on Ethiopia in 1935. When the threat of an Italian invasion of Egypt arose in June 1940, it prompted a clash between the British and Mussolini's forces in North Africa. Italian defeats in both Africa and the Balkans brought Germany into the Mediterranean theatre of war drawing troops away from Europe and lending some credibility to Churchill's Mediterranean strategy. However, the Allies would find that fighting fascism in the Mediterranean was no easy task.

The Italian campaign, which began with the invasion of Sicily in 1943, was a particularly bitter fight that would be waged by the Allies for 18 months and cost 250 000 lives. Although the Italians surrendered in September 1943, after the Allied invasion of the mainland, the struggle for control of Italy was far from over. Following the collapse of the Italian army, the Germans stepped in to ensure an Allied victory in Italy would be no easy feat. Making full use of Italy's terrain the Germans were able to mount a stubborn defence. The only easy means to advance inland was via the narrow coastal plains that were often flooded in winter or easily blocked by German defences. This left only the treacherous mountain passes, which guaranteed that every kilometre the Allies advanced would have to be the result of a tortuous battle against a well-entrenched German army.

Canadians played a crucial role in the hard fought struggle for Italy. After their initial baptism in fire in Sicily, Canada's 1st Division became the spearhead in the Allies drive toward Rome. The Canadians encountered German resistance unlike anything they had seen before. The fierce fighting around the small Adriatic town of Ortona was described in the following way: "Amid the olive groves and vineyards, every farmhouse became a bastion. Every yard of ground was ravaged by shellfire. The rain pelted down. Mines were everywhere." CBC war correspondent Mathew Halton's report of the fighting around Ortona read: "Soaking wet, in a morass of mud, against an enemy fighting harder than he's fought before, the Canadians attack, attack, and attack. The enemy is now fighting like the devil to hold us. He brings in more and more guns, more and more troops. The hillsides and farmlands and orchards are a ghastly brew of fire..."

The persistence of the Allies, especially the Canadian troops, eventually paid off. The road to Rome was eventually opened and after 10 months of fighting victory was at hand on June 5, 1944, one day before the massive D-Day landing at Normandy. Unfortunately, neither the capture of Rome nor the successful D–Day invasion would bring an end to the fighting in Italy. The stubborn German army would fight on until the spring of 1945. By the end of the war the Italian campaign claimed the lives of over 5000 Canadian and left over 25 000 wounded.

These members of the Edmonton Regiment were part of the street fighting that took place in Ortona in December 1943.

During the war few questioned the morality or the effectiveness of strategic bombing. However, historians have since questioned the effectiveness of this strategy, suggesting the money used could have been better spent on tanks and in support of the army, which, in the end, brought about the defeat of the German army. Some, too, criticize the morality of total war, questioning the Allies use of terror to ensure victory.

The Teheran Conference

The first meeting of all three leaders of the major Allied nations, Stalin, Roosevelt, and Churchill, took place during November 1943, in Teheran, Persia. By this point in the war, events had turned decidedly in the favour of the Allies, and the leaders of the Big Three were able to work toward planning the final defeat of Nazi Germany. Churchill pressed for continued support for his Mediterranean strategy arguing that fighting Germany from the south through Italy and the Austrian Alps would ensure the greatest success. Stalin had grown tired of the delays in the opening of a second front in the west to relieve pressure in the Soviet Union and now he had support from Roosevelt. Through negotiation, a reluctant Churchill was convinced to agree to an invasion from the west. The cross-Channel assault would take place in the late spring or early summer of 1944. Despite Churchill's agreement to take part in Operation Overlord, as the cross-Channel invasion was code–named, he did not abandon his Mediterranean policy and Allied soldiers would continue to fight in this theatre of war.

The *Teheran Conference* also marked the beginning of planning for the end of war by the Big Three powers. The three leaders agreed that when the war was over the Soviets would be allowed to move their borders west at the expense of Poland. Poland, meanwhile, would be given a part of Eastern Germany as compensation. Although no details were worked out at Teheran, it was apparent that a defeated Germany would be harshly dealt with by the Allied powers. In return, Stalin assured Roosevelt that once Germany had surrendered, the Soviet Union would enter into the Pacific war to bring about a rapid defeat of Japan.

Operation Overlord: The Allied Invasion of Normandy

Immediately following the Teheran Conference the British, Americans, and Canadians began planning for the cross-Channel invasion. At a conference held earlier in 1943 at Quebec between Churchill and Roosevelt, American General Eisenhower was appointed supreme Allied commander. In preparation for the launching of the second front, Eisenhower directed British Field Marshal Bernard Montgomery to prepare detailed invasion plans and act as commander of the invasion ground forces. The invasion of France across the English Channel would be supported by a naval bombardment and fighter cover from American and British planes, using British airfields as their base. The crossing would be no easy feat. The English Channel can be a difficult body of water to cross at the best of times, and the Germans had constructed a formidable series of defences along the northwestern coast of France. The Allied invasion was supported by their success at disguising their intentions. The most logical place for an invasion would be at the Straits of Dover where the Channel is the narrowest and the beaches flat. Needing to defend all coasts, the German defence was hampered by spreading their infantry and armoured divisions too thinly.

By the time the attack on the beaches of Normandy came in the early morning of June 6, 1944, the Allies had amassed one of the largest invasion forces in history. The 156 000 British, American, and Canadian troops were transported under the cover of heavy air bombardment to Sword, Juno, Gold, Omaha, and Utah beaches. The convoy transporting the troops and armoured vehicles comprised 6500 naval and transport craft, divided into 75 convoys, while the air support was made up of 12 000 aircraft. The Germans could muster only 425 fighters. By nightfall the Allies had secured all beachheads and defeated an attempted counterattack by the Germans. By June 10, the separate beachheads had been consolidated giving the Allies a solid base from which to begin pushing back the German army.

Throughout July the Germans would mount a determined resistance, especially the Twelfth SS Hitler Jugend (Hitler Youth) who were fanatical and would take no prisoners nor would they surrender. Hitler refused to allow his armies to retreat and launched several desperate counterattacks in an attempt to stem the tide against his armies. During the Allies drive into France the Germans unleashed a new weapon, the first missiles. These pilotless bombs proved to be inaccurate and therefore of little consequence. Meanwhile, Allied strategic bombing during the summer of 1944 was beginning to bear fruit as the productive capacity of

Landing on beaches in Normandy.

Germany began to weaken. German scientists scrambled to develop a superweapon to save the Third Reich from imminent collapse. No such weapon would be developed in time to save Hitler's crumbling empire. By the end of July 1944, the Allied forces had secured the area around Caen and were able to begin their drive toward Paris. The successful landing at Normandy would spell the beginning of the end for Nazi Germany; defeat was now only a matter of time.

Hitler's Last Desperate Attempts To Avoid Defeat

In the six weeks following the Normandy invasion the Allies had managed to consolidate their position and begin their drive eastward. Hitler's armies were now being squeezed both from the east, where the Soviet Red Army had pushed the Germans back to the Polish frontier, and by the Allied armies which were driving hard from the west. Many of his top military commanders knew defeat was inevitable, but Hitler, with the support of the state police (the Gestapo) and the SS, continued to control military and political decision making. Hoping to negotiate peace before Germany was crushed, a group of army officers attempted to assassinate Hitler. On July 20, 1944, Colonel Claus von Stauffenberg placed a briefcase containing a bomb beside Hitler prior to a meeting in the map room of his

East Prussian headquarters. Just before the bomb detonated, Hitler moved the briefcase to the other side of the table leg. Although injured, Hitler miraculously survived the blast. The repercussions of this failed attempt were immediate and severe. At least 5000 officers and suspected conspirators were executed, among them were Field Marshal von Kluge, the Normandy commander–in–chief and Erwin Rommel, who had earned the nickname "Desert Fox" for his heroics in Africa.

Despite the dramatic turn of fortunes against the Third Reich and the rapidly declining morale among German troops, Hitler refused to admit defeat. To complement Operation Overlord, the Allies launched an invasion of southern France on August 15 and began driving northward. By late fall Paris had been liberated as had Belgium and the Netherlands. Yet Hitler stubbornly refused to accept defeat and the Allies would consider nothing less than an unconditional surrender. Although defeat was certain, Hitler would launch one final counter-offensive and drag the war on a further six months, bringing about the total destruction of Germany and the loss of millions more lives.

Hitler had conceived the idea of a winter counter-offensive even while his armies were reeling in defeat during the Normandy invasion. Gathering what strength the German army had left in the west, Hitler launched an attack on the Ardennes region, along the German Belgium border on December 16, 1944. Although the counter-offensive met with some initial success, the strength of the Allies soon overwhelmed what remained of the German army. In January, 1945, 180 Russian divisions crossed the Vistual River into Germany as the German defences collapsed, while in the west the Western Allies crossed the Rhine by March. From this point onward there would be no pause in the Allied offensives in the east and west until Germany surrendered.

The Yalta Conference

With victory all but certain, Churchill, Roosevelt, and Stalin met one more time at Yalta, in the Crimean Peninsula, from February 4 to 11, 1945. This would be the last meeting of the three leaders, as Roosevelt, who suffered from polio, was gravely ill. Unlike their previous meeting, during which they mapped out a strategy to bring about the defeat of Germany, the focus of the *Yalta Conference* was to decide the fate of a defeated Nazi Germany.

The peace settlement imposed on Germany would be harsh. Roosevelt had declared earlier that "the German people as a whole must have it driven home to them that the whole nation has been engaged in a lawless conspiracy against the decencies of modern civilization." Stalin certainly agreed with Roosevelt's sentiments, insisting that Germany pay 20 billion dollars in compensation for the destruction they had brought to Europe and that half of this be given to the Soviet Union for the carnage the Nazis had caused in Russia. Furthermore, Stalin reminded Churchill and Roosevelt of the Teheran agreement to partition Poland and compensate it with part of Eastern Germany. Churchill, suspicious of the Soviet leader, balked at agreeing to this demand. Although Roosevelt was more accepting of Stalin's request, the three decided to put off any final decision until the war ended.

The major agreement to come out of Yalta was that a defeated Germany would be demilitarized and denazified. Furthermore, Germany was to be divided into four zones of occupation, a zone for each of the Big Three powers and a zone for France. Berlin would be similarly occupied.

The Founding of the United Nations

The other major development to come out of the Yalta Conference was the foundations for a new organization to replace the failed League of Nations. The countries allied against the Axis powers were to be invited to a meeting in San Francisco in April 1945. Wanting to be part of the emerging new world order, several countries joined in the war against Germany in the last few months. The new organization, known as the *United Nations Organization* would replace the League of Nations and its mandate. It would comprise a General Assembly, in which all member countries would have equal voting rights, and a Security Council of five permanent members; Britain, United States, China, the Soviet Union, and France. The Security Council would be given the power to decide if the United Nations should intervene in disputes that may threaten international peace and security. Each member of the Security Council had a veto, or the right to overturn a decision.

Two other organizations would also play a crucial role in rebuilding of Europe and bringing about stability and order in the postwar world. Following a meeting at Bretton Woods, in the United States, in 1944, the Americans and British set up the World Bank and the International Monetary Fund. The function of the International Monetary Fund was to lend money to countries whose economies were in trouble in order to prevent the wild fluctuations in world currencies that had played such havoc to world economies in the 1930s. The World Bank would lend money to war-torn Europe to assist in the rebuilding and to poor countries for economic development. It was hoped that these two organizations would help to ensure stability and prosperity in the postwar era and avoid the chaos and destruction that had plagued the first half of the twentieth century.

Hitler's Final Demise

The Third Reich, which Hitler had boasted would last 1000 years, had completely crumbled by the spring of 1945. During the final days, Hitler wavered between plans to continue resistance or withdraw his remaining troops to the Alpine areas of southern Germany and Russia. In the end, he decided to remain in Berlin where he attempted to implement scorched earth orders and contemplated the use of new and deadly gases as well as the massacre of all prisoners. Finally, on April 22, Hitler seemed to realize his defeat and, in a fit of temper, abandoned all his powers, only to resume them the next day. On April 25, Soviet and American troops met at Torgau on the river Elbe in central Germany. By this time the Italian front had also collapsed, leaving only a few blocks of Berlin as the remnants of the former Nazi empire.

On April 30, Hitler with his mistress Eva Braun withdrew into the air-raid shelter of the Reich Chancellory in Berlin. With the sounds of the Soviet Red Army advancing in the background, Hitler nominated Admiral Doenitz as his successor; then he and Braun committed suicide. Their bodies were never recovered from the bombed shelter. On May 7, the German forces surrendered unconditionally. Germany was left without a government, its cities and factories lie in ruins, its transportation system destroyed, and its fate in the hands of the victorious Allies.

The Holocaust

World War II was not just a war of territorial conquest or an ideological clash; it was a war of racism and genocide unlike anything the world has seen before or since. The people who would suffer the greatest during the 12 years of Nazi reign were European Jews. When the war began, Europe was home to approximately 12

The Hossbach Memorandum:

During the Nuremberg Trials, a piece of evidence was produced that significantly altered the trials as well as coloured the way in which World War II would be recorded by historians. This piece of evidence was the Hossbach Memorandum: notes recorded by Colonel Hossbach at a meeting held in Berlin on November 5, 1937. At the Nuremberg Trials, Hermann Göring, Commander-in-Chief of the Luftwaffe, found the Hossbach Memorandum used as the key piece of evidence against him, proving him guilty of war crimes as well as proving that Hitler had premeditated World War II. Since then, historians have been divided into two camps: those who argue that the Memorandum reveals Hitler's blueprint for war and those who argue that the conference that produced the memorandum was not a war council and was not responsible for World War II. The extracts below were taken from the Hossbach Memorandum. From what is presented here, do you believe Hitler premeditated the war and that this is in fact his blueprint?

Minutes of the Conference in the Reich Chancellery, Berlin, November 5, 1937, from 4:15 to 8:30 P.M.

Present: The Führer and Chancellor;
Field Marshal von Blomberg, War Minister;
Colonel General Baron von Fritsch, Commander-in-Chief, Army;
Admiral Dr. Erich Raeder, Commander-in-Chief, Navy;
Colonel General Göring, Commander-in-Chief, Luftwaffe;
Baron von Neurath, Foreign Minister;
Colonel Hossbach

The Führer began by stating that the subject of the present conference was of such importance that its discussion would, in other countries, certainly be a matter for a full cabinet meeting, but he—the Führer—had rejected the idea of making it a subject of discussion before the wider circle of the Reich Cabinet just because of the importance of the matter.

The Führer then continued:

The aim of German policy was to make secure and to preserve the racial community [*Volksmasse*] and to enlarge it. It was therefore a question of space...

Germany's problem could only be solved by means of force and this was never without attendant risk. If one accepts as the basis of the following exposition the resort to force with its attendant risks, then there remain still to be answered the questions "when" and "how."

Case 1: Period 1943–1945

After this date, only a change for the worse, from our point of view, could be expected.

The equipment of the army, navy, and Luftwaffe, as well as the formation of the officer corps, was nearly completed. Equipment and armament were modern; in further delay there lay the danger of their obsolescence. In particular, the secrecy of special weapons could not be preserved forever. The recruiting of reserves was limited to current age groups; further drafts from older untrained age groups were no longer available.

Our relative strength would decrease in relation to rearmament, which would by then have been carried out by the rest of the world. If we did not act by 1943–1945, any year could, in consequence of a lack of reserves, produce the food crisis, to cope with which the necessary foreign exchange was not available, and this must be regarded as a waning point of the regime. Besides, the world was expecting our attack and was increasing its countermeasures from year to year. It was while the rest of the world was still preparing its defences that we were obliged to take the offensive.

Nobody knew that day what the situation would be in the years 1943–1945. One thing only was certain, that we could not wait longer. On

Hitler's Blueprint for War?

the one hand, there was the great Wehrmacht and the necessity of maintaining it at its present level; on the other, the prospect of a lowering of the standard of living and of a limitation of the birthrate, which left no choice but to act. If the Führer was still living, it was his unalterable resolve to solve Germany's problem of space at the latest by 1943–1945.

Actually, the Führer believed that almost certainly Britain, and probably France as well, had already tacitly written off the Czechs and were reconciled to the fact that this question would be cleared up in due course by Germany. Difficulties connected with the empire, and the prospect of being once more entangled in a protracted European war, were decisive considerations for Britain against participation in a war against Germany. Britain's attitude would certainly not be without influence on that of France. An attack by France without British support, and with the prospect of the offensive being brought to a standstill on our western fortifications, was hardly probable. Nor was a French march through Belgium and Holland without British support to be expected; this also was a course not to be contemplated by us in the event of a conflict with France, because it would certainly entail the hostility of Britain. It would of course be necessary to maintain a strong defence on our western frontier during the prosecution of our attack on the Czechs and Austrians. In this connection it had to be remembered that the defence measures of the Czechs were growing in strength from year to year and that the actual worth of the Austrian army also was increasing in the course of time. Even though the populations concerned, especially of Czechoslovakia, were not sparse, the annexation of Czechoslovakia and Austria would mean an acquisition of foodstuffs for 5 to 6 million people, on the assumption that the compulsory emigration of 2 million people from Czechoslovakia and 1 million people from Austria was practicable. The incorporation of these two states with Germany meant, from the politico-military point of view, a substantial advantage because it would mean shorter and better frontiers, the freeing of forces for other purposes, and the possibility of creating new units up to a level of about 12 divisions, that is, one new division per million inhabitants.

In appraising the situation, Field Marshal von Blomberg and Colonel General von Fritsch repeatedly emphasized the necessity that Britain and France must not appear in the role of our enemies, and stated that the French army would not be so committed to the war with Italy that France could not at the same time enter the field with forces superior to ours on our western frontier. General von Fritsch estimated the probable French forces available for use on the Alpine frontier at approximately 20 divisions, so that a strong French superiority would still remain on the western frontier, with the role, according to the German view, of invading the Rhineland. In this matter, moreover, the advanced state of French defence preparations [*Mobilmachung*] must be taken into particular account, and it must be remembered apart from the insignificant value of our present fortifications—on which Field Marshal von Blomberg laid special emphasis— that the four motorized divisions intended for the West were still more or less incapable of movement. In regard to our offensive toward the southeast, Field Marshal von Blomberg drew particular attention to the strength of the Czech fortifications, which had acquired by now a structure like a Maginot Line and which would gravely hamper our attack.

General von Fritsch mentioned that this was the very purpose of a study which he had ordered made this winter, namely, to examine the possibility of conducting operations against the Czechs, with special reference to overcoming the Czech fortification system; the General further expressed his opinion that under existing circumstances he must give up his plan to go abroad on his leave, which was due to begin on November 10. The Führer dismissed this idea on the ground that the possibility of a conflict need not yet be regarded as so imminent. To the Foreign Minister's objection that an Anglo-French-Italian conflict was not yet within such a measurable distance as the Führer seemed to assume, the Führer put the summer of 1938 as the date which seemed to him possible for this. In reply to considerations offered by Field Marshal von Blomberg and General von Fritsch regarding the attitude of Britain and France, the Führer repeated his previous statements that he was convinced of Britain's non-participation, and therefore he did not believe in the probability of belligerent action by France against Germany. Should the Mediterranean conflict under discussion lead to a general mobilization in Europe, then we must immediately begin action against the Czechs.

million Jews. By war's end half of the Jewish people in Europe had been exterminated by the Nazis. Millions more were homeless and had spent several years in deplorable conditions in concentration camps where they had been used as slave labour by the Third Reich. Only 10 percent of the Jewish children living in occupied Europe would survive the *Holocaust*, the name given to the attempted genocide of the Jewish people. Every European Jew suffered in one way or another from the atrocities caused by Hitler and his regime.

The Holocaust is generally seen to have gone through three phases; deportation, ghettoization, and finally extermination. The first phase of deportation occurred prior to the outbreak of war as the German government attempted to drive Jews out of Germany. Once the war broke out and Germany began to roll over much of Europe, millions more Jews came under the grip of the Third Reich. Initially, Hitler's reaction was to concentrate Jews in huge ghettos such as the Warsaw ghetto in Poland. These ghettos were guarded by German soldiers and tightly regulated. Finally, the Nazis put into effect the Final Solution.

The Final Solution

The Final Solution refers to the Nazi's plan to exterminate all European Jews. At a meeting in January 1942, in the Berlin suburb of Wansee, top SS officials gathered to work out the details of the *Endlosung* or "final solution of the Jewish problem." What was the most efficient means to kill large numbers of people? What could be done with the bodies? Did someone with one Jewish parent or grandparent qualify as a Jew?

While there is a general consensus among historians as to the horrors perpetrated on the Jewish people by the Nazi's Final Solution, a wide gulf exists over when and why the extermination of the Jews took place. Lucy Dawidowicz has argued that the Holocaust was a part of Hitler's grand design as early as 1919. Certainly, *Mein Kampf*, which Hitler wrote in 1925, contains numerous examples of anti-Semitism, and Jewish Germans faced terrible persecution throughout the 1930s under the Third Reich.

Christopher Browning accepts that anti-Semitism played a role in the eventual attempt at genocide but rejects Dawidowicz's view that the Final Solution was already a fixed goal before the war began. Instead, Browning argues that the Final Solution was a product of a series of events over a number of months with the period between the fall of 1941 and the spring of 1942 being the critical transition to genocide. Brown stated: "The intention of systematically murdering the European Jews was not fixed in Hitler's mind before the war, but crystallized in 1941 after previous solutions proved unworkable and the imminent attack upon Russia raised the prospect of yet another vast increase in the number of Jews within the growing empire." Historian Arno Mayer has suggested that the Final Solution came about even later. He contends that the Final Solution was a result of the failure of Operation Barbarossa. With Nazi Germany stretching its resources to the limit, it could no longer afford to guard and feed Jews in concentration camps and ghettos.

Once the decision was made to carry out the extermination of the Jews, the Germans wasted little time in putting their plans into operation. Specialized death camps, such as Auschwitz, were set up to handle the mass murders that were to take place. The first Jews to be selected for the gas chambers were those who were too young or frail to work. Others were used as slave labour, given little to eat, and later, when their strength was wasted, were sent to the gas chamber. Some were even used as human guinea pigs in medical experiments. The decision to use the gas chamber as the

The faces of these two Jewish prisoners show the anguish suffered by millions at the hands of Nazi Germany.

means of mass execution resulted from the psychological problems that grew out of middle-aged family men (Nazi soldiers) being required to shoot women and children repeatedly. The use of the gas chamber provided a more humane method for those carrying out the murders. The use of gas to commit murder was first conceived in September 1939, to carry out the Nazi policy of euthanasia to rid Germany of "unworthy life," in other words, those in mental hospitals.

Adolf Hitler is the obvious explanation for the Holocaust. Too often the blame for the atrocities are placed on him and to a lesser extent on his top officials. While the Nazi leadership may have decided on the physical extermination of the Jews, it was the willing collaboration of numerous individuals that allowed for the plan to be put into effect. The Final Solution was the product of many people's co-operation in expressing their anti-Semitism in the ultimate form, genocide. Hitler may have given the orders for the extermination of the Jews, but numerous others must also be held accountable in the archives of history.

At war's end the death toll was staggering. Aside from the 6 million Jews who died as a result of the Holocaust, nearly 14 million Russians, 6 million Poles, and 1.7 million Yugoslavians died as a result of the war. As well, 600 000 French, 357 000 British, 405 000 Americans, and 109 000 soldiers from British Commonwealth nations lost their lives. When these staggering numbers are added to the loss of life in Axis countries, the death toll for World War II approaches 40 million people. The age of total war had brought widespread death and destruction to Europe and the world.

Preparing for the Postwar Era

The Potsdam Conference

As the defeat of Nazi Germany came increasingly closer, postwar realities began to emerge. The Soviet Union would undoubtedly emerge as a great power. Furthermore, their critical role in the defeat of Germany and their desire to ensure postwar security would lead to aggressive Soviet demands at the diplomatic table. These realities forced the Western Allies to once again adapt their view of the Soviet Union. In a few short years Western perceptions of the Soviet Union and Joseph Stalin had gone from evil to hero to suspicious ally. By 1944 ,the Western Allies, aware of the crucial role of the Soviet Union in bringing about the defeat of the Third Reich, were becoming aware of the potentially dominant force the Soviet Union could play in the postwar world. This would lead both Britain and the United States to view the Soviets with some caution and lead to the beginning of Cold War rhetoric that would dominate postwar diplomacy and international politics.

When the three Allied leaders, Stalin, Churchill, and Truman (Roosevelt's replacement), met at Potsdam, near Berlin on July 17, 1945, major changes were in the wind. The Americans had just tested the world's first nuclear weapon in a remote part of New Mexico, and Winston Churchill had been ungratefully defeated in a general election. His seat at the **Potsdam Conference** would be filled by the newly elected British prime minister, Clement Attlee. As the sole surviving member of the Big Three powers left at the diplomatic table, Stalin would attempt to use the sudden changes to his advantage. He had already established a puppet government in Poland and had ruthlessly dealt with any opposition. The Soviet Union clearly would act to consolidate gains in Eastern Europe regardless of the opposition voiced by the West.

Little was actually accomplished at the Potsdam Conference. The administration of Germany was to be by a Control Council made up of the four military commanders in the occupied zones. As well, the decision was made to arrest former members of the SS and wartime leaders of the Nazi Party. They would be tried before a special tribunal, which was to be set up at Nuremberg, Germany. Each power was allowed to take what it wanted from their zone of occupation as reparation payment, while the Soviet Union would also be allowed to seize a quarter of the industrial equipment in the British and American zones. For the most part the tone of the Potsdam Conference was one of a declining alliance, not one that promised postwar harmony among the great powers. In fact, there were no discussions over the fate of Eastern Europe or Germany. These issues had been settled by the positions of the Allied armies when Germany surrendered. Europe was now clearly divided between the communist-controlled East and democracies of the West. Churchill, prior to the Potsdam Conference, lamented the fate of Europe when he wrote to Truman "I view with profound misgivings... the descent of an iron curtain between us and everything to the eastward." For the next four decades this iron curtain would stand between the East and the West as the age of the Cold War descended upon Europe and the world.

Victory in the Pacific

Immediately following the Potsdam Conference and the defeat of Germany, the world leaders turned their attention to the Pacific where the war against Japan dragged on. Since the bombing of Pearl Harbor, the Americans, British, Australians, and New Zealanders had waged a relentless and tiring war against the Japanese. Over the course of the war fierce fighting

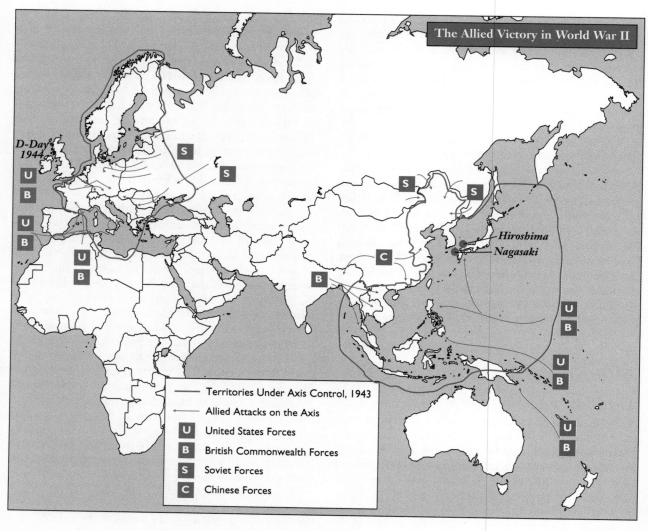

The Allied Victory in World War II

D-Day
1944

Hiroshima
Nagasaki

Territories Under Axis Control, 1943
Allied Attacks on the Axis
U United States Forces
B British Commonwealth Forces
S Soviet Forces
C Chinese Forces

had spread through the jungles of Burma and Borneo and the numerous islands of the South Pacific, reaching as far as the Aleutian Islands off the coast of Alaska. Concerned that an invasion of Japan could cost a further 2 million American lives, President Truman called for Japan's surrender on July 26 or warned they would face "prompt and utter destruction." Japanese Prime Minister Kantaro Suzuki replied that his government would *mokusatsu* the Allied demand — "kill it with silence."

Truman and his military advisors weighed their options and in the end decided against a demonstration of the atom bomb's force. Instead they would bomb a Japanese city. On August 6, 1945, Hiroshima, Japan

became the world's first target of a nuclear attack. At 8:15 a.m., an American B-29 bomber, called the *Enola Gay*, dropped a 3.2-metre-long bomb that exploded in the air above Hiroshima. Soundless lightning followed by a supersonic shock wave and a fireball hot enough to melt iron spread across the land. The blast was so powerful it tore a hole in the air, reversing the wind. People at the centre of the blast were immediately vaporized, while others suffered agonizing deaths as their clothes ignited and their skin melted from their bodies. By the end of the day 70 000 had died, some from radiation burns, others buried in the rubble of collapsed buildings. Another 61 000 were injured, many of whom would die from their wounds. By the

Hiroshima: blackened by fire after the world's first atomic bomb exploded over the Japanese city.

end of the year the death toll in Hiroshima would reach 140 000 as radiation, burns, and infection claimed numerous lives. When the Japanese failed to announce an immediate surrender, a second bomb claiming 40 000 more lives was dropped on the city of Nagasaki. Much controversy surrounds Truman's decision to drop the second bomb. Many feel the bombing of Nagasaki had little to do with pressuring Japan into surrender but was intended as a show of force to the

Soviet Union to keep the communists in check in the immediate postwar years.

Following the mass destruction of Hiroshima and Nagasaki, Japanese Emperor Hirohito accepted the Allied terms of surrender. On August 14, 1945, the war in the Pacific was over. Six years of brutal warfare had come to an end. The United States, which had won the war in the Pacific, would dictate the peace. Japan was to be demilitarized and democracy put in place under the guidance of a military government headed by General Douglas MacArthur, supreme commander for the Allied Powers.

Reflections

The world in 1945 was quite different from the one that had preceded the war. It was now a world divided between the communist East and the democratic and capitalist West; it was a nuclear world in which future wars could spell the end of civilization as we know it. Peace had been restored, but it was again a tenuous peace. This time, however, it would last. The world had entered World War II reluctantly, still mournful over the heavy losses of war a generation earlier. By the time peace had returned, the nuclear age had made future world war virtually unthinkable. The development of the nuclear bomb would lead to an uneasy peace in the new era known as the Cold War.

Key Concepts, Figures, and Events

Appeasement
Neville Chamberlain
Munich Agreement
Phony War

Miracle of Dunkirk
Operation Barbarossa
Teheran Conference
Yalta Conference

United Nations Organization
Holocaust
Potsdam Conference

Topics for Further Thought

1. Neville Chamberlain has often been criticized by historians for his policy of appeasement. Were his attempts to secure peace a valiant effort or a naïve response to the rising Nazi threat? Be sure to reflect on the Versailles Treaty and its implications when responding to this question.

2. The Spanish Civil War has been referred to as "The Last Great Cause." In what ways was this conflict a microcosm of the world war which was to follow?

3. In 1939, the world was stunned by the Nazi-Soviet Pact. To many, the fact that fascist and communist powers would sign such a pact suggested the "death of ideologies." Others, however, maintain that in signing the Pact, both sides furthered their ideological goals in a very practical manner. Does an agreement between diametrically opposed powers suggest that ideologies have no real meaning in the real world of politics?

4. During World War I, Germany's attempted invasion of France bogged down in the trenches for three years. In 1940, despite the Maginot Line, France fell quickly to the armies of the Third Reich. How can the surprisingly quick fall of France be explained?

5. Hitler's planned invasion of Britain, code-named Operation Sea Lion, never managed to get off the ground. How can Germany's failure to invade England successfully be explained? What would be the long-term consequences of this failure for the Third Reich?

6. It has often been said that while Hitler was a genius in directing the overall war effort, he would have made a poor general because of his inability to direct specific battles. What evidence supports or refutes this statement?

7. Germany's invasion of the Soviet Union, code-named Operation Barbarossa, began with stunning success but ultimately ended in failure. How can this reversal of fortunes be explained considering the actions of both the Nazi army and the Soviet Union? Should the failure of Operation Barbarossa be seen as a crucial turning point in the war? Explain your answer.

8. In recent years, the use of strategic bombing has been criticized by some for the indiscriminate harm it does to civilians. Can the use of strategic bombing be morally justified? Should military strategists advocate total war or should they be considered war criminals for their attacks on civilians?

9. The Holocaust can be seen in terms of victims and victimizers. Who were the victims? The victimizers? Should those who knew what was happening but said nothing, those who were following orders, or those who drove the train loads of people to the death camps bear some of the guilt? What is the relevance of the Holocaust for us today?

10. Despite six years of war and the loss of millions of lives, World War II concluded with an uneasy peace and an unstable world. Respond.

Topics for Further Research

1. As in World War I, Canadians distinguished themselves in the Spanish Civil War and World War II. Research one of the following topics with a focus on the contribution made by Canadians:

Norman Bethune
Mackenzie-Papineau Regiment (Spanish Civil War)
Sicily
Ortona
Normandy

2. With the Axis powers prepared for an aggressive war, many of the Allied powers took defensive measures as they too prepared for war. Research the war preparation carried out by one of the following countries:

Soviet Union	France	Germany
Britain	Italy	Japan
United States		

3. Research the impact of war on one of the following countries not covered in detail in the chapter:

Greece	Yugoslavia	North Africa	Turkey

4. Despite the Nazi triumph over much of Europe by 1941, resistance movements arose to continue the struggle against fascism. Research the resistance movement in one of the following countries, focusing on its leadership, objectives, tactics, and what became of it after the end of the war:

Greece   France   Yugoslavia
Netherlands

5. The strength of the Nazi army is often attributed to the superb military generals who served under Hitler. Research one of Hitler's generals. Use your research to prepare a biographical sketch and to explain his role in the Third Reich. Be sure to assess to what degree the general played a crucial role in the success or failure of the Nazi war effort.

Erwin Rommel   Adolf Eichmann
Heinrich Himmler   Rudolph Hess

6. Research an aspect of the Holocaust. Prepare a summary of the events to help our understanding of racism, intolerance and inhumanity toward fellow human beings:

Kristallnacht
Death Camps
Wansee Conference
Warsaw Uprising
Nazi Treatment of the Handicapped, Gypsies,
  and Homosexuals

Responding to Ideas

1. In *Origins of the Second World War*, English historian A. J. P. Taylor wrote: "The First [World] War explains the Second, and in fact, caused it, insofar as one event causes another. The link between the two wars went deeper. Germany fought specifically in the Second War to reverse the verdict of the First and to destroy the settlement that followed." This interpretation of history suggests that World War II was a product of the age, rather than part of a grand design by Hitler and his generals. In *Hitler's War Aims*, Norman Rich challenges this view, suggesting that Hitler carefully planned for war. Was World War II a product of historical events or did Hitler intentionally bring it about?

2. Few atrocities in the history of humanity compare to the Holocaust in scope or in the legacy left behind. While there is a general consensus among historians as to the horrors and destruction perpetrated on the Jewish people by the Nazi Final Solution, a wide gulf exists over when planning began and why the extermination of the Jews took place. Christopher Browning's *Fateful Months* dealing with the emergence of the Final Solution presents a "moderate functionalist" view by accepting that Hitler's anti-Semitism played a role in the eventual attempts at genocide but he rejects the intentionalist view that the Final Solution was already a fixed goal before the war began. Along with suggesting that the fall of 1941 to the spring of 1942 was a transitional period in Nazi policy in regard to the Jewish question, Browning also attempts to show that a true understanding of the forces that shaped the Final Solution requires a close examination of the middle and lower echelons of Germans and a move away from the traditional Hitlercentric focus. Browning states: "The intention of systematically murdering the European Jews was not fixed in Hitler's mind before the war, but crystallized in 1941 after previous solutions proved unworkable and the imminent attack upon Russia raised the prospect of yet another vast increase in the number of Jews within the growing empire. The Final Solution emerged out of a series of decisions taken that year." From your understanding of the events leading up to the Holocaust, do you agree with the intentionalist or the moderate functionalist view? Support your answer.

Art, Music, and Literature in the Early Twentieth Century

CHAPTER HIGHLIGHTS

- The art of the turn of the century: symbolism and Art Nouveau

- A rebellion against tradition: the Fauves and the Expressionists

- European music and the rise of nationalism

- Writers react to the Victorian era

- New forms in poetry

Introduction

It is remarkably difficult to comment on the arts of the twentieth century because we are still so much a part of it. The development of technology has catapulted all aspects of the arts and sciences into a new realm, confusing and ambiguous, often frightening. We are bombarded with new sensations, new ideas, new controversies, new troubles. As science reveals new realities we are bound to find the foundations of society rocked again and again. In response to this onslaught of the new, artists in every discipline have tried to reconstruct reality through works. Yet there is no one stable truth or reality on which to base their expression. Artists often turn to their own personal life experience make sense of a very unstable world. This has resulted in an immense variety of styles, techniques, subjects in every branch of the arts.

Consider the political and historical details of the first half of this century: the incredible devastation of World Wars I and II, the atomic bomb, and the incredible advances in science and technology. Lives have been taken, lives have been given back.

Europe in the second half of the twentieth century has not been free from war either. Although no concerted world war has occurred, the whole continent is full of conflicts. The breakdown of communism has created civil wars that offer no hope of ending. Conflicts that began hundreds of years ago are still shattering the peace. And we witness them in our very homes on television. For example, people watched the Gulf War as they would the Super Bowl. It became a "media event." With so much reality brutally imposed upon us, surely there has been an effect on our collective psyche. Depression, anger, stress-related diseases are common. How can we hope to find beauty in such a world? It is possible that every generation of artists has tried to answer this question through its art. In our century, perhaps we have to find a new sense of beauty, what Yeats called "a new and terrible beauty," in order to satisfy our creative instincts and our need to make sense of a chaotic world.

Art of the Early Twentieth Century

Symbolism and Art Nouveau

Symbolist art was a carryover from the romantic period. As the Impressionists looked to Asian art for inspiration, the symbolists looked not only to Asian art but also to the arts of other cultures: the South Pacific, the Middle East, or past European eras: medieval and Byzantine. Symbolist art searched for a form of expression other than that of a picture in a frame. In their paintings, figures or objects decorate a flat surface. There is no sense of perspective. The figures may be realistic, but they do not create a reality, rather a world of dream.

This reaction against realistic picture making, coupled with the influence of non-Western art, led to the movement known as *Art Nouveau*, which dominated art and decoration up to the time of World War I. This art in a way echoes the romantics' reaction to the Industrial Revolution. Art Nouveau sought, like Rococo art, to achieve beauty in a world that was becoming mechanized and, to the minds of these artists, ugly. The crafts of other cultures became an influence. In a world leading up to a terrifying war, people seemed to need to find beauty in simple, domestic objects that were treasured and easily understood.

Fauvism and Expressionism

The symbolist and Art Nouveau movements were a continuation of the art of the late romantics. The first real art movement that wholly belonged to the twentieth century involved a group of artists who called themselves *Les Fauves* (wild beasts in French). They considered themselves to be wild and rebellious, defying the traditions and aesthetics of the previous century. *Fauvism* signalled a definite change from the predominant styles of late romantic art. The Fauves overrode the Impressionists and post-Impressionists in their technique and use of colour. They rejected the

Oskar Kokoschka: *The Bride of the Wind*

———————————————————————
⚓

"beauty" of pre-Raphaelite painters and the dream-like images of the symbolists. Their art, also coming at a time when academic, classical art was still predominating, is comparable to the bold, experimental work of English landscape painter Joseph Turner.

As with Turner, colour became the subject of Fauvism because it expressed deep emotion. The Fauves wanted to convey deep feeling through bright colour and strong imagery. On its own, Fauvism did not last long. However its main proponent, *Henri Matisse*, was faithful to its aesthetic. His art expressed a continuation of the basic Fauve principles of colour and form.

In a way, Fauvism and Expressionism, which involved the expression of intense feeling and emotion, were highly intellectual. On a literary level, the work of these artists may be compared to the literature of James Joyce, which employed the "stream-of-consciousness" technique. The Expressionists' aesthetic is highly complex. However, it is unnecessary to understand this philosophy in order to enjoy the beautiful colour and the simplicity of the subjects. Viewing their work may be related to the pleasure of viewing a painting by pre-Impressionist Jean-Baptiste Chardin.

The Fauves had an influence outside of France. In Germany a strong school of Expressionist painters emerged. These paintings, characterized by dark colours and violent imagery, are in the tradition of the German style as far back as the medieval and Renaissance periods. Consider Kokoschka's *The Bride*

Max Beckmann: *The Departure,* 1932-33

————————————————— ᚠ —————————————————

of the Wind: the two lovers are surrounded by menacing clouds which swirl violently around them, yet they seem immune to the storm, even though they exist in the eye of the hurricane. Their love transcends the threatening environment.

The Bride of the Wind symbolizes the political situation which, of course, influenced all European painters during the build-up to World War I and subsequently World War II. German and Austrian painters explored the disasters, distress, and suffering of people through bizarre, chaotic paintings that reflect the political and social chaos brought on by the war and the rise of Nazism. These paintings were considered degenerate by Hitler and many artists had to flee Germany. One such artist was Max Beckmann, who served as a medical orderly in World War I. He was, naturally, deeply affected by the suffering and death he witnessed. His paintings reflect his war experience and the loss of his country.

Beckmann is best known for his disturbing symbolic work *The Departure*. He has structured the work in three panels, based on the medieval art form known as a **triptych**. The middle panel depicts the departure of a royal family. The "king" figure has turned his back on the viewer, and thus on the world. In the same panel, a person with a covered head reaches for a net with fish, perhaps symbolizing lost souls. This central panel is flanked by panels depicting horrible scenes of bizarre torture. The king may represent all Jews, trying to escape the persecution and torments of Hitler's Germany.

Russian painting, too, was affected by the new Expressionist movement. The work of the Russian painter *Wassily Kandinsky* shows amazing courage in its complete abandonment of any recognizable subject matter. Again we may compare his aesthetic to that of Turner, or Igor Stravinsky in music, or Joyce and D. H. Lawrence in literature. As Turner saw colour as symbolic of emotional states, Kandinsky saw colour as relating to the artist's subconscious. According to the nineteenth-century philosopher Nietzsche, civilization is simply a lie, used to cover up the reality of our primitive, irrational human nature. In creating or expressing the irrational through colour on the canvas, the artist expresses the truest reality of himself or herself, and thus human nature in general.

The twentieth-century art movement that really left behind the artistic convention that began with the Renaissance was *cubism*. Cubism took its inspiration from the work of Paul Cézanne in the nineteenth century. Cézanne intellectualized nature into geometrical forms to fit them onto a two-dimensional canvas. This aesthetic philosophy was promoted by two extremely influential and important painters: Spanish painter Pablo Picasso and French painter Georges Braque.

To get a sense of the major trends in modern art, one need only look at the works of Picasso. He was a modern painter because he constantly experimented and changed styles, matching the philosophies and the historical "isms" of late-nineteenth and twentieth-century Europe—a world in upheaval and transition itself. Picasso began his painting career in a realistic mode but his work gradually became more and more abstract. In the early 1900s, he became influenced by the art of Africa and Oceania, as did so many artists and musicians. This influence allowed him to break away from the Western tradition. Like Cézanne, he began to reduce what he saw into abstract planes.

This breaking of objects into planes allowed the cubists to give many viewpoints to convey what they considered a more complete reality. This style mirrors the literary movements of the time. Authors such as James Joyce, Virginia Woolf, and William Faulkner attempted to convey as many points of view as possible in their novels to achieve a more truthful vision. Words, like brush strokes, create an experience as complete and realistic as possible. Needless to say, the cubists' intellectual, almost scientific approach, created stylistic limitations. Nevertheless, cubism broke apart

Picasso's
Guernica

Picasso was not simply an abstract painter, working in the cubist style. Throughout his painting career, he experimented with many different styles, techniques, and forms. His works reveal the influence of a variety of traditional, realistic painters such as Raphael, Rembrandt, and Ingres. One of Picasso's most deeply moving and passionate works is his mural entitled *Guernica*. The painting is an indictment of the 1937 bombing of the small Basque town of Guernica during the Spanish Civil War. Hitler's Luftwaffe practised their bombing techniques at the expense of the population; the painting, done in somber black and white, depicts the resulting carnage.

The painting may be viewed as a triptych, separated into three "movements." Its design echoes the medieval triptych form used by Max Beckmann in *The Departure*. It even bears a similarity to the bas-relief sculpture of the Renaissance, in which the sculptor creates a sense of the passage of time through telling the story by placing an image in several dimensions of sculptural space. The painting has also been compared to a crucifixion, with the tormented horse in the center of the painting representing Christ. This, then, leads us to also compare *Guernica* to Goya's *Third of May, 1808* in Unit 2.

In both paintings we see the same figure whose upthrust hands convey the same climactic gesture as Goya's peasant who is about to die. Abstract modernism may be considered a movement away from engaging the feelings of the observer. Not so with *Guernica*. Although modern—and indeed abstracted from our usual notions of realism—*Guernica* has become a universal memorial to all those who suffer at the hands of a cruel aggressor.

Salvador Dalí: *The Persistence of Memory*, 1931

the structure of art so that the possibilities for representations of form became endless.

All the new "modern-art" movements of this century try to deal with those possibilities. To discuss each significant modern-art movement in detail could be far too cumbersome a task. However, there are people and movements that must be mentioned as they reflect the parallel trends in the political and social histories of this century.

In a reaction to the horrors of World War I, artists in Europe and the United States decided to create a non-art movement. Their prevailing question was: How could the great cultural centres of the Western world, the very countries which had produced wonderful and beautiful works of art in every form, now be intent on destroying each other? This anti-art movement is known as *Dadaism*. Dada is a nonsense word, perhaps reflective of the first sounds that babies make. The champions of Dadaism were French painter *Marcel Duchamp*, who was a futurist (cubist) painter, and German painter Karl Schwitters.

Dadaism, rather like Fauvism, set out to shock the viewing public. An example of Dada art is Duchamp painting on a huge piece of glass and then mounting it on a piece of wood. When the glass accidentally shattered, he was not concerned; rather, he felt that the breakage became part of the work of art. (In a way he prefigures performance art of the last decades of this century.) When dust collected on the glass, he spread it around, considering the dust also to be part of the

artistic effect. Schwitters even took garbage and created a collage of it. Yet another artist, Meret Oppenheim, created a fur teacup!

The Dada movement came to an end, but it allowed the purely intellectual direction of modern art to change. A sense of humour, a satiric aspect, was added to art as a whole. This led to an even greater type of artistic freedom. This time it occurred in the realm of fantasy and dream.

Another extremely important art movement in the early twentieth century is *surrealism*. As stated, the emergence of psychology as a new science or mode of thinking, was a powerful influence on all aspects of the arts. The discovery of new realities by scientific research was paralleled by the discovery of the inner realities revealed by exploration into the psyche. A whole new plane of existence, altered states of consciousness, became the subject matter for all aspects of the arts. Indeed art became an effective method for self-discovery and revelation. Surrealism, then, was a movement designed to explore altered states of consciousness through many forms of the arts.

Surrealism even had a manifesto written by French poet André Breton in 1924. The man who inspired the movement was the Italian Giorgio de Chirico. His paintings usually involve various types of architectures as he plays with space, creating and recreating perspectives to produce the landscapes of dreams. The painter we most associate with surrealism is Spanish painter *Salvador Dalí*, whose work redefines our sense of beauty. His paintings, in one sense, are lyrical, colourful, and romantic as they present almost perfect objects placed together in bizarre relationships. They exist in and of themselves in gorgeous but ineffably strange landscapes. This description of course is an attempt to describe a dream. How can images from a dream make any sort of sense to anyone but the individual who has dreamed them? Yet Dalí's work captures the essence of all dreams. His paintings may be appreciated for their allegorical significance or for their strange and compelling beauty. Certainly they are mesmerizing for the imagery they offer.

No less interesting, but completely different in style, is the work of Marc Chagall. He too paints a world of dream. However, unlike Dalí's often mysterious and melancholy imagery, Chagall's work is full of the joy of life. There is no mystery in a Chagall painting, other than his playful attitude towards space and people's place in it. He paints life in the obscure Russian village where he was born and raised. Chagall's art is not confined to painting. The great Gothic cathedral of Metz in northern France suffered from bomb damage in World War II and lost many of its medieval stained glass windows. Chagall was commissioned to replace some of them. The result is a gorgeous array of biblical stories framed in glass of truly incredible colours. Chagall's mastery of colour and his joyous style do not suffer at all in the translation from canvas to glass.

The great modern artists of the time, up to World War II, are numerous. Therefore, we are unable to do them justice here. In every Western country, there was an outpouring of genius in every genre. And there was a huge expansion in the art of sculpture. Auguste Rodin had the greatest influence on modern sculptors. His rebellion against the classical world and the expressionistic character of his works attracted young sculptors who wanted to break new ground. Many painters tried sculpture as well. Impressionists Degas, Renoir, and the more modern Matisse, Joan Miró, and Picasso, all produced interesting sculptural representations of the imagery found in their paintings. Alberto Giacometti, Constantin Brancusi, and Henry Moore are among the most famous of early to mid-twentieth-century European sculptors.

The work of Giacometti creates a tormented world of stringy, elongated figures. Some even recall survivors of concentration camps, hopelessly in need of physical and emotional nourishment. In contrast, the enormous, full, smooth figures of a Henry Moore reveal a more peaceful, nurtured vision of existence. However, Moore's works do contain the odd sharp edge to keep us aware of the harder realities of twentieth-century life. Constantin Brancusi's works fall somewhere in between Giacometti's and Moore's. The smooth, clean lines of these sculptures prefigure the shapes of modern aircraft or rockets. All of these artists, through their sculpture, are presenting abstractions in a three-dimensional, concrete form. The magic of their works is that, although concrete in shape and texture, they are able to express ideas which are timeless and universal abstract ideas.

The two World Wars, which defined the art of the first half of the twentieth century, still have an influence on contemporary art. The physical devastation has been thoroughly explored and the psychic fallout on the generations since World War II is still being felt. These conflicts are still giving artists a backboard from which to bounce themselves back and forth in hundreds of new directions. The question is: Will there be a strong new direction or style in art as we move into a new century? Considering the dynamics of our world at present, the answer is probably: No.

Music of the Early Twentieth Century

In 1889, the World Exposition in Paris ushered in the beginning of a new century and thus a new era in all aspects of life. We have seen the new directions in the art world. A similar and inevitable change took place in the world of music. However, many composers still followed a traditional middle course. The romantic age was followed by a period known as the **post-romantic** era, which lasted about 20 years (1890–1910). The music of **Gustav Mahler**, the great Austrian conductor and composer, may be considered a bridge between the romantic and the modern eras. His music may be compared to Beethoven's in that he too composed a series of deeply intense, emotional symphonies often including choral pieces. Mahler did work in a traditional vein.

It was the work of Impressionist composers that really ushered in the twentieth century. Impressionism was the bridge into the twentieth century. Just before the onset of World War I, there was a reaction against romanticism. This desire for change affected all the arts. Painters presented new planes of existence; writers presented new points of view. In music, the traditional major-minor scale began to be considered obsolete. Impressionist composers and musicians looked to the construction of the religious music of the Middle Ages for inspiration. Non-Western music was also a strong influence in

Gustav Mahler

music as it was in the arts. Japanese and Chinese instruments were incorporated into Western works. **Dissonance**, or non-harmonic music, became a value unto itself and new sounds and tones became acceptable. Composers put together unusual combinations of sounds and tones just as Monet put unusual combinations of paint colours to create his vision.

Impressionist composers, like the painters, let themes and melodies flow into each other subtly. Unlike romantic concertos and symphonies, which are full of climaxes and mood changes, Impressionist works used short lyric forms such as **preludes**, **nocturnes**, and **arabesques**. These titles were often used for paintings as well. And, as in painting, Impressionist music had many romantic qualities: lyricism, an incorporation of painting and poetry, and an emphasis on mood and atmosphere.

Just as French painters dominated the painting scene, so did French composers dominate the music scene, replacing the Austro-Hungarian Empire as a source of music. **Claude Debussy** (1862–1918) is considered the most important of the French Impressionist composers. He was a child prodigy, entering the Paris Conservatoire at 11. The music he composed was shockingly contrary to the strict academic rules of the Conservatoire. He wanted to compose music for his own pleasure. This ties in to the late-nineteenth-century aesthetic, "art for art's sake." However, his music had a strong intellectual base in that he wanted to communicate ideas as well as feelings. Debussy was influenced by the French symbolist poets. Their literary movement tried to present poetic images through symbolism, similar to the art of the symbolist painters. They wanted to move language away from its intellectual purpose—conveying a meaning—to its symbolic purpose—presenting an idea. Their free verse forms were echoed by Debussy's musical language.

Debussy, like the Impressionist painters, felt that art, particularly music, was a sensory experience. He reacted against the romantic expression of powerful emotions. Instead, he created subtle pieces of music that suggested feeling and mood, rather than stating them. His best known orchestral works are *Afternoon of a Faun*, *La Mer*, and *Nocturnes*. Debussy also experimented with pieces for solo piano. As did the Impressionists, Debussy sought to capture a moment in time through his abstract and utterly beautiful pieces. His most famous piano work is *Clair de Lune*, which tries to capture the beauty and evanescent quality of moonlight. By the time World War I broke out, Debussy was very ill with cancer. He was extremely upset by the carnage of the war and the devastation of his country. He kept working in an attempt to transcend the horrors of the war through the beauty of his music. Debussy died in 1918, perhaps as exhausted as his country.

The greatest of the French post-Impressionist composers was **Maurice Ravel**. He achieved recognition after World War I. Like Debussy, Ravel was attracted by the art of the Impressionists. He was influenced by Spanish music and the music of the nineteenth-century romantics. He was also deeply affected by World War I. Although over 40, he served as a driver in the army but had to be discharged due to ill health. One of his most famous works is his *Concerto for the Left Hand*, written for a concert pianist who lost his right hand in the war. In his later years Ravel became ill with a brain disease which afflicted his ability to speak and move. It became impossible for him to compose. Naturally, he became horribly depressed that he still had so much music within him. He died, during an operation, in 1937.

Maurice Ravel

German Expressionism

In Germany, the Expressionist movement extended to music as well as to literature and art. It reached its peak during the time of the Weimar Republic. As Impressionists focused on nature for their inspiration, Expressionist composers, like their artistic counterparts, looked inside the human psyche for subject matter. Their music is characterized by several unusual features, for example, drastic changes in melody and extreme highs or lows on the register. These features were designed to reflect the emotional highs and lows of the human soul.

Igor Stravinsky and *The Rite of Spring*

One of the greatest influences on twentieth-century music was the work of Igor Stravinsky. Stravinsky was born near St. Petersburg in 1882 and was brought up to play the piano and appreciate music as his father was a professional musician. However, his parents wanted him to study law rather than music. Thus, he became a lawyer but kept composing and eventually found success in a musical career.

Sergey Diaghilev, the artistic director of the Russian Ballet in Paris, which featured the dancing of Nijinsky, commissioned Stravinsky to write a score for the ballet *The Firebird* and a year later for *Petrouchka*. The success of these productions ensured Stravinsky's position as a major modern artist. His most important and controversial work was his 1913 music for the ballet *The Rite of Spring*. Much like the reception of Rodin's statue *Balzac*, *The Rite of Spring* was met with horror and derision. Audiences considered it an insult to all art. Yet a year later, it was met with approbation and excitement. Such is the up-and-down nature of the public. When one considers the story told by *The Rite of Spring*, one may understand the outrage it engendered. All art in this time was influenced by the music

and imagery and mythology of the New World. *The Rite of Spring* celebrates primitive, pagan ritual and sacrifice. It is divided into two parts: *The Adoration of the Earth* and *The Sacrifice*.

The Adoration of the Earth, which depicts the birth of spring, features a group of young male and female dancers who move slowly before a "sacred mound." These movements gradually become interwoven to suggest a physical union between the dancers. Part I ends with complete abandonment to the physical as the men and women perform the *Dance of the Earth*. Part II is *The Sacrifice*. One of the women is chosen to be the sacrifice to fertility. After a slow movement, which builds up the tension of the impending death, the ballet climaxes as the chosen woman dances herself to death and is offered

to the earth. Her body is born aloft by the young male dancers and presented to the mound. The ballet is over.

The music accompanying this outrageous ballet employs a new type of musical language involving dissonance and many layers of tones and rhythms. Stravinsky also used an enormous orchestra. When watching a performance of *The Rite of Spring*, one is always amazed to see the number of extra violins and timpani drums moved onto the stage before the bassoon begins its long, plaintive wail that signals the start of the piece. Whether performed as a ballet or an orchestral piece, *The Rite of Spring* is a powerful and evocative work that still amazes and even shocks contemporary audiences.

In 1914, with the outbreak of World War I, Stravinsky and Diaghilev were no longer able to stage these types of productions. Stravinsky and his family moved to Switzerland, where he worked at smaller, more intimate pieces. After the Russian Revolution of 1917, he could not return to Russia and so moved to France. He lived there as a conductor and performer until 1939, when he went to the United States to lecture at Harvard. The outbreak of World War II caused him to move permanently to California. He lived there until he died in New York in 1971.

Igor Stravinsky

A further reaction to the romantic movement was seen in a revival of the classical style in the early 1920s. It is interesting that during the period of post-war problems in every sphere of life, artists should look to a time of order and harmony to express themselves. These composers felt that the duty of the composer was not to express emotion but to manipulate abstract combinations of sound. Russian composer *Igor Stravinsky*, one of the most significant artists of the early twentieth century, used abstraction to establish order. The focus of such music, like the artwork of the cubists or the literature of James Joyce, was on form and technique rather than content.

Nationalism in Music

The years after World War I saw a revival in musical nationalism, perhaps congruent with the rise in political nationalism. It is worth noting the composers who looked to their musical heritage for new and further inspiration saw the old music as a means of moving away from conventional musical styles. In France, Erik Satie and Francis Poulenc, among other composers, wrote songs, symphonic poems, ballets, and operas that subtly defied convention in subject matter and form. In Russia, *Sergey Rachmaninoff's* powerful symphonies and piano concertos defined a new romanticism. *Dmitri Shostakovich*, on the other hand, experimented with the symphonic form to create a completely new style for post-revolutionary Russia.

In England, prominent composers were Edward Elgar, Frederick Delius, and Benjamin Britten. Perhaps the most important was Ralph Vaughn Williams who incorporated the folk songs of England in his music. In Hungary, the composers Béla Bartók and Zoltán Kodály, in Czechoslovakia Leoš Janaček, in Spain Manuel de Falla, and in Finland Jan Sibelius, all used their national musical heritage as inspiration. With the approach of World War II, there was an outpouring of music that sought to celebrate the traditions of each European country. Perhaps these artists felt a need to gather their traditions around them before the horrible destruction of all they held precious began.

Literature of the Early Twentieth Century

As we have seen in the fields of music and art, the modern era, which we usually associate with the twentieth century, had its beginnings in the last decades of the nineteenth century. These bridging years were characterized by several features that signalled the coming change from an old world into a new. In these years, there was a weakening of the traditions and values so firmly upheld in the Victorian era. This reaction affected all aspects of European society. In the world of the arts, artists no longer wanted to associate themselves with the establishment. There was a strong movement to isolate themselves from the middle class. One method was physical isolation: artists deliberately lived in poor areas, in poor housing. This is when the idea of the "starving artist" arose. Irish writer James Joyce and, on the Continent, French and German writers, depicted the artist as a bohemian who rejected society. Artists did not want to think of themselves as catering to the philistine tastes of the middle class.

Another method was to provoke outrage. In England, the "art-for-art's-sake" movement, championed by the playwright Oscar Wilde and painter Aubrey Beardsley, produced works that were designed to shock and anger the late Victorian public. The behaviour of artists often mirrored their outrageous art. In England, the growth of a large, unsophisticated reading public gave way to newspapers and literature that catered to them. This created a huge gap all over Europe between popular art and literature on the one hand and highbrow or sophisticated art on the other.

Another feature of late Victorian literature was an almost Shakespearean spirit of pessimism. Thomas Hardy's fatalistic novels, such as *Tess of the d'Urbervilles*, portray characters who see themselves as pawns in a huge chess game, perpetual victims of fate.

As the Victorian age drew to a close, there was an even stronger reaction against its strictures and conservatism. People were in the mood for a freer society. The political situation in England added fuel to this fire. People protested the Boer War and imperialism in general. Writers too became involved in these issues. For example, Irish playwright George Bernard Shaw championed women's rights. The Irish struggle for independence was supported in the works of James Joyce and *William Butler Yeats*. They also worked hard to keep Irish culture alive by encouraging a renaissance in Irish literature.

Despite the death of Queen Victoria and the reaction against traditional Victorian society, life for the established order in England continued as ever. The upper classes continued to rule in the style to which they were accustomed. The Edwardian and Georgian periods in Britain, obviously named for the ruling monarchs, occurred from 1901 to 1914, just before World War I. This rather peaceful period may be considered the lull before the storm. A contemporary film, *The Shooting Party*, written by Harold Pinter, portrays the nature of the time perfectly.

However, underneath the seemingly perfect exterior of English country life, there was a sense of restless energy signalled by experimentation in all branches of the arts. We have already seen how the personal and national agonies that afflicted all European nations during World War I were manifest in the art and music of the time. Needless to say, the horrors of the war redefined the consciousness of many writers who survived the experience and lived to write again.

New Forms in Poetry

Imagist Movement

During the early years of the twentieth century, the legacy left by the romantic movement in poetry was still felt in the continued use of traditional poetic styles. ***Imagist poetry*** arose in reaction to the emotional qualities of romantic poetry. As a literary movement, it coincided with similar movements in the visual and performing arts. There are parallels in abstract painting, particularly cubism, in the musical compositions of Igor Stravinsky, and in the work of the Russian filmmaker Sergey Eisenstein. Just as Debussy and Picasso were influenced by Oriental rhythms and African motifs, imagist poets used Oriental forms such as the haiku to express in a deceptively simple manner their very complex vision.

Consider this imagist poem written by the American poet ***Ezra Pound***. The poem was inspired by a scene he experienced in a Paris subway station. It is called "In the Station of the Métro."

> The apparition of these faces in the crowd;
> Petals on a wet, black bough.

Note the simplicity of this poem, yet the language reflects the beauty and texture of the image. These movements toward intellectualizing poetry were also seen in France in the work of ***French symbolist*** poet ***Charles Baudelaire***.

Poets began to experiment with language: they juxtaposed poetic language with the language of everyday conversation, including slang. The result was a highly intellectual attempt to create poetry that reflected the emotional qualities of real life as much as possible. The poet ***T. S. Eliot*** spearheaded this movement, which revolutionized the way artists wrote and people thought about poetry for the rest of this century.

T. S. Eliot is considered the foremost English-speaking poet of the twentieth century. Like Ezra Pound, he was an American, but Eliot lived and worked in England. Eliot started with the intellectual, imagist approach but took it many steps farther. His poetry is compelling for its ability to stir both the emotion and intellect of his readers. He experimented with poetic forms, language, and the structure of poetry, even playing with how a poem actually appeared on the page.

For example, one of his greatest works, "The Love Song of J. Alfred Prufrock," is actually a journey or odyssey of a man who feels isolated and alienated in a society for which he feels no affinity and yet he longs to be part of it. The poem's structure meanders over the pages on which it is printed, just as its narrator wanders through "certain half-deserted streets" in search of love or at least companionship. The poem combines rich and beautiful language and imagery with grotesque, bizarre scenes or bits of colloquial conversation. The poem forces the reader to think and yet the reader is always so conscious and sympathetic to the painful self-consciousness of the narrator, Prufrock, as he sits at a coffee party, trying desperately

T. S. Eliot

to make conversation. He feels he has "measured out... life in coffee spoons." His whole demeanour is that of a man in a middle-age crisis. Yet Eliot was only in his early 20s when he wrote the poem. It is amazing that one so young should have such a complex and mature vision of contemporary life.

The other extremely influential and important poet of the twentieth century was W. B. Yeats, who was Irish. He began his career in the 1890s, at the time when the "art for art's sake" aesthetic dominated the literary scene. Yeats soon developed his own particular aesthetic and style of poetry. Like the eighteenth-century poet and forerunner of romanticism William Blake, he developed his own particular mythology and symbolism based on Byzantine and Celtic imagery. His interest in Irish mythology led him to become a champion of the Irish independence movement. His poem "Easter 1916" commemorates the attempted Irish nationalist revolt against the British government in 1916. The poem ends with reference to the men involved in the uprising some of whom were known to Yeats:

> MacDonagh and MacBride
> And Connolly and Pearse
> Now and in time to be,
> Wherever green is worn,
> Are changed, changed utterly:
> A terrible beauty is born.

The line, "a terrible beauty is born," is prophetic of all the subsequent horrors inflicted not only on Ireland but on the whole of Europe in the twentieth century. One of Yeats's most interesting and controversial poems is "The Second Coming," written in the early 1920s.

> Turning and turning in the
>   widening gyre
> The falcon cannot hear the
>   falconer;
> Things fall apart; the centre
>   cannot hold;
> Mere anarchy is loosed upon
>   the world,
> The blood-dimmed tide is
>   loosed, and everywhere
> The ceremony of innocence is
> drowned;
> The best lack all conviction, while the worst
> Are full of passionate intensity.
> Surely some revelation is at hand;
> Surely the Second Coming is at hand.
> The Second Coming! Hardly are those words out
> When a vast image out of Spiritus Mundi
> Troubles my sight: somewhere in sands of the
>   desert
> A shape with lion body and the head of a man,
> A gaze blank and pitiless as the sun,
> Is moving its slow thighs, while all about it
> Reel shadows of the indignant desert birds.
> The darkness drops again; but now I know
> That twenty centuries of stony sleep
> Were vexed to nightmare by a rocking cradle,
> And what rough beast, its hour come round at last,
> Slouches towards Bethlehem to be born?

It is a powerful, esoteric poem containing biblical allusions and references to political events such as the Russian Revolution. It has also been seen to prophesy the rise of fascism in the 1930s. The lines "The best lack all conviction, while the worst/Are full of passionate intensity" seem painfully close to describing Chamberlain's attempt at appeasement just before the outbreak of World War II. The poem's menacing vision of an approaching anti-Christ foreshadows the prospect of yet another world war and perhaps all the other conflicts that plague our time.

Several poets who experienced World War I wrote many powerful poems which, although traditional in style, still move us very deeply with their powerful evocations of the horror of the war. Rupert Brooke wrote "The Hill and The Soldier." He was killed in the war at 27. Wilfred Owen's piece "Dulce et Decorum Est" is one of the most graphic descriptions of a mustard-gas attack. The poem is full of what Yeats called "a terrible beauty." And of course, no one can forget "In Flanders Fields" by John McCrae. No matter how many times we hear this poem on Remembrance Day or any other

Virginia Woolf

day, it still evokes the image of the millions of young people who gave their lives for so many countries.

T. S. Eliot's poem "The Waste Land" describes the spiritual wasteland that existed in Europe between the wars. Just as artists reacted by art movements such as Dadaism and Expressionism, many writers, disillusioned and horrified by the loss of so much life, looked to the political left for some sort of justification for existence. Many intellectuals from all over Europe joined the Republican army in the Spanish Civil War. However, it became obvious that their stand against the ultra-right was ineffectual: World War II broke out. The exhaustion and depression most people felt with the onslaught of yet another horrible conflict found a parallel in the character of European literature. This was a time of stagnation and fatigue. Thus, there were few significant changes or developments in literary techniques during this time.

The Novel

The novel underwent a transformation in the early twentieth century. Four of the most important English novelists of this time were **Joseph Conrad**, **James Joyce**, **D. H. Lawrence**, and **Virginia Woolf**. In keeping with the new psychological theories of Freud and Jung and with the changes in poetics, these novelists sought to develop a technique that allowed them to truly capture a sense of the human condition. One way was to present a narrative or situation in layers using multiple points of view. This allowed the novelist to present a totality of experience.

In one of the most important novels of this century, *Heart of Darkness*, Joseph Conrad's framed narration allows a character to explore his psyche and the human condition in general, through conversational narrative. Like the Ancient Mariner of Coleridge's poem, the narrator, Marlow, feels compelled to tell the tale of his extraordinary experience to a group of his friends. Marlow discovers his own "heart of darkness" through the telling of his story just as we discover our "hearts of darkness" through listening to it. He confronts a man, Kurtz, who has abandoned the hypocrisy of civilization for a life amidst the reality of the jungle where he has established himself as a god figure who dominates the people through terrorism and torture. Despite Kurtz's complete abandonment to "darkness," Marlow identifies with him and defends his name and honour to his family in Europe. In doing so, Marlow has to lie, an action which is an abomination to him.

Yet Marlow cannot bear to admit the truth of how civilization is merely a thin veneer with which we clothe ourselves against our darkness. Conrad uses conversational language, digression, flashbacks, and leaps forward in time to reflect the reality of one person telling a story to another. The result is a narrative which turns in on itself. The narrative is a form of psychotherapy as it allows Marlow to express his pain and guilt over his experience as he confronts his dark side. Conrad's narrative style anticipates the **stream-of-consciousness** style that arose in the early 1900s.

Virginia Woolf used multiple points of view to express a total reality in her novel *The Waves*. The novel tells the story of six children who move from childhood to adulthood. Each character presents his or her viewpoint of certain situations. The reader puts these situations together to obtain a complete picture of the life surrounding the characters and a realistic picture of the characters themselves.

James Joyce's novel *Ulysses*, based on Homer's classical epic written around 850 B.C.E., *The Odyssey*, details an extraordinary day in the life of an ordinary man as he journeys through Dublin having various adventures. The whole novel is one experiment with technique after another. For example, in one chapter, Joyce bases his narrative on the musical score of a Bach fugue. Indeed Wagner's concept of a leitmotif (recurring theme) is expressed through repetition of words and rhythms throughout the entire novel. The last 70 or so pages of the novel are pure stream-of-consciousness technique. Joyce eliminates all punctuation in an attempt to record the actual thought patterns of Molly Bloom, the wife of the hapless hero.

James Joyce

Beatrix Potter

One of the most enchanting museums one could possible visit is located in a small farm in the village of Sawrey in the English Lake District. This farm belonged to Beatrix Potter, the author and illustrator of the story of Peter Rabbit and a host of other wonderful animal tales which are loved by children worldwide.

Beatrix Potter was born to a well-to-do family in London in 1866. Like many young girls of this time she was raised by nannies, educated at home by governesses, and had little contact with her parents. She spent long periods on her own and had few friends. When Potter was six, her brother Bertram was born. He was to become a good friend to the young Beatrix. He too had a gift for drawing and shared an interest in animals. They kept a menagerie of pets in their schoolroom, including lizards, mice, and bats and these they drew and studied. However, her experience with the natural world opened up when her parents took their children away on holidays in Scotland and the Lake District. Both children loved the change from their urban existence and became passionate students of plant and animal life.

These holidays continued as the children became adults and it was through these holidays in Scotland that Potter became interested in fungi. She made hundreds of botanical drawings and paintings and formulated a new theory on the germination of spores. Her uncle, impressed by her work, took Potter and her drawings to the Royal Botanical Society. However, because of her age—but mostly because she was a woman—she was not taken seriously. Undaunted, she submitted a paper on her findings to the Linnean Society; however, she faced a setback again, as women were not allowed to deliver papers or attend meetings. Her paper was presented by someone else and received a lukewarm reception. We now know that her discovery was indeed a new and important one.

After this disappointment, Potter decided not to pursue her scientific interests and instead concentrated on the animal illustrations for which she was to become best known. Around this time she wrote an illustrated letter about her pet rabbit, Peter, to the sick child of a friend and former governess. The children loved it and she submitted a manuscript based on this to several publishers; it was rejected by all of them.

Beatrix Potter

Undeterred, she paid to have it printed herself. It was a huge success and every copy sold. Eventually in 1902, the publisher Frederick Warne agreed to publish it. Since that day, *The Tale of Peter Rabbit* has been continuously in print. With the proceeds of the book, she bought a little farm in the Lake District. It was here that most of her other books were written. Most of her tales are set around the Lake District, a few at Hill Top and the settings for her illustrations still remain recognizable today.

Potter became good friends with Norman Warne, the son of her publisher and he proposed marriage. Potter knew that her parents would not approve but, before they could announce it, Norman died of pneumonia. To recover from this sadness, she threw herself into the running of the farm and concentrated on her writing. At the age of 47, she eventually married a local solicitor, William Heelis, and she became well known in the Lake District as a farmer, a breeder of Herdwick sheep, and a conservator of the English countryside. For over 30 years, Potter bought local land to ensure that it didn't get into the hands of developers. Upon her death, she bequeathed this land to the National Trust together with her own farm, Hill Top.

Beatrix Potter's tales have been translated into over 15 languages. Thus, children around the world, some of whom may have never seen an actual rabbit, hedgehog, or squirrel, are still able to enjoy the simple stories and the marvellous characters that Potter has left behind as a timeless legacy to children and adults alike.

In this novel, theme becomes secondary to technique. We simply revel in Joyce's brilliant escapades with language. Yet, just as we have feelings for T. S. Eliot's Prufrock, so do we come to feel great empathy for the experiences of the antihero, Leopold Bloom, as he struggles to deal with his lack of confidence and his problematic marriage.

D. H. Lawrence was more concerned with exploring human relationships than technical experimentation. He was interested in all combinations of relationships: mother and son, lover and lover, friend and friend. Lawrence had a Freudian approach to human sexuality. In his novels *Lady Chatterley's Lover*, *The Rainbow*, and *Women in Love*, he openly describes the physical as well as emotional experiences of women during sexual relationships.

These four novelists laid the foundation for modern writing. However, they are only four of many whose works have become the building blocks for literature of successive generations.

Drama of the Twentieth Century

The works of Oscar Wilde, George Bernard Shaw, and Hendrik Ibsen bridged the gap between the Victorian and modern periods of drama. After these playwrights, drama existed in pockets of brilliance: Noel Coward in England for social satire, and Sean O'Casey and J. M. Synge, for exploring Irish problems. In the 1950s, the plays of John Osborne brought a new vitality to the theatre. His play *Look Back in Anger* raised the public's awareness of the frustrations and social problems existing in post-war England.

The other great movement in drama in the twentieth century is the *Theatre of the Absurd*. This movement tried to reflect the absurdity of modern life by dramatizing situations that had no plot basis but merely offered a slice of human existence.

The works of **Samuel Beckett**, **Harold Pinter**, and Bertold Brecht are akin to the art movements of post-war Europe. They portray characters with Dada-like names, such as Didi and Gogo from Beckett's *Waiting for Godot*, who indulge in meaningless conversations over impossible problems to arrive at no solution. Of these playwrights, Harold Pinter is perhaps the most approachable. He has worked in film as well as theatre, writing interesting screenplays for his own dramas in film and for film versions of novels.

Plays such as Beckett's *Waiting for Godot*, novels such as Joyce's *Finnegans Wake* or poems such as Eliot's *The Four Quartets* signal the dramatic change in the structure and function of classic literary styles and themes. Just as artistic and musical forms became more and more abstract, so did literary styles. In the latter half of the twentieth century, form came to equal or even replace theme as the predominant feature of a piece of literature. Whole new genres and styles have developed to suit our contemporary consciousness.

Reflections

The most profound influence on the arts of the second half of the twentieth century was World War II. The physical and psychological trauma of the war has faded, but it lingers in all facets of today's society. The movement toward the expression of the inner reality of human nature, begun by artists such as Joyce, Eliot, Picasso, Kandinsky, and Stravinsky, continues in the works of the post-war artists who continue to question our increasingly complex world through their artistic expression. As the new century approaches, the questions multiply, but answers are few and far between.

ART
Key Concepts, Figures, and Events

Symbolist Art	Fauvism	Wassily Kandinsky	Dadaism	Surrealism
Art Nouveau	Henri Matisse	Cubism	Marcel Duchamp	Salvador Dalí

1. Find some examples of Art Deco pieces or Art Deco buildings and discuss their particular style. Compare them to some of the Art Nouveau paintings. How do they seem to relate?

2. Another great painter of the Fauvist movement was André Derain. Compare his *London Bridge* to one of Monet's studies of London, such as *Waterloo Bridge* or *Westminster Bridge*. Discuss how a comparison of these two paintings demonstrates a dramatic shift in colour and technique between the late nineteenth and early twentieth centuries.

3. Consider various art pieces by Emil Nolde, Käthe Kollwitz, or George Roualt painted around World War I. How does their art reflect this particular frame of time?

4. Georges Braque and Fernand Léger were two very influential cubist painters. Research some of their works and discuss how their type of abstraction compares to that of Picasso.

5. Joan Miró and Max Ernst were surrealist painters whose styles differed greatly from that of Salvador Dalí. Study their works and describe what is particulary unusual about each one's surrealist vision Can you find common images or themes?

6. Edvard Munch created a series of very powerful paintings that detail the slow death of his sister by tuberculosis. Locate several of these and discuss how each one reveals a progression from realism to the pure abstraction of his grief and pain over her impending death.

MUSIC
Key Concepts, Figures, and Events

Post-Romanticism	Dissonance	Maurice Ravel	Serge Diaghilev	Dmitri Shostakovich
Gustav Mahler	Claude Debussy	Igor Stravinsky	Sergey Rachmaninoff	

1. Listen to several pieces of Debussy's piano music and discuss how he was influenced by Oriental music.

2. Compare a piece of music by Debussy and a painting by Monet.

3. Listen to Ravel's *Daphnis et Chloé* and Debussy's *La Mer*. How are these pieces characteristic of early-twentieth-century styles and themes? Do they in any way relate to the art of the time?

4. Compare Mahler's *Resurrection Symphony* with *Beethoven's Ninth*. How does the late romantic piece of music differ from the early romantic piece?

LITERATURE
Key Concepts, Figures, and Events

William Butler Yeats
Harold Pinter
Imagist poetry
T.S. Eliot

Ezra Pound
French Symbolists
Charles Baudelaire
Joseph Conrad

James Joyce
D. H. Lawrence
Virginia Woolf
Stream of Consciousness

Theatre of the Absurd
Samuel Beckett

1. Locate some translations of original Japanese haiku. Compare them to some of the imagist poems of Ezra Pound and some of Debussy's piano pieces.

2. Research and study examples of the poetry of World War I and World War II. Do you notice any change in theme or style?

3. Charles Baudelaire published a series of poems called *The Flowers of Evil*. How do these works relate to the philosophy of symbolist poets? Compare several of Baudelaire's poems to some of Edgar Allan Poe's.

4. One of T. S. Eliot's most significant poems is "The Hollow Men." It opens with a quotation from Joseph Conrad's *Heart of Darkness*. It is very interesting to read both works and show how they relate to one another.

5. *Apocalypse Now* is a film version of Joseph Conrad's *Heart of Darkness*. Francis Ford Coppola, the director, uses the song *The End*, by the Doors, to begin the movie. Discuss how one or both of these two modern genres are metaphors for Conrad's message in *Heart of Darkness*.

6. Read several of Yeats's poems that deal with the Irish question. What do they reveal about the political situation at the time they were written? What do they reveal about Yeats's perception of the Irish consciousness of the time?

7. Virginia's Woolf's diaries reveal interesting details not only about her life and ideas about literature but also about the way common people felt during World War II. Cite some excerpts from these diaries and describe her attitudes and those of her friends toward World War II.

8. The plays of George Bernard Shaw are extremely humorous and powerful. They are wonderful to see performed and most enjoyable to read. Within a group, read and perform one of Shaw's plays such as *Heartbreak House* or *Major Barbara*. Discuss how the play you chose reflects his vision.

9. Henrik Ibsen's two most powerful plays are *Hedda Gabler* and *A Doll's House*. Try to see a performance, live or on video. Discuss how these plays show the struggle of women to escape the repressive society of Victorian Norway.

Skills Focus

Avoiding Historical Fallacies

One of the dangers faced by historians and students of history is the use of historical fallacies. A fallacy is an error in reasoning that can render an argument logically invalid. When history essays are based on or include historical fallacy, the argument being presented is often weakened to the point of not standing up to scrutiny. This can be a very unfortunate error on the part of the student because, despite having carefully carried out the research and presenting credible facts, flaws in reasoning can limit the effectiveness of the essay.

An example of a fallacy of history which is commonly heard is that history repeats itself. While the study of history can assist us in detecting trends and predicting future events based on our understanding of the past, history never repeats itself. Another common fallacy is to refer to events as inevitable. No incident can be said to have been inevitable as many factors can affect the course of events. A chain of occurrences can be said to have rendered an event highly likely, but it is never accurate to say an occurrence could not have been avoided or could not have happened differently had events unfolded differently. Below are a list of other common fallacies; make sure that you clearly understand them. Once you have read and understood the fallacies listed, review a piece of historical writing you have done in the past. Does any of these fallacies exist in your argument? How could you alter your argument to avoid the fallacy? Exchange a piece of historical writing with a friend and see if you can detect errors in logic in each other's work. Try to help each other strengthen the essays by eliminating the use of historical fallacies. This is an excellent exercise to go through before handing in a major term paper. It can help to improve the strength of your essay and your overall grades, aside from helping to build your analytical skills.

Historical Fallacies

1. Post hoc, propter hoc
This fallacy occurs when it is assumed that event A alone caused event B. For example, slaves in Jamaica revolted in 1831, leading Britain to decide to end slavery in the British Empire. In fact, there were many other causes leading to this decision.

2. Reductive Fallacy
Oversimplifying an event. For example, World War I was caused by nations being competitive.

3. Fallacy of Indiscriminate Pluralism
This fallacy occurs when a variety of events is listed without considering the significance of each. Some causes may have been of tremendous importance, while others were insignificant. They should not be given equal weight in the argument.

4. Fallacy of Mechanistic Cause

This fallacy suggests that the sum of a sequence of events must equal the cause. This is not always the case. The cause of an event may not be the result only of preceding events. For example, an event may occur randomly.

5. Fallacy of Reason as Cause

This fallacy occurs in situations where it is assumed the historical character's actions must have been based on rational decisions and/or motives. It cannot always be assumed that people's actions are carried out for rational reasons. For example, attempting to explain all of Napoleon's military decisions based on the assumption he always acted rationally may not be valid.

6. Fallacy of Responsibility

This occurs when there is confusion between "who is to blame" and "why an event happened." For example, Adolf Hitler is blamed for the Holocaust, yet this does not provide a sound explanation for why it happened.

7. Cleopatra's Nose

This fallacy is also known as "what-if history." Speculating as to what would have happened if events had been different produces bad history. For example, what if Cleopatra would have had a big nose, then perhaps Mark Antony would not have fallen in love with her and then....

Suggested Sources for Further Research

Adamthwaite, Anthony, *The Making of the Second World War* (Unwin Hyman, 1979)

Bessel, Richard, *Life in the Third Reich* (Oxford University Press, 1987)

Browning, Christopher, *Fateful Months* (Holmes & Meier, 1985)

Deutscher, Issac, *Stalin* (Oxford University Press, 1967)

Eksteins, Modris, *Rites of Spring* (Lester and Opren Dennys, 1989)

Ellis, John, *Eye Deep In Hell* (Pantheon Books, 1976)

Fussell, Paul, *The Great War and Modern Memory* (Oxford University Press, 1975)

Gilbert, Felix, *The End of the European Era, 1890 to the Present* (Norton, 1991)

Gilbert, Martin, *The Holocaust: The Jewish Tragedy* (Collins, 1986)

Gill, Anton, *The Journey Back From Hell* (William Morrow and Co., 1988)

Keegan, John, *The Second World War* (Viking, 1990)

Liddle, Peter, *Voices of War* (Lee Cooper, 1988)

Marwick, Arthur, *Women at War 1914-1918* (Fontana Paperback, 1977)

Massie, Robert, K., *Dreadnought: Britain, Germany and the coming of the great war* (Random House, 1991)

Riasanovsky, Nicholas, *A History of Russia* (Oxford University Press, 1984)

Rich, Norman, *Hitler's War Aims* (Norton, 1974)

Terraine, John, *The Smoke and the Fire: Myths and Anti-Myths of War, 1861–1945* (Sidgwick & Jackson, 1980)

Tuchman, Barbara, *The Guns of August* (Dell, 1962)

UNIT 4

Europe in the New World Order

After a generation of war, much of Europe and its people lay in ruins. The task of rebuilding the devastated cities and countryside would be a monumental one. The superpowers of the past few centuries, Britain, France, Germany, and Austria, had suffered too greatly in both world wars to be able to dominate the post-war world: by 1945, they were eclipsed by the United States and the Soviet Union.

The post-war world was divided along ideological lines: Western democracies against East European communism. With the advent of atomic weapons, confrontation became a threat to humankind: for the first time in the history of the world, humans possessed the capability of annihilating the human race. The decades following 1945 were thus a time of uneasy peace in Europe, a time when the cost of open warfare between the major powers—annihilation—was too high, resulting in limited wars between smaller states.

The changes which were reshaping Europe were also impacting on much of the world. The age of European colonialism had finally come to an end. In the decades following World War II, European empires were dismantled and former colonies were granted their independence. The process of decolonization proved volatile as ethnic rivalries often erupted into civil war. Former empires split into independent states, many of which, in turn, joined trading blocs in order to survive.

Perhaps the least tangible but nonetheless most profound change to occur since 1945 has been in our perception of the world: our religious beliefs, assumptions about family structures, the roles of the sexes, the role of science in society, and the nature of education have all come under scrutiny in the past few decades. Space travel, feminism, existentialism, the emergence of a global village, and the computer revolution have all contributed to our rethinking of the way the world operates and our place in society. While the Renaissance and the Scientific Revolution laid the foundations for the modern world, the latter half of the twentieth century has paved the way for the dismantling of the modern age.

	Political/Military	INTELLECTUAL	Cultural
1942			Albert Camus: *The Stranger*
1944	IMF/World Bank is established		
1945	Yalta Agreement ends World War II		Emily Carr dies
	United Nations is formed		
1947			Jackson Pollock: *Lucifer*
1948	Communists take over Czechoslovakia		Andrew Wyeth: *Christina's World*
	Civil war in Greece		
1949	Mao Zedong comes to power in China	Simone de Beauvoir: *The Second Sex*	George Orwell: *1984*
	NATO is established		
1950	North Korea invades South Korea		
1951			Arnold Schönberg dies
1953	Stalin dies	Ludwig Wittgenstein: *Philosophical Investigations*	
1954			Samuel Becket: *Waiting for Godot*
			Karlheinz Stockhausen: *Electronic Studies* finished
1955	Warsaw Pact is signed		
1956	Suez Crisis		
1957	Soviets launch *Sputnik* satellite		
1958			Jean-Paul Sartre: *No Exit*
			John Cage: *Fontana Mix*
1960			Harold Pinter: *The Caretaker*
1961	Berlin Wall is erected		
1962	Cuban Missile Crisis		Andy Warhol: *Marilyn Monroe*
1963		Betty Friedan: *The Feminine Mystique*	
1964	Vietnam War begins	Marshall McLuhan: *Understanding Media*	Margaret Laurence: *The Stone Angel*
		Herbert Marcuse: *One-Dimensional Man*	
1965			Edgard Varèse dies
1967	Arab-Israeli Six-Day War		The Beatles: *Sgt. Pepper's Lonely Hearts Club Band*
1969		American astronauts land on the moon	
1973	Oil crisis		
1974			Duke Ellington dies
1975	Helsinki Agreement signed		
	Vietnam War ends		
1976			Philip Glass: *Einstein on the Beach*
			Christo: *Running Fence*
1989	Soviet communism collapses		
1994			Michael Ondaatje: *The English Patient*

17

Contemporary Europe, 1945–1995

CHAPTER HIGHLIGHTS

- The role of new global financial institutions

- The emergence and impact of a bipolar world

- The nature of post-war Western European economy, culture, and society

- The importance of new philosophical movements, such as existentialism and feminism

- The positive and progressive results of scientific and technological innovation and their environmental impact

- The nature of economics and politics behind the Iron Curtain

- The European themes of the 1960s and 1970s: politics, terrorism, oil crises, racism, and Thatcherism

---

Anyone observing the European scene at the end of World War II would have noticed two things. First of all, seven years of fighting had thoroughly devastated the Continent. "What is Europe now?" asked British prime minister Winston Churchill mournfully. "A rubble heap, a charnel-house (morgue), a breeding ground of pestilence and hate." The second striking point, though less immediately obvious, had to do with Europe's international status. Decisions regarding Europe's future lay in the hands of two superpowers: the Soviet Union and the United States. The Soviets, with several million soldiers in Eastern Europe, dominated the Continent militarily; the Americans dominated economically. During World War II, the need to defeat Nazi forces had made allies of two very dissimilar nations. But their wartime collaboration was an uneasy one and, once the fighting stopped, the profound differences that separated them complicated the process of drawing up a post-war settlement.

Thanks to American aid and to their own strenuous efforts, the nations in Western Europe recovered relatively quickly. Eastern Europe, under Soviet domination, got on its feet more slowly. In international affairs, however, tensions between the two superpowers erupted into a cold war whose crises dominated European and world politics for a generation after 1945. Only when communism collapsed in 1989 did the cold war finally come to an end. At that time, many people looked forward to a new era of peace and prosperity; unfortunately, as we shall see, such hopes proved to be overly optimistic. Economic uncertainty and ethnic unrest have created a new set of problems for Europe to deal with as the twenty-first century draws near.

Rebuilding the Continent

At the end of World War II, conditions in Europe were far worse than after World War I. The invention of the long-range bomber had made it possible for both Allied and Nazi forces to launch massive air raids on each other's territories. Practically every major city in Europe was devastated; bridges and railroads in many areas were non-existent; vast stretches of Central and Eastern Europe resembled a lunar landscape. In addition to the material damage, there was an immense human tragedy. About 40 million Europeans died in World War II, four times the number in the previous war; 6 million of the dead were Jewish victims of the Holocaust. A year after hostilities ended, millions had to survive on rations providing 6300 kJ or less per day.[1] Millions (40 to 50) of displaced persons fled their homes, among them 10 million German-speaking refugees from Eastern Europe.

Planning for the future began in 1944, when representatives from 44 Allied countries met in the New Hampshire resort town of Bretton Woods to discuss financial policy. They set up institutions that still function today. The ***International Monetary Fund*** (IMF) (a kind of international insurance fund) helped stabilize world financial systems, while the World Bank provided low-cost loans for economic reconstruction. The countries present at the conference agreed to contribute funds in order to start up these organizations; however, since the U.S. contributed about one third of the total, they dominated both bodies. American predominance was symbolized by the fact that headquarters for both the IMF and the World Bank were located in Washington, D.C. and the American dollar became the currency standard against which others were measured.

Another key contribution to European economic recovery was the European Recovery Program, more commonly known as the ***Marshall Plan***. Proposed in 1947 and named after George C. Marshall, American secretary of state from 1945 to 1947, the Plan made over 13 billion U.S. dollars available to rebuild industry with up-to-date technology. Such aid, along with food and raw materials, was crucial in the years immediately following the war. Recovery was slow, and political turmoil in France, Italy, and other Mediterranean countries threatened the stability of a world only recently at peace. Aid offered under the Marshall Plan was not merely a handout. The Americans insisted that Europeans take responsibility for planning their economic recovery:

This photograph captures the impact of the Marshall Plan as a typical French family admires their new tractor acquired under the plan. The horse-drawn farm implement provides a stark contrast.

"The initiative must come from Europe," declared Marshall, "the role of the U.S. should consist of friendly aid." All European nations were invited to participate. Participating nations had to allow the U.S. government to supervise their budgets and to agree to purchase American exports. Not unexpectedly, the Soviet Union refused to take part in the Plan. Soviet leader Joseph Stalin would have accepted American financial assistance only if it came with no strings attached. Soviet allies in Eastern Europe took their cue from the Soviets and also turned down Marshall Plan assistance. Moscow organized a rival organization, COMECON, which integrated the economies of Soviet bloc countries.

The United States took on the lion's share of responsibility in helping to reconstruct European economies for several reasons. Compassion (the impulse to help people in distress) certainly played a part; so did economic and political considerations. The war had made the United States the world's richest nation, accounting for 50 percent of the world's gross national product. American leaders realized that the U.S. could not prosper for long in a ruined world.

---

1 A moderately active woman, age 20–50, requires 7980 KJ per day; a moderately active man requires more.

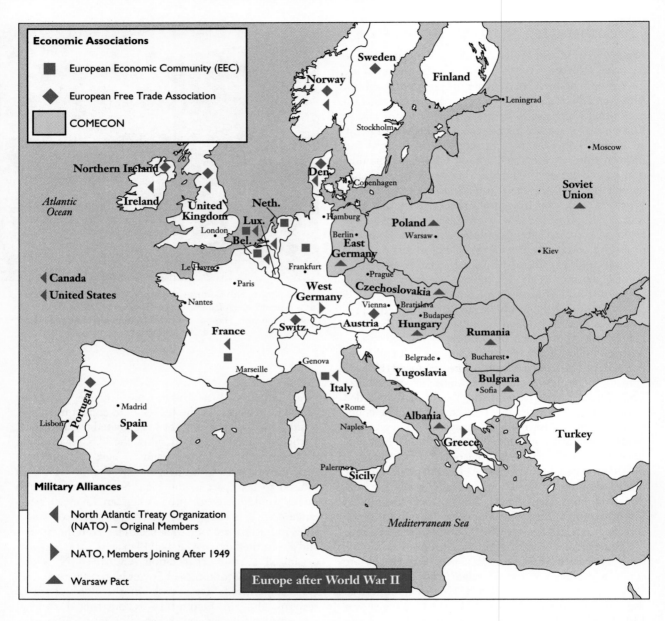

Economic Associations

- ■ European Economic Community (EEC)
- ◆ European Free Trade Association
- ▭ COMECON

Military Alliances

- ◀ North Atlantic Treaty Organization (NATO) – Original Members
- ▶ NATO, Members Joining After 1949
- ▲ Warsaw Pact

Europe after World War II

Moreover, the beginning of the cold war and the dismal prospect of communist dictatorships persuaded American legislators to grant the billions needed to help return Europe to normalcy.

The Marshall Plan is one of the most successful foreign-aid programs ever undertaken by any country. It also served as a model for Western European cooperation in other areas. In 1951, France, West Germany, Belgium, Luxembourg, the Netherlands, and Italy formed an organization to coordinate the production of steel and coal. Seven years later, this body, known as the European Coal and Steel Community, expanded into a free-trade area called the ***European Economic Community*** (EEC). With the creation of a large, tariff-free market, businesses could cut costs, lower the prices of consumer goods, and raise the standard of living. By the late 1960s, Western Europe had become an economic powerhouse. The creation of the EEC was also significant because it showed that European states, most notably the long-time enemies France and West Germany, could put aside national rivalries in the interest of their common welfare.

The Emergence of a Bipolar World

Constructing a stable international order in 1945 was another important issue on the Allied agenda. A number of questions had to be resolved: What could be done to prevent future wars? What should happen to Germany? What kind of border changes should be drawn in Central Europe? There was profound disagreement on these issues between Stalin on the one hand, and Roosevelt and Churchill on the other. Reaching a consensus would not be an easy task.

World Peace and the United Nations

American president Franklin Roosevelt believed that maintaining world peace required an international body that could restrain aggressors effectively. "All nations of the world must be guided in spirit to abandon the use of force," he had declared in 1941. At the Dumbarton Oaks Conference in Washington, D.C. in 1944, Roosevelt outlined his idea for a new international organization, later to be called the **United Nations** (UN). In some ways, it was similar to the League of Nations created in 1920: all members had a seat in the General Assembly. In addition, there was a Security Council of the world's most powerful nations; this body would have the authority to punish aggressors with "immediate bombardment and possible invasion" if necessary.

The nucleus of the UN was the Security Council, in which China, France, Britain, the United States, and the Soviet Union received permanent seats. (Six seats were allotted to smaller powers who held office for two-year terms.) The permanent delegates had a veto power over Security Council decisions. This arrangement was made to accommodate Stalin, who opposed any scheme that would have given smaller powers an opportunity to restrict Soviet freedom of action in international affairs. Since the Americans and the Soviets almost always disagreed, joint action to restrain aggressors proved to be almost impossible. Too often, the United Nations became an arena for verbal confrontation between the superpowers and their allies.

The German Problem

Within Europe itself, the most pressing question was what to do with Germany. Stalin wanted to deindustrialize Germany and return it to a kind of primitive agricultural state. His allies went along with this goal at first, then decided that a modernized, demilitarized Germany under Allied control would be a better guarantee for peace. In accordance with the 1945 Yalta agreement, the Allies divided Germany into four zones of occupation. (At British insistence, France was allotted a zone of occupation.) The former German capital, Berlin, was partitioned in a similar fashion. Once Germany was de-Nazified and a suitable system of government put in place, the occupying forces could withdraw. The whole process, it was hoped, would take no more than four years.

Unfortunately, friction between Allied leaders scuttled those plans. The issue of how much Germany should pay in reparations provoked dissension. A figure of 20 billion dollars was agreed upon, half of which would go to the Soviet Union. The Soviets, however, wanted more than money. In defiance of their allies, they began to confiscate all the German industry and factories they could lay their hands on; and, in order to speed up the expropriation process, they widened the gauge of German railroads to correspond to the Soviet gauge. In the Soviet view, German property represented the spoils of war, to which they were entitled as victors.

Meanwhile, the Western Allies took steps that alarmed the Soviets: they instituted a new currency system in their zones and encouraged German leaders to start drafting a new democratic system of government. After the Berlin blockade of 1948 (in which the Soviet Union blockaded the land routes leading to the Allied sector of Berlin), the Americans, British, and French merged their zones of occupation into one unit, creating the Federal Republic of Germany. The Soviets, in turn, established the communist German Democratic Republic in the area that they controlled. The city of Berlin, which lay inside the communist German Democratic Republic, was also divided, so that East Berlin was communist-controlled while West Berlin was in the hands of the Federal Republic of Germany. This created the awkward situation of a free and democratic West Berlin surrounded by communist-held territory.

What would be done with former Nazis? There were quite a few of them, almost 8 million officially

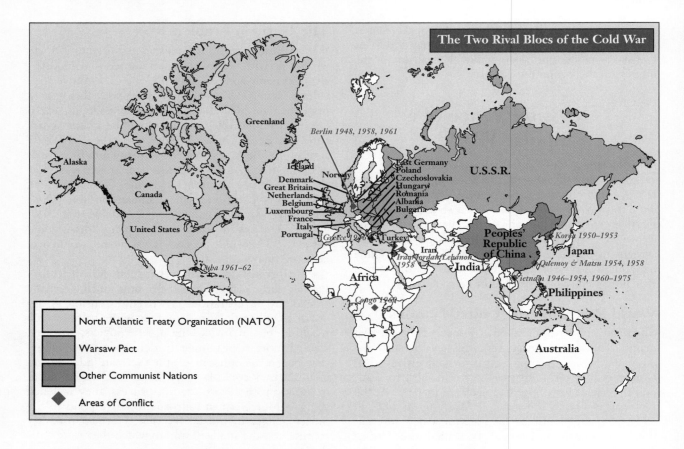

The Two Rival Blocs of the Cold War

Greenland

Berlin 1948, 1958, 1961

Alaska

Iceland
Norway
Denmark
Great Britain
Netherlands
Belgium
Luxembourg
France
Italy
Portugal

East Germany
Poland
Czechoslovakia
Hungary
Romania
Albania
Bulgaria

U.S.S.R.

Canada

United States

Cuba 1961–62

Greece

Turkey

Iran
Iran/Jordan/Lebanon
1958

Peoples'
Republic
of China

Korea 1950–1953

Japan

Quemoy & Matsu 1954, 1958

Vietnam 1946–1954, 1960–1975

India

Philippines

Africa

Congo 1960

Australia

North Atlantic Treaty Organization (NATO)

Warsaw Pact

Other Communist Nations

◆ Areas of Conflict

registered, from all walks of life: ordinary citizens, business and academic leaders, judges, and key officials in the civil service. Stalin, who preferred brutal and quick solutions, suggested rounding up 50 000 Nazi leaders and simply shooting them. After much wrangling, the Allies set up a War Crimes Tribunal in the German city of Nuremberg. They identified three categories of crimes: crimes against peace, crimes against humanity, and war crimes. Of the 24 Nazi leaders tried in Nuremberg in 1945–1946, three were acquitted, 12 condemned to death, and the rest sentenced to life imprisonment. Other trials followed of less important Nazis. The Soviets and French went after the more serious criminals, while the Americans and British examined thousands of individual cases.

When the cold war began, the West shifted its attention to fighting communism. As a result, many former Nazis quietly resumed their lives and hid the details of their criminal past. Much the same happened in East Germany. The Soviets were not inclined to

look into people's past as long as they agreed to co-operate with communist regimes.

Dividing Eastern Europe

Another source of friction concerned the fate of Eastern Europe, which was determined by Soviet needs and demands. One of Stalin's goals was to regain the territory that Russia had lost at the end of World War I. The three Baltic republics—Estonia, Lithuania, and Latvia—which had once been part of czarist Russia, were incorporated into the Soviet Union along with a large part of Eastern Poland. By way of compensation, Poland received a slice of Eastern Germany. The Soviets also took over Czechoslovakia, Rumania, and Finland. With these changes, the boundaries of the Soviet Union were more or less the same as those of czarist Russia in 1914.

National security was a second Soviet concern. The German invasion in 1940 marked the second time in the twentieth century that Russian soil had felt the tread of German troops. Getting rid of the invaders cost millions of Soviet soldiers and citizens their lives. Nazi occupiers had treated Slavic peoples very brutally. Their attitude can be seen from a remark made by the sinister head of the Gestapo (Nazi secret police), Heinrich Himmler. "If ten thousand Russian females die of exhaustion digging an anti-tank ditch, that interests me only insofar as the ditch is dug." Nazis drove millions of Ukrainian and Russian civilians into slave labour camps, where they manufactured goods for the German war effort.

Given the Russian experience with German brutality, it is not surprising that Stalin wanted a protective barrier of "friendly" states in Eastern Europe in the event of another invasion. He was successful in attaining this objective: by 1949, a buffer zone of six satellite states—East Germany, Poland, Czechoslovakia, Rumania, Hungary, and Bulgaria—existed on the Western Soviet border. For a time, it seemed that Yugoslavia would also be part of the Soviet Empire in the eastern part of the continent, but Yugoslav communist leader Josip Broz, known as Tito, successfully challenged Stalin's attempt at domination by asserting Yugoslavia's independence. Finland also managed to retain its independence.

The Western Allies did not like the changes that the Soviets had imposed upon Central and Eastern Europe. But short of going to war, there did not seem to be much that they could do. The presence of several million Soviet troops meant that Eastern Europe was part of the Soviet sphere of influence.

Politics: The Revival of Democracy

The process of rebuilding the Continent had a political dimension. Germany and Italy had been ruled by fascist dictators and France had been a German puppet state. These countries now had to refashion their systems of government along democratic lines.

In 1948, the three Western Allies directed German leaders to begin drafting a new system of government. The Basic Law guaranteed German citizens fundamental rights and provided the framework for a democratic constitution. A federal system of government was put in place with a Bundestag, or lower house elected by the people, and an upper house representing the states. One important provision of the Basic Law stipulated that a party had to win 5 percent of the popular vote before its delegates could sit in the Bundestag; in addition, courts had the power to outlaw extremist parties. The framers of the Basic Law wanted to prevent the kind of chaotic situation that had characterized the Weimar Republic, where a large number of small antagonistic splinter parties destabilized the political process, giving Hitler an opportunity to gain power. Consequently, both communists and neo-Nazis were prevented from sitting in the Bundestag. The parties that dominated West German politics were the Christian Democratic Union and the Social Democratic Party.

For 17 years, from 1946 until his resignation in 1963, Christian Democratic chancellor Konrad Adenauer dominated West German politics. Adenauer's goal was to restore respect for Germany by cooperating with the U.S. and with Germany's neighbours. Under Adenauer's leadership, Germany took responsibility for the atrocities of the past and offered an apology along with financial compensation to Holocaust survivors. West Germany also adopted a very generous asylum law allowing refugees from other parts of the world to enter freely.

Italy too underwent a profound change. In 1946, Italian voters decided to abolish the monarchy in favour of a republican form of government. Italian politics were characterized by constant changes of government, although the Christian Democratic Party remained dominant.

After its liberation from Nazi rule, France adopted a new constitution, known as the Fourth Republic. In contrast to the stable West German situation, the French political scene was volatile: a multitude of parties resulted in a series of short-lived coalition governments and virtual decision-making paralysis. In 1958, war in its Algerian colony brought the Fourth Republic to the brink of collapse. General ***Charles de Gaulle***, who had been the leader of the French Resistance to Nazi Germany during the war, was called by the army to assume the position of president. De Gaulle supervised the preparation of a new constitution, that of the Fifth Republic, increasing the power of the president.

President Charles de Gaulle was not a humble man: "When I want to know what France thinks, I ask myself." He was confident that he represented the mind of the French electorate. Restoring respect for his country was de Gaulle's primary goal, just as it was for Adenauer in Germany. First, he stabilized the French franc, encouraged state-controlled enterprises, and took other measures to strengthen the economy. Under de Gaulle, the French economy achieved one of the highest rates of industrial growth in Europe. But whereas Adenauer made Germany into a loyal ally of the U.S., de Gaulle rejected "American hegemony." De Gaulle took France out of NATO (North Atlantic Treaty Organization), developed an independent French nuclear force, and tried to make France into a "third force" in international politics. He was only moderately successful in achieving this objective.

As far as the political situation in the rest of Western Europe is concerned, in the immediate post-war period there was a move toward the left: socialist parties formed governments in Britain, Italy, and the Scandinavian countries. By the 1950s, the mood of the voting public shifted to the right and conservative parties came to power—but they did not dismantle the socialist states and they accepted the need for government control of the economy. During the 1960s, socialist parties once again found themselves in office but they had to adjust to their new situation. Automated factories cut down on the number of blue-collar jobs. The number of white-collar workers (technicians, researchers, clerks, health care workers) increased. In effect, a new class structure had emerged. Under these new circumstances, socialist politicians could no longer rely on appeals to class struggle or revolution in order to win votes. They realized that their political platforms had to appeal to a broad range of the electorate.

It is interesting to note, however, that until the 1970s, communist parties managed to hang on to popular support. Communists had been very active in the resistance against the Nazis and their efforts earned them a great deal of prestige. Growing tensions between East and West diminished the appeal of communism but did not eliminate it entirely as a political force. This is especially true of France and Italy, but there were also significant differences between them. The French Communist Party followed Moscow; the Italian Communist Party, by contrast, rejected Moscow's domination. They worked hard to come up with practical election platforms that addressed voters' concerns. Though Italian communists were never elected to national office, they regularly won municipal elections.

Whatever the form of government or party in power, the politics of post-war Western Europe reaffirmed the values of parliamentary democracy. The two notable exceptions were Spain and Portugal, where dictatorships remained in place until the 1970s. In Spain, Generalissimo Francisco Franco ruled with an iron hand until his death in 1975, when, under the guidance of newly restored king Juan Carlos, Spain made a peaceful transition to a democratic system of government. In Portugal, a revolution overthrew the dictator Antonio Salazar in 1974 and opened the way for a democratically elected republic.

The Cold War

"From Stettin in the Baltic to Trieste in the Adriatic, an iron curtain has descended on the continent," declared Winston Churchill in a speech in Fulton, Missouri in 1946. This famous speech marked the beginning of the cold war, which can be described as a period of tension and confrontation between the Soviet Union and the United States short of actual war. Allied disagreements at Yalta in February 1945 and Potsdam had already foreshadowed the cold war; Soviet refusal to join the Marshall Plan, and the disputes over Germany and Eastern Europe described earlier made it a reality. Until its end in 1989, the cold war was the most critical feature of international politics.

Why did the cold war begin? Whose fault was it? Could it have been avoided? Until the former Soviet archives have been completely opened, no definitive answers to such questions can be given. Nevertheless, it is possible to point out several factors that contributed to this conflict.

In the prewar years, Americans had been very suspicious of the Soviets and relations between the two nations had not been cordial. The need to defeat Hitler made them allies and, for a while, much good feeling existed. American political leaders convinced themselves that Stalin, whom they nicknamed "Uncle Joe," was essentially a reasonable person. But the Soviet attempt to infiltrate Iran, and then Turkey, at the end of the war irritated the Americans. During the war, the Allies had agreed that the people of Eastern Europe would be allowed to establish "democratic institutions of their own choice." When Stalin, in total defiance of this aim, forcibly installed communist governments in one state after another, the West was alarmed. Press reports from journalists who had spent time in the post-war Soviet Union made it clear to the American public that the Soviet Union was a repressive dictatorship. This was not exactly new information, but the friendly feelings inspired by fighting a common enemy had made people forget about the nastier aspects of Stalin's rule.

The Soviets, for their part, distrusted the West and misinterpreted any Western Allied action. For example, the delay in starting the second front against Germany during World War II was a sore point. The Soviets felt that the Western Allies did not show sufficient concern for the tremendous human and material losses Soviet people suffered in pushing back Nazi armies and turning the tide of the war into eventual victory. No bombs had hit American factories; no invading armies had crossed its borders. The U.S. had indeed prospered as a consequence of war. In the Soviet view, American prosperity had been gained by Soviet sacrifice. Consequently, Stalin denounced the Marshall Plan as an American plot to extend American economic domination over Europe. He also believed that American capitalism was doomed to collapse.

On a more general level, the cold war represented the clash of two rival world views. Each superpower felt that it had a special role to play in history. The American sense of uniqueness had its roots in the experience of the sixteenth-century Pilgrim Fathers, who had arrived in New England in order to find religious freedom. In the eighteenth century, the American *Declaration of Independence* offered a model for other nations; it guaranteed individual rights, political freedom, and free enterprise. Many Americans felt they had a mission to spread their form of democracy to the rest of the world. As for the Soviet Union, it too had a sense of mission dating from the past. Since the fifteenth century, Russia regarded itself as a "Third Rome" and a successor to the ancient Christian capitals of Rome and Constantinople. After 1917, communist leaders envisioned a global proletarian revolution under their leadership. The organization of the Communist Information Bureau (COMINFORM) in 1947 united all European communist parties under Moscow's dominance and was regarded by the West as a confirmation of sinister Soviet intentions.

Whatever the reasons for its outbreak, the cold war divided first Europe and then the rest of the world into two rival blocs headed by superpowers. It was a war punctuated by a series of crises, all of which kept international relations at boiling point for a number of years.

The year 1948 was particularly critical. Communists took over Czechoslovakia, the one country in Eastern Europe with a democratic tradition. In Greece, an ongoing civil war pitted communist guerrillas (supported by the Soviet Union) against forces loyal to the Greek government. American president Harry Truman regarded communism as "bacteria" that had to be "contained" before the infection spread to the whole world. Truman dispatched a naval squadron to the Mediterranean and began to supply arms to the Greek government. Faced with the prospect of war with the U.S., the Soviets stopped supporting the guerrillas. Truman's policy of containment, as it was named, became the basis for American policy toward the USSR in the years that followed. In addition to sending

military assistance as they had done for Greece, the Americans made arrangements with other countries, allowing them to build military bases around the world. From these bases, the U.S. could launch bombers against the Soviet Union. The Soviets, of course, regarded containment as a threat to their security.

The most dramatic crisis in 1948 was undoubtedly the Berlin blockade and the Allied airlift. When the Western Allies merged their zones into a new country called West Germany, the Soviets responded by closing roads and railways linking West Berlin with West Germany. For almost a year, Allied planes flew in massive supplies to the besieged population. At one point, cargo planes landed every few minutes in the Templehof airport 24 hours a day. After 300 days, when they realized that the Allies were not going to back down, the Soviets gave up. Such confrontations, along with the victory of Mao Zedong in China in 1949 and the North Korean communist invasion of South Korea in 1950, persuaded many people in the West that communism had become a major threat to the free world.

In response to the communist danger in 1949, the United States, Great Britain, France, Canada, Portugal, Italy, the Netherlands, Luxembourg, Norway, and Iceland formed the **North Atlantic Treaty Organization** (NATO). (Greece and Turkey were admitted in 1952, West Germany in 1955, and Spain in 1982.) The members of NATO agreed to come to one another's assistance if attacked. The decision to allow Germany to join NATO in 1955 prompted the communist countries into a similar alliance of their own: the Warsaw Pact. Barely ten years after the end of World War II, Europe was again divided into hostile alliance systems just as it had been so many times in the past. Contact between the two blocs dwindled to a minimum; trade dried up; no tourism was allowed; Western books and newspapers were banned and Western radio programs jammed.

A rapidly escalating arms race accompanied the political activity. The Soviets exploded their first

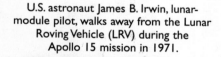

U.S. astronaut James B. Irwin, lunar-module pilot, walks away from the Lunar Roving Vehicle (LRV) during the Apollo 15 mission in 1971.

atomic bomb in 1949; the Americans countered with a much more powerful hydrogen bomb in 1951; and the Soviets followed suit over a year later. In 1957, the race moved into space when the Soviets launched the *Sputnik* satellite. Both superpowers developed sophisticated intercontinental ballistic missile systems (ICBMs). Soon, enough firepower existed to destroy the world several times over.

Confrontation in Asia

During World War II, Korea had sided with Japan and the other Axis powers against the Allies. Like Germany, Korea was partitioned into American and Soviet zones, the dividing line being the 38th parallel. When the superpowers withdrew from Korea, they left behind two heavily armed, mutually hostile governments: a Soviet-supported regime in the north and an American-supported regime in the South. Both claimed the right to govern the whole Korean peninsula.

In 1949, troops from North Korea invaded South Korea and captured its capital, Seoul. The American government saw this action as proof of the Soviet intent to extend its power in the Far East. American president Harry Truman declared that Korea was "the Greece of the Far East" and that "if we aren't tough now, there won't be any next step." Because the Soviet delegate was boycotting the Security Council, the U.S. succeeded in persuading the UN Council to send military assistance to help South Korea repel the northern invaders. Led by American general Douglas MacArthur, the UN troops achieved their goal.

When MacArthur decided to penetrate deep into North Korea and unify the two Koreas, the Chinese became alarmed. In August 1951, 200 000 Chinese "volunteers" crossed the Yalu River separating North Korea from China and reversed the tide of battle. Unwilling to continue a lengthy war, President Truman decided to seek a negotiated settlement. The Soviets, who feared that the Korean conflict might escalate into a major war, also gave their support to a cease-fire. In the end, after 50 000 American and 1 million Korean and Chinese dead, the border between the two Koreas remained roughly at the 38th parallel. In Europe, the impact of the Korean War was to strengthen the military influence of NATO and to accelerate rearmament.

Vietnam proved to be a bloodier battleground than Korea. Initially it was part of the French empire in Indochina. At the end of World War II, Vietnam was

Between 1964 and 1975, United States involvement in the unsuccessful Vietnam War cost tens of thousands of lives and polarized American public opinion over the morality of the war.

partitioned into a communist-ruled North supported by China and a non-communist South supported by France. In 1950, at the height of the Korean War, the U.S. decided to help their French ally; by the last stages of French occupation, the U.S. was underwriting more than half of French military expenditures in South Vietnam.

When the French withdrew from Southeast Asia in 1957, the U.S. assumed France's role as supporter of the non-communist South. The government was corrupt and repressed civil rights; nevertheless, the U.S. did not feel that it could be abandoned due to the domino theory: if one country in Southeast Asia fell to communism, neighbouring states would also fall. The U.S. dispatched increasing numbers of military advisers in order to bolster the South Vietnamese government.

In 1964, North Vietnamese warships fired on American vessels in the Gulf of Tonkin and the nature of American participation changed dramatically. The Gulf of Tonkin incident persuaded the American Congress to accept President Lyndon Johnson's plan to bomb the North. Two years later, the U.S. had over half a million soldiers in the region. In the course of hostilities, the U.S. dropped more bombs on Vietnam than the Allies had dropped on Germany and Japan combined during World War II.

Television coverage of the war and its horrors eroded support for American involvement both in the U.S. and throughout the world. Corruption in the South Vietnamese government destroyed its image. In 1968, the Vietcong, as the communist rebels were called, undertook the Tet Offensive into the South; it was repelled but the fact that the Vietcong could launch such an attack showed that their power had not declined. It was the beginning of the end of the war. In 1972, a generation after the U.S. first became involved in Vietnam, they began peace talks and pulled out entirely in 1975.

From Cold War to Détente

A second Berlin crisis occurred in 1961. Throughout the previous decade, nearly 3 million East Germans, many of them well-educated, had fled to the West through Berlin. In order to halt the flow of escapees, East German authorities erected a concrete wall separating the two sectors of Berlin and then constructed barriers all along the border with West Germany.

The most critical event of the cold war occurred a year later in Cuba, where the Soviet-supported government of Fidel Castro was in power. From photos taken by spy planes, American intelligence learned that the Soviets had constructed missile silos on the island, only 150 km away from U.S. territory. President John F. Kennedy ordered a naval blockade against Cuba. After six very tense days, the Soviet leader Nikita Khrushchev capitulated and agreed to remove the offending weapons.

The *Cuban Missile Crisis* had brought the world shockingly close to nuclear war. Both the United States and the Soviet Union took steps to reduce tensions. They set up a hotline between the White House and the Kremlin in order to improve communication between the two governments. In 1963, the United States agreed to sell wheat to the Soviets and other trade agreements followed. Tourism and cultural exchange between the two countries were encouraged.

In 1963, Soviet and American leaders (along with those of several other nations) signed a treaty to limit the testing of nuclear weapons in the atmosphere, in outer space, and under water. However, the Soviets continued to strive for nuclear parity with the Americans, and they succeeded because of American involvement in Vietnam. In 1972, the two superpowers signed a Strategic Arms Limitation Treaty (SALT), under which they agreed to limit the production of defensive missiles. When Soviet leader Leonid Brezhnev visited Washington to sign the treaty, some optimistic observers declared that the cold war had ended and a new era of world peace had dawned.

These hopes, proved to be premature: the arms race continued under a new guise. The superpowers intensified the firepower of existing weapons and developed new ones, such as the stealth bomber, the low-flying cruise missile, the neutron bomb (which destroyed people rather than property), and laser beams. By 1978, the arms race reached the *MAD* (Mutually Assured Destruction) stage. It meant that each side had the capability to destroy one quarter of the enemy's population and one half of its industry.

New sources of disagreement fuelled international tensions: American president Jimmy Carter's crusade for human rights; the Soviet invasion of Afghanistan in 1979; the American boycott of the Moscow Olympics in 1980; President Ronald Reagan's description of the Soviet Union as "an evil empire" and his projected Star Wars defence system. But, despite these and other conflicts, the temperature of international relations had not dropped to the frosty depths of the early post-war period. Various factors worked to bring about moderation. Some historians believe that the reality of MAD and the large-scale destruction that it would entail restrained the U.S. and the Soviet Union from actions that might result in war. The rise of China as a communist power in 1948 challenged Soviet predominance in the communist world. During the 1960s and 1970s, trade between the two blocs increased: Western nations began to export technology and extend loans to countries in Eastern Europe. Attempts at détente were made by West German chancellor Willy Brandt, the creator of *Ostpolitik*, or reaching out to the East. In 1972, the two Germanies signed a treaty recognizing each other's borders. In 1975, East and West signed the Helsinki Agreement guaranteeing human rights. Such non-military developments helped build bridges between West and East.

The European Response

For Europeans, the Cuban Missile Crisis underlined the fact that foreign policy was decided in Moscow and Washington. Western Europeans were very much the junior partners in NATO, which was headed by American generals. In his handling of the Cuban crisis, President Kennedy had not consulted with NATO governments and, although they supported his position,

Euro Disney:
American Cultural Imperialism?

The age of imperialism is generally associated with the eighteenth and nineteenth centuries; some scholars consider the United States as the imperialist nation of the late twentieth century. It has specialized in exporting ideologies of capitalism and its own brand of democracy to developing countries in order to pave the way for its export of goods and import of raw materials from those countries. It has also exported its culture, mainly in the form of Hollywood movies and television, which portray various aspects of American life and create a demand among other cultures for the products that will allow them to simulate the American lifestyle. South and East Asia now receive via cable television over 30 channels that broadcast popular American sitcoms and soap operas. The United States was on the verge of a serious trade war with China in 1995 partially as a result of the difficulty American movie companies were facing in penetrating the Chinese market.

Euro Disney is Walt Disney's second theme park outside of America (the first one opened in Tokyo). The French spent freely wining and dining Disney Studios to obtain the coveted concession (Spain had also wanted it but lost to France). Since Euro Disney opened in April 1992, this replica of the Magic Kingdom built on the farmlands of the Seine-de-Marne department just east of Paris has been surrounded by both hype and resistance. French intellectuals have protested the arrival of Euro Disney, calling it a "cultural Chernobyl." It is described as "a horror of cardboard, plastic, atrocious colours, solidified chewing-gum constructions, and idiotic folk stories that come straight out of cartoon books ....." American journalists perceive this to be simply the snobbish chattering of French intellectuals about what is pure, clean fun.

It has also been suggested that comic strips and the stories they tell constitute important cultural rituals that developed from defined belief systems and codify acceptable social behaviour, business conduct, and moral values in simplistic terms. Thus, Mickey Mouse and Donald Duck represent characters that know good from bad and behave accordingly, in a humourous way.

A great deal of the resistance to Euro Disney can also be attributed to the financial environment in which the park exists. Walt Disney (U.S.A.) owns 49 percent of the French theme park and has put together a business deal that seems to guarantee that even when the park is losing money, the company will still be making a profit. Euro Disney was a financial disappointment. It received 20 percent fewer visitors than it hoped for and sold at least 10 percent less merchandise. These problems are due to a variety of factors, including advertising techniques, entrance fees, and miscalculations regarding the Europeans' desire to buy souvenirs. In the face of disheartening fiscal prospects, Walt Disney is still receiving a 3 percent management fee (which rises to 6 percent in 1997), a 10 percent royalty on admission, 5 percent on food, etc. It is estimated that by 1997, 57 percent of Euro Disney's operating profit will go to its parent company in the United States.

Are French complaints really related to the fact that, financially, they are stuck with a raw deal? Or is their objection to the alleged imposition of American culture justified? The answer probably lies in a combination of the two but as American culture continues to reach to the farthest corners of the globe, these questions will have to be answered again and again.

they were alarmed at the possibility that Europe could become a nuclear battleground. But European nations were unwilling to build up their armies to counter the Soviet troops massed in Eastern Europe, so they tacitly accepted the American nuclear umbrella.

The Good Times: Economy, Society, and Culture, 1950s–1970s

During the first post-war generation Europe enjoyed what someone jokingly called a **helicopter economy**: all figures measuring economic activity climbed. By 1949, industrial production had regained the levels of ten years earlier and continued to climb for the next 20 years. Between 1953 and 1964, West Germany led the way with an annual growth rate of 6 percent. Considering the destruction inflicted by bombing during the war, this growth rate seemed like an economic miracle. The same term could be applied to Italy, whose economy expanded at a rate of 5.6 percent during this period. France followed with 4.9 percent, and Britain with 2.7 percent. In the words of one historian: "Never in its history had industrial Europe made such striking advances."

Translated into personal terms, the "helicopter economy" meant a shorter work week, higher wages, and longer paid holidays. Prosperity created a demand for all kinds of household appliances, consumer goods, and, above all, automobiles. In Europe, the state-owned French company Renault was the first to develop an auto industry catering to a mass market. Its four-cylinder vehicles (all painted desert-sand yellow with paint confiscated from Germany's Afrika Korps) began to roll off assembly lines in 1947. The Renault's success was followed by the Volkswagen in Germany, the Morris Minor in Britain, and the Fiat in Italy. By 1960, the European auto industry had produced 45 million cars, up from 5 million in 1940. Owning a car was no longer a privilege enjoyed by the well-to-do.

A mass market in autos required roads, and all European nations either expanded or constructed a network of superhighways. The most famous were the German Autobahnen, four-lane highways along which people could zip at speeds of up to 220 km/h.

There was virtually no unemployment during the 1950s and 1960s. In fact, the demand for labour was so great that Western Europe became a magnet for people in search of a better life. Italians and Portuguese found work in France and Germany. East and West Indians migrated to Britain; Turks went to Germany as guest workers; Arabs and West Africans migrated to France.

The Americanization of Culture

A shorter work week and longer holidays allowed people more time for leisure activities. One of the most popular amusements in the immediate post-war years was going to movies and watching the latest Hollywood films (often directed or produced by refugees from Nazi-dominated Europe). The "American way of life" portrayed in movies of the time had an appeal that went beyond entertainment. America was perceived as a free society where every person had a chance to succeed, a society very different from that of class-conscious Europe. America stood for democracy, which was what the Allies had fought for. American society was prosperous and looked to the future; such were the goals that many Europeans aspired to attain. The casual approach to life in the U.S. seemed so much more attractive than the stiffness and formality still prevalent in much of European society. American music—jazz and pop music—was also well liked by Europeans. Not all Europeans appreciated what they called the Americanization of European culture, but the presence of American troops in Europe and American Armed Forces Radio made it difficult to avoid American music and films.

Italy and Sweden developed their own film industries, which captivated North American audiences. Sometimes, Europeans adapted American forms and produced hybrids that were re-exported across the Atlantic. The history of rock-and-roll is one example of American-European cultural mixing. In the late 1950s, the music of Elvis Presley, Little Richard, and Chuck Berry swept through Europe. The British group the Beatles reinterpreted the rock idiom, creating a musical explosion whose echoes reverberated throughout the whole world. The Beatles' 1967 album *Sergeant Pepper's Lonely Hearts Club Band*, declared one critic, was "the greatest force for bringing European civilization together since the Congress of Vienna." The Beatles' success encouraged other groups, such as the Who and the Rolling Stones, who achieved great popularity in Britain during the late 1960s. The Rolling Stones were more outrageous than the Beatles

Pop Art and Economics

10:35 Marilyn Monroe, Coca-Cola, Mickey Mouse, and Campbell's soup—these familiar, everyday images were the subject of paintings that represent the overwhelmingly successful art movement of the 1960s known as pop art. These are the images that made artists such as Andy Warhol, Robert Rauschenberg, Jasper Johns, and Claes Oldenburg famous, their paintings valued today at amounts up to $3.5 million. How can we account for the huge success of a painting that is the exact reproduction of a label of a soup can or of a comic strip? Some writers have said that art cannot be studied or analyzed as isolated pieces but must be understood in the greater context of the society at the time. In this case, pop art was a direct reflection of society's relatively recent shift toward consumerism. The artwork itself, the method in which it was marketed, and the response it garnered from the public showed that it was not only a symbol but a product of America's consumer culture.

A consumer culture has been defined as "one in which the activities and ethics of a society are determined by patterns of consumption." Consumerism is a relatively recent development. As an economic theory, its roots are in the writings of British economist John Maynard Keynes, a revolutionary thinker of the 1930s. Economists, who have always been concerned with developing theories and policies that will maintain the economic stability and growth of a nation, had traditionally focused on manipulating the production of goods—which was in the hands of the suppliers—in order to achieve a healthy economy. Keynes revolutionized economic theory by concentrating on understanding and then managing the consumption of goods—which is directed by the buyer. This shift in ideas led to changes in foreign economic policy, government legislation, and corporate behaviour. It also led to a manufacturing strategy that produced goods that did not last and, therefore, continually had to be replaced.

Advertising fuelled the demand for more goods and kept the production going.

Into this general framework, the strange phenomenon of pop art fits very neatly. The images portrayed by pop art were taken directly from the shelves of supermarkets and the silver screen; the style was directly linked to the contemporary mass media and their advertising techniques. It is said of one woman who visited a gallery at which pop art was being displayed in 1964 that she "came in... took one look, and ran out... screaming. She said that it reminded her of her mother's grocery store."

Not only the images, but also the marketing techniques surrounding this new art movement, reflected the emerging consumer age. The role of art critics dwindled and in their place surfaced an important network of artists, dealers, and collectors who sold and promoted artwork in a manner similar to big business.

Pop art of the 1960s was a purely American phenomenon but its legacy lives on today as the value of these artists' work continues to climb and their pieces are exhibited in renowned galleries around the world, where they continue to influence other artists.

The art of Roy Lichtenstein epitomizes pop art and mass culture.

McDonald's arrival in Moscow was a clear sign of the thawing of the cold war and the increasing global influence of U.S. culture.

and the themes of their music more sexually suggestive, reflecting the permissive, sexually liberated society that began to emerge in the 1960s.

By the 1970s, an increasingly large number of people were spending their leisure hours in front of the television. American exports, such as the soap opera *Dallas*, drew large audiences. The British Broadcasting Corporation (BBC) found that imports cost one tenth the price of producing homegrown programs. To counterbalance the American cultural invasion, government-regulated networks in all European countries began offering a variety of domestic programs. Some of these, such as *Monty Python's Flying Circus*, were well received by viewers in North America. And everywhere, sports telecasts, especially soccer, attracted ever-expanding audiences. As one historian put it: "The age of television turned the game into great theatre and the soccer players into superheroes. The teams had their own battle colors, legends, superstitions, groupies, and sacred victories."

Government and the Welfare State

As European leaders planned the post-war economic recovery, they were determined to avoid the economic catastrophe that had marked the years after World War I. Governments adjusted tax rates to encourage investment, regulated the money supply, and imposed price and wage controls to control inflation. One of the first steps taken in 1945 by the newly elected British Labour government was to nationalize the Bank of England, the coal and steel industries, public transport, and utilities. Other European nations followed suit.

Britain also took the lead in developing the welfare state. Parliament passed the National Health Act to help the unemployed, the aged, and other less fortunate members of the country. Subsidized housing, assistance to the handicapped, and improved educational opportunities followed later.

The post-war welfare state covered people "from the cradle to the grave," and grew out of a conviction that society as a whole was responsible for the welfare of its members. This seemed only fair. Since all citizens had shared in the hardships of wartime, all should share in the benefits of peace.

Elsewhere in Europe, governments followed the British example. Old age pensions, health care, family allowances, unemployment benefits, state-supported child care became commonplace. So did improved access to education. All over Europe, new universities were built and financial support was extended to all students qualified to attend. Between 1940 and 1960, student enrollment tripled in Europe, with many of the students now coming from the middle and lower classes. Going to university was no longer an upper-class privilege as had been the case in previous generations. Social programs had to be paid for with higher taxes, but they were highly popular with the electorate in all countries and no government dared to tamper with them.

The changes described above (the welfare state, greater prosperity, more open access to education) made European society more egalitarian. Class barriers remained but were less pronounced. The population grew and society became more urbanized. Automobiles made society more mobile as well, and it was common to commute long distances to work. The workplace changed: women entered the work force in increasing numbers, particularly in the growing government and social-service sectors. Automation lightened the burden of blue-collar or manual work and, in some cases, eliminated jobs. Over time, the number of peasant farmers declined, while the number of industrial and service workers rose.

Alienation, Protest, and Revolt

A sense of pessimism pervaded Europe in 1945. Europeans had lived through two wars, a depression, and fascism. The early stages of the cold war and the Iron Curtain did not do much to dispel their sombre mood. George Orwell's novel *1984*, with its bleak vision of a totalitarian society ruled by Big Brother, captured the sense of anxiety felt by many. So did the new existentialist philosophy. With the prosperity of the 1950s and 1960s came various protest movements: neo-Marxism, the feminist movement, youth protests, and environmentalism, all of which challenged prevailing values to an unforeseen degree.

Existentialism

What is *existentialism*? A philosophy? A way of life? A cultural mood? Existentialism is not a body of rules, like the Ten Commandments, that can be clearly and succinctly stated. Its forerunners include nineteenth-century thinkers such as German philosopher Friedrich Nietzsche and Danish philosopher Søren Kierkegaard. Existentialism is very much a product of the post-war world. The name existentialism is a translation of German *Existenzphilosophie* (philosophy of existence) current during the 1930s. Its most important exponents in the years after 1945 were French writers Jean-Paul Sartre and Albert Camus.

Existentialism proposes that, like the character Roquentin in Sartre's 1938 novel *Nausea*, we are alone in a universe that is totally indifferent to our needs and wants. Neither religion, philosophy, nor traditional values can guide us. Life has no predetermined meaning: it is absurd. This is a profoundly depressing truth, but it is also a liberating one. "Life begins on the other side of despair," wrote Sartre. We may be alone but we are also free: free to determine our own destiny, free to choose the kind of person we wish to be. There are limits... but within those limits we can still make choices. To make excuses is to be guilty of what some existentialists termed "bad faith." Sartre said at one point, "Make up your own mind; just be sure you are totally sincere and do not live by rules made by others."

There was a great deal of ambiguity in Sartre's advice. It could lead one person to choose a life of terrorism, another to seek peaceful reform within the existing social system. Sartre, who had fought in the Resistance to Nazism in France, eventually became a communist. His choice was not an unusual one for the time. As has been mentioned earlier, communism enjoyed a great deal of support after the war. Only when the Soviet Union invaded Hungary during the Hungarian Revolution of 1956 did Sartre abandon the communist cause. For Albert Camus, the disillusionment with what he called the "concentration-camp socialism" found in the Soviet Union came much earlier. Camus affirmed a belief in human dignity in a universe filled with evil. For other existentialists, commitment involved a renewed religious faith.

Another critique of society, which overlapped to some extent with existentialism, came from a new brand of Marxism, called neo-Marxism or the New Left. Among the more popular neo-Marxist writers was Herbert Marcuse, an exile from Nazi Germany who had found refuge in the United States. Marcuse's immensely popular *One-Dimensional Man* presented a wide-ranging critique of contemporary capitalism and its "contradictions." As an economic and technological system, capitalism was immensely productive and efficient but, ultimately, it debased human values. Instead of making it possible for people to live rich, multifaceted spiritual and intellectual lives, capitalism transformed people into willing conformists and docile workers. It bought people off with material goods. Capitalism led people, in Marcuse's words, to "find their soul in their automobile, hi-fi set, split-level home, kitchen equipment." The emphasis on individual values within capitalism brought about a breakdown in the sense of social cohesiveness: people were "alienated" from one another.

What thinkers such as Marcuse would have put in the place of capitalism was not entirely clear. Nor did criticism of Western capitalism translate into admiration for Soviet-style communism. Neo-Marxists regarded it as even more repressive and dehumanizing than Western capitalism, and a perversion of genuine Marxism. Their philosophy, with its numerous insights into the depersonalized nature of modern industrialism, was a critique of society rather than a blueprint for change.

The Feminist Movement

Women had taken an active part in the war effort but, once the fighting was over, they resumed traditional roles. Social attitude—the belief that a woman's place was in the home—reinforced their traditional roles. Legislation encouraged women to stay home and raise a family; fashion also reinforced traditional femininity

Simone de Beauvoir and *The Second Sex*

The advantage man enjoys, which makes itself felt from his childhood, is that his vocation as a human being in no way runs counter to his destiny as a male. Through the identification of phallus and transcendence, it turns out that his social and spiritual successes endow him with a virile prestige. He is not divided. Whereas it is required of woman that in order to realize her femininity she must make herself object and prey, which is to say that she must renounce her claims as a sovereign subject. It is this conflict that especially marks the situation of the emancipated woman....

In so far as a woman wishes to be a woman, her independent status gives rise to an inferiority complex; on the other hand, her femininity makes her doubtful of her professional future. This is a point of great importance. We have seen that girls of fourteen declared to an investigator: "Boys are better than girls; they are better workers." The young girl is convinced that she has limited capacities. Because parents and teachers concede that the girls' level is lower than that of the boys, the pupils readily concede it also... She will attribute [her weaknesses in academic matters] not to the mediocrity of her training, but to the unjust curse of her femininity; by resigning herself to this inequality, she enhances it....

Simone de Beauvoir published these words in 1949 and has since been considered the mother of the modern feminist movement. She was a French intellectual whose ideas were clearly ahead of their time. Challenging the Freudian premise that "biology is destiny," she wrote in *The Second Sex* that the image and status of women had been institutionalized in society rather than predetermined according to their gender. She was an existentialist who was concerned with woman's destiny as a human being, which she saw as being hindered and suppressed by her social role as a wife and mother.

De Beauvoir rejected these traditional roles; she chose not to have children and remained the lifelong companion and colleague of existentialist philosopher Jean-Paul Sartre. During her lifetime, she rejected her strict Catholic upbringing in a bourgeois family and pursued a career in teaching until she was fired from her position by the Nazis in 1941. After this, she became involved, along with Sartre, in the French Resistance.

Her personal resistance to the role of "other" assigned to women by society was taken up by leading feminists everywhere; it was popularized and made accessible to ordinary women by U.S. feminist writer Betty Friedan, who described the status of the suburban American housewife in *The Feminine Mystique*.

The feminist movement is a multifaceted attempt at reforming the role of women in society. Some feminists reject the traditionally female roles of wife and mother; others propose that true equality will come by elevating the physical and spiritual attributes of women to a higher level.

Simone de Beauvoir's *The Second Sex* was one of the sparks that set off this passion and urgency which drive the modern day women's movement almost half a century ago and is still considered essential reading for those studying woman's role in society today.

under the name of the New Woman—with her tiny waist and full skirt. When French writer **Simone de Beauvoir** published her book *The Second Sex* in 1949 it did not provoke much of a response outside of France. Today it is a classic.

The perception of women's roles would change by the 1960s as a militant feminist movement appeared throughout Europe. To a great extent, women's grievances had an economic basis: women entered the European work force in ever-increasing numbers only to be concentrated in poorly paid jobs. Fighting for higher wages and access to better paying jobs was an important goal of the women's movement. It was, however, only part of the feminist critique of society, as can be seen from the following statement issued by a British Women's Liberation Workshop in 1969: "We are economically oppressed: in jobs we do full work for half pay; in the home we do unpaid work full time; commercially exploited by advertisements, legally we often have only the status of children. We are brought up to feel inadequate, educated to narrower horizons than men. This is our special oppression as women."

In order to bring about change, women's groups organized marches and demonstrations and pressured politicians to abolish repressive laws. They opened shelters for abused women and their children. They published newsletters, agitated for women's studies courses, and organized consciousness-raising sessions to make women aware of injustices dealt them.

Feminist agitation raised the consciousness of society as a whole. Several countries passed legislation granting women pay equity, wider access to abortion, and day-care. Changes in social attitudes made it easier for women to pursue non-traditional careers, such as newscasters, surveyors, engineers, and auto mechanics. Women found employment in the service sector, especially in the new computer technology. Family life began to evolve. As more women worked outside the home, they opted for later marriage and fewer children. In short, the feminist movement helped bring about what is probably the most important social revolution of our times.

In Eastern Europe, the status of women lagged behind that in the West. On paper women had the same rights as men but the realities of Soviet life made it impossible to enjoy such rights fully. Stalin had insisted on the importance of motherhood. Even more than in the West, Soviet women shouldered the double burden of housework and full-time jobs outside the

Marches such as this one in Toronto have helped to raise consciousness about women's issues in Western societies.

home. Standing in line for food consumed hours of their time. Occupations such as medicine and teaching were dominated by women but suffered from low prestige. As in the West, the sphere of politics was reserved for males.

Youth Revolt

Europe had a lively tradition of student protest dating back to the mid-nineteenth century. But the generation that reached maturity in the 1950s was not inclined to take to the streets or erect barricades. After years of depression and war, the chance to have a job and a settled life was very appealing.

In the 1960s, young people began to criticize the materialism of their parents' generation, adopting to a great extent the neo-Marxist critique of capitalism. Herbert Marcuse and Jean-Paul Sartre became the heroes of the student avant-garde. Many students supported and demonstrated in favour of national liberation movements in developing countries. American students protested their country's involvement in the Vietnam War, encouraging European students to launch their own protests.

The most dramatic student protest broke out in France. In November 1967, students and professors at the newly built university of Nanterre, in the outskirts of Paris, went on strike. Overcrowded classrooms and

This barricade was erected on a Parisian street at the height of the 1968 student revolt.

too few professors made learning difficult. In addition, they objected to the theoretical subject matter being taught, which they felt was irrelevant to a modern society. In the course of their revolt, students gathered support from intellectuals, ordinary citizens, and young workers who had their own grievances against the system. In the new year, 10 million workers went on strike. Trains did not run, airplanes were grounded, and post offices were shut down. In the cafés of Paris, a carnival atmosphere reigned; patrons felt that they were witnessing the first stages of a cultural revolution that would usher in a more democratic world. The collapse of President de Gaulle's government seemed imminent. But when police moved to restore order, the revolt collapsed almost as suddenly as it had begun.

The collapse of the revolt can be attributed to various factors. Vandalism and destruction of property, which were rampant in the poorer sections of Paris, alienated potential supporters. Students started out by asking for specific reforms in university life but proceeded to demand the destruction of the whole capitalist system, frightening a significant sector of the population, especially since the students had no clear vision of the new social structures that would replace capitalism. A split appeared between students—many

of whom came from affluent middle-class families—and the workers who sought job security: they wanted to have a secure place within the system, not to overturn it.

If the 1968 student revolt in Paris did not bring about a cultural revolution, it certainly caused significant changes. The French government introduced long overdue reforms in the educational system. The revolt contributed indirectly to the resignation of President de Gaulle, who left office within a year. Shock waves from the revolt reverberated throughout Europe encouraging similar—though less dramatic—events elsewhere. It also accelerated the decline in communist political influence. Party members came from an older generation and did not have much sympathy for the young rebels who, in turn, no longer looked to the Left for leadership or inspiration.

Science and Environmentalism

The years after 1945 were years of scientific and technological innovations. It is not possible to cover, or even mention, all of them. One major technological development was the computer. The precursor of the modern computer was devised in the seventeenth century by French philosopher Blaise Pascal. It was an adding machine. German mathematician Gottfried Wilhelm Leibniz devised a calculator that could multiply as well as add. During World War II, British mathematician Alan Turing helped design a computer that was used by the Allies to decode German intelligence messages and helped them win World War II. The first computer was nicknamed Colossus because it was huge, slow, and noisy; when in operation, it sounded like "a roomful of people knitting away with steel needles."

Rapid advances in computer technology soon made Colossus look like an antique from a bygone age. Digital electronic circuits embedded on tiny microchips replaced the radio tubes used in earlier generations of computers. The microchip shrank the size of computers; from the size of a gymnasium in the 1940s, to that of a small desk in the 1970s and a brief case by the 1980s. Not only were computers smaller, they also became more powerful and inexpensive enough for ordinary consumers to purchase.

Dramatic advances in biology also took place. In 1951–1953, based on the work of British biophysicist Rosalind Franklin, British and American scientists Francis Crick and James Watson uncovered the molecular structure of DNA (deoxyribonucleic acid), a component of every cell of an organism. Their discovery made possible the manipulation of genes, the hereditary units of living things, and, ultimately, the eradication of disease. Lasers moved out of the realm of science fiction into daily life; one particularly useful application was in microsurgery. New materials, such as plastics and glass fibre, appeared on the market and were put to numerous uses. Chemical fertilizers increased agricultural yields dramatically. Antibiotics were mass-produced and many infectious diseases became curable. The contraceptive pill gave women greater control over fertility. Sixteenth-century thinkers had dreamed that science would allow people to control nature and improve human life. At no time did this dream seem closer to reality than in the first generation after World War II.

The down side of technological progress soon became apparent. The runoff from farms using chemical fertilizers damaged streams. Genetic engineering facilitates biological warfare. Because of the cold war, scientific research was geared overwhelmingly to military purposes. Acording to one estimate, one quarter of all scientists in the U.S. and the USSR were conducting military research.

The economic miracle also had its dark side. The millions of cars on European roads gave their drivers mobility, but they also contributed to traffic congestion and air pollution. Nitrous oxide emissions and factory gases fell as acid rain that killed lakes, rivers, and forests. Environmental damage was more marked in Eastern Europe, where heavy industry was concentrated, but such damage marred the Western landscape as well.

Many thoughtful people began to question the values of industrial society. "The modern industrial system," wrote British economist E. F. Schumpeter in his popular book *Small but Beautiful*, "consumes the very basis on which it has been erected." It does so through wasteful use of fossil fuels and other natural resources. What was needed was a new lifestyle, which relied on "small-scale... relatively non-violent technology" that Schumpeter described as "a technology with a human face." Schumpeter's message found a growing audience. By the late 1970s, a variety of groups began to raise their voices in protest against environmental degradation. Not all environmental groups had the same goals: some were conservationists; more radical groups envisioned a return to a simple way of life; still others felt that it was possible to balance economic growth with a concern for the environment. The environmental movement attracted veterans of the 1960s student movement, women's groups, and peace activists. Environmental activists became—and still are—a major political force.

Life Behind the Iron Curtain

Economic reconstruction became a top priority in the Soviet Union after 1945. The task was colossal, given the degree of destruction inflicted by the war, particularly in Ukraine, Belarus, and parts of European Russia. Stalin insisted that Soviets would rebuild their country through their own efforts. A series of Five Year Plans set out the economic goals that various sectors of the economy were expected to achieve, with emphasis placed on heavy industry, the military, and exports.

Restoring the economy, Soviet people were told, required sacrifices equal to those of war. As a result, the standard of living was barely better than it had been early in the century. Because so many men had died in the war, much of the burden fell on Soviet women, who performed up to 40 percent of heavy labour. Producing for export left little to invest in consumer goods or home construction. Urban workers lived in one-room apartments with a communal kitchen and bathroom. Those were the lucky ones: many workers had to make do with shacks built of earth, cardboard planks, or anything else they could find. During the war, agriculture had been privatized to some degree and peasants hoped that this trend would continue. Stalin, however, insisted on reinstating the collective farm system, with its low prices and quotas for the state. No exceptions were allowed under any circumstances. In 1946, drought hit Ukraine, which was the main grain-producing area of the Soviet Union. "We are sure that the State and the Party won't forget us and that they will come to our aid," wrote one group of peasants who had nothing left after dispatching their allotment. Their hopes were dashed: they were left to starve. In some areas, conditions were so bad that reports of cannibalism began to circulate.

Even without natural disasters, agricultural productivity never did rise significantly under Stalinism. At the time of his death in 1953, grain production had dropped to 1913 levels and there were fewer head of cattle than in 1916. The only sectors that showed improvement were heavy industry: iron, steel, and weapons.

Realizing the gravity of the situation, Stalin's successor, **Nikita Khrushchev**, undertook an energetic program of economic reform. Khrushchev decentralized the economy and put more emphasis on the manufacture of consumer goods. He raised the prices paid to peasants and permitted them a greater degree of independence in managing the collective farms. Some of his initiatives were not too well thought out. In order to boost grain production, Khrushchev pushed through a plan to turn the virgin grasslands in Central Asia into wheat fields. Low rainfall and overproduction turned the project into a economic flop and an ecological disaster. During his visit to the U.S., Khrushchev was impressed by the vast fields of corn in the American Midwest. He encouraged Soviet farmers to plant corn to be used as cattle feed. Because the Soviet climate was colder than the American Midwest, most of the corn froze. The Soviet Union found itself in the embarrassing position of having to import grain from its capitalist rivals: the U.S. and Canada. Nevertheless, Khrushchev's reforms did bring improvements in the Soviet standard of living. The number of housing units doubled and more consumer goods did become available.

Khrushchev's successor, Leonid Brezhnev, did not do much better. The command economy with its Five Year Plans designed in Moscow was too rigid and could not be fixed by piecemeal reforms. "They pretend to pay us and we pretend to work," was how workers described the communist system. Soviet citizens devised their own ways of coping and a flourishing underground economy developed. Private plots, which made up 2 to 5 percent of the agricultural land, produced 25 percent of the Soviet Union's food supply.

Life was better in Eastern Europe, but not by much. Moscow attempted, with varying degrees of success, to integrate the satellites' economies into the Soviet system, giving rise to resentment in satellite states.

Communist leaders tried to persuade their people that socialism was a more just way of life and that capitalism was too materialistic. Because no contacts with the West were allowed, many Soviet citizens were persuaded that theirs was a superior system. By the 1970s, however, as channels of communication with the West opened and as the cold war thawed, such propaganda became less and less convincing.

Politics: The Dictatorships

On paper, the Soviet Union had one of the most democratic constitutions in the world. In reality, the Communist Party dominated the political system. It was a very select group comprising about 10 percent of the population. Within the party, the post of general secretary was the most important. From 1922 until the time of his death from a heart attack in 1953, this post was filled by Joseph Stalin.

To maintain his power, Stalin used a variety of techniques. He made himself the centre of a unique personality cult: every book, film, or article published paid tribute to Stalin, the great war hero. Stalin rewarded the members of the party whose loyalty was unquestioned very generously. They enjoyed many privileges: jobs, good apartments, country homes, travel privileges, better education for their children, access to shops selling Western goods. But privileged positions depended on Stalin's whim. A secret police force reporting directly to Stalin kept tabs on potential dissenters. A misstep of some kind, a remark made to the wrong person could result in instant dismissal, trial, a sentence to a labour camp, even death. The prosecutors realized that they too could end up behind bars. Even those who were close to Stalin never knew if their position was secure. "You come to Stalin's table as a friend, but you never know if you'll go home by yourself or if you'll be given a ride to prison," said one of his chief ministers. Not even his family was exempt; Stalin sent his sisters-in-law to prison for writing a memoir that he considered did not treat him respectfully. Toward the end of his life, he became convinced that there was a conspiracy against him.

Control, intimidation, and terror were the norms for all of Soviet society. Literature, music, art, and science all had to serve the needs of the state and glorify Soviet communism. Soviet citizens had little freedom of movement. Peasants could not leave their farms because they lacked the necessary papers giving them permission to move, and workers had to carry their job record with them at all times. Many Soviet soldiers came home from German prisoner-of-war camps only to find themselves shipped off to labour camps. In Stalin's view, soldiers who surrendered—even if they had no choice but to do so—were traitors whose exposure to Western ways undermined their loyalty to the Soviet system. After the Iron Curtain descended, contact with non-communist countries was severely restricted. No dissent of any kind was tolerated. Children were encouraged to inform on their parents; neighbours on one another. And yet, when Stalin died, thousands of people thronged the streets of Moscow to mourn him and hundreds were trampled to death in the rush. Even prisoners in concentration camps wept. Stalin had dominated Soviet society and government for so long that people could not imagine life without his leadership.

Nikita Khrushchev succeeded to the post of secretary of the Communist Party in 1954. Born to a peasant family, he had risen through the ranks to the post of party secretary in Ukraine. In style, Khrushchev was quite different from Stalin: he mingled with people on the street, laughed, joked, and argued with them; he was a "Western-style" politician.

The differences went beyond a question of political style. This became clear when Khrushchev delivered his 1956 "secret speech" to the 20th Party Congress. To a largely unbelieving audience, Khrushchev denounced the cult of personality fostered by Stalin. He described in gruesome detail the cruel repression, the mass arrests and deportations, the executions without trial that had decimated party ranks during the 1930s. He exposed Stalin's refusal to believe the intelligence reports warning of German invasion in 1941. He accused Stalin of perverting the Leninist heritage. Khrushchev made no mention of the millions of ordinary people who had died in the camps but, even so, the news of his secret speech leaked out and shook Soviet society. A policy of de-Stalinization followed.

Khrushchev ended Stalin's politics of terror. He dealt with two of his rivals by sending one as ambassador to Outer Mongolia and the other to manage a hydro-electric station; Stalin would have shot them. Stalin's portraits and statues disappeared from public places; history books were rewritten; people were released from labour camps and their reputations rehabilitated. More freedom of thought was permitted. "Readers should be allowed to make their own judgements," declared Khrushchev, and certain authors had their works published for the first time. Alexander Solzhenitsyn's novel *One Day in the Life of Ivan Denisovitch* overwhelmed readers with its description of life in a labour camp. Poet Yevgeny Yevtushenko published *Babi Yar*, a poem describing the slaughter of Jews by Nazis during the war and their burial in a mass grave near Kiev. Indirectly, it suggested that

anti-Semitism still prevailed in the USSR, since their grave was being used as a garbage dump.

Such changes marked a thaw in repression, not the creation of an open society. Dissidents criticizing the system were still persecuted. They were confined to psychiatric hospitals for re-education, ridiculed by the press, or, as in the case of the physicist Andrei Sakharov, exiled to a remote town. Khrushchev's tastes in art were very conservative: he preferred socialist realism, a style that celebrated some aspect of Soviet life.

Khrushchev's de-Stalinization program contributed to his downfall: it threatened the privileges and position of high party officials, many of whom had gone along with Stalin's terror. His rather crude political style was not always in good taste. When he pounded his shoe on the podium to make a point during a speech to the UN General Assembly in 1960, his colleagues cringed with embarrassment. The details of his secret speech leaked out to Soviet satellites and encouraged a move to rebellion. Strikes and demonstrations broke out in Poland. Hungary rose in revolt in 1956 and Soviet troops invaded to restore order. Khrushchev failed to prevent rupture with China in 1961. The confrontation over Cuba in 1962 ended in a humiliating retreat for the Soviet Union. His attempts at economic reform did not live up to expectations. For these reasons, Khrushchev's colleagues in the Communist Party ousted him from his position as party secretary. The official party newspaper denounced Khrushchev's "harebrained schemes."

One of those who conspired against Khrushchev was his eventual successor, Leonid Brezhnev. His tenure as general secretary of the Communist Party and premier of the Soviet Union (1964–1982) marked a trend toward a more collective style of leadership. The good-natured Brezhnev collected luxury cars and believed in "live and let live." What this meant in practice was that Communist Party members enjoyed more privileges. He did not continue Khrushchev's de-Stalinization policy but he did not fill up the labour camps again. His greatest failure was the invasion of Afghanistan in 1979, a war that, for the Soviets, was the counterpart to the American intervention in Vietnam.

In the mid-1970s, public confidence in the communist system plummeted. The Soviet Union was unwilling or unable to suppress dissent by force. Developing nations lost faith in the communist system.

Overly centralized economies had not proven successful in improving standards of living. Defectors to the West, among them Alexander Solzhenitsyn, all had their own stories of persecution to tell. *Samizdat* (secret publication) books, articles, and newspapers linked dissenters in an underground network of opposition. Many Soviet citizens became increasingly disturbed by the growing corruption in the Communist Party and very cynical about the values of communism. The momentum for change was picking up steam; the climax would come with Mikhail Gorbachev.

The Soviet Bloc

All Soviet satellites had a common post-war experience: initially, Soviet troops were welcomed as liberators from Nazi brutality but liberation soon turned into occupation and imposition of a communist government. The process went through three stages: first, communists cooperated with other parties to form a "popular front," then coalition governments were formed in which communists held key posts. The last and permanent stage was a communist-dominated government led by a "little Stalin," a puppet approved by Moscow. A Hungarian communist leader nicknamed this political process (in which non-communists were gradually cut out of power) "salami politics."

What made the process of imposing communist governments easier was the lack of democratic traditions in Eastern Europe. Nevertheless, it was not possible to repress all opposition. Strikes and demonstrations did break out from time to time, although they were suppressed by force if necessary. In Poland, the Catholic Church served as a focus for opposition. In all countries, an underground literary network similar to that in the Soviet Union began to grow in importance. On occasion, Soviet-bloc countries introduced policies that ran counter to Moscow's initiatives. Khrushchev's secret speech on de-Stalinization prompted Hungarian leaders to decollectivize agriculture in 1956, leave the Warsaw Pact, and declare Hungary a neutral state. The Soviet response was an invasion and a return to the old system.

Another poignant example was that of Czechoslovakia. In 1968, Alexander Dubček decided to introduce what he called "socialism with a human face." The purpose was not to eliminate the communist system but to liberalize it. And, with the Hungarian experience in mind, Dubček declared that Czechoslovakia would remain within the Warsaw Pact. Even so, Moscow became alarmed. The period of reform, the so-called "Prague Spring" ended abruptly when Soviet tanks rolled into Czechoslovakia. The Soviets justified their intervention by the Brezhnev doctrine. "Every communist party was responsible not only to its own people but to those of other socialist countries": the Soviet Union had the right to intervene in order to bring any wavering satellite back into line.

Europe from the 1970s to 1990s

The so-called "helicopter economy" took a turn downward in the mid-1970s. The Middle Eastern oil crisis of 1973 marked a turning point. Egypt and Syria attacked Israel, hoping to regain territory lost in the 1967 Six-Day War. Their offensive failed but the oil-producing countries of the Middle East, OPEC, put an embargo on crude-oil shipments to Europe to show their dissatisfaction with the support that Western nations had provided to Israel. OPEC eventually lifted the embargo but raised oil prices considerably. The price of oil went from $2 a barrel to $30 within a few years. The higher price for oil soon translated into higher prices for consumer goods and greater wage demands. In addition to the oil price hike, other factors contributed to the recession that ensued. The demand for consumer goods, which had fuelled the European economy in the post-war period, slowed down. European manufacturers found themselves competing against more aggressive manufacturers in Southeast Asia and Japan. Factories shut down and people lost jobs, with the result that unemployed workers could not buy consumer goods. The end result was "stagflation": a stagnant economy and rising prices.

Some measure of prosperity returned in the 1980s but not all sectors of European society benefited. High unemployment, averaging 11 percent, persisted. "Deindustrialization" began to transform the European workplace. New computer-assisted technologies needed fewer workers, and the workers whom they did employ had to have different skills. The businesses that realized this in time, such as the Italian clothing manufacturer Benetton, did well; those who failed to adapt faced bankruptcy.

Politics

By the end of the 1970s, a growing number of people, especially the unemployed, felt alienated from a society that had no place for them. Respect for traditional institutions declined. In one country after another, people felt a growing sense of frustration with the political system, which did not seem to offer voters much choice. Over the years, both socialists and conservatives had moved their platforms toward the middle of the political spectrum: conservatives supported the welfare state while socialists accepted capitalism.

Frustration found various outlets. In Italy, the so-called "hot autumn" of 1969 brought with it a wave of strikes and demonstrations. Terrorist activity also became common during the 1970s. The Baader-Meinhof Group in Germany attacked American army bases there and assassinated industrialists, judges, and political leaders. Computerized tracking of suspects brought an end to the movement. In Italy, a similar fate befell the terrorist Red Brigades. Like the German youth terrorists, Brigade members came from affluent middle-class families and believed that, without revolutionary terrorism, capitalism would never change. The climax of their terrorist campaign came in 1978, when they kidnapped and killed former Italian prime minister Aldo Moro. This act of terror turned public opinion against them. Organizations such as the Irish Republican Army (IRA) and various terrorist groups with Middle Eastern connections carried out random acts of violence in order to draw attention to their demands.

As recession deepened, attitudes toward foreign workers turned sour. The economic miracle in Germany and other European states depended on many thousands of guest workers from Turkey, Algeria, and the West Indies. They had been tolerated but they had never been truly welcomed. When recession hit Europe, they were accused of taking away jobs. But these immigrants could not be sent away: their children knew no other home or culture. The outcome in a number of cities was violence and a rise in racism.

The appearance of various ecologically oriented parties throughout Europe signalled yet another political trend. The Green Party in Germany was first elected to the Bundestag in 1983. The Green movement included peace activists, feminists, and veterans of the 1960s student movement as well as environmentalists. Their preference for dressing in jeans and their casual manner shocked German politicians from other parties. The unconventional dress symbolized their determination not to act like a regular political party. But unlike the student radicals of the 1960s the Greens rejected confrontational tactics.

Government reports into the environment had shown that an alarming number of trees were sick or dying; much of the famous Black Forest in Southern Germany was damaged. Initially, the Greens attracted support from the German public but they failed to maintain it. Divisions persisted in the movement between those who wanted fundamental changes and those who were prepared to work within the system. By the 1990s, the Greens and their allies were still a part of the German political scene, but their concerns did not dominate to the extent that they had in the 1980s.

Yet another significant political trend was a re-evaluation of the welfare state. A depressed economy and an aging population made it more expensive to maintain, while a declining birth rate lowered the tax base. Governments faced a dilemma: either cut back on the benefits provided by the state or raise taxes.

Just as Britain had led in the post-war introduction of the welfare state, so it led in its partial reversal. In 1979, the Conservative government of Margaret Thatcher trimmed health and unemployment benefits and cut back on university funding. Prime Minister Thatcher also abandoned interventionist economic policies. She sold off municipal housing to working-class people and privatized industries. She went on to defeat the coal miners' union in the course of a long and bitter strike. At first, the British economy responded to the "Iron Lady's" hard medicine and productivity soared. By the 1990s, however, Britain was once more in a recession. Thatcher's arrogance and a failed attempt to introduce an extremely unpopular poll tax forced her to resign. Nevertheless, her neoconservative approach found followers even in socialist circles. Governments in other parts of Europe began to adopt similar policies. In France, the socialist government of François Mitterrand began its 14-year term of office in 1981 with a socially progressive political program but was forced to modify much of it. In Sweden, where the welfare state had been most highly developed, cutbacks were also imposed.

Regardless of the political turmoil that Europe experienced during the 1970s and 1980s, the commitment to democracy remained firm. Social and economic problems did not lead to dictatorships. In France, Georges Pompidou succeeded de Gaulle after the 1968 student revolt but the Fifth Republic did not fall. Despite the rise of neo-Nazi groups, Germany remained committed to democratic values and integrated into Europe. Italy was plagued by corruption and constant changes of government but no Mussolini stood in the wings to exploit such a situation. This stands in marked contrast to the events of the 1930s, when some European nations had found authoritarian solutions to their political and economic problems.

The Collapse of Communism and the End of the Cold War

Events in Eastern Europe and the Soviet Union stand in marked contrast to the course of history in the West. In the former, fragmentation, rather than unity, characterized the political scene in the 1980s. The collapse of the communist system in the USSR and the Soviet-dominated East bloc was one of the most dramatic and unexpected events of the twentieth century.

The impetus for change came from the Soviet Union. By the late 1970s, the economy of the Soviet Union had deteriorated dangerously. The military consumed the GNP; collective agriculture failed to feed the country; consumer goods were in short supply; and long line-ups at food stores became more and more common. Widespread industrial pollution, low morale in the work force, and alcoholism further depressed the quality of life. Politically, the government, headed by an aged and sick Brezhnev, lost credibility and respect. "What has become of us?" asked a young poet, capturing the mood of many people in Soviet society.

By the time of Leonid Brezhnev's death, conditions in the Soviet Union had deteriorated further still. Despite attempts at reform, the country remained economically backward as compared to Western Europe. The problems within Soviet society seemed endless and unsurmountable: too much spending diverted into military purposes, the failure of collectivized agriculture, and inefficient central planning. It was against this kind of backdrop that **Mikhail Gorbachev** came on the scene. No one could guess that the likable party man Gorbachev was a revolutionary in the making. He believed in the superiority of communism but, at the same time, he was ready to confront his country's problems and did not doubt that they could be overcome. He had charm and made skillful use of the mass media in trying to get his views across. After his election in 1984 to the post of Communist Party secretary, Gorbachev began to implement reforms.

Gorbachev's "second revolution," as he described it, was based on two principles. One was *glasnost*: openness. It meant free expression of political opinions, the loosening of centralized Communist Party structures, and more democracy in political life. The second principle was *perestroika*, or rebuilding. It entailed decentralizing the Soviet economy, putting more stress on personal initiative, and curtailing vodka sales. Taken together, the changes proposed by Gorbachev amounted to the most important reform package since the ill-fated attempt by Khrushchev to change Soviet society 20 years earlier.

Unfortunately, what happened was "catastroika." Stalin had established a centralized command economy. No one republic was self-sufficient; all had to rely on others for goods and services. For example, all of the Soviet Union's locomotives were assembled in Ukraine but 800 different factories throughout the Soviet Union supplied the parts. The problems involved in transforming this method of manufacturing were tremendous. Gorbachev did propose a 500-day plan in 1990 to privatize 80 percent of the economy but he encountered a great deal of opposition from party officials opposed to reforms. The transition to privatization risked throwing many out of work.

Named Man of the Century by *Time Magazine*, Mikhail Gorbachev's attempt at reform eventually led to his own fall from power in the Soviet Union.

Mismanagement and distribution problems worsened the situation further. In some areas, crops rotted in the fields; in others, farmers withheld grain from the market. As a result, the Soviet Union experienced the worst economic conditions since 1945. The visible signs of this deterioration included beggars in the streets, shortages of housing, food, basic commodities, and a decline in the quality of health care.

In the end, it seemed that perestroika brought nothing but mass confusion. Bad though the old system may have been, at least people enjoyed a minimum level of services. The Chernobyl nuclear disaster in 1986 and the withdrawal of the Soviet army from Afghanistan added to the demoralization in Soviet society. Gorbachev became a hero in the West, but to Soviet citizens he was a failure.

Before long, Gorbachev lost control of the situation. Glasnost led ultimately to a rejection not only of Stalinism but also of Leninism and the communist system. In 1990, **Boris Yeltsin**, chairman of the Russian parliament, took Russia out of the embattled Soviet Union and resigned from the Communist Party. The following year, he was elected president of the Russian Republic. Disgruntled army officers attempted to reverse the reform process by forcing Gorbachev from office. Yeltsin became the focus of resistance, and the revolt collapsed. The Communist Party was disbanded and Gorbachev, premier of a non-existent Soviet Union, and head of an illegal party, was out of a job.

The USSR was a multi-ethnic empire consisting of 92 nationalities and 112 languages. The Communist Party in Moscow repressed religious, ethnic, and national feelings with an iron hand and used propaganda to promote the concept of the Soviet citizen. With glasnost and the relaxation of central control, old tensions surfaced. Nationalist movements called for independence. Fourteen former republics obtained independence, including the Baltic areas, Ukraine, Belarus, Georgia, and Muslim republics in the south. The Soviet Union was dismembered in 1991 and replaced with the Commonwealth of Independent States.

The end of communism brought sighs of relief. In their euphoria, however, people failed to realize how hard it would be to transform a command economy into a free-market system. In the meantime, the output of Russian factories has fallen dramatically since 1990. For many Russians, especially for the poor and elderly, living conditions continue to worsen. Inflation has made their savings worthless; crime continues to be a social problem. Alcoholism has reached critical proportions.

To complicate matters, Russians have had to devise a democratic political system at the same time as they reform their economy. They have had no democratic traditions in their past to guide them. With free elections, all kinds of splinter parties have appeared, creating confusion and cynicism among the people. Not surprisingly, a nostalgia for Stalin and the days when the Soviet Union was a feared and respected superpower prevails among many people.

Reflections

In the post-war generation, Europe experienced a bewildering array of changes. Wartime devastation was followed by a spectacular economic recovery, domination by the superpowers, tensions arising from the cold war, and challenges to established values and social structures.

Then, in the 1970s, the U.S. became a debtor nation and lost its post-war claim to economic dominance. The Soviet Union began its slide into eventual break-up. New areas of the globe assumed greater prominence. And, of course, the march of technology continues to affect everyday life. What does the future hold for Europe? Making predictions is difficult: no one—not even the most optimistic observer—would have predicted that communism would collapse as quickly as it did and with so little resistance. But the historical process is complicated by unexpected events and influenced by the personal impact of leaders and the choices made by individuals.

Key Concepts, Figures, and Events

International Monetary Fund (IMF)
United Nations (UN)
North Atlantic Treaty Organization (NATO)
Cuban Missile Crisis
Helicopter Economy
Simone de Beauvoir
Marshall Plan

European Economic Community (EEC)
Charles de Gaulle
Mutually Assured Destruction (MAD)
Existentialism
Nikita Khrushchev
Mikhail Gorbachev
Boris Yeltsin

Topics for Further Thought

1. Following World War II, Europe was in shambles and millions of people were homeless. In such situations, what moral obligations do other nations of the world have to assist in the rebuilding process? Is it reasonable for countries offering the aid to attach conditions and to expect economic gain in the long run?

2. Early in the sixteenth century, Niccolò Machiavelli wrote "The end justifies the means." Given the experiences of the Soviet Union during World War II, was Stalin justified in his actions to protect the Soviet Union in the post-war years? Did he provide effective leadership in rebuilding the Soviet Union in the immediate post-war years?

3. Democracy has emerged as the favoured political system of the Western world in the second half of the twentieth century. Reflecting on the achievements of countries in Western Europe since 1945, to what degree could it be argued that parliamentary democracy has been responsible for the stability and general prosperity enjoyed by most of Western Europe?

4. Was the cold war the product of clashing superpowers, intent on empire building, or clashing ideologies that made co-operation and understanding virtually impossible. Could a world divided along diametrically opposed political lines have found a way to work harmoniously?

5. During the 1970s and 1980s, a debate emerged over whether deterrence (MAD) or disarmament was the best means to ensure peace. Which do you believe was more important in preventing a major conflict between superpowers: the concept of MAD or efforts such as the SALT talks to limit the production of weapons?

6. While consumers around the globe eagerly embrace icons of American culture—from Big Macs and Coke to Hollywood movies—there are those who decry the Americanization of European culture. Do you think the export of American products poses a real threat to other cultures? Should governments provide funding for "home-grown" entertainment or block the importation of American culture as protective measures or should such actions be seen as antidemocratic?

7. The years following World War II witnessed the emergence of the "welfare state," in which the government played a much more active role in the economy to ensure greater stability and to assist the less fortunate members of society. Today, as governments struggle to trim deficits, the welfare state is under fire. How can we explain this reversal? Has society evolved so that the welfare state is less necessary? Are the cost-saving measures being implemented regressive? Was the welfare state a costly mistake from the outset?

8. Youth of the 1960s was militant in its belief that the world could be a better place. The generation since has been far less active in pursuing change. How can we explain this? Were the young of the 1960s naïve idealists or did they manage to bring about real and lasting change? Is today's youth skeptical because of the failure of the sixties to bring about the kind of utopian society they spoke and sang about?

Topics for Further Research

1. In recent years, the political map of Eastern Europe has been transformed by the collapse of communism and the emergence of new independent states. Research the current status of one of the following new republics, focusing on economic conditions, current political status, and major social changes:

Slovenia	Macedonia
Slovakia	Poland
Romania	Latvia
Bulgaria	Lithuania
Hungary	Serbia

2. During the cold war, several events occurred that heightened tensions between East and West. Research the origins, outcome, and significance of one of the following events:

Berlin Blockade	Korea
Building the Berlin Wall	Vietnam
Cuban Missile Crisis	Afghanistan

3. During the 1960s, several bands and singers became symbols of the youth movement. Research one of the following groups or soloists and prepare a biographical sketch that also assesses their importance to the 1960s and youth culture:

The Beatles	The Grateful Dead
The Rolling Stones	Joan Baez
The Who	Bob Dylan
The Doors	Neil Young

4. The decades immediately prior to and following World War II produced some of the most thought-provoking literature of the century. Prepare a biographical sketch including a summary of the most important ideas of one of the following writers:

Jean-Paul Sartre	Simone de Beauvoir
Albert Camus	Samuel Beckett
Herbert Marcuse	Franz Kafka
Bertolt Brecht	

Responding to Ideas

1. When new information about a historical character is brought to light, historians often must look critically at long-held views of the individual. The revelations about Stalin made by Khrushchev at the Twentieth Congress in 1956 forced a critical re-evaluation of Stalin. However, upon reflection, Stalin's biographer, Isaac Deutscher, had this to say about Stalin: "Unfortunately, those revelations have added nothing to the account given in this book of Stalin's rise to power.... I do not accept Khrushchev's assertion that Stalin's role in the Second World War was virtually insignificant. This allegation was obviously meant to boost Khrushchev himself at Stalin's expense." What do Deutscher's words tell us about the writing—and especially the rewriting—of history? What precaution must be taken when responding to new information?

2. Throughout this textbook, there has been an emphasis on ideas that have shaped the world. Roland Stromberg, in the conclusion to *European Intellectual History Since 1789*, wrote: "If the most urgent task confronting us is the organization of our ideas that they may be creatively used, and if these ideas indeed are 'the invisible powers that govern men,' then the systematic study of ideas... would seem to be not the least important of the many studies currently pursued." Do you agree with Stromberg's assessment of the importance of the study of ideas? Defend your answer.

Europe and the Global Village

CHAPTER HIGHLIGHTS

- The importance of independence movements in European colonies and the collapse of colonial empires

- The nature of the process of decolonization and the problems facing newly independent, post-colonial nations

- The emergence of new international organizations

- The new unifying imperatives governing these relations: resources, ecology, the market, and information

---

In 1964, Canadian professor Marshall McLuhan published *Understanding Media*. One phrase from the book has become part of everyday language: ***global village***. McLuhan predicted that as communications systems became more efficient, people would be brought closer together and cultural distinctions would diminish, creating a world community: a global village.

McLuhan's prediction has become a reality to some extent. Satellite communication enables television networks to deliver instantaneous coverage of world events to millions of TV viewers. Stock exchanges from Tokyo to Vancouver and from New York to London are linked into one global 24-hour financial market. Multinational corporations do business without regard to national boundaries.

Environmental problems are also globally shared: the fallout from the Chernobyl nuclear catastrophe in Ukraine spread 50 tonnes of radioactive waste over Northeastern Europe and the fallout in the soil contaminated the food exported from there to different countries. We seem to have become a "McWorld tied together by technology, ecology, communications and commerce," wrote Benjamin Barber in the *Atlantic Monthly* of March 1992.

But, for every force that brings the human community together, an opposite force operates to tear it apart. The global village is under attack by discord and opposing economic, cultural, and political interests. These divergent processes of unity and separation are as old as history itself.

The First Global Village

The prototype of McLuhan's global village appeared in the sixteenth and seventeenth centuries, as Europeans leapfrogged throughout the globe, establishing trading posts and colonies. By the eighteenth century, the Americas, Australia, and New Zealand were settled by European populations, while European plants and animals such as the dandelion, clover, pig, horse, and rabbit competed for space with native species.

In the nineteenth century, Africa and Southeast Asia were carved up into European colonies and spheres of influence. China, though nominally independent, was forced to make humiliating concessions to European and American powers anxious to penetrate the Chinese market. By the beginning of the twentieth century, Western nations controlled nearly five sixths of the globe. The race for empire brought into being a network of global villages connected by a web of railroad lines, telegraph cables, and steamship routes. European languages, systems of government, social structures, and values dominated, pushed aside, or blended with non-European cultures.

Twentieth-Century Collapse

European empires began to crumble after World War I, and the process of decolonization picked up momentum after 1945. By 1975, most former colonies, representing about one third of the world population, were independent of their European masters. The reasons for such a startling collapse were related to two sets of factors: (a) colonial peoples (African, Arab, Asian) organized independence movements against European rule and (b) there were changes in European attitudes toward empire.

Forces for Colonial Independence

Ironically, Europeans themselves planted the seeds of national resistance. As European nations extended their power over the globe, non-European powers, such as the Moguls in India, the Ottoman Turks in the Middle East, and the Manchu rulers in China, proved unable to resist Western advance. Europeans were convinced that their power rested on their racial superiority: Arabs were "devious"; Orientals were "clever, crafty, and cruel"; Indians were "lazy and backward." Blacks ranked the lowest in European estimation. Take, for example, this shocking entry from a British explorer's journal. "Human nature, viewed in its crude state as pictured amongst African savages, is quite on a level with that of the brute, and is not to be compared with the noble character of the dog."

Civilization was viewed as a race up a mountain in which Europeans had already reached the peak, while allegedly lesser races had barely started. Given these circumstances, Europeans had a moral duty to help their colonies catch up. The British government took over India in 1858 and built railroads, developed industry, and educated Indian students for positions in the Indian civil service. British authorities put an end to *sati*, the practice of burning widows on their husbands' funeral pyre. They repressed *thagi*, the ritual assassination of travellers by roving bands who sacrificed for their goddess. The British unified the many small states of the Indian Subcontinent by imposing law and order and, perhaps most significantly, their language.

Force was viewed as a necessary part of the civilizing process: "The moment there is a sign of revolt," noted one European administrator, "it is wise to hit the Oriental straight between the eyes, and to keep on hitting him thus, till he appreciates exactly what he is, and who is who." In South Africa, after a raid against a group of blacks, a British soldier wrote in his diary: "All over the place it was nothing but dead or dying niggers. We burnt all the huts and a lot of niggers that could not come out were burnt to death; you could hear them screaming, but it served them right."

Except for the Spanish and the Portuguese (who intermarried with the native populations of their empires), Europeans set up barriers between themselves and the peoples they ruled. British settlers in India lived in their own separate compounds, freezing out even the best-educated or most refined Indians. The relations between other colonial powers and their subjects were no different. In certain Chinese cities, Europeans inhabited separate quarters and were governed by their right of extraterritoriality, which meant they were not subject to Chinese laws. Independence movements owed much of their original energy to European-educated leaders who were slighted and scorned and maltreated by Europeans. Memories of such arrogant and discriminatory attitudes continue to poison European relations with other peoples in countries where the populations did not blend through intermarriage.

Economic exploitation intensified the bitterness aroused by racism and insensitivity. Imperial powers extracted the resources of their colonies for their own

Marshall McLuhan:
The Medium is the Message

Marshall McLuhan stands out among the great intellectuals of the late twentieth century. Born in Edmonton, Alberta in 1911, McLuhan became internationally famous during the 1960s for his pioneering work as a communications theorist.

McLuhan's work focused on the effects of the mass media on thought and behaviour. His contributions in this field have been compared to the works of Darwin and Freud for their universal significance. The extract below is from his book *Understanding Media*, which earned him world-wide acclaim.

In a culture like ours, long accustomed to splitting and dividing all things as a means of control, it is sometimes a bit of a shock to be reminded that, in operational and practical fact, the medium is the message. This is merely to say that the personal and social consequences of any medium—that is, of any extension of ourselves—result from the new scale that is introduced into our affairs by each extension of ourselves or by any new technology. Thus, with automation, for example, the new patterns of human association tend to eliminate jobs, create roles for people, which is to say depth of involvement in their work and human association that our preceding mechanical technology had destroyed. Many people would be disposed to say that it was not the machine, but what one did with the machine, that was its meaning or message. In terms of the ways in which the machine altered our relations to one another and to ourselves, it mattered not in the least whether it turned out cornflakes or Cadillacs. The restructuring of human work and association was shaped by the technique of fragmentation that is the essence of machine technology. The essence of automation technology is the opposite. It is integral and decentralist in depth, just as the machine was fragmentary, centralist, and superficial in its patterning of human relationships.

The instance of the electric light may prove illuminating in this connection. The electric light is pure information. It is a medium without a message, as it were, unless it is used to spell out some verbal ad or name. This fact, characteristic of all media, means that the "content" of any medium is always another medium. The content of writing is speech, just as the written word is the content of print, and print is the content of the telegraph. If it is asked, "What is the content of speech?," it is necessary to say, "It is an actual process of thought, which is in itself nonverbal." An abstract painting represents direct manifestation of creative thought processes as they might appear in computer designs. What we are considering here, however, are the psychic and social consequences of the designs or patterns as they amplify or accelerate existing processes. For the "message" of any medium or technology is the change of scale or pace or pattern that it introduces into human affairs. The railway did not introduce movement or transportation or wheel or road into human society, but it accelerated and enlarged the scale of previous human functions, creating totally new kinds of cities and new kinds of work and leisure. This happened whether the railway functioned in a tropical or a northern environment, and is quite independent of the freight or content of the railway medium. The airplane, on the other hand, by accelerating the rate of transportation, tends to dissolve the railway form of city, politics, and association, quite independently of what the airplane is used for.

benefit, leaving the native populations to a life of poverty. Among the most cruel instances of economic exploitation was that of the former Belgian Congo (today Zaire), which during the 1880s was the private property of King Leopold II. He allowed private developers to conscript natives into labour gangs to work the mines and rubber plantations. Often, however, the growth of a European-dominated world economy integrated non-Europeans into an economic system over which they had no control: the Chinese silk industry produced silk to suit the tastes of the European consumer and the specifications of European textile mills; Kenyan farmers gave up their traditional agriculture in order to produce cash crops for an overseas market; in India, cheap cotton manufactured in England flooded the Indian market during the nineteenth century, throwing many village craftspeople out of work.

Fighting Back

The expulsion of European occupiers became the goal of resentful colonial peoples throughout the globe during the twentieth century. Violence was common. One particularly bloody example was the 1899–1900 Boxer Uprising in China. Disgusted by the way in which Europeans and Americans had divided China into their own economic spheres of interest, and ashamed of their government's weakness, the "fists of righteous harmony" (Boxers) rose up against the "foreign devils." The Chinese government suppressed the rebellion but only with military assistance from Europe and the U.S.

In some cases, European disdain of non-European culture aroused a reaction in defence of historic ways of life. Indian spiritual leader **Mohandas Karamchand Gandhi** urged Indians to reject British culture and return to traditional Indian lifestyles. Gandhi set an example by weaving his own cloth and dressing in traditional native clothing. In contrast to traditionalists such as Gandhi, modernizers such as Gandhi's successor, Jawaharlal Nehru, believed that adapting to the modern world was a more effective way of dealing with European imperialism.

In Turkey, a group calling itself Young Turks sought to build a thoroughly modern, secular Turkish society. Their role model was Japan, whose dazzling surge to world power status showed that it was possible to beat the whites at their own game.

After American Commodore Matthew Perry blasted his way into Tokyo Bay in 1853, Japan undertook a thorough reconstruction of its political, military, and educational systems. Reform began in earnest after 1868 and is known as the Meiji Restoration. Borrowing and adapting extensively from the West, Japan transformed itself into a modern industrial nation without abandoning its own religion, traditions, and culture. The takeover of Formosa from China in 1884–1885 propelled Japan into the ranks of imperial powers. Much to everyone's surprise, the Russo-Japanese War of 1904–1905 ended in a decisive Japanese victory and destroyed the myth that European nations could not be conquered.

In the Middle East, the **Muslim Brotherhood** won many followers during the 1950s and 1960s. Rejecting the European way of life, the Brotherhood envisioned a just society based on Islamic values as outlined in their sacred book, the Koran. The leaders of the Muslim Brotherhood came from educated elites and attracted Arabs who had been shut out of English or French society.

Frantz Fanon, a West Indian psychoanalyst and social philosopher from Martinique, spoke eloquently in the 1960s of the need for a "counter-culture" based on ideals radically different from those of European society. The conclusion of his book *The Wretched of the Earth*, published in 1975, reads:

> The European game has finally ended; we must do something different. We today can do everything, so long as we do not imitate Europe, so long as we are not obsessed by the desire to catch up with Europe.... The Third World today faces Europe like a colossal mass whose aim should be to try to resolve the problems to which Europe has not been

Thousands of Muslim worshippers pray at the Al-Aqsa mosque near the Dome of the Rock in Jerusalem.

able to find answers.... If we want humanity to advance a step further, if we want to bring it up to a different level than that which Europe has shown it, then we must invent and we must make discoveries.

Changes in Europe

Colonial peoples' desire for independence coincided with shifts in European attitudes. In the years following World War II, imperialism was no longer as fashionable as it had once been. In Europe during the 1970s, Fanon's message captured the imagination and support of many intellectuals and student protesters. How could Europeans, who prided themselves on being democratic, and who had just fought a brutal war to defend freedom, justify a claim to rule other peoples? In 1948, 50 countries had signed the UN Universal Declaration of Human Rights, which, among other things, recognized "the equal rights of... nations large and small."

A second reason for ending imperialism was financial. As discussed in Chapter 17, European nations faced the enormous expense of economic reconstruction after 1945. Building the welfare state took priority over maintaining an imperial presence abroad. The economic miracle of Germany and Italy, countries that had no colonial empires, proved that colonies were not vital to prosperity.

The Process of Decolonization

The process of decolonization can only be outlined in this chapter. The examples considered below focus on the two major imperial powers of the twentieth century: Great Britain and France. Sometimes the route to colonial independence was relatively peaceful; on other occasions violent. Much depended on whether a colony had a large European settlement or not. The cold war often complicated the process of decolonization.

India: The Jewel in the British Crown

Britain was the greatest imperial power at the beginning of the twentieth century. In one form or another, its empire encompassed territory all over the globe. Canada and Australia were self-governing dominions. Rhodesia enjoyed a limited degree of self-rule. Hong Kong, seized from China during the Opium War of 1841–1842, was a crown colony administered by a British governor, as were West Indian islands. Egypt was a protectorate, in theory an independent state but in practice subject to British military and financial control. Of all British possessions, however, the Indian Subcontinent was the largest—the "jewel" in the British crown. British India consisted of India proper, present-day Pakistan, Myanmar (formerly Burma), and present-day Bangladesh. A British viceroy ruled the Subcontinent with the assistance of an Indian civil service.

In the 1880s, a nationalist movement under the leadership of the Congress Party won the backing of many educated Indians. Mohandas Gandhi, an upper-class Indian trained as a lawyer in Britain, became the Congress Party's leader in 1925. He had already earned a reputation as a champion of immigrant Indian labourers when he was living in South Africa. It was in Africa that Gandhi developed his revolutionary idea of peaceful protest.

Gandhi realized that the success of the independence movement depended on mass participation. In order to build a broad base of support, he visited towns and villages all over India. He welcomed all castes, women, and Muslims to join the cause of independence. Gandhi's philosophy of life, known as *satyāgraha*, called for non-violence, individual spiritual renewal, and moral awakening, which, in Gandhi's view, formed the only sound basis for national independence and stability.

Gandhi was not only a philosopher but also a shrewd political leader. He was quick to realize that, during the interwar years, the mass media were playing an increasingly influential role in political affairs, as can be seen from his highly publicized 1930 protest against the salt tax. Gandhi argued that a tax on such a basic commodity not only burdened poor people, it violated civil rights. To protest the repressive salt tax, Gandhi and a group of followers began a 300 km march to the Indian Ocean. Led by Gandhi, they waded into its waters, filled a pitcher, and boiled it down to extract the salt. This symbolic action was the signal for a nationwide strike and a boycott of British goods. The resulting press coverage generated widespread public support for self-government, while the boycott threw textile workers in Britain out of work and added British political pressure to the campaign for Indian independence. Gandhi had become a revered holy person, or *mahatma*, to his own people and an admired hero to many British people, who threw their support behind

Mahatma Gandhi's cause. The outbreak of World War II, however, delayed Indian independence until 1947.

With India gone, self-rule for other parts of the empire was only a matter of time. Well before the outbreak of World War II, British colonial authorities drew up plans to prepare their colonies for self-rule. They thought that the process might take several decades but the rising tide of post-World War II nationalism and the cold war forced them to speed up their schedule. Soviet propaganda blamed the West for the misery in which many colonial peoples lived. Fear of communism and the possibility of anti-Western pro-Soviet uprisings prompted British leaders to grant early independence to several colonies.

The Gold Coast, renamed Ghana, was the first African colony to break colonial ties with Britain. The year was 1957. Soon others followed. In Egypt, charismatic leader Gamal Abdel Nasser engineered a revolution in 1952 that eventually forced Britain to end its protectorate over Egypt. The major exception was the crown colony of Hong Kong, which is to be returned to Chinese sovereignty in 1997. The British Empire, upon which at one time the sun never set, was reduced to a few pinpricks on the globe.

The French Experience

After Britain, the second largest imperial power was France. Most of its possessions were in Africa and Southeast Asia. Long before the Americans became involved in Southeast Asia, Vietnam had been a battleground between a French government intent on keeping its colony and Vietnamese rebels (Viet Minh) determined to overthrow the French. The French established their empire in Indochina (Southeast Asia) after 1858. During World War II, Japanese armies overran Indochina. After Japan surrendered, France repossessed Vietnam bit by bit, occupying Saigon in 1945 and Hanoi a year later. At the same time, the French government reached an agreement with Ho Chi Minh, the Viet Minh leader, to grant independence to the North. Eventually, it was hoped, the whole Vietnamese peninsula would become united under an independent government. The fact that Ho Chi Minh was a communist did not seem to matter at the time.

Some French leaders objected strongly to this arrangement. The humiliating German occupation of France in 1940 probably contributed to the French determination to retain their overseas empire in the post-war period. In defiance of official government policy, the French viceroy in Vietnam allowed local leaders to set up a separate state South Vietnam. Peace talks broke down and confrontation between the Viet Minh and French troops followed. When a French warship fired on the port of Haiphong, killing 6000 people, the communists declared a war of liberation.

Three years later, in 1949, the situation became more serious as China, under Mao Zedong, became communist and began supporting Vietnamese rebels. A year later, the Korean War broke out. With the cold war raging in Europe, the U.S. came to the aid of the French in order to counterbalance Chinese forces. The domino theory guided their thinking: if one country succumbed to communism, others would follow. Before long, the U.S. was financing about 80 percent of the French military budget in the Vietnam. This aid served to prolong the war.

In 1954, the French military decided to make a stand at the fortress of Dien Bien Phu, which sat astride the Viet Minh supply route to China. An overconfident French commander made mistakes in planning Dien Bien Phu's defences and, after three months of fighting, the French conceded defeat. Out of an occupying force of 20 000, only 3000 survived. The whole Dien Bien Phu episode was a political as well as a military catastrophe. France had no choice but to withdraw from Indochina. The eight-and-a-half-year-old Vietnamese War cost France 8.5 billion dollars and over 200 000 casualties. Indochina suffered approximately 43 000 casualties.

Algeria

French society had barely enough time to recover from the Vietnam debacle before the country found itself fighting to keep Algeria. Few French nationals had settled in Vietnam. Algeria, on the other hand, was an overseas department of France that had elected delegates to the National Assembly since 1871. It had close economic and cultural links with France but in truth was controlled by the French minority.

Nationalist groups had begun to agitate against the French presence in Algeria in the last months of World War II. Tens of thousands were killed by the French army. A well-organized and dedicated Muslim-led independence movement, known as the Front de Libération Nationale (FLN), gathered force in the years after the war and began a campaign of violence in 1954, fuelled by French economic exploitation and

Mahatma Gandhi

Mahatma Gandhi stands out among the famous people of the twentieth century. His commitment to peaceful resolutions and to his selfless service to his country and people continue to shine as an example to us all nearly half a century after his death. Gandhi was born in 1869 in the state of Porbandar, in Western India. In 1888, he was sent to London to complete his education, after which he went to South Africa to practise law. Gandhi worked tirelessly to gain rights and protection under the law for Indians in South Africa. It was during this period that Gandhi, in part influenced by Russian novelist Leo Tolstoy, developed his idea of *satyāgraha* (Hindi, "truth force"), a component of which is passive resistance, or *ahimsa* (the Sanskrit word for "non-injury"). Word of his work in South Africa preceded his return to India in 1915. Upon arriving home, Gandhi found himself to be much sought after by Indian political leaders who were struggling for independence from Britain. Gandhi immediately became an instrumental force in the drive for Indian independence. He was able to bring about this goal without the use of violence, although his entire dream has never been fully realized. Gandhi had dreamed of a united India, with its economy and society based on the traditional Indian village community, and its national spirit united by a concept of selfless service that would transcend the boundaries of caste, faith, race, and wealth. The extracts below are from letters written by Gandhi. What do they reveal about his ideas? Would his approach be viable today?

Stick to Non-Violence

At last the long-expected hour seems to have come.

In the dead of night, my colleagues and companions have roused me from deep slumber and requested me to give them a message. I am therefore giving this message, although I have not the slightest inclination to give any.

Messages I have given enough already. Of what avail would this message be if none of the previous messages evoked a proper response? But information received until this midnight leads me to the belief that my message did not fall flat, but was taken up by the people in right earnest. The people of Gujarat seem to have risen in a body, as it were. I have seen with my own eyes thousands of men and women at Aat and Bhimrad, fearlessly breaking the Salt Act. Not a sign of mischief, not a sign of violence have I seen, despite the presence of people in such large numbers. They have remained perfectly peaceful and non-violent, although Government officers have transgressed all bounds.

Here in Gujarat, well-tried and popular public servants have been arrested one after another, and yet the people have been perfectly non-violent. They have refused to give way to panic, and have celebrated the arrests by offering civil disobedience in ever-increasing numbers. This is just as it should be.

If the struggle so auspiciously begun is continued in the same spirit of non-violence to the end, not only shall we see *Purna Swarāj* (Hindi, "home rule") established in our country before long, but we shall have given to the world an object-lesson worthy of India and her glorious past.

Swarāj won without sacrifice cannot last long. I would, therefore, like our people to get ready to make the highest sacrifice that they are capable of. In true sacrifice all the suffering is on one side—one is required to master the art of getting killed without killing, of gaining life by losing it. May India live up to this mantra!

At present, India's self-respect, in fact her all, is symbolized as it were in a handful of salt in the satyagrahi's[1] hand. Let the fist holding it therefore be broken, but let there be not voluntary surrender of the salt.

Let the Government, if it claims to be a civilized Government, jail those who help themselves to contraband salt. After their arrest, the civil resisters will gladly surrender the salt, as they will their bodies, into the custody of their jailors.

But by main force to snatch the salt from the poor, harmless satyagrahis' hands is barbarism pure and simple and an insult to India. Such insult can be answered only by allowing our hand to be fractured without loosening the grasp. Even then the actual sufferer or his comrades may not harbour in their hearts anger against the wrongdoer. Incivility should be answered not by incivility but by a dignified and calm endurance of all suffering in the name of God.

Let not my companions or the people at large be perturbed over my arrest, for it is not I but God Who is guiding this movement. He ever dwells in the hearts of all and he will vouchsafe to use the right guidance if only we have faith in Him. Our path has already been chalked out for us. Let every village fetch

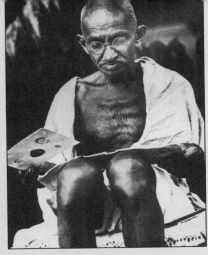

Mahatma Gandhi in his plain cotton attire.

or manufacture contraband salt, sisters should picket liquor shops, opium dens and foreign cloth dealers' shops. Young and old in every home should ply the *takli* [2] and spin and get woven heaps of yarn every day. Foreign cloth should be burnt. Hindus should eschew untouchability. Hindus, Mussulmans [3], Sikhs, Parsis [4], and Christians should all achieve heart unity. Let the majority rest content with what remains after the minorities have been satisfied. Let students leave Government schools and colleges, and Government servants resign their service and devote themselves to the service of the people, and we shall find that *Purna Swarāj*, will come knocking at our doors.

Young India, August 5, 1930

---

1 Someone who follows the principle of *satyāgraha*.
2 Hindi: small spindle used to produce cotton yarn
3 Muslims
4 Persians (today, Iranians)

My Dream

Before I ever knew anything of politics in my early youth, I dreamt the dream of communal unity of the heart. I shall jump in the evening of my life, like a child, to feel that the dream has been realized in this life. The wish for living the full span of life, portrayed by the seers of old and which they permit us to set down at 125 years, will then revive. Who would not risk sacrificing his life for the realization of such a dream? Then we shall have real *Swarāj*. Then, though legally and geographically we may still be two States, in daily life no one will think that we were separate States. The vista before me seems to me to be, as it must be to you, too glorious to be true. But like a child in a famous picture drawn by a famous painter, I shall not be happy till I have got it. I live and want to live for no lesser goal. Let the seekers from Pakistan help me to come as near the goal as it is humanly possible. A goal ceases to be one when it is reached. The nearest approach is always possible. What I have said holds good irrespective of whether others do it or not. It is open to every individual to purify himself or herself so as to render him or her fit for that land of promise. I remember to have read, I forget whether in the Delhi Fort or the Agra Fort, when I visited them in 1896, a verse on one of the gates, which when translated reads: "If there is a paradise on earth, it is here, it is here, it is here." That Fort with all its magnificence at its best was no paradise in my estimation. But I should love to see that verse with justice inscribed on the gates of Pakistan at all the entrances. In such paradise, whether it is in the Union or in Pakistan, there will be neither paupers nor beggars, nor high nor low, neither millionaire employers nor half-starved employees, nor intoxicating drinks nor drugs. There will be the same respect for women as vouchsafed to men and the chastity and purity of men and women will be jealously guarded. Where every woman except one's wife will be treated by men of all religions as mother, sister or daughter, according to her age. Where there will no untouchability and where there will be equal respect for all faiths. They will be all proudly, joyously and voluntarily bread labourers. I hope everyone who listens to me or reads these lines will forgive me if stretched on my bed and basking in the sun, inhaling life-giving sunshine, I allow myself to indulge in the ecstasy. Let this assure the doubters and sceptics that I have not the slightest desire that the fast should be ended as quickly as possible. It matters little if the ecstatic wishes of a fool like me are never realized and the fast is never broken. I am content to wait as long as it may be necessary, but it will hurt me to think that people have acted merely in order to save me. I claim that God has inspired this fast and it will be broken only when and if He wishes it. No human agency has ever been known to thwart, nor will it thwart, the Divine Will.

cultural domination. French settlers, or *colons*, and their descendants formed 10 percent of a population of 9 million. Most *colons* were poor but those at the top owned the best land and controlled most of the industry. French was the language of instruction imposed on the Arab majority. The two largest cities, Algiers and Oran, were mainly French in culture: the mosque in Algiers had been turned into a cathedral.

When the FLN began its campaign of terror, the *colons* retaliated in kind. The colons undertook "rat-hunts" against rebels as reprisals for FLN café bombings in Algiers. The FLN cut off noses of Muslims suspected of sympathizing with the French. The *colons* threatened to upset any French government inclined to grant concessions to the Muslim rebels. A demoralized French government could not cope with the situation. President de Gaulle, who initially seemed to favour the *colons*, ended the war by negotiating Algerian independence. In doing so, he had the support of most mainland French who felt that keeping Algeria was not worth the expense. In any case, independence did not dissolve the economic links between Algeria and France.

In contrast to the Algerian blood bath, two French colonies in North Africa, Morocco and Tunisia, as well as French colonies south of the Sahara, became independent by negotiation. Their leaders, who were educated in France, cooperated with French authorities in the transition to self-government.

Other imperial powers retreated from their overseas possessions. The United States withdrew from the Philippines in 1946 and pressured its European allies to grant independence to their colonies. The Netherlands gave up their control of the Dutch East Indies (today Indonesia) in 1950; Belgium left the Congo (today Zaire) in 1960, and Portugal reluctantly withdrew from Angola, Mozambique, and Guinea-Bissau in the mid-1970s. The nineteenth-century network of nations with their "capital" in Europe became a relic of the past.

Problems of Independence

Unfortunately, political independence did not result in a better life for the people of the newly independent countries. In too many cases, it brought chaos and fragmentation. Precolonial Africa had been a jumble of city-states, small kingdoms, and tribal territories. Europeans, in carving out their empires in Africa, paid no attention to existing arrangements, often including

long-time enemies and people of different ethnic backgrounds in their new divisions. Ethiopia, for example, encompassed many ethnic groups and languages. The period of colonial rule had been too short to impose any kind of unifying set of traditions.

With the end of imperialism, long-repressed hatreds burst out. Angola, a former Portuguese colony, turned into a bloody battleground between rival political groups. In the 1970s, Ugandan dictator Idi Amin expelled Asian Ugandans en masse. A bloody civil war broke out in Nigeria, the most populous country in Africa, when the more prosperous and Christian South attempted to secede from the less prosperous and largely Muslim North. The fighting that broke out in 1993 in the Central African country of Rwanda also has origins in intertribal rivalry.

Failure to resolve the major Hindu-Muslim conflict forced Britain out of India. The creation of a separate Muslim state, Pakistan, to the east and west of India brought a temporary peace. Gandhi, the Hindu champion of non-violence, was shot by a Hindu fanatic who thought he was too soft on Muslims. After independence, various minority groups agitated for greater autonomy and religious freedom. When Sikhs living in the Punjab failed to obtain greater autonomy, they turned to violence. In 1971, civil war ripped through Pakistan and the eastern portion of the country emerged as Bangladesh.

The American withdrawal from Vietnam did not bring peace to Indochina, where feuding between competing communist groups meant continued warfare for that troubled region. In Cambodia, radical communist leader Pol Pot and his Khmer Rouge ruthlessly murdered 1 million people and dispossessed many others. In Ceylon (today Sri Lanka) friction between the Buddhist Sinhalese majority and the Hindu Tamil minority sparked a guerrilla war.

The pattern of violence has been endlessly repeated in many former colonial territories with the end of the cold war. Rapidly growing populations, poverty, economic stagnation, and political corruption have worsened the situation.

The Middle East

Religious and political interests have clashed repeatedly in the Middle East, the crossroads between the East and the West. Under the tolerant Ottoman rule, Muslim, Christian, and Jewish communities coexisted peacefully. In the nineteenth century, an intellectual import from the West—the idea of the nation-state—spread throughout the Middle East. The Young Turks, under the leadership of Kemal Atatürk, ruthlessly Westernized Turkey. Nationalism also inspired various Arab groups. Meanwhile, in Europe, the Jewish people, who were still subjected to widespread anti-Semitism, began to dream of establishing a Jewish state where they could live without fear of persecution. For historical reasons, the most natural location for a Jewish homeland was Palestine, which was under British rule since 1919.

Dreams of nationhood, whether Turkish, Arab, or Jewish, clashed with European imperial plans. As Ottoman Turkish authority weakened in the last decades of the nineteenth century, Britain and France seized the opportunity to extend their influence in the Middle East. They wanted to protect their access to the Suez Canal, which lay on the route to India and the Far East, where both countries had imperial possessions. The discovery of oil in the region added to its importance.

In 1915–1916, the British planted the seeds for the Arab-Israeli conflict which still plagues Middle Eastern politics. Secret negotiations between the Arab ruler of Mecca in the Arabian peninsula and the British government encouraged him to believe that Arab independence would follow when the fighting in Europe was over. (The British fostered anti-Turkish feelings among the Arab countries ruled by the Ottoman Turks because they wanted to bring them into the war against Germany.) The secret Sykes-Picot Agreement between Britain and France divided the Middle East between these two powers.

The ***Balfour Declaration*** of 1916 announced British support for "a national home for the Jewish people" in Palestine. Though not specified in the Declaration, many people, both Jewish and non-Jewish, assumed that "national home" meant an independent state. The Arab majority of Palestine was not consulted. A small number of Jewish people had always lived in Palestine, but the Arabs constituted 90 percent of the population and they too had inhabited the region for centuries. A wave of Jewish immigration from Europe during the 1920s and 1930s raised the Jewish population considerably. The Arabs regarded Jewish immigrants as Western intruders.

Since Palestine was a British protectorate, the British needed to balance competing Arab and Jewish claims. In 1939, even though Jews were being persecuted by the Nazis, Britain decided to limit the Jewish population in Palestine to one third of the total and to restrict Jewish land purchases. The Holocaust changed public opinion in the West in favour of the creation of an independent Jewish state in Palestine. In the meantime, Jewish settlers were moving into the area in defiance of British attempts to keep them out. Terrorist attacks made it increasingly difficult for the British to maintain order and Britain appealed to the UN. The UN proposed that Palestine be divided into Arab and Jewish sectors, with the city of Jerusalem, which was sacred to both Jews and Muslims, remaining an international zone. All three sectors would be linked in an economic union.

The Jews reluctantly accepted this proposal, but the Arabs did not because it gave them less land than they currently occupied. In frustration, the British simply pulled out in 1948. Immediately after their departure, the Arab residents attacked and the first Arab-Israeli War broke out. In the midst of hostilities, the Jews announced, on May 14, 1948, the creation of the independent state of Israel, with David Ben-Gurion as its president. When the fighting stopped, the Israelis had expanded their territory by one third. Thousands of Arab Palestinians fled to the Gaza Strip and the West Bank (of the Jordan River), where they set up huge refugee camps. The Israelis regarded the refugees as potentially disruptive, while the Arabs believed they should be returned to their homelands.

Embittered by Israeli success, Arab nations refused to recognize the state of Israel and tensions continued to simmer. One of the most dramatic episodes in Arab-Israeli relations was the Suez Crisis in 1956. That year, Egyptian president Gamal Abdel Nasser nationalized the Suez Canal. His action infuriated British and French investors, who owned shares in the Canal. The Israelis suspected that Egypt was supporting Palestinian guerrillas. A combined Israeli, British, and French force landed in the Canal zone. The rest of the world was shocked at British and French intervention, and in a rare show of agreement, both the U.S. and the USSR expressed strong disapproval of the British-French action. Mediation by Canadian External Affairs minister Lester Pearson paved the way for the arrival of a UN peacekeeping force, whose presence allowed British, French, and Israeli troops to withdraw peacefully.

No peace treaty was signed after the Suez Crisis and both sides expected that a war would flare up again

Following the Gulf War in 1991, hundreds of oil wells in Kuwait were set on fire by the retreating Iraqis and burned out of control.

———————— ⚓ ————————

at some point. In 1967, Nasser demanded the withdrawal of the UN peacekeepers and called for a joint Arab (Egypt-Jordan-Syria) attack against Israel. The Israelis moved swiftly and decisively to defend themselves against their enemies before they even had a chance to mobilize. In the course of what became known as the Six-Day War, they captured the Golan Heights from Syria, the Sinai peninsula and adjoining Gaza strip from Egypt, and the West Bank, tripling the size of the Israeli state and increasing the numbers of Palestinian refugees. It was a humiliating experience for the Arab countries involved. As a result, the *Palestinian Liberation Organization* (PLO), a terrorist organization founded in 1964 to reclaim the Palestinian homeland from Israel, became more militant. The UN called for the Israelis to withdraw from the occupied territories in return for Arab recognition of Israel's right to exist, but the Arabs refused to recognize Israel and guerrilla fighting continued.

A decade later, in 1973, on the eve of Yom Kippur, a high holy day in the Jewish religion, Egypt and Syria again attacked Israel and again Israel succeeded in driving them back. In retaliation, the largely Arab Organization of Petroleum Exporting Countries (OPEC) imposed an oil embargo against Europe and

the U.S. Attempts to find a negotiated settlement went on for several months until Egyptian president Anwar Sadat took a dramatic and courageous step: he made a personal visit to Jerusalem and addressed the Knesset (Israeli parliament). This was the first time an Arab leader had travelled to Israel. His goal was peace. Eventually, thanks to the patient mediation of American president Jimmy Carter, Israel and Egypt met at Camp David in the U.S. in 1979 and signed a peace treaty. Israel handed the Sinai back to Egypt and Egypt recognized the existence of the state of Israel. The Camp David Accord did not resolve the Palestinian refugee problem, nor the dispute over who owned the Gaza Strip; however, it showed that, given good will, resolution of differences was possible.

Limited as was the Camp David Accord, it angered the Arab world. From the Arab point of view, Egypt had betrayed the Arab cause. President Sadat was assassinated in 1981 but his successor, Hosni Mubarak, continued the policy of peace with Israel. It was not until 1991, after the Gulf War, that Israel and the PLO began to negotiate.

Organizations for Unity

As the European colonial system fell apart, new forms of international organization took its place. One example was the *British Commonwealth of Nations*, which consists of 49 independent nations (representing one quarter of the world's population) and is symbolically headed by the British monarch. Most former colonies joined the Commonwealth, the major exception being Burma (today Myanmar).

The English language provides the unifying basis of the Commonwealth. In multilingual India, for example, English remains the official language of law, commerce, government, and education. Cultural and sports events, such as the Commonwealth Games, academic scholarships, conferences on topics of common interest (e.g. agriculture, technology, medicine), create bonds between widely different peoples.

Britain is no longer a leader; it is a member of the European Union. It has very close relations with its former colony, the U.S. Canada is a partner in a North American Free Trade Agreement (NAFTA) which includes the three countries of North America (Canada, the U.S., and Mexico). Although meetings between government heads to discuss issues of common

1989: A Year of Upheaval in Eastern Europe

interest are common, peace and harmony do not always prevail in the Commonwealth. When Commonwealth leaders condemned South Africa's apartheid policy, South Africa angrily left the Commonwealth in 1961. Economic sanctions enforced by the Commonwealth led South Africa, under Frederik W. de Klerk, to dismantle apartheid. With the democratic election of Nelson Mandela to the presidency, South Africa again joined the Commonwealth in 1994.

Like Great Britain, France now relates to its former colonies on an equal footing but, unlike Great Britain, France continues to maintain close economic and cultural ties with its former African colonies. The community of French-speaking countries is called *La francophonie*.

Former president of South Africa F. W. de Klerk and former African National Congress deputy-president Nelson Mandela discuss the dismantling of apartheid.

The United Nations

The UN is undoubtedly the most prominent organization of the twentieth century. From its initial membership of 50 countries, the UN has grown to over 160 members, many of whom were former colonies. Some of them took on new names to symbolize the rejection of an unpleasant past: Zaire is the former Belgian Congo; Zimbabwe is the former Rhodesia; Sri Lanka is the former Ceylon; and Myanmar is the former Burma. In the UN General Assembly all members, regardless of size, have a vote and a voice. Major decisions are made by the Security Council, but the Assembly, which is a kind of global-village meeting, provides a forum for small countries to express their points of view.

For the UN, however, acting as a world community is another matter. Restraining aggression was one of the original goals of the UN but the UN has rarely intervened against aggressors. In 1950, the UN dispatched an army under American general Douglas MacArthur to help South Korea, which had been invaded by the North. United action was possible because the Soviet Union boycotted the Security Council vote on this issue. The UN force sent in response to Iraq's invasion of Kuwait in 1991 was under UN sponsorship. As in the Korean case, Americans provided the bulk of the troops for the Gulf War, but unlike in Korea, the Soviet Union joined with other nations in supporting military action against Iraq. Between 1945 and 1978, over 25 million people have died in guerrilla and civil wars in Africa, Asia, and Latin America.

United Nations peacekeeping, rather than action against aggression, has gained mounting significance since 1945. Peacekeeping forces, which consist of troops from many countries, separate belligerents so they can work out a peaceable solution to their dispute. UN troops have intervened in many trouble spots, including the Congo, Kashmir, along the Pakistan-India border, and Cyprus. When Yugoslavia disintegrated, UN peacekeepers intervened to provide humanitarian aid to civilian populations.

Unfortunately, persisting national and ethnic rivalries frequently frustrate UN efforts at peacekeeping. Intervention in the Suez Crisis did not bring peace to the Middle East. Thirty years after UN forces entered Cyprus in 1963, they still remain policing the so-called Green Line dividing Turkish and Greek sectors. Nevertheless, despite such setbacks, in 1988 UN peacekeepers were awarded the Nobel Peace Prize, an award which acknowledged the importance of their work.

More successful but less spectacular is the UN's role in improving people's lives throughout the globe. The World Health Organization (WHO), United Nations Relief and Rehabilitation Agency (UNRRA), United Nations Children's Fund (UNICEF), Food and Agriculture Organization (FAO), and World Population Fund are all UN organizations staffed and supported by member nations.

Hundreds of non-governmental organizations (NGOs), such as Greenpeace, the Red Cross/Red Crescent, Amnesty International, and Oxfam, link peoples from different parts of the world for humanitarian purposes. Religion can also be a major force for world unity: the Catholic, Protestant, Islamic, and Jewish religious communities include people fom all parts of the world.

Europe: Unity and Fragmentation

Ever since the Middle Ages, the vision of a united Europe has haunted the European imagination. Unfortunately, bitter rivalries—economic, religious, and national—have repeatedly frustrated dreams of a united Europe.

Western Europe

Two immensely destructive world wars, caused in part by national rivalries, changed people's thinking. Peace could become a reality if Europeans could construct a European federation capable of resolving tensions before they reach a danger point. Secondly, the superpower confrontation that resulted from the cold war brought home the uncomfortable truth that Europe was at the mercy of the two superpowers (the U.S. and the USSR) and their competing interests. Only by building a new European nation could Europe regain some measure of independence.

As mentioned in Chapter 16, a first step was the European Steel and Coal Community (ESCC), which by integrating West Germany, France, and other nations economically, diminished the long-standing fear of German dominance. The 1957 Treaty of Rome transformed the ESCC into a wider economic union: the European Economic Community (EEC), initially consisting of its founder, France, plus West Germany, Italy, the Netherlands, Belgium, and Luxembourg. Steps toward political unity followed with the creation of a European Parliament in 1962. The EEC's economic success was the model for the European Free Trade Area (EFTA), the so-called "outer six" made up of Britain, Ireland, Denmark, and the Scandinavian countries.

Progress toward European unity hit occasional obstacles. National rivalries did not subside easily. France, under President de Gaulle, twice opposed Britain's entry into the EEC. Only in 1973 did Britain, Ireland, and Denmark succeed in joining. During the 1980s, the EEC inched toward a more integrated economic community with uniform product standards and freer circulation of money, goods, and services. In 1992, delegates from 12 European nations met in the Dutch city of Maastricht to hammer out the

Originating in Vancouver, Greenpeace has become an international organization dedicated to the preservation of the environment. Controversial actions, such as saving baby seals from the hatchets of hunters by spraying them with paint, have become the hallmark of Greenpeace.

foundation for a closer federation. The treaty increased the powers of the European parliament, introduced the basis for a common currency (the *écu*), a common banking system, and a common passport, all of which are functioning today. Delegates also dealt with a broad range of social/cultural issues. They drew up policies protecting workers' rights, regulating television programming, pollution controls on automobiles, and even standardized health warnings on cigarette packages. Based on the idea of French political economist Jean Monnet (who was the first president of the ESCC), the European union created by the ***Treaty of Maastricht*** was a federal system similar in many respects to the existing Canadian confederation.

On July 1, 1994, the European Union (EU) was proclaimed. It was a tremendous historical development. The EU rivals North America and Japan in terms of its potential economic clout. It has a large territory with many resources and a highly educated population. It controls one third of the world's trade and is home to some of the largest banks and insurance companies. Seven of the world's top ten trading nations are European. European auto, pharmaceutical, and engineering industries are world leaders. The Treaty of Maastricht provides for the inclusion of other nations, extending into the Mediterranean basin, Eastern, and Central Europe. But the European community has forces of fragmentation within its own ranks: Britain and France ratified Maastricht with only narrow margins of support; Denmark rejected it the first time. The reluctance to ratify the Treaty of Maastricht and the lukewarm support for the EU in Scandinavian countries reveal the strength of national feelings in Europe.

Formulating a common foreign policy is another potential area of dissension in the EU. When Canada (illegally but justifiably) apprehended a Spanish trawler fishing outside Canadian waters in 1995, the EU put up a united front in protest against Canadian action. However, Europeans were not united in their response to the Gulf War and have no consensus on how to deal with the problems resulting from the breakup of Yugoslavia.

1989: Year of Revolution

In 1989, as discussed in Chapter 17, the Soviet Union collapsed. The ensuing turmoil was replayed elsewhere in the Soviet bloc. In the case of Poland, where hatred of Soviet domination went back to the early post-war period, the unravelling of communism had begun before Gorbachev came to power. The Catholic Church in Poland, which claimed the allegiance of 25 million people out of a population of 28 million, served as a rallying point for Polish dissent. In 1978, the election of Polish pope John Paul II enhanced the prestige of the Church. A visit by the new pope to his homeland the following year gave moral support to a trade-union movement, *Solidarity*, which had originated in the Gdansk shipyards. Its leader, Lech Walesa, demanded recognition of Solidarity as an independent (non-communist) trade union. As had happened in the past, the government countered with repressive measures and outlawed Solidarity in 1981.

During the 1980s, the Polish government failed to govern effectively and to crush the Solidarity movement. As a last resort, Polish communist leaders called upon the Soviet Union for help. But, unlike previous Soviet leaders, Gorbachev refused to intervene. He advised the Polish communist government to solve its own problems, repudiating in effect the Brezhnev doctrine. There would be no repetition of the invasion of Hungary in 1956 or of Czechoslovakia in 1968. Polish leaders had no choice but to legalize Solidarity and hold free elections. To no one's surprise, Lech Walesa was elected president. His government successfully negotiated a peaceful end to communist rule in June 1989. Such an outcome would have been unthinkable a decade earlier.

Elsewhere in Eastern Europe, a similar pattern appeared as one communist government after another collapsed. In November 1989, East German authorities dismantled the Berlin Wall, preparing the way for German reunification a year later. The transition from one-party rule to democracy in Czechoslovakia was so smooth that it was called "the Velvet Revolution." Bulgaria, Hungary, and Albania also managed to transfer power from communist to non-communist parties relatively peacefully. The only exception was Rumania, where dictator Nicolae Ceausescu's refusal to leave office led to an armed revolt and his summary execution.

No one would have predicted that communist systems could have collapsed so suddenly with so little resistance. Europeans were euphoric, for it seemed that an era of peace and reconstruction had finally replaced communism and the last lingering tensions of the cold war.

Ethnic Tensions

As in the former Soviet Union, the sober reality of rebuilding society dissipated some of the optimism created by the fall of communism. One of the most intractable problems was that of ethnic tensions, which caused Czechoslovakia to break up into two independent states. Rumanians turned against their Hungarian minority. But undoubtedly the most tragic example of the impact of ethnic unrest is that of the former Yugoslavia.

The independent Kingdom of Yugoslavia came into being in 1921. It fell apart during World War II but emerged again in 1945 as an independent republic. The Yugoslav federation consisted of six republics: Serbia, Croatia, Bosnia, Montenegro, Slovenia, and Macedonia. The people were Slavic (Yugoslav means

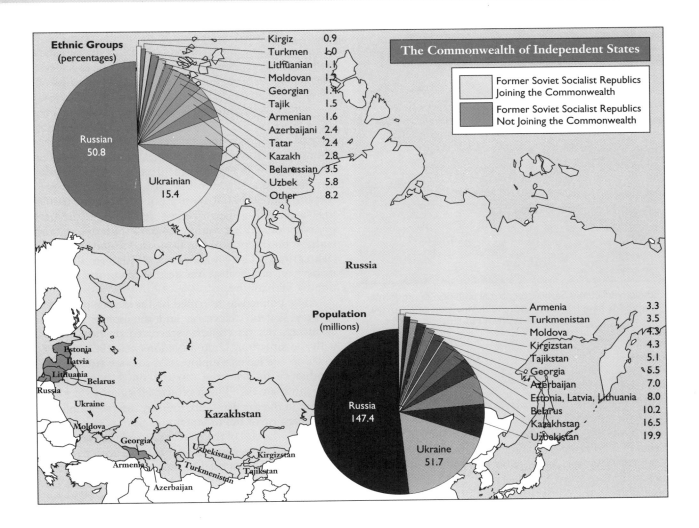

Ethnic Groups
(percentages)

Kirgiz	0.9
Turkmen	1.0
Lithuanian	1.1
Moldovan	1.2
Georgian	1.4
Tajik	1.5
Armenian	1.6
Azerbaijani	2.4
Tatar	2.4
Kazakh	2.8
Belarussian	3.5
Uzbek	5.8
Other	8.2

Russian 50.8

Ukrainian 15.4

The Commonwealth of Independent States

Former Soviet Socialist Republics Joining the Commonwealth

Former Soviet Socialist Republics Not Joining the Commonwealth

Russia

Population
(millions)

Armenia	3.3
Turkmenistan	3.5
Moldova	4.3
Kirgizstan	4.3
Tajikistan	5.1
Georgia	5.5
Azerbaijan	7.0
Estonia, Latvia, Lithuania	8.0
Belarus	10.2
Kazakhstan	16.5
Uzbekistan	19.9

Russia 147.4

Ukraine 51.7

Estonia
Latvia
Lithuania
Belarus
Russia
Ukraine
Moldova
Georgia
Armenia
Azerbaijan
Kazakhstan
Uzbekistan
Kirgizstan
Turkmenistan
Tajikstan

South Slav) of three religions: Orthodox, Catholic, and Muslim. Its undisputed leader was a staunch communist, Josip Broz, known as *Tito*.

A major problem facing Tito and his country was nationalist tension. Its roots lay deep in history but most serious was the post-war animosity between Serbs and Croats. During the war, Croatians, and some Muslims, had collaborated with the Nazis to exterminate an estimated 1 million Jews and Serbs. In trying to overcome the legacy of bitterness, Tito (a Croat) insisted that Yugoslavs put the past behind them. He preached a message of "brotherhood and unity" and

tried to balance the interests of major ethnic groups. He reduced Serbian influence in Belgrade and promoted Serbs to power in Croatia. Tito was a skilled politician and, in addition, he was personally popular because of his wartime leadership of the Partisans, who resisted the Nazis. He took Yugoslavia out of the Soviet orbit in 1948, an impressive move that appealed to Yugoslav national pride. He decentralized the economy to an extent unknown in Soviet-bloc satellites and established links with the West. Though authoritarian and cruel, Tito's regime was not as brutal as Stalin's. Yugoslavia's ambassador to the EEC stated that, under

Ethnic conflict and Serbian territorial ambition in the former Yugoslavia have led to widespread destruction and carnage, especially of Bosnian Muslims.

Tito's government, Yugoslavia enjoyed relative "prosperity, stability, and respectability."

Nevertheless, tension began to mount in the last years of Tito's rule. A feeling grew that Yugoslavia was dominated by the Serbs, who filled many of the key posts in the army, civil service, and police forces. Revisions to the constitution did not go far enough to forestall ethnic discontent. The Serbs, who were the majority, felt that their rights outside of their republic were not respected.

After Tito's death in 1980, the tensions repressed by his authoritarian regime exploded. Tito's successors lacked his political skill. Moreover, they failed to deal decisively with the country's economic problems. Tito's major failing was probably his unwillingness to transform the nation into a truly democratic society. Communism had served as a repressive glue that held enemies together. In the 1980s, communism lost its appeal. For want of a unifying ideal, local leaders fell back on strident nationalism, which served to divide Yugoslavia further. Slovenia declared its autonomy in 1991, followed by Croatia, then Bosnia, reducing Yugoslavia to Serbia, Montenegro, and Macedonia, which constituted 40 percent of its former territory.

Serbian president Slobodan Milosevic aimed to build a greater Serbia on the ruins of Tito's Yugoslavia. He incited the Serb minorities in Croatia and Bosnia to rebel and demand Serbian protection. Initially, most Serbs did not respond to his nationalist propaganda but an intense media campaign changed their minds. Croatia's Nazi past and murder of thousands of Serbs did not help the cause of reconciliation. The Bosnian declaration of independence prompted Serbian military intervention. Ostensibly Milosevic acted to protect Bosnian Serbs but a brutal policy of "ethnic cleansing" against Bosnian Muslims accompanied military intervention. What resulted was a brutal war with ruthless destruction of the Bosnian Muslims and their rich heritage. The Bosnian capital, Sarajevo, a jewel in its heritage and beauty, was destroyed beyond recognition by Serbian fire.

The public was horrified by the degree of brutality they saw on television and the policy of ethnic cleansing, but no consensus evolved on how to deal with the situation. United Nations peacekeepers tried to set up safe havens; diplomats made one attempt after another to mediate the dispute; the UN distributed humanitarian aid. These efforts all came to nothing. Unlike in the Persian Gulf, military intervention is difficult because of the mountainous terrain.

With the end of the cold war, people hoped that the world could enter a new era of peace and prosperity. Yet the tragedies in Yugoslavia, the continuing tensions in the Middle East, the ethnic and religious rivalries elsewhere remind us that the era of peace has not arrived.

Toward a New World Order

To complicate matters further, forces beyond the control of nations are in the process of transforming human society. These include the following four forces: the resource imperative, the ecological imperative, the market imperative, and the information imperative.

The Resource Imperative

The European dream of economic self-sufficiency proved to be impossible to realize. Products for European consumers were not always available nearby, or they had been exhausted. Depletion led to a search for new sources which in turn led to new trading

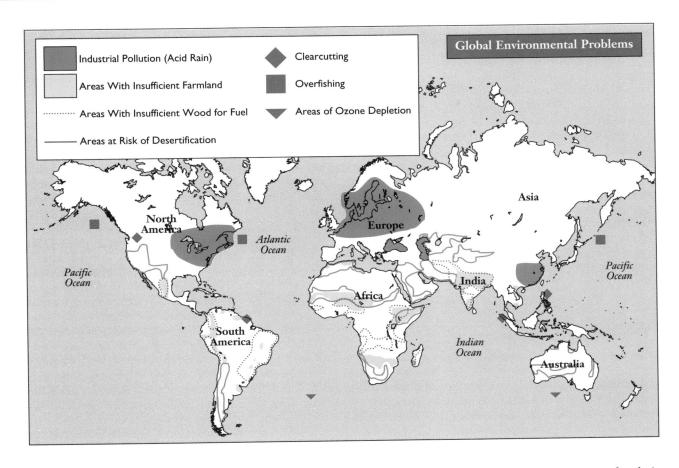

Global Environmental Problems

Industrial Pollution (Acid Rain)

Areas With Insufficient Farmland

Areas With Insufficient Wood for Fuel

Areas at Risk of Desertification

Clearcutting

Overfishing

Areas of Ozone Depletion

relationships between Europeans and other peoples. When the Europeans exterminated their own beaver populations, they found an alternative supply in the New World. The resulting fur trade brought together native hunters, European merchants, and consumers into a trading network.

In the sixteenth century, Europeans acquired a taste for sugar. To satisfy this demand, sugar plantations spread throughout the Caribbean. At the height of the plantation system, a three-cornered trading pattern linked Europe (source of trade goods) with Africa (source of slaves to work the plantations) and the Americas. By the mid-nineteenth century, Britain could not grow enough grain to feed its population and was obliged to import it from Russia and North America. In the 1960s, the Soviet Union, despite efforts to grow more grain during the Khrushchev years, had to buy wheat from North America.

Conflict can arise when nations compete for their share of a declining resource. European appetite for fish and the depletion of herring stocks in the Baltic by the sixteenth century prompted sailors from France, Spain, Portugal, and England to sail for the Grand Banks of Newfoundland, where they found abundant swarms of cod. For centuries, there was enough cod for everyone, but by the end of the twentieth century, intensive fishing techniques and a growing world appetite for fish had depleted the supply of many fish stocks, including the once plentiful cod. Competition for remaining fish stocks off the Newfoundland Grand Banks has led to confrontation between Canada and Spain. As coal reserves in Europe dwindled during the post-World War II period, Europeans imported oil from the Middle East to meet their growing needs. In 1973, OPEC imposed an oil embargo on oil exports from the Middle East; the scarcity caused the price to shoot upward, traumatizing the European economy and sending shock waves throughout the world.

The resources of the world's oceans may be worth trillions of dollars. Whom should they benefit? Industrialized nations who have the technology to exploit them? Should industrialized nations share resources with poorer countries? At the Law of the Sea Conference convened in 1974 to discuss ocean resources, the Maltese delegate, Dr. Arvido Pardo, suggested that the ocean beds be declared the "common heritage of humankind" and their riches diverted to a UN agency to help the poorer countries. He was opposed by developed nations determined to defend their national interests. When the *International Law of the Sea Treaty* came into effect in 1994 after 20 years of negotiations, it gave maritime countries (such as Canada) jurisdiction over the continental shelf along their borders. Dissension over resources divides nations just as needs and wants bring them together through trade.

The Ecological Imperative

Ecological issues are related to the question of resource utilization. The list of ecological concerns keeps mounting. With tourism, germs can hitch rides to all parts of the globe. Ballast dumped by ocean-going merchant vessels introduces species to new territories where they have no natural predators to keep their populations in check. The zebra mussel, which has invaded the Great Lakes from its native Europe, is one such instance. Proliferation of nuclear wastes, oil spills in ocean waters, deforestation, and industrial emissions are other examples of transnational environmental problems caused by human activity.

Global warming is probably the most alarming example of ecological interdependence. The primary contributor to warming is carbon dioxide (CO_2), followed by methane and chlorofluorocarbons (CFCs). Human activities from all parts of the globe contribute to atmospheric warming. Factory and automobile emissions and coal burning release CO_2 into the atmosphere. Deforestation and overgrazing by animals remove the plant cover that utilizes CO_2.

Reforestation programs, the use of alternative energy sources, energy-efficient technologies, and responsible forms of agriculture could minimize the effects of global warming. Energetic action to stop emissions requires global cooperation, which is politically difficult to accomplish. Citizens of rich countries are reluctant to make lifestyle changes. Very few would readily turn in their cars for ecologically friendly bicycles. Developing countries that want to enjoy a higher standard of living resent being told by wealthier nations that they must adopt costly environmental regulations. The *Rio Summit* in 1992 made these differences quite clear. Brazilian delegates insisted that the industrialized world had no right to demand that Brazil stop cutting the Amazonian rain forest, since *they* were contributing the lion's share of pollutants to the atmosphere with their excessive use of energy.

Environmental priorities vary widely from one part of the globe to another. For the industrialized world, control of population is a primary concern because of the strain huge numbers of people put on resources. In the Third World, however, large families are needed to ensure survival of the family unit. In the developed world, many people are worried about global warming and the resulting hole in the ozone layer. For poor peasant families in many areas of the world, however, the most pressing environmental problem is getting enough clean water, food, and firewood to survive.

In the former Soviet bloc, decades of rapid industrial growth ruined vast tracts of forest and polluted many rivers. Irrigation schemes diverted rivers flowing into the Aral Sea, which threatens to reduce it to a gigantic salt flat. The costs of reversing the damages are horrendous. As in developing countries, the need to clean up the environment takes second place to the need to extract resources in order to gain foreign exchange for survival.

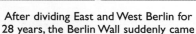

After dividing East and West Berlin for 28 years, the Berlin Wall suddenly came down in November 1989.

The Market Imperative

When Europeans disbanded their colonial empires in the post-war period, they retained economic links with the newly independent countries. Trade knits together consumers, producers, suppliers, and governments from diverse countries into a single economic system. Globalization blurs the distinction between a product made in one country as opposed to another. Consider the case of Chevrolet's Geo Metro. This car was designed in Japan and built in Canada using Canadian and Japanese parts at a Canadian factory managed by Japanese executives. Is the Geo Metro Canadian or Japanese?

The vehicle for economic globalization is the large international, or multinational, corporation. McDonald's, with its 3000 franchises throughout the world, is one very well-known example, as are Boeing, General Motors, Nissan, Northern Telecom, and others whose names appear on newspaper business pages. To operate successfully, multinationals require an open business environment. It is no coincidence that the integration of the world economy has marched in step with international accords promoting free trade. The best known is the General Agreement on Tariffs and Trade (GATT), now known as the World Trade Organization (WTO). Its aim is to eliminate tariff barriers and other trade restrictions between member nations. The North American Free Trade Agreement (NAFTA), the European Union (EU), and Asia-Pacific Economic Cooperation (APEC) are instances of regional agreements to reduce barriers to trade.

"Once they hear some of our music and they get a pair of Levis," notes an American business executive, "the next thing they want is a hamburger. And the next thing you know, they're eating our kind of food." And the appetite for televisions, VCRs, cars, and clothes leads to an appetite for American culture. Brand-name advertising and American television programs offer non-Western peoples an idealized view of the American lifestyle. On the surface at least, the outcome of global trade is a world culture far more homogeneous than anything envisioned by nineteenth-century imperialists. To oversimplify somewhat: "McDonald's in Moscow and Coke in China will do more to create a global culture than military colonization ever could."

Is globalization a good thing? Enthusiastic supporters claim that, in a global market, consumers have greater choice and lower prices. Since business requires stability, globalization can be a force for peace and international cooperation. But multinationals can exert a great deal of extraneous influence on the economies of all nations. If a government imposes a restrictive tax or limits the movement of money, a multinational can switch its operations to a more hospitable country. Though its head office is in a particular country, the responsibility of a multinational is ultimately to its shareholders—not to the nation that hosts its head office or branch plants. To a great extent, the multinational corporation is a new kind of superpower, not amenable to democratic control. Multinationals may make attempts to be good corporate citizens wherever they are based but, in the last analysis, a concern for social justice will usually take second place to the need to make a profit.

In developing countries, multinationals and the world economic system are often regarded as a sophisticated form of Western imperialism, or a kind of neo-colonialism. In order to obtain badly needed foreign exchange, developing nations grow crops in demand in the West even if doing so is at the expense of feeding their own people. In the Philippines, for example, half the bananas, sugar, and pineapples are exported, while many Filipino children are malnourished. In Africa, land that could be used to sustain local populations is used instead to produce goods such as tea, coffee, cacao, and palm oil for export.

Developing nations cannot escape the requirements of a worldwide financial network. During the 1970s, Western banks extended loans to several developing countries who had immense reserves of oil. The price of petroleum fell during the 1980s. A rise in the prices of manufactured goods and imported food aggravated the situation. Debtor countries could not repay their loans on schedule. They renegotiated loans through the International Monetary Fund (IMF), but the IMF demanded politically unpopular measures: austerity programs, balanced budgets, and free markets. Such structural reforms weigh most heavily on the poorer sectors of society. Global markets may give the consumer greater choice and cheaper prices but the benefits of greater choice are available only to a small proportion of the world's population. The gap between rich and poor continues to widen. In 1960, the average annual income in the poorest countries was estimated at one thirtieth of the income in the wealthiest; by 1990, it had widened to one sixtieth.

It is not surprising that, in the non-Western world, the response to globalization and progress has sometimes taken violent forms. A good example is the 1979 Iranian revolution. From his exile in Paris, Ayatollah Ruhollah Khomeini masterminded a well-organized campaign to overthrow the government of Shah Mohammad Reza Pahlavi, who was committed to Westernizing Iran. Khomeini wanted a society governed strictly by the rule of Islam. Upon his triumphant return to Iran after the Shah fled, Khomeini decreed that women take up the veil and adhere strictly to Islamic law. Khomeini's revolution achieved international media exposure when a group of militants held American embassy staff hostage for more than a year. Further notoriety resulted when, later on, he called for the death of Indian author Salman Rushdie for allegedly being disrespectful to the Prophet Mohammad, founder of Islam, in his book *Satanic Verses*. But Iran is not the only nation where Islamic fundamentalists have called for a rejection of Western ways. In Pakistan, Bangladesh, Malaysia, Islamic movements have replaced British civil and criminal codes with Islamic law, or *shari'a*.

The Information Imperative

During the cold war, the Iron Curtain separated Eastern Europe from the West. Little news of the outside world got through to Soviet citizens and the West knew little of Soviet life. But it is highly unlikely that an iron curtain could work today because

Thomas Homer-Dixon:
Modern Day Malthusian or Predictions of the Apocalypse?

 Overpopulation and the rapid depletion of the earth's natural resources are two concerns that have reached the forefront of the environmental, economic, and human-rights debate over the future of the world that we live in. Recently, these two global problems have also entered the discussion of international politics and the causes of war thanks to Canadian scholar Thomas Homer-Dixon.

Homer-Dixon, a native of Vancouver Island and political scientist at the University of Toronto, has extensively studied the causes of war and has developed a theory that is directly related to the concerns shared by environmentalists and human-rights groups. He explains that the foundation of his theories is the straightforward fact that "humans cannot survive unless we harvest the earth's resources and exploit our environment, and yet we will not survive for long unless we use our resources sparingly." This fact is coupled with the analysis that what seem to be positive economic growth rates in some developing countries, such as China, are really phenomena that are confined to the advanced urban areas of those countries. In the rural sectors, abject poverty, uncontrolled population growth, and water and land shortages have led to or will lead to worker uprisings, loss of government control, and general civil unrest. Furthermore, these conditions will soon reach such an accelerated state that the unrest will spread beyond national borders and threaten international security.

Much controversy has surrounded Homer-Dixon's work. Some have labelled him a modern-day Malthusian, after Thomas Malthus, the English economist who predicted the detrimental effect of overpopulation two centuries ago. Malthus, too, was a controversial figure who was assailed by the criticism of those who objected to his proposals to limit reproduction and his reasoning that natural disasters reduce population to more manageable levels. Writers such as Malthus and Homer-Dixon have been called both pessimistic and pragmatic but, either way, they present a frightening vision of the future.

Homer-Dixon's vision of the possible causes of future international tension has become of great interest to the government of the United States. He has been invited on more than one occasion to speak with Vice-President Al Gore, with the director of the CIA, and with the head of the U.S. Agency for International Development.

Whatever the future holds in the way of government policy, it is difficult to deny that the earth's rapidly growing population, coupled with the excessive use of various non-renewable resources, forecasts a grim future unless new solutions are found soon.

the contemporary world has witnessed an explosion of communications technologies: television, tape recorders, videos, fax machines, and personal computers. All of these contribute to a worldwide exchange of information beyond the control of governments.

A French satellite photographed the 1986 Chernobyl nuclear disaster and broadcast the photos to all parts of the world. Despite their government's attempts to limit access to satellite signals, Soviet citizens improvised ingenious ways to bypass these restrictions, such as fashioning satellite dishes from the seats of children's sleds. Television captured the Tiananmen Square Massacre in China. The images of demonstrators and tanks were seen all over the world, including China. Information flooded into China in the form of fax messages and electronic mail. In Europe, during the Year of Revolution (1989–1990), television coverage of the destruction of the Berlin Wall built up an unstoppable momentum for change. By showing images of a successful black professional family, the American situation comedy *The Bill Cosby Show* helped discredit the policies of apartheid in South Africa.

Other communications technologies add to the impact of television. After the Polish government banned the anticommunist Solidarity movement in 1981, members organized an underground information network. They circulated audiocassettes and videos with antigovernment songs, interviews with Solidarity leaders, political lectures, and other materials. By these means, Solidarity built an underground network of people determined to change the system. In South Africa, the imprisoned African National Congress leader Nelson Mandela used the fax machine to negotiate the terms of his release and to communicate with his supporters.

These examples offer evidence for the claim that the media can serve as a catalyst for democratic change: authoritarian governments cannot hide their human-rights violations and economic failures. Yet a word of caution is in order: the message is not always one which most people in the West would admire. In the immediate post-war years, audiocassettes spread the gospel of communism to nations that resented Western colonialism. The Iranian revolution was masterminded very effectively from Paris by Ayatollah Khomeini. His propaganda, centred on the demand "The Pahlavi dynasty must go," was recorded on cassettes and smuggled into Iran. Religious leaders broadcast his words to worshippers in mosques; instructions to students on organizing marches, demonstrations, and protests were transmitted the same way.

The impact of media, of course, goes beyond politics. Computer systems incredibly more powerful than those developed in the Second World War make it possible to transfer vast amounts of information across the world. In the world of finance, such information technology enables investors, bond dealers, and speculators to exchange vast sums of money electronically. The computer has begun to change the workplace because it makes it possible to work at home. The Internet links many millions of people in a sprawling computer information network. Users can exchange information on almost any topic: how to plan a vacation, obtain information about investments, find a companion, discuss ideas. The potential exists to link all people on earth electronically. More than any other medium of communication, the computer makes possible the global village. Or does it? Paradoxically, such technologies may lead to greater social atomization and a diminished sense of community. Until more time has passed, it is not possible to draw any conclusions about the long-term impact of the communications systems on humanity.

A striking example of the effect of television on international affairs was the CNN (Cable News Network) coverage of the 1991 Gulf War. "The Gulf War," claims one media expert, "established CNN as an entirely new kind of global information system—an intelligence system that serves not only 70 million households but also world leaders." Knowing that American chiefs of staff watched CNN, Iraqi officials often delayed press conferences until CNN reporters arrived. American officials did much the same.

A world audience from 103 countries watched the Gulf War. As the U.S. bombed military targets near Baghdad, a dazzling show of fireworks lit up the Baghdad sky. This was followed by pictures of Scud missiles exploding; computer-generated images of "smart" bombs targeting Iraqi cities. Periodic commentary by CNN reporter Peter Arnett, against the backdrop of Baghdad, allowed viewers to keep track of events.

Networks increasingly rely on "parachute journalism" (sending a video team to an ongoing-news spot) because it is cheaper than maintaining a foreign news bureau. It also means that reporters no longer need to establish their own local contacts and must rely on official sources for information. None of the CNN reporters covering the Gulf War could speak Arabic or knew much about military affairs. Their ignorance of such matters left them ill-equipped to question the UN and U.S. military, who had learned how to present the military viewpoint using the latest TV technology in a very sophisticated way. Thus, instead of contributing to greater understanding, TV reporting can cause misunderstanding.

Reflections

In 1918, an unknown German high-school teacher, Oswald Spengler, published *The Decline of the West*. Spengler believed that, like living organisms, civilizations go through a cycle of birth, growth, and decline. European civilization, which began to take shape in the Middle Ages, had reached the final stage of its development: it lacked vitality and its creativity was gone. Spengler's book became a spectacular best seller in the 1920s and was translated into many languages. Its gloomy tone coincided with the pessimism that pervaded Europe after the Great War.

Had Spengler lived to see the carnage of World War II, he might have been too appalled to write. The destruction inflicted on the European Continent, in both human and material terms, exceeded that of World War I. The emergence of two superpowers, the United States and the Soviet Union, diminished Europe's international influence to a point lower than that of 1918. The process of decolonization further undercut European **hegemony**. Although European nations recovered some degree of their former power in the post-World War II period, the forces working toward the creation of a global village make impossible the kind of world domination Europe enjoyed at the turn of the century. Other regions (China, Japan, the Americas) have emerged as powerful competitors for global dominance.

Does this mean that European/Western civilization is doomed? And has it been possible, as Franz Fanon hoped, to take a step beyond Europe? As we struggle to formulate an answer to these questions, we should keep in mind two generalizations: cultural change is ongoing, and cultures do not evolve in isolation. The Europe of the 1990s is far different from the Europe of 500 years ago, when explorers and adventurers from this continent began the process of world conquest and domination. What we know as European civilization is an amalgam of cultures. The values, ideas, and structures that have characterized European civilization will almost certainly persist, though in forms that will depend on future generations. Whatever shape world civilization may take, elements of Western culture will be found within it.

Key Concepts, Figures, and Events

Global Village
Balfour Declaration
Treaty of Maastricht
International Law of the Sea Treaty

Mohandas Gandhi
Palestine Liberation Organization
Solidarity
Rio Summit

Muslim Brotherhood
British Commonwealth of Nations
Tito

Topics for Further Thought

1. In *The Wretched of the Earth*, Frantz Fanon claims that "the European game has finally ended...." Do you agree with his assessment of the current direction the world is taking? Does he offer sound advice to people of developing nations? Explain your answer.

2. Why did the process of decolonization differ depending on the size of the European population in the colony? Can this be explained by the nature of the political institutions or does it reflect inherent racism?

3. The end of the colonial era, while it may have brought independence to many countries, has often not brought prosperity or stability. Why have many former European colonies experienced difficulties? Are these difficulties a lasting legacy of European imperialism?

4. In recent years, peace talks in the Middle East have edged cautiously forward as we continue to look for solutions. Given the ethnic and religious make-up of the regions and the history of conflict in the twentieth century, do you believe peace is a realistic possibility in the Middle East? Explain your answer.

5. "McDonald's in Moscow and Coke in China will do more to create a global culture than military colonization ever could." Explain why you agree or disagree with this quote by making reference to each of the four imperatives (market, resource, ecological, and information) as explained in this chapter.

6. When trying to understand the collapse of communism in Eastern Europe, in particular in the Soviet Union, can we find answers in the first three decades following 1945? Did Gorbachev's ill-fated reforms bring about the demise of communism or simply speed up a process that was already under way? Explain your answer with support.

Topics for Further Research

1. Many countries have only recently (during the past half century) won their independence from colonial empires. Research a country from one of the following areas of the world. Try to find out when the country gained independence, the present state of its economy, its current political system, and any major changes that have occurred since independence:

Caribbean   Asia
Middle East   Africa

2. In several areas of the world, independence has been accompanied by violence. Research the eruption of violence and attempt to provide an explanation for it for one of the following:

Angola   Uganda (under Idi Amin, 1970s)
Nigeria   Rwanda (1993–)
Pakistan (1971)   Sikhs in the Punjab
Sri Lanka

3. Tensions in the Middle East have led to many conflicts in the twentieth century. Research one of these conflicts and attempt to explain its origins, the main events, and the lasting significance of the event:

Suez Crisis   Six-Day War
War of Yom Kippur   Gulf War

4. The United Nations has not limited its role to maintaining peace but has also sought to assist in improving lives of people around the world. Research one of the following UN organizations and explain its objectives, methods, and degree of success:

World Health Organization (WHO)
United Nations Relief and Rehabilitation Agency (UNRRA)
United Nations International Children's Emergency Fund (UNICEF)
Food and Agriculture Organization (FAO)
United Nations Educational, Scientific and Cultural Organization (UNESCO)
United Nations Environment Programme (UNEP)

5. Over the past decade, the world has moved toward freer trade, with several large trading blocs being formed and restrictive tariffs being lowered globally. Research one of the following trade agreements or organizations and explain the nature of the agreement or organization as well as the results to date (or projected) for the countries involved:

World Trade Organization (formerly GATT)
North American Free Trade Agreement (NAFTA)
European Union (EU)
Asia-Pacific Economic Cooperation (APEC)

Responding to Ideas

1. Ever since the Scientific Revolution, Western society has viewed history as progressive and maintained the belief that the world can be immeasurably improved through the acquisition of knowledge and the application of science. This is often referred to as the "modernization theory." Cyril Black, in *The Dynamics of Modernization* (1966) defended this theory in light of the technical advancements made since 1945. He wrote: "We are experiencing one of the great revolutionary transformations of mankind. Throughout the world, in widely differing societies, man is seeking to apply the finding of a rapidly developing science and technology to the age-old problems of life. The resulting patterns of change offer unprecedented prospects for the betterment of the human condition." How do you think non-Western readers would respond to Black's assessment? Do you share his optimism about the future based on the potential of modernization?

2. Too often, the study of intellectual thought in our schools focuses on Western philosophy and excludes the philosophy of other cultures, despite the important contributions non-Western philosophers have made to the development of Western thought. One explanation for the exclusion of non-Western philosophy suggests that European imperialism was intellectually justified on the grounds that those brought under the rule of European powers were inferior. Hence, to pay tribute to Latin American, African, or Asian writers would be to acknowledge them as intelligent and rational peoples, rather than as inferiors. Given what you have learned about European imperialism and colonialism from 1500 to the twentieth century, do you think this is a valid conclusion? Explain your answer.

19

Contemporary Western Society

The second half of the twentieth century has seen tremendous change in Western societies. Spurred by unprecedented economic growth and a baby boom in the two decades following the end of World War II, European and North American societies embarked on a spending spree that gave rise to widespread consumerism. Many businesses targeted their new products at the emerging youth market, the baby boomers, in the 1960s. The birth of rock-and-roll owes much to the fact that teenagers, who comprised a large segment of the population in the 1960s, had more freedom and more money to spend than ever before. Catering to the tastes of the baby boomers continues to be an important factor in our consumer-driven economy: in the late 1980s, Toronto radio station CHUM dropped its top-40 format in favour of "oldies." The number of products related to preserving a youthful look, health fads, retirement and nursing homes—even the sale of tombstones—can expect a significant rise in the years to come as the demographic shift continues in North America and Europe.

The shift in women's role is another factor that has drastically altered the face of the twentieth century. As more and more women enter the workplace and occupy positions within the upper echelons of the business world, the marketplace is evolving to meet their needs. As well, the family unit is expanding to include two-income families, single-parent families, and step-families. Rapid technological progress has also caused changes in family life. The number of technological innovations that have invaded our homes since 1945 is staggering: televisions, VCRs, microwave ovens, home

As late as the 1950s, women in Italy gathered at public fountains to wash clothes.

computers, fax machines, etc. Try to imagine your home 50 years ago without these devices; how would your life have been different in 1946 than in 1996?

The changes witnessed by North Americans and West Europeans pale in comparison to the revolutionary changes that have swept through Eastern Europe. At the end of World War II, most of Eastern Europe was under the repressive grip of communism. Consumer goods and freedom were rare commodities. Suddenly, without anyone having suspected it—let alone predicted it—communism was dismantled in Eastern Europe. What have been the social implications for Eastern Europe and for the rest of the world?

Life in Post-War Europe

Historians will undoubtedly describe the second half of the twentieth century as a period of rapid social change in the Western world, during which unprecedented wealth created an age of materialism. While this image is appropriate for North America from the 1950s onward, it is a valid perception of much of Europe only after the 1960s. Rebuilding war-torn Europe was an arduous process and many people continued to live in refugee camps for up to a decade after the war ended. The advances in home comfort enjoyed by a majority

of North Americans during the first half of the twentieth century were not available to most Europeans until the 1960s and 1970s.

A Revolution in Living Space

A census carried out in France in 1954 gives a clear picture of the primitive state of housing throughout France at the time. Of 13.4 million homes, only 58.4 percent had running water; 26.6 percent had indoor toilets; and 10.4 percent had a bathtub or shower. People continued to rely on public fountains and hydrants for water. The startling results of the French 1954 census prompted the government to encourage new home construction by offering subsidies. Under new government regulations, apartments were required to contain a kitchen, a living room, a master bedroom, at least one bedroom for every two children, a bathroom including bathtub and toilet, and central heating. Within 20 years of the census, modern comforts had become available to the vast majority of French citizens. By 1973, 97 percent of all homes had running water, 70 percent had indoor toilets, 65 percent had a bath or shower, and 49 percent had central heating. The state of housing in France since 1954 gives us an indication of European living conditions in the decades following World War II.

Privacy and Intimacy

Improved housing conditions brought about significant changes in the lives of Europeans. Intimacy was a luxury enjoyed by the middle and upper classes. In the crowded conditions of the lower classes, many people had to dress and wash in front of others who, when decency required, would avert their eyes. When people bathed, which occurred rarely, they did so with the help of a family member in the common room, or outside, and they seldom were able to wash the whole body at once. Even sleeping offered no privacy as most people slept several to a room and even several to a bed.

A clear illustration of how differently the middle and working class regarded privacy is the social attitude toward the wedding night. For the middle class, the wedding night and honeymoon were closely guarded secrets to protect the privacy of the newlyweds. By contrast, the custom among peasants and workers in much of France until recently has been for the wedding party to visit the bride and groom in their bed in the middle of the night and to present them with a mixture known as *la rôtie*, containing white wine, eggs, chocolate, and biscuits delivered in a chamber pot. It is obvious that, until the very recent past, family life in Europe afforded little individual privacy. In the past few decades, individual privacy is no longer a luxury but a right due the majority of Europeans.

The Evolution of the Family

Since World War II ended, the family has undergone such significant changes as to render it almost unrecognizable to someone from the 1950s. American television in the 1950s portrayed the typical if somewhat idealized family in programs such as *Leave It To Beaver*, which can be viewed as a sociological study of the time. Ward Cleaver represented the hard-working professional, bread-winner father; his wife, June, was the ever-pleasant homemaker; Wally and Beaver were the children, growing up with high expectations for their future careers.

By the 1980s, families such as the Cleavers would represent a mere 15 percent of North American homes. Almost half of the children born in the 1980s would spend some of their early years in a single-parent environment; the number of couples choosing to live together rather than marry quadrupled; and the proportion of women postponing sexual intercourse until marriage dropped from 50 percent to 20 percent. Changing employment patterns also did much to alter the family. By 1988, the percentage of married women working outside the home had risen to 60 percent (45 percent of the women who had pre-school children).

Today, we have developed a much broader concept of family, and children are less often burdened with the stigma of being "bastards" or coming from a "broken home." Some moralists see these changes as a loss of universal family values and blame the ills of society on the changes to the "traditional family." Ironically, this is a common refrain heard throughout history as the family has evolved. The fact that our concept of family has had to undergo change to keep pace with the realities of our society should not surprise those who understand the past. Change, as in all areas of life, allows for revitalization and growth. Hence, what we perceive as common behaviour and acceptable family arrangements will continue to change as societies undergo change.

After World War II most women still remained at home full-time caring for the children.

Advances in Science and Technology

The Marriage of Science and Technology

Among the profound and lasting effects that World War II had on the world is the marriage between science and technology. Prior to the war, pure (theoretical) science and applied science (technology) largely operated independently of each other. Scientists generally worked in university laboratories, doing research aimed at discovering the laws of nature. Improving machines and developing new inventions remained the domain of tinkering technicians and engineers who were most often employed by large corporations. The war years brought together scientific research and technical expertise in an attempt to provide solutions to military problems. Major scientific breakthroughs, like radar and the atomic bomb, were achieved during the war. In the post-war years, the close cooperation between science and technology continued to lead to the explosion in new technology that has revolutionized the world in which we live.

Some of these advances have come at an enormous financial cost. In fact, the cost of so-called "big science"

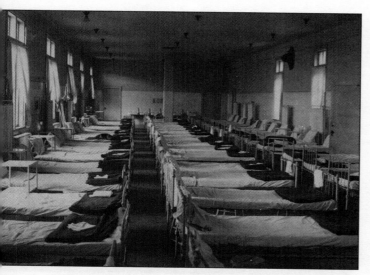

Hospitals in the 1950s offered little privacy to their patients.

in the post-war years can only be met by large corporations and governments. Consequently, there has been an increasing link between science and taxpayers. By 1965, 75 percent of the money spent in the United States on scientific research came from the government. An example of the marriage between pure science, technology, and large sums of government capital, all aimed at producing practical results, is the U.S. space program. In 1961, the Soviet Union sent the world's first cosmonauts into space. Not to be outdone, the U.S. immediately committed huge sums of money to its own space program. By 1969, the U.S. succeeded at landing a spacecraft on the moon. Neil Armstrong, after taking his first few steps on the moon, declared he had taken "one small step for a man, one giant leap for mankind."

The Age of Consumerism

A result of the rapid scientific and technological advances made in the past half-century has been a proliferation of consumer products. These new products have come about not only because of the practical application of science, but also because of high consumer demand. Wartime savings and higher post-war wages created a demand for consumer products that continues unabated to this day. In fact, the affluence

enjoyed by many North Americans and Europeans has steadily increased until the 1990s. Many now feel the bubble may have burst and that the youth of today cannot expect to live a life as comfortable as that of their parents.

The affluence and technological innovations of the latter part of the twentieth century have combined to create a consumer society in which the three basic questions of economics—what to produce, how much to produce, and how to distribute production—are largely determined by the desires of society. Some see *consumerism* as a healthy expression of the democratization of Western culture; others condemn it for its materialistic focus and the resulting loss of spiritual and moral values.

The high level of disposable income now enjoyed by many North Americans and Europeans has created a market for luxury items such as virtual reality and designer fashions. It has also led to an explosion in the service industry as, more than ever, people are eating at restaurants, travelling to foreign destinations, keeping fit at health clubs, and seeking entertainment at theme parks such as Disney World, Paramount Canada's Wonderland, or Euro Disney.

The Computer Revolution

Perhaps the most fundamental change to affect Western industry and society in the past half-century has been the advent of computers. In every aspect of life—from the workplace to the shopping place, from the home to the battlefield—computers are revolutionizing our world. Maurice Estabrooks, a senior economist with the federal government of Canada, wrote: "Events such as these will be seen as a metamorphosis on the grandest of scales that gave rise to a new social and economic order in which intelligent machines emerged to mediate all the essential activities of the new society." In industry, computers are being used from the design and simulation stage right through to the manufacturing. New car plants, such as the Honda plant in Alliston, Ontario, are highly automated and use robotics to ensure consistent quality and levels of production. Computers have also allowed for major advances in telecommunications. As a result of sophisticated processing and intelligence capabilities, we now have the ability to voice-store and forward-call. Computers are improving the quality, comfort, and efficiency of our hospitals as they assist in everything from diagnosing, managing hospital admissions, tracking

Jurassic Park:

Science Misused?

In his blockbuster novel *Jurassic Park*, American author Michael Crichton uses the manipulation of biotechnology and genetic engineering as the basis for a "techno-dino" thriller. In his story, scientists using the latest scientific research are able to extract DNA from a dinosaur egg. Using the DNA and supercomputers for gene sequencing, Jurassic Park scientists hatch dinosaurs and fill with them a park that will attract millions of thrill-seeking tourists. Only something goes terribly wrong.... One could argue that the problem begins with the misuse of science, an issue of very real importance in our world today. Genetic engineering is a rapidly growing field, where advances in science just may be running ahead of our moral and ethical development. Have we, as a society, thought enough about the implications of the scientific breakthroughs that are being made? Are we abusing science for our own greed and in the end creating potential for disaster? In the following excerpt from *Jurassic Park*, Malcolm, a mathematician who specializes in chaos theory, attacks the misuse of science as he outlines why he believes Jurassic Park should not have been built:

"You know what we are really talking about here," Malcolm said. "All this attempt to control....We are talking about Western attitudes that are five hundred years old. They began at the time when Florence, Italy, was the most important city in the world. The basic idea of science—that there was a new way to look at reality, that it was objective, that it did not depend on your beliefs or your nationality, that it was rational—that idea was fresh and exciting back then. It offered promise and hope for the future, and it swept away the old medieval system, which was hundreds of years old. The medieval world of feudal politics and religious dogma and hateful superstitions fell before science. But, in truth, this was because the medieval world didn't really work any more. It didn't work economically, it didn't work intellectually, and it didn't fit the new world that was emerging."

Malcolm coughed.

"But now," he continued, "science is the belief system that is hundreds of years old. And, like the medieval system before it, science is starting not to fit the world any more. Science has attained so much power that its practical limits begin to be apparent. Largely through science, billions of us live in one small world, densely packed and intercommunicating. But science cannot help us decide what to do with that world or how to live. Science can make a nuclear reactor, but it cannot tell us not to build it. And our world starts to seem polluted in fundamental ways—air, and water, and land—because of ungovernable science." He sighed. "This much is obvious to everyone."

There was a silence. Malcolm lay with his eyes closed, his breathing laboured. No one spoke, and it seemed to Ellie that Malcolm had finally fallen asleep. Then he sat up again, abruptly.

"At the same time, the great intellectual justification of science has vanished. Ever since Newton and Descartes, science has explicitly offered us the vision of total control. Science has claimed the power to eventually control everything, through its understanding of natural laws. But in the twentieth century, that claim has been shattered beyond repair. First, Heisenberg's uncertainty principle set limits on what we could know about the subatomic world. Oh well, we say, none of us lives in a subatomic world. It doesn't make any practical difference as we go through our lives. Then Gödel's theorem set similar limits to mathematics, the formal language of science. Mathematicians used to think that their language had some special inherent trueness that derived from the laws of logic. Now we know that what we call 'reason' is just an arbitrary game. It's not special, in the way we thought it was.

"And now chaos theory proves that unpredictability is built into our daily lives. It is as mundane as the rainstorm we cannot predict. And so the grand vision of science, hundreds of years old—the dream of total control—has died, in our century. And with it much of the justification, the rationale for science to do what it does. And for us to listen to it. Science has always said that it may not know everything now but it will know, eventually. But now we see that isn't true. It is an idle boast. As foolish, and as misguided, as the child who jumps off a building because he believes he can fly."

"This is very extreme," Hammond said, shaking his head.

"We are witnessing the end of the scientific era. Science, like other outmoded systems, is destroying itself. As it gains in power, it proves itself incapable of handling the power. Because things are going very fast now. Fifty years ago, everyone was gaga over the atomic bomb. That was power. No one could imagine anything more. Yet, a bare decade after the bomb, we began to have genetic power. And genetic power is far more potent than atomic power. And it will be in everyone's hands. It will be in kits for backyard gardeners. Experiments for schoolchildren. Cheap labs for terrorists and dictators. And that will force everyone to ask the same question: What should I do with my power?—which is the very question science says it cannot answer."

drug use, and food distribution to forming part of new life-monitoring and life-support systems such as CAT (computer axial tomography) scanners and PET (positron emission tomography) scanners.

Scientific research has also greatly benefited from the computer revolution as computers allow scientists to probe the innermost depths of matter, to examine, simulate, and manipulate. The effect computers will have on our society is only beginning to be understood. As we edge toward the twenty-first century, we are rapidly leaving behind the society of past generations to enter a bold new world with computer technology at its core.

Facing Our Moral Dilemmas

The research carried out in the past few decades has led to amazing breakthroughs in many areas. The atomic bomb, developed during the war, ushered in the atomic age of nuclear reactors and of nuclear bombs capable of annihilating the world. The development of chemical fertilizers has allowed record crop yields but has also led to the poisoning of rivers. Breakthroughs in genetic engineering have helped us to cure diseases but have also given us the potential to create dangerous new life forms. The virtual elimination of malaria-carrying mosquitoes by the use of the organic insecticide DDT (dichlorodiphenyltrichloroethane) greatly lowered death rates in tropical areas, but also poisoned waters and extinguished bird species. Francis Bacon could have been referring to the second half of the twentieth century when he wrote in 1620: "Knowledge and human power are synonymous."

The combined forces of science and technology have given humanity incredible control over the physical environment. This control has come with a price tag: population explosion, environmental degradation, and deadly weaponry are but a few examples. The application of science to our world without consideration given to the implications for the delicate balance which exists can have deadly results. Perhaps one of the greatest threats facing the world in the twenty-first century is that science is rapidly outstripping the social sciences; in other words, we are learning how to manipulate our physical environment before we develop the ethics to protect society from potential abuses of the new developments.

Contemporary Feminism

During the late nineteenth and early twentieth centuries, the first wave of feminism focused its energies on achieving legal and political equality for women. Central to this struggle was obtaining the right to vote and to be recognized as equal citizens under the law. Women in North America and many European countries fought for the right to participate in the political process and had begun to earn the legal recognition which would allow them equal rights with men. The Great Depression of the 1930s slowed the wave of feminism as people turned their attention to surviving a major economic calamity. Then came World War II and its aftermath, during which women and men made great sacrifices to defend liberty and justice against tyranny and oppression. By the 1960s, the second wave of feminism was well under way. Having achieved political and legal equality, feminists now focused their energies on achieving social and economic equality.

American feminist **Betty Friedan**, author of *The Feminine Mystique* (1963), is often credited with providing the impetus for the second wave of feminism. In

During the past few decades, increasing numbers of family women are pursuing professional careers.

her influential book she argued that women led unhappy and unfulfilled lives because they were trapped by the societal belief that the only desirable role for women to play in society was that of wife, mother, and housekeeper. Friedan's voice was joined by several other prominent feminists such as Germaine Greer and Gloria Steinem, all of whom claimed that the existing society was based on domination and oppression of women by men.

A radical feminist organization known as The Redstockings succinctly stated the primary objectives of the second wave of feminism in their 1969 manifesto, which stated: "We cannot rely on existing ideologies, as they are all products of male-supremacist culture. We question every generalization and accept none that are not confirmed by our experience. Our chief task at present is to develop female class consciousness through sharing experiences and publicly exposing the sexist foundation of all our institutions." But, despite the efforts of feminist groups and a wide variety of victories in many fields, women continue to be underrepresented in politics in all Western nations. Sweden has the highest percentage of women in parliament (41 percent), while other countries continue to lag far behind. For example in Germany, Canada, the United States, and France the proportion of women in parliament is 26 percent, 18 percent, 9.9 percent and 5.7 percent, respectively.

Today, the feminist movement has become quite fragmented. While some feel that the struggle for equality is far from over, others believe that the militant feminism of the 1960s and 1970s has lost both its appeal and its usefulness. Public attitudes toward women's role in society have changed significantly in the past few decades. Old notions of women's work versus men's work are fast becoming relics of the past. Between 1986 and 1991, the number of female lawyers in Canada jumped by 71 percent and that of female economists by 65 percent. Women have also made significant inroads into several other areas, including architecture, engineering, and sports. Steadily, the wage gap between men and women is narrowing and, increasingly, women are occupying powerful positions within government and business organizations. Betty Friedan believes that it is time for women to move beyond the first stage of achieving full participation, power, and a voice in the main institutions of society and on to the second stage:

> The second stage cannot be seen in terms of women alone, our separate personhood, or equality with men. The second stage may not even be a women's movement. Men may be at the cutting edge of the second stage.... If we can eliminate the false polarities and appreciate the limits and true potential of women's power, we

Naomi Wolf's works, such as *The Beauty Myth,* have established her as one of the most prominent feminists of the 1990s.

will be able to join with men—follow or lead—in the new human politics that must emerge beyond reaction. And this new human liberation will enable us to take back the day and night, and use the precious, limited resources of our earth and the limitless resources of our human capital to erect new kinds of homes for all our dreams...

Naomi Wolf, American feminist and author of *The Beauty Myth* and *Fire with Fire*, represents a new breed of feminists who share Friedan's belief that it is time for the women's movement to move forward from the ideological to the pragmatic stage. Wolf asserts that women are far more powerful than they realize and have the potential to bring about significant change. "To do so, however, women must stop seeing themselves as the passive victims of history and understand that they can determine not only their own fate but that of the rest of the world." This is not to suggest that women's struggle for equality is over but that women now have, in the democracies of the Western world, the political clout to effect real change. Consequently, women must become proactive in implementing the changes desired rather than blaming the ills of society on male oppression.

In *The Beauty Myth*, Wolf explores why modern women, who have gained legal and reproductive rights, pursued higher education, made significant inroads into professions, and overturned beliefs about their limited social roles, still do not feel free. It is Wolf's belief that what she terms the "beauty myth" continues to hamper women's pursuit of full and equal participation in society. "We are in the midst of a violent backlash against feminism that uses images of female beauty as a political weapon against women's advancement." Wolf supports her argument by noting that, during the past decade, when women have made significant advancements in society's power structure, eating disorders have skyrocketed, cosmetic surgery has become the fastest-growing medical specialty, and pornography has burgeoned into a billion-dollar industry. Wolf summarizes the apparent paradox of contemporary women in the following paragraph:

> More women have more money and power and scope and legal recognition than we have ever had before; but in terms of how we feel about ourselves physically, we may actually be worse off than our unliberated grandmothers. Recent research consistently shows that inside the majority of the West's controlled, attractive, successful working women, there is a secret "underlife" poisoning our freedom; infused with notions of beauty, it is a dark vein of self-hatred, physical obsessions, terror of aging, and dread of lost control.

Often referred to as "outrageous and compelling," a third American feminist, **Camille Paglia**, offers a radical new form of feminism based on libertarian principles that oppose the intrusion of the state into private affairs. Paglia unabashedly proclaims that she is fervently in favour of abortion, sodomy, prostitution, pornography, drug use, and suicide. Regarding the rape issue, she opposes university-campus grievance committees. According to Paglia, women who are raped on a date read the rapist's messages wrong and are therefore equally at fault. She argues: "We should teach general ethics to both men and women, but sexual relationships themselves must not be policed. Sex, like the city streets, would be risk-free only in a totalitarian regime." Among her more controversial statements are "Had civilization been left in the hands of women we would still be living in grass huts" and "Madonna is the ultimate feminist." She responds to critics who claim Madonna degrades womanhood by arguing that contemporary feminism is bankrupt because it is based on the false premise of male oppression and females as sex-object victims. Paglia argues:

> Woman is the dominant sex. Women's sexual glamour has bewitched and destroyed men since Delilah and Helen of Troy. Madonna, role model to millions of girls world-wide, has cured the ills of feminism by reasserting woman's command of the sexual realm.... Madonna has made a major contribution to the history of women.

Paglia has her following but she has undoubtedly earned the scorn of many women's groups. She has boldly and brazenly offered a new kind of feminism which emphasizes personal responsibility and which is,

in her own words: "bawdy, streetwise, and on-the-spot confrontational." The divergent views of contemporary feminists Friedan, Wolf, and Paglia are indications that the feminist movement lacks the cohesiveness of earlier days.

Life in Eastern Europe Before and After the Collapse of Communism

The 1930s and 1940s were difficult years for the former Soviet Union. Stalinist purges, famine, and war took the lives of nearly 40 million people. For the survivors, they were lean and hard times during which the entire country was in a state of quasi-military mobilization, a state in which all resources—both natural and human—were focused on building up Soviet industry and creating a strong army. Even agriculture, under forced collectivization, was industrialized and the produce sold for hard currency badly needed in Stalin's plan to rapidly industrialize the Soviet Union. Despite the Non-Aggression Pact of 1939 between the Soviet Union and Nazi Germany, war arrived on Soviet soil in 1940, leaving a deep scar on the people and the state. In the post-war years, Soviet citizens continued to experience severe shortages. Having emerged a superpower, the leadership was determined to consolidate military supremacy and create a buffer zone of satellite states that would help to ensure that future wars would not be fought on Russian soil.

The post-war generation has been referred to as "the generation of hungry children," for whom hard work, poor housing, food shortages, and few available consumer products were the norm. While North Americans and Europeans rebuilt their economies and revelled in an unprecedented economic boom, much of Eastern Europe stumbled along, enjoying living conditions little better than in the previous half-century.

The Two Worlds of Communist Societies

By the 1970s, a very clear division between those who enjoyed the good life and those who continued to eke out an existence had developed in the Soviet Union. This division was based on their position in—and loyalty to—the Communist Party. The average

Slovenia:
Facing the Challenges of Tomorrow

The past decade has brought significant change in many parts of the world. This is especially true in Eastern Europe, where the collapse of communism led to the splintering of the former Soviet Union and to the creation of numerous new republics. The former state of Yugoslavia also fell prey to the end of communism in Europe. Created in the aftermath of World War I, Yugoslavia was a state comprised of several ethnic groups: Slovenians, Croatians, Bosnians, Serbians and Macedonians. Such diversity made Yugoslavia a difficult country to govern although, for nearly four decades, the communist leader Marshal Tito managed to unite Yugoslavs. Few were surprised at the quick disintegration of Yugoslavia following Tito's death. Without his strong hand to unite the diverse ethnic groups, war soon broke out as various regions struggled to establish their independence.

The Republic of Slovenia emerged from the chaos created by the collapse of the former Yugoslavia. Nestled between Croatia, Austria, and Northern Italy, Slovenia is a tiny republic of 20 000 km² with a population of 2 million. Following a plebiscite in which the citizens voted overwhelmingly in favour of creating an independent and sovereign state, Slovenia proclaimed its independence on June 26, 1991. Finally, after over 1000 years, Slovenians were once again an independent people. Prior to this they had been governed by Bavarian, Frankish, Czech, and Habsburg rulers.

Independence has brought with it many benefits as well as challenges. Having abandoned communism in favour of capitalism, Slovenia is already reaping the benefits of trade with Western Europe. As a member of the European Community, Slovenia has enjoyed a surge in exports and is fast becoming a popular destination for tourists. Described as "the sunny side of the Alps: young state, old culture, fantastic scenery," Slovenia offers excellent skiing, restful spas, tranquil villages, and exciting caving in its 15 000 caves, many of which are world famous.

But the benefits of independence have been accompanied by many challenges for Slovenians. The end of communism and the influx of foreign investment have also brought foreign influence. Will this tiny nation be able to withstand the powerful forces of Western culture? As more and more homes acquire television sets, Western programs are increasing in popularity. Already English is the second most popular language spoken and taught in Slovenia, despite the close proximity of Austria and Italy.

Also, how will Slovenians handle the shift to a capitalist system? Teachers who have taught under a communist system for decades now must suddenly change their

---

❦

Slovenia's past and present. These two homes reflect the changes sweeping through Slovenia. On the top is a 300-year-old home in the small village of Klenik, which, until recently, had no running water or electricity. On the bottom is a modern home in the village of Zagorje, which has most amenities found in North American homes.

practices, particularly in business and economics courses. Stores, also, must work hard to reform their business practices. In department stores, customers are still required to select the item they wish to purchase, have a receipt written up by a store clerk, then take this receipt (without the item) down to the bottom floor, where they pay for the item. The customers then return to the floor on which they selected the item to pick it up. Obviously, this onerous and inefficient system needs to be overhauled. But change is coming quickly to Slovenia. Walk down the main shopping district in the capital city of Ljubjana and you soon notice McDonald's, Dairy Queen, and other Western chain stores.

In the countryside, you see the clearest evidence of a nation in change. Here you can find centuries-old homes, often with plumbing only recently installed, standing beside comfortable new homes that have most modern conveniences. These new homes can be a misleading indicator of the average wealth enjoyed by Slovenians. The average monthly salary earned by factory workers is approximately $400 CDN, while an average new home can cost up to $200 000. Consequently, many new homes are built over many years with much of the labour being provided by families and friends. Also, the investment Slovenians make in their homes is intended to benefit future generations. Most families today have only one child, who will often remain in the home after marriage and eventually inherit the family home.

Slovenians, like other citizens of newly independent republics in Eastern Europe, face many challenges as they adapt to new economic and political systems. They must endeavour to protect their culture and heritage in a competitive global village as they seek to become an active member of the international community. Although the road to freedom may be an arduous one, it is an exhilarating journey for Slovenians, who have for so long toiled under the rule of foreign governments.

Soviet citizen lived in congested apartments and had to stand in long lines to acquire limited amounts of substandard food. Having lived through harder times in their childhood, many were content to say: "Give us food, a roof over our heads, and work—and do whatever you want politically. Give us the material minimum. We won't ask for more." Few Soviet citizens complained openly of their situation. Many were content with a system that provided low-cost housing, free medical care, education, and a guaranteed job. A Muscovite expressed Russian contentment as follows:

> We know life here is not as good as it is in America, that your best workers make three and four times as much as ours, and your apartments and homes are bigger than ours. But we don't have to save for unemployment here. I bring home my pay and give it to Lyuba [wife] and she organizes the household. What do I have to worry about? There is enough pay... I never have to worry. I don't have to worry about the future....

There was no shortage of material goods for the elite members of the Communist Party. Stores, open only to a select few, were abundantly shelved with luxury foods and items imported from the West, such as Belgian chocolate, French wine, Scotch whisky, American cigarettes, Italian ties, and Japanese stereos—all at cut-rate prices. The homes of the party elite also betrayed the revolutionary ideals of equality. Party leaders lived in large mansions provided free of charge by the state. These stately homes, often hidden from view, were surrounded by several hectares of land. Some even had private beaches.

By the 1970s, rumblings of discontent were beginning to be heard among the youth of the Soviet Union. Not having experienced the hardships of earlier generations, the youth of the 1970s and 1980s were less willing to accept the long lines and lack of material goods, nor were they as willing to ignore the obvious discrepancies between the Communist Party elite and the majority of Soviets. Although the authoritarian nature of the regime allowed little room for protest, the seedbed for change had been planted.

Adjusting to Life After Communism

Suddenly and unexpectedly, in 1989 the Soviet Union began to crumble and the communist system collapsed. The revolutionary turn of events left the former Soviet Union and its satellites in disarray. Throughout Eastern Europe, the collapse of communism has brought about a resurgence of nationalism and the promise of a free and democratic future. This change was not without its costs and challenges, as a close look at the former Soviet Union reveals.

In some ways, the collapse of communism was an even more radical change for Russians than was the revolution in 1917 (which brought the communists to power). For over five centuries, from Czar Ivan the Terrible to the last communist regime, Russians have been governed autocratically. The authoritarian rule of czars and commisars has left the Russian people for the most part submissive and conservative. The vast majority of Soviet people had come to expect the state to look after their needs. The end of the communist regime and the introduction of democracy and free enterprise thrust Russians into a world of choices completely new to them. The challenges they face in the coming decades, as they embrace the virtues and vices of free enterprise and individual freedoms, will more profoundly reshape Eastern Europe than any other event in the past five centuries.

The end of communism was accompanied by a host of difficult problems. No longer did people have the security they once enjoyed. As Russian industry attempts to survive on the competitive global market, the inefficiencies of the old system have to be eradicated. This invariably leads to massive layoffs. The uncertainty over Russia's economic future led to the collapse of the ruble, causing rampant inflation, which further eroded the already low standard of living of many Russians. As people found their jobs in jeopardy and their buying power eroded, they became increasingly impatient with the economic reforms that promised to bring about a better life. In the face of such uncertainty, the former communist regime, for some at least, began to take on a mythical image as a time of stability and order.

Eastern Europe sits on the threshold of radical change as millions of people begin to experience capitalism and democracy. The absence of a powerful centralized government has left power vacuums, in some cases filled by crime, in others leading to violent clashes between rival groups. How the collapse will affect the daily lives of those living in countries such as Lithuania, Poland, and Russia is something we will only know as history unfolds.

Reflections

The rate of change over the last 50 years has been astounding. Advances in science and technology have affected our daily lives in ways too numerous to mention. Technology has turned the world into a fast-paced global village. Family structures and roles of women, men, and youth continue to evolve and to blur long-held assumptions. The more rapidly our world changes—be it technologically, politically, or socially— the more we as individuals must show the capacity to adapt and change. It is no longer possible to make assumptions about the society in which we live based upon the experiences of past generations. If we can learn anything from the study of social history over the past half-century, it is that the only constant factor is change. Adapting to change is the surest way for individuals to survive and thrive in the twenty-first century.

Key Concepts, Figures, and Events

Consumerism   Betty Friedan   Naomi Wolf   Camille Paglia

Topics for Further Thought

1. Since 1945, the quality of living space for most Europeans has greatly improved. Do these changes reflect greater equality among European social classes? Has the revolution in living space produced a more homogeneous mass culture, less divided along class lines than in previous centuries?

2. Moralists who decry the high divorce rate in Western societies often look to the past when describing the ideal family. Why is it dangerous to assume that the family structure of the past was superior to that of today? Is it fair to assume that changes in family structure reflect an erosion of values and morals in society? Explain your answer.

3. A common criticism of Western culture is that it is too materialistic. Could it be argued that materialism is necessary for sustained economic growth and that it is a natural extension of democracy? Further, could it be said that those who promote free enterprise and democracy but are critical of materialism are inconsistent in their views? Defend your answer.

4. In recent years, feminism has come under fire and it has become increasingly common to hear women distance themselves from the feminist movement. Why has this change in attitude come about? Have many of the objectives of the earlier women's movement been met, rendering feminism less relevant? Were earlier feminists too radical, promoting disunity rather than harmony and equality, and therefore alienating moderate women? Have women become too comfortable and complacent in society to have the drive to carry on the struggle?

5. After the collapse of communism, Eastern Europeans face many challenges as they learn to live under new political and economic systems. Under free enterprise, individuals will have the opportunity to earn wealth unlike before, but also unlike before, they will have to face the uncertainties of the marketplace without the security formerly provided by the state. Will freedom from oppression be enough to compensate for this loss of security? What measures would you recommend to East European governments to make the transition bearable for all citizens and avoid a backlash against new reforms? Is it possible that democracy and capitalism may fail in countries such as Russia? What would account for such a failure?

Topics for Further Research

1. Television programs can give interesting insights into the society that produced them. Watch a popular television program that deals with family issues from the 1950s or 1960s and one from the 1990s. Using the programs as socio-historical documents, what changes can you detect in family structure and attitudes over the past 30 years?

2. The application of science to society has caused a revolution in the twentieth century. Research an issue related to science and ethics and suggest guidelines that should be followed to ensure that science does not outrun social science. Be sure to identify the potential problems or dangers that accompany the application of science you are researching. Some possible issues are:

Genetic Engineering
Development of Advanced Weaponry
Organic Insecticides
Chemical Fertilizers
Eradication of Disease
Depletion of the Ozone Layer and Global Warming

3. Research one of the prominent feminists of the movement's second wave. Prepare a biographical sketch, including her major contributions to the feminist movement. Some of the possible feminists are:

Germaine Greer	Gloria Steinem
Betty Friedan	Naomi Wolf

Responding to Ideas

1. In recent years, scholars commenting on the present condition of the world have offered quite pessimistic views. One of the leading proponents of the pessimism of the future is economist Robert Heilbroner. In his 1980 book, *An Inquiry into the Human Prospect*, Heilbroner summarizes the current challenges to the world as follows: "We are entering a period in which rapid population growth, the presence of obliterative weapons, and dwindling resources will bring international tensions to dangerous levels for an extended period. Indeed, there seems no reason for these levels of danger to subside unless population equilibrium is achieved and some rough measure of equity reached in the distribution of wealth among nations..." Has the world taken steps toward addressing concerns such as those that Heilbroner outlines in the 15 years since these warnings were made? Do you share Heilbroner's pessimism regarding the future?

2. The family, both in North America and Europe, continues to change and respond to the challenges served up by a rapidly changing world. Social historian Elaine Tyler May notes: "In spite of the persistence of many of its features, the American family continues to evolve. The wide diversity of family structures that exist today has profoundly challenged beliefs about the "ideal" or "normative" family. Divorce has become so common that today's families are frequently arranged around relationships between exspouses and stepparents, stepsiblings...." What evidence do you see in your community of the evolving nature of the family? Is there evidence to suggest that the changes which are occurring are a detriment to society or an adjustment to the new realities of our society?

20

Contemporary Art, Music, and Literature

Contemporary Art

The twentieth century is almost over. It is difficult to assess the art of the past 50 years because we are still so close to it. It seems that art movements are simply reactions to previous art. We are still building on a foundation set by the "modern" painters and sculptors at the beginning of this century.

Since World War II, art has taken many directions. There is the work of abstract artists who rely on clean, yet rigid, lines to create an organized, intellectual composition. There is also the work of those abstract artists who convey the fractured, violent aspects of the modern world through dynamic composition and strong colour. What aspects about art have changed? Artists are still concerned about people,

politics, society, beauty, and truth. And we are still seeing a polarization between classical and romantic art.

Where do realist painters fit into the modern world? On the American scene, Andrew Wyeth continues to paint extremely intellectual, realistic paintings that portray the human condition in a most subtle, even reverent manner. Edward Hopper portrayed stark, beautifully lit images of urban America that recall the seventeenth-century Dutch masters, such as Vermeer, or the eighteenth-century painter Chardin. In Canada, Robert Bateman leads a group of nature artists who, in tune with the current ecological movements, celebrate the natural heritage of North America.

Post-modernism is an art movement that reacts against "modern" art for its formal abstraction, its lack of feeling, and its rigid, almost academic rules. Here we

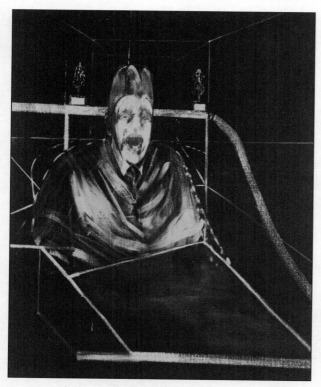

Francis Bacon: *Number VII from Eight Studies for a Portrait,* 1953.

in the environment that has dominated Western consciousness in the last two decades.

New Expressionist Abstraction

The end of World War II signalled a new direction in European art. The horrors of the war and its aftermath had a profound effect on all the arts. Although still painting in an abstract vein, artists longed to bring back a personal quality to their art. In keeping with existentialist philosophy, artists explored the concept of the individual's freedom in the face of alienation. Art became a way of purging the depression and sense of loss left after the war. This art became known as ***new expressionist abstraction***. It is simply abstract art that expresses feelings. And artists became concerned once more with the effects of the war on humanity. However, unlike the humanism of the Renaissance, which celebrated the human body, these artists pictured humanity as tormented, fractured, and full of suffering. Consider the sculpture, *City Square*, by Alberto Giacometti. Note how his figures are elongated and tormented. They have been reduced to the essence of humanity, stripped to the bone, exposed to a harsh reality.

Other artists depicted cruel and startling—even macabre—images. A work by ***Francis Bacon***, *Study for a Pope*, depicts a screaming church official, seemingly at the moment of his execution in the electric chair. Like Goya, Bacon condemns church and state. Bacon's negative, even repulsive vision of the human condition expresses the effect of war on all the arts of Europe. Having lived so long with the anguish brought on by two such appalling world conflicts, the artists of the late 1940s and 1950s considered suffering as an integral part of humanity. Painters sought to alleviate the suffering through painting or sculpture. There is a perverse sense of beauty in these works, recalling the art of Goya or Dalí. Did the world wars annihilate and reform our sense of beauty forever?

The second generation of post-war European artists freed itself from the first by establishing a Dada-like movement in art. For the most part, straight pictorial representations were abandoned. Artists made use of objects taken from everyday life, industry, and nature. ***Performance art*** had its beginning here with elaborate, theatrical presentations often involving other media.

see a similar reaction to that of the romantics to the strictures of the rules established by Louis XIV. Post-modernists—like the romantics—do not enjoy being labelled. They feel a need to seek new directions, new paths, perhaps by looking to the old ways. However, there still exists a plurality of styles and post-modernist artists still look to abstraction, formalism, and expressionism to express themselves.

Regardless of how or what new directions are taken, artists of the late twentieth century are still trying to express the multitude of social upheavals that affect our lives. Images of war, political and urban, abound and yet there has been a return to the landscape genre. Perhaps this is in part due to the interest

The main art movements during this time were new realism, pop Art (popular art), constructive abstraction, op art (optical art), and kinetic art. The new realism involved the use of stark, shocking images often presented as pieces of theatre or sculptures made up of scrap or "junk." An interesting example of new-realist art is the work of Bulgarian artist *Christo*, who produces art "projects" involving the urban and natural environment. In 1968, he wrapped a building in Switzerland with 8300 m of synthetic material tied with rope. Since then, he has produced many such "events" which sometimes involve bridges or miles of landscape.

Although American pop art receives most of the attention, pop art actually began in England in the 1950s. A group of artists and critics became obsessed with popular culture as seen in advertising and signs. *David Hockney* and Allen Jones are two of the most important of the English pop artists. Their art forms a bridge between "high" art and the tacky, commonplace subject matter of pop art. English pop art became a significant movement in the 1960s, coinciding with the emergence of the Beatles.

In the face of all these new and experimental art forms, a group of artists, the *concrete abstractionists*, continued to express art in a rigid, intellectual style involving hard, clean lines. As ever, art continues to express the old polarity between classicism and romanticism.

In an attempt to get a sense of contemporary art as well as contemporary aesthetics, a group of grade 12 students visited the Vancouver Art Gallery. They saw the regular collection, which contains the work of Emily Carr and other nineteenth-century Canadian artists. There was one whole floor dedicated to the work of Jochen Gerz. His exhibition is entitled People Speak. He combines videos, photos, text, and concrete objects to present a comment on Nazi Germany. There was also a display of American prints of the 1960s, including works by Andy Warhol, Jasper Johns, and Robert Rauschenberg. After the visit, the students wrote down their impressions of the art they saw:

The afternoon excursion to the Vancouver Art Gallery exposed me to a style of art with which I am very much unfamiliar. I expected to see classical, European paintings, Impressionist art, cubist art, and other classics. But what I saw was totally unexpected. Art and beauty were given a new

Alberto Giacometti: *City Square*, 1948.

meaning when the things displayed ranged from technical charts to a piece of bread. I never considered these objects artwork because they lacked the aesthetic qualities and were unappealing to the eye. To a philistine such as myself, I am unable to appreciate these works of art. If only there were museum guides to show me around, I think that I would have found the message that these artists wanted to convey. If such abstract art work is merely presented without any explanation, I am afraid that the essence that it is supposed to capture may get lost.   *Anna de Vera*

Upon my visit to the Vancouver Art Gallery, I was exposed to many forms of "art." I saw contemporary art, performance art, Inuit art, and some American prints of the 60s. However, what I found most interesting and intriguing were the abstract paintings. I liked them because they allow me to stop and ponder the meanings of the painting. There would be clues within the painting, but the conclusions could only be drawn by me. That is not to say there is only one definite meaning for the painting because there is not. The meaning is interpreted as whatever I want it to be. After all, it is abstract and with abstract art, it is whatever I would like it to be. I also enjoyed the innovative sculptures that were there; for example, the sculpture of Venus built from light bulbs. I like these innovative pieces of art because I admire the artists' creativity, of which I consider myself to possess very little. All in all, it was a worthwhile experience!   *Trever Siu*

After the class visit to the art gallery, I stepped out thinking, what really is art? Seeing the various pieces of art on display from abstract to realist, made me feel very small, very unimportant. As I walked past each painting, each photograph, each "whatchamacallit," I asked myself, what does this mean? Sometimes I got an answer, sometimes I didn't. Sometimes I couldn't even answer the question, what is this? I think the trip to the art gallery altered my previous definition of art. Art used to be either a painting, a sculpture, a structure, or music. Classical art could easily have been placed in one of those four categories. Now I have learned that art can also be a mixture of two or more categories. I think what is more important now, is not what art means, but how it makes me feel.   *Anita Hui*

The unique situations of everyday life are the ebb and flow of modern day art. Modern art can be both pleasing and repulsive to see, feel and sometimes hear. Whether it is a painting depicting a spring surrounded by trees or a room filled with instruments of war, the visceral sensations are still present. The media which are used reflect the state of industrialization and mechanization in our society today. I was happy to see things portrayed with uniqueness and creativity, compared to some of the more traditional and conservative methods. These new and exciting media add to the sensations that the artist tried to evoke in the piece of art. The strides that modern day art has taken in style, medium and content is very symbolic of how far civilization has advanced to this point.   *Scott Laliberté*

We are at the turn of another century. It is practically impossible to make any concrete judgements about our most recent artistic trends or make any valid predictions about the future. The Impressionists at the turn of the century probably felt the same way about their art and future as do our contemporary generation of artists—full of a desire to make a change, a statement, an impact, in the face of overwhelming odds. The "odds" against us are much the same as 100 years ago—new technology, new industry, less community, less sense of one's self. In the huge array of artistic styles, techniques, ideas, one truth exists—that all art portrays an adventure into or out of the human condition. No matter how abstract, how computerized, how objective the work of art is, it is a human being who is at the centre of the creation. Art reflects the nature (society) of its time—but it is always reflective of the actual humans who create it. And one wonders how much has changed in our deepest essence, since the first Cro-Magnon attempted to paint a cave wall in France. Maybe he painted for some equivalent to what we call money, but more likely he created his work to fulfil a need that exists beyond any understanding or definition. And in that way, he is the same as any artist today.

Emily Carr: *Forsaken*

Contemporary Music

The music of the second half of the twentieth century may be considered as having three prongs: classical, jazz, and rock. Each prong maintains a singularity of style, but no one of them exists in isolation from the other two. All three have influenced each other and continue to do so. The new directions we have seen taken by the art world have been paralleled by new directions in "classical" music. Indeed, many modern composers have been influenced by modern painters. Contemporary compositions are highly intellectual. They may employ traditional instruments but forge new musical ideas. For example, some composers employ several instruments at once, each playing its own rhythm, which fluctuates at its own pace.

Other composers use instruments such as flutes or saxophones, rather than violins, to express the emotional character of a piece. Still others try to create a geometric pattern in their scores, reminiscent of the severely intellectual paintings of Piet Mondrian. Some combine these avant-garde elements with traditional pieces. All these new ideas, textures, and sounds reflect the various trends in contemporary painting and sculpture. There seems to be no limit to the variety of sounds, rhythms, and instruments that can come together to create contemporary classical music.

In the decades after the war, in keeping with the new classicism in abstract painting, a movement developed to give greater structure to sound. The chief progenitor of this movement was the German composer Arnold Schönberg. The result is an ultrarational form of music based on very strict organization of all aspects of the piece. In a completely opposite direction, there is the music of American composer *John Cage*. French painter Marcel Duchamp's desire to let his artwork change or develop by chance is similar to John Cage's aim to create music by chance. Cage is best known for his highly experimental works. For example, he may simply set a radio between stations and allow the resulting static to be his composition. In these types of works, the emphasis is on form. As in many types of contemporary art, content or meaning plays no role at all in the composition. The artist desires to express absolute freedom; therefore, the work of art creates its own pattern, its own structure.

Electronic Music

In the years following World War II, there was a technological revolution in the field of music. The first great advance was the use of magnetic tape to record sound, which made the manipulation and recording of sound much easier. Now artists could use not only natural sounds but also artificial ones. This, then, led to the development

Scott Joplin

of instruments and equipment to create these sounds. One of the chief proponents of this experimental technique was *Karlheinz Stockhausen* in Germany in the early 1950s. Production studios sprang up in Europe and the United States. Composers immediately took advantage of these new opportunities to create new music.

The invention of synthesizers allowed composers to make sound and play with it all in one system, which made it faster to compose music; of course, smaller synthesizers could actually be played on stage. Today, the computer has become an important factor in musical composition of all genres, from classical to rock to jazz. It allows composers greater flexibility and the creation of new sounds. One of the greatest proponents of electronic music was *Edgard Varèse*. He was born in France in 1883 and studied music there but moved to the United States in his thirties. For 20 years, he did not compose; rather, he studied the new trends in music and started composing again when electronic music was accepted and understood. Varèse rejected sounds made by traditional instruments: he wanted to create musical sounds that had never before been heard. He used a great deal of percussion to emulate the sounds of the urban landscape: horns, sirens, industrial tools at work. His music has been compared to abstract painting in its layering of sounds and rhythms.

In contrast to this harshly intellectual approach to composition and performance is the soft music of the *new romanticism*. The new romantic composers want to take music back to its traditional roots and appeal to the emotions once again. Some composers of note are Samuel Barber, Ned Rorem, and Thea Musgrave.

The new freedom and the great variety of styles and techniques available to us may make it difficult to understand contemporary art and music. The computer has led to new types of composition, new instrumentation, and the production of new sounds. The musical world has expanded, yet the most intellectual art and music is not very accessible to the public. The regular concertgoer is not always able to appreciate the highly experimental music that continues to be composed.

Blues and Jazz

One of the most important types of contemporary music is jazz. This genre continues to grow in style and technique as it too has been influenced by the post-war technology boom. It is interesting to consider the roots of jazz in order to come to an understanding of it as a musical genre. At the beginning of the twentieth century, African American music began to have a profound influence on the music of Europe and America. One of the first black American composers was *Scott Joplin*. Joplin was born in 1868, to an ex-slave. His mother and father were both musical, so Joplin began his musical career playing guitar. Later, he changed to piano when he was given free lessons. He worked his way around the southern United States as a pianist in bars and ended up in St. Louis, a centre of *ragtime* music. The word ragtime refers to the "ragged" rhythms of this type of piano playing. Unlike the traditional rhythm of Bach, where the downbeat is at the beginning of the measure, ragtime rhythms are **syncopated**: the downbeat occurs on the second and fourth beats of the measure. Scott Joplin made ragtime famous. His most famous compositions are *The Maple Leaf Rag* and *The Entertainer*. He even wrote an opera based on ragtime forms. Stravinsky and Debussy were two European composers who were influenced by Joplin's music.

Blues developed from Afro-American folk music and spirituals. It is a simple, repetitive type of music that comes from the songs that American slaves sang at work. Blues varies in style from region to region in the United States. For example, the blues of the Mississippi delta, sung by men such as Robert Johnson, has different characteristics from that of Chicago blues.

Jazz was born of a combination of blues, ragtime, and spirituals and is a music based on improvisation. New Orleans was the first great centre of jazz. Some of the most famous and influential musicians to come out of New Orleans were **Louis Armstrong** and his band. These names may not be familiar but they recall giants in the history of jazz: Sidney Bechet on saxophone and "Jelly Roll" Morton on piano. Louis Armstrong was a wonderful trumpet player but he is also famous for his highly distinctive, gritty vocal style.

The early 1920s, a time of relaxation and freedom after the horrors of war, came to be known in musical circles as the **big-band era**. Big bands involve a much larger number of instruments than ragtime or jazz bands. There is usually a number of saxophones, trumpets, trombones, and lots of percussion. Big-band music is international, but it was the United States that again exerted the greatest influence. **Duke Ellington** was a brilliant pianist; he was also a composer and orchestrator because the development of big bands meant that the music had to be written down. Other big bands of note are those of Tommy Dorsey, (who hired young Frank Sinatra as a singer), Woody Herman, and Glenn Miller.

The next important movement in jazz was **bebop**, which developed in the 1940s in reaction to the music of the big bands: bebop jazz involved much smaller groups of musicians and much more improvisation. Great bebop musicians are Charlie Parker, Thelonious Monk, and Dizzy Gillespie. Their work is still a major influence in jazz today.

Duke Ellington

Jazz is an important genre of contemporary music, comparable, in its multiplicity of styles, to modern art. Some jazz artists remain faithful to big-band or to bebop; others take those styles as their base and fuse jazz with rock or classical music. Some musicians use only acoustic instruments; others experiment with all types of electronic equipment to find new sounds. Contemporary jazz continues to grow internationally: a jazz musician can travel to any part of the world and feel comfortable playing his or her music. Perhaps this is because there are no rules, no restrictions with jazz. It is a type

Elvis Presley

 It is fair to say that the twentieth century has been a period of rich and diverse artistic achievement. Of the numerous important artists to emerge from this period, there is one who personifies the aesthetics of the twentieth century particularly well: pop icon Elvis Aron Presley. He became an incredibly influential force in Western society.

Elvis was born on January 8, 1935, in Tupelo, Mississippi. His musical talents were apparent at an early age; at 18, he was recording his own music. The rise to popularity was meteoric for Elvis, beginning with music and progressing to an acting career. For decades, he was the most popular entertainer in the world. However, fame was not kind to the man known as the "King of Rock'n'Roll": in his middle age he became ill and depressed. Elvis Presley died alone at his Memphis estate on August 16, 1977.

But how did a rock-and-roll and movie star have such a profound influence on twentieth-century aesthetics? It all began with the revolution that rock-and-roll brought to the forefront of society. Before Elvis, popular music had tended to be conservative and liked by young and old. Elvis's liberal music paved the way for further change and experimentation in the musical world—currently, these values are a main goal of most influential musicians. Widespread public exposure allowed society to absorb the message that accompanied Elvis's music. It was a straightforward message of rebellion for the young to seek out their own

❧

Elvis Presley

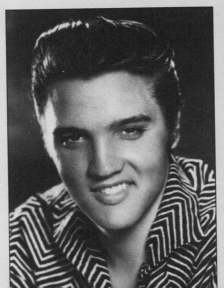

emotional expression—be it musical, literary, or artistic—free from the chains of parental or societal influence. Young people inspired by Elvis became some of the most significant artists of the century: the Beatles, Andy Warhol, and Jack Kerouac, for example. Elvis's music, a blend of Negro rhythm-and-blues and white country music, also helped to harmonize the two races in the U.S.A., by bringing black music to the young people who otherwise would not have been exposed to it.

Elvis's popularity had another effect on the aesthetics of the time: a change in popular lifestyle. His daring fashions and overall look influenced many, helping to shift accepted fashion from a suit and tie to much more outlandish and "fun" clothing. Many people who idolized Elvis took up the renegade lifestyle that he embodied; for example, the popularity of Harley-Davidson motorcycles is attributable to Elvis, because of the many public appearances and publicity shots of him on motorcycles.

The Beatles

⚓

of music which is as individual as the artist who plays it and the listener who loves to hear it.

Rock-and-Roll

We have considered two of the prongs of contemporary music: classical and jazz. The third prong is, of course, rock or pop music. Like jazz and classical music, **rock-and-roll** has evolved to include a wide variety of styles, themes, and instrumentation. Rock-and-roll had its roots in American music and became a genre unto itself in the 1950s with artists such as Elvis Presley, Chuck Berry, and Buddy Holly. It appealed, for the most part, to youthful audiences and became, in one sense, a voice for youth. It was, and perhaps still is, a way for youth to express concerns about emotional problems.

From the mid-twentieth century onward, every decade seems to have its own great rock movement. The music of the 1950s changed dramatically in the 1960s with the "British invasion" led by the Beatles. In the U.S., the late 1950s and early 1960s saw a revival of folk music. The advent of the hippie movement in the

United States led to psychedelic music. And, of course, all of these styles interacted with each other. The music of the 1970s has been denigrated for its disco movement. In the late 1960s and early 1970s, popular music took a very serious turn when some musicians used it as a vehicle for protest against the war in Vietnam. The impetus for this protest was the huge rock festival at Woodstock in New York. For three days, thousands of people gathered to celebrate life and music and give vent to the frustrations that had been voiced by the various protest movements of the 1960s, such as feminism, the struggle for civil rights, and the peace movement.

The 1980s saw a continuation of the serious styles of the 1970s and a strong movement known as New Wave, or punk rock, which had its roots in England. ***Alternative music*** has come to refer, in a broad sense, to music that is not in the mainstream of popular culture. In the U.S. specifically, alternative music refers to the "garage bands," such as Pearl Jam. However, there is also a powerful alternative movement in the popular music of Europe. In the mid-1990s, there continues to be a variety of styles, from a revival of regional folk music, to the birth of grunge and the popularity of rap music. Grunge is a label for a musical style. Rap music had its roots in street music in the African American ghettoes, probably in the 1950s. African music, especially that of South Africa, is having a strong influence on all musical styles. Nevertheless, all musicians since the post-war era owe a debt to rhythm-and-blues which remains a strong, steady force in music while fads and stars come and go.

It has been said that the music one listens to and loves during high school will remain with one forever. Consider the popularity of "oldies" stations. Songs from these years are evocative of a time that is a blend of heartfelt joys and pains. In 20 years, the people studying this textbook will hear a piece of music from their high school years and feel the same emotions then as they do now.

Contemporary Literature

New forms of literature have led to a new way of looking at literature. In the latter half of this century, literary criticism has become a genre unto itself. The various movements of literary criticism parallel similar movements in the art world. It is useful to discuss these movements, rather than try to discuss actual authors and works for two reasons. First, the literature of the last decades of the twentieth century is difficult to discuss in objective terms because we are still trying to place it in a context relevant to us. Second, many movements under critical discussion are linked to social and political movements and so are relevant to a study of history. As we consider some of these critical theories which try to make sense of current literature, try to draw parallels with the various movements in twentieth-century art and music that we have already discussed

Theories of Literary Criticism

What is a work of literature? We have seen how important form was to the writers of the eighteenth and nineteenth centuries. Form—or lack of it—defined the literature of these centuries. Writers in the eighteenth century had definite boundaries within which to explore their ideas, writers in the nineteenth century had those boundaries to react against. Modern literature may be compared to a satellite that has lost its orbit and is spinning off into space. Perhaps literary criticism is a way to bring it back to find some relationship with our world, our reality.

Objectivism

Some critics regard a work of literature as existing wholly unto itself, having no connection to its author or its reader. It is very difficult to read a novel, for example, and not project ourselves into it in some way; perhaps it is impossible. Objectivist critics want the reader to view the text as having its own language or set of sign posts, ones we have not encountered before. They think that our approach to literature should be similar to our approach to mathematics. According to the objectivist critic, we should be engaging in a new, wholly intellectual endeavour when we read a literary work.

Formalism

Formalism is a critical theory that began in Russia at the start of World War I. Russian formalists felt that literary scholarship had become bogged down in the companion studies of history, psychology, sociology, and philosophy, to name a few. They felt that the actual work of literature had become secondary to all these other aspects. They felt that a work of literature needs no outside influences to give it meaning since its very existence gives it meaning. The form, rather than the content of the work, is its most important feature. The ideas begun by the Russian formalists spread to other parts of Europe: Czechoslovakia, Germany, and France.

New Criticism

However, by the mid-twentieth century, another theory called new criticism came to dominate literary criticism in Europe and the United States. This movement began early in the twentieth century with the critical theories of T. S. Eliot. Generally, the new critics believe that every word, image, line, and feature of a text contributes to its overall meaning. To fully understand a text, the reader must systematically analyze all these aspects. New critics focus on meaning as well as form. For them, literature refers to the greater reality of nature or humanity.

Structuralism

Another school of formalism is **structuralism**. Like the Russian formalists, structuralists focus on the actual work of literature and its meaning, only as it exists upon a page. Structuralism had its roots in linguistics, a discipline of which a chief exponent was **Ferdinand de Saussure,** early in the twentieth century. He believed that languages are systems made up of signs and form their own reality apart from that of the outside world. Structuralism, which did not become a movement until the 1960s, was built on this idea. Structuralists, such as Claude Lévi-Strauss and Roland Barthes, think that literature, as expressed through a language system, creates a new self-contained reality. Creativity does not enter into structuralist thought. Authors are not considered in the study of texts: the reader needs to be completely objective while analyzing a work of literature; only then can he or she find the truth of a text. This rigid objectivity led to a reaction against structuralism.

Post-Structuralism

Although scientific and objective, post-structuralist criticism opposed the idea that any text can be truly reliable, given the many layers of meaning there are to even one word. Deconstruction is a post-structuralist form of literary criticism which, as opposed to construction or structure, proposes that no text can have any definite meaning: the text is actually created by a reader as he or she reads it. In similar fashion, composer John Cage expects the listener to create and interpret his music while listening to it.

The most famous proponent of deconstruction is Jacques Derrida. His theory is that texts, by their very structure, deconstruct their meanings to become neutral or static. The reader is then free to create his or her personal interpretation within the confines of the text. Many deconstructionists have strong affiliations with radical political movements, especially with those of France in the 1960s. Literary critics with interests in other disciplines, such as sociology, feminism, and psychology, use deconstruction as a base from which to examine literature.

Subjectivism

Just as expressionism opposes abstraction in art, in literature, subjectivism opposes objectivism. Subjectivism is a type of criticism that involves the reader as well as the author in the analysis of a literary work.

Pyschological Criticism

Pyschological criticism involves the psyche of the author. For these critics, literature needs to be interpreted according to its revelation of the psychology of its characters, symbols, and author. For example, a Freudian approach involves an understanding of Freud's psychological theories and applies them to the behaviours of the characters in a work. Jungian criticism, based on the psychology of Freud's contemporary, Carl Jung, sees us all as sharing a universal or collective unconscious which is formed from universal images called archetypes. These archetypes surface in literature to help us form our interpretation. We are then able to look beyond the surface meaning of the text to a greater universal understanding.

Jung's theory of psychology sees humanity as having three levels of consciousness. The first level—the persona—refers to the face or mask we put out to the world. The second level—the unconscious—refers to our world of dreams and memories. The third level—the collective unconscious—is a state of mind that has its origins in our ancestral past and, thus, is common to all humans.

The collective unconscious is made up of universal images, or archetypes, which act as patterns or moulds that may be traced through many cultures. Archetypes find expression in works of art and literature and come to symbolize a deeper meaning than their literal one. An example of an archetype would be a female deity that we see represented in various cultures, from the Venus figurine of the Cro-Magnon era to Aphrodite from Greek mythology and the Virgin Mary from Christianity. Another archetypal image is that of the garden, as seen in the Garden of Eden, the idyllic island in William Golding's *Lord of the Flies*, and the garden described in Andrew Marvell's seventeenth-century masterpiece *The Garden*.

One of Canada's greatest writers, Robertson Davies, uses Jungian psychology and symbolism in his *Deptford Trilogy*. The three novels are powerful stories in themselves but an understanding of Jung's theory of personality and archetypes makes them even richer.

Historical Criticism

Historical criticism looks at literature in, naturally enough, a historical context. In this century we have four main approaches that involve history and culture.

Dialoguism

Dialoguism is a critical approach that sees all language as a form of conversation, both outer and inner. Each person has a personal language made of personal attributes and cultural features. Thus, language is a product of a certain time and place. Therefore, by studying the historical context of a work, one gains greater insight into its meaning. Allied to this is sociological criticism.

Marxist Criticism

Marxist criticism sees literature as a product of the class struggle in any given historical place and moment. For Marxist critics, language is heavily endowed with economic or class values, those which have initiated the class struggle. They believe that art should not be considered above or apart from our day to day existence but as an expression of the political struggle of a culture—whether positive or negative. In the last ten years, two other schools of critical thought have become very powerful issues: feminism and new historicism.

A Glimpse into Contemporary Literature

There are so many approaches to literary analysis that often a student of literature feels overwhelmed. There is great joy in reading works that completely transport us into the reality defined by the text. A great work of literature is one in which the reader may become wholly absorbed. The following excerpts are from two different writers who are recognized for their marvellous ability to transport the reader into another world. The two excerpts given below contain descriptions of scenes, so one is able to appreciate the power of the writing without having to know the narrative context from which they are taken.

Michael Ondaatje is one of Canada's most revered writers. His poetry and novels combine two worlds: his Asian heritage and his Canadian experience. Ondaatje was born in Sri Lanka, went to school in England, and came to Canada in 1962. His poetry has won him the Governor General's Award and his first novel, *Coming Through Slaughter*, won him the Books in Canada award for first novels. His autobiographical work, *Running in the Family*, tells of his experience in Sri Lanka as he traces his family roots. His latest novel, *The English Patient*, has won him worldwide acclaim. This poem is an example of his ability to evoke a particular mood through simple, yet powerful, descriptive language.

The Agatha Christie Books by the Window

In the long open Vancouver Island
    room
sitting by the indoor avocados
where indoor spring light
falls on the half covered bulbs

and down the long room light falling
onto the dwarf orange tree
vines from south america
the agatha christie books by the
    window

Nameless morning
solution of grain and colour

There is this amazing light,
colourless, which falls on the warm
stretching brain of the bulb
that is dreaming avocado

American writer Toni Morrison does in prose what Ondaatje does so well in poetry. In her unusual, intense novels, she tells haunting stories of the African American experience that, because of their abstract nature, make that experience both universal and particular. She won the 1993 Nobel Prize for her fiction. Her most recent novel is *Jazz*, whose narrative structure is like a musical piece of jazz: improvisational, moody, taking the listener or reader into unknown worlds. As you read the passage from *Jazz*, at right, consider its musical qualities.

But I have seen the City do an unbelievable sky. Redcaps and dining car attendants who wouldn't think of moving out of the City sometimes go on at great length about country skies they have seen from the windows of trains. But there is nothing to beat what the City can make of a nightsky. It can empty itself of surface, and more like the ocean than the ocean itself, go deep, starless. Close up on the tops of buildings, near, nearer than the cap you are wearing, such a citysky presses and retreats, presses and retreats, making me think of the free but illegal love of sweethearts before they are discovered. Looking at it, this nightsky booming over a glittering city, it's possible for me to avoid dreaming of what I know is in the ocean, and the bays and tributaries it feeds: the two-seat aeroplanes, nose down in the muck, pilot and passenger staring at schools of passing bluefish; money, soaked and salty in canvas bags, or waving their edges gently from metal bands made to hold them forever. They are down there, along with yellow flowers that eat water beetles and eggs floating away from thrashing fins; along with the children who made a mistake in the parents they chose; along with slabs of Carrara pried from unfashionable buildings. There are bottles too, made of glass beautiful enough to rival stars I cannot see above me because the citysky has hidden them. Otherwise, if it wanted to, it could show me stars cut from the lamé gowns of chorus girls, or mirrored in the eyes of sweethearts furtive and happy under the pressure of a deep, touchable sky.

To really get a sense of contemporary fiction, read further works by Ondaatje and Morrison. If you loved to hear stories that your grandparents used to tell you about life in Canada's past or the pasts of Europe, Asia, or Africa, read stories by Canadian Alice Munro or Chilean Isabel Allende, the quietly political spinner of marvellous South American tales. A genuine work of literature should be like a precious many-faceted gem to which one may return again and again for further reflections upon and into the human experience.

Feminist Criticism

Feminist criticism believes that literature reflects society and has had an influence on that society. Feminist critics draw attention to women. French feminists are influenced by modern psychoanalysis and the poststructuralists' emphasis on language rather than on theme. American and Canadian feminist critics try to revive literature written by women from the past, including poetry, novels, diaries, and letters: they support all kinds of women's literature.

New Historicism

New historicism sees written material as evidence of culture and society. Whereas feminist or Marxist critics may view certain texts as politically injurious to women or to social struggle, these critics consider all literature as worthy of attention, even that deemed for mass consumption. All literature, popular and academic, should be studied as part of "popular culture."

After considering these many ways of approaching literature, which one seems the most interesting, most appropriate to your way of thinking? Certainly all are valid. There is even a movement to try to combine all these ways of thinking into a single, pluralistic, school of thought. Perhaps for the general reader, the worth of a work of literature is in the amount of intellectual and emotional pleasure it affords.

Reflections

As we approach the end of another decade and century, we are beset with such a variety of genres in all aspects of the arts. How do we relate to experimental music? How can we truly appreciate abstract art? Are we still able to read a piece of literature for the beauty of the language or do we constantly strive for a deeper meaning? One cannot help thinking that a similar situation existed at the turn of the last century. People clung to traditions in the face of enormous social, technical, and industrial changes which impacted on them as much as the changes affect us today. We still celebrate the works of the Impressionists, the sculpture of Rodin, and the highly intellectual work of James Joyce. Although they are as much as a century old, these works have a universal importance which is as strong today as it was when they were first produced, perhaps even more so. Therefore, we should be open to all artistic endeavours, rejoice in what we find wonderful, and be ojectively critical of what we reject.

Consider this famous statement by Alphonse Karr: *"Plus ça change, plus c'est la même chose"* (the more things change, the more they remain the same). In 20 years, consider it again and the truth of it will ring as clear then as it does now.

ART
Key Concepts, Figures, and Events

Post-Modernism
Performance Art
Concrete Abstractionists

New Expressionist Abstraction
Christo

Francis Bacon
David Hockney

I. Compare and contrast paintings by Jackson Pollock and Piet Mondrian as examples of romantic and classical art.

2. The following twentieth-century architects have had a great influence on contemporary architecture in general. Choose and research one in order to discuss the individual's style and influence.

Antonio Gaudí, Spain
Frank Lloyd Wright, United States
Arthur Erickson, Canada
Le Corbusier, France
Walter Gropius, Germany
Ludwig Mies van der Rohe, Germany

3. Photography has become an important art form. Consider the work of artists such as Ansel Adams, Annie Leibowitz, or Yousuf Karsh. How is photography similar and different to the art of painting?

4. Modern sculpture is as diverse in style and theme as modern painting. Choose a sculptor whose work appeals to you, e.g. Henry Moore, Constantin Brancusi, Vladimir Tatlin, Umberto Boccioni, or Jacques Lipchitz. Consider several works by the artist you choose and discuss how they reflect the concerns of modern society.

5. Visit an art gallery and participate in a general tour. Record your immediate reactions to what you have seen. You may want to go back and concentrate on a particular exhibition or single work of art that caught your attention. Again, record your impressions and, in essay form, discuss how the work or works you have chosen to observe are characteristic of the time and society in which they were created.

6. The earliest paintings known are of animals, found in caves of Lascaux, France and Altamira, Spain. Find prints of these extraordinary pieces. How do these pieces fit into the aesthetics of this century?

7. Do not confine yourself to studying the art of Western Europe. Find examples of art from Africa, Latin America, or Asia and compare them to art of Europe, the U.S., and Canada.

MUSIC
Key Concepts, Figures, and Events

John Cage
New Romanticism
Blues
Duke Ellington
Alternative Music

Karlheinz Stockhausen
Scott Joplin
Louis Armstrong
Bebop

Edgard Varèse
Ragtime
Big Band Era
Rock-and-Roll

1. Oscar Peterson is a great Canadian musician. He not only plays brilliant interpretations of standard jazz but also has composed beautiful pieces that are distinctly Canadian. Find a recording of his *Nova Scotia Suite*. In what way is this jazz Canadian?

2. An interesting way to hear contemporary alternative music is to listen to the CBC program *Brave New Waves*, which broadcasts international music. How is alternative music different from mainstream music? Can you find any common themes, styles, or instrumentation?

3. Compare and contrast the contemporary genre of large musicals in a Broadway style to classical opera. How has one genre borrowed from the other? Compare *Les Misérables* by Andrew Lloyd Webber to *Fidelio* by Beethoven or *Phantom of the Opera*, also by Webber, to *Peter Grimes* by Benjamin Britten.

4. Listen to the music of the American composers George Gershwin and Aaron Copland. How are their works a blend of classical and jazz?

5. Two of the greatest musicians of post-war jazz were John Coltrane on saxophone and Miles Davis on trumpet. Both were highly experimental in their playing styles and compositions. Try to find recordings of their early and late work and see how their styles and techniques developed as they moved from bebop into contemporary jazz.

6. Joni Mitchell is a great Canadian musician whose work spans three decades. Her music does not fit into one genre as she blends elements of folk, rock, jazz, and classical in her compositions. Her lyrics stand alone as pure poetry. Locate some recordings of Joni Mitchell's work. Before you listen to her music, analyze several of her works as poetry. Then discuss them as music.

LITERATURE
Key Concepts, Figures, and Events

Formalism
Psychological Criticism
Marxist Criticism

Structuralism
Historical Criticism
Feminist Criticism

Ferdinand de Saussure
Dialoguism
New Historicism

I. Consider the novels of the existentialist philosophers, Jean-Paul Sartre: *Nausea*, Franz Kafka: *The Trial*, and Albert Camus: *The Stranger*. How do these works reflect the despair and fragmentation of society after the war?

2. Simone de Beauvoir is a feminist and an existentialist. Read her short novel, *A Very Easy Death*, and comment on her attitude to life and death, perhaps in comparison to the philosophy of her lifelong companion, Jean-Paul Sartre.

3. Günter Grass is a great contemporary German novelist. Read *The Tin Drum*, which gives an extraordinary picture of life in northern Germany during the Nazi years as seen by a child. There is also an excellent film of the novel available in video.

4. A great deal of interesting literature and film has come from Italy. Read Umberto Eco's historical novel *The Name of the Rose*, or some short stories by Italo Calvino.

5. Some of the greatest films made in the late twentieth century are Italian. Look at the works of Fellini, such as *Amarcord* or *Satyricon*. Lina Wertmüller, a German filmmaker, made *Seven Beauties*, which is a fascinating study of World War II from the point of view of an Italian prisoner of war.

6. An outstanding novelist and short-story writer is Chilean author Isabel Allende. She is from the Allende family who were ousted from Chile by the military junta in the 1970s. She now lives in Caracas, Venezuela. She is a marvellous creator of character and a wonderful teller of tales. Her work is a blend of the New World and the Old and gives interesting insights into the rich and poor of South American society. Read *House of the Spirits* or any of her collections of short stories and prepare a class presentation.

7. Try to get a sense of the literary scene that surrounded Picasso in Paris in the early years of the twentieth century. Read either Ernest Hemingway, F. Scott Fitzgerald, Gertrude Stein, or Alice B. Toklas. Compare their ideas to those of British novelists, such as Virginia Woolf and James Joyce.

8. Canadian novels reflect the regional differences in our country. Read Margaret Laurence, Alice Munro, or Margaret Atwood. How do their works reflect the specific regions of Canada in or about which they write?

9. Michael Ondaatje is a Canadian author whose work portrays multiculturalism. Read *The English Patient* or his autobiography, *Running in the Family*, in which he explores his Sri Lankan heritage. How does this exploration affect his identity as a Canadian?

Skills Focus

Is History a Science?

 This may seem an odd question to ask when dealing with developing historical skills, but the answer to such a question sheds much light on the nature of historical studies. That is not to imply, however, that the answer is either simple or straightforward. Attempting to explain the similarities between the study of science and history helps us understand how historians operate; it also helps us understand science.

Firstly, let us deal with the similarities between history and science. Both the historian and the scientist gather data, the scientist from experiments or observations in the field or laboratory, the historian from documents in libraries. Based on their preliminary observations, scientists formulate a hypothesis through rigorous experimentation or analysis. Similarily, historians formulate questions based on their preliminary reading on a topic and attempt to answer them by carrying out more in-depth research. Both the scientist and the historian look for general trends or patterns and, based on the evidence gathered, formulate theses or theories of wider—possibly universal—scope. Finally, both scientist and historian must communicate their findings in writing.

As we can see, the methodology of scientists and historians is similar: it goes from the specific to the general—it is inductive—and it is based on objective evidence. And yet, the nature of the two disciplines is quite different. One of the most obvious differences between history and science is that scientific experiments must be repeatable, whereas a historian cannot ask for repetition of the past. Even though similar events may occur, the historian can never find events which are exact recreations of other events. Consequently, scientists can formulate universal laws; historians cannot. Nor can historians predict the future with any certainty; they must limit themselves to educated speculation based on their knowledge of the past.

Historians are just as systematic and critical in their research as are scientists. The crucial difference between history and science lies in the nature of the phenomena they study: whereas the scientist is concerned with physical objects, the historian is concerned with human experience.

How can an understanding of the difference between history and science assist you in your study of history?

Firstly, it can help to ensure that you do not fall into a trap, such as attempting to understand the past based on universal historical laws. Secondly, it should alert you to the fact that each historical event is unique and must be studied as such. Thirdly, it should be pointed out that both historians and scientists should publish their findings so that the public can share their knowledge. By sharing information, both historian and scientist attempt to contribute to the advancement of humankind.

Review the process you followed in preparing a research essay for this course. Did you follow the method set out above? How was your methodology similar to your experiences in a science class? How did the application of your research in history differ from the use of information gathered in science? Did you gather information that would be helpful to others in understanding a historical event? Write a one-page response to these questions. Remember: this is a reflective rather than a factual piece of writing, in which you should discuss the historical process rather than historical events.

Suggested Sources for Further Research

Drakulic, S., *The Balkan Express: Fragments from the Other Side of War* (W. W. Norton, 1993).

Gerner, D. J., ed., *One Land, Two Peoples: The Conflict Over Palestine* (Westview Press, 1994).

Goff, R., *The Twentieth Century: A Brief Global History* (McGraw-Hill Ryerson, 1994).

Hughes, H. S., *Sophisticated Rebels: The Political Culture of European Dissent, 1968–1987* (Oxford University Press, 1988).

Hyland, W. G., *The Cold War: Fifty Years of Conflict* (Random House, 1991).

Kennedy, P., *Preparing for the Twenty-First Century World* (HarperCollins, 1993).

Keylor, W., *The Twentieth-Century World: An International History* (Oxford University Press, 1992).

Laqueur, W., *Europe in Our Time: A History, 1945-1992* (Penguin Books, 1993).

Weigall, D. and Stirk, P., *The Origins and Developments of the European Community* (Leicester University Press, 1992).

Looking Toward Tomorrow

We sit poised on the brink of a new millennium. The modern age, generally agreed to have arrived with the Renaissance, is quickly fading into the past as a new era dawns. The modern age was one of certainties about values and conventions; it placed tremendous faith in the potential of rational human thought. There was also much emphasis on the acquisition of knowledge and the belief that history was unfolding in a progressive manner. Generation upon generation built upon the discoveries and experiences of their forebears to edge the world forward. The modern age has been an age dominated by the Western world and by capitalism, by a belief in the invariable triumph of freedom, and by Christian values. A recent American textbook dealing with modern European history concluded as follows:

> Perhaps our Western heritage may even inspire us with pride and measured self-confidence. We stand, momentarily, at the end of the long procession of Western civilization winding through the ages.... Through no effort of our own, we are the beneficiaries of those sacrifices and achievements. Now that it is our turn to carry the torch onward, we may remember these ties with our forebears.

Statements such as these are riddled with potential problems, for they assume that we can apply a set standard of values as we evaluate both the past and the direction for the future. Many intellectuals now question such assumptions, claiming that there is no irrefutable body of truths and that the assumed leadership of the Western world, accompanied by its ideals and sense of moral superiority, may not fit the entire world that is presently unfolding. Furthermore, we are not the culmination of history but rather a mere part of the time continuum that goes on unravelling. History has and will continue to unfold randomly: there are no set patterns, and we cannot claim to predict the future.

An often-heard phrase is that history repeats itself. This is in fact a fallacy: although study of the past can help us to understand the present and prepare for the future, it can never enable us to predict the future with any certainty. Through the study of history, we can identify certain relationships and trends that allow us to plan our actions accordingly. For example, history teaches us that arms races tend to lead to war, yet the nuclear arms race has so far not led to a confrontation between superpowers. Will a nuclear war eventually break out? This question can only be answered by the future.

Another fallacy of history is that certain events were inevitable. Nothing that occurs in the past, present, or future is ever inevitable. Certain factors can render an event likely, but to suggest inevitability is to imply the historical process is predestined. This would deny the role of chance occurrence and of human participation in history. Hence, we can do no more than study history to learn the past, hoping to develop appreciation for the accomplishments of our forebears. This way, we can more clearly grasp the forces that shape our lives today.

Post-Modernism

In a broad sense, the Renaissance can be seen as the historical period during which there was a fundamental break with Europe's medieval past. Hence, the period from the fifteenth to the eighteenth century came to be known as the early modern period. The advent of the Enlightenment, followed closely by the French Revolution and the Industrial Revolution, brought the Western world into the modern era. While some revisionist historians reject these labels, they do provide a convenient framework from which to address the post-modern world. The defining features of the early modern and modern eras in European history were their search for truth, beauty, and goodness; the confidence that it was possible to understand everything; and the faith that, through the application of human knowledge and rational thought, we could perfect society. The very belief that society could achieve some kind of utopia implies a common set of goals and values. This assumption is no longer valid and the Western world must come to grips with the fact that it does not have a monopoly on what defines good government or the moral foundations of society. Irish author James Joyce described the post-modern cosmopolitan mind as "Europasianized Afferyank."

Post-modern is a difficult term to define and understand. Essentially, post-modernists reject the earlier premises that there are universal truths or standards of goodness and beauty, so they embrace plurality. They no longer accept that individuals are capable of understanding everything because they recognize that the realm of knowledge has become too vast for any one mind to grasp. Furthermore, post-modernists reject the West's centuries-old quest for common values and accept that in the present and future world there will be diverse moral codes, each equally valid. This attack on individualism and rationalism can be dangerous, as it reduces individuals to mere cogs in an incomprehensible machine and removes the foundation upon which Western societies have been built. Yet, if we reject the pluralism of post-modernism, who will be the arbiter of what is best? By what standards will they judge? Historian Roland Stromberg points out that: "The encounter between the European West and Africa and Asia, begun long ago, has now reached the stage of a true syncretization of cultures...."

Post-modernism presents us with many challenges as it forces us to rethink the ways in which we respond to the world around us. Its most visual representation is in architecture, where old conventions have been abandoned in favour of "premeditated chaos," which brings together a wide variety of styles in any possible combination. The winning entry in a recent architectural contest on homes was a Manitoba design that incorporated a metal tepee with a wooden silo and a glass home. Such eclecticism has become the hallmark of post-modernism. The impact of post-modernism on history, philosophy, and literature is that it is no longer possible to affirm absolute values. In the teaching of history, it becomes impossible to establish the "essentials" of a course as there are, theoretically, no fundamental truths and therefore no events of universal significance. Rather, what have long been considered milestones of history must now be acknowledged as favourite topics of the teacher. To argue that it is more important that the events of the French Revolution be studied than the downfall of the Chinese emperor Pu Yi, is to impose a Western bias on history. In an attempt to redress this issue, this textbook has tried to present the history of Europe including Western civilization's place in the broader world from several perspectives. Post-modernists could question the value and accuracy of much of the material covered in these pages: such is the nature of viewing history from an eclectic perspective.

Facing the Challenges of Tomorrow

The preceding discussion of post-modernism is relevant over and beyond the intellectual exercise of coming to grips with its meaning. The post-industrial world in which we live, linked by satellites, international trading agreements, and the constant threat of global warming, nuclear war, and rampant disease, is no longer a world in which we can turn a blind eye to events outside of Canada. We live, for better or worse, in a global village where our actions and the actions of others have implications beyond our borders. Terrorism, environmental degradation, poverty, and disease are threats to all of us. No longer can we afford to view events from the narrow perspective of the Western world.

To respond to the challenges that lie before us, we must accept the pluralism of our world and work toward a common harmony that embraces religious and cultural differences. In the final unit of this textbook, you were introduced to many of the critical issues that face our world in the coming century. Population explosion, poverty, global warming, wars prompted by rising nationalism, ethnic cleansing, and unregulated advances in science, are but a few of the problems that now confront us. As students bound for university, you are the future leaders of society and on you falls the burden of helping to lead the world to a stable and prosperous future.

The study of history is an important tool in preparing for your future role as leaders in society. Understanding the past will give you a clearer picture of the present and assist you in planning for the future. Learn from the triumphs and failures of the past. Through your knowledge of history, you will be well aware of the potential for human creativity and the limitless opportunities that lie ahead. You should also be aware of the human capacity for evil. As we continue the elusive search for meaning in life, look to the past for guidance on how you can play a productive role in shaping the future.

GLOSSARY

aesthetic A philosophy of the perception of beauty. The study of the qualities of a work of art that make it beautiful.

annex To add, as an addition or minor part, to existing possessions; particularly used in the context of the government of a country seizing, taking over, invading, and claiming as its own parts or the whole of another country.

apartheid Racial segregation and discrimination supported by government policy, as against non-whites in the Republic of South Africa.

appeasement The policy of making territorial or other concessions to potential aggressors in order to maintain peace.

arabesque In music, an intricate musical piece using stylized motifs, based on a flowing, ornate, usually floral pattern in painting, as found in Islamic art.

archaic Outdated; no longer in use; belonging to a former period.

archetype The original type or model from which copies are patterned. For example, in Western Christianity, the snake is an archetypal image of evil.

conquistador The Spanish conquerors of the Americas in the sixteenth century (from Spanish *conquistadores*).

dialectic The art or practice of examining statements logically, as by questions and answers, in order to establish validity.

dramatic monologue A first-person poem in which the narrator, in supposed conversation with a silent listener, reveals his or her character to the reader.

elegy A work of literature that may be a memorial to a dead person or simply a sad, contemplative lyric.

emancipation The release/freedom from bondage, oppression, or authority.

evangelical Of or relating to the four Gospels of the New Testament; the doctrine of Protestant churches that salvation is attained chiefly by faith in Christ.

franchise The right to vote; suffrage.

fraternal Brotherly. (Note: a fraternal order—a brotherhood of men organized to further their mutual benefit or to attain a common goal.)

guild Association of merchants or craftsmen established in medieval times to provide economic protection for their members and to regulate their practices.

hegemony Domination or leadership, especially the predominant influence of one state over others.

indigenous Having originated, developed, or been produced in a particular land, region, or environment.

inveterate Firmly established by long continuance; deep-rooted.

KGB The Commission of State Security of the Soviet Union: an agency charged with detecting and countering security threats from abroad.

metropolis The central country, city, region, etc. of an imperialist system which directly or indirectly controls other areas where it may have colonized, established trade, or exploited that area's natural resources.

nation-state A geographical area that is usually inhabited by a ethnically homogenous people and that is politically autonomous.

nocturne A short, lyric piano piece of the nineteenth century. It literally means "of the night" in French. There is often a melancholy aspect to nocturnes.

nouveau-riche A person who comes by wealth through commerce rather than title or inheritance. The nouveaux-riches were often resented and spurned by the aristocracy.

oratorio A sacred piece of music, which usually narrates (through song) a story from the Bible. A religious opera.

pagan Non-believer, heathen; often said by Christian Europeans of the ancient Greeks and Romans.

paternalist Used to describe a country, community, group of employees, etc. that is cared for or controlled in a manner suggestive of a father looking after his children.

periphery Countries, regions, villages, etc. that are controlled through colonization, exploitation of natural resources, and trade by the metropolis within an imperialist system.

philanthropist One who embodies and demonstrates good will toward humanity by performing charitable or benevolent acts.

plebiscite An expression of the popular will by means of a vote by the whole population.

precept A rule prescribing a particular kind of conduct or action; a proverbial standard or guide to morals.

prelude In music, a short introduction to a larger piece; a short lyrical piece.

proselytism The making of converts to a religion, sect, or party.

quasi-military mobilization The organization of society in a manner similar to that which may be necessary at the time of war; usually in reference to Russia under Stalin.

reconnaissance in force A military strategy of launching an initial assault primarily for the purpose of gathering information for a future attack upon the same site.

salon A room where an intellectually oriented hostess would entertain selected guests.

secular Not religious; worldly.

stalemate A tie or deadlock in a war or competition.

syncopate To play a musical rhythm by starting a note on an unaccented beat and continuing on the accented.

tithes A tenth of the yearly agricultural yield; personal income or profits paid as a tax or donation for the support of the church and clergy.

triptych A set of three panels side by side with pictures or carvings, often an altarpiece.

universal suffrage The condition under which all members of the population have the right to vote.

ILLUSTRATION CREDITS

Giraudon/Art Resource, N.Y.; **page 330** DALI, Salvador. *The Persistence of Memory* [Persistence de la mémoire]. (1931) Oil on canvas, 9 1/2" x 13" (24.1 cm x 33 cm). The Museum of Modern Art, New York. Given anonymously. Photograph © 1995 The Museum of Modern Art, New York; **pages 331 and 332 and 333** The Bettmann Archive; **page 335** National Portrait Gallery, Smithsonian Institution/Art Resource, N.Y.; **page 336** The Bettmann Archive; **page 337** Hulton Deutsch Collection; **page 338** Courtesy of private collection, c/o The Warne Archive, reproduced by permission of Frederick Warne & Company; **page 347** The Bettmann Archive; **page 354** National Aeronautics and Space Administration (NASA); **page 355** Canapress; **page 359** © Roy Lichtenstein 1995/VIS*ART Copyright Inc.; **page 360** © MacDonald's; **page 363** Canadian Women's Movement Archives, University of Ottawa Library Network, item P534, Nancy Adamson, photographer; **page 364** Wide World Photos/Canapress; **page 370** The Bettmann Archive; **page 377** The Bettmann Archive; **pages 381 and 384 and 386** The Bettmann Archive; **page 387** Courtesy of Greenpeace; **page 390** Canapress Photo Service (Peter Northall); **page 392** The Bettmann Archive; **page 400** The Bettmann Archive; **page 401** Public Archives of Canada, PA71362; **page 402** The Bettmann Archive; **page 404** V. Henry/Canapress; **page 405** *The Toronto Star*/C. McConnell; **page 407** Garfield Newman; **page 412** BACON, Francis. *Number VII from Eight Studies for a Portrait.* (1953) Oil on linen, 60" x 46 1/8" (152.3 cm x 117 cm). The Museum of Modern Art, New York, Gift of Mr. and Mrs. William A.M. Burden. Photograph © 1995 The Museum of Modern Art, New York; **page 413** GIACOMETTI, Alberto. *City Square [la Place].* (1948) Bronze, 8 1/2" x 25 3/8" x 17 1/4" (21.6 cm x 64.5 cm x 43.8 cm). The Museum of Modern Art, New York, Purchase. Photograph © 1995 The Museum of Modern Art, New York; **page 414** Courtesy Vancouver Art Gallery; photo Trevor Mills; **page 415** The Bettmann Archive; **pages 416 and 417 and 418** Canapress.

We would like to thank Garfield Newman for contributing numerous photographs.

TEXT CREDITS

INDEX